W.A. MACKINTOSH

CARLETON LIBRARY SERIES

The Carleton Library Series publishes books about Canadian economics, geography, history, politics, public policy, society and culture, and related topics, in the form of leading new scholarship and reprints of classics in these fields. The series is funded by Carleton University, published by McGill-Queen's University Press, and is under the guidance of the Carleton Library Series Editorial Board, which consists of faculty members of Carleton University. Suggestions and proposals for manuscripts and new editions of classic works are welcome and may be directed to the Carleton Library Series Editorial Board c/o the Library, Carleton University, Ottawa K1S 5B6, at cls@carleton.ca, or on the web at www.carleton.ca/cls.

214 *Inventing Canada*
Early Victorian Science and the Idea of a Transcontinental Nation
Suzanne Zeller

215 *Documents on the Confederation of British North America*
G.P. Browne

216 *The Irish in Ontario*
A Study in Rural History
Donald Harman Akenson

217 *The Canadian Economy in the Great Depression* (Third edition)
A.E. Safarian

218 *The Ordinary People of Essex*
Environment, Culture, and Economy on the Frontier of Upper Canada
John Clarke

219 *So Vast and Various*
Interpreting Canada's Regions in the Nineteenth and Twentieth Centuries
Edited by John Warkentin

220 *Industrial Organization in Canada*
Empirical Evidence and Policy Challenges
Edited by Zhiqi Chen and Marc Duhamel

221 *Surveyors of Empire*
Samuel Holland, J.F.W. Des Barres, and the Making of The Atlantic Neptune
Stephen J. Hornsby

222 *Peopling the North American City*
Montreal, 1840–1900
Sherry Olson and Patricia Thornton

223 *Interregional Migration and Public Policy in Canada*
An Empirical Study
Kathleen M. Day and Stanley L. Winer

224 *How Schools Worked*
Public Education in English Canada, 1900–1940
R.D. Gidney and W.P.J. Millar

225 A Two-Edged Sword
The Navy as an Instrument of Canadian Foreign Policy
Nicholas Tracy

226 *The Illustrated History of Canada*
25th Anniversary Edition
Edited by Craig Brown

227 *In Duty Bound*
Men, Women, and the State in Upper Canada, 1783–1841
J.K. Johnson

228 *Asleep at the Switch*
The Political Economy of Federal Research and Development Policy since 1960
Bruce Smardon

229 *And We Go On*
Will R. Bird
Introduction and Afterword by David Williams

230 *The Great War as I Saw It*
Frederick George Scott
Introduction by Mark G. McGowan

231 *The Canadian Oral History Reader*
Edited by Kristina R. Llewellyn, Alexander Freund, and Nolan Reilly

232 *Lives in Transition*
Longitudinal Analysis from Historical Sources
Edited by Peter Baskerville and Kris Inwood

233 *W.A. Mackintosh*
The Life of a Canadian Economist
Hugh Grant

W.A. Mackintosh

The Life of a Canadian Economist

HUGH GRANT

Carleton Library Series 233

McGill-Queen's University Press
Montreal & Kingston • London • Chicago

ISBN 978-0-7735-4638-7 (cloth)
ISBN 978-0-7735-9762-4 (ePDF)
ISBN 978-0-7735-9763-1 (ePUB)

Legal deposit fourth quarter 2015
Bibliothèque nationale du Québec

Printed in Canada on acid-free paper that is 100% ancient forest free (100% post-consumer recycled), processed chlorine free

This book has been published with the help of a grant from the Canadian Federation for the Humanities and Social Sciences, through the Awards to Scholarly Publications Program, using funds provided by the Social Sciences and Humanities Research Council of Canada.

McGill-Queen's University Press acknowledges the support of the Canada Council for the Arts for our publishing program. We also acknowledge the financial support of the Government of Canada through the Canada Book Fund for our publishing activities.

Library and Archives Canada Cataloguing in Publication

Grant, Hugh M. K. (Hugh Murray Kenneth), 1956–, author
W.A. Mackintosh: the life of a Canadian economist/Hugh Grant.

(Carleton library series; 233)
Includes bibliographical references and index.
Issued in print and electronic formats.
ISBN 978-0-7735-4638-7 (bound). – ISBN 978-0-7735-9762-4 (ePDF). – ISBN 978-0-7735-9763-1 (ePUB)

1. Mackintosh, W. A. (William Archibald), 1895-1970. 2. Economists – Canada – Biography. I. Title. II. Series: Carleton library series; 233

HB121.M33G73 2015 330.092 C2015-904306-9
C2015-904307-7

This book was typeset by Interscript in 10.5/13 Sabon.

To Claire Gwyneth Watson, Neil Duncan Watson,
Reese Alison Morgan, and Griffyn Ieuan Mackintosh Morgan,
who carry on a proud tradition.

Contents

Acknowledgments

When Mel Watkins first suggested that a biography of W.A. Mackintosh was long overdue, I was not entirely convinced that he was serious. Was not Mackintosh of Queen's the antithesis of the University of Toronto tradition that Mel had spent a career extending through his reinterpretation of Harold Innis's contribution to Canadian political economy? For anyone with the slightest association with the University of Toronto to suggest that a biography of a Queen's man was in order struck me as highly suspect. But Mel made a compelling case for Mackintosh's importance to the development of economics as an academic discipline in Canada and for his material contribution to the well-being of Canadians through policy work. I was sufficiently persuaded to spend a few days in the Queen's University Archives and was quickly convinced that W.A. Mackintosh was indeed a very remarkable man.

One comment on an aspect of the work involved in this project is necessary. Because of an apparent conspiracy to misspell "Mackintosh" in a variety of creative ways, there were no research shortcuts. It was not possible, for instance, to scan the secondary literature using book indexes, or to rely with confidence on electronic keyword searches, without exhausting a host of variations in spelling. Even his public-service file with the federal government is labelled "W.G. McIntosh" and a keyword search for senior officials of the department of finance on the Library and Archives Canada website turns up "W.A. McIntosh" but no "W.A. Mackintosh" (since corrected). In 1927, "W.E. MacIntosh" was invited to work on the Advisory Board on Tariff and Taxation but "W.C. Mackintosh" received the formal appointment. Nonetheless, Hector McKinnon persisted in addressing his correspondence to "W.A. McIntosh," and one senses that the replies to "H.B. Mackinnon" may have been deliberately misdirected. Newspapers, however, can be counted on to get the spelling right, and a keyword search through the records of the *Globe and Mail* proved remarkably efficient – that is, until Mackintosh Toffee began advertising regularly in the 1920s and Shirley Mackintosh emerged as an accomplished ten-pin bowler in the 1950s. At some point, it is tempting to change the name to accord with the historical record. For instance, there is scarcely any account of Mackintosh's brother in the records of the University of Toronto; however, John Cowie McIntosh's service to the Literary and Athletic Society at University College is preserved for posterity on the oak-panelled walls of its Junior Common Room. In this instance, at least, it would seem easier to change the family's surname. Alternatively, consider the advice of O.D. Skelton. Having to correct by hand the typist's rendering of Mackintosh's name on a memorandum, Skelton added a postscript: "Shouldn't an [Order in Council] be passed under the War Measures Act compelling the Mac's Mc's and M's to get together?"

In the course of the research, I acquired a number of debts to people who, in many instances, have moved on to other undertakings: Tom Mitchell (Archivist, Brandon University); Kyle Carey (Reference Assistant, Harvard University Archives); Melissa Richer (Canadian Baptist Archives); Tim Hutchinson (University of Saskatchewan Archives); Lewis Stubbs (University of Manitoba Archives); Suzy Martin (Town of Gravelbourg) and Jody Kennedy (RM of Shamrock) in Saskatchewan; and the staff at the Library and Archives of Canada, Princeton University Archives, Glasgow University Archives, the Bank of Canada Archives, and the Parliamentary Library of Canada. Paul Banfield, Heather Home, Deidre Bryden, Gillian Barlow, Susan Office and others at the Queen's University Archives provide rich professional and uniquely convivial assistance to scholarly research in Canada. I had the privilege of speaking with Mac Urquhart, David McQueen, David Slater, Simon Reisman, Arthur Kroeger, James Coyne, and Alan Green about their recollections of Mackintosh. My colleagues in the department of economics at the University of Winnipeg listened patiently whenever I insisted that Mackintosh had played an indirect, yet nonetheless influential, role in their own lives as academic economists in Canada. Mel Watkins, who has provided a lifetime of intellectual and personal guidance,

Bruce Daniels, bon vivant and mentor in all things involving good taste, and Mark Golden provided examples of scholarly commitment and excellence. David Wolfe, Rae Fleming, Duncan McDowall, and Ieuan Morgan, lent their assistance and insights. Mrs J.J. Deutsch's admonishments to finish the book did not go unheeded. Philip Cercone and the staff at McGill-Queen's University Press demonstrated an inordinate patience that no aspiring author has the right to expect. Patricia Kennedy, as copy editor, was tireless in correcting my grammatical shortcomings, and turned an otherwise tedious task into what was for me a most pleasant learning experience. Gretta Grant has provided a lifetime of care and Denise Maharaj unbounded indulgence.

Financial support was received from the Department of Economics, Queen's University (thanks to James G. MacKinnon), the Social Sciences and Humanities Research Council of Canada, and the University of Winnipeg.

The epigraph on page 25, "The Country North of Belleville" by Al Purdy, *Beyond Remembering: The Collected Poems of Al Purdy,* edited by Sam Sdecki, 2000, Harbour Publishing, www.harbourpublishing.com, appears with permission.

Finally, my most heartfelt thanks are extended to Alison Mackintosh Morgan. My admiration for W.A. Mackintosh is wholly biased by her warmth, charm, and "easy social graces," which I infer to be inherited gifts.

William Mackintosh (Courtesy of Queen's University Archives/H.K. Smith)

Agnes Cowie Mackintosh (Courtesy of Alison Morgan)

Young Bill in front of the Madoc home (Courtesy of Queen's University Archives)

Studying in a Kingston rooming house (Courtesy of Queen's University Archives)

Pioneer family (possibly the Vigors), Wiwa Hills (Courtesy of Queen's University Archives)

A young W.A. Mackintosh (Courtesy of Queen's University Archives)

Brandon College circa 1912 (Photo by Davidson & Gowen, courtesy of S.J. McKee Archives, Brandon University, Alf Fowler Collection, 6-1999.9)

O.D. Skelton with W.L. Mackenzie King and King's sister Jennie (Mrs H.M. Lay) at Kingsmere, 1923 (Courtesy of Library and Archives Canada, C-026031)

A young Harold Innis (Courtesy of University of Toronto Archives, B1972–003/034 (56))

Arthur B. Purvis (Courtesy of McGill University Archives, PR027602)

Norman McLeod Rogers (Courtesy of National Film Board of Canada; Phototheque/Library and Archives Canada, C-081525)

J.L. Isley (Courtesy of Walter Stoneman, Library and Archives Canada, R4515-29, e006608788)

King and cabinet, September 1939. (*Front, L–R*): W.D. Euler, T.A. Crerar, Raoul Dandurand, W.L. Mackenzie King, Ernest Lapointe, P.J.A. Cardin, J.L. Ralston. (*Rear, L–R*): J.A. Mackinnon, J.G. Gardiner, Norman Rogers, J.L. Ilsley, Ian Mackenzie, C.G. Power, J.E. Michaud, C.D. Howe, N.L. McLarty (Courtesy of National Film Board of Canada; Phototheque/Library and Archives Canada, C-090191)

R.B. Bryce, 1959 (Courtesy of Lingard/Library and Archives Canada, PA-129000)

With Brooke Claxton, minister of national health and welfare, at the UN Economic and Social Council meetings, New York, 1946 (Courtesy of National Film Board of Canada/Library and Archives Canada, PA-129003)

Meeting of the Canada–US Joint Economic Committees (Courtesy of Queen's University Archives)

Mackintosh, Donald Gordon, and Milton Friedman debate Canada's postwar economic policy on NBC radio, 1948 (Courtesy of Queen's University Archives)

Mackintosh accepts the congratulations of Charles Dunning upon being installed as the 12th principal of Queen's University (Courtesy of Queen's University Archives)

Mackintosh with senior administrative team (Queen's University Archives/Wallace Berry, Cinema-Television Productions)

Walking to work accompanied by Sam, the family dog (Courtesy of Queen's University Archives)

At home in Summerhill with Jean and Alison (Courtesy of Queen's University Archives)

James Coyne and his wife, Meribeth Riley Coyne, leaving Parliament after Senate hearings, 1961 (Courtesy of Canadian Press, 620925)

Bank of Canada, board of directors (Courtesy of Queen's University Archives)

W.A. MACKINTOSH

Preface

May I say to you ... sourpusses, misanthropes and hollow cynics – here is a great man. He has ideas, sweep of mind.

Grant Dexter, 1944[1]

On an otherwise grey and rather drab day in the fall of 1951, Queen's University treated Kingston, Ontario, to a colourful procession. The event lacked none of the pageantry of the royal visit by Princess Elizabeth and the Duke of Edinburgh just two weeks earlier, and for Queen's the day would be "at once, one of the most solemnly impressive and one of the most spontaneously joyous occasions in the university's history." An imposing roster of politicians, civil servants, bankers, industrialists, and academics were in attendance. The prime minister of Canada, Louis St Laurent, would not arrive until later in the evening, but Ontario's premier, Leslie Frost, and the future governor general, Vincent Massey, were present, as was Brooke Claxton, Canada's minister of defence, "so swathed [in academic regalia] that he looked for all the world like Joe Louis entering the ring in his robe and towels."[2] These luminaries gathered not to honour a titan of industry, a cultural icon, a visiting foreign dignitary, or an eminent politician; instead, they paid regal tribute to a demure man, unassuming both in appearance and behaviour, near the end of the academic procession as it entered Grant Hall. For William Archibald Mackintosh, the ceremony crowned a journey that had started in Kingston some forty years earlier. When he first arrived at Queen's in 1912, it was as an undergraduate student, but on this day he was to be installed as the university's twelfth principal.

If not a natural outcome, this triumph seemed all but inevitable in retrospect. Mackintosh had been raised in "Queen's country," in the eastern-Ontario town of Madoc, and he confessed to his Toronto colleague, Harold Innis, that Queen's "has been rather bred in my bones."[3] After receiving his MA from Queen's, he obtained his doctorate in economics from Harvard in 1922, his studies there interrupted by two years of teaching at Brandon College in Manitoba. He joined the department of political and economic science at Queen's in 1920, ascended to department head in 1927, to dean of arts in 1946, vice-principal in 1947, and now stood poised to begin what would be a ten-year term as principal and vice-chancellor. With a further five-year tenure as vice-chancellor eventually added to his resumé, he would spend a total of forty-five years working at the university, a run only broken by seven years of wartime service with the Government of Canada.

Among the assembled guests were several people with whom Mackintosh's life had intersected at various stages. Graham Towers, governor of the Bank of Canada, had been a fellow student at St Andrew's College in Toronto in 1912; George Earle Wilson, professor of history at Dalhousie University, had been his closest friend since their undergraduate days at Queen's and later at Harvard; Jacob Viner, the Montreal-born professor of economics at Princeton, hailed as "the greatest all-rounder" in his discipline, was in the same graduating class at Harvard; J.R. Evans, president of Brandon College, was a colleague in Brandon from 1917 to 1919; the chancellor, Charles A. Dunning, formerly the premier of Saskatchewan and Canadian minister of finance, had assisted with his doctoral research some thirty-five years earlier; Frank Knox, Clifford A. Curtis, and Mac Urquhart had shared in the development at Queen's of the foremost department in applied economic research in the country, while other colleagues from Queen's held the same lifelong commitment to education. Only a series of three recent heart attacks and the intervention of his physician could have prevented William E. McNeill, the loyal servant of Queen's, from attending.[4] J.L. Ilsley (chief justice of the Supreme Court of Nova Scotia), Louis Rasminsky (future governor of the Bank of Canada), Norman Robertson (clerk of the Privy Council), Walter Gordon, St Laurent, Claxton, Dunning, and Towers were part of the remarkable group that oversaw the wartime effort in Ottawa. W.C. Clark, deputy minister of finance, in attendance despite his failing health, would simply state with tears in his eyes that "This is really grand," while John J. Deutsch, a student, colleague, and wartime associate, "conceal[ed] his affection behind apparent stolidity."[5] The ceremony was also graced by the presence of Isabel Skelton, widow of Mackintosh's lifelong mentor O.D. Skelton, as well as by "a young woman in a dark fur jacket and a smart turquoise hat, and the girl beside her, Mrs. [Jean Easton] Mackintosh and daughter Alison."[6]

A fanfare of trumpets heralded the academic procession as it made its way to the platform of Grant Hall. After the singing of the traditional hymn, "O God, Our Help in Ages Past," a prayer, and introduction of delegates from various universities and colleges, the formal installation proceeded. Mackintosh, now fifty-six years old, the retreat of his hairline well advanced and a few extra pounds on his otherwise slight five-foot-eight-inch frame, "quietly and earnestly" recited the pledge to uphold the traditions and principles of Queen's University. As he donned the white-and-silver-trimmed black brocade of the principal, "the sun burst through the clouds of a wide October day, and filled the whole interior of hallowed Grant Hall with a golden light. It was almost as if the higher power himself had decreed that the choice was the right one."[7]

But as he stepped to the front of the platform to begin his inaugural address to this august gathering (broadcast locally by the university radio station and nationwide the next day by the CBC), a "mighty Queen's yell" interrupted the proceedings, accompanied by the sounds of bells and whistles and the release of confetti and paper streamers from the side balconies. Opinions differ on whether two pigeons that appeared were invited or came of their own accord. Newspaper accounts record that "some of the distinguished officials and guests on the platform looked rather shocked at the student boisterousness," and many could not help but notice a pigeon feather slowly fluttering down to light on the head of Sir James Dunn. Unperturbed, Mackintosh departed from his prepared text to thank his "warm-hearted supporters in the gallery" by quoting Adam Smith on the generosity of students: "So far from being disposed to neglect or despise the instructions of their master, provided he show some serious intention of being of use to them, they are generally inclined to pardon a great deal of incorrectness in the performance of his duty, and sometimes even to conceal from the public a good deal of gross negligence."[8] When asked afterwards what he thought of the interruption, he replied, with all of the candour and pith for which he was renowned among his academic and government colleagues, and with his constant admonishment not to take oneself too seriously, "It was great!"[9]

The story of how this quiet, self-effacing man climbed the ranks to become principal of one of Canada's leading academic institutions and to be honoured by the presence of so many accomplished Canadians is much like the man himself: on first glance rather unexceptional, but in substance, most remarkable.

BY SKELTON, OUT OF SHORTT

During an invited lecture given at the University of Toronto in 1938, Mackintosh paid homage to his fellow economist, Harold Innis: "If we ever come to the time when *Who's Who* includes the intellectual pedigrees of scholars, there will appear an item: Innis, H.A., by Veblen, out of Shortt."[10] In this spirit, a second entry would surely read: Mackintosh, W.A., by Skelton, out of Shortt.

The teaching of political economy in Canada began in 1878, when John Watson lectured on the topic as part of the moral philosophy curriculum at Queen's. It might have begun much earlier had John Rae, one of the foremost contributors to the development of economics in the mid-1800s, not been turned down for a chair in natural philosophy at Queen's in 1841.[11] Nonetheless, it was not until Adam Shortt was appointed as lecturer at Queen's in 1887 that the subject received systematic treatment.[12] Shortt would become the John Leys Professor of Political Science, and during the course of the next twenty years would begin building the tradition of "Queensian economics" with its strong bent for applied, policy-oriented studies.[13]

There were three distinct phases to Shortt's career. A philosophical approach to economics and politics informed his early teaching. He then shifted to empirical research on the historical background to Canadian institutions and problems, and finally he entered public service as one of the first two members of the Civil Service Commission of Canada. Although never a student of Shortt's, Mackintosh wrote that: "[M]y own generation remembers him chiefly at the Archives, as one who was always interested, always ready to give advice and to share his knowledge. We remember engaging him in argument as he sat in his familiar Morris chair with his desk across his knees, his white Van Dyck beard and his heavy fingers punctuating sentences. The arguments all followed one course: a carefully nourished and cherished generalization on the part of the youth fell into fragments under a barrage of information so wide in origin and so precise in form that youth subsided smothered but admiring."[14] Mackintosh appreciated the "marked independence," "driving curiosity," and "appeal to the facts of history" that Shortt brought to bear on the study of the Canadian economy, and a similar impartiality and practical judgment that he exercised in his duties as a public servant.[15] At the same time, however, he was frustrated by Shortt's lack of interest in "the search for generalities" and his incapacity "to digest or to mark out essential lines of development."[16] He characterized him as "a journeyman who wrought mightily in his chosen craft, and whose work will have enduring influence in Canada."[17] It was Shortt's integrity as a scholar that was, according to Mackintosh, his legacy to Queen's: "To the University from which he started he left a cherished tradition. As I have apprehended it, it is one of honest and untrammelled inquiry. It is a tradition of attack on Canadian problems and the pushing of inquiry where it leads, and choosing the appropriate tools, regardless of changing intellectual fashions; a tradition which makes imitativeness and intellectual self-consciousness cardinal sins. But, beyond these easily identifiable influences the results of his devoted and unremitting work go on in scores of unidentified ways and places, a kind of immortality which belongs to the teacher."[18]

O.D. Skelton came from a similar background and followed in much the same direction as Shortt. Born in Orangeville, Ontario, in 1878, he entered Queen's University in 1896 and left five years later with his MA, having completed the honours requirements in English, Latin, and Greek, and capturing gold medals in Latin and in Greek. After a year studying Greek at the University of Chicago and three years as assistant editor of *Booklover's Magazine* in Philadelphia, he re-entered the University of Chicago to study political science. There, he completed the bulk of his doctoral dissertation (later published in 1911 as *Socialism: A Critical Analysis*) before returning to Queen's as a lecturer in 1907. One year later, he succeeded Shortt as head of the department of political and economic science and was appointed dean of Arts in 1919. During his time at Queen's, he strengthened its role as a training ground for applied economics – adding extramural courses in commerce to serve the needs of the banking and accounting professions – while his own scholarship extended the historical analysis of Canadian public policy. He left Queen's in 1924 to join the Canadian civil service, serving as under-secretary of state for external affairs from 1925 until his death in 1943.

If Mackintosh's admiration of Shortt was subject to qualification, there was no equivocation in his effusive praise of Skelton's "acute and sensitive mind," his "amazing powers of synthesis and balanced judgment," and his mastery of the written word, "marked by his command of compressed, forceful phrases, and his swift, accurate draftsmanship."[19] His fierce loyalty to Skelton – whose portrait was always prominently displayed in Mackintosh's study – stemmed from a deep personal affection. As he wrote on the occasion of his mentor's death: "We have known a great Canadian of capacious and humane mind, of profound insight, wise in counsel, who walked humbly and served, unmindful of self, who believed passionately in human liberty, in tolerance, in the dignity of the individual, and in the pursuit of learning. Down the years, we shall remember."[20] This echoed the sentiments of others who described Skelton in the same terms that Skelton assigned to Sir Wilfrid Laurier: "The finest and simplest gentleman, the noblest and most unselfish man, it has ever been my good fortune to know."[21] Upon Skelton's death, Mackintosh took over the duty of completing a short paper that Skelton left unfinished. In doing so, he wrote: "This is not the first time that I have had the honour of taking over tasks from O.D. Skelton. But it is the last assignment. There will be no more. I shall accomplish it as I have the others with little of his rich judgment and none of his brilliance. But what store of competence I can muster on this or any other occasion, he more than anyone else gave me."[22]

Mackintosh started down the same path as Shortt and Skelton. His scholarship focused on the institutional aspects of the Canadian economy, where he picked up the "staples" argument implicit in Shortt's work and cast it into one of the most compelling themes of national economic development. He then turned from strict academic scholarship to public service when, summoned to Ottawa by his long-time friend and former colleague W.C. Clark, he served in various capacities during World War II. Yet unlike Shortt and Skelton, Mackintosh never intended to remain in the civil service and repeatedly reassured Principal R.C. Wallace that, "My stay here [in Ottawa] is purely temporary."[23] True to his word, Mackintosh turned down several appointments – including a senior post in external affairs, as deputy minister of the department of reconstruction, and as Canada's representative to the International Bank for Development and Reconstruction – to renew his commitment to education at Queen's in 1946.

When he was named as a companion of the Order of Canada, it was observed that the only similarity between "Mackintosh and all of Gaul" was that each could be divided into three parts.[24] For the former, the first part was as a scholar who contributed to the development of an indigenous approach to economics in Canada; the second was as a temporary public servant, in which role he was central to bringing Keynesian analysis to bear on Canadian economic policy; and the third was as an academic administrator who nurtured and guided Queen's University and higher education in Canada, institutions he publicly and privately cherished. In each capacity, his service was marked by humility, generosity to others, and, above all else, an outstanding record of accomplishment.

MACKINTOSH AND INNIS: THE DEVELOPMENT OF CANADIAN ECONOMICS

An honour that fell to Mackintosh in his capacity as vice-president of the Canadian Political Science Association in 1935 was to pay tribute to the American Economic Association on the occasion of its fiftieth anniversary. Among those gathered at the New Yorker Hotel for the event were four surviving founding members of the association – J.B. Clark, E.R.A. Seligman, Richard Ely, and Davis R. Dewey – as well as the who's who of the American profession, including Frank Taussig, Edwin F. Gay, J.M. Clark, Irving Fisher, Jacob Viner, and a very young Milton Friedman. When it was Mackintosh's turn on the roster of speakers he gracefully acknowledged the close relationship of the discipline in the two countries, with Canadians benefiting from graduate training in the United States, and the American profession profiting from the large number of Canadian émigrés in its midst. But he reminded his American hosts of the independent roots of economics in Canada: "Last evening Dr. Ely spoke of the stimulus which the founding of the American Economic Association had given to the study of economics in this and in other countries. Whether from this stimulus or not, it was in the eighties that economics in Canada left the parental control of Moral Philosophy. The appointment of Adam Shortt to a lectureship in Political Economy at

Queen's University in 1887 and of W.J. Ashley to a chair in the University of Toronto in the following year marks the beginning of its independent existence."[25]

This gentle reminder to his American colleagues reflected the growing confidence of the discipline in Canada. Between the First and Second World Wars, an indigenous school of political economy would emerge, concerned with explaining the country's unique pattern of growth and contributing to the search for an effective national policy. As his fellow economist Kenneth Taylor writes: "The main bulk of economic writing directly or indirectly came out of the complementary schools of economics at Toronto and Queen's, or to be more accurately personal, they reflected the work and influence of our two leading economists, Innis and Mackintosh. To these two men we owe a very large part of the growth and the trends in Canadian economics, at least up to about 1950."[26] In a similar vein, John H. Dales describes the period between 1925 and 1950 as "the era of Mackintosh at Queen's and Innis at Toronto ... It was a firm theoretical underpinning that gave value to the writings of both men."[27]

Many similarities united Innis and Mackintosh. Born in rural Ontario less than a year apart, they acquired their first degrees in Canada before completing their doctoral studies in the United States (Innis at the less conventional University of Chicago, where he was heavily influenced by Thorstein Veblen, and Mackintosh at the more orthodox Harvard under the chairmanship of Frank Taussig).[28] Their dissertations (Innis on the Canadian Pacific Railway and Mackintosh on the cooperative movement in the western grain trade) led each to consider the geographical background of Canadian economic development and the importance of primary commodity exports to that development. They returned to Canada to accept academic appointments in 1920 (Innis at the University of Toronto and Mackintosh at Queen's), only to lament the paucity of Canadian material for the teaching of economics and, in research, to find fault with the indiscriminate application of traditional economic theory to distinctively Canadian problems.[29] They thus shared a sense of purpose in trying to remedy the situation by producing the fodder of data from which an interpretation of Canada's economic history would be possible. Innis's contribution lay primarily in his books *The Fur Trade in Canada* and *The Cod Fisheries*, and Mackintosh's in his volumes *Prairie Settlement* and *The Economic Problems of the Prairie Provinces*.

Their early scholarship "co-discovered" the staple thesis – heralded as Canada's foremost contribution to the literature of economics – that emphasized the unique geographical and institutional setting to Canadian economic development based upon the exploitation of successive export commodities. In 1922, Mackintosh, in concert with Shortt, arranged for a graduate seminar in Canadian economic development to be given during the summer at the Public Archives of Canada in Ottawa, and his lectures formed the basis of his seminal article, "Economic Factors in Canadian History," published in 1923.[30] "The broad thesis of the lectures," Mackintosh explained, "was that Canadian economic, and indeed national, development, had been delayed and frustrated because we had been able to achieve no more than intermittent and marginal staple exports until the wheat trade achieved a firm basis at the turn of the century."[31] When Innis credited these lectures with arousing his own interest in the export staple, Mackintosh characteristically downplayed his own contribution: "Innis clearly exaggerated the influence of this lecture on his own thought, since it represented no more than obvious application to the facts of Canadian history of the generalizations that had been made by Adam Smith and Guy S. Callender. Further, he had himself in his work on the Canadian Pacific Railway fixed his attention on the export staple. It is quite clear that he noted with special emphasis an article which was concerned with ideas already formed in his own mind."[32] Whatever the case, Mackintosh had laid out the first broad strokes to the staple thesis.

Innis's interest in Canadian history became part of a much larger theoretical agenda. Ian Parker argues persuasively that Innis's staple studies were not about the specific characteristics of each export commodity per se, but with its relationship to the general social and economic structure, and the qualitative differences in its capacity to reproduce these systems over time, or, in the opposite case, to specify the contradictions that led to a system's collapse. His interest in the "dialectics of historical change" marks the continuity between Innis's early research in Canadian economic history and his later writings on communications, and took him well beyond "the capacity of conventional economic theory."[33]

Mackintosh's work had no such grand ambitions. His early writings reflect his intellectual progression from a rudimentary view of a staples economy in a "pioneer" setting to a detailed exposition of wheat as a staple in the early twentieth century, and then to an effort to cast the staple thesis as an explanation for national economic development. This work culminated in his "masterly volume" *The Economic Background of Federal-Provincial Relations*, produced for the Royal Commission on Dominion-Provincial Relations in 1939 and described as the best single synthesis of Canada's economic development and the concomitant search for an effective national policy.[34]

Partly due to these differences in methodology and scope, a significant breach arose between the two men in their willingness to offer policy solutions to the relevant economic problems of the day. While Mackintosh was continually engaged in policy work, Innis's focus on long-term change made him increasingly critical of the "present-mindedness" of economic scholarship during the 1930s. Carl Berger does Innis a disservice in suggesting that he was preoccupied with the "intractability of forces at work ... Innis appeared to dwell excessively on what men could not do. His political economy, in its recognition and preoccupation with deterministic features of economic life, had an anti-reform bias."[35] Instead, as Alexander John Watson emphasizes, Innis objected to the "perversion" of the social sciences by an adherence to a particular doctrine and its application to immediate economic problems with the expectation that it would yield clear policy prescriptions.[36] Much of Innis's displeasure was directed towards the League for Social Reconstruction and its argument for state planning (a hostility that Mackintosh shared in his denouncement of the "zealots of the 1930s"), but he expressed equal disapproval of the "parade of travelling comedians disguised as economists" offering policy advice. (One wag responded that "they aren't that funny."[37]) When Frank Underhill dubbed Canadian economists as "the intellectual garage mechanics of capitalism," he no doubt included Mackintosh among those playing "the humble self-imposed role of minor technicians, never questioning the major purposes of the capitalist system in which they found themselves, never venturing any opinions about the general planning of the machine or the power of its engines, pottering around with their little statistical measuring instruments, doing occasional odd repair jobs on Royal Commissions, such as putting new brake linings into the financial mechanism."[38] Innis would later exempt himself from this indictment, preferring to describe himself as "one of the sons of the Hittites."[39]

Despite the divergence in their interests, the writing of Canada's economic history was very much a shared project. This broad sense of purpose was present in the resuscitation of the Canadian Political Science Association in 1929, and the creation of the *Canadian Journal of Economics and Political Science* in 1935. The annual meetings of the association and the journal became the outlet for the first generation of Canadian-born scholars to present and discuss their research on the country's political economy. Innis and Mackintosh were central to this discussion and played a major role in setting the agenda. In the more specific case of the staple thesis as expounded in the 1920s and 1930s, W.T. Easterbrook writes that it "achieved an integration in thought which, under the heading of Political Economy, brought to an end the early era of empiricism overdone and linked in close harmony the economics of Queen's and Toronto. The techniques were somewhat different, but the vision was the same."[40]

The vitality and unity of thought that existed within Canadian political economy, however, was to be short-lived. Internationally renowned political theorist C.B. Macpherson argues that two events interrupted the grand agenda for working out Canada's unique economic development. The first was the publication of John Maynard Keynes's *General Theory* in 1936, which promised universal solutions to economic problems without recourse to an economy's specific institutional setting and, by implication, brought into doubt whether a uniquely Canadian approach could and should survive. The second, World War II, not only produced a profound economic transformation in Canada, with new industries and changing patterns of trade and capital movements, but also drew a number of Canadian economists into wartime service in Ottawa. By the time they returned to their university departments, if in fact they did return, the world was a very different place and the research questions very different as well.[41]

Innis and Mackintosh reacted to these events in strikingly different ways. For his part, Innis had little to say about Keynes. His comments were limited to a perfunctory note in his Idea File: "Keynes the triumph of economics over politics, and of common law over customary law." In anticipation of "the changing climate of thought and policy,"[42] his attention turned to the much larger project of examining the bias of communication in determining the rise and decline of civilizations. Innis survived the onset of Keynesian economics only by superseding it, but at the cost of becoming increasingly irrelevant to immediate policy debates.[43] As for wartime participation, Innis took to the pages of *Queen's Quarterly*, of all places, to voice a rather caustic complaint: "It has been said that Canadian birth, participation in the last war, and non-attendance at Queen's University present a combination practically precluding an appointment with the federal government."[44]

Mackintosh took a very different road. It fell upon him to address the implications of Keynes's writings for economics in Canada and, through his involvement in coordinating the war effort, he would articulate a postwar vision for the Canadian economy along Keynesian lines.

MACKINTOSH AND KEYNES: HOW KEYNESIANISM CAME TO CANADA

John Kenneth Galbraith asserts that, by virtue of the federal government's 1945 White Paper, *Employment and Income, with Special Reference to the Initial Period of Reconstruction*, Canada was perhaps the first country formally to declare an adherence to Keynesian stabilization policy.[45] The various paths by which Keynes's ideas gained currency in Canada are discussed in Part III; however, it is possible to suggest, as David McQueen does, that Mackintosh, as principal author of the 1945 White Paper, was *the* Canadian Keynesian. If so, the evolution of his thought during World War II provides the clearest explication of how Keynesianism came to Canada.

Mackintosh's interest in Keynes's writings stemmed from a need to address specific problems as they arose in the Great Depression and during World War II. No epiphany burst forth from a reading of the *General Theory*; instead, Keynes's influence was transmitted through his journalistic contributions in the *Nation*, the *New Statesman*, and the *Times*, which were directed at shaping policy discussions in Britain. From the early 1920s, Mackintosh avidly read Keynes's shorter policy pieces, such as those collected in *Essays in Persuasion*, and his more academic *Treatise* appeared on Mackintosh's reading list at Queen's in 1936. Through discussions with academic colleagues such as Frank Knox, Robert "Pete" McQueen, and John Deutsch, Mackintosh acquired a growing appreciation for the *General Theory* during the later 1930s, and he benefited from his association with his wartime colleagues in Ottawa, R.B. Bryce and

A.F.W. (Wynne) Plumptre, who had studied with Keynes at Cambridge in the early 1930s.

As important as his reading of Keynes was, Mackintosh's conversion to Keynesian economic policy occurred largely as a process of learning-by-doing during World War II. Each solution to the steady parade of pressing economic concerns – mobilizing the necessary resources for the war effort, financing government purchases, choking off domestic consumption, preventing rampant inflation, curtailing imports to save on scarce foreign exchange, managing an equitable distribution of the costs of the war effort, and reforming international trade and currency institutions – carried Canadian economic policy a step closer to embracing a Keynesian framework. When it came to defining a program for postwar reconstruction, Mackintosh would serve as the principal advocate of managing the Canadian economy within an explicit Keynesian context.

Entering the federal civil service in December 1939 as special assistant to the deputy minister of finance, Mackintosh served in several capacities. He chaired the powerful Economic Advisory Committee, participated in the drafting of several wartime budgets, became director general of research in the department of reconstruction and, during W.C. Clark's illness, was acting deputy minister of finance. His resumé also includes the chairmanship of the Canadian Committee of the Joint Canada–US Economic Committees, the National Joint Council of the Public Service of Canada and the Unemployment Insurance Advisory Committee, along with membership on numerous other committees, included the Foreign Exchange Control Board and the Wartime Prices and Trade Board. These responsibilities entailed a close working relationship with several other economists and, in particular, Bryce. Moreover, Mackintosh's involvement in international reconstruction negotiations brought him into contact with leading American and British economists who were heavily influenced by Keynes's writings. Through various government forums, he met frequently with Harry Dexter White, Carl Bernstein, Charles Kindleberger, Lauchlin Currie, Walter Salant, and especially Alvin Hansen, while during Commonwealth negotiations he often crossed paths with Lionel Robbins, Dennis Robertson, James Meade, Austin Robinson, Richard Stone, and, of course, Keynes himself.

Mackintosh had a profound admiration for Keynes, but also some misgivings. On one occasion he referred to him as "a spoiled brat."[46]

Prior to World War II, he held that Keynes often misjudged his audience and insulted the very people he was attempting to win over: "To intellectuals, Keynes was compellingly persuasive both as a writer and a speaker. He wrote with great charm, economy, and vigour. His metaphors and similes were apt and lit up with a sense of fun and mischief. He had an artist's sense of the essentials and of balance. He had a magnificently resonant voice. To the man of affairs he was less persuasive (or at least so it seems to me). His argument was usually provocative. He conceded little or nothing to his opponent's case. Opposition frequently seemed to him to spring from stupidity or prejudice. Beset with a complexity of problems, businessmen and politicians were unconvinced that the answers could be as simple as Keynes's lucid explanation made them or that others could have been so completely wrong as Keynes made them out to be." But during the exigencies of war, Mackintosh observed how a change in Keynes's attitude brought his powers to their greatest point. "As a result of this change and his own generosity and superhuman work, he seemed to me to lift those about him to the highest pitch of quality and output. He was a star who inspired rather than disrupted the company of players."[47]

Among the cast on this international stage, Mackintosh played a central role. During the multinational negotiations for postwar reconstruction, he made a significant contribution to the formation of the International Monetary Fund and the International Bank for Reconstruction and Development (the former name for the World Bank) and, to a lesser extent, the United Nations. Indeed, a fitting testimony to his part in shaping the postwar world came at the final plenary of the Bretton Woods conference. The honour of placing the motion to adopt the "Final Act" was bestowed upon Keynes; and it was Mackintosh who stood on behalf of the Canadian delegation to second the motion.

The transformation in Mackintosh's economic thinking began during his work with the National Employment Commission in 1936–38, evolved during the Rowell–Sirois Royal Commission of 1938–39, and reached its zenith in the 1945 White Paper. The paper's unequivocal statement that the federal government accepted responsibility "to maintain a high and stable level of employment and income" – a phrase borrowed from the British white paper on *Employment Policy* issued one year earlier – ushered in a new period in Canadian economic policy. Writing in 1959, Mackintosh modestly stated that "there was nothing either radical or novel in the White Paper." It merely placed many of the wartime economic initiatives into a coherent framework in order to provide "an unusually comprehensive statement of economic and fiscal policy."[48]

But the Canadian White Paper did much more than that. First, it was a superbly crafted political document aimed at addressing the perceived electoral strength of the Co-operative Commonwealth Federation (CCF) and the apparent incapacity of the Liberal government to provide a clear alternative. Second, it remains an important academic document that translated Keynes into an open-economy model applicable to a federal state. In essence, Mackintosh successfully wedded the staple thesis to a Keynesian aggregate-demand framework appropriate to a small, open economy. Third, and above all, the White Paper was an important policy document because of its power to persuade. Just six years after his *Economic Background of Dominion-Provincial Relations* provided a definitive statement of Canada's recent economic history, Mackintosh would articulate a compelling vision of the future of the Canadian economy.

MACKINTOSH AND QUEEN'S: MAPPING THE FUTURE OF CANADA'S UNIVERSITIES

Despite his identification as a wartime economic policy advisor, Mackintosh was first and foremost a "university man," and, as Rector Leonard Brockington would pronounce, "the ideal Queen's man."[49]

Mackintosh's conviction of the importance of education was instilled in him at an early age; indeed many of his pronouncements on the role of education echo the sentiments of his father, a legendary public school inspector for north Hastings County. Absorbing his father's view that the role of public schools in the nineteenth century was to instil the moral judgment that was the foundation of citizenship, Mackintosh defined the objective of education in the twentieth century as providing students with the necessary tools to contribute to civil society.

During his first two decades as a faculty member at Queen's, Mackintosh brought to fruition Skelton's ambitious plans to build the Department of Political and Economic Science into the foremost department in the country, dealing with affairs of immediate relevance to Canada. In this respect, Queen's growing reputation as the "nursery for the civil service" was well justified, but through the expansion of the first program in Commerce it was equally important as a nursery for those in private industry. In both cases, the objective was to serve the public interest. Under Mackintosh's leadership, industrial relations, sociology, and geography would be added into the mix. This emphasis on applied research, particularly within economics, was not without its critics. Both John Dales and Harry Johnson, for instance, argued that the drain of talented individuals into policy work retarded the development of the academic discipline generally, and particularly in areas of economic theory. But it is difficult to quarrel with the contribution of "Queensian economics" to public service in Canada.

Mackintosh's return to Queen's in 1946, as the dean of the Faculty of Arts, and sho rtly after as vice-principal, involved him in "five years of frantic improvisation to meet the emergency needs of the ex-service students."[50] In 1951, the challenges facing Queen's were even more imposing than those of the previous five years, but they were accompanied by the promise of greater resources and the opportunity to engage in longer- term planning. At the time of Mackintosh's installation as principal, the report of the Massey Commission recommended increased federal funding of universities to meet the anticipated growth in enrolment, Ontario government operating and capital grants were poised to increase significantly, and private fund-raising efforts and accumulated reserve funds added to the war chest. What followed was "the most active decade in the history of Canadian universities."[51] In this context, the hallmark of Mackintosh's principalship was his steadfast commitment to quality. The challenge was to maintain a high level of teaching and scholarship when there was tremendous pressure – and a tremendous temptation – for growth. Mackintosh's ability to manage this growth in a manner that preserved the autonomy of the faculty and the integrity of its teaching and research is his most enduring contribution to Queen's. The underlying continuity between his earlier scholarship and policy work and his service as a university administrator was observed by his colleague Glen Shortcliffe: "We do not separate Mackintosh the scholar and public servant from Mackintosh the Principal and Vice-Chancellor. Indeed ... we take pride that in W.A. Mackintosh has been exemplified the finest in his own conception of the head of a university: that of chief scholar in a community of scholars."[52] Moreover, Mackintosh's influence over the direction of higher education would extend beyond Queen's in his roles as president of the National Conference of Canadian Universities (forerunner of the Association of Universities and Colleges of Canada) and as president of the Association of British Commonwealth Universities (the first non-Brit to hold this august post).

LEGACY

W.A. Mackintosh's contribution to public life was appropriately recognized during his lifetime. His standing among his peers is also recorded for posterity. To the journalist Bruce Hutchison, he was the "quiet and homespun ... economic handyman" of the wartime civil service.[53] Mitchell Sharp praised him as "an elegant and economical draftsman," Vincent Massey referred to his "characteristic clarity and urbanity and skill," while Lester B. Pearson recalls his "brilliant performance" as a public speaker.[54] Walter Gordon describes him as a man with "a judicious disposition ... good judgement, and ... a wonderful *raconteur* with a delicious sense of humour."[55] Beryl Plumptre "always referred to him as one of my favourite people ... Everyone mentions his contribution to Canadian public life, but then adds that his kindnesses and humour is what they best remember and cherish."[56] To Simon Reisman he was quite simply "Canada's greatest economist."[57]

Yet the sum of the attention paid to Mackintosh falls well short of the whole that it deserves. There is no single volume that draws together the various strands of his life – from academic scholarship through public service to university governance – and provides an assessment of its impact.

Nor has the relationship between his personal qualities and his record of accomplishment been sufficiently explored. In his history of Queen's, F.W. Gibson provides a portrait of Mackintosh's character cast largely in relation to Skelton's. "Perception and balance, integrity and generosity, self-respect and tolerance, loyalty to friends and love of country – all the qualities which Mackintosh admired in Skelton – these he cultivated in himself and in his university." He cautions, however, that there was another side to Mackintosh.

> Cool and deliberate though he usually appeared, he was not at bottom, and he never entirely became, the gentle, serene man of sweet disposition that he so admired in O.D. Skelton.

> "Imperturbable" was Principal Wallace's favourite word for Mackintosh, but there were, nevertheless, quite definite limits to his patience ... He was, in fact, a man of strong feelings, passionate and intense, holding the deepest loyalties and most decided aversions. One senses, now and then, that Mackintosh's customary demeanour was a triumph of self-control over temperament. Duplicity enraged him and so did incompetence, stupidity and pretension. To such offences his response could be scathing ... For the most part, however, Mackintosh's inner tensions found gentler release. He was blessed with a lively sense of the ridiculous – termed by Wallace "his saving grace of quiet humour" – and there is no doubt that his wit, irony, and abundant store of anecdotes frequently rescued him from exasperation and relieved many a difficult academic meeting.[58]

Grant Dexter, the Ottawa correspondent of the *Winnipeg Free Press*, offered a similar account of Mackintosh's character: "He was often called an excessively modest man or a shy man. He is neither. But he is a man of patience and of kindliness who always looks for bright spots and is slow to criticize and rarely if ever imputes ill motives. These traits, perhaps more than his great abilities, account for the scope of his service."[59] Alex Corry observed "a great capacity for friendship, testified to by scores of those who prized it as precious. At the same time, he was a very private person. He had an inner life that was revealed but little, and that little mostly to a few ... The privacy into which he could retreat was the source of his strength, of his rich qualities, and of his attractiveness – the engaging mystery of personality. One can only speak of what was revealed ... What was revealed was treasure enough."[60]

This biography, therefore, is an attempt to take the measure of the man by establishing the relationship between Mackintosh's personal experience and his contributions to academic scholarship, public service, and university government. That this is an account, with rare exceptions, of a male, Anglophone, and Protestant Canada is a reflection of the time in which Mackintosh lived as well as the limitations of the historical records. With this qualification in mind, it has three primary objectives. The first is to place his scholarship in appropriate context. Just as Dales invites us to read Mackintosh's *Economic Background* in a critical fashion so as to challenge and question the powerful myths of Canadian economic development that it helped to create, this biography seeks to do the same with the entire body of Mackintosh's academic writings. Second, an assessment of Mackintosh's service with the federal government is the best vehicle for examining the transmission of Keynesian economic policy to Canada and adds to the understanding of not only the development of modern economic thought in Canada but also the reciprocal relationship between the academic discipline and the policy process. Third, it assesses Mackintosh's role in Canadian educational history through the lens of his lifelong service to Queen's. Each of these aspects of Mackintosh's career has been examined piecemeal by other able scholars, but the totality of Mackintosh's life is greater than the mere sum of its parts. This biography, then, seeks to contribute to Canadian intellectual history and recent Canadian economic thought by examining the full, rich life of an outstanding Canadian economic scholar, policy advisor, and educator.

PART ONE

Beginnings

One of the few surviving stories about W.A. Mackintosh's life growing up in Madoc concerns a debate he had with a friend. Twelve or thirteen years old at the time, he insisted that, if a person was shot in a specific part of the leg, the bullet would pass cleanly through the flesh without causing significant injury. His theory being met with scepticism, the obvious means of resolving the issue was to have his friend shoot him in the thigh. When his friend complied, as the story goes, young Bill insisted he was unhurt, staggered a few paces, collapsed, and passed out.

However implausible the story, one might argue that it serves to suggest the early formation of several aspects of Mackintosh's character: an inquiring mind, the need to accumulate facts to test theories, a sense of determination, and, above all, the need to better channel innate intellectual curiosity. But before it can be dismissed as merely apocryphal, it bears noting that, in a notation on his military service card of 1917, there is a reference to "a large round scar from scald back and inner side left leg."[1]

1

Educational Pioneering in Old Ontario: Madoc, 1895–1912

The need of our time is well-trained, educated men and women,
equipped morally, intellectually, and physically, to be of service to Society
and the State, men who, in the discharge of duty, know what is right
and dare to do it.

William Mackintosh, Sr, 1892[1]

Yet this is the country of defeat
where Sisyphus rolls a big stone
year after year up the ancient hills
picknicking glaciers have left strewn
with centuries' rubble.
  backbreaking days
  in the sun and rain
when realization seeps slow in the mind
without grandeur or self-deception in
  noble struggle
of being a fool

Al Purdy, "The Country North of Belleville"[2]

William Archibald Mackintosh was born in Madoc, Ontario, on 21 May 1895. This was in the year that the opening of European markets to prairie wheat ushered in an era of unprecedented prosperity in Canada. Under the guise of nation-building, the economy was to be radically transformed by the development of new export commodities, an inflow of labour and capital, an expanded transportation infrastructure, and rapid industrialization and urbanization. Two world wars and a deep, prolonged depression might suggest that the approaching century did not belong to Canada in just the manner Laurier had envisioned, but Mackintosh would later describe it, in typically Canadian terms, as a period of "vigorous survival."[3]

If Mackintosh's timing was right, his sense of place may have been less than ideal. Madoc was an attractive enough town of about a thousand people, but never achieved the economic aspirations of its founding families. Located in Hastings County, on the southern edge of the Laurentian Shield, its farmland was of marginal fertility and its gold and iron-ore deposits produced only fitful mining ventures with far more busts than booms. Hopes of becoming a regional centre in the 1850s had rested on the construction of the Hastings Colonization Road, "the last pioneer trek in Old Ontario."[4] Extending north from Madoc for over a hundred miles, nearly to the edge of present-day Algonquin Park, it was designed to open up the interior to settlement. But as Mackintosh would write in 1926: "For a period of seventy-five years the attempt of agriculture to move into the Laurentian country of Ontario has failed wretchedly, with lamentable social costs."[5] Only its stands of white pine provided any form of livelihood: when the timber trade spilled out of the Ottawa Valley in the latter part of the nineteenth century, logs were harvested by teams of lumberjacks and driven down the Moira River to the sawmills of Belleville, and lumber was shipped from there to the United States. Local farmers depended upon the sale of potatoes, oats, and cheese to the lumber camps, but when this trade collapsed during the Depression of 1873, "the settlers found themselves stranded and marketless." What remained of Madoc's ambitions was finally dashed when the town was bypassed by the Ottawa–Toronto line of the Canadian Pacific Railway in 1880, dooming it to remain part of the "back country" of Belleville.[6]

Mackintosh would quip that he was the only person born in Madoc to have escaped.[7] There were, however, at least two other prominent people exported from Madoc Township, albeit each of rather dubious distinction. Perhaps Mackintosh's success helped to expunge the town's memories of Allan Roy Dafoe, the attending doctor at the birth of the Dionne quintuplets (and a participant in their subsequent exploitation), or of Thomas Scott, famous only for being shot, executed during the Red River resistance of 1869–70.

This sense of place would play an important part in his later writings. The Laurentian Shield as an imposing barrier to economic development and Canada as a country created "in defiance of geography" were contentions he drew, at least in part, from personal experience. At the same time, the hardships of pioneer life and the ingenuity displayed in the effort to adopt institutions designed to overcome the geographical setting, played a prominent role in his perception of Canada's rise to nationhood.

"A HOME WHERE INTELLECTUAL LIFE WAS HONOURED"[8]

W.A. Mackintosh was the youngest child of William Mackintosh, Sr, and Agnes Cowie, both of Scottish descent. His father's family, of Highland stock, traced its roots back through several generations to Lachlan Morrison McIntosh, the sixteenth chief of the clan. By the early nineteenth century, William McIntosh (W.A.'s grandfather), was residing in the working-class district of Gorbals on the south bank of the River Clyde in Glasgow, and from there he departed with his wife, Mary McNeil, for Montreal in 1839. William Mackintosh, Sr, was born there five years later. Agnes Cowie's parents, John and Helen, had sailed from Leith to Montreal in April 1833, and then travelled by Durham boat to Toronto. Three years later they settled on a farm in the Kirkwall area of Beverly Township, Wentworth County, Ontario.[9] William and Agnes met while he was the school inspector for North Hastings and she the first teacher in the Madoc model school. They were married in 1879 – when he was thirty-five and she twenty-two years of age – and in the same year built the family home at 213 St Lawrence Street East, a handsome two-and-a-half stories of red brick in the "Ontario Classic" style. They had eight children: twin brothers William McNeil and James Cowie (1880), Mary Elizabeth (1883), Helen (1885), Jean (1888), Margaret (1890), Agnes (1892), and William Archibald (1895). The death of William McNeil at the age of two, in 1882, explains why W.A. Mackintosh carried the time-honoured paternal family name for the first-born son.[10]

William Mackintosh, Sr, was a man of significant accomplishment. Stricken by polio in his youth, he was undeterred from embarking on a teaching career when he was eighteen. After one year educating the youth of Thorah Township, he obtained his first-class certificate at the Toronto Normal School and then taught for a further nine years in Thorah Township, Brock Township, Mariposa, Baltimore Village (Northumberland County), and Campbellville. He then obtained his inspector's certificate and was appointed inspector of public schools for the northern part of Hastings County, a position he held for over forty-one years. In all, he spent fifty-one years working in the Ontario public school system, retiring at the age of seventy-one in 1915.[11]

Travelling by horse and buggy, or horse and cutter in the winter, he was a prominent figure in the region. One student recalls the "scary visits" of the school inspector: "Mr. Mackintosh was a lame man but could go faster on crutches than anyone I ever saw. It is said he could go quicker than a horse could trot. I remember at the old red School when Mr. Mackintosh would visit the school, the door would be open and with just four leaps on his crutches he would be on the platform. He would tell two boys to take his horse." Curiously, he had poor penmanship. "One time he wrote about something to one of the teachers, but she could not read the letter. She kept it, after she had showed it to the trustees who weren't able to read it either, for the school inspector's next visit. When he arrived some months later and looked at the letter he could not read it either and he had forgotten what he had written. During his inspectorate he brought the schools under his charge up to efficiency until they were second to none."[12]

George Newcombe Gordon, a lawyer who served one term as the member of parliament for Peterborough West and was briefly the minister of immigration in the King government, recalls the elder Mackintosh's rather stern treatment of individuals who displayed only a passing attachment to the teaching profession. While working in Toronto, Gordon contracted typhoid and, upon his physician's advice, decided to attend a model school as a form of rest. He later described to W.A. Mackintosh the encouragement he received in abandoning teaching: "Your father, apparently, was rather curious to know why I had come all the way from Toronto to Madoc and one day, collared me, and with true Scotch canniness, asked me if I intended to stay in the teaching profession. Naturally, this forced a statement from me that I had no such intention, but was enjoying the Model School training during a period of convalescence ... Your father made the rather unflattering remark to me that he thought it was probably the best thing for me, from which I took it he meant not to remain in the Teaching profession, but afterwards to go into law."[13]

Being the school inspector in a newly settled region of the province was no simple task. He was responsible for overseeing more than a hundred schools, many in remote areas, where it was difficult to recruit qualified teachers. In the district of Dungannon and Faraday, for instance, he reported to the Department of Education in 1888 that: "I do not know of a single qualified teacher without a situation excepting two or three who have graduated recently from Normal School and will not take such a school as the one referred to. It is, at least, 75 miles north of Madoc, away from any leading road, and is poor in every way … [I]t will, for years, be difficult to get any teachers but those accustomed to life in the more recently settled and poorer districts. In such Sections the boarding places are very uncomfortable. Nothing short of necessity will induce a young girl from the more favourable districts to take such a school."[14] He had only admiration for the commitment to education in poor and remote northern townships of the county. One inspection tour in 1875 took him 125 miles over water and road to Bangor Township, to visit a new school housing sixteen pupils. His recorded observations bear a striking resemblance in style to his son's later writing, conveying a precise description, an appreciation for the pioneering spirit of the local settlers, and the inability to resist a wry comment at the end. "With the exception of the door, window sashes and teacher's desk, the whole owes its construction to the chopping and broad axe. Floor, benches, and desks are made of planks hewn from logs. The interior I found scrupulously clean and ornamented with spruce branches. The windows, not extensive affairs, were provided with curtains formed from newspapers – which in every part of the province is a certain indication of a lady teacher … Much of its success is due to the perseverance and intelligence of a few of the settlers. Mr. Whalen, the tavernkeeper, never loses a fitting opportunity for pressing the claims of the school upon his guests."[15]

Among the sixteen students who benefited from the tavern keeper's initiative was the nine-year-old John Wesley Dafoe. The legendary editor of the *Winnipeg Free Press* still had a vivid recollection of the school inspector's visit some sixty years later: "I can see him yet, a brisk eager valiant man hopping into the school room on his crutches and putting us through our paces. That he … made a lifelong impression on a youngster is testimony to his personality."[16] W.A. Mackintosh would consistently claim his links to Dafoe, and describe him in terms befitting his North Hastings origins: "Dafoe looked like a pioneer – big, untidy and oblivious of it … But Dafoe never posed as the rugged pioneer; he never posed as anything; his mind was wholly on the matter at hand. It was another of his qualities that, ardent protagonist though he was, he had respect for the realities of experience. He had his visions, but his feet never left his native earth."[17] This esteem for the enterprise of individuals struggling to make a living, and his disdain for pretentiousness, were to endure throughout his life.

His father interpreted his duty as school inspector as being to oversee the moral and intellectual training of students for "preparation for citizenship and for the duties and responsibilities of life." This required teachers to impart not only the "mechanical virtues, punctuality, regularity, obedience," and the "practice of the great duties of self-control, of temperance, of restraining the passions, of ruling the spirit," but, more importantly, the "social duties of honesty, truthfulness, justice, fidelity to trust, courage, honor, magnanimity, toleration, sympathy, and charity, the sacred obligations of citizenship." Accordingly, he placed greater importance of having "the law of veracity lodged in a boy's mind, than to teach him how to factor algebraic expressions, how to solve arithmetic conundrums ... To train children to be truthful, honest and trustworthy is of far more importance than to make them brilliant scholars or even successful money makers."[18]

Accomplishing these objectives was hindered by the poor quality of teachers. He spread the blame for this among the department of education, local trustees, and parents and teachers alike. The department of education placed too much emphasis on training teachers to impart bits of information and facts, and not enough time developing their faculties for critical and independent thought. Trustees in some sections took too little care in the selection of teachers, "far less than is deemed necessary for the selection of a cheese maker or a farm laborer. The manner in which the children of some sections are sacrificed would dishearten any one." Teachers and parents were faulted for too little concern for the formation of character and intellectual development in favour of the results of written examinations "as an indication of educational progress." The problem was further compounded by the difficulty in retaining teachers for more than four or five years, such that the relatively youthful body of teachers lacked the maturity of character and experience to be "efficient."[19]

The commitment of William Mackintosh, Sr, to educational reform led him to play a formative role in the Ontario Teachers' Association. In 1890 he became the association's president – a position formerly held by the likes of Egerton Ryerson and Goldwin Smith – and in his presidential address he credited the association with fostering the most important improvements in provincial school laws and regulations. He advocated a more practical curriculum, but was generally opposed to legislative efforts that encroached upon local decision making.[20] Despite his personal preference for more direct Biblical teachings in the schools, for instance, he was against legislation to introduce religious instruction in favour of promoting a secular notion of "the rarer and more precious virtues of veracity and purity of thought." The solution was to educate the public as to its correct sense of duty, rather than introduce legal intervention. "That legislation, the making of laws by Parliament, is the sovereign panacea for all the ills which affect the body politic is one of the superstitions of the Anglo-Saxon race. We cry aloud to the legislative power to remedy evils that can, at times, be cured without his aid." More importantly, he saw the association as providing an intellectual forum that, among other things, encouraged teachers "to look upon themselves as members of a great brotherhood engaged in a most ennobling and patriotic (if poorly paid) vocation."[21]

The longevity of his career is testimony enough to his worthiness for the position. School inspectorships were not above (or below) considerations of political patronage, and his steadfast support for the Liberal Party meant that his uninterrupted tenure did not go unnoticed. So commented George Ross in 1905, a week after his defeat as premier of Ontario. A former school inspector himself, he wrote to his former colleague: "How you have lived so long in that Tory riding and kept your standing is a mystery which, if you had explained it to me, might have assisted me in keeping my standing in the face of the great onslaught of last week. However, a government must go under some time, and I have only to accept what I first anticipated when I became Premier. I know I have had the support of the best educationalists of the Province and particularly my old comrades in the inspectorate."[22]

"A PROPER SCOTTISH FOUNDATION"

The emphasis on moral training – a shared responsibility of family, church, and school – also dominated W.A. Mackintosh's early childhood. His mother was a devote Christian and his father an elder in Madoc's St Peter's Presbyterian Church. Both sons and daughters were imbued with a strong sense of the importance of moral and intellectual development. Among the girls, Margaret would note that a "woman's capacity was never looked down upon."[23] Three daughters attended Queen's University, with which they maintained a lifelong allegiance.[24] Helen completed her senior matriculation year at Galt Collegiate Institute, received her MA from Queen's in 1906, and then completed two years of postgraduate work at the Sorbonne. She returned to Queen's in 1919 to obtain her high-school teaching certificate and taught for several years at Humberside Collegiate in Toronto before being appointed as the editor of *Glad Tidings*, the journal of the Women's Missionary Society of the Presbyterian Church of Canada.[25] Agnes, the youngest daughter, completed high school in Madoc, entered Queen's in the same year as her younger brother, and left four years later with the gold medal in German. She also became a high-school teacher. Margaret would finish her secondary schooling in Belleville, where she earned an entrance scholarship to Queen's in mathematics. She graduated in 1912 with an honours degree in history and English. When she opted for a career in government, she did so against the advice of her father, who warned that she would spend the rest of her life "kicking against the pricks." She would assume a prominent role in Canada's department of labour, where she was acknowledged as Canada's leading authority on labour and industrial-relations legislation and, if not for her gender, likely would have become deputy minister.[26]

There were, however, subtle differences in the expectations placed on the sons. While the local university was deemed suitable for the girls, the boys were expected to attend the more prestigious University of Toronto. John Cowie Mackintosh was sent from Madoc to Owen Sound Collegiate Institute – one of the prized public schools in the period – where he completed his matriculation year and earned the Prince of Wales Scholarship for entrance into the University of Toronto. He enrolled in 1898, as a student of University College, where he was to win the Edward Blake Scholarship in Chemistry and Mineralogy. His yearbook entry suggests that although a "man of science ... when he gets his pipe lit is ready to talk on any subject from politics to theology."[27] Graduating in 1902, he pursued a career as an industrial mineralogist in northern Ontario before dying of typhoid fever in 1910.

W.A. Mackintosh was expected to follow his brother to the University of Toronto. His early education was in the local public schools; he began public school at age seven and when he was twelve entered Madoc High School, which boasted four rooms and an auditorium in the attic.[28] As one of his classmates would recollect, "our little group of five banded together for self-protection in the Madoc High School (Jessie, Bunnie, Ted – and the two Bills)."[29] The other Bill was William Dafoe, who became, like his father, a physician. There is no record of what happened to Jessie, Bunnie, or Ted, but even without their contribution, the two Bills constituted a graduating class of some accomplishment, perhaps because they posed such a formidable group. As a former "fourth former" wrote to Mackintosh fifty years later, "Do you remember Jack Nayler and Bill Dafoe who with yourself and some other very young First-Formers comprised the 'Pee-Wee Gang'? Woe to anyone who laid a finger on any one of you!"[30]

Mackintosh's youth was not restricted to the dour pursuit of moral and intellectual training that might be implied by being raised by the local school inspector and devout parents. Tending to the horses was his family responsibility, but one which he took to with some zeal. He was also an ardent fisherman. When he returned to Madoc for a testimonial dinner in 1963, he spoke fondly of Henry Mitchell, an aboriginal man living in a one-room cabin on Moira Lake, who would take Mackintosh and other young boys fishing.[31]

In preparation for university, Mackintosh was dispatched to St Andrew's College in September 1911 for his final year of high school. St Andrew's, formed as a "haphazard adventure" of several prominent Scotch Presbyterians, is described as the "last [Canadian private] school to be founded during the era of Christian gentility." Built in 1899 in the Toronto suburb of Rosedale, it quickly ascended into the ranks of the "Big Little Four," joining Upper Canada College ("so large, so near, and so snooty"), Bishop Ridley College, and Trinity College among the more prestigious boys' schools in Ontario. In short order, St Andrew's became "a strong contender in the education of the sons of Canada's Establishment families."[32] It was of sufficient repute to gain the patronage of both halves of the Massey–Harris merger, with Vincent Massey and Lauren Harris counted among its most celebrated graduates during the first ten years of its existence.

The school – from its curriculum, its emphasis on rugby, cricket, and other sports as a means of building character, its integration of morning prayers into the daily routine, its prefect system, and even its kilted cadet corps – was based on the British public school model. Inheriting some of the obligations of the church, it defined its mandate in terms similar to those defined by William Mackintosh, Sr: its duty was not just to educate but to "maintain the moral and religious culture of a Christian home, to promote manliness, integrity, and a high sense of honour and truthfulness, and to inspire boys with a generous respect for all that is sacred."[33]

One can speculate on why his parents chose to send him there. The family could certainly afford private-school tuition. Despite the modest salary of a public school inspector – the elder Mackintosh's pay rose steadily from $445 in 1875 to nearly $900 by 1912 – inherited wealth and a penchant for shrewd financial investment left the family with abundant resources.[34] However, for a public school inspector of important social standing within the educational community to send his youngest son to a Toronto private school seems, on the face of it, to be an unlikely choice. Three reasons are suggested for choosing a private school in this era: to attend a denominational school, to obtain a higher quality of education, or to join the social elite.[35] If these motivations indeed applied in this case, then his father was surely disappointed on at least two of three counts. Whether because of his experience at St Andrew's or for other reasons, Mackintosh retained a strong sense of moral commitment but escaped established religious conventions in favour of agnosticism. Moreover, he continued to carry with him a deep and abiding animosity towards pretence and snobbery, especially British, and did not acquire the same "private-school gloss" that Graham Towers, one class behind at St Andrew's, did.[36]

For whatever reason he was dispatched to St Andrew's, his stay was brief and its impression upon him scant. Upon agreeing to serve on the college's advisory committee some forty-three years later, he confessed that, "if I have any place on the records it is probably only because of a severe case of Scarlet Fever which constituted an achievement in itself." In February 1912, he was placed in quarantine for six weeks and left the college.[37] He returned to Madoc for "private tuition in home"[38] and, contrary to his father's wishes, announced that he would not attend the University of Toronto. What his father failed to appreciate is that, as Frank Knox would later observe, W.A. Mackintosh had chosen to be born in Queen's country.[39]

2

Queen's Undergraduate: Kingston, Wiwa Hills, and Indian Head, 1912–1916

His all round training, genial, yet serious disposition, and firmness of purpose, bespeaks for him a career that shall be "worth while."

Queen's *Year Book*, entry on W.A. Mackintosh, 1916[1]

Queen's University in the latter-nineteenth and early twentieth centuries is often depicted in idyllic terms that dwell on the simplicity of everyday life. If Canada was part of a "well-ordered, static world," largely untouched by the advent of the automobile, radio, and telephone, life in Kingston was particularly serene because of its small population and relative isolation from major urban centres. Four passenger trains passing between Toronto and Montreal each day stopped in Kingston, but a one-way trip between the two larger cities took twelve hours to complete. As it was unusual for students to leave the city during the academic term, life at Queen's was "more its own."[2] In the absence of dormitories, fraternities, or dining halls, students resided in boarding houses, where most meals were taken. Otherwise, "town-gown" relations were limited, save for the regular trips to one of the many laundries run primarily by Canadian-Chinese families[3] and the occasional boisterous night on Princess Street. Every other aspect of student life – academic, as well as athletic and social – centred on the university, where Queen's sought to "train her sons and daughters to be polite members of society." During the day men were expected to be neatly dressed – "stand up collars, stiff cuffs, high-button coats, laced boots" – and women "covered from neck to heel in 'blouse and skirt.'" For the frequent dances in Grant Hall, consisting of waltzes and two steps, men were attired in boiled shirts and tail coats, and arrived by horse-drawn cab.[4]

However romanticized this portrait of the halcyon days of the Queen's undergraduate, two significant events in the early twentieth century would disrupt it. First, students in this period were children of the wheat boom, and the transformation wrought by the rapid pace of settlement on the Canadian prairies reverberated throughout the country, Kingston being no exception. Located at the junction of the St Lawrence River and Lake Ontario, much of the city's raison d'etre had been as a shipping entrepôt, with the grain elevators of Richardson's Company dominating its waterfront. Western expansion would transform both the national economy and Kingston's place in it. Second, World War I brought a dramatic change in outlook. This was especially the case for male university students who were immediately forced to confront their sense of obligation to the country and the British Empire, a consideration that was not merely an intellectual exercise but involved the profound decision of whether to enlist for active duty. With the Canadian Officers Training Corps conducting regular drills and buildings transformed into makeshift hospitals, university campuses offered no escape from the reality of the war.

Both of these changes encroached upon Mackintosh's life during his undergraduate days. The dynamic nature of the prairie economy – with its pioneering spirit and experimentation with new economic institutions – immediately captured his imagination. In his later writings, he would often speak of the lure of the St Lawrence in drawing men to the West at various points in history. In his own case, the call of the prairies took the form of a stint as a summer-school teacher in rural Saskatchewan, a first-hand experience that would influence his thinking throughout the rest of his life. More demanding, on a personal level, was the need to make sense out of World War I. Nineteen years old when Canada became a combatant, he was of prime age for enlisting. Whether to do so was not an easy decision, and he would weigh a deep sense of duty as a citizen against his growing conviction that the war was an unjust one.

O.D. Skelton played a guiding role as Mackintosh grappled with these changes. It is easy to exaggerate the influence that a professor exercises over a student, but not in this case. Skelton's commitment to the importance of education and public service resonated with

Mackintosh's own upbringing in Madoc, and he would seek to emulate Skelton's application of balanced judgment and reasoned argument to understand the changing nature of the world. It was under Skelton's tutelage that he would not only gain the intellectual background and outlook that he brought to bear on world affairs, but also come to grips with changing international events at a personal level. The outcome of Mackintosh's reflections on these events was articulated in his curious, yet nonetheless provocative, honours thesis in political economy, "The Social and Political Teachings of Count Leo Tolstoy." The writings of Tolstoy served as a useful vehicle for commenting on both the Canadian prairies and the war. Mackintosh's thesis would not only strengthen his admiration for the pioneering spirit of western farmers, but furthered his conviction that Canada should play no role in World War I.

STUDENT LIFE

In 1912, Queen's had some fifteen hundred students in the faculties of Arts, Applied Sciences, Engineering, and Medicine.[5] Begun as a Presbyterian college in 1841, it had just relinquished its formal denominational ties and established a national presence seeking to rival Toronto and McGill in reputation. Most of the students were drawn from the immediate vicinity of eastern Ontario, with roughly a third coming from Toronto and parts further west.[6]

The fall term ran from the beginning of October until the middle of December, and the winter term from the beginning of January until the end of April. Classes were held Monday through Friday, predominately in the morning, leaving the afternoon free for study in the library or for participation in the many campus activities. There were clubs for music, drama, and debating, and intramural and intercollegiate clubs and competitions in a host of sports (rugby, football, hockey, basketball, tennis, shooting, cross-country running, and assault-at-arms). In addition to the students' Alma Mater Society, each faculty had a student society, staging frequent lectures and social evenings. Campus life was largely organized around a student's graduating class (by faculty and year), which held regular meetings that would typically dispense a few formal deliberations, follow with a talk from the faculty member serving as honorary class president, and end with a musical soloist, oration, and poetry reading. In addition, the Levana Society organized events for women, and, for those so inclined, there were the Missionary Society and the YMCA/YWCA.

Mackintosh was seventeen years old when he entered Queen's, sporting "a very boyish look, a ruddy complexion, and a quiet, almost shy manner."[7] He described himself as a "diffident and coltish student," but engaged in every aspect of student life. Taking up residence in a boarding house (the first year at the corner of Mack and Alfred streets, his second year on Johnson Street west of Albert Street, and later on University Avenue), he was a charter member of the "Eat-a-Pie" group of students that also included John McNab, future editor of the *Presbyterian Record* in Toronto. His name first appears on the pages of the student *Journal* during his sophomore year, when he was elected a "constable" in the Arts Concursus. Later in the year he helped organize the Arts '16 skating party, worked on the yearbook executive, and was recording secretary for the YMCA and assistant editor of the *Journal*. In his final year, he was elected class president for Arts '16, beating out Watson Kirkconnell, future president of Acadia University. This was likely the only graduating class in a Canadian university to boast two future university heads.[8]

For a man who later in life showed little interest in sports – he would decline invitations to play golf on the grounds that he had "misplaced his clubs" – he demonstrated a great zeal for and competence in athletics. With each class in the Arts, Science, and Medical faculties expected to field intramural squads in a variety of men's and women's sports, all hands were on deck. Mackintosh played his part as goalie on the Arts '16 soccer team and as a member of its rugby team, but he found his true calling as a fencer, and served as vice-president of the Boxing, Wrestling, and Fencing Club. His stirring 5–4 victory ensured Arts the 1913–14 interfaculty Assault-on-Arms Championship and, a year later, he was the university fencing champion. "McIntosh [*sic*] has improved wonderfully as a fencer," reported the *Journal*. "He has no nerves at all."[9] He would earn his Queen's "Q" as a member of the intercollegiate Assault-on-Arms team in 1915 and even ran, unsuccessfully, for election as "Athletic Stick" in his senior year.[10] In 1915, he helped to organize an Assault-on-Arms exhibition as a fundraiser for the Dr Ross Horse Ambulance. The evening included boxing and fencing exhibitions and the somewhat dubious Tremblay-versus-Herman match for the wrestling lightweight championship of the world. As the *Journal* reported on the event, "Herman has long been looking for Tremblay's scalp …

Herman wrestled barefoot, and is truly a Wildman on the mat – one worse than the famous Cazeaux. His chief expression was 'I don't care,' which he repeated upon each case of warning for hairpulling, strangling, and jumping with both feet on Tremblay's back."[11]

Fun and games aside, the primary reason for being in Kingston was to gain a formal education. After passing his senior matriculation examinations, Mackintosh had been granted standing in Junior Latin and English history. He then embarked on the four-year, twenty-course program towards an honours BA. With the exception of one course in mathematics and one in philosophy (the first term taught by John Watson), his undergraduate education was restricted to languages, history, and political economy. He completed two pass courses in each of French, English and Greek, and one in Latin (in which W.C. Clark was his tutor). His grades were generally good, although Greek did not appear to agree with him (he achieved a woeful ranking of second last out of twelve students in Senior Greek). He also took one pass and two honours courses in history; a pass course in each of economics and politics; and two honours courses in political economy. In terms of full-course equivalence, then, his specialist training amounted to five courses in history and six in political economy (where honours courses were equivalent to two pass courses). Needless to say, Mackintosh excelled in both honours fields, claiming the prize in honours history in his third year, and in political economy in his final year.

History, rather than political economy, was his first choice upon arrival at Queen's. The department was the domain of W.L. Grant, Douglas Professor of Canadian and Colonial History, and John Lyle Morison. Grant, son of the former principal and father of George Parkin Grant, was a noted and prolific scholar in his own right. He would leave Queen's to become principal of Upper Canada College after his service in World War I. Mackintosh acknowledged Grant's "discerning kindness which set many of us decisively on our way,"[12] however, he expressed a greater affection for Morison, a graduate of Glasgow University who taught at Queen's from 1907 to 1922 before returning to Scotland. He was a prominent figure on campus, offering regular Sunday-morning bible classes and frequent campus talks. He was a true iconoclast, and the *Queen's Journal* reported its appreciation for his "breezy candour and independence," which challenged students, but expressed reservations about some of his more unconventional views. When he spoke against co-education,

Table 2:1 W.A. Mackintosh's Undergraduate Record

Year	*Course*	*Grade*	*Instructor*	*Topic*
1912–13	Jr French	78		
	Sr Latin	70		
	Jr Mathematics	79		
	Jr English	72		
	European History	69	Morison	The Renaissance and Reformation
1913–14	Sr French	54		
	Sr English	63		
	Politics	66	Skelton	Comparative National Government; History of Political Theory
	Prelim. Honour History	80	Morison; Grant	Whig and French Revolutions (Morison); British Colonial Policy, 1783–1900 (Grant)
Summer 1914	Jr Greek	60 – "not to count"		
	Prep Greek	50		
1914–15	Economics	83	Skelton; Swanson	Principles of Economic Theory; Economic Geography
	Prelimin. Honours Political Science	77	Skelton; Swanson	Canadian Constitutional Law; Social and Charitable Work; Money and Banking; Corporation Finance
	Final Honours History	85	Morison; Grant	Some Problems in Sixteenth and Seventeenth Century History; Nineteenth Century Canadian History
1915–16	Sr Greek	42		
	Jr Philosophy	61	Watson; Symons	History of Modern Philosophy; Lectures on Psychology and Logic
	Final Honours Political Science	86	Skelton; Swanson	Commercial Law, 1st term (Skelton) Russia: Its Political and Economic Problems. 2nd term. Swanson. Economic Theory … from John Stuart Mill to the present.

Note: The "Determination of Standing" was for Pass Courses: Division 1 (70+), Division 2 (55–69) and Division 3 (40–54); for Honours Courses, Class I (75+), Class II (66–74) and Class III (50–65).

Source: Queen's College and University, *Calendar*, 1912–16; QUA, Mackintosh Transcript.

favouring instead to limit the teaching of women to music and the arts, the *Journal* confessed that, at times, "he seems to us almost Shavian in his lack of balanced judgment and of tact."[13] Mackintosh found him to be "an extraordinarily good lecturer," who showed a keen interest in his students, but also acknowledged that he was "sometimes erratic." One senses that Morison's intellectual influence was overshadowed by the eccentricities of this Scotsman, who, noted for "his prowess as a walker," cut a striking figure "striding along in his tweed hat and flying cape." Later in life, Mackintosh would take the opportunity to visit his old professor in Scotland: "I walked with him in the early morning along Hadrian's Wall with the mist which might have concealed the Picts and Scots driving across the hills."[14]

Mackintosh's prowess in history allowed him to obtain his first taste of intellectual life in Ottawa. Under a program created by the Public Archives of Canada, he received a scholarship of $50 a month to spend part of the summer of 1915 conducting research on a topic of his choice – "Political and Constitutional Growth Under Bagot" – under the guidance of the archives staff.[15] Housed on Sussex Avenue, the archives was an intellectual hub for a generation of young scholars, primarily in history but also in the social sciences.[16] He took advantage of his time in Ottawa to hear Borden and Laurier in the House of Commons, to enjoy the company of his sister, Margaret, and to experience the tutelage of James Bonar.

A renowned British scholar, Bonar gave up an academic career to join the British civil service and eventually become the first master of the Ottawa branch of the Royal Mint in 1907. He was one of Adam Smith's most ardent admirers ("Smith should be read and read hard"), and Mackintosh relished the opportunity to discuss with him the virtues of the *Wealth of Nations*. As Mackintosh would later write: "There are few men who in their later years produce such pleasant works of graceful scholarship as come from the pen of the former Deputy Master of the Royal Mint at Ottawa, Dr. James Bonar. A philosopher and an economist of wide repute."[17]

It was Skelton, however, who came to dominate Mackintosh's undergraduate life. With Adam Shortt's departure for the Civil Service Commission in 1908, Skelton assumed the John A. Macdonald Chair and, with it, responsibility for the department of political and economic science. The department had a major presence in the university, with some 180 majors and an enrolment of over 300 full-course-equivalent students.[18] Barry Ferguson makes the compelling case that Shortt's objective was to create a department at Queen's that would further the development of a liberal democratic tradition in Canada.[19] This entailed cultivating the skills of social scientists who, through their research and/or direct involvement in government work, could contribute to the shaping of rational government policy. Both expertise and the accumulation of knowledge were necessary to understand the nature of capitalist institutions and how they might be reformed to allow for greater equality and the full participation of citizens. What differentiated political economy at Queen's from the subject at the larger universities of Toronto and McGill was its interest in current Canadian economic and political issues and the freshness of thought that came from relying more on home-grown faculty than on imported academics from Britain.[20] As Mackintosh later observed, "The bearded James Mavor at Toronto found a congenial and safe field of study, not disturbing to the local Establishment, in pre-revolutionary Russia. At McGill, Stephen Leacock turned his infectious humour on the innocents of Orillia and left the vast comic resources of St. James Street and Westmount untouched."[21]

If Skelton inherited this tradition from Shortt, he did so, according to Mackintosh, "in ways more adapted to his own talents."[22] This was a polite way of saying that Skelton elevated the study of political economy at Queen's to new heights. Despite Shortt's "profound knowledge of the detail of Canadian history, he had little capacity to digest or to mark out essential lines of development." In contrast, Skelton added to his remarkable breadth of knowledge the "amazing powers of synthesis and balanced judgment," and a pen that "ran swiftly and with a craftsman's sure precision."[23] Indeed, it was Innis's impression that Skelton had a greater influence on Shortt than vice versa.[24] A true renaissance figure who only turned to the study of political economy after undergraduate and graduate studies in Greek and Latin, he brought to bear an extraordinary range of thought to the study of Canadian economic and political issues. His closest friend from his undergraduate days, J.F. MacDonald, who spent seventeen years teaching English at Queen's before moving to the University of Toronto, emphasized how Skelton's love of literature informed his political thought: "His liberalism was based not merely on Veblen and John Stuart Mill but more deeply on Carlyle and Arnold and the great Greeks. The talks with him I remember best of past years were two or three in which he lamented that he had so little time for Sophocles and the haunting lyrics in Euripides which touched the depths of aspiration and sorrow."[25]

Skelton was thirty-five in 1913 and was in the early stages of his most prolific academic period. One senses in Mackintosh's description of him a mixture of awe and admiration for a man who epitomized the scholar. "A vagrant lock of his rather colourless hair was likely to slide forward over his prominent forehead. His heavy long eyebrows protruded inquiringly over his thick-lensed eye-glasses. His mouth was sensitive and mobile, now pursuing in considered judgment, now diffidently smiling as his own comic paraphrase of a well-known quotation, or encouragingly at an inarticulate student."[26] Comfortable in the knowledge that his reputation as a scholar could secure him other academic appointments, Skelton refused to be intimidated by efforts to constrain his academic freedom, despite occasional "heresy hunting" among the trustees. Here was the Ontario Orangeman who worked through a clearly reasoned argument to arrive at his support for bilingual schools, and who would later publicly criticize the "blundering and disastrous fashion" in which conscription was imposed, particularly in Quebec, where the unwillingness to allow a voluntary system to work was "a most unpardonable piece of Prussianism."[27]

Mackintosh conceded that Skelton had "comparatively few of the accepted pedagogical arts" as a lecturer or in leading classroom discussion. Instead, his students learned by a "sort of contagion. The stimulus came from being able to follow the workings of a master-mind." He served as an "authoritative guide" on issues such as constitutional law, public finance, and income distribution, but as a "fellow explorer" when working through various strands of contemporary political thought. He was drawn to thinkers with "radical but rational points of view … Hobhouse, Graham Wallas, Veblen, H.N. Brailsford, Walter Lippmann, and Wells were turning up new points of view and he shared with his students the excitement of them." This was combined with a respect for his students. "He had as a great asset in his teaching a most generous, optimistic belief in the capacity of young people. Occasionally, it led him into errors of judgment, but what was more important, it was a tremendous stimulus to many to stretch their slender powers to the limit. More than anyone at the University in my time, he really shaped students' minds. Others entertained, and stimulated, but he, in any number of cases, left his students with a particular way of thinking and judging which was peculiarly his own."[28]

A specific tool that students were expected to acquire was polished writing. Mackintosh presumably arrived well-equipped, given his father's influence, but the required language courses, coupled with the emphasis on writing in other disciplines, certainly strengthened whatever capacity he already possessed. A common practice was for students to rewrite their lecture notes in prose form, and Mackintosh's surviving notes for his final honours history course (Development of Modern European Nations) reads like a short, dense textbook.[29] Exercises of this nature contributed to the development of terse, effective writing and, again, it was Skelton who led by example.

From Skelton, then, Mackintosh came to prize the virtue of intellectual honesty, the importance of research, exploring views from a wide range of sources, incisive writing, and public service. He was not alone in holding Skelton in high esteem. For Clifford Clark, who preceded Mackintosh as an undergraduate at Queen's and as a graduate student at Harvard before taking up an appointment at Queen's in 1916: "He was my teacher, colleague, guide, philosopher and friend, and no one could match him in any of these capacities. He was responsible for practically every major turning point in my life and at all times he was my ideal and my inspiration ... the affection which I had for him was that of a son for a father." Bryce Stewart, a Queen's undergraduate who completed his graduate work at Columbia in 1914, wrote in similar terms: "At Queen's for four years I attended Oscar Skelton's classes. He made one over from a callow sentimental youth into a person with some understanding of the seriousness of life. He gave one the will to work for the common good and most of such equipment as I have for the task came from him." For Frank Knox, he was "a major factor in shaping my life."[30] Skelton's influence also extended to the students of other universities, especially Jacob Viner: "While I met Skelton for the first time in 1939, he had been my examiner (external) during my last year at McGill and in consequence thereof I had some correspondence with him at that time (1914) of so generous a nature on his side that I have always had a feeling of admiration for him."[31] Many years later, Mackintosh would simply state that "whatever I have of balance, detachment, and tolerance, I owe in large measure to O.D. Skelton."[32]

WORLD WAR I

The declaration of war had an immediate impact on daily life at Queen's. The Canadian Officers Training Corps (COTC) organized military training, the Engineers Corps was formed and sent a battalion overseas, while medical students were recruited to serve in the 5th Canadian Stationary Hospital which served in Egypt and France. Women were engaged in Red Cross work, while Grant Hall and Kingston Hall were later converted into military hospitals. Even so, Principal Gordon took to the pages of the *Queen's Journal* to question why students were so slow to volunteer for military training on campus. He indicated that the senate was preparing to grant credit for COTC training and reminded students that Canada was a member of the British Empire and that the war was "a fight for freedom ... for righteousness; for national existence."[33] A month later, students convened a mass meeting in Grant Hall to discuss the war and their apparent apathy towards drilling. An editorial in the *Journal* reminded Principal Gordon that a good proportion of students had participated in training, others sought to postpone training until classes were over, and that "to others it is a plain duty to remain at home and it would be simply mock heroism to sign for drilling." Many students objected to the decision about participation in training being taken out of their hands; nonetheless, within a year of the outbreak of the war, it was reported that four in ten undergraduate men at Queen's were in uniform, most to eventually serve overseas.[34] Mackintosh would not be among them.

The national debate over Canada's responsibility to the Empire played out in public lectures at Queen's with Grant and Skelton, despite being close friends, as the principal antagonists. Prior to the war, Grant spoke to the Political Science Club on the "Fallacy of Nationalism" and chided Skelton for having a book by J.S. Ewart ("the great apostle of nationalism") on his reading list.[35] Grant was one of the foremost proponents of closer Canadian links with the British Empire, which he justified on several grounds, including its role in ameliorating French–English conflict within Canada and the spectre of Canada's collapse and its annexation to the United States, and as a means of curbing the materialism of North America. More important were the superior moral virtues of the Anglo-Saxon world and, insofar as the war was concerned, it was necessary to demonstrate the will to assert its leadership role. In explaining "why we must fight to the finish," he argued that, "We must indicate our own character as a fighting race, and show the whole world, not Germany alone, that the British Empire is a factor to be reckoned with on land as well as at sea. The recognition of this will go far to secure peace throughout the world."[36] Grant, like Morison, was a man of conviction. Both would enlist and see active service in the war, Morison as a lieutenant with the British Expeditionary Force and Grant (at the age of forty-two) as a captain and then major in the Canadian Expeditionary Force's 59th Battalion.

For his part, Skelton argued against blindly following imperial policy in favour of an independent Canadian foreign policy.[37] He held that imperial relations were largely economically motivated and shared Shortt's view that Canada should not be content to be merely the supplier of foodstuffs to the Empire.[38] Thus, while Grant was convening the Home Missions Committee and lecturing to the OTC on military strategy, Shortt addressed the Political Science Club to explain why many economists had thought that war was unlikely because of the degree of economic integration, and Skelton spoke on the "Economic Factors of the War" and "Laws of the War," in which he argued the Allies had an economic advantage.[39] Skelton stopped short of opposing the war, instead protesting Canada's automatic involvement because of its imperial relations. Mackintosh would echo these sentiments on Canadian independence. As he would write in 1919, "we fell into a war which, however much we supported it, was none of our getting."[40] However he transcended his mentor's views, during his undergraduate studies and later as a graduate student, to express his increasing conviction that the war was an unjust one.

EGGS, THREE TIMES A DAY

Mackintosh may be excused for being initially oblivious to the war. When it was first declared he was teaching school in an area of Saskatchewan so remote that it took three weeks for news of the conflict to reach the community.

Teaching in prairie schools proved to be a popular vocation for Queen's students – so much so that the university offered a short four-lecture course to better prepare them as teachers.[41] With the benefit of a month spent teaching school in his father's district of North Hastings during the summers of 1914 and 1916, Mackintosh accepted the more challenging, and definitely more exotic, task of teaching in rural Saskatchewan. With as many as two hundred rural schools being created annually, the demand for summer teachers on the prairies was so great that several recruitment agencies were established, including one with a sub-agency in Kingston run by W.C. Clark.[42] The pay was also attractive: $80 per calendar month compared favourably to salaries in rural Ontario in the order of $500 for an entire year. The student would pay for transportation west, but, as Mackintosh recalled, "if he was a resourceful fellow, he bought for very little, though illegally, the return stub of someone who had come out on a harvesters' excursion and had decided to stay."[43] Mackintosh acquired a provisional Saskatchewan teacher's certificate on the strength of his undergraduate studies and the payment of a $5 fee.[44]

His first posting was Wiwa Hills School #1207 in the south-central part of the province, roughly a hundred kilometres south-west of Moose Jaw. The area had not been settled until 1908, because it was in the semi-arid agricultural zone and was some distance from the nearest railway. This was a rather foreboding area, truly on the "baldheaded prairie," where the virtual absence of trees for building material, the numerous sloughs, and the ominous saline Lake Chaplin to the north made transportation particularly difficult. The prospect of homestead land, however, drew settlers from England, Ireland, Scotland, Germany, and Russia, as well as Ontario, North Dakota, Iowa, and Minnesota. They were obliged to transport their grain along primitive roads to Morse, some sixty-five kilometres to the northwest, a round trip taking two to three days, until a branch line reached Gravelbourg, forty kilometres to the southeast.[45] Telephone service did not arrive until 1917.

Local farmers successfully petitioned the department of education for a school in 1912 and raised $2,400 in debentures to be repaid through a school tax of $16 per quarter-section. A school was constructed in the summer of 1914, thus giving Mackintosh the distinction of being its first teacher. Near the end of April, armed with his summer reading and the material for his extramural course in Greek, he boarded a CPR train from Kingston to Moose Jaw, connected to Morse, and then made has way by wagon to Wiwa Hills, a trip of five days in total. In the absence of a "teacherage" – not constructed until 1918 – Mackintosh billeted with the Vigors family. This left little room for idealizing agrarian life. His most vivid recollection of these summers was the frequency with which the basis of his three square meals a day consisted of eggs, eggs, and eggs. But the job also had its fringe benefits, the most appealing to him being access to a horse and wagon as his regular means of transportation.

Among the families of the original homesteaders – Armson, August, Dales, Doering, Erickson, Merriott, and Taylor – were some forty children of school age (six to fifteen years old), many of whom had to ford Wiwa Creek on horseback in order to attend.[46] While the schoolhouse was new, other amenities were lacking, with students sitting on overturned apple boxes in lieu of desks and chairs.[47] The janitor would arrive each morning to light the furnace and supply drinking water. Mackintosh's duties included the purchase of books for the "library" – a cupboard with three shelves – from an annual fund of $10, and the counting and sorting of gopher tails presented by students as part of a provincial campaign to rid the area of unwelcome residents.[48]

His second prairie summer, in 1916, was spent near the town of Indian Head, roughly forty kilometres east of Regina, a more accessible and prosperous area in the southeastern corner of Saskatchewan. If the newly settled area surrounding Wiwa Halls heightened his appreciation for the pioneering spirit of farmers, then the second summer underscored for him their capacity to organize in an effort to remedy their disadvantageous place in world grain markets. Indian Head was less than twenty kilometres from Sintaluta, the centre of the prairie farmers' movement, where Edward Partridge and others formed the first cooperative marketing venture, the Grain Growers' Grain Company, in 1906, and two years later launched the *Grain Growers' Guide* as the voice of the prairie farmer. In the preface to his doctoral thesis, Mackintosh would acknowledge his indebtedness: "Much more perhaps is owed to friends in certain sections of Saskatchewan where as a rural teacher the writer had the opportunity to observe conditions which gave rise to the [farmers'] movements described in this essay."[49]

Mac Urquhart emphasizes the importance of this experience in Mackintosh's life for "the evidence of the nature and impact of the settlement was everywhere to be seen at first hand."[50] Some forty-five years later, while giving the convocation address at the University of Saskatchewan in 1959, he referred to the importance of his summers teaching on the prairies: "I am a timid fellow who early learned that it is safer to speak only of what he knows. I have, of course, the limitations of one, most of whose life was spent, as you may feel, within the narrow horizons and in the parochial complacency of the Province of Ontario. Yet I had some early experience in this province, beginning when this University was barely five years old, experience which I valued greatly but which yielded no observable benefits to the province."[51] If nothing else, the time spent in the West equipped Mackintosh with a storehouse of tales of the prairies which he imparted to "effete" Easterners in the years to follow as the honorary chair of the Western Club at Queen's. To convey the harshness of the fierce windstorms, he liked to recount solemnly the story of the "unfortunate pedestrian ... who was blown up against a board fence and before the wind abated enough for him to break away he had starved to death," or of the gopher that saw the pile of sand blown away from its burrow and leaving just "the hole sticking up in the air."[52]

TOLSTOY, AGRARIANISM, AND THE WAR

With the rapid development of the Canadian prairies and the war serving as the important background to Mackintosh's undergraduate years, it is not surprising that he took the opportunity to reflect on both in his honours thesis in political economy. Under the old "Edinburgh" system, students with first-class standing in two honours subjects and who completed an honours thesis in each were awarded an MA. The history department had recently dropped its honours thesis requirement, meaning that a thesis in political economy was the only remaining requirement for Mackintosh's master's degree. Thus, while his thesis was technically an honours paper, the claim that Mackintosh wrote the first MA thesis in political economy at Queen's is substantially correct.

The writings of Leo Tolstoy as the subject of the thesis reflects Skelton's interest in Russia and his encouragement to range across economic, political, social, religious, and literary material for insights. However, it is worth noting that it was William W. Swanson who taught the course on Russia during Mackintosh's final year.[53] In any case, there is no mistaking Mackintosh's reverence for the Russian. "Count Leo Tolstoy has been the greatest figure in literary and religious creative thought of the last century." If this was not sufficiently clear, with the self-assurance and uncompromising terms of an undergraduate, he added that "The representatives of other nations sink into insignificance beside him."[54] Mackintosh's reading of Tolstoy, though not original, is an intriguing expression of a young man seeking to make sense out of rapidly changing world. This invariably meant deriving some practical lessons from the encounter. Mackintosh's objective was to distinguish those aspects of Russian institutions that were relevant to a western, and, more specifically, an Anglo-American, setting. Accordingly, the last chapter of the thesis is entitled "An Application of Tolstoy's Teachings from a Western Standpoint."

Mackintosh embraced the uncompromising terms of Tolstoy's indictment of Russia's tsarist regime, contrasting the "outworn and corrupt" autocracy and its bloated bureaucracy with the "vitality" of local self-government in outlying rural areas. The most important institution in the latter was the reconstituted *mir*, which had emerged as a post-feudal institution to distribute, and frequently redistribute, land communally, according to family size. He was also attracted by Tolstoy's version of secular humanism, which he interpreted as a rejection of the dogmas of established churches and, "without the interminable ramifications of theological writings," entailed "unremitting search and piercing criticisms applied to the teaching of Christ." In particular, Tolstoy examines the Sermon on the Mount and translates its five commandments into principles that "startle the Western mind": non-resistance of evil, no government, no church, no human law, and no private property. Stripped of all forms of coercion imposed by civilization, Tolstoy returns to the "natural man" and reinforces the view of the *mir* as the natural form of communal organization.[55] Mackintosh was hardly willing to accept Tolstoy's indictment of modern society and glorification of the naturalism of peasant life. In particular, while he saw the *mir* as an important vehicle for cooperation, it came at the expense of individual initiative and efficient agricultural practices, since there was little incentive to improve the land. Nor did Tolstoy recognize the role of industrialization in creating a larger middle class and economic growth, as well as the conditions for social and political stability. Yet it still remained for the West to learn from Tolstoy's central tenet about the virtues of cooperation: "We can temper our Anglo-Saxon individualism with Russian cooperation; we can modify our love of race to love of fellow men; we can break down British snobbery and sham with Russian sincerity." The lesson for North Americans, then, was the need for an appropriate combination of

Anglo-Saxon "dynamic power" with Russian "cooperation in labour." In Mackintosh's view, "cooperation is the cart and the harness, and initiative is the horse."[56]

Equally fascinating is Mackintosh's application of Tolstoy's concept of non-resistance of evil as it applies to war. He bristled at the depiction of Tolstoy as a "sentimental pacifist," as distinct from Norman Angell and others who argued against the war on economic grounds. "To apply the word 'sentimental' to a man who upholds peace because it is peace and a natural state, is incongruous. Which was sentimental, in the Eastern question, Gladstone or Disraeli? Is Cramb more rational than John Morley? Is there more sentimentality about the Kaiser and Crown Prince or Karl Liebknecht? Rudyard Kipling or John Burns? Theodore Roosevelt or Woodrow Wilson?" One wonders to what extent he had W.L. Grant in mind when he asked, "How much patriotism is mere jingo?" or when he asserted that "Intellectual sincerity is the only 'respirator' with which nations can fight the poisonous gas exuded by its Kiplings and their tawdry imitators." When he concluded that "non-resistance is not the doctrine of a weakling," he surely had his own personal circumstances in mind.[57]

The emphasis on the relationship between cooperation and initiative was hardly a detailed blueprint for economic and social success; however, the inspiration drawn from his reading of Russian history, as interpreted through Tolstoy, is readily apparent. Nor was it to be abandoned. Though Mackintosh makes no explicit reference to his experience on the Canadian prairies in his Queen's thesis, his endorsement of arrangements that combined individual initiative with the virtues of cooperation, when not at the expense of efficiency, he would later express with respect to the farms of western Canada. There Mackintosh would find the ideal vehicle for studying just such a combination of individualism and cooperation in an agrarian setting.

But his return to the prairies – both intellectually and physically – was interrupted by a year in Cambridge, Massachusetts. At the urging of Skelton, he would pursue graduate studies at Harvard University.

3

Harvard's Traditional Philology and the Unfenced Prairie: Cambridge and Brandon, 1916–1919

On this day after one semester at Harvard and being now thoroughly imbued in the 'new systematism,' I have resolved each day to record my thoughts and events in my daily life in order to note the diminishing returns to systematic study.

W.A. Mackintosh, Diary, 16 February 1917[1]

Mackintosh arrived at Harvard University in the fall of 1916 as a Thayer's Scholar – a scholarship awarded on the basis of scholarly merit and financial need – in the division of history, government, and economics in the Graduate School of Arts and Science.[2] He did so as part of a proud tradition of Queen's graduates taking up residence in Conant Hall and studying in Cambridge. In particular, he followed in the wake of W. Clifford Clark, also steered towards Harvard by O.D. Skelton in order to study economics under Frank Taussig. Clark would distinguish himself by being awarded the Ricardo Prize Scholarship (based on an essay in political economy) and the Henry Lee Fellowship, and by endearing himself to Taussig "who always spoke of [Clark] with almost parental pride and affection."[3] Mackintosh, however, found the Harvard experience to be less ideal. This was, in Jacob Viner's blunt assessment, a "dead period" in the otherwise distinguished history of Harvard's economics department.[4]

It is not altogether surprising, then, that Mackintosh's first stay at Harvard proved to be relatively brief. After completing eight months' of coursework, he accepted a position at Brandon College, where he would remain for two years. Despite a heavy teaching load and light salary, his time in Brandon provided a rich experience. Living in the student residence as a surrogate don, marching with the local Canadian Officers Training Corps, assisting with the college journal, organizing social and intellectual events, and speaking at various town functions, he was fully engaged in college and community life. It was the political climate, however, that left an indelible mark. The upsurge in labour militancy in western Canada during the latter stages of World War I added to his belief in the folly of the war – in this instance because of misguided domestic policy that imposed an unequal burden on workers – and served to reinforce his conviction that economists had an important role to play in developing a more just economy.

HARVARD'S "TRADITIONAL PHILOLOGY"

Under the successive headship of Charles Dunbar and Taussig, Harvard's economics department in the latter nineteenth and early twentieth centuries remained firmly within the orthodoxy of the discipline. It had largely resisted pressures to extend the discipline to applied subjects beyond the conventional concerns with trade and currency issues, such that its curriculum in the late-nineteenth century is described as "Mill, more Mill, and currency."[5] In contrast, for Richard Ely, John Commons, and other forerunners of American institutionalism, the discipline had an obligation to address the growing social problems associated with industrialization and urbanization; indeed, it was in the context of the Social Gospel movement that the American Economic Association (AEA) was formed in 1884. Notably, Dunbar and Taussig initially refused to join the AEA because its "Statement of Principles" included a positive role for the state: "We hold that the conflict of labor and capital has brought into prominence a vast number of social problems, whose solution requires the united efforts, each in its own sphere, of the church, of the state, and of science."[6] In a similar vein, the creation of the *Journal of Political Economy* at the University of Chicago in 1895 as an alternative to the Harvard-edited *Quarterly Journal of Economics* reflected the struggle between the new and the old schools in American economics.

By the time Mackintosh arrived, the economics curriculum at Harvard grudgingly accepted the expanded scope of the discipline.

In addition to traditional offerings in economic theory, the history of thought, economic history, international trade, public finance, and monetary economics, there were newer courses on statistics, agricultural economics, transportation, labour and industrial relations, socialism, and sociology (see Table 3.1). Notwithstanding Joseph Dorfman's claim that in Taussig, Thomas Nixon Carver, and C.J. Bullock, the department had an outstanding group of theorists, its strength was in applied economics, boasting the likes of J.S. Davis (agricultural economics), Edwin F. Gay (economic history), Benjamin Anderson (monetary theory and policy), William Zebina Ripley (labour and agricultural economics), and Ezra Edmund Day (the statistician who would go on to become president of Cornell).[7] Mackintosh's coursework took advantage of the department's relative strengths. He enrolled in two one-semester courses in economic history (European Industry and Commerce in the Nineteenth Century, and Economic History of the United States) taught by Gay with the assistance of Arthur H. Cole; a one-semester course (The Single Tax, Socialism, and Anarchism) and a two-semester course (The Economics of Agriculture), both taught by Carver; and Harvard's traditional rite of passage, Taussig's famous Economic Theory seminar. He rounded out his year with a two-semester course on the history of England during the Tudor and Stuart periods from Roger Merriman of the department of history.

Taussig was at the height of his powers and influence. He was editor or the *Quarterly Journal of Economics* and author of the influential textbook, *Principles of Economics*, first published in 1911. Defying easy categorization, he is often described as the "American Marshall" in the sense that he brought neo-classical economics to the United States in a fashion similar to that played by Alfred Marshall in England. Others see Taussig as a "mid-Victorian," who, despite rejecting the formalism of the marginal revolution, maintained an insular narrowness in his approach to economic questions, in which his first impulse was towards deductive reasoning at the expense of incorporating institutional considerations. His opposition to institutionalism, coupled with his defence of the gold standard and his free-trade bias, placed him on the conservative side of the discipline. Applying modern standards, Robert Fogel argues to the contrary, describing Taussig as "the prototype of a policy-oriented academic economist. Although primarily an applied theorist, he was comfortable in handling empirical evidence. He recognized that

Table 3.1 Course Offerings in Economics, Harvard University, 1916–1917 (including Mackintosh's courses and grades in italics)

UNDERGRADUATE AND GRADUATE COURSES			
No.	*Course Title*	*Instructor*	*Grade*
1b	Statistics	J.S. Davis	
2a	*European Industry and Commerce in the Nineteenth Century*	*Edwin F. Gay*	*B+*
2b	*Economic History of the United States*	*Edwin F. Gay*	*A-*
3	Money, Banking and Commercial Crises	Anderson	
4a	History of Transportation	Ripley	
4b	Economics of Corporations	Ripley	
5a	Public Finance, exclusive of Taxation	Bullock	
5b	The Theory and Method of Taxation	Burbank	
6a	Trade Unionism and Allied Problems	Ripley	
6b	The Labor Movement in Europe		
7a	Economic Theory	Taussig	
7b	*The Single Tax, Socialism, and Anarchism*	*Carver*	*A*
8	Principles of Sociology	Carver	
9	*Economics of Agriculture*	*Carver*	*A-*
PRIMARILY FOR GRADUATES			
No.	*Course Title*	*Instructor*	*Grade*
11	*Economic Theory*	*Taussig*	*A*
12 hf	The Distribution of Wealth	Carver	
13	Statistics: Theory, Method, and Practice	Day	
14	History and Literature of Economics to the year 1848	Gay	
15	German and French Economists of the Nineteenth Century		
16 hf	The Theories of Contemporary Socialism	Anderson	
17	Economic Theory: Value and Related Problems		
18a	Analytical Sociology	Anderson	

Source: Harvard University. *Courses of Instruction offered by the Faculty of Arts and Science for the Academic Year 1916–17*. 2nd ed. Cambridge, 1916); Harvard University Archives, UAV 161.272.5. Official Student Record Card: W.A. Mackintosh.

when applying economic theory to issues of public policy, numerous concerns, not strictly economic, had to be addressed. Hence the application of economics to public policy was an art rather than a science."[8] Taussig's work in international trade and tariff policy is his most enduring contribution to the discipline.

His influence on Mackintosh was not inconsequential; after all, Mackintosh learned his economics at Queen's using the first edition of *Principles of Economics*, and achieved first-class standing in his seminar at Harvard. He deemed Taussig to be a "great teacher" and would come to echo some of his thoughts on human behaviour that incorporated a richness that extended beyond the normal motivations often ascribed by economists.[9] Elsewhere he described Taussig as "so cautious an economist" – by no means a bad quality – in citing his view of the New York Stock Exchange as "the greatest of gambling hells."[10] But the most lasting impression was indirect: Taussig demonstrated the important policy role for economists, and Mackintosh's later call for a Canadian tariff board, as an independent regulatory agency to relieve political pressures on tariff policy, was surely a reflection of Taussig's experience as the first head of the US Tariff Commission.

Carver is also difficult to classify within the economics discipline. Born on an Iowa farm, educated at Iowa Wesleyan, University of Southern California, Johns Hopkins, and Cornell, he joined the faculty at Harvard in 1900 and, at the time of Mackintosh's arrival there, had ascended to the role of president of the American Economic Association. He wrote prolifically on a variety of topics – from birth control to anarchism – and his courses on social reform "attracted every kind of radical that the student body could furnish" as he "battled valiantly for the souls of the unenlightened."[11] The main body of his work earned him a reputation as the foremost agricultural economist in the United States. Much of his analysis focused on the terms of trade between agriculture and industry, where he argued that, because of the immobility of land as a resource, agriculture was prone to overproduction, and farmers faced chronically low prices and low incomes. Since farmers themselves had little avenue for addressing their adverse position in a commodity market, Carver was a proponent of a strong role for the state and other institutions in order to ameliorate potential social conflict.[12]

Gay was among the most prominent economic historians in the country. He spent twelve years engaged in postgraduate studies in

Europe, where he completed his doctorate in economic history at Berlin under Gustav Schmoller, "the last notable representative of the historical school of economics."[13] He took up an appointment at Harvard in 1902, and assumed the role of dean of the newly created Graduate School of Business Administration in 1908 (only after the president was dissuaded from offering the position to Mackenzie King).[14] Mackintosh deemed his Ec2a to be an excellent course; however, a classmate "made extended reference to the 'Prussian' manner in which the course was conducted. Gay was much taken aback and hurt, since at that time 'Prussian' was rather an offensive word. Actually the course was somewhat mechanically done, but since the sergeants were Oscar Ryder, the chairman of the United States Tariff Commission at the time, and Arthur Cole, the rigour of the regime was not very pronounced." According to Mackintosh, Ec2b on American economic history, in which he wrote a paper on the impact of the American tariff on the Canadian pulp-and-paper industry, "was not particularly good as he [Gay] had no knowledge of it." Nonetheless, Mackintosh would remember Gay "with great respect and something short of affection. I never got to know him intimately."[15]

It is unlikely that Mackintosh had much patience with Merriman. Described by one former student as a "colorful, salty personality of the old school, passionately devoted to aristocratic Britain,"[16] he personified the Oxbridge snobbery that so rankled Mackintosh. He survived the course with a grade of "B," for which there was no shame, given Merriman's reputation as being unsympathetic to students. According to one commentator, "when Roger B. Merriman (1876–1945) was a Harvard PhD candidate, he failed at an oral history examination. Afterwards, he delighted in failing PhD candidates, and was little loved in Conant Hall. When he was a candidate for president of Harvard in 1920, it was pointed out that Merriman had some enemies, who were probably the students he failed, as well as their thesis directors. In the end, Merriman did not become president."[17] Mackintosh was more forgiving. When writing to Gerald Graham, a Queen's graduate studying at Harvard in 1927, he asked: "Have you been doing any work with my friend Roger Merriman? ... He is a peculiar fellow but is a great pusher if he really gets behind anything, and in the art of effective wire-pulling he is a marvel."[18]

On paper it is hard to imagine a better combination of economists than Taussig, Carver, and Gay for guiding the work of a student interested in the economic history of farmer organizations, but in reality, Mackintosh's experience at Harvard fell short of the implied potential. Viner's description of World War I as "a dead period" in the department is due in part to the immersion of Taussig, Carver, Gay, and others in government work. The same year that Mackintosh arrived at Harvard, Taussig was appointed chairman of the newly formed US Tariff Commission, and he departed a year later to serve in a variety of wartime capacities in Washington, including the Price-Fixing Committee of the War Industries Board.[19] Herbert Heaton, in a short biography, describes Gay's academic career as "distracted and dislocated." Preoccupied with the administration of the business school, engaged too heavily in advising governments and generally unable to say no to outside opportunities. "Gay had elements of ruthlessness in driving both himself and others. It is a pity he did not confine his sphere of operations to Harvard Yard or some such innocuous place. There were many elements of tragedy in his story."[20] Mackintosh had expected to do his thesis under Gay's supervision, only to see him leave for a temporary position with the New York *Post*.[21] As for Carver, who remained at Harvard throughout the war years, his former student and colleague Edward Mason observed that he was increasingly "indolent in his application to teaching."[22]

Despite doing well on his courses, Mackintosh was disappointed with his own work effort. In a diary he kept during the year, he was constantly cajoling himself in the evening to work harder, to "live positively with interest and enthusiasm if possible," only to record the next day, more often than not, his failure to do so. He despaired, "May I be kept from degenerating into a grubber!"[23]

This state of dejection stemmed in part from the death of his father on 11 December 1916. At the age of seventy-two, he had been retired for little more than a year when he suffered a fatal stroke. His son hurried home at the end of the first term to help put the estate in order. More distracting was the war. Mackintosh followed the news intently as the United States inched its way toward becoming a combatant and, as it did so, his opposition to the war became more ardent. On reading H.G. Wells's, *Mr. Britling Sees It Through*, he wrote in his diary: "Is the war bringing no religion? Are we being flung hard back upon reality or upon materialism? Is not the essence of war a ghastly sham and its tragedy that we think it reality? There is no tragedy in a sordid war, in the war of Kings, of Kaisers, bureaucracies or snob-ocracies but there is a tragedy in the war of men unalterably convinced of the rightness of their right of the highness of their duty, with hearts steeled to hatred against those who watch the same star from another hilltop, who see the same shield from another side, who pray to the same God in another tongue."[24] Over a two-day period in February he wrote "Some Observations on the American Situation," his first published work, which would appear in *Economic World*. In it he speculated on public support for the war.[25] In his diary he recorded that "Country behind Wilson but quite a distance behind him. The melting pot of nations is not melting. Decided pacifist feeling among Southerners and Westerners. N. England more bellicose. Several fear of Japan."[26] A month later, after observing a large rally on Washington Street, he was convinced that public support was unified and that America would "go the whole hog. Crowds now very much excited. The war is still 3,000 miles away. Universal military service asked for. Will it come without demand? It means a tremendous turnover if it does within the last few weeks. If it is accepted it shows the volatile character of the American public and the tremendous power of the President at war."[27]

The chapel provided some consolation, where many of the leading theologians of the day including Albert Parker Fitch (Andover Theological Seminary), Harry Emerson Fosdick (the liberal Baptist of the Union Theological Seminary), Walter Rauschenbusch (Rochester Theological Seminary) – held forth. Sermons that addressed the pressing political issues of the day – including the war and socialism – were particularly to his liking.[28]

Harvard also offered an abundance of male companionship. Mackintosh roomed with Charles Owen, a Queen's graduate studying Classics, while George Wilson, his closest friend from Queen's, who shared both Mackintosh's interest in Tolstoy and his opposition to the war, lived down the street in the Canadian Club.[29] Many evenings were spent in Conant Hall reading poetry, playing cards, or debating the issues of the day. He also reported on a dinner date with a Miss Sinclair ("Had a very interesting evening"[30]). Neither male nor female companionship, however, served to raise his spirits. Seeing the seventy-two-year-old Sarah Bernhardt in *Camille* offered a "break in the even tenor of my path," but when he went to see William Faversham in *Getting Married* the next day, he wrote that "I am tired of Shaw. One finds it hard to laugh at the world when it is too horrible to laugh at. One can only be cynical when things don't matter."[31] He particularly bemoaned the bellicose attitude of most New Englanders. Even a flower show could not shake his depression. "Poor flowers to be so beset with swarming human beings. The place stunk so with Back Bay perfume one could not detect the scent of the flowers. Tinselled dames showed their bedaubed cheeks against pure roses and had not even the grace to blush."[32]

All things considered, Mackintosh's first sojourn to Harvard was not a happy one. Its narrow academic confines and intellectual pretense hardly suited his demeanour. When he learned in April that he had not been awarded a scholarship for the following year, he "was rather sour at first,"[33] but then considered his alternatives. Years later he noted that Paul Shorey, professor of Classics at the University of Chicago, "had forsaken Harvard's traditional philology for the unfenced prairie."[34] For Mackintosh, it would be Brandon, Manitoba, that offered such an escape.

BRANDON COLLEGE

Mackintosh was twenty-two years old when took up his first academic appointment at Brandon College in September 1917. The college's annual report observed that: "Mr. William A. MacIntosh, MA, a graduate of Queen's, and a post-graduate of Harvard, has taken the lectureship in Political Economy." He was deemed "a worthy and efficient man," although the misspelling of his name might suggest that this assessment was based more on speculation than a rigorous job screening. When he left two years later, the president still could not spell his name correctly. In his annual report on the college's affairs, the departure of its young economist is tersely noted: "Mr. W.A. MacIntosh, Lecturer in Economics, after two years' successful teaching, resigned, in order to complete his advanced post-graduate work at Harvard University."[35] Reminiscing years later, one of his Brandon colleagues referred to him as "another McIntosh," yet a further variation in spelling, in deference to the institution's most renowned faculty member, D.C. McIntosh, who became dean of theology at Yale's Divinity School.[36] But whatever impression he may have had on Brandon, the climate there provided him with a rich experience.

Brandon, Manitoba, with a population of approximately fifteen thousand people in the mid-1910s, was an unlikely spot for an institution of higher learning. Located on the main line of the Canadian

Pacific Railway, some two hundred kilometres west of Winnipeg, and with spur lines running north and south, the city was a minor transportation and commercial centre for the surrounding agricultural community. The college was founded in 1899 by the Baptist Union of Western Canada, and was housed in two handsome buildings on a fifteen-acre site in the town centre. The original four-storey building was erected in 1901, while Clark Hall (the "Ladies Building," which included a women's residence and music rooms) was added in 1906. The college offered to some four hundred students programs in arts and theology (with degrees granted through its affiliation with McMaster University in Toronto), an academic department (covering grades nine through twelve), as well as a program in "music and expression" that was intended "to develop womanly regard for the right way of thinking and acting."[37] Reflecting the immigrant population of the region, it also boasted what must have been the country's only Scandinavian department.

This might seem like an inauspicious place to begin an academic career; however, academic opportunities for Canadians were exceedingly sparse in economics. As a relatively new discipline, Canadian departments were largely dependent on British-trained (and British-born) academics. The number of Canadians in American graduate programs was increasing, particularly at the University of Chicago (including McMaster's celebrated undergraduates, Harold Innis, Duncan MacGibbon, W.J.A. Donald, and Norman Ware) and Harvard (Jacob Viner, W.C. Clark, and Mackintosh), but it remained difficult to have any firm expectations for an academic position in Canada. When Clark was studying at Harvard in 1915, for instance, he aspired to a job in one of the provincial universities in western Canada; indeed, he was reluctant to give up a tutorship at Harvard for a temporary position at Queen's in the event that it might harm his chances for such a permanent appointment in western Canada.[38]

Yet despite its modest size, Brandon College had a very capable faculty. MacGibbon, whom Mackintosh replaced, observed that "Although the teaching load was heavy and salaries exiguous the college was successful in enlisting a group of teachers that would compare most favourably with larger and more pretentious institutions." He later noted, somewhat immodestly, that the college had a particularly strong record in Economics, where "a succession of four young instructors … subsequently became the heads of departments in the subject in four Canadian universities, three in Ontario and one in Alberta."[39] The first of these was MacGibbon himself, who was aptly described as "probably the ablest economist in the West."[40] He came to Brandon College in 1908 fresh from a BA in political economy at McMaster, completed the work for a McMaster MA during his first year at Brandon, and then took a leave of absence in order to obtain his PhD from the University of Chicago. He resigned in 1917 to enlist, at the age of thirty-six, in the Canadian Tank Battalion. After the war, he assumed the chair of political economy at the University of Alberta. Mackintosh followed, and was succeeded by H.A. Logan, who spent two years in Brandon before becoming the chair at the University of Western Ontario, and later joined the faculty at the University of Toronto. Logan's replacement, Burton Hurd, taught at Brandon from 1922 to 1935, before accepting a position at McMaster, where he became chair of the economics department and then dean of Arts and Science. The names of H. Clare Pentland and W.T. Easterbrook, can also be added to the list. Pentland, an undergraduate at Brandon, became head at the University of Manitoba, while Easterbrook taught briefly at Brandon College before joining the department of political economy at the University of Toronto and eventually becoming its head.[41]

Much credit for the quality of the faculty can be given to the shrewd recruitment by the college's president, Howard P. Whidden, and his predecessors. Brandon College attracted a number of young academics who were beginning their careers and proved to be fertile ground for staffing McMaster University, also a Baptist institution. Whidden himself departed for McMaster in 1923 to assume its presidency. Although a Baptist minister, he was "less noted for his spiritual gifts"[42] than for his worldly activities, which included serving one term as the federal member of parliament for Brandon under the Union Government (1917–1921). He has been both praised, and especially vilified, for contributing to the secularization of both Brandon and McMaster. According to George Rawlyk, for instance, "closely associated with the Ontario business elite, an active Mason and a committed Conservative, Whidden was perceived by many members of McMaster's Board of Governors ... as just the man to lead the university ... into the mainstream of North American bourgeois success and respectability."[43] This tendency towards secularization may have been a blessing for Mackintosh. The college asserted that "In every department the professors and teachers must be members of some evangelical church."[44] This was obviously untrue, but in any event, its religious bent was depicted as "not ostentatious or over aggressive, but the positive, strong kind."[45] This included a daily assembly of staff and students in the chapel for announcements and congregational singing. For Mackintosh, who enjoyed church services as an outlet for reflection and for music, such obligations were not onerous.

He was "domiciled" in a private room in the student residence on the top floor of the main college building, which housed up to seventy male students in rather spartan circumstances: at least two to a room, each of which contained iron beds, tables, chairs, and bureaus. Students were required to provide their own bedding, towels, and, for a touch of refinement, a "table napkin ring." (A ban on alcohol, gambling, and tobacco in the residence, if it extended to faculty members, was only an imposition on Mackintosh with respect to his cigarette smoking.) Despite being as young as many of the university students, he exercised an important don-like role for, as the college journal noted, "his quiet presence and gentlemanly bearing are influences that cannot fail to be recognized."[46]

He was not without his misgivings about leaving Harvard: "Have been here more than a week now. Not very settled yet. Think I will like the place though it is small and rather strait laced for a heretic like me. I am afraid I will explode some day. Probably I can hold on till spring however, if I am allowed to."[47] When he received a letter from George Wilson, back in Cambridge for the winter term, Mackintosh briefly questioned whether he should have returned with him, but then dismissed the thought with a perfunctory "*alea jacta est!* [the dye is cast]." However, he would still reflect on some of his fonder memories of the year past, reminiscing about "the evenings at 41 Conant when we ... sat around the fire and read poetry or familiar essays. 'The days that are no more.' My Sunday evenings this year! Where?" His ability to stay in Brandon depended with the state of the war. When the Military Service Act implemented conscription in August 1917, Mackintosh duly reported to the medical board and was placed in "Medical Category C," unfit for overseas service. He confided in his diary that he was "Somewhat relieved because of reports of lax methods. It would be awful however to spend a year on Home Service. Hope I can now settle down for the winter."[48]

Brandon would come to provide a congenial atmosphere. Within a week of his arrival, Reverend Mr Nicol of St Paul's Presbyterian Church (a fellow student of Mackintosh's brother, John, both at

Owen Sound Collegiate and the University of Toronto) paid a visit, and Mackintosh would spend most of his Sundays sampling the sermons offered at St Paul's and other churches in the city.[49] His colleagues also extended their hospitality to him – often at weekend brunches and teas – and he relished talking with Louis Wright, the music instructor, about his experiences in Germany. He also found an amiable companion in Evangeline Cline, the instructor in "expression," with whom he enjoyed good company and bad tennis.

During his two-year stay in Brandon, college life was largely dominated by the two important events of the era: the war and the outbreak of Spanish influenza. Over two hundred students and graduates of the college served in World War I: a college platoon, formed as part of the Western Universities Battalion, had embarked for France a year earlier, and a further sixty men were enrolled in the Canadian Officers Training Corps (COTC). With the COTC going through its paces on the college lawns, Mackintosh did his part, earning his "stripe" as a corporal.[50] As the war was nearing a conclusion, the flu pandemic in the fall of 1918 affected some fifty students and staff, and the college was placed under quarantine. Mackintosh was not spared, complaining of "a rather sharp attack ... of this very troublesome plague."[51] Otherwise, the college sought to operate as normally as could be expected.

Mackintosh's status as an "exceedingly influential"[52] member of the staff derived from his extensive involvement in campus and community activities. He presided over the Political Science and International Polity Club and participated in ad hoc meetings of students and faculty in the chapel to discuss important events of the day. He also served as "Consulting Editor" to the *Brandon College Quill*, for which he penned an intriguing article "On Humor and the Humorous." On the social front, he organized a skating party, rounding up "a sufficient number of 'nonfluites' and germless students" for a two-mile hike to Lake Percy that was declared the "liveliest and best outing of the season." He also cut a striking figure in the "The Masquerade" given by the Literary Society, where "Wonder was expressed at the fact that Mr. Mackintosh in his French uniform did not beat a double retreat from the overtowering Russian Cossack who always seemed to stick close to him."[53]

The teaching duties were onerous. As professor of political economy, Mackintosh was a one-person department, which, judging by the courses offered, meant teaching the equivalent of five two-semester courses each academic year. Students majoring in political economy were required to take six full courses and a one-term, fourth-year seminar in the subject, plus a course in history. A second-year course in "Elementary Principles of Political Economy" (covering Seager's *Principles of Economics*, Hayes's *Problems and Exercises in Economics*, and Smart's *Theory of Value*) and a third-year course "Principles of Commerce" (more akin to a modern course in International Trade, based upon Bastable's *Theory of International Trade*, Fisk's *International Commercial Policies*, and Ashley's *Modern Tariff History*) were offered annually. In 1917–18, he also taught courses in accounting and sociology, "Principles of Finance" and "Money, Credit, and Banking." The following year offered courses on "Labour Problems," "Public Expenditure and Taxation," and "Transportation," the latter dealing with "the basic principles of land and marine transportation, with particular reference to the industry and foreign trade of Canada." The topic of the senior seminar was "Socialism." If nothing else, there was ample opportunity to hone one's lecturing skills.

SUMMER WORK IN OTTAWA

However congenial the climate was in Brandon, there was no avoiding the fact that it was far removed from the centre of research activity on the Canadian economy. In particular, it was a long way from Ottawa, where Mackintosh was convinced that the important research in applied economics needed to take place. An outlet for this interest came in the form of employment with the dominion government during the summer months. In the summer of 1917, prior to taking up his appointment at Brandon, Mackintosh had worked with the department of labour's prices and wages division under the direction of C.W. Bolton. (It is probably no coincidence that his first opportunity came in the department where the deputy minister, F.A. Acland, was a former associate of Skelton during their days with the *Booklover's Magazine* in Philadelphia, and in the same division where Margaret Mackintosh was employed.[54]) Nearing the end of his first academic year at Brandon, he wrote to R.H. Coats, inquiring about the possibility of working with the newly formed Dominion Bureau of Statistics (DBS): "I have been considering taking up government work if possible during this summer. My experience at the Department of Labour, and personal interest would give me some foundation for work with index numbers. Have you some such work which could be 'rounded up' in two and a half or three months beginning the latter part of June? If there is some such work to be done, I think we could come readily to terms, for I am anxious to keep busy during the summer at any reasonable remuneration if the work is needed."[55] Coats was anxious to involve university faculty in research, and Mackintosh joined S.A. Cudmore of the University of Toronto, Humphrey Michell of Queen's, and W.C. Clark working in Ottawa in the summer of 1918. None got wealthy from the experience, since the remuneration was three dollars per day, but it afforded the opportunity to engage in policy research. Coats put Mackintosh to work on wholesale prices for the new internal trade division, and later congratulated him on the work he produced: "It is exactly the treatment we wanted."[56]

Despite his enthusiasm for teaching, the low pay and heavy course load at Brandon left Mackintosh questioning whether an academic career was worth pursuing. His annual salary was $1,000 (plus room and board) in his first year and, despite being raised to $1,200 in the second, was roughly half of what a senior statistician's position was paying at the DBS. Thus, when he inquired about employment for a third summer, he also told Coats that he would entertain a permanent position. "It is unlikely that I will return to Brandon another year (this is private). I have consented to consider an offer from McMaster University but the matter will probably not be closed for 10 days more. Unless their offer is more favourable than I anticipate, I would consider on equal terms, an offer of $1,800 for work similar to that which you outlined last autumn."[57] Just two weeks after inquiring about a permanent job, however, Mackintosh informed Coats that "I have ... decided to stay with my teaching work [at Brandon] for next year."[58] Coats would later offer him the position of editor of the *Canada Year Book*, which would include responsibility for a monthly "barometrics" bulletin. "I don't know if this would appeal to you. I think we could open the position in the $1,600–$2,100 class with an assurance with a year or so of promotion to the $2,100–$2,800 class. We would like someone at the end of the year, but it could wait for a few months longer."[59] But Mackintosh had renewed a commitment to completing his graduate studies. "If the war comes to a conclusion this winter or next spring, I wish to return for next winter to Harvard to finish up some work there for my doctor's degree. That I feel I must do before I can settle down to anything approaching a permanent position, even though the temptation is great to take up work at a time when there is so much of it to be done that it is going begging."[60]

It was Skelton who steered Mackintosh back on course towards an academic career. While working in Ottawa during the summer of 1918, he had occasion to talk to Skelton while walking home from dinner at W.C. Clark's residence. He noted in his diary, "discussed economic thesis subjects, Industrial subjects, etc. He gives a man a fresh start to talk to him a while. Suggested possibility of help in research at Queen's."[61] In May 1919, on the eve of leaving his position at Brandon College, his plans had crystallized, and this entailed a renewed focus on research leading to his doctoral thesis. In declining another summer of employment with the DBS, he explained to Coats that: "I think I spoke to you about the possibility that I would be doing some work with Dr. Skelton this summer. I have had an arrangement with him for some time and he wrote me last week that he had been able to make provision for having the work done. I suspect therefore that I shall be at that work for the greater part of the summer. I was counting on being in Ottawa but this work will probably necessitate my being in the West."[62] With Skelton's encouragement, he was committed to returning to Harvard for the fall of 1919.

ECONOMICS, PRICES, AND THE WAR

Before leaving Brandon, Mackintosh wrote his first academic paper, "Economics, Prices and the War," published in the *Queen's Quarterly* and as a Queen's University research bulletin.[63] The central concern of the paper, the unequal distribution of the burdens of the war caused by rapid inflation, reflects three important influences on Mackintosh's thinking: his studies at Harvard; his work with the department of labour and the DBS on price indexes; and, most importantly, his first-hand experience with the growing labour militancy leading up to the Winnipeg General Strike.

His first year at Harvard informed his approach to applied economics. Like Taussig, he was not particularly troubled by the behavioural axioms underlying traditional economic analysis. This position was stated more explicitly in a paper written in 1923, "The Psychologist and Economics," that drew upon the work of Taussig and Zenas Clark Dickinson's thesis written under Taussig's supervision.[64] Mackintosh acknowledged that "assumptions that men do act on a purely rational basis will lead to grave mistakes of policy," but argued that the economics literature had always had a richer portrait of human behaviour. Specifically, he credited Veblen with developing an analysis based on "complex present-day situations rather than upon simple eighteenth century unrealities." Failure to account for such complexities would lead to "nonsense on stilts." He concluded that "On the whole the self-interest posited by the economist still holds true" and served as a useful "working generalization, a reliable basis on which to shape policy."[65] Similarly, his reading of how markets functioned began with a simple Marshallian approach to price determination. The price of a commodity ranged between its long-run supply price (average cost of production) and demand (marginal utility), with the actual short-run price determined by the relative bargaining power of producers and consumers. Economists, however, had applied this theory indiscriminately and had not realized what was patently obvious to the public: a model based upon perfect competition was of little assistance in understanding the complexities of a real-world economy. Inequalities in market power left some groups vulnerable. In this respect, he clearly drew upon the teachings of Carver. It was the "lack of organized resistance" to price increases by workers, farmers, and consumers which left them in a weak bargaining position, such that inflation benefits the "business man more largely than any other classes."[66]

The shortcomings of economics in Canada were not so much that the theory was inadequate, but that there was not the accumulated "body of facts" upon which to base "practical advice." While economists eschewed price controls as an ineffective and unnecessary interference with market forces, they ignored equity considerations arising out of the redistribution of income caused by inflation. Mackintosh thus shared Innis's evaluation of the state of economics in Canada. Both adopted the traditional dichotomy between theory and history, where it was the role of the latter to provide the "facts" upon which to amend theory. The task of Canadian economists was to embark on detailed analysis of the country's industries and identify the market frictions and rigidities in order to provide a more informed application of theory to contemporary problems.

This view was reinforced by his work with the DBS. Documenting the rise in wholesale prices, however mundane, was a small step in gathering the necessary fodder for informed economic policy. Work of this nature had largely gone unheeded: the Canadian government "with few exceptions ... asked and received but little aid from Canadian economists." Indeed, it was not until W.C. Clark's appointment in 1932 that an economist was employed in the Canadian civil service. This stood in sharp contrast to the situation in the United States, where economists – including, from Harvard, Taussig, Carver, and Day – assumed important advisory roles with the federal government during World War I.

It was the human cost of this neglect, readily apparent in the labour unrest throughout western Canada, that provided the context for Mackintosh's paper. Life in Brandon forced him to confront the class complexity of the prairie economy, and he could not help but observe the hardship faced by workers, due to the sharp decline in real wages and high rates of unemployment. Brandon's economy was more industrial in character than its rural setting might suggest. Its two largest employers were the city itself and the Canadian Pacific Railway, but a number of light manufacturing enterprises were also present. Accordingly, the city had a sizeable working-class population, with largely British immigrants occupying the working-class neighbourhoods to the east and south, while the north-end "Ghetto" housed central and eastern European unskilled immigrants.[67] The increasing militancy of workers was expressed through traditional organizations such as the Brandon Trades and Labour Council, the Social Gospel movement, and the legislature.[68] Capital-labour conflict had escalated during the later stages of the war, leading up to a walkout by civic employees in late April 1919 and followed a month later by a broader sympathy strike with workers engaged in the Winnipeg General Strike.[69] Less than two months before the Winnipeg General Strike, Mackintosh gave a public address under the auspices of the Brandon Educational Society, in which he argued for the "betterment of the present industrial order." This included safer factories, proper housing conditions, a living wage, a shorter workday, and insurance against accidents and unemployment. These reforms could be achieved, not through conflict ("indignation is no substitute for reason"), but through existing institutions. Thus he called for an Industrial Relations Commission equipped with a permanent research staff.[70]

Mackintosh's first publication, then, is a lament for the absence of economists in contributing to the important issues of the day. At a time when inflation was threatening to undermine not only Canada's economic stability, but social stability as well, economists had little useful advice to offer. He concludes by outlining the research agenda for economics in Canada. "Unemployment, industrial organization, the tariff, the possible period of depression: for the solution of these problems it is the basis of fact that is required. Until by government or private initiative these facts are acquired, economists are but stirring the dust which obscures them."[71] Just what was obscured – the facts or the economists – is ambiguous, but it was mostly likely both.

If his treatment of the difficulties faced by workers because of wartime inflation was a tempered one, largely addressed to academic and policy audiences, he was soon more emotionally engaged in the politics of the moment. When he resigned his position at Brandon College, he embarked for Winnipeg on 17 June 1919 in order to meet with people involved in the grain trade and gather material for Skelton and for his own doctoral thesis. Instead, he found himself in the midst of the Winnipeg General Strike on the day its leaders were arrested, and he spent most of the next three days "tramping around the city" in order to observe the extent of the conflict. He would depart one day before the strike reached its climax on "Bloody Saturday," June 21, when two people were killed and several injured as the Royal North West Mounted Police first charged and then fired upon a demonstration of strikers on Main Street. He returned to Winnipeg six weeks later, however, to attend the sedition trials of the strike leaders, accompanied by W.C. Clark.[72] In one day they travelled by jitney to attend a speech by William Pritchard in the Labour Church in Transcona; to Norwood to listen to William Ivens; and finally to the Columbia Theatre to hear Salem Bland, the social-gospeller recently dismissed from his position at Winnipeg's United College because of his radical stance.[73] A few days later he had lunch with Ivens and A.A. Heaps. He spoke sardonically of "hunting Bolsheviks," only to find Ivens and Heaps to be altogether sensible men, and he noted that Clark had much the same opinion of the other strike leaders, James Winning, R.B. Russell, and Pritchard: "Much impressed by absolute decent character of former and cleverness and decentness of latter two. Good econ. students and ardent socialists." He also added the intriguing comment, based upon Pritchard's account, that "At BC University only 2 classes – Bolsheviks and Mensheviks."[74]

This experience in Winnipeg reinforced the conclusions reached in "Economics, Prices, and the War," but heightened Mackintosh's sense of outrage. He drafted an eight-page commentary on the "Revolution in Winnipeg,"[75] in which he addressed three main issues: the circumstances leading up to the conflict, the legitimacy of the workers' demands, and the appropriate resolution. In each case, his views were anything but temperate.

First, the conflict, if not caused by the government actions, was certainly heightened by them. His criticism of wartime government policy was all the more scathing. "In matters of fiscal policy at least, the Canadian government was reactionary at the outset. A fiscal policy making reckless use of loans and credits brought with it all the evils of inflation, rising prices, the slow racking of the poor between soaring prices and slow rising wages, and the demoralization of the captains of industry in a situation where 'any fool could make profits.'"[76] Moreover, the financing of the war primarily through taxes on consumption had imposed an unfair burden on workers, and their militant reaction was all too predictable.

Second, despite the propaganda circulated by both employers' organizations and governments about the revolutionary objectives of the strike leaders and of the One Big Union (OBU), the issue at hand was the right to bargain collectively. The conflict began when workers represented by the metals- and building-trade councils walked off the job in order to press their demands for collective bargaining, and escalated when some thirty thousand workers also went on strike in sympathy. The support garnered by the OBU was in large part a result of the intransigence of the craft-based unions affiliated with the American Federation of Labor in refusing to embrace the interests of unskilled workers. Mackintosh not only endorsed the legitimacy of the right to collective bargaining in the metals and building trades, but also of the sympathy strike.

> Paradoxically a sympathetic strike is only possible in so far as it is not sympathetic in essence. In the average industrial community a sympathetic strike over wages is not practicable. There is not enough interest, solidarity to carry it through. Only where unionists are convinced that not this or that union but the whole fabric is at stake, will the sympathetic strike persist. The worker must be assured not that such and such a group needs his help, but that he and his group are attacked through other groups. He is not fighting to help another union any more than Platoon No. 1 is fighting to help Platoon No. 2. Both are fighting, for a common object, as necessary to the one as to the other. Refusal to recognize one organization of workers, in the eyes of the unionist, strikes at the whole fabric of unionism and hence is as much his affair as that of the other.[77]

Third, the most far-reaching argument posed by Mackintosh was that the community was not a passive victim of the conflict but bore a direct responsibility for it. "There is much being said as to the right of the community in the matter of industrial disputes. Much more should be said as to the responsibility of the community. Winnipeg and Canada were not innocent bystanders in the recent struggle. There were not only interested but responsible parties. The way for a community to save itself the enormous cost of a general strike is not to read the Riot Act, but to shoulder the responsibility for industrial relations, so that a widespread strike is not needed to wake it up to its duties."[78] The community's obligation was to recognize the legitimate demands of workers for union recognition and the right to bargain collectively in order to redress the inequality inherent in the employer-employee relationship. Organized labour, then, was a progressive force in Canada, and legislative reform was required to manage industrial conflict, and to provide for a more just economy. With Canada's growing economic maturity in the early twentieth century, and with appropriate institutional reform and effective state management of the economy, the legitimate demands of labour could be accommodated within the existing constitutional framework. As a corollary, the nascent radicalism of labour in western Canada would subside.

These observations on the conditions faced by workers near the end of World War I did much to shape Mackintosh's attitude towards industrial relations and economic policy generally. He was a strong advocate of Canada's Industrial Disputes Investigation Act and credited Shortt's astute administration with what early success it achieved in ameliorating industrial disputes.[79] Like Skelton, he was also a strong proponent of the right to collective bargaining, but stopped short of endorsing public-sector unionism or any actions that threatened the "constitutional authority" of government. Reflecting these concerns, Mackintosh would create the first Industrial Relations program in a Canadian university, at Queen's in the 1930s, and his experience in Manitoba at the end of the war would inform much of his work on labour policy during World War II.

"THE PASSING RAINBOW OF COLLEGE FELLOWSHIP"

Mackintosh's time at Brandon College was a curious refuge from the turmoil of war. Amid the larger problems in the world, he devoted his energies to the education of students at a small prairie college. As honorary president of the Arts '18 class, his address to the graduating class cited Irene Parlby, farm leader and future member of the Alberta legislature: "The mind is not a vessel to be filled, but a hearth to be lighted."[80] In his last duty at the college, he reported on "Class Day," where "having freely received lectures, degrees, sermons and advice in quite inedible quantities" from the faculty, the graduating Class of 1919 returned the favour. Students and faculty gathered in the chapel to hear poetry, a song, a few skits, and the valedictory address. For the graduating class, as well as for Mackintosh, it brought to an end a period of fellowship "unobtrusive, yet all-pervasive, which remains in the very fibres of life after much else of college acquirement has disappeared." Given the occasion, he can be excused for being overly sentimental in referring to "the passing rainbow of college fellowship before it faded in the mingling cloud and light of the world's work."[81] For Mackintosh, this work was not to happen in Brandon; instead, he would resume his graduate studies at Harvard.[82]

4

Agricultural Cooperation in Western Canada: Cambridge and Sintaluta, 1919–1920

We are no longer denizens of a hamlet, but citizens of the world.

E.A. Partridge, 1906[1]

If the end of World War I marked Canada's loss of innocence and its preparation for playing a larger, independent role on the world stage, the same can be said for Mackintosh. Leaving the relative quietude of Brandon, he would return to Harvard for more coursework, and then complete the rite of passage into the academic world, his doctoral thesis.

Submitted to Harvard in 1921, his dissertation was for all practical purposes the first Queen's PhD thesis in Economics. In the preface to the published version, which appeared in 1924, he generously acknowledged his "indebtedness to Professor F.W. Taussig of Harvard University for his advice and encouragement in regard to this particular work is but a small part of the debt of a student to a great teacher." It was Queen's, however, that provided the topic, funding, research advice, and editorial help. "Dean Skelton originally suggested the subject and without his aid and advice the work would scarcely have been completed. Professor W.C. Clark ... generously shared the results of his own researches in the grain trade. Numerous suggestions as to the form of presentation have been offered by Principal R. Bruce Taylor, who undertook the dull task of reading the manuscript."[2] Needless to say, there are not many books derived from doctoral theses to which a university principal offers editorial assistance.

The resulting output, *Agricultural Cooperation in Western Canada*, examines what he declares to be the "most significant phase of the economic history of America."[3] The settlement of the Canadian prairies captured many people's attention as the dynamic margin upon which much of the nation's growth was based. For Mackintosh, it was more than that. It was also the celebration of the capacity of Canadian farmers to create economic organizations to address what they perceived to be their unequal position in domestic and international markets. Finding themselves involved in one of the most complicated markets in the world, and one beset by monopoly elements that left them in an inequitable position, they developed institutions to facilitate cooperation among producers, based upon prudent management and the education of members. In essence, Mackintosh would find in western Canadian farm organizations the very combination of eastern cooperation and western enterprise that he had argued for in his honours political economy paper at Queen's.

RETURN TO HARVARD

After spending the summer in western Canada, Mackintosh set aside his research and was back at Harvard by the end of September 1919. With the war over, his state of mind was much improved over what it had been two years earlier. As he would record in his diary, "To visit the past helps one to see that the clods of the present are not mountains."[4] He was soon hard at work preparing to meet his language requirement in German ("a most damnable lingo"[5]) and registering in five courses: the History of Economic Thought and Public Finance (both taught by Charles Jessie Bullock), the Economics of Agriculture and International Trade and Tariff Problems (both with Thomas Carver), and Problems of Labour (taught by William Zebina Ripley).

An improved attitude notwithstanding, his courses were no more satisfying than before. Bullock could be amusing ("Thinks there is a God who looks after fools and the United States, save a number of instances of injustice under income tax"[6]), but Mackintosh found him "most tiresome at times with his damning everything right and left."[7] Edward Mason, who was in the same class, commented on "the increasing sterility of [Bullock's] instruction … his lecture notes had a distinct tinge of yellow."[8] Another graduate student in economics in the early 1920s refers to Bullock's "intolerance for ideas other than his own," and asserted that his "emotional outbursts … converted no one to his reactionary position."[9] Mackintosh aspired merely to "scrape along" in the course.[10] Ripley's instruction was no more inspiring. After completing the final examination, Mackintosh noted that he could have done just as well if he had written it before the course began. On hearing that the grades were uniformly low, he expressed the hope that "the old witch didn't put me below a B"; however, when he obtained a grade of only C+, he concluded that "the class is simply sacrificed." He went to see E.E. Day, the acting chair of the department, who assured him that "it would make no difference. Hinted that Mr. Ripley was in a very bad way. Told me I would get a letter of 'apology' ... Ripley also wrote a letter to Haskins asking him to disregard the grades sent in. I have less respect than before for such crawfishing. He must be a poor specimen in the essentials."[11]

Outside the lecture hall, Mackintosh was zealous in absorbing the life that Harvard, and Boston generally, had to offer. The Canadian Club, the Harvard Club, and the Economics Seminar hosted a series of evening speakers, including William Jennings Bryan, Beatrice and Sidney Webb (he was intrigued by Beatrice's cigar smoking), Taussig, back on campus urging the acceptance of the international trade provisions that arose as part of the Paris Peace Treaty, and J.L. Morison, his old history professor at Queen's, who spoke to the Harvard Club. "It was great to hear the old chap once more," wrote Mackintosh. "He quite took the crowd."[12] He took less solace in Sunday sermons than on his previous sojourn to Harvard: his attendance was less frequent and, when he did go, his tastes continued to run towards more secular views. In particular, he embraced the talk given by Johnston Ross on the role of the church. "Very fine. Showed its function and where the church fell short of it in its professionalized ministry. Could dispense with one-third of them. Mummies! No need to urge men to go into the Church. No modern religious poetry – the dactylic jazz of the modern revival hymn. Need for better hymnology – for more place for the layman." The concept of God was not to be limited to ecclesiasticism. "No narrow graven image. A God that is in Science and Business not leading a tubercular existence within the ecclesiastical confines. H.G. Wells had the naïve audacity to create a God important enough to explain the duration of the war. God is not smiling geniality and sentimentality. The Holy Ghost would feel as much at home in a laboratory as in prayer-meeting. Nor yet a tribal provincial God. Need for mysticism, all pervading Deity that expresses himself in all the forms of life."[13]

With George Wilson now teaching at Dalhousie University, Mackintosh's closest friends were three history students who would go on to long and distinguished academic careers: Frederick Merk, James B. Hedges, and Paul Bigelow Schaeffer. Merk, who would spend much of his career at Harvard, had hardly created a positive first impression when Mackintosh met him in 1917, when Merk lived next door in Conant Hall. After a long argument on religion, Mackintosh dismissed him as a "pseudo-savant," "atheist," and materialist," who raised "boresome arguments" and often "talked ranting socialism of the most insane kind. Has hardly much originality for a graduate."[14] He would come to reverse his opinion and to appreciate greatly Merk's companionship and, as well, his much prized Victrola. Hedges, who expressed his displeasure with Harvard's "chronological school of history," earned his PhD in 1924 before taking a job at Clark University and then at Brown.[15] Schaeffer's studies at Harvard were interrupted by service in World War I. After graduating in 1923, he taught at the University of California (Berkeley) for thirty years. The four men passed a great deal of time in each other's company, taking long walks, occasionally skating on the Charles River, talking, reading the poetry of George Meredith, and listening to Merk's Victrola.[16]

Mackintosh was less kind in his diary about other graduate students. On Frederick Binkerd Artz, who went on to a long career at Oberlin College, he commented: "Newman, Arnold and Marcus Aureluis are his idols. He is soaked to the ears in Babbitt's doctrines. Prattles of nothing but principles though most of his practices he admits must be based on expediency."[17] Ralph Macdonald Spankie (a Queen's graduate studying law) fared no better: "a heavy witted individual to be sure ... I think it would be conducive to quiet if I saw little of him."[18] Nor did his fellow Canadian, Duncan Clark Hyde, escape unscathed: "rather important little fellow not overly modest ... For a graduate student of very good record he has the most immature mind I ever struck. A queer mixture of old religion, mossback reactionism and assumed superiority. Very much down on Bolshevist-minded women, especially at Radcliffe. How does economics seem to produce such persons?"[19]

In the company of Schaeffer, Mackintosh became a devotee of the arts, regardless of the weather ("Bitter blustery morning not fit for man or beast or even a Canadian so Schaeffer says"[20]). The symphony increasingly supplanted the chapel as his favourite Sunday venue, and he often rushed from weekday classes for an afternoon concert in Boston. He took in several operas (*Il Trovatore*, *Aida*, *Tales of Hoffmann*, and *The Taming of the Shrew*), a "movie," and even the occasional vaudeville act. The theatre, however, became his most ardent pursuit, and he attended at least one play a week at one of Boston's grand stages, where he saw many of the leading stage actors of the day, including William Gillette, Leo Dietrichstein, Minnie Maddern (Mrs) Fiske, Grace George, Helen Hayes, Ruth Chatterton, and Laura Crews. Indeed, so absorbing was the theatre that Mackintosh turned down a date with a Radcliffe woman: "Note from Miss Cruickshank inviting me to a dance on Friday. Had to decline on account of theatre engagement with Schaeffer (Mrs Fiske). Awfully decent of Miss Ray to invite me. Sorry I can't go."[21] He remained unimpressed with Boston audiences, complaining of "silly shop girl tittering audiences" and puzzled by "the curious type of Back Bay Duchess whom one always sees at a risqué performance." But the arts were important. "Every town should have a repertory theatre," he confidently asserted. "It would help the theatre and the public both."[22]

In his return to Harvard, then, Mackintosh still found his coursework wanting, but, whether engaged in discussion with his colleagues, attending lectures, the occasional sermon, and arts performances, or munching on his usual late-night diet of an egg sandwich at the Waldorf in Cambridge Circus, the overall experience was more gratifying.

However, it all came to a rather abrupt halt. This is reflected in his official transcript for the 1919–1920 academic year.[23]

This dubious record (a C+, an incomplete, two "absent," and an ambiguous " – ") is due to the fact that Economics 14 and 31 were two-semester courses, Economics 32 and 33 were second-term courses commencing in January 1920, and Economics 34 was a one-semester course in the fall term. In other words, Mackintosh completed his fall coursework, but left Harvard before the end of the winter term. With Day's assurance that his coursework was adequate, he departed for western Canada to continue research on his dissertation.

THE SAGE OF SINTALUTA

There was a not-so-coincidental relationship between Skelton's research interests and Mackintosh's dissertation topic. During the summer of 1919, Mackintosh had been dispatched by Skelton to Regina, Winnipeg, and points in between, to gather material on

Table 4.1 Summary of Mackintosh's Student Transcript at Harvard

Course	*Title*	*Instructor*	*Period*	*Grade*
Economics 14	History of Economics to the Year 1848	Bullock	MWF 11	incomp
Economics 31	Public Finance	Bullock	MWF10	–
Economics 32 (second term)	Economics of Agriculture	Carver	TuThSa 12	abs
Economics 33 (second term)	International Trade and Tariff Problems	Taussig	TuTh 2:30	abs
Economics 34	Problems of Labour	Ripley	TuTh 1:30	C+

Source: HUA, Official Student Records, "William Archibald Mackintosh," UAV 161.272.5.

farmers' cooperative organizations for the handling and marketing of grain. The primary fodder for this research was newspaper accounts, company records, trade journals, and Hansard transcripts; however, he also had occasion to interview many of the key participants in the prairie cooperative movement. Largely unimpressed with George Chipman, editor of the *Grain Growers' Guide* ("a rather a brusque self-centred individual"[24]), he had abundant respect for several others: T.A. Crerar, president and general manager of the United Grain Growers, who became the federal minister of agriculture in 1917; C.A. Dunning, an English-born homesteader, the first manager of the Saskatchewan Co-op Elevator Company before becoming premier of Saskatchewan and later minister of finance in Mackenzie King's cabinet; and W.R. Motherwell, the first president of the Territorial Grain Growers' Association in 1901, then Saskatchewan's minister of agriculture, and eventually leader of the Progressive Party.[25] Crerar and Dunning would both figure prominently in his later work with the Government of Canada and, by coincidence, it would be Dunning, as chancellor of Queen's University, who would bestow upon Mackintosh the robes of the principal at his installation in 1951.

But if one man was responsible for educating Mackintosh on the nuances of the farmers' movement, it was the iconic and iconoclastic "sage of Sintaluta," E.A. Partridge. Born in Dalston, Ontario, in 1861, Partridge completed secondary school and then taught school in Saskatchewan while homesteading near Sintaluta. Despite suffering much personal tragedy, including the loss of a leg in a farm accident, the drowning of one of his three daughters, and the death of both of his sons serving overseas during World War I, Partridge was tireless in his efforts to promote the interests of prairie farmers. Described by one as "an unsuccessful farmer, an unsuccessful businessman and an unsuccessful editor," he was the moving force behind the creation of "a mammoth business and a national farm magazine."[26] It was through Partridge's efforts that farmers first successfully challenged the railways' control over grain handling; it was also Partridge who was primarily responsible for the *Grain Growers' Guide* and was its first editor; and it was Partridge who laid the groundwork for the formation of the United Grain Growers as the farmer-owned grain-marketing outlet. Personal wealth escaped him, however, and he ended his life in virtual poverty.

Mackintosh had first met Partridge while teaching near Indian Head in the summer of 1915, and he renewed the acquaintanceship in 1919. He travelled to Sintaluta to meet Partridge and they toured the wheat fields in the region by car.[27] As a testament to his affection and admiration for the self-described "Ruskinite," a personal touch is added in one footnote to Mackintosh's thesis: "It is a far cry from 'The Political Economy of Art' to the Canadian Grain Trade, yet the initiators of successful cooperative selling of grain in Western Canada drew from Ruskin much of his inspiration and not a few of his ideas."[28] On reading the thesis, Partridge would counsel Mackintosh that: "As a Doctor of Philosophy should, you refrain from prophesy – a dangerous position these days if one cares for one's reputation for economic wisdom." He added that "You see I am still a Ruskinite." He would later write *A War on Poverty: The One War that Can End War* (1925), which included his utopian vision of "Coalsamao" a cooperative commonwealth extending from British Columbia to northwestern Ontario. He died in Victoria in 1931, apparently taking his own life.

AGRICULTURAL COOPERATION

Mackintosh begins his thesis with his first published reference to "staples," a concept that he credits to the Yale economist, Guy Callender. "In the settlement of new countries one problem takes precedence over all others – the problem of discovering a staple product with a ready market. The world makes a path to the doors of those regions fortunate enough to possess such a product, and all commodities of other countries are obtainable in exchange." Wheat had the "all-essential quality of a pioneer staple": it was a cash crop well-suited to the growing conditions on the Canadian prairies, reducible to standard grades, compact and thus capable of long-distance shipping in bulk form, and valuable once transportation costs had fallen sufficiently to allow western wheat to compete for the markets of Europe. As such, "a commodity which is produced on the agricultural frontier, under extensive cultivation and with the resulting wide scattering of population and rural isolation, enters into one of the most intricate of world marketing organizations."[29] But those looking for the kernel of the staple thesis will be disappointed. There is no concern with the relationship between wheat exports and Canadian economic growth, and no analysis of the production process. Instead, Mackintosh focuses on new institutions created by farmers to overcome the obstacles they faced in getting their grain to market. In particular, there were three challenges in "bridging the gap" between their own productive activity and international markets: the monopoly power (or more properly, monopsony power) of railways, elevator companies, and the Winnipeg Grain Exchange. Farmers addressed each in step by pressing for legislative reforms and by developing their own marketing institutions to take over the role of the middleman.

The first problem encountered was the CPR's practice of leasing sites for track elevators and guaranteeing them a local monopoly. Initially, grain was transferred from wagon to railway box car on a loading platform at a "flat warehouse." Subsequently, grain elevators emerged, because they had superior storage facilities to meet seasonal variations in grain shipping and because their more capital-intensive form of weighing, unloading wagons, and loading cars by hopper gave them a distinct cost advantage. When the CPR prevented farmers from loading grain directly onto cars or using flat warehouses for temporary storage, farmers had little option but to sell their grain to a local merchant or dealer. In most cases, this merchant function was in the hands of the elevator company. Farmers' organizations, such as the Territorial Grain Growers' Association (1901; renamed the Saskatchewan Grain Growers' when Saskatchewan attained provincial status in 1906) and the United Farmers of Alberta (a consolidation of rival farm organizations) proved their worth in challenging the power of the CPR. Their political agitation led to the Manitoba Grain Act of 1900 – for Mackintosh the "true Magna Carta of the West" – requiring dealers to be licensed and railways to build flat warehouses when petitioned by a sufficient number of farmers to do so. This gave the farmer an alternative to selling "on track" to the local elevator company, thus, in theory, breaking the monopoly of the line companies as purchasers.

While this reform opened up the possibility for greater competition from independent commission agents, the large millers, exporters, and "line" elevator companies continued to dominate the industry. They enjoyed a decided cost advantage over independent buyers who were dependent on the direct loading of grain cars at flat warehouses. Moreover, their size enabled them to extract concessions on transportation and banking services and, through the Northwest Grain Dealers' Association, they exercised considerable influence over prices on the Grain Exchange. Farmers had a "vague sense" that something was wrong, although they were unable to demonstrate that collusion occurred in the fixing of street prices.

The question for farm organizations was how best to respond. They considered building their own elevators, but rejected this option, fearing that, without substantial capital, predatory pricing on behalf of the line elevators would drive them into bankruptcy. Moreover, a farmer-run elevator would not address the needs of smaller farmers unable to fill a complete grain car and thus in need of flat warehousing facilities. Instead, it was Partridge who first proposed cooperative marketing, as distinct from the ownership of elevator facilities, as the means of overcoming monopoly control. A farmer-owned agency selling on a consignment basis in Winnipeg would allow farmers an alternative to the Northwest Grain Dealers' Association, which was seen to be manipulating street prices. Partridge thus formed the Sintaluta Grain Growers with a limited amount of capital and bought a seat on the Winnipeg Grain Exchange. Although his membership was suspended by the exchange after just six weeks – among the reasons was his inflammatory propaganda against the exchange's rules – he was readmitted after the province intervened and he thus laid the groundwork for the Grain Growers' Grain Company.

Only after establishing a major presence in the cooperative marketing field did farmers enter the elevator business. In 1911, the Saskatchewan Co-operative Elevator Company, Limited, was formed with the assistance of government loans for up to 85 per cent of elevator costs and grants for administrative expenses. "It attempted to do what the Grain Growers Grain Cooperative had done in the commission field – provide another competitor in the field and allow farmers to gain first hand knowledge of elevator problems." This led to the emergence of two large farmer-run elevator companies, the United Grain Growers Ltd and Saskatchewan Co-operative Elevator Company, which was soon handling up to a third of the grain on the prairies.[30]

Through these successive steps, farm organizations achieved the degree of vertical integration necessary to compete effectively in world markets. "It is in the great grain companies that the cooperative movement of Western Canada centres," wrote Mackintosh. "There the most substantial achievements have been made, the greatest financial success has been attained, and the experience gained and the model given for further cooperative enterprises. They have become the largest grain companies in Canada and among the most powerful on the continent. At every stage of the marketing process, country elevators, commission houses, terminal elevators, and export, the farmers' companies are powerful and effective competitors."[31]

Two features distinguish Mackintosh's account of the rise of farmer organizations in western Canada. The first was his emphasis on the "prudent" leadership that adopted a pragmatic approach to cooperation. Individuals such as Crerar, Dunning, and Motherwell were farmers with abundant personal ability and business training. These were men with common sense, who sought cooperation not out of a romantic or idealized notion, but as a pragmatic solution to the problems they encountered. This enabled them to make the wise choice of the point of entry – the commission market – where higher profits and low capital requirements allowed them to take advantage of the existing grain exchange instead of competing with it. Mackintosh would later write that "people are subject to agrarian movements as children are subject to measles," but show little patience for "sermons" on the cooperative spirit: "The truth is that successful cooperation must be adapted to the business facts of its community ... Farmers' movements, to make substantial progress, must be far sighted rather than idealistic, and their programmes, or at least the essential parts of them, must be practical as plumbing."[32] In contrast, he would depict Aaron Shapiro as "the not always-discriminating apostle of cooperation."[33] The second feature emphasized by Mackintosh was the importance of educating farmers about international markets and about cooperation as necessary to address the inequitable position in which they found themselves. "One of the professed objects of cooperative marketing was to enlighten that ignorance and permit the effective participation of thousands of producers in the marketing process ... This educational benefit in the marketing of grain is more important than any other. This is so because of the wide gap between many producers in a frontier agricultural region and the ultimate market for wheat in Europe, with the consequent greater difficulty of relating producer to market."[34]

When published in 1924, *Agricultural Cooperation* received modest attention and qualified praise. Humphrey Michell, in his review for the *Canadian Historical Review*, applauded it as "a distinctly valuable contribution," but struggled when it came to appreciating the style of an economic history that departed from the norms of Canadian historiography. He complained of an annoying tendency for over-documentation and some of the analytical methods: "Is it really necessary to give ninety-six references in one chapter of sixteen pages? ... And what will the poor mathematical readers make of 'adjusted medians of percentages of monthly average prices of no. 1 northern wheat?'"[35] Henry Vivian, in the *Economic Journal*, observed that, from a European perspective, "there are many lessons to be learned from the remarkable development of agricultural cooperation with which this study deals," but rightly criticized Mackintosh for referring to the "yardstick of the Rochdale system" (or the principles that had evolved based on the British Rochdale Society of Equitable Pioneers founded in 1844) as a basis for comparison, since it entailed cooperation among consumers rather than producers. Vivian does, however, single out the importance of Mackintosh's underlying thesis: that the strength of the cooperatives rested less on eliminating the exploitation of middlemen as it did the farmers' accumulation of knowledge and sound business practice necessary for running a large organization efficiently.[36] E.G. Nourske, in a brief piece in the *American Economic Review*, echoed Vivian's sentiments. He wrote that "there is an admirable insistence upon the relations between the distinctive features of organization and practice and the peculiar conditions of time, place, and the existing economic organization out of which they grew." But he was correct to point out that, "While the concluding chapter professes to present 'The theory of agricultural cooperation,' this title seems overambitious and the content of the chapter is disappointing."[37]

Mackintosh's thesis has no grand theory of cooperation; however, it does provide a compelling account of the success of farmer organizations on the Canadian prairies in which cooperation was the essence of reform. Small farmers, isolated geographically, could only effectively compete in the market through cooperation and vertical integration. The organizations that emerged were successful because of prudent and moderate leadership, efficiency rather than ideology as the guiding principle, education of the farmer on the rudiments of grain marketing, and recourse to the state to enact appropriate legislative reform. Cooperation, therefore, was neither a retreat nor a rebellion against the market, but a more effective means of linking farmers to their final market. "The complete commercialization of agriculture to which agricultural cooperation is a means, and often an indispensable means, constitutes an Agricultural Revolution of far-reaching significance."[38] In this regard, there is an obvious continuity between his honours political economy paper and his doctoral dissertation. What Mackintosh celebrated was the capacity of prairie farmers to combine the lessons of cooperation of the sort outlined by Tolstoy with western "enterprise," the result being a more vibrant and equitable economy.

PART TWO

Canadian Political Economy and the Origins of the Staple Thesis

Economic scholarship in English Canada truly "came of age" in the interwar period.[1] Much of the credit for this can be attributed to the remarkable esprit de corps that emerged among Canadian economists. There was recognition that they were engaged in a common undertaking in writing Canada's economic history for the first time and, through this, gaining an understanding of the challenges facing the nation during the Great Depression. This spirit was most readily apparent in the revival of the Canadian Political Science Association and the subsequent creation of the *Canadian Journal of Economics and Political Science* as a forum for research. In 1932, R.H. Coats could justifiably claim that "Economic research has not only been born, it has attained firm foothold, if not vigorous growth, in Canada."[2]

Mackintosh was central to the developments in the discipline. In his administrative role as head of the department of political and economic science at Queen's, he furthered its role as the centre for applied economic research on Canadian economic issues, and as director of the commerce program, he oversaw the expansion of the first bachelor of commerce degree in the country. Outside of his department, he supported the work of his colleagues, through his involvement in the Canadian Political Science Association, as editor of the *Journal of the Canadian Bankers' Association* where he published their papers, and as director of the Canadian Pioneer Problems Committee, which provided an outlet for their research in the *Frontier of Canadian Settlement* series.

But his main contribution came through his own scholarship. Beginning with his 1923 paper on "Economic Factors in Canadian

History," he outlined the geographical and economic determinants of Canadian history both before and after Confederation. In doing so, he defined for himself and the discipline generally a program of study for writing Canadian economic history. In this shared endeavour – undertaken primarily in concert with Innis but also including other members of the academic community in Canada – Mackintosh's personal contribution was in explaining the role of prairie wheat production as the driving force in Canadian national development in the early twentieth century. He would then provide the first attempt to articulate the staple thesis – heralded by many as Canada's greatest contribution to the discipline of economics – as an explanation for Canadian economic history, as well as a model for export-led growth in developing countries.

5

Queensian Economics: Kingston, 1920–1928

If all the comforts we enjoy
Are based on pain of others,
And social gain can come when we
Have trampled on our brothers,
How shall we, then, with any sense
Proclaim our faith in Providence?

Anonymous translation of
W.A. Mackintosh into verse, 1928[1]

Canada's future depends much upon [Mackenzie King's] wisdom and much upon a good crop.

W.A. Mackintosh, 1922[2]

In the fall of 1920, Mackintosh returned home to take up an appointment as assistant professor in the department of political and economic science at Queen's University. The ensuing decade would see the growth of a department that would define "Queensian economics": continuation of a strong tradition in undergraduate teaching in economics and political science; development of the country's first degree program in the complementary field of commerce; and a record of applied research with strong ties to both the public and private sectors. In joining O.D. Skelton and W.C. Clark as the junior member in the department, Mackintosh had every reason to anticipate playing an active role in its development, but he could not have expected just how much so. With the departure of his two senior colleagues within four years of his arrival, he would assume the directorship of what would eventually become the School of Commerce and, three years later in 1927, would ascend to the John A.

Macdonald Chair as department head. At the age of thirty-two, Mackintosh was directing one of the two most important political economy departments in the country, and would bring to fruition Skelton's vision of a degree program in commerce taught within a liberal-arts context.

At the same time, Mackintosh built a personal research program that extended his thesis work on the wheat economy into a more general exploration of the geographical background to Canada's economic development. Adding to this several commentaries on current economic issues in *Queen's Quarterly*, editorship of the *Journal of the Canadian Bankers' Association*, and summer work with the Government of Canada, he emerged as one of Canada's leading economists. But his administrative and government work did not come without some cost in terms of his academic scholarship. In 1923, Mackintosh's paper on the "Economic Factors in Canadian History" provided a path-breaking analysis of the geographical and economic determinants of Canada's history. He described his argument as tentative and "susceptible of proof" but requiring much further research to establish its veracity. With his time largely consumed in teaching, administration, and government work, it would take another decade before this skeleton to the staple thesis would be fleshed out.

THE DEPARTMENT OF POLITICAL AND ECONOMIC SCIENCE

In the early 1920s, Queen's University was not much larger than when Mackintosh was an undergraduate: some 1,500 students were taught by a faculty complement of 110.[3] Where the Faculty of Arts was concerned, Skelton asserted that it was "unquestionably stronger than that of McGill or any of the Maritime universities, and it will on the whole still rank ahead of any Western faculty."[4] The department of political and economic science had the largest enrolment in the faculty, and offered a surprising range of courses, given that in 1920 it had only three permanent members, a temporary appointment in commerce, and two chartered accountants, responsible primarily for extramural courses.

The normal teaching load was the equivalent of three eight-month courses, each composed of three lectures a week, either on Monday, Wednesday, and Friday, or on Tuesday, Thursday, and Saturday.

Skelton enjoyed no relief despite his duties as department head and dean of Arts, teaching the full-year Introduction to Political Science and four half-courses on the politics side (Socialism and the Relation of the State to Industry, the Government of Canada, National Problems, and Commercial Law). Clark handled the bulk of the economics courses, including Introduction to Economics, second-year courses on Agricultural Economics, Money and Banking, and the Canadian Banking System, and an upper-level course, Corporate Finance. Mackintosh taught a comparatively light load of four half-courses in his first year: the Economic History of Canada, Economic Geography, Economics of Transportation, and Social Problems.[5] J.W. Ballard, also hired in 1920, taught marketing and accounting in support of the commerce program.

Pressure on teaching increased with the newly minted commerce program, the first such degree offered in the country. When the Canadian Bankers' Association (CBA) was formed in the 1890s, it expected to provide the type of special courses for junior bank employees that were the norm in many other countries. No action was taken on the matter until Skelton proposed to the CBA that Queen's assume responsibility. Commencing in 1914, three correspondence courses were offered: an associate course for junior staff, taught through the Shaw Correspondence School of Toronto, and an advanced course and a supplementary course, taught by Queen's. Enrolment was slow to take off because of World War I, but afterwards became an important part of both the CBA and Queen's.[6] Building on the extramural courses in banking, the commerce program, created by Skelton and Clark in 1919, offered business training within a liberal-arts education. Students were required to take the full-year introductory courses, Economics and Politics, Economic History, Money and Banking, and either Socialism and the Relation of State to Industry or Labour Problems. Required business courses included Marketing, Commercial Law, and two courses in accounting.

The commerce program was not without controversy. J.M. Macdonnell, an influential trustee, protested against the introduction of a "vocational spirit" into the liberal-arts curriculum and urged that the university would "do well to eradicate it as speedily as may be."[7] Clark responded that business training was needed and was best addressed within an arts faculty.[8] Mackintosh elaborated on Clark's sentiments in a 1923 paper on "The Psychologist and

Economics." He found a similarity between Taussig's concept of the "instinct of contrivance" and Veblen's "workmanship," in that both suggested a predisposition to creativity free from any motive of self-interest. Accordingly, he did not see entrepreneurial drive as singularly related to the pursuit of profit: "Business is to some extent a game and the score is counted in dollars. Not the profit but the success which the profit stands for is in many cases the incentive to life-long activity. There is some truth in the socialist's claim that we have bound together accumulation and business success when they need not have been so bound."[9] The challenge facing commerce programs was to professionalize business – just as law, engineering and medicine had been professionalized – so that "profit and executive success will no longer be correlated. Inequality of wealth will, of course, not disappear, but something of the money-making age, 'the acquisitive society,' will pass from us."[10] Writing in 1930, Mackintosh acknowledged that this argument was self-serving to the extent that one of his motives for a commerce program was as a vehicle for expanding the scope and size of economics departments. Nonetheless, it remains the case that the introduction of commerce courses was designed to prepare students for social service. "The only legitimate object of a course in Commerce is to train young people so that they may serve, in business or closely related vocations, a more useful social purpose than would be probable if they entered the field of business with no university training or with some other type of university training of equivalent attainment."[11] In this vein, he would repeatedly remind graduating classes that "Native shrewdness and burning ambition will still carry a man far in business, but there is need for an enkindled imagination, there is even greater need for a broader and more sophisticated system of business ethics, if business is to serve and not to enslave the world in our day."[12]

Extramural courses in accounting were added in 1920 when Skelton reached an agreement with the Institute of Chartered Accountants of Ontario. To qualify as a chartered accountant in the province required four years of articling and successful completion of three examinations. In preparation, students took voluntary courses through for-profit correspondence schools. Skelton proposed that the course be delivered by Queen's, which would prepare the course material and regular assignments based on the curriculum set out by the institute. In return, students would require one less year of articling and avoid taking the preliminary examination.

When 275 students signed up in the first year, it was quickly apparent that Skelton's ambitions outstripped the department's resources, such that he travelled to Great Britain during the summer of 1922 in order to recruit new faculty members. Queen's low salaries made it difficult to attract senior academics, so Skelton was on the lookout for "promising young men [who are] more readily detached and will fit more regularly into Canadian ways than dons of mature years." He reported to President Taylor his success in securing the services of R.G.H. (Rex) Smails and C.A. Ashley, two men in their late twenties "of distinct individuality and promise." Smails was appointed assistant professor of accounting on the strength of two years of professional practice and teaching with the Institute of Chartered Accountants in Manchester. "He strikes me as having a good general education and background, has a very clear orderly mind, isn't afraid of work, and while a man who distinctly knows his own mind, should be a congenial colleague." Ashley was hired as assistant professor of commerce to replace Ballard. "Ashley seemed to best meet our needs; he is a B.Com., of Birmingham, and has just passed his final C.A. here; he has experience which will fit admirably for busi ness and factory organization courses. He is quite a bit like his fellow Midlander – both slight in build, and a good deal of initiative, I think – organized the National Union of Students here, was an artillery captain at twenty-one, has travelled a good deal in Europe lately on student affairs."[13] With the arrival of the "two young Englishmen who don't wear hats," as they came to be known, "Skelton created academic accountancy in Canada."[14] With the addition of another chartered accountant, C.E. Walker, in the same year, Skelton ranked Queen's program highly by British standards: "I think there is no doubt that with our work and staff as it will be organized next year, our Commerce course will be easily ahead of Edinburgh, Leeds, or Sheffield, as good as Manchester, and nearly as good as Birmingham; London has immensely greater potentialities which are, however, not yet fully coordinated."[15]

The volume of administrative work accompanying the extramural courses placed a strain on the department's already inadequate facilities. The commerce staff was located in the New Arts Building, with one room serving as a general office and another as "executive" office, where Clark, as director, and his team of accountants "would be seated on kitchen chairs at two collapsible tables."[16] Smails complained that, upon his arrival, the piles of unmarked assignments littering the floor were so thick that it made it difficult to open the office door.[17] The lack of a telephone, as well as office furniture to put it on, led Clark to issue a curt appeal: "May I suggest that one of the sundries [in the budget] might be a telephone. There is, I believe, real need for a telephone service for the banking and accounting office; the continual running up and downstairs is not only annoying but represents a serious waste of my time and the time of my staff."[18]

With the permanent staff in place – Skelton, Clark, Mackintosh, Ashley, Smails, and Walker – Mackintosh had every reason to expect that he would settle into a department under the leadership of his senior colleagues. But this was not to be the case. Clark's resignation in 1923 to join a firm of investment bankers in Chicago was described by Skelton as "an irreparable blow," noting that "Dr. Mackintosh is going to be fully as good a man, but one is not two."[19] Then came the unthinkable. In the summer of 1924, Skelton took a one-year leave of absence and subsequently resigned, "after months of swithering,"[20] to join the department of external affairs in Ottawa. As he recorded in his diary, "I found it hard to leave on account of the deep interest and responsibility in Queen's; the constant opportunity of developing youngsters of promise and helping them to count for something hereafter; the friends in the university; the possibility of doing more in the future; while on the other hand, lack of faith in the direction of affairs under the present Principal; some resentment of affairs like Sandwell's appointment [in the English department] or J.M. Macdonnell's Commerce inquisitions, lack of opportunity of late for writing; a salary that left no margin."[21] The appointment of B.K. Sandwell as provisional head of the English department was an affront to Skelton on both a personal and an academic level. Though a respected journalist, Sandwell had no experience teaching English and little acquaintance with university affairs. His selection prompted the resignation of J.F. Macdonald, an extremely popular instructor, established scholar, acting head, and a close friend of Skelton. Macdonald was quickly hired by the University of Toronto, while Sandwell was not reappointed at the end of his two-year term.[22]

"The prospect of a whole session without Dean Skelton is rather difficult to contemplate," wrote Mackintosh to Principal Taylor, "but I suppose we will have to make the best of the situation."[23] However, he helped assemble a credible staff to replace Clark and Skelton. Frank Knox, who received his BA from Queen's in 1923, interrupted his graduate studies at Harvard to assume responsibility for some of the teaching in economics. He would remain at Queen's for forty years and, although he never completed his doctoral work, Mackintosh would herald him as the greatest teacher of economics in the country.[24] W.B. Wynne, who received his BA (1918) and MA (1919) from Queen's, studied Law at Oxford as a Rhodes Scholar and then taught at Trinity College, Cambridge, was hired primarily to teach Skelton's courses in political science.[25] When Ashley left after only one year, H.G. Caldwell, an undergraduate classmate of Mackintosh's, was recruited to teach statistics and to assist Smails and Walker on the commerce side.[26] To augment this group during Skelton's one-year temporary absence, a "special lecturer" was also sought, and the list of potential candidates speaks highly of Queen's international prominence. Skelton elicited the interest of Matthew Brown Hammond (Ohio State and future president of the American Economic Association), while Mackintosh, when travelling to Scotland, sought out R.H. Tawney (who "looked very favourably on the possibility for some time but finally decided he couldn't forego the London School of Economics or the Labour Party") and Alfred Zimmern (Oxford). He then alerted Taylor to the availability of Herbert Heaton. The English-born and -trained economic historian was spending much of a sabbatical year away from the University of Adelaide teaching at Oxford, and planned to tour North America in what was effectively a year-long job search: "there is a very able man in Economic History – Heaton who has been over here for a year and who is returning to his post in Australia via Canada, who would be glad of an opportunity (remunerative). He is giving lectures at Toronto, Harvard, Chicago, Manitoba, and Alberta. His particular subjects are Economic History and Labour & Social Problems in Australia."[27] When suitable arrangements could not be made with Hammond, Tawney, or Zimmern, Skelton noted that "thro' [Mackintosh], [C.R.] Fay, [William] Beveridge, secured Heaton of Australia for part of semester."[28]

Responsibility for the commerce program fell into Mackintosh's "surprised and inexperienced hands,"[29] and he found himself, at the age of twenty-nine, and just four years after arriving, as the senior scholar in the department. Yet Skelton had the pride of a surrogate parent when, on a visit from Ottawa, he observed that his former protegé "handled the executive work with a quiet efficiency which has been a pleasure to watch."[30] Consistent with Skelton's conviction that Queen's "cannot under our conditions secure ready-made men; we must grow our own,"[31] he left with the assurance that, despite the youth of Mackintosh, Knox, and Wynne, the department was in good hands.

MORE HEATON THAN LIGHT

Selecting a replacement for Skelton as department head proved a different matter. On Adam Shortt's recommendation, C.R. Fay was the first choice of the trustees and Mackintosh the second. It was hard to dispute this ranking: Fay, despite being an economic historian when a political scientist was required, was a distinguished scholar who had interrupted his career at Cambridge to spend ten years at the University of Toronto during the 1920s. Skelton noted in his diary that Mackintosh "seemed to take the offer to Fay philosophically."[32] In speaking to Principal Taylor, Mackintosh indicated that "I would prefer to continue my work at a salary of $3,000 in a strong progressive Department rather than receive $4,000 as the Head of a weaker Department." At the same time, he added that, because Fay was also an economic historian, "there would be little room for me to continue indefinitely at Queen's in the work in which I had been endeavouring in the past nine years to specialize and that it would be but a matter of time and a favourable opportunity until I took a position elsewhere."[33] But with everyone anticipating that Fay would decline the appointment, Mackintosh left his interview with Taylor expecting to become department head.

The plot thickened when Fay, in declining the offer, suggested Heaton in his stead. "A good sort," observed Skelton, "but not thorough or well balanced and with no knowledge of Canada. [Dean] Matheson asked my opinion, of course I strongly recommended Mack. Matheson said he felt equally strongly and would recommend his immediate appointment."[34] When the trustees opted for Heaton, Skelton declared the selection "inexplicable" and "preposterous." He wrote to Mackintosh that "The only explanation I can give is that after the wrecking of the English Department it has been felt that it would be invidious not to wreck the Economics Department also." This decision Mackintosh did not accept philosophically. Given that Principal Taylor had twice insisted that no outside candidate other than Fay was under consideration, Mackintosh deemed Taylor's actions "a grave breach of ordinary good faith" and conveyed his sense of personal betrayal to Taylor in no uncertain terms: "The strong claims which Queen's has had on my loyalty and services have all but dissolved."[35] The intensity of this reaction appears surprising, for Heaton proved to be a first-rate scholar who eventually became president of the American Economic Association. But Mackintosh questioned Heaton's commitment to Queen's: "Now it seems that he is making offers to Heaton, who is likely to accept depending, I should think entirely on two things, how much he calculates the cost of coal would increase the cost of living in Canada as compared with South Australia, and secondly, the chances of Fay getting a post in England in a few years and Heaton succeeding Fay. Heaton is a very likeable chap in many ways, but the service which he gave us at Queen's was worth, I should say, about 40 per cent of the money which he was paid."[36] Moreover, since Queen's had developed a strong empirical orientation, focusing on Canadian issues, bringing in an English-trained "Australian" was a clear departure from the department's established direction. Mackintosh's anger was heightened by the treatment of Wynne, who was "gracelessly dropped" to make way for Heaton, on the rationale that another "Queen's man" was undesired.[37]

On hearing officially of Heaton's appointment, Mackintosh expressed to Skelton his strong inclination to resign, but that he would not leave the university in the breach with insufficient time to fill his vacancy. He took a week-long trip to Cambridge with George Wilson in order to escape the gloomy atmosphere in Kingston, but returned feeling no differently about the situation. Six months later, he was still considering resigning, despite Vice-Principal William McNeill's pleas to the contrary. As Mackintosh wrote to Clark: "McNeill's suggestion is that I shed the work in Commerce and get some increased financial allowance that would permit me to get some help in research; in fact, he rather challenges me to name any suitable conditions and give him a chance to see if they cannot be met. I may say the whole business of using one's position to extract a pound of flesh is rather a disgusting one to me and I am very loath to commit myself to any conditions under which I might stay. The fact is, I did not know how weary I was until I actually began to anticipate relief at the end of the present term. There is a very great deal of reason in what McNeill says, but I am loath to sacrifice my glimpse of freedom at present."[38]

The appointment of Heaton reverberated throughout the university community. On a visit to Ottawa in the fall, McNeill had dinner with Skelton, and the latter reported that his former colleague "apparently has no idea of widespread distinct opposition to RBT[aylor]. Said he had been raked over coals at Trustees' meeting for way in which Heaton appointment made (tho Nickle and Macdonnell equally responsible) and later lectured by Nickle at Shortt's request – but bobbed off serenely next day."[39] McNeill's serenity was shattered a few months later at a fractious meeting in Toronto as part of the university's endowment campaign, where he was forced to defend the administration's handling of both the English and economics departments. Mackintosh confessed to being indirectly responsible for "for a good deal of the bomb-throwing," having earlier appealed to Neil Leckie and D.I. McLeod – both trustees – to consider a review of the university's administration.[40]

The turmoil abated when Heaton resigned after two years to become head of the department of history at the University of Minnesota. (When canvassed for his opinion of Heaton by the University of Minnesota, Skelton was prepared to recommend Mackintosh for the position.[41]) There was little debate as to Heaton's successor, and Mackintosh was appointed as department head and Sir John A. Macdonald Chair of Political Economy in 1927. On hearing the news, Skelton was "much pleased and particularly so as it came without any effort or wrangling on my part."[42]

"CANADA IS A NATION CREATED IN DEFIANCE OF GEOGRAPHY"

After submitting his doctoral dissertation in 1921, and turning it into a book, published in 1924, Mackintosh remained interested in the institutional aspects of grain marketing, and, specifically, the emergence of the wheat pools. But his attention turned to the broad geographical factors underlying Canadian economic history. His seminal article "Economic Factors in Canadian History," published in 1923, provides the first broad strokes of the staple thesis. The paper sets out to correct the "constitutional bias" in the writing of Canadian history: preoccupation among historians with British colonial policy not only ignored the underlying geographical and economic factors that shaped government decision making, but also led to a neglect of the importance of continental influences. He thus offers an account of Canadian history based not on political events per se, but as the response to underlying changes in the international economic conditions in relation to the country's fundamental physical characteristics.

He begins with the evocative statement that "North America faces Europe": the Atlantic seaboard was more accessible by virtue of its coastal plain and navigable river systems, such that colonization was more likely from Europe than Asia. Subsequent settlement of the interior was shaped by two imposing barriers, the Laurentian Shield over the northern half of the continent and the Appalachians, each making it difficult to reach the fertile Central Plains. He then draws upon Guy Callender's observations to assert that "The prime requisite of colonial prosperity is the colonial staple ... Nothing is more typical of colonial development than the restless, unceasing search for staples which would permit the pioneer community to come into close contact with the commercial world and leave behind the disabilities of a pioneer existence." The tidewater settlements were fortunate in finding products that were in demand in Europe and the West Indies – tobacco, indigo, naval stores, furs, cod, and timber – and that could be transported cheaply enough to garner a share of the market. These staple products could be either "good or bad" in the sense that could find a ready market and stimulate economic diversification or not. In New France, for example, the fur trade failed to generate significant domestic linkages and attempts to develop an agricultural staple were in vain, such that that colony increasingly took on the appearance of a subsistence economy.[43] It was the two principal "gaps" in the Appalachians – the St Lawrence River and the Mohawk Valley – that lent Montreal and New York their commercial importance as rival trade centres.[44] Both endeavoured to extend their influence into the unified region of the St Lawrence and Mississippi valleys by developing staple products that could bear the cost of expensive interior transportation in order to be marketable in Europe. Once divided politically by the American Revolution, westward expansion on the northern and southern halves of the continent followed divergent paths. The United States, once through the Appalachians, faced no geographical obstacles to the settlement of the Mississippi Valley and beyond; however, to the north were the "impassable barriers of the Laurentian highlands" and progress to the Canadian prairies was effectively blocked for half a century.[45]

Commercial policy in British North America thus evolved in relation to this geographic setting. Beginning in the later eighteenth century, the attempt to recreate the colonial system through the preferential tariff treatment of timber and wheat largely failed because of Canada's inability to produce a sufficient volume of foodstuffs to displace New England's role as a supplier to the West Indies. More importantly, "One looks in vain in Canadian history in the first half of the nineteenth century for any such triumphant movement of western forces ... There was no Jacksonian democracy and no Jackson in Canada because up to 1850 western development was doubly frustrated, at the east by the difficulties of the St Lawrence route, and the European market for bulky staples, and at the west by the impassable barrier of the Laurentian highlands."[46] Although responsible government and the Reciprocity Treaty of 1854 provided some relief from this "frustration," it was not until the grand development strategy of the national-policy period and the fortuitous events near the end of the nineteenth century ushered in a period of rapid economic growth based on western expansion that the conditions for nationhood were created. Mackintosh thus concludes with his oft-cited observation that "Canada is a nation created in defiance of geography," and adds that "the geographical and economic factors have had a large place in shaping her history."[47]

In 1926, he elaborated on the theme of the St Lawrence plateau as the dominant feature of Canadian economic history. The more easily accessible Mississippi Valley had received American settlers for some 150 years, and "the frontier has placed its stamp on American life and history."[48] In contrast, Canada faced the "rugged and forbidding" Precambrian Shield that tended to deflect settlers to the south.[49] When settlement of the western prairies did occur, there remained the "great traffic desert" between the Red River Valley and Georgian Bay that imposed higher transportation costs because of the distance that had to be traversed and the heavy one-way traffic west to east. Canadian development thus lagged behind that of the United States because of the "stubborn conditions which the Pre-Cambrian region has imposed upon us."[50] This forbidding region, rather than the wheat-bearing prairies, eventually held the future of Canadian economic development by "what the Pre-Cambrian area ... will produce in the way of natural resources for industry."[51] In this he included the Sudbury nickel-copper deposits and other minerals, the stands of forests for the pulp-and-paper industry, and the "perpetual annuity of water power."[52] His argument thus did not rest on geographical determinism. As he later stated, "Resources may be laid down by glaciers, but they are also, in a measure, created by knowledge."[53] Instead, it was the interplay between geography and human initiative – "the resistance and the opportunities which that area offers to our industrial development" – that would be "likely to mould to a considerable degree the distinctive characteristics of future Canadians."[54]

This geographical background also contributed to "sectionalism" as a central aspect of Canada's distinctive cultural development. In an earlier commentary in *Queen's Quarterly* on "The General Election of 1921," Mackintosh interpreted the distribution of seats as more a reflection of economic and regional conditions than of party politics. That Liberals were elected from Ottawa eastward, the prairies were dominated by the Progressive Party, and the Conservatives retained seats in Ontario and British Columbia only by virtue of "inertia, personal considerations and local political traditions," was largely due to the "stubborn facts of geography." Sectionalism arose out of the conflicts inherent in a new and expanding economy, and was exaggerated by the distance between the western frontier and older communities to the east. In this context, he downplayed cultural differences between English and French Canada. (In another paper, he masterfully dispenses with the old argument that the tradition-bound, quasi-peasantry of New France accounted for the colony's lack of progress: "it is not at all sure that … the orthodox, respectable colonists of New France were not in many ways preferable to the radicals and malcontents which made up New England."[55]) While acknowledging that nationalism in Quebec had roots other than economic, he maintained that the "problems of the immediate future are dominantly economic. In the face of them there is likely to be greater solidarity among Western farmers than among representatives of the widely differing constituencies of Quebec."[56]

The scope of Mackintosh's analysis, and his treatment of the relationship between geography, economics, politics, and culture, was a bold and provocative statement in the context of Canadian historiography at the time. He cautioned that his treatment of geographical factors was speculative and required much further research in order to establish its validity and flesh out the skeleton of the argument. Unfortunately, other demands on his time would postpone his pursuit of this research agenda and a fuller statement of the staple thesis.

COMMENTATOR, EDITOR, AND PRIVATE CONSULTANT

The life of an academic economist in Canada entailed a range of activities in addition to teaching and research. A reflection of the applied focus of the Queen's department was the contribution of its faculty to debates on the issues of the day. In particular, *Queen's Quarterly* provided an outlet for short papers as well as commentaries on political and economic affairs in its "Current Events" (later named "Political Affairs") section. These commentaries, varying from two to ten pages in length, were mostly written by faculty members at Queen's (and often identified with only the author's initials). Between 1921 and 1927, Mackintosh contributed seven short pieces on a range of topics: "The General Election of 1921," "Banks and Banking," "Canadian Politics," "The Situation in the United States," "A World Problem," "The Return to Gold," and "Economic Conditions in Europe."[57] He also wrote longer articles on "The Psychologist and Economics (1923)," "The Wheat Pools" (1925), and "Adam Smith on Education" (1927).

Other duties and opportunities arose as an extension of his role as the director of the commerce program after 1924. Mackintosh assumed two important editorial responsibilities. The first was the books published by Ryerson Press under its "Business Studies" series, which would form the basis of the commerce curriculum at Queen's. He edited and wrote introductions to John D. Falconbridge, *The Law of Negotiable Instruments in Canada: A Handbook* (1923); R.G.H. Smails and C.E. Walker, *Accounting Principles and Practice* (1926); W.A. McKague, *Investment* (1931); and E.L. Stewart Patterson, *Canadian Banking* (1932). The other editorial task was with the *Journal of the Canadian Bankers' Association* (renamed *Canadian Banker* in 1936). The journal, which appeared quarterly, had a long association with the courses taught at Queen's for the CBA. A succession of four Queen's professors served as editor between 1919 and 1967 – Skelton, Mackintosh, Knox, and David Slater – while Adam Shortt contributed over nine hundred pages of text on Canada's monetary history. Mackintosh took over Skelton's duties in the fall of 1924 and retained the practice of writing a long editorial section, which began with a broad series of observations on international and domestic affairs under the heading "The March of Events" and followed with shorter editorials on other subjects. The topics discussed in the October 1926 issue are representative of the scope of the issues surveyed: Germany Enters the League, M. Poincare Again, Mussolini Still, Abyssinia Aroused, An International Steel Trust, War Debt Cancellation, The Crisis in China, Church and State in Mexico, and The General Election. Aside from his observations on international affairs (which included postwar reparations and Keynes's criticisms of British banking and monetary policy), he provided regular commentaries on Canadian matters, including the wheat industry and business conditions generally, industrial relations, monetary policy, and federal politics. Add to this his own reviews of publications, under the heading of "The Banker's Bookshelf," and he would write some dozen pages in each issue that gave ample outlet for his range of interests.

Mackintosh also tried his hand at private consulting when he testified in front of the Board of Railway Commissioners in 1926 on behalf of Bell Telephone's application for a rate increase.[58] He reviewed the pattern of wholesale prices in Canada from 1890 to 1925 and related the changes to the stock of gold and adherence to the gold standard, changes in the banking system and credit expansion, and the level of industrial production. A general upward trend in prices from 1890 to 1920 (interrupted by the 1907 crisis and post–World War I deflation) was attributed to the discovery of new gold fields, financial deregulation, and shifts off the gold standard during World War I, which increased the credit-gold ratio, such that purchasing power generally outstripped the expansion in productive capacity. This was followed by a "slow and painful readjustment," as countries generally returned to the gold standard after the war, and by rising industrial production. Canada's resumption of gold payments implied that its prices would be tied to world prices, albeit at a higher level, because of the large capital inflows. He arrived at the conclusion, generally supportive of the telephone company, that "taking into consideration all the factors which are commonly understood by economists to affect this problem, the tendency will be for the price level for the next five years to be relatively stable, with a slight upward tendency." In what was one of the first instances of a professional economist offering testimony in a quasi-judicial setting in Canada, the commissioners struggled with the nature of the evidence, unable to embrace fully his analysis, replete with thirteen charts, as more than "theory and opinion." He presumably found a more sympathetic audience when he published his report as a paper in the *Journal of the Canadian Bankers' Association*.[59]

One venture that did not reach fruition was a proposed regular newsletter on "barometrics." Interest in statistics relating to the business cycle had increased throughout western economies, and Canada was no exception: in 1918 the Dominion Bureau of Statistics (DBS) began constructing data, a project on which both Mackintosh and Humphrey Michell (then at Queen's) had worked during the summer. A few years later, Skelton secured financial support from Queen's for a Canadian Statistical Service. When Michell left Queen's for McMaster University, the two schools planned a joint undertaking, but Michell then muddied the waters by approaching Charles Bullock, Mackintosh's former Harvard professor, about cooperating with the fledgling Harvard Economic Service. Michell's proposal – to investigate the entire field of economic statistics in Canada and to "present to the financial and commercial world a comprehensive and authoritative review of current statistical indices of industry, finance and commerce"[60] – left Mackintosh displeased on several counts. He complained to Michell that its scope was enough to "keep us busy for the next decade without being hampered at all," and that the purpose of cooperation was that "nobody would be rushed into hasty publication before the whole field had been thoroughly gone over." He added, "We would want to put out not simply a set of statistics modelled on the Harvard plan but something distinctively Canadian and of use to Canadian subscribers for the Harvard Service. I am not sure that the business cycle in Canada is just the same thing as in the United States. In fact it seems rather apparent that it is not."[61] Skelton noted that during the summer of 1923 Mackintosh was still endeavouring to "educate Michell on statistics,"[62] but, for whatever reason, the project was dropped, and probably fortuitously, for the Harvard Economic Service lost all credibility when it failed to forecast the Great Depression.[63] The one legacy of the Queen's–McMaster collaboration was the publication of *Statistical Contributions to Canadian Economic History* (Toronto: Macmillan, 1931), edited and introduced by Mackintosh and with chapters written by Michell, Clifford Curtis, and Kenneth Taylor.

POLICY ADVISING

While Queen's involvement with the CBA and the Charter Accountants established important connections to the private sector, the department was also busy cultivating a regular flow of traffic between Kingston and Ottawa for government work. Mackintosh took advantage of his earlier association with R.H. Coats to make annual inquiries about summer jobs at the DBS for Queen's students.[64] It also became commonplace for younger faculty members to seek summer employment, not only to supplement their relatively low academic salaries, but also to participate in policy work. In 1926, for instance, Mackintosh informed Coats that: "There is going to be difficulty in getting men here as our staff are pretty well tied up for the summer. Heaton and Caldwell are doing Summer School work, Walker is working for the Bell Telephone Company, Knox is continuing some postgraduate work at Chicago, and I already have several irons in the fire."[65] He did, however, recommend Smails for summer employment. One year later, Mackintosh arranged for Knox to spend the summer at the DBS working on the international balance of payments accounts, for his proposed doctoral thesis under Jacob Viner was to extend the time framework to Viner's own study of Canada's international indebtedness.[66] He also sought a full-time position for Caldwell, "a particularly decent and loyal colleague," who had taught statistics in the department for four years before suffering a nervous breakdown.[67]

One of the irons in the fire for Mackintosh was work under the Combines Investigation Act, which, at the time, fell into the domain of the department of labour. In the shadowy history of anti-combines legislation in Canada, one of the rare instances of effective government intervention concerned the Proprietary Articles and Trade Association (PATA). The PATA was formed in 1925 by virtually every firm in the Canadian pharmaceutical industry, including 157 manufacturers, 28 wholesale druggists, and 2,732 retail druggists (80 to 90 per cent of all retailers). Copying a similar British organization, it was designed to maintain retail prices on over 600 patent medicines and other articles. Manufacturers were expected to adhere to the PATA price list – which allowed for a 16.7-per-cent margin for wholesalers and a 33.3-per-cent margin for retailers – and not to sell to "price cutters." Following a formal complaint to the Combines Investigation Act in 1926, it was necessary to determine not only if there was in fact a tacit or formal agreement to fix prices, but also if the organization was "to the detriment of or against the interest of the public." Mackintosh, hired to assist F.A. McGregor, registrar of the Combines Investigation Act, produced a lengthy brief that formed the basis of the *Interim Report* issued in September 1926.[68]

Mackintosh provided an analysis of the impact of new, mass-merchandising techniques on the relationship among manufacturers, wholesalers, and retailers. The rise of "branded" products, new sales techniques typically identified with monopolistic competition, and the growth of retail chain stores was undermining the traditional position of the wholesaler. Manufacturers were now engaging in extensive advertising campaigns to increase brand-name identification, and were increasingly selling to new types of retailers, chain stores such as Tamblyn Drug Company and department and grocery stores with large pharmacies. The role of wholesaler, which had depended on the large number of unbranded end products purchased by retailers in small lots, was thus being usurped by direct manufacturer-to-retailer sales. In addition, the small drugstore was finding it difficult to compete with the new retailers who were able to obtain a volume discounts from manufacturers. The PATA was thus seen as a reaction against radical changes in distribution and a way to preserve the traditional manufacturer-wholesaler-retailer relationship. While the *Interim Report* expressed its sympathy for the position of wholesalers and smaller druggists, there was no question that the PATA was engaged in price maintenance that resulted in higher prices and was, therefore, detrimental to the public interest.

The *Interim Report* drew predictable criticism from industry sources. In the trade journal *Hardware and Metal*, E.H. Morrow (who was briefly Mackintosh's colleague at Queen's before becoming head of the commerce department at the University of Western Ontario) described the report's conclusion as a "hasty decision."[69] Less reserved was an editorial in the *Canadian Pharmaceutical Journal*, which objected that the report amounted to "virtually branding almost the entire drug trade of the Dominion as fit subjects to be indicted as criminals – an *ex partes* and biased statement sent out evidently for the purpose of spreading propaganda antagonistic to the fair trading methods adopted by the PATA." It added that the investigation was "unBritish" for not recognizing that the PATA was merely mimicking accepted practices in the British industry.[70] In contrast, an editorial in the *Canadian Forum* held that: "Much credit is due to Mr McGregor and Mr MacKintosh [*sic*] for the excellent way in which the enquiry was handled, and the report is everything a blue book should be, concise and well-reasoned, scrupulously fair in the presentation of both sides of the case, and containing, in addition to all the facts in connection with the operation of the PATA, a brief summary of modern developments in distribution, particularly such aspects as had a direct bearing on the inquiry."[71]

Cognizant of the need to give the industry an opportunity to respond, the department of labour appointed a full commission of investigation. When its report concurred with the interim one, and was later deemed by the Privy Council not to be ultra vires, the PATA voluntarily disbanded.

The next summer, Mackintosh was at work for the Advisory Board on Tariff and Taxation. Established in 1926 to advise the minister of finance "on all matters pertaining to tariff and other forms of taxation,"[72] the board was empowered to investigate specific matters referred to it by the minister and to hold public sittings before offering recommendations. It was to operate with a small staff and rely upon the assistance of "economists of national reputation,"[73] in order to provide a higher standard of public discussion than had previously accompanied politically charged tariff deliberations. This was a significant step towards greater involvement of economists in Ottawa; as Bryce reminds us, there were not even any economists in the department of finance prior to 1930.[74] As a student of Taussig at Harvard, Mackintosh was an obvious choice to turn to for expert advice, and he accepted an offer to work with the advisory board during the summer of 1927. His first assignment was to examine the tariff schedule on "hides, skins, and their products," and at the end of his first week of service he reported that "I have been engaged here since Monday in trying to disguise myself as an expert on leather."[75] It must have come as a surprise one week later that his responsibilities were considerably enlarged. William H. Moore, the head of the board, wrote to Mackintosh that: "I am inclined to think that possibly your first service, and best service to the Board, would be, as suggested, a regrouping of the whole Tariff Schedule. This, it seems to me, should be done as early as possible inasmuch as we will have different men working on different groups, and out of your rearrangement might come suggestions for them."[76] Mackintosh responded warily: "The ultimate desirability of re-classifying the items in the tariff schedule has become apparent, even in my brief examination of some of the items. On the other hand, however, I am very doubtful of the desirability of my starting in on the problem of re-classification at this particular stage of my ignorance of the intricacy of the tariff." But he accepted the task of coming up with a "working classification" for the board's own purposes, rather than as a recommendation for changes to the Tariff Act. In doing so, he sought out the advice of the tariff commissioner, for "I am quite sure, at present, he could readily and effectively ridicule any classification of items I might produce."[77]

This tentativeness gave way as he became further immersed in the minutiae of the tariff schedule. By early August he had produced a preliminary memorandum on "woollens" and promised a second missive, in which "the main proposals will be the setting-up of two new groups – leather and rubber, as I have already explained to you – and the reduction by this and other means of the miscellaneous group from 156 to 110."[78] He then grappled with the commodities grouped under "vehicles" ("While they are all vehicles, there really is no competition between aeroplanes and baby carriages, nor, for that matter, any significant competition between buggies and automobiles"), while showing more verve in proposing a new classification under "Exotic Vegetable Products."[79] When he returned to the issues of woollens, he sought out the advice of Ford W. Fridinburg of the Cobourg Knit Wear Limited. As for the mill manager's response, it is sufficient to advise discretion about reading a seven-page letter than begins by expressing a "desire to give you a little background to yarn, and its construction."[80]

Everyone, it is said, has to start somewhere. Having earned his spurs, Mackintosh was asked to comment on the rates of tariff protection, beginning with woollens and food products. He approached the subject with two objectives in mind: the first to achieve greater simplicity (such as avoiding the "irksomeness of the Drawback regulations") and the second to identify areas where the duty could fall without removing the protection enjoyed by domestic producers.[81] At the same time, he was aware of items subject to a pure revenue tariff, since there were no domestic producers (such as in his "Exotic Vegetable Products" category, which included coffee, tea, and spices). This work continued on an intermittent basis throughout the fall of 1927, with Mackintosh travelling to Ottawa at least once a month for the monthly public sittings of the board. His memorandum on "Suggested Revisions of Tariff Items Covering Woollen Yarns and Fabrics" was welcomed by Moore as "more nearly in line with what we want than anything I have yet had," while a second memorandum, on "Suggestions for Increasing the Flexibility of the Canadian Tariff," received even heartier praise as "exactly along the lines I wanted."[82]

The following summer of 1928, Mackintosh returned to full-time work with the board, on this occasion addressing matters in the iron and steel industry. In this capacity, he was sent to observe conditions at the troubled British Empire Steel Corporation (BESCO) in Sydney, Nova Scotia, which had been the source of significant labour unrest a few years earlier and had since fallen on financial hard times. To this assignment, Mackintosh brought his conviction that management-labour disputes could be resolved by finding the underlying source of the problem. At the time of the BESCO strike in 1925, he wrote in the *Journal of the Canadian Bankers' Association* that "No industrial crisis of the magnitude of the Nova Scotian strike arises unless there is a serious industrial problem at the base." The appropriate task was to avoid trying to assign the blame: "They are both right. It is not a case of giving a decision for the plaintiff or the defendant but of finding a solution to a difficult industrial problem."[83] But his investigation in 1928 dampened his optimism. Mackintosh made note of the mill operators' complaint that the wages paid were high relative to their European competitors and of their insistence in the "need for an improved attitude on the part of the miners before any hope of reducing costs could be maintained." He conceded that "discipline and morale are lax," but placed the blame for BESCO's financial woes elsewhere. "The greatest handicap with which the plant seems to contend is its location in reference to its markets." BESCO was having increasing difficulty meeting European competition in its traditional export markets, while "its location is distinctly disadvantageous from the point of view of domestic trade." Moreover, its ability to compete in Central Canada was compounded by the "large number of drawbacks or special free items under which iron and steel are brought into Ontario and Quebec for further manufacturing." He was, however, forced to conclude that there was no simple solution to be found: "The troubles ... seem to be much more numerous than the hopes."[84]

He continued to work intermittently for the board until October 1929, largely concerning its hearings on the iron and steel industry. The experience for Mackintosh was a positive one. As he would write in an editorial for the *Journal of the Canadian Bankers' Association*, "it may not be out of place to say that the hearings conducted before the Canadian Advisory Board on Tariff and Taxation are distinctly more comprehensive, more thorough, and have provided a larger body of authoritative information than have the Washington hearings before the Ways and Means Committee."[85] When the budget of 1928 made use of the committee's research, he held that judgments about the relative merits of tariff protection were, for the first time, based on a wealth of information, and that "good administration" was more important than any tinkering with the tariff schedule.[86]

MARRIAGE

Until 1928, Mackintosh enjoyed the life of a bachelor, with a comfortable income and rented rooms at 310 University Avenue. His salary from Queen's had risen from $2,000 to $4,000 by virtue of promotion to professor and his stipends as head of the department and director of the commerce program. In addition, as editor of the *Journal of the Canadian Bankers' Association*, he garnered $500 annually, and he received an average of $1,600 a year between 1925 and 1928 for his work with the dominion government.[87] His financial circumstances had been further bolstered in 1920 with the receipt of a small inheritance of $4,800 from his father's estate, held in trust until he reached the age of twenty-five. With this Mackintosh embarked on a career as a small, albeit cautious, investor, which yielded additional annual income in the range of $500.[88]

His social life revolved around his students and colleagues at Queen's, a favourite haunt being the Victoria Restaurant on King Street, where Jewly Lee would serve up egg sandwiches and coffee while Mackintosh gathered with friends such as Austin Cross, Les Stevenson, and Paul Glasgow (his future brother-in-law) to discuss the affairs of the day. He also remained close to his sister Margaret. In 1923, they enjoyed a brief boat trip ("a very pleasant trip indeed up the lakes and back again being much the larger part of the time on the boat, although I was two days in Port Arthur with my sister and a part of a day in Detroit on the way back. It was the best sort of rest possible and did me all sorts of good"[89]) and the next summer they travelled overseas. "Scotland has provided me with a delightful holiday," he informed Principal Taylor, "even though it did not provide my grandfather with a living."[90] A distant relative, Archibald Sinclair, had died in Scotland and left a small legacy to his Canadian cousins rather than to his brother, for whom he "had a spleen against." Meeting with the executor, Mackintosh and his sister opted to give £2,000, or the bulk of the estate, to the aggrieved brother. The executor remarked that the amount "was far beyond any sum which I might have reasonably expected," while the fortunate brother wrote to his "Dear Cousin William Mackintosh" that "you are a long suffering, forgiving generous soul and ought to be canonized but as presently pronounced your name does not seem to fit in."[91]

The relatively healthy state of Mackintosh's finances afforded him the indulgence of a new car, purchased in 1925. Skelton's diary contains a portrait, meticulous if not poignant, of the two men sharing the drive from Kingston to Ottawa: "Mackintosh has bought a new Essex coach (which is now in Canada $1,395 as against $895 in the US), and as he was planning to run to Ottawa invited me to go along. We left at 1:30 and reached Ottawa at 5:45; a very pleasant trip, smooth riding, no vibration – only contretemps was taking a short cut from Smith's Falls, via Frankford, which involved 10 miles of very bad road."[92] Mackintosh's frequent trips to Ottawa also offered the advantage of an active social and intellectual scene, dominated by Queen's graduates, and centring on Skelton. In his diary, Skelton describes a typical Sunday afternoon in the summer of 1926: "tea at the Shortt's – Mrs. S, Muriel Clarke (with Betty, Donald, Katherine), W.A. Mackintosh and Margaret, Charlotte Whitton and Margaret Grier, Wrong of the Bureau of Statistics and Mrs. Wrong, Scott an instructor at the U. of Michigan, then back to the house driven by Miss Whitton, a letter to Isabel and some bills and insurance cheques dashed off, then back to the Whitton-Grier establishment in Dr. Wodehouse's and with Mackintosh to the P.O. and back again in a pleasant drive and chat."[93] The following day, it would be lunch at the parliamentary restaurant, "with Mackintosh and Brinley Thomas, who is working in the archives on his thesis; met W.C. Ford[?] coming out, then Dr. Bryce, and later George Wilson of Dalhousie, just up to finish his Baldwin thesis."[94] The Archives were an important meeting point for scholars, not just in history but in political economy as well. Indeed, it was there in 1927 that Mackintosh first met Lester B. Pearson, a young history professor at the University of Toronto, and passed his name on to Skelton as a man with the potential to make a greater potential contribution to external affairs.[95]

If Mackintosh needed any further reason for maintaining a hand in government work in Ottawa, it was the presence in the city of Jean Easton. Born in Renfrew, Ontario, she followed in the footsteps of her sister, Kathleen, receiving a scholarship to attend Queen's in 1923. She graduated in 1926 with a degree in commerce (one of four women in a class of twenty-six), and it was an open secret in Kingston that Mackintosh carried a torch for her. Among her numerous virtues, she was related to Skelton by marriage, Isabel Skelton being her aunt. After graduating, she took up temporary residence in the Ottawa Ladies' College and Mackintosh arranged for her to work in a clerical capacity with the Advisory Board on Tariff and Taxation in

September 1927.[96] She continued with the board until the end of July 1928, when she resigned for what was at the time a common reason: she had accepted Mackintosh's proposal of marriage. On 11 August 1928, they were married in a small ceremony in Renfrew, Ontario, with George Wilson serving as best man.

During the first decade of his career at Queen's, Mackintosh had come a long way very quickly. He was head of his department, director of the commerce program, and an important contributor to public policy and debates on current affairs. Publication of his doctoral dissertation and journal papers established him as scholar of note, which was acknowledged in his election to the Royal Society of Canada in 1929.[97] Yet there was an awkward pause in his research work, as the analytical framework for the staple thesis which he articulated in his 1923 paper on "Economic Factors in Canadian History" was left largely undeveloped. Commentaries in *Queen's Quarterly*, editorial work for the *Journal of the Canadian Bankers' Association*, private consulting, and policy advising in Ottawa were outlets for his wide-ranging capacity as an economist, but they were, by his own admission, a distraction from his more scholarly work. When offering his services to the Tariff Board in the summer of 1928, he did so with some reluctance. "I have, however, some research work of my own which badly needs doing and if the need for additional assistance is not pressing I can make progress with some of my own work, which has been badly delayed during the past year or so."[98] From his perspective, there was much work to be done in Ottawa, and he found it difficult to resist contributing his expertise to important policy concerns. Allowance too must be made for the fact that he had fallen in love and got married – a concession one must allow even the most dedicated of scholars.

6

Wheat as Staple: Kingston and Europe, 1928–1936

The story which I like best is of [C.R. Fay's] visit to the Peace River when he urged a farmer who was driving him to take him further and further north until finally he was assured that, aside from the odd trading post, there was no settlement between him and the Arctic, whereupon Fay sat down on the running board of the car and wrote one of his famous post-cards to Maynard Keynes which ran: Dear Maynard – Ricardo was right. I sit on the margin of cultivation, my feet on no rent land.

Mackintosh to Gerald Graham, 1961[1]

Professor Mackintosh has done suggestive work as a Canadian in pointing out that Canada only developed as a nation with the production of wheat as a staple.

Harold Innis, 1929[2]

While working for the Advisory Board on Tariff and Taxation in the summer of 1927, Mackintosh was invited to attend the meetings of the US Social Science Research Council (SSRC) in Hanover, New Hampshire. "I am not anxious to spend the time," he told Hector McKinnon in explaining that he would be absent from Ottawa for a few days, "but they are offering to spend a considerable sum of money in a project of research which affects this country, and it is difficult to refuse their invitation to discuss it with them."[3] He was undoubtedly ingenuous in expressing regret about being away from his painstaking work with tariff schedules to consider an ambitious project, especially in light of the limited monies and outlets for publication of academic research in Canada. Whether he required much convincing or not, his selection to head a group of social scientists and historians in an ambitious study of Canada's agricultural settlement that would take over a decade to complete thrust Mackintosh into a leading role in the development of Canadian political economy. It gave him the opportunity to pursue part of the research agenda he identified in his 1923 paper on "Economic Factors in Canadian History," and would serve as the catalyst to his most prolific period of academic scholarship. His analysis of the prairie wheat economy would be the definitive study of the application of the staple thesis to the Canadian economy in the early twentieth century and, in concert with Innis, he would contribute to a general theory of development based on resource exports. The staple thesis became the central focus of a generation of scholars during a particularly vibrant period in the history of the discipline.

That the staple thesis would be fully articulated during the Great Depression was only partly happenstance, for the collapse of export markets heightened awareness of the vulnerability of a resource-dependent economy. The depression intensified the need to make sense out of Canada's place in the world economy, as well as the search for policy initiatives that might realistically ameliorate the burden imposed on a small open economy. In his discussions with department members, in his participation in national academic forums, and in his role as editor of the *Journal of the Canadian Bankers' Association*, Mackintosh struggled to understand the scope of domestic fiscal, monetary, and trade policy in light of rapidly changing international circumstances. Part of this search took him to Europe, where he investigated first-hand the rising political turmoil leading up to World War II. In his search for answers, he was intrigued by the observations of Keynes and others on the efforts of various governments to address the slump in output and employment; nonetheless, Mackintosh and his Canadian colleagues were unable to offer much compelling advice in response to the challenges presented by the Great Depression.

THE PRAIRIE WHEAT ECONOMY

A "scientific study of the land question" in western Canada was the idea of Isaiah Bowman, director of the American Geographical Society. With $45,000 in funding from the SSRC, the Canadian Pioneer Problems Committee was established to oversee a five-year program of research. The interest of the SSRC was piqued by concern that available arable land in the United States was diminishing; indeed, Bowman has been recently characterized as an instrument of American foreign policy. Everyone concerned, however, was careful to emphasize the autonomy exercised by the Canadian committee.[4] The grant allowed Mackintosh, as coordinator of the research, to take a partial leave from his duties at Queen's during the 1929–30 and 1930–31 academic years in order to spend time in the West securing members of each prairie agricultural college to conduct field surveys and to arrange other research.[5] The committee commissioned studies from an impressive roster of academics, including William Allen (farm management, Saskatchewan), W.A. Carrothers (history, Saskatchewan), A.B. Clark (economics, Manitoba), C.A. Dawson (sociology, McGill), G.E. Elliott (economics, Alberta), H.C. Grant (economics, Manitoba), Harold Innis (political economy, Toronto), Arthur Lower (history, United College), Duncan MacGibbon (economics, Alberta), Chester Martin (history, Toronto), D.A. McArthur (history, Queen's), A.S. Morton (history, Saskatchewan), R.W. Murchie (sociology, Minnesota), William Swanson (eonomics, Saskatchewan), and Eva R. Younge (sociology, McGill). The Macmillan Company of Canada agreed to publish the studies as the Canadian Frontiers of Settlement series for a subsidy of $1,000 per volume. Although it was planned as a nine-volume series, by the time the project was wrapped up in 1940, only eight had made it into print.[6]

The first and fourth volumes, written primarily by Mackintosh, proved to have the most enduring impact. Volume 1, *Prairie Settlement: The Geographical Setting,* outlines the "physical facts" to which the farmer was forced to adapt. The western Canadian agricultural frontier is defined as the northern part of the greater interior plain of North America, bounded by the Rocky Mountains to the west, the forty-ninth parallel to the south, the Precambrian Shield to the east, and the Mackenzie Delta to the north. The entire region was characterized by extreme temperatures and sparse precipitation, but within it there was significant diversity. Lying to the west of the fertile Red River Valley were the "dirty" hills extending to Moose Jaw and the broken topography of coulees and hills from Moose Jaw to the foothills of the Rockies. The variations within the region are treated in detail, replete with 160 figures, including maps indicating soil qualities, topographical features, rainfall levels, and temperature ranges. Settlement followed careful investigation of the each area's agricultural possibilities, the most notable being the relatively pessimistic view of the Palliser Expedition (1857–60), which distinguished between the fertile belt in the valleys of the Red, Assiniboine, and North Saskatchewan rivers and the semi-arid lands of the "true prairies." After the American agricultural frontier was "virtually closed" by 1890, and the development of early maturing varieties of wheat to deal with the short growing season and dry-farming techniques suitable to semi-arid lands, the pace of settlement in Canada intensified. Commercial viability, however, largely awaited improved transportation to European markets in 1895: "Only with modern railways and cheap ocean transportation can the frontier produce bulky staples, such as wheat, for metropolitan markets, and, without markets, the pioneer fringe is condemned to a low and rude standard of living, a precarious existence in which man, unarmed, pits his strength against relentless nature." He cautioned that the "wheat farmer in Western Canada is engaged in a business subject to unusually sharp fluctuations, imposed on it in greater or lesser degree by pronounced variations in rainfall and the other climatic conditions of wheat growing, and by the necessity of competing in a far distant world market for the sale of a raw material."[7]

Volume 4, on the *Economic Problems of the Prairie Provinces*, addresses the "more complicated and more difficult" problem of interpreting the "economic factors of settlement." Settlers were not "a tradition-ridden peasantry but farmer-entrepreneurs," who "like other business enterprisers, must accept business risks." Land-rich but capital-poor, and thereby dependent upon capital borrowing, farmers promoted policies that encouraged an inflow of capital, that lowered the cost of transportation and other infrastructure, and that facilitated efficient marketing practices. Accordingly, "it is in the conditions which promote the outflow of the staple product and the inflow of the capital that the mainsprings of economic development are found." In this specific instance, "Wheat is the export staple of the Canadian prairies. Prosperity and stimulus came through wheat, as did depression and discouragement." With lower transportation costs opening up access to European markets, Canada was producing 12 per cent of the world's wheat by 1902, and accounted for as much as 60 per cent of world exports during World War I.[8]

The pace of long-term growth and short-term fluctuations around this trend were largely dictated by the price of wheat and transportation costs, both factors lying outside of the control of the farmer. The timing of settlement – the false start (1883–95), rapid settlement (1896–1911) and its extension during World War I, the postwar slump, and the renewed expansion of 1926–29 – was treated in terms of the trends in wheat prices and transportation costs. These conditions, in turn, were reflected in the value of land and determined the amount of debt farmers were obliged to absorb: "The record of the prices of land is, therefore, at one and the same time an index of the expectations which settlers have of the profitableness of settlement, and also an index of the fixed investment which settlers who undertake settlement in a particular year must assume. The price of land at the time a farm enterprise is begun determines to a high degree the amount of indebtedness which rests on the farm."[9]

The fundamental problem that the farmer faced was dependence on a staple product subject to large overhead costs but yielding a highly variable income. Gross farm income fluctuated with the price of wheat, as well as with variations in yields and grade (especially in semi-arid regions). Since variable costs (for binder twine, hired labour, and threshing) were comparatively small relative to the fixed costs associated with own-farm labour and the indebtedness assumed in the purchase of capital goods and land, net farm income was even more variable than gross income. Returning to the themes developed in his doctoral thesis, Mackintosh repeated his account of the innovations that farmers undertook in grain handling and marketing in order to counter the monopoly position of the private grain companies and railways – "All charges which intervene between the producer and his market and which fluctuate with the quantity sold but not to any great extent with the price are never outside the circle of the prairie farmer's attention" – but the vagaries of wheat prices and yields remained largely outside their control.[10]

What was true for the farmer was also true for the entire prairie economy. Farmers bore a large share of the risk, but so too did governments by subsidizing the cost of railway construction as well as education, health, and social-services infrastructure. "The whole economic organization of the Prairie Provinces is, as it were, suspended from the railway network" and both "governments and communities willing to mortgage their future income for the necessary capital goods." Mackintosh estimated that provincial and municipal debt was in the range of $650 million, roughly equal to the amount of private farm debt, and, taken together, interest payments accounted for 40 per cent of gross farm income. Farm credit and capital markets generally were ill-equipped to deal with such a circumstance: "It is an axiom of finance that heavy fixed charges and highly fluctuating income are incompatible. The rapid expansion of agricultural settlement led to the assumption of heavy fixed charges; highly fluctuating incomes make them difficult to carry."[11] With the catastrophic collapse of wheat prices in the Great Depression, the difficulties facing the prairies arrived with a vengeance. Mackintosh concluded that "The wheat farmer in Western Canada is engaged in a business subject to unusually sharp fluctuations, imposed on it in greater or less degree by pronounced variations in rainfall and the other climatic conditions of wheat growing, and by the necessity of competing in a far distant world market for the sale of a raw material. In these facts of a commercial agriculture in which a high degree of variability is inherent will be found the centre of the economic problems of Western Canada."[12]

Looking forward, Mackintosh was skeptical about the potential for absorbing more settlers, as marginal lands posed greater obstacles in the form of a shorter growing season, less fertile soils, and higher transportation costs. While he suggested that land under cultivation might increase by 20 to 30 per cent under favourable economic conditions, he anticipated that further mechanization and scale economies would dampen the inflow of labour. Under prevailing economic circumstances, he was doubtful if the record crop of 1928 would again be reached. Thus he argued the need for "social planning" to provide greater knowledge and to avoid unwarranted settlement: "The development of the potential agricultural lands of the northern fringe calls for the greatest forethought and care. Policies based on insufficient knowledge are likely to lead to heavy financial and social costs."[13] This caution proved appropriate, for it would not be until 1951 that the 1928 level of wheat production was exceeded (Figure 6.1). Ironically, a project that was expected to outline the potential of the Canadian frontier for further settlement instead documented what was effectively the end to the "wheat boom" era.

The Canadian Frontiers of Settlement series was well received and Mackintosh's authored volumes particularly so. Irene Biss (Spry), who praised Volumes 1 and 4 in a review for the *Journal of Political Economy*, used them as a travel guide as she crossed the prairies by train on her own research trip. "I am glad I read Mackintosh before I started," she wrote to Innis. "The scenery means something."[14]

Figure 6.1 Wheat production in Canada, 1890–1975

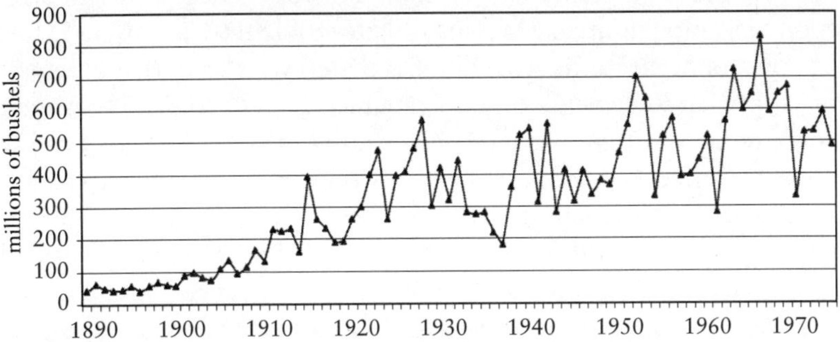

Source: derived from Statistics Canada, *Historical Statistics of Canada*, 2nd ed. (Ottawa, 1983), Series M301-309.

Other colleagues in Canada were equally laudatory. C.R. Fay and Lorie Tarshis commended the series for carrying the writing of Canadian economic history "a further stage forward"; Vincent Bladen recognized the relevance of Mackintosh's "admirably developed" thesis to an understanding of Canadian economic development; and O.D. Skelton told Mackintosh privately that Volume I was "incomparably the best survey of the physical conditions of the prairie settlement we have ever had."[15] A decade later it was hailed by Griffith Taylor, the University of Toronto geographer, as exemplifying "the specific contribution that a geographer can make to the general body of knowledge."[16] International praise came from M.J. Bonn of the London School of Economics and Political Science: "Canadians may well be proud of the work of their researchers." A review in the British *Geographical Journal* lauded "this impressive piece of team work" and Mackintosh's first volume for providing the "skeleton and connecting tissue" for the series, while a review in the *Australian Geographer* stated that the series "sets a standard for such work [on frontier studies]."[17] For his efforts, Mackintosh was honoured with a lifetime membership in the American Geographical Society.[18]

THE STAPLE THESIS WRIT LARGE

By 1934, Innis and Mackintosh had completed their major studies of specific Canadian staple industries: Innis on the fur trade and cod fisheries, and Mackintosh on wheat. The enthusiasm each expressed for the other's work reflects a common desire to understand the broad patterns to Canadian economic history. Their written correspondence was limited. Mackintosh later told S.D. Clark that "Most of my communications with him have been very brief scribble notes or cryptic endorsements on papers which he sent to me."[19] In their correspondence that survives, they shared information on locating government records and, as heads of their respective departments, commented on the suitability of individuals for various university appointments. The discussion of each other's scholarship instead took place through published work and conference presentations. Mackintosh hailed Innis's *The Fur Trade in Canada* (1930) as "the greatest single contribution that has been made to the interpretation of the economic history of this country" and "a great book in economic history."[20] (In contrast, George Wilson, Mackintosh's friend from his undergraduate days at Queen's, in reviewing Innis's book, provided an example of why one should never commit predictions to print: "The book will, however, never be popular except with historians and economists who may be drawn to the subject. While Mr. Innis may be well satisfied to leave the romantic side of his subject to the novelist, it would not injure the fur trade in any way if the facts of its history were presented with somewhat more ease and grace."[21]) For Mackintosh, a key aspect of the *Fur Trade* was Innis's recognition of the vulnerability of a staple economy: "a perpetual Canadian economic problem of great significance, that of carrying heavy overhead costs and with variable income and with relatively unproductive seasonal periods."[22] Innis, in turn, was quick to appreciate Mackintosh's extension of this theme to the analysis of the prairie wheat economy. In a lengthy review of the Volumes 1, 2, and 4 of the Frontiers of Settlement series, Innis focused on Mackintosh's contribution both as editor of the series and as author of two of the volumes. As the ultimate compliment, he cites frequently from the texts, and even reproduces several of its maps and figures. Indeed, Innis largely summarizes Mackintosh's findings and then, in classic Innisian style, offers a concluding paragraph under the heading of "The Broad Significance."

> It is impossible even in an extended review to convey an appreciation of the significance of the work carried out under the project represented by the volumes under review. The authors have been concerned primarily with the immediate problems of

> western Canada, but their work provides a fundamental basis to the problems of Canada as a whole. Throughout the volumes the problem of the adjustment of burdens between established and fringe areas has been of vital concern and emphasis has been placed on methods by which the burdens may be kept under control and reduced. But in many ways Western Canada is to the industrial center of Canada what the fringe is to the center within the western provinces, and a provincial regional problem becomes a Canadian problem. These volumes constitute a first preliminary attack on the difficulties of provincial-federal relations, and their importance is enhanced by the opportune date of the study and their appearance in the years of the depression. No economist or historian or geographer can continue to write intelligibly about diminishing returns, the frontier theory, and other related concepts without a through appreciation of their implications.[23]

Mutual respect did not however deter each from criticizing the other's work, or using it as a foil. Innis's oft-cited phrase from *The Fur Trade in Canada* that "the present Dominion emerged not in spite of geography but because of it" is an obvious reference to Mackintosh's 1923 statement that "Canada was created in defiance of geography."[24] For Innis, the post-Confederation development of Canadian economy based on transcontinental railways and western settlement was an extension of the unity created by the fur trade and the east-west flow of traffic carried along water routes. But there was certainly agreement among the two men that the barrier of the Laurentian Shield contributed substantially to the overhead cost of staple exploitation. Mackintosh, for his part, felt free to criticize Innis's *Problems of Staple Production in Canada* (a collection of earlier papers) for failing "to achieve the desired unity" and for offering no solutions to the current depression.[25]

The sense of a common purpose in writing Canada's economic history extended beyond the Innis–Mackintosh relationship and was apparent in the resuscitation of the Canadian Political Science Association (CPSA). It had been founded in 1912 by Canadian economists attending the meetings of the American Social Sciences Association in Boston, where Adam Shortt was elected president and O.D. Skelton secretary-treasurer. Designed for "encouragement of the investigation and study of governmental, economic, and social problems," the term "political science" was chosen, since "social science" was "not yet respectable in Canada."[26] After its first annual meeting in 1913, the CPSA lapsed into inactivity until 1929, when, under the initiative of Duncan MacGibbon, economists attending the National Conference of Canadian Universities agreed to re-form the association with Skelton as president and Mackintosh serving on the executive committee. The CPSA brought a new energy and focus to research on the Canadian economy. Annual meetings were held to coincide with those of the Canadian Historical Association and the Royal Society of Canada and, while this gave the meetings a decidedly central-Canadian bias, they still garnered wide representation from academics in the West (such as MacGibbon, Carrothers, W.B. Hurd, W.J. Waines, Robert "Pete" McQueen, and George Britnell) and the Maritimes (R.A. MacKay, W.C. Keirstead, A.B. Balcolm), as well as the involvement of government officials (such as Skelton and R.H. Coats) and journalists (W.A. Dafoe and George Ferguson). Publication of the annual proceedings provided a new forum for completed research. While there had been other print outlets, such as the Queen's Bulletin series (1910–28), generalist journals (*Queen's Quarterly*, *Dalhousie Review*, *University of Toronto Quarterly*), and the *Journal of the Canadian Bankers' Association* (where as editor Mackintosh published the writings of several colleagues, including Hurd, MacGibbon, McQueen, Herbert Heaton, C.R. Fay, F.A. Knox, K.W. Taylor, and H. Michell), none matched the annual proceedings of the CPSA as a forum for discussion within the discipline. Indeed, the meetings proved sufficiently vigorous to lead to the creation of the *Canadian Journal of Economics and Political Science* in 1935. The emerging writing style of economists did not receive universal approval. Upon reading a 1938 issue, Arthur Lower wrote to Vincent Bladen, the editor, complaining that the articles "all reach a new low in incomprehensibility, obscurity and banality of expression. If economic writing is to go on like this in Canada, it will be nothing short of sinful, for economists seem to be developing a tradition of the worst sort. Sentences limp, then fall down, with their limbs spread out in all directions."[27]

Mackintosh and Innis would assume a leadership role in the affairs of the CPSA – Mackintosh served as president in 1936 and Innis one year later – and this helped to forge a closer working relationship. At the 1931 meetings, Mackintosh presented "Gold and the Decline of Prices," which Innis would later praise and draw from it the observation that, during World War I and afterwards, "the state has become a more effective monetary device."[28] Mackintosh, in turn, served as the discussant on Innis's "Transportation as a Factor in Canadian Economic History," and summarily concluded that "Dr. Innis's paper is so complete and so convincing that it is much easier to congratulate him on his work than discuss it."[29]

At the 1935 meetings of the CPSA, Mackintosh presented "Some Aspects of a Pioneer Economy,"[30] in which he made the first attempt to generalize the findings on specific staple industries into a more comprehensive framework for understanding the development of Canada, and "new countries" in general. "It is, then, in the history of new countries that the economics of development can best be studied," he wrote. "I suggest that the fully operating open economic system is best exemplified in new, pioneer countries." He defined four basic features of a pioneer economy. First, countries characterized by plentiful resources need to find a staple product that "adapted to the basic geographical facts" and was in demand in metropolitan markets. Second, the scarcity of labour and capital necessitated an inflow of labour (through immigration, indentured servitude, or slavery), use of the "industrial arts of mature economies" (or "mature techniques" to use Innis's term), and capital borrowing. The latter implied a high rate of investment and indebtedness, and a high propensity to save if the interest payments on debt were to be met. Third, the nature of the production function, or the technological and institutional conditions under which the staple commodity is produced, had broader implications not only for the economy as a whole, but for political and social institutions as well. Fourth, the conflict between highly variable income from staple exports and heavy overhead costs left the economy vulnerable to wide fluctuations in the rate of economic growth. The staples economy thus faced periodic tests of the capacity of export earnings to carry the growing debt charges and to pay for imports.[31] Together these factors give rise to "that familiar circular flow which is the life-blood of the pioneer economy – merchandise exports, capital imports, merchandise import balances, a high rate of investment, full employment in spite of heavy immigration, profit inflation, and rising property values." The concentration on a single staple product had cumulative effects which influenced the capacity to transformation from an immature to mature economy. During period of growth, factors prices tend to adjust as the inflow of relatively scare labour and capital drive down wages and interest rates respectively and increase the price of land. "Rising prices and falling interest rates are the attendants of pioneer prosperity." When the inflow of capital eventually declines, there must be sufficient export earnings to fund imported consumer goods and establish the basis for domestic capital accumulation, particularly in secondary industries, to help spread out the social overhead costs. Only then can the economy "pass from the pseudo-prosperity of the settlement boom to the genuine prosperity of a fully functioning economy."[32] This paper would serve as the starting point for his larger treatment of *The Economic Background of Dominion-Provincial Relations*, written in 1938.

Innis served as a discussant on the paper and was sufficiently intrigued to invite Mackintosh to speak at the University of Toronto in March 1936. He then wrote "Notes on the Problems of Adjustment in Canada" for the *Journal of Political Economy*, beginning with the statement that "Professor W.A. Mackintosh raises problems of fundamental importance in the Canadian economy which warrant emphasis and comment."[33] Upon receiving an offprint of Innis's paper, Mackintosh wrote in response: "You develop so many implications from my talk that I am beginning to be complacent about it." As a gesture of collegiality, Mackintosh declined to cash the small cheque that he had been given to cover his expenses. "Please do not think that this is generosity on my part," he wrote to Innis. "Just bear in mind that you or some of your colleagues now owe us a visit, and that your chance of getting your expenses paid is probably of the second order of small."[34]

Their paths would increasingly diverge over the course of the later 1930s. For Innis, the basis for knowledge was fragile and the search for bias was an essential step to gaining self-knowledge; he cited James Ten-Broeke, his philosophy professor from his undergraduate days at McMaster, "Why do we attend to the things to which we attend?"[35] Questioning the basis for one's own convictions was, if not the route to detached objectivity, at least the grounds for obtaining a perspective on the subject. It did not, however, provide a reliable basis upon which to offer expert policy advice. His scathing review of the Rowell–Sirois Royal Commission in 1939[36] – whose *Final Report* Mackintosh had a large hand in drafting – underscores Innis's increasing isolation from the majority of his fellow economists. Mackintosh was no less introspective, despite consistently expressing a matter-of-fact approach to intellectual inquiry and the capacity to apply "common sense" to a body of accumulated facts. He subscribed to no simple inductive method; rather, "It is that wealth of knowledge which tempers logic with intuition and enables the competent economist to judge the quality of imprecise facts, to exercise what we may call his economic sense."[37] He acknowledged that "as an individual of experience he will doubtless have strong prejudices and inherited tastes," but believed that scientific detachment was possible. "Men must have a philosophy of some kind no matter how poor or contradictory a thing it is, but it is essential that we keep our philosophy separate from our scientific thinking, or rather that our philosophy should always be ready to retreat before science."[38]

In Mackintosh's presidential address to the CPSA, the methodological gulf between the two men is quite apparent. In responding to Underhill's assertion that economists should drop the pretence of scientific detachment, Mackintosh acknowledged that "In all quarters one gathers the impression that the general public is disappointed in economists, is distrustful of them, is unimpressed with the complexity of the subject, or considers them out-moded and outworn receptacles of a bourgeois ideology, the product of a particular historical epoch." But he defended the economist's role as a policy expert as long as one resisted the pressure to "abandon his scientific method and become a propagandist." In this respect he endorsed Keynes's view, which he described as the trusting of a technical man to do a technical job according to good professional standards. "Just as engineering principles do not lay down the form and structure of a bridge apart from the particular facts of span, weight, strength of materials, etc., so economics enunciates no policy apart from the particular facts of the problem." Thus, as Innis lamented the growing division within the social scientists, Mackintosh championed the scientific foundation of economics with the proviso that "the economist must remember that he is an expert in but *one* of the social sciences."[39] He was equally adamant that "any social science must ultimately be justified by the basis which it affords for policy … unless economics and other social sciences are to be justified by policy they become mere chess games, to be classed as recreation, wholesome recreation if you will."[40]

Whatever differences emerged between the two men, Mackintosh's loyalty to Innis never waned. Vincent Bladen recounts the story of his "generous support" in the effort to have Innis appointed as head of Toronto's department of political economy. "When we were discussing the election of Mackintosh as president of the CPSA, he asked me what Innis's prospects were. I replied that they were good, but uncertain and there might be yet another year's delay. Mackintosh then urged us to elect Innis as President as a form of manifesto directed at the Board of Governors. He, Mackintosh, could wait for election at a later date."[41] In a similar vein, when in 1936 Henry John Cody, president of the University of Toronto, inquired about the possibility of recruiting "some outstanding Canadian Economist such as … McIntosh [sic]," Urwick, the head of the department, responded that "[Mackintosh], I am quite sure, would not come if his coming in any way interfered with Innis's prospect of being appointed Head of the Department."[42] When invited to give one of a series of lectures at the University of Toronto to celebrate the fiftieth anniversary of the department of political economy in May 1938, one year after Innis's appointment as head, Mackintosh took the opportunity to state that: "Distinguished as its history has been, at no time has the Department … commanded more respect among economists and political scientists than it does at present."[43]

CORPORATE SOLIDARITY

The cohesiveness that characterized the economics discipline in Canada during the 1930s was particularly evident within the department at Queen's. Under the financial exigencies of the Depression and Treasurer William McNeill's legendary austerity measures, there were not ample resources to be dispersed; however, the money generated through the extramural banking and accounting courses lent the department of political and economic science great clout within the institution. This enabled Mackintosh, in 1930, to secure the Home for Friendless Women and Children on Union Street to house the department's nine teaching staff and six secretaries (who largely handled correspondence for extramural courses). Rex Smails credits the physical closeness of the staff – previously scattered throughout Kingston Hall and the Old Arts Building – as contributing to "the quite unique sense of corporate solidarity which has characterized the Department, been the admiration of its friends and the despair of its enemies."[44]

A modest growth in staff also occurred. Clifford A. Curtis, who obtained his PhD from the University of Chicago, had been hired in 1927 and, together with Knox and Mackintosh, would form the "illustrious triumvirate" on the economics side of the department for two decades.[45] Political science was reinvigorated with the appointment of Norman McLeod Rogers in 1929. An Acadia undergraduate and Rhodes Scholar, who had studied law at Oxford, Rogers returned to Acadia to teach for five years before spending two years as secretary for Privy Council affairs under Mackenzie King. He would lecture at Queen's for six years before being elected to the House of Commons as the member of parliament for Kingston. To fill Rogers's vacancy, Mackintosh wrote to President Murray of the University of Saskatchewan, to warn of his "poaching expedition" – which proved successful – to recruit J.A. Corry.[46] In commerce, Smails and Walker were aided by the return of W.C. Clark in 1931, but he left after only one year to join the dominion civil service, and in short order become deputy minister of finance. J.L. MacDougall, who had filled in on a temporary basis for two years during the absences of Curtis and Clark, was appointed assistant professor of commerce in 1934, while Lawrence G. Macpherson (BA, CA) was hired as instructor in accounting in 1933.

The final addition to the department before World War II was the industrial relations section, the first such venture in a Canadian university. Modelled after similar programs at Princeton, the University of Michigan, and Stanford, the section's objective was to provide a teaching and research forum on employer-employee relations.[47] The initiative came in part from the Industrial Relations Counselors Inc., New York, a non-profit organization established in 1926 by John D. Rockefeller II, where Bryce Stewart, a former Queen's undergraduate, was director of research. It also resulted from Mackintosh's long-standing conviction that capital-labour conflict could be managed through collective bargaining and "constitutional" avenues. The sympathy he expressed with the Winnipeg General Strike was based on his support for union recognition and free collective bargaining; however, he had no interest in trade unionism as part of a broader social movement. As a case in point, he hailed Samuel Gompers as "one man who clearly saw the reality in the chaos of 'isms,' vain imaginings and sloppy sentimentality which characterized the day of the Knights of Labor before Gompers and his new Federation emerged victorious from their war to the death with the rival organization."[48] With the emergence of the CIO and increasing labour unrest spilling over into Canada during the latter half of the 1930s, he continued to support the right to bargain collectively, but considered it "a matter of great concern if the attitudes and policies developed under the unfortunate conditions obtaining in certain areas of the United States are transferred to Canadian territory where they have little or no application." He was emphatic that "lawlessness in industrial disputes cannot be tolerated" and that capital-labour relations could be managed through legislative channels. "One would like to see on the part of both employers and employees much less appeal to prejudice, much less use of catchwords, and a great deal more frank assessment of the facts of each case." Negotiated settlements were thus to be achieved by "orderly business agreements ... [not] small civil wars dividing whole communities."[49]

After a successful conference was held in 1936, money was sought to support an institute at Queen's. James A. Richardson appealed to Sam McLaughlin of General Motors for a contribution, partially on the strength of Mackintosh's reputation. "Principal Wallace writes me that there has been a great deal of criticism, and some of it from university circles and much of it ill informed, about the relationship between capital and labour. He thinks the university should do something about it, and he believes that Queen's University is in a unique position to make a worthwhile contribution ... The University, as you know, holds an outstanding position in Canada in the field of banking, commerce, political economy and business administration and Professor Mackintosh, as an economist, enjoys the confidence of banking, industrial and business interests in a way not enjoyed I believe by any other economist in Canada."

McLaughlin was not persuaded. According to Richardson, he "states they have a very happy family in Oshawa which was working out very nicely in the interests of all concerned, but it was badly upset by the CIO last winter, and they are now endeavouring to restore again the relationship which used to exist between the company and the men ... He has talked over the contents of my letter with some of his colleagues and they have come to the conclusion that they would not wish to make a contribution or associate themselves with the work contemplated at Queen's, and in coming to this conclusion he referred to the work of the college economists who had been associated with President Roosevelt."[50] But other companies were forthcoming, and a total of $11,000 was secured from a dozen of Canada's leading corporations, including Imperial Oil, Bell Telephone, Northern Electric, Canadian Westinghouse, Canada Cement, Canada Packers, Imperial Tobacco, Moore Corporation,

International Nickel Corporation of Canada, Canadian Industries Limited and Sun Life.[51] This was sufficient to establish the section on a five-year experimental basis, with a director and two staff people. Stewart declined the position of director, urging instead the appointment of an "industry man," on the grounds that companies needed to innovate in order to address the growing government involvement in the field. After Harry Cassidy and Gerald Riddell were considered for the post, James C. Cameron was hired.[52] Despite its corporate sponsorship, other companies would come to complain of the section's "pro-labour sentiments."[53]

With this appointment the department complement rose to nine: Mackintosh, Smails, Walker, Knox, Curtis, MacDougall, Macpherson, Corry, and Cameron. What it may have lacked in faculty numbers – particularly in comparison to Toronto's department of political economy – it made up for in terms of harmony. Frank Knox's diary entries covering the latter part of the 1930s provide a flavour of the "congenial intellectual atmosphere" that prevailed. Department members took turns hosting evening meetings as often as twice a month to discuss their own research or issues of the day; the Arts and Science Club met at least once a month on Tuesday evenings; and the appetite for academic discussion was sufficient to add monthly evening meetings of the Saturday Club, much to the consternation of faculty spouses (or more specifically wives, as there were no women faculty members), who saw it as a further infringement on family life. Topics at the Saturday Club ranged from "Religion with a God" (by J.M. Shaw) to European Affairs (Mackintosh) and the ensuing discussion freely crossed disciplinary lines. For instance, when G.B. Reid spoke on rate of scientific improvement, Mackintosh, Curtis, and Reginald Trotter (History) felt free to "attack the factual analysis."[54] Thus, when persuading Robert "Pete" McQueen to spend the summer of 1936 in Kingston, Mackintosh could describe a vibrant community of scholars. "I shall be here myself having agreed to do a spell of Summer School. Knox will be in the vicinity as well as most of the others. Whether federal politics will draw Curtis to Ottawa or municipal politics keep him in Kingston, I could not predict. Archie Reid is going to work here during the summer, and [E.F.] Beach, one of our students who is finishing his second year at Harvard, is also going to spend the summer here. Thus, there will be a fairly good group conferring from time to time in the Commerce Building."[55]

McQueen was a treasured addition to the academic milieu. The son of a Presbyterian minister in Edmonton, he laid claim to being Canada's first prairie-born economist, despite never completing a university degree in the subject.[56] After dabbling in engineering, he completed a BA and MA in philosophy at the University of Alberta, and then studied economics at Alberta (with Duncan MacGibbon), the London School of Economics (where he was influenced by Hobhouse, Walls, Cannan, Dalton, and Laski), the University of Chicago (with Jacob Viner and Frank Knight), and Columbia University (Alvin Hansen); however, he never completed his LSE dissertation. In 1924 he was appointed assistant professor of economics at the University of Saskatchewan, where he established a reputation as a gifted lecturer and an incisive commentator on a range of economic issues. In 1929, Mackintosh described McQueen as "a first-class man," but added that "I do not think he has quite found himself yet."[57] Over the course of the next few years, however, primarily through their involvement in the CPSA, they developed a close friendship. When Mackintosh was looking for someone to fill in during his sabbatical leave in 1934–35, the financial woes of the University of Saskatchewan made McQueen available. Salaries had been cut by 22 per cent, and with the department expecting to be asked to "sacrifice a man," spending a year at Queen's was an appealing opportunity for McQueen, not only for his own benefit but also to ease the financial pressure on his department. It would prove to be "an obvious landmark in his life. Not since his time in England had there come the daily joy of contact with economists of distinction and reputation ... The confidence he acquired in that single session at Queen's was lasting and good."[58] McQueen returned to teach summer school in Kingston in the following two years, and reported to Principal Wallace in 1940 that "I may safely say that the happiest and most profitable period of my academic life was spent at your institution."[59]

The esprit de corps that Smails observed in the department was most readily apparent in a series of papers published in the *Queen's Quarterly* in 1933 and 1934, with the authorship given as "members of the Economics Department, Queen's University."[60] The publication of four policy papers – "Financial Manipulation: A Project of Reform" (addressing the regulation of securities market), "Canadian Trade Policy in a World of Nationalism" (making the case for trade liberalization), "Financial Problems of our Federal System" (reiterating the long-held view that the Dominion-Provincial fiscal arrangements defined at the time of Confederation never properly functioned), and "The Proposal for a Central Bank" (providing the clearest justification for the formation of the Bank of Canada) – as a joint product of all the members of an academic department was surely an unprecedented event. The latter three papers would define the essence of the focus at Queen's on applied economics – international trade, public finance, and monetary policy – and spoke to the central policy issues of the Great Depression.

ADDRESSING THE GREAT DEPRESSION

Irving Brecher of McGill suggests that the debate over Canadian economic policy in the 1920s and 1930s was shaped by the demands of western farm organizations for monetary and other economic reform. Particularly vulnerable to periods of tight credit or high domestic inflation, farmers were willing to consider radical approaches – ranging from social credit to under-consumption theories of the business cycle – that departed from the concern with "sound money" and implicit acceptance of the quantity theory of money. Canadian economists, save perhaps the few associated with the League for Social Reconstruction, deviated little from the monetary and fiscal orthodoxy during the period: as a staples exporter, Canada required exchange-rate stability and prudent debt management, even if this meant a loss of autonomy over monetary and fiscal policy.[61] The potential hardship created through greater domestic price volatility – evident in the effects of post-WWI inflation on the standard of living of Canadian workers and of the subsequent deflation on the real cost of debt that farmers faced – was a consequence that had to be borne.

Mackintosh did not depart from this monetary orthodoxy. Commenting on the testimony before the banking committee of the House of Commons in 1923, he rejected Irving Fisher's proposal for flexible exchange rates (his "compensated dollar" proposal in which the gold-to-currency exchange rate would be adjusted to maintain stable prices) as ineffective in a staples-based economy where the main source of price fluctuations was found in overseas export markets.[62] Similarly, he rejected the calls by C.H. Douglas and George Bevington, advocates in the social credit movement, to tie credit expansion to increases in productive capacity by reciting the quantity theory of money: "Any scheme for the financing of long term credits by the issue of paper money inevitably brings as a result rising prices (or inflation) with its inevitable day of reckoning when liquidation must take place. A policy of 'easy money' or of restrictions on loans may hasten or postpone that day, it cannot avoid it." In this regard, economists had little assistance to offer: "The cyclical or rhythmic movement of industry with its recurring and successive periods of boom and depression is the major economic problem of the world today ... There is no easy way out, for as yet we know but little of the causes and course of the business cycle."[63]

Mackintosh's regular commentaries in the *Journal of the Canadian Bankers' Association* and *Queen's Quarterly* provide a unique perspective on the thinking of Canadian economists in the period. On the eve of the Great Depression, he saw "abundant signs of prosperity past and future,"[64] but expressed several qualifications. In April 1929, he wrote on "The Problems of Reparations" as the central economic and political issue in Europe since the end of World War I. In tracing the history of the financial penalties imposed on Germany in the Treaty of Versailles (Keynes's "Carthaginian peace"), and revised by the Dawes Plan of 1924 and the Young Plan of 1929, he accepted Keynes's view that the disabling of the German economy had impeded European economic growth and raised political tensions (evident, for instance, in the French occupation of the Ruhr to enforce its claims for retribution).[65] Second, he warned of the long-term trend towards protectionism that began in the 1870s, when latecomers to the Industrial Revolution used tariff barriers as a means of supporting domestic manufacturers, and accelerated after World War I when the realignment of international production created similar attempts by countries to claim a greater share of industrial output. He could only record his dismay with President Hoover's commitment to increased protectionism, despite the United States already having among the highest tariff rates in the developed world.[66] The American proposal to increase the duty on raw sugar in support of its domestic sugar-beet industry he described as "one of the most astonishing recent instances of economic nationalism gone mad" and expected that it would destroy the economy of Cuba, a country in which "American 'imperialism' has most completely operated."[67] In the October 1929 issue of the *Journal of the Canadian Bankers' Association* – written before the stock-market crash at the end of the month – he expressed his reservations over excess capacity in key American industries, the weakness of the pound sterling, and Canada's bad wheat crop. He then posed the ominous question: "Must Depression Follow?"[68]

When depression did indeed follow, he rejected monetary theories that said a shortage of gold and other mediums of exchange was the underlying cause. Instead, he subscribed to the view of a fundamental disequilibrium in prices and terms of trade dating back to the sharp expansion and global redistribution in the production of food and raw materials during World War I. Protectionism and currency devaluation only aggravated the problem. As the United States replaced Great Britain as the world's largest creditor nation, it increased neither its foreign lending nor its imports to allow debtor countries to meet their international obligations.[69] In Charles Kindleberger's words, "the British couldn't and the United States wouldn't" assume responsibility for ensuring that world trade was maintained.[70] What followed was a series of countries devaluing their currency and adopting higher tariffs in an effort to protect their domestic markets. Writing in 1936, Mackintosh observed that "During the past sixteen years and especially during the past six, deliberately planned artificial obstacles to international trade have been fantastically increased in height, in complexity and in instability … It is the unprecedented *magnitude* and *swiftness* of the changes in competitive positions that have characterized the postwar period."[71] With the collapse in world trade, no amount of monetary expansion could stimulate an economic recovery until the "accumulated maladjustments" were resolved.[72]

In October 1932 he speculated that the worldwide panic brought on by currency devaluation might be over, and that the world had returned to a "normal level of depression." With an easing of credit in short-term capital markets, it was a matter of awaiting a recovery in confidence; at the same time, he expected that, given the glut in resources and foodstuffs, as well as persistent beggar-thy-neighbour policies, "the road back to recovery is likely to be a long road."[73] He continued to hold some hope that international arrangements for currency management and trade liberalization might be on the horizon; however, with the failure to reach any international agreement at the 1933 Monetary and Economic Conference (which "after a lingering illness, finally departed this life") and hopes of US tariff reform dwindling, he could only recommend the use of a social psychologist "who would discover ways of relieving nations and mobs of the fears under which they act irrationally. Fear lies at the basis of competition in armaments and of excessive trade restrictions."[74]

As far as Canada was concerned, there was little to do but sit and wait out the storm. Having mortgaged its future income from natural resources in order to obtain the capital for their exploitation, the collapse of world trade exposed the vulnerability of the Canadian economy, as it lacked the export revenue to meet the interest charges on its large fixed debt. Revenue earned in the wheat sector, for instance, fell by 68 per cent between 1928 and 1932, as European markets closed against Canadian exports.[75] Fault could be found in the "amiable co-operation in folly by governments, industrialists, and financiers [who] recklessly and deliberately overdeveloped" Canada's newsprint industry, and in the overexpansion in railways that had saddled the government with a large burden of debt. Yet most factors affecting the national economy were beyond domestic control. "Canada as a nation is peculiarly bound up in the international fabric. We, of all countries, cannot pull ourselves up by our own bootstraps, but must in large measure await the recovery in the international markets on which we depend for the sale of our exports and for the provision of our capital requirements."[76] Assessing "The Progress of Canada's Recovery" in 1935, he deemed the economy to be 35 to 40 per cent of the way back to pre-Depression levels. The volume of construction, newsprint, and other industrial production had been restored, although prices had not, while the development of new mining industries and hydroelectric power had improved matters. There would be no sustained upturn, however, without a good wheat crop and an improvement in world commodity markets. "In the final analysis," he wrote, "we can recover our position as a prosperous country only through the recovery of international trade."[77]

If this left little room for policy initiatives, it was possible for Canada to remove existing impediments in order to facilitate renewed growth once an upturn in world trade occurred. This involved appropriate trade, fiscal, and monetary policy.

As far as trade policy was concerned, the election of the Bennett government in 1930 was not greeted by Mackintosh with enthusiasm. It went "whole hog" in increasing protectionism, converting Canada into a country of high and unstable tariff rates.[78] His early optimism that the Advisory Committee on Tariff and Taxation would lead to a more rational consideration of trade policy dissolved in light of anti-dumping legislation that imposed arbitrary valuations of commodities, justified on the basis of "the shopworn and bedraggled formula on which the United States Tariff Commission has operated."[79] For the same reason, he objected to the Ottawa Agreements of 1932, which strengthened the system of imperial preferences, largely through raising tariff rates against non-British countries and thereby merely diverting rather than expanding trade.[80] In "Canadian Trade Policy in a World of Nationalism," one of the four papers co-authored by the members of the Queen's department, the only rationale for tariffs was for infant industries, and this required a "judicious selection of infants." More generally, protectionism in Canada penalized its export industries – such as in the case of increasing the cost of agricultural implements for wheat farmers – leading to the assertion that Canada should undertake a unilateral reduction in tariff barriers.[81] As Mackintosh made the case in another paper, "Ricardo once said that the way to resume specie payments was to resume them. All our discussing methods of reducing barriers to trade must not obscure the simple truth, particularly important on this continent, that the way to reduce barriers to trade is to reduce them."[82] On this basis he welcomed the Anglo-American trade agreement of 1937 as the basis for wider multilateral cooperation and insisted that Canada needed to make concessions by ceding some imperial preferences incorporated into the Ottawa Agreements. Reminding readers of the *Journal of the Canadian Bankers' Association* that the world needed to view trade "as a benefit not a menace," he insisted that "our position would be happier if we contributed a smaller fraction of a much enlarged world trade."[83]

Nor did Mackintosh deviate from the orthodoxy that government fiscal policy should be as neutral as possible in order to balance the budget and maintain Canada's international credit-worthiness.[84] As an "economically immature" country, dependent on staple exports and heavy foreign borrowing, it had to control the size of the public debt, regardless of the state of the business cycle. During periods of relative prosperity, such as in 1924, he held that "clearly the present is a time when no extravagance should be tolerated and when government expenditures should be pared to the bone." Five years later he complained that "every period of rapid business expansion has been a period of waste, of declining business ethics and the appropriation by a few of the major rewards of expansion" and that, in light of the upsurge in government revenues, "It behooves both the electors and the government to scan critically every proposal for expenditures so that large revenues may not beget foolish waste."[85] Recessions also dictated fiscal restraint. Though he applauded Roosevelt, who acted "swiftly and decisively" in implementing the "first" New Deal in 1933 and cautiously supported deficit financing of public works because of the soundness of the US treasury, he perceived the situation in Canada to be quite different.[86] Recessions brought the ill effects of foreign borrowing – the large fixed commitment to meet interest and dividend payments at a time of a slump in export earnings – which required a greater rate of saving, both public and private.[87] This "burden of debt" was the "deep-rooted problem of our national life."[88]

The significant obstacle to fiscal prudence was Canada's federal system. On the revenue side, an outmoded system of taxation, only slightly modified during World War I, placed undue emphasis on customs revenue and indirect taxation, as opposed to corporate and personal income taxes. With less ability to adjust taxation to economic circumstances, fiscal policy aggravated rather than alleviated the business cycle. Yet he was more damning of the expenditure side of the ledger, where he saw conditional grants to the provinces as a built-in mechanism for excessive spending. "Financial Problems of our Federal System" (written by the Queen's economists) reiterated the long-held view that the dominion-provincial fiscal arrangements defined at the time of Confederation never properly functioned. Income transfers to the provinces were needed, but the absence of a clearly defined principle for transfer payments left the process open to political manipulation and "political bribery on a lavish scale as a means of securing or retaining the support of disaffected provinces."[89] Mackintosh had never minced words on the topic, and the paper echoed his earlier sentiments. In 1929 he complained of "repeated raids by provinces on the Dominion Treasury for increased subsidies ... [W]hen the Confederation Debates were going on the eminent lawyer, Christopher Dunkin, criticized the proposals, because he foresaw that the provinces would consider the Dominion Government 'an enormous milch cow' to which they would 'return again and again with a most calf-like appetite.' No criticism of Confederation has been more clear-sighted nor has any prophecy been borne out further by facts of our half century of history."[90] Conditional transfers led not only to wasteful spending, but provided an "incitement to further provincial expenditures" at a time when the dominion government was seeking to impose greater spending restraints.[91]

The one concrete measure called for was the creation of a central bank to regulate the money supply. Canada's adherence to the fixed exchange rates of the gold standard prior to 1914 occurred without any discretionary actions on the part of the banking system: all debts were legally discharged in gold, all currency was readily convertible to gold, and there were no restrictions on the international movement of gold. Since commercial banks held reserves chiefly in the form of dominion notes and gold, and their chief means of obtaining gold was through redemption of dominion notes, they had no avenue for increasing credit domestically. When Canada shifted off the gold standard in 1914, the department of finance was authorized to advance dominion notes to commercial banks on the basis of suitable collateral, and this lending authority was made permanent in the Finance Act of 1923. This "revolutionary legislation," by giving the commercial banks a domestic vehicle for increasing their reserves, proved incompatible with Canada's return to the gold standard in 1926. The Canadian dollar was soon trading at a discount to the US dollar, prompting the commercial banks to arbitrage by redeeming dominion notes for gold and exporting gold to the United States. Since nothing prevented the banks from further borrowing of dominion notes from the department of finance and repeating the process, Canada's gold reserves were significantly reduced. The department of finance was forced to institute an unofficial embargo on gold exports, tantamount to Canada effectively abandoning the gold standard, and, by default, leaving monetary policy in the hands of the chartered banks.[92]

"The Proposal for a Central Bank," written by Mackintosh and his department colleagues, thus championed the cause of a Bank of Canada to control the money supply. So vociferously did they argue the case that it was widely referred to as the "Queen's position" during the deliberations of the Macmillan Royal Commission in 1932.[93] Clifford Curtis took the lead in placing the argument in front of the commissioners, while Knox and Mackintosh elaborated on aspects of it during their testimony. Knox suggested that a central bank – with the traditional controls over rediscounting, buying, and selling of foreign exchange, and the enforcement of interest-rate policy – was necessary to maintain exchange-rate stability, but that it was beyond Canada's capacity to carry out "any kind of a purely domestic policy such as price stabilization, while the variations in the value of our raw material exports and in the volume of capital imports will subject us continually to the shocks."[94] For his part, Mackintosh dismissed the alternative of returning to the pre-WWI days of the gold standard, since

> the relatively stable conditions, the favourable trends, and the dominance of the London money market and the Bank of England policies within which the pre-war system worked, can never be recaptured. It would be unwise to expose the Canadian economy, without any intervention of deliberate control, to the full force of fluctuations of any international monetary standard which is likely to be adopted in the near future ... It is not contended that a central bank could perform miracles; that it could restore prosperity, solve the western debt problem, or revive depressed industries. In the carrying out of sound policies to meet these problems, however, it would be a valuable and indeed essential aid. Canadian prosperity is dependent to a peculiar degree on world prosperity. Effective cooperation with other nations in climbing back to prosperity requires the existence of a central bank of Canada ... A central bank is no panacea. It is merely an instrument to perform certain well-defined functions which must be performed whether intelligently or unwittingly.[95]

He insisted, however, that a central bank should be left under private control: "Surely only an over-enthusiasm for government control and operation would lead to the establishment of such an institution within the confines of an administrative department of government. Such a central monetary authority would be lacking in prestige, misunderstood abroad, and seriously subject to political influence."[96]

As far as the economics discipline in Canada had come during the 1930s, its analysis of the Great Depression was, to used Irving Brecher's terms, "fragmentary, fatalistic and confused."[97] Its fragmentary and confused nature came from an incomplete understanding of the cause of business cycles. Despite the call for a central bank and the need for greater domestic control over the money supply to ameliorate fluctuations imported from abroad, a general adherence to the quantity theory of money left little room for monetary policy to exercise an important influence over the level of real output. Nor, in an era prior to Keynes's *General Theory*, was there much appreciation of the potential for fiscal policy to influence the level of income and employment. The overriding characteristic was fatalism, which derived as a corollary of the staple thesis: since external markets set the pace for domestic growth, there was little avenue for domestic monetary and fiscal policy to influence economic conditions while waiting for international commodity markets to recover. The irony is that just when the discipline had developed the staple thesis as a unifying theme to explain the pace and pattern of economic growth, the Great Depression raised a host of other questions for which the staple thesis had, at best, partial answers.

Mackintosh was not immune from these criticisms and his own views reflected the discipline's search for new answers. Part of this search took him to Europe, with the intent of observing the attempts of various national governments to explore new solutions to the Great Depression; through the pages of the *Journal of the Canadian Bankers' Association* and *Queen's Quarterly*, he would comment on the political events as the world first stumbled and then, at a "dizzy pace," raced towards World War II.

EUROPE: "THE SWIFT SLIDE DOWN THE STEEP SLOPE OF CATASTROPHE"[98]

Upon completion of his work on the Frontiers of Settlement series, Mackintosh wrote to Principal William Hamilton Fyfe: "I have been at the University for the past fourteen years and during the past five years have been engaged in the administration of a research project which has kept me constantly at work for twelve months each year. I feel that the University would gain, not less than I, if I were given an opportunity of physical and mental change." Fyfe acquiesced, granting a sabbatical leave (unpaid as was the standard of the time) for the 1934–35 academic year.[99] Mackintosh would use the time to travel to Europe, still a sufficiently rare event to make the social pages: on 6 September 1934, the *Toronto Star* reported that, among the passengers sailing for England aboard the *Duchess of Bedford* were Professor and Mrs Mackintosh.[100] Using London as a base, they toured through England, Scotland, and France. They then gave up the "fog and brussel sprouts" of London for the "sun and oranges of Malaga."[101] After travelling through southern Spain, they took a coastal boat to Sicily, and then made their way north through Italy,

Switzerland (where they first met Lou and Lela Rasminsky in Geneva[102]), and Germany, eventually returning to London.

On the state of the European economy, Mackintosh first commented on "The Recovery of Britain."[103] Struck by the degree of optimism in the country, he attributed its recent economic improvement to the abandonment of the gold standard (adopting Keynes's argument that, in its resumption in 1925, it had placed the pound sterling at too high a level of parity), tariff protection, and subsidies extended to agriculture. These actions allowed Britain to avoid deflation by stimulating the domestic market, but discouraged a recovery in its exports, and came at the expense of "confusion" in the rest of the world. In Paris, he noted the declining public morale in France. Left to hold up a crumbing gold bloc, as country after country abandoned the gold standard, it too resorted to protectionism as an alternative to either devaluation (which was politically unacceptable to those living off their savings) or deflation (which might induce social unrest). Of all of Mackintosh's European experiences, Mussolini's Italy made the most powerful impression. He could not avoid marvelling at the institutional expressions of the myth of Italian supremacy: the emphasis on youth and athletics, the power of the fascist militia, the modern statues, and even the traffic officers all served to recreate the country around the themes of national unity, discipline, and efficiency. Mussolini himself was self-consciously a powerful aspect of this myth, with his apparent strength and vitality emblematic of the new Italy. Also striking were the workings of a fascist "corporatist state," which Mackintosh likened to a medieval city state with private property rights and incentives maintained but directed towards the state's interests. Tripartite boards of employer, employee, and state representatives were organized on an industry basis and placed under the direction of an "energetic, honest, and resourceful administration." The state also undertook sizable infrastructure spending on electrification, railways, and irrigation to support agriculture and industry. All of this was designed to further the quest for international prestige and power, which also led Italy to expand its presence in East Africa and, in particular, to erase the embarrassing defeat of earlier efforts to colonize Abyssinia. It was a similar identification of the value of the lira with national prestige that dictated much of Mussolini's economic policy during the depression. Following the devaluation of the pound sterling and the franc, Italy pursued a policy of deflation to defend the lira, seeking to cut wages, rents, and other prices uniformly to avoid income redistribution. He noted, however, that Mussolini had eliminated graft and corruption, and had converted chaos to order, only by creating an army of one million men in an electorate of ten million.[104]

Upon his return to London, Mackintosh accorded himself the pleasure of a visit with James Bonar, who had returned to England upon retiring in 1919 from the Royal Mint in Ottawa. "You will be right welcome, already by no means a stranger," stated Bonar. Mackintosh thus sojourned to Hampstead to pay his respects and, no doubt, to avail himself of one last occasion to discuss and debate with Bonar the virtues of Adam Smith's *Wealth of Nations*.[105] He then delayed his departure from England in order to attend the Economic and Monetary Conference held at Chatham House in London, where he rubbed shoulders with leading European scholars and partook of some of the finer features of European academic life. He would lunch with Sir Austen Chamberlain and, at the closing banquet held at Claridge's Hotel, he was seated at a table with Sir William Collins, Sir Karl Knudsen (the Norwegian-born British shipping magnate), Ivison S. Macadam (director general of the Royal Institute of International Affairs in London), Ramsay Muir (a prominent member of the Liberal Party in England), René Seydoux (dean of the École des sciences politiques in Paris), Hartley Withers (former editor of *The Economist*), and Alfred Zimmern (Montague Burton Professor of International Relations at Oxford). The conversation was unlikely as exotic as the seven-course meal, which began with Caviar Malossol, passed on to Tortue Verte au Sherry, Dame de Saumon d'Écosse Grimod, Selle de Baby Lamb au Romarin, and Poularde de Surrey Souvaroff, and ended with rather frightening sounding Bombe Marie Stuart.[106]

By the time of his return to Kingston, economic matters in Europe were overshadowed by political affairs. Mackintosh recognized at an early stage that the rise of Hitler in 1932 marked a transformation in European politics. The fragile peace in Europe rested with France's concern over national security: intent that Germany remain economically weak and be prevented from rearming, it was the most vociferous defender of the Treaty of Versailles. In contrast, the "muddling unreliability of British foreign policy," led it to eventually accept that further war reparations were "unsporting," since Germany was a valuable customer and repayment was unlikely to occur in any event. "Though to a very considerable extent the Hitler movement rose out of the resentment at the wrongs of the Peace Treaty, it would be a mistake to think that it could be appeased and civilized merely by rectification ... [I]t is a tragedy that they were righted only in the face of German force." With Germany's repudiation of the arms clause in the Treaty of Versailles ("logical and legal but not sensible"[107]) and the League of Nations' unwillingness to respond decisively, there would be no more German conciliation in its dealings with the "Versailles League."[108]

Italy's colonization of Ethiopia ("at first a mere side-show in the colonial exploitation of Africa it has now become a central problem of international politics"), the Spanish Civil War ("the increasing slaughter in Spain continues"), the "undeclared war in China," "crisis after crisis," as Germany extended its territorial control into the Balkans, and the succession of "Parliaments [that] disappeared before dictators"[109] were further evidence of the failure of the League of Nations. He added his voice to those criticizing the league for responding too slowly in Ethiopia, arguing that "had Britain and France stood together and acted promptly and persistently, the League of Nations policy would have been successful." Instead, "British prestige never stood higher than last year at the time of the Jubilee; since then it has dropped like a plummet."[110]

In 1936, Mackintosh still held out hope that a reinvigorated League of Nations could play an important role by evolving from an institution concerned with enforcing the terms of the Treaty of Versailles into one that might achieve currency stabilization and "the making of a peace which it would be in the interest of the vanquished to maintain."[111] But Germany's territorial expansion in central Europe exposed other shortcomings in the 1919 peace accord. "It is trite to say that the Treaty of Versailles gave to the problem of Central Europe only a dangerous half-answer." The division of the Austro-Hungarian Empire was based on nationality rather than economics, while Czechoslovakia failed to achieve a workable federated state, leaving Vienna as "a vast metropolis without a hinterland." With Germany's march down the Danube marking the obvious failure of Chamberlain's policy of appeasement and the efforts of the League of Nations, Mackintosh embraced the "clear and courageous line" expressed by Roosevelt in his "quarantine the aggressor" speech. With a sense of resignation, he accepted that "force and the threat of force must be used not to deny German expansion but to oppose the settlement of disputes by war."[112]

HAVE YOU EVER THOUGHT OF MACKINTOSH?

The early 1930s was the most prolific period of academic scholarship in Mackintosh's life. His research on the prairie economy brought him to the forefront of his discipline, while his observations on domestic and international affairs gave him an increasing presence as a public speaker and commentator. This did not go unnoticed in university circles.

Upon their return from Europe and at the urging of Vice-Principal McNeill, the Mackintoshes moved in next door to Principal Wallace, in the west wing of Summerhill, on the university grounds overlooking Stuart Street and the Kingston General Hospital. Designed as a grand country villa in the early 1840s, it boasted an impressive two-storey centre block, with three sweeping staircases inside and adorned with towering colonnades and a broad veranda. The adjoining wings were one-storey in height. Summerhill had served in a variety of capacities other than a private residence, including the domicile of members of parliament during Kingston's brief reign as the seat of government. When taken over by Queen's in 1854, it also filled several purposes, from gymnasium and lecture rooms to housing for the medical library, theology department, faculty offices, and rooms for the principal.[113] Eventually, the centre block became the principal's residence, with the east and west wings rented to senior faculty members. The ambitions of Summerhill exceeded its grasp, the rather "tired" décor with its "muddy tan and brown" walls left much to be desired. But what it lacked in grandeur was made up for in location, and it would be the Mackintoshs' residence for the next thirty years.

The move would foreshadow future events. When Principal Fyfe resigned from Queen's in 1935, he listed W.E. McNeill and James Macdonnell as possible replacements, and then added: "Have you ever thought of Mackintosh? During my time here he has *grown* most remarkably both in grasp and in reputation. I believe he is almost the only academic economist whom bankers trust. He has built up, manages and inspires an excellent department. I am confident that he would go on *growing*. And that's what one wants." Macdonnell, in his capacity as a trustee, forwarded the recommendation to James A. Richardson, but expressed the reservation that Mackintosh had not "enough energy, initiative, decisiveness and readiness if necessary to take a strong stand on a controversy."[114] R.C. Wallace, president of the University of Alberta, would be appointed principal at Queen's.

Macdonnell was clearly expressing a minority view. Indeed, Mackintosh's candidacy had been solicited for the presidency of the University of Manitoba in 1934[115] (and would be again in 1944), and in September 1936 he was identified as a replacement for Wallace at the University of Alberta. Premier William Aberhart invited him to visit Edmonton "to the end that we might get acquainted and learn how far our ideas of university development might coincide." The invitation was gracefully declined on two grounds: "In the first place, the Presidency of a University is very much a full time job and anyone undertaking it must be prepared to bid good-bye to his work as a serious scholar. Faced with a definite choice it has become quite clear to me that I am not prepared to do so at this point. I want to push my work as an economist a bit farther." His second reason was to avoid any possible embarrassment to himself or the government, for "I should inevitably find myself in disagreement with the Government of the Province on matters of economic policy."[116] Six months later, he completed a prairie trifecta when the presidency of the University of Saskatchewan became vacant. Macdonnell would lament that "the name of MacKintosh [sic] I suppose will come up again," and on this occasion he was correct. Mackintosh, however, declined to be considered, again citing his reluctance to give up his work as an economist.[117] It would be another fifteen years before he would entertain an appointment as a university head.

PART THREE

How Keynesianism Came to Canada

In 1936, W.A. Mackintosh embarked upon a career in public service that would see much of the next ten years of his life immersed in policy work for the Government of Canada. This began on a part-time basis with his appointment to the National Employment Commission (NEC) and was followed immediately by research for the Royal Commission on Dominion Provincial Relations in 1938. Then, in December 1939, he took a leave of absence from Queen's in order to work on a full-time basis in the department of finance for the duration of the war. He would not return to Queen's until September 1946.

During this decade of service, Canadian economic policy underwent a rapid and profound transformation. In 1936, as the Great Depression dragged on into its seventh year, the Canadian government muddled along, stubbornly refusing to change course and striving to adhere to the traditional "balanced budget" orthodoxy of public finance. Jack Pickersgill, who joined the prime minister's office in 1937, writes that there was "scarcely a hint of a Canadian New Deal in the official Liberal program of 1935," and adds that "it is doubtful if Mackenzie King had ever heard of Keynes's *General Theory* and he would have been horrified if he had not least because he would have not thought it moral."[1] Similarly, Robert Bryce notes that, in the May 1936 budget speech, just weeks before the publication of Keynes's *General Theory*, Finance Minister Dunning stated the orthodoxy: "the declared purpose of the government is to end in the shortest practicable time the era of recurrent deficits."[2] Yet ten years later, the Government of Canada had firmly embraced a commitment to Keynesian stabilization policy.

There were several avenues through which Keynes's influence spread to Canada. The first, and direct, route was through the presence of three prominent Canadians – Wynne Plumptre, Bryce, and Lorie Tarshis – among the "Cambridge circus" in the early 1930s.

Plumptre was an undergraduate at the University of Toronto before studying under Keynes at King's College between 1928 and 1930. Described by Keynes as "one of the best young economists we have had in the place in recent years,"[3] Plumptre returned to Toronto as a lecturer in 1933. He went on to a distinguished career in the Canadian civil service, as financial attaché in the Canadian embassy in Washington, secretary of the Wartime Prices Board, as head of the economic division of the department of external affairs, and in the department of finance, where he became deputy minister in 1954. He returned to academic life in as principal of Scarborough College, University of Toronto, between 1965 and 1972. Perhaps his most enduring academic contribution to economics is preserved only in a footnote. In the wake of the appearance of Keynes's *General Theory*, D.H. Robertson offered his important critique of Keynes's treatment of interest-rate determination as "the grin on the Cheshire cat." In his correspondence with both Roy Harrod and Keynes, Robertson states that "I have seen an effective criticism by Plumptre along these lines."[4] No such paper by Plumptre has ever surfaced, and the substance of his critique remains a minor puzzle in the history of economic thought.

Bryce completed a degree in mining engineering at the University of Toronto in 1931, before his interest turned to economics. He enrolled in a master's program at Cambridge, under the supervision of Joan Robinson, where he attended the Political Economy Club and Keynes's lectures from 1932 to 1934.[5] Quickly converted to Keynes's ideas, he incorporated them in a paper written in 1935, and became a self-appointed emissary. He solicited the opportunity to present his paper to Friedrich Hayek's LSE seminar, where he was accorded a polite reception, and then dispatched himself to Harvard for six months to undertake its indoctrination. Both Joseph Schumpeter and Paul A. Samuelson comment on the significance of Bryce's arrival at Cambridge, Massachusetts. Bryce's own view of his stay at Harvard is more modest: "I hesitate to say that it gave them a running start on the *General Theory*, but at least I had softened things up a bit by the time the book came out."[6] He joined the Canadian department of finance in 1938 and spent the next thirty years in public service. From the perspective of the academic discipline, Charles P. Kindleberger describes Bryce as "one of those brilliant civil servants whose names are largely unknown."[7]

Tarshis also spent his undergraduate years at the University of Toronto, where, as a student of Plumptre, he was "reared on [Keynes's] *Treatise on Money*."[8] He then studied for a second undergraduate degree in economics at Trinity College, Cambridge, under the supervision of Maurice Dobb, Robertson, and Colin Clark. He too became a member of Keynes's Political Economy Club and attended Keynes's lectures during the formative period of *The General Theory*. He wrote the Economics Tripos after two years and then enrolled in a PhD program, eventually earning his doctorate in 1939. Accepting an appointment at Tufts, Tarshis became "an influential member of the colony of 'bright young things' in Cambridge, Massachusetts, who brought Keynes to Harvard."[9] But he did not have a major influence upon the direction of the economics discipline in Canada for two reasons. The most obvious one is that he spent most of his academic career in the United States, not returning to Canada until he was sixty. Despite the fact that he canvassed for a job in Canada in the 1940s, no offers were apparently forthcoming.[10] It was not until 1971, "sickened by the Vietnam War and the growing illiberalism of the United States," that he left Stanford to accept the offer of his former mentor Plumptre to assume the chair of the division of social sciences at Scarborough College, University of Toronto.[11] The second reason is the sad fate that befell his 1947 textbook, *The Essentials of Economics*. This story, though by now well-known, merits retelling. Tarshis began it prior to enlisting in the US Army during World War II and completed it while at Stanford. Samuelson acknowledges that: "It was a good book; a very good book. Maybe in 1945 I would have stuck to my mathematical-economics knitting if the Tarshis text had then been available."[12] It was not the appearance in print of Samuelson's *Economics* one year after that doomed Tarshis's *Essentials* to the remainder bin, but an odious censorship campaign. The story, recounted several times, is that an anti–New Dealer, Merwin K. Hart, and the writer Rose Wilder Lane appealed to the trustees of every American university against adopting the book because of the perceived radical nature of the

Keynesian content.[13] Canadian universities were unlikely part of this campaign; however, it doubtlessly contributed to the fact that no copies of Tarshis's textbook were ever sold in Canada.[14]

In addition to the influence of Canadian students among the Cambridge circus, a second path by which Keynesianism was transmitted to Canada was that blazed by Mabel Frances Timlin. Her route to an academic career has achieved minor folklore status. After teaching in Wisconsin and several Canadian prairie schools, she completing a business course at a private college and accepted a secretarial position at the University of Saskatchewan in 1921. Over the next eight years she completed her undergraduate degree and then obtained her doctorate at the University of Washington – both while attending to her full-time secretarial duties. Upon completion of her thesis, "Keynesian Economics – A Synthesis," in 1940, she was appointed assistant professor at the University of Saskatchewan.[15] The published version of her thesis, *Keynesian Economics*, which came out in 1942, is identified by Harry Johnson as one of the earliest contributions to pure theory by an economist working in Canada.[16] Despite being favourably reviewed outside the country, its impact on the Canadian economics community – dominated by economic history and institutional analysis, by men, and by universities located in Ontario and Quebec – was modest.

Instead, it was Mackintosh who played the most important role in the transmission of Keynesian ideas to Canada. With his experience of the Great Depression and World War II, his personal views were to undergo a change that would, in turn, inform his contribution to Canadian economic policy. While Mackintosh was conversant with Keynes's criticisms of the British Treasury and with his academic writings, it was in responding to the pressing economic challenges of the moment that his appreciation for Keynesian economics emerged. Though initially circumspect about applying some Keynesian policy prescriptions to a staple-based economy, he would eventually recast the staple thesis in terms of an open-economy Keynesian model applicable to Canada.

The process by which Canadian economic policy came to adopt a Keynesian perspective, as well as the degree to which it adhered to it, is open to debate.[17] There are several assertions as to the timing of the changes in Canadian economic policy. According to Blair Neatby, for instance, "John Maynard Keynes had arrived in Canada" with the NEC's *Final Report*; similarly, both Donald Smiley and Neil Bradford suggest that the final report of the Rowell–Sirois Royal Commission reflected Keynes's influence.[18] While none of these assertions is wrong, there is a need to clarify the use of the term Keynesian and to distinguish the various meanings it has acquired.

In its broadest sense, what Robert Skidelsky calls "Keynesian politics," Keynesianism refers to the expanded role of the state in managing a capitalist economy. As such, it serves as both a description and a rationale for the expansion in social security, government expenditure, public ownership, and regulatory interventions that characterized the post-WWII economy in most western countries.[19] One could also include in this sense of the term the new political culture that redefined the relationship between citizens and the state, with the latter assuming greater responsibility for the livelihood of individuals.[20] In this context, the labour-relations policy that evolved piecemeal during World War II in Canada played an important role in managing capital-labour conflict during the next three decades.[21]

A second connotation identifies Keynesianism more narrowly with counter-cyclical fiscal policy: the expansion of government spending and transfer payments (and/or a reduction in taxes) during a recession to offset a decline in private-sector spending and, concomitantly, a reduction in government net outlays during a period of prosperity. In a historical context, this issue most frequently arose in debates over the use of public-works projects to "prime the pump" during a recession to alleviate unemployment (as was Keynes's argument in his 1929 pamphlet *Can Lloyd George Do It?*) and over the appropriateness of government budgetary deficits. It implied the recognition that, in addition to the traditional tools of trade and monetary policy, government fiscal adjustment might also play a role in stabilizing economic activity. While this is certainly an important aspect of Keynesian economic policy, it is not necessarily unique to it. Douglas Owram, for instance, points to the concise and lucid justification for counter-cyclical fiscal policy provided by O.D. Skelton in 1909, predating Keynes by at least two decades.[22]

A third meaning, then, refers more directly to Keynes's academic writings and, in particular, to the theory of effective demand as the "central message" of the *General Theory*.[23] It was one thing to suggest that public works could create employment and might be invoked to hasten the rate of economic recovery at a particular point in the business cycle; however, it was quite another to argue at a theoretical level that such actions were necessary because there were no automatic forces ensuring that an economy tended towards equilibrium at a full-employment level of output. A concrete reflection of the growing acceptance of this view was the recasting of national income accounts into expenditure categories that occurred in many countries during World War II. Equating a nation's output with the sum of total spending – divided between personal consumption, private investment, government expenditures, and net exports – followed logically from the conviction that governments had a responsibility to stabilize aggregate spending in the economy and national income accounts were a requisite tool for this purpose.

A fourth and more restrictive definition rests on a complete model of national income determination. For James Meade, Keynes's Cambridge colleague, the crucial aspect of a Keynesian model was the causal relationship between saving and investment. Following Say's Law, it was commonplace to see the interest rate as a means of equilibrating savings and investment: an excess of savings would drive down the interest rate and induce greater investment until the two were brought into equality. For Keynes, interest rates played no such role in ensuring that planned investment would equal total savings. Investment was instead largely determined by the state of long-term expectations held by entrepreneurs ("the news of the day"), while saving was a function of the level of national income. Meade's focus on the investment-savings relationship may be extended to include the third of John Hicks's "fundamental equations" (where the interest rate is set by the equilibrium between liquidity preference and the money supply) to identify the analytical core of a Keynesian model.[24] This leads to an entirely different conception of the equilibrating forces in the economy, with obvious implications for policy. Wage and price flexibility were insufficient for ensuring that the economy would reach full employment; instead, it was necessary to manage the various aspects of aggregate demand to ensure that the necessary adjustments in the quantity of employment and output would occur. Equilibrium was thus to be achieved through output, not price, adjustment. Accordingly, the appropriate policy focus was on managing the level of aggregate demand rather seeking to bring labour and product markets into equilibrium through encouraging greater wage and price flexibility.[25]

These four uses of the term "Keynesian" are mutually compatible, but become progressively more specific in the order presented above. They also provide a helpful criterion for assessing how quickly, and how completely, Canadian economic policy adopted a Keynesian stance.[26] At the risk of grave oversimplification, the diffusion of Keynesian ideas in Canada progressed in the same order – as a general rationale for greater government involvement in the economy, to an acceptance of the efficacy of countercyclical government fiscal policy, followed by the recognition of effective demand as the determinant of the level of national income, and finally to a more robust analytical model of the determinants of various components of aggregate demand. Interpreted in this manner, the argument presented in the next five chapters is that, both for Mackintosh and Canadian economic policy, the adoption of a Keynesian perspective increased progressively during the National Employment Commission, the Rowell–Sirois Royal Commission, and World War II, and reached its fullest expression in the 1945 White Paper on *Employment and Income, with Special Reference to the Initial Period of Reconstruction* and the *Proposals of the Government of Canada* (or the "Green Book") presented at the Dominion-Provincial Conference on Reconstruction in 1945.

7

The Queen's Conspiracy and the National Employment Commission: Ottawa, 1936–1938

When we come to a general election … the Tory Party will make the [National Employment] commission's recommendations a plank in its platform, purely for the sake of gaining power. In that event, we stand a good chance to be beaten, and Rogers, Mackintosh, Purvis, et al., will find that all they have succeeded in doing is putting the Liberal Party out of office perhaps for the rest of their days.

Mackenzie King (1938)[1]

If Canadian economic policy during the 1930s lacked any innovative attempts to remedy the economic downturn, there was no reason to expect that the National Employment Commission (NEC) would be any different. Its creation in May 1936 arose out of a veritable dog's breakfast of goals and objectives. Proposed by Mackenzie King as early as 1930, while in opposition, it was the centrepiece of the Liberal's 1935 election campaign as an alternative to the "New Deal" posturing of the Bennett administration. The NEC, combined with the Canada–US Trade Agreement enacted the same day, shouldered responsibility for addressing the problem of unemployment upon the Liberal Party's return to power. Indeed, King wrote in his diary that "I knew by these measures I had on the one hand helped to bring millions of dollars in work and wages to homes. – In reduced cost of living to families all over Canada, and while helping to provide work save the Treasury & thereby the taxpayers many millions of dollars as well, if one takes account of the means taken to restore control by Parl't over expenditures, etc. I felt it was worth all the strain and stress of public life."[2]

Despite this grand portrayal, the NEC was primarily expected to address one nagging and dubious concern, and one very urgent and real problem. The former was King's conviction that there was tremendous waste in the system of unemployment relief, where dominion grants to the provinces were being misdirected for purposes other than the alleviation of hardship among idle workers and farmers. "Chiselers" – among individuals, municipalities, and provinces – were to be exposed at great saving to the dominion government, a cynical perspective reinforced by the cuts to grants-in-aid to the provinces for relief that immediately followed the announcement of the NEC. The urgent political problem was the rising social unrest among the unemployed, punctuated by the "On-to-Ottawa Trek" and the Regina Riot in the summer of 1935. It was recognized that the relief camps had been an unequivocal failure and had to be shut down, and the responsibility for coming up with an alternative became the responsibility of the NEC. As Frank Underhill notes, these were dangerous times.

The mandate given to the NEC, therefore, was a confusing array of administrative tasks and directives for policy advice. Among the administrative assignments, it was to carry out a national registration and classification of unemployed persons in receipt of relief and to improve the coordination of the relief effort, which included responsibility for the allocation of public-works funds. In an advisory capacity, it was to offer recommendations for immediately increasing employment, including special attention to the problems faced by youth and women. Though its mandate was apparently broad-ranging, the significant and overriding constraint on the NEC was the provisos that it would result in a "lessening [of] the burden of taxation" and that no new major public-works initiatives would be undertaken.[3] In essence, the NEC was expected to save money by better monitoring the transfer of relief money to the provinces, and to find a short-term palliative solution once the announced closure of the relief camps was enacted. The additional task – to formulate "long-range plans of national development for the purpose of ameliorating the effects of future depressions"[4] – appears seemingly as an afterthought.

The mainstream press strongly endorsed the direction given to the NEC. The *Globe and Mail* argued that "The unemployment problem in Canada is too long standing, too entangled with the problems of trade and industrial expansion. Nor has the Commission unlimited resources and the powers to go New-Dealing all over the country with elaborate work projects and farm rehabilitation schemes. It must proceed within the framework of the present system and confine its plans to sound and meritorious schemes that are within the limitations of the public purse."[5] It also accepted King's view that the villains in the scenario were the provinces and the unemployed themselves: "It is proposed to curb racketeering, the padding of relief rolls, etc., which have scandalized taxpayers and public men, including the present Prime Minister. The day of the 'blank cheque' and the indiscriminate handouts is gone. The hatchet is to be raised against imposters."[6]

For the *Financial Post*, the NEC was a personification of its chairman, Arthur Blaikie Purvis. It found in Purvis the business leadership necessary to remedy floundering public efforts to address the economic malaise. As president and managing director of Canadian Industries Ltd. (an affiliate of Imperial Chemical Industries in the UK and Dupont in the US), he was hailed as Canada's leading business executive and just the man "to put the emphasis on character – the maintenance of self-reliance, the restoration of self-respect, and the stimulation of the will to work."[7] He was also embraced for having "shown little sympathy with the recent American experiment 'to buy back prosperity with unlimited expenditures for the public purse,' with 'deliberate monetary manipulation in an effort to adjust the debt burden,' and with running of industry by the government itself ... Such steps he believes only result in spreading the area of stagnation and lowering the confidence and character of the people."[8]

The *Financial Post* was also enthusiastic about the supporting cast. A. Neil McLean, a former bank manager and president of a fish-packing firm, was "noted for his insistence that there is somewhere – and he thinks he knows where – a monetary cure for the depression." Alfred Marois was a Montreal shoe manufacturer and head of the Quebec Board of Trade, who had "demonstrated his business acumen by keeping his company afloat in the wreck-strewn boot and shoe industry." E.J. Young, a Saskatchewan farmer and a former Liberal MP from 1925 to 1935, was lauded for his "ability to reduce intricate problems to a didactive simplicity [that] rivals that of Henry Ford and Sir Norman Angell, and whose dissentient *Price Spreads Report* is already a classic in Canadian business literature." Tom Moore, president of the Trades and Labor Congress from 1918 to 1935, was described as "an honest, sincere, middle-of-the-road fellow of great common sense, known in every part of Canada and respected by employers and workers alike." Mary Sutherland was the former associate editor of the *Grain Growers' Guide* and a Liberal Party loyalist. As for Mackintosh, he was described as "steeped in the lore of political economy." The *Financial Post* added, with a sense of comfort, that he was "not the traditional pipe smoking academician but a practical-minded economist, a clear sane thinker and a most prodigious worker."[9]

Mackintosh had gained public prominence through his Canadian Frontiers of Settlement research and his public speaking on domestic and international affairs, while his credentials were further bolstered by his participation on the Unemployment Research Committee of Ontario in 1935.[10] It was likely his status as president-elect of the Canadian Political Science Association that led to his formal nomination to the NEC (by Duncan MacGibbon, past president of the CPSA).[11] Whatever the case, he was a late addition to the roster of commissioners, at least as far as King was concerned. After having failed to recruit William Rundle, former general manager of the National Trust Company, as late as May 7, King had T.J. Bradshaw, president of North American Life, pencilled in as the Ontario representative. When Purvis accepted the appointment as chair, he expressed "some doubts in regards to one of the names mentioned which I would like to express to you and Mr. Rogers at the appropriate time."[12] Whether the objection was to Bradshaw or someone else, Mackintosh was placed on the commission, no doubt on the urging of Norman McLeod Rogers, the minister of labour and Mackintosh's former Queen's colleague.

Even if the mandate for the NEC had been clear – despite the differing expectations for success – to understand the deliberations on the NEC and its eventual results, it is necessary to appreciate the intervention of its minister, Rogers, the personality of its chairman, Purvis, and Mackintosh's self-perceived role as a "policy expert." Rogers was the rising star in the cabinet, where he was a strong and progressive voice for increased spending, in opposition to Finance Minister Dunning's attempts to avoid a budgetary deficit. When he was appointed minister of labour, King expressed the view that "Rogers is the best all round man in the Cabinet; (if he has the strength, he may yet be the Party Leader & P.M.)."[13] Purvis had staked much of his personal reputation on getting some tangible results, and would grow increasingly impatient with the cabinet's inaction on several of the NEC's recommendations. For his part,

Mackintosh worked tirelessly – over his already well-worn path between Ottawa and Kingston, he would make more than fifty round trips and spend ninety-four days working on the NEC in the first year alone – and was not about to see these efforts to achieve some economic reform go for naught.[14] Given the scope of the tasks and limitations placed on its resources, it is remarkable that anything remotely coherent emerged. That something did is a testament to the efforts of these three men.

ECONOMIC FUNDAMENTALS OF RECOVERY

Much of the reasoning underlying the NEC's approach to the unemployment problem was outlined in a series of memoranda drafted by Mackintosh. The first of these, on the "Economic Fundamentals of Recovery," was prepared for discussion at the end of July 1936.[15] It provided a concise account of the causes of the Great Depression and the course of a "normal" recovery, and then outlined the scope of initiatives that the NEC might undertake. He began by arguing that the current economic crisis was not due to any inherent weakness in capitalism, but due to the failure of national economies to undertake "the magnitude of adjustment" required after World War I. The war not only left many countries with large public debt and, in the case of Germany, large reparation payments, but also brought a reordering in the international division of labour with the relocation of manufacturing activity and the expansion in primary commodity production. Failure to reach international trade and currency agreements to accommodate these changes eventually resulted in the beggar-thy-neighbour policies that curtailed economic growth.

Canada's vulnerability was due to its primary role as a staple exporter and the collapse of international commodity markets: the slump was transmitted to Canada through an abrupt decline in demand for its exports and a reduced inflow of foreign savings. "To countries such as Canada," Mackintosh wrote, "an economic depression, by which we mean not merely a decline in the national income but a decline associated with idle means of production, particularly unemployed labour, is communicated through the chief activities which tie it to the rest of the economic world, namely, its exports of merchandise, its imports of capital, and to a lesser extent, its imports of merchandise."[16] These international problems, over which Canada could exercise little influence, were exacerbated by overproduction in the country's two largest export industries, wheat due to misguided economic policy, and newsprint due to "gross financial mismanagement" in the private sector.

A normal recovery, he argued, occurred as inventories of raw materials and finished goods gradually diminished, and as accumulated savings sought outlets for profitable investment. Renewed investment first occurs in the replacement of obsolete capital stock and gains momentum as new techniques of production emerge in response to the drive to lower costs. Recovery in the capital-goods industry is typically followed by renewed investment in the production of consumption goods as business confidence and employment recovers. While there was little that Canada could do to stimulate business investment, Mackintosh cautioned against public initiatives that might interfere with private-sector spending once an international recovery was under way. He did allow for one exception: "I am prepared to consider offering special inducements for investment ... in fields where there are special social benefits to be derived as, for example, in the case of housing."[17]

There were other things that Canada could do to take advantage of opportunities as the world economy recovered. Foremost in this regard were the removal of barriers to trade, in order to facilitate exports, and an appropriate monetary policy to keep interest rates low, in order to accommodate investment when business expectations improved. While both of these measures were outside the purview of the NEC, Mackintosh was reasonably satisfied that appropriate steps had been taken. What remained for the NEC, then, was ensuring that there were no obstacles to increased employment when exports and investment increased: "There will still remain an extensive field of work in seeing that employables are brought into jobs which have been opened for them ... It may be that in certain industries and in certain areas the commission may have to consider the problem of transferring workers."[18]

The focus of the NEC, therefore, was to identify the scope of the unemployment problem and to ensure that the supply of labour was adequately prepared when economic fortunes improved job opportunities. The registration of relief recipients – and their classification by whether they were employable or non-employable, duration of unemployment, gender, and age – was an obvious and important first step. As a corollary, it might then identify a more efficient means of providing relief and save the dominion government money if provinces were found to be using relief funds for inappropriate purposes. Other initiatives were required to address the deterioration in both work skills and morale among individuals who had experienced long bouts of unemployment. Specifically, a rehabilitated Employment Services under dominion control, youth training, and apprenticeship programs would help to match the unemployed to job openings when they occurred. The emphasis on administrative efficiency was also reflected in the NEC's responsibility for administering relief funds. In place of public-works projects, largely conceived to be tainted by local party politics and municipal patronage, it solicited from each province "alternative plans" for public works which met the NEC's criteria for labour-intensive infrastructure projects that would support private development in areas like tourism, mining, or forest conservation.

A second memorandum, written by Mackintosh in February 1937, provided the argument for rejecting a large-scale increase in public works as a stimulus to economic growth. In response to increasing provincial requests for dominion funding of public projects, he conceded that the "work for relief" was intuitively appealing when compared to the simple dole, but suggested the make-work projects were not an efficient means of job creation, as only one out of every three dollars was paid out in wages. More generally, his views were based on the premise that a "normal recovery" was already under way. Acknowledging the logic to counter-cyclical fiscal policy, he expressed caution with respect to the timing of great public spending:

> There is sound economic ground for urging a policy under which public expenditures might be expanded and contracted to offset fluctuations in private expenditures, but any such policy must be subject to the most careful management and good judgment lest it create more problems than it solves. Such a programme is usually associated with public works but only because expenditures on public works, in contrast with other expenditures, are probably more capable of being postponed and made in the proper economic circumstances without thereby reducing the value of the work ... It should not be lost sight of, however, that the essential of any stabilizing policy of this sort is the expansion and contraction of public expenditures to the end that total expenditures (public and private) may be made more stable.[19]

To its credit, the NEC did recommend government expenditures on public infrastructure – tourist development, mining roads, reforestation projects, and land clearance for land settlement – but the overriding concern was that public spending would "crowd out" private investment by competing for skilled workers. "At this stage in the recovery," Mackintosh argued, "employment will be stimulated more by a substantial reduction in public works expenditures than by an increase therein. This is because of the encouragement to industry which would be likely to result from such a reduction in Government expenditures."[20] Public works, at the time, would merely reallocate wealth within the country by creating jobs in a specific locale at the expense of a higher debt burden in the country generally. In keeping with this argument, Purvis advised Rogers in January 1937 that "A very substantial reduction in the total of all Government expenditures for Public Works projects ... can in its viewpoint be very safely made for the fiscal year starting 1 April 1937, without disturbing the expectation of materially decreased unemployment, and with the added advantage of ameliorating Government competition with industry for the services of skilled workers."[21] This point would be reiterated in the NEC's *Interim Report* of July 1937.

The one exception to the NEC's reluctance to offer short-term economic stimuli was in the area of housing. Mackintosh stated the case in an August 1936 memorandum: "Direct government stimulation of investment in private competitive industry is extremely difficult to devise without grave inequities and a strong probability of finally frustrating private investment. In the field of Housing, on the contrary, the direct benefits of government stimulation are widespread, the inequities can be reduced to negligible proportions, and the indirect benefits of improved public health and moral[e] alone are incalculable ... Bold and concerted attempts to attack the housing problem on several fronts will have not only the advantage of more popular support than any other employment policy will win, but the virtue of striking at the root of the present unemployment."[22] In theory, housing was a magic elixir for employment: it targeted for assistance the relatively labour-intensive construction industry; it did not compete with the private sector for scarce resources to the extent that the construction trades were suffering from particularly high rates of unemployment; there was a large backlog of deferred investment in new construction and repairs during the depression; it required very little outlay of government funds if based on modest subsidies to mortgage lending; and it provided an overriding social benefit in the form of improved accommodation, health, and sanitation. Mackintosh estimated the "housing backlog" to be substantial. Given that there were some two million homes in Canada with roughly a fifty-year lifespan, and taking into consideration the rate of population growth, he concluded that an adequate rate of investment in residential housing would be 30,000 homes per year, which, at an average cost in the order of $3,300, would imply an annual investment of $100 million. Since new home construction over the previous five years was roughly half of this amount, this left a backlog of 75,000 houses, amounting to approximately $245 million.[23]

To address the backlog, a three-pronged approach was proposed. First, the Home Improvement Plan (HIP) was to provide low-interest loans to homeowners for renovation and rehabilitation work. Based upon a successful US program, residential property owners could borrow up to $2,000 from approved lending institutions, with the government insuring against losses of up to 15 per cent of the aggregate value of the loan. Interest rates were set at 3.5 per cent on a one-year loan, repayable in monthly instalments, so the effective annual rate was 6.32 per cent. Second, amendments to the Dominion Housing Act (1935) were proposed to make it easier for "relatively affluent" potential homeowners to obtain mortgage financing. Existing regulations, which provided mortgage funds at a 5-per-cent rate of interest for up to 80 per cent of the value of the home, had proved to have little effect, because its cumbersome procedure resulted in little cooperation from lending institutions, particularly in rural areas.[24] Third, a low-rental plan to subsidize the construction of rental accommodation for poorer families was proposed as a form of slum clearance. Mackintosh justified government subsidies in this area on the grounds that they did not compete with private builders and were an important social investment in public health. An amount of $10 million was to be set aside to subsidize municipal housing authorities or limited-dividend housing corporations[25] for up to one-third of the cost of constructing low-income rental accommodation. The projects were required to have at least a hundred units, and the cost could not exceed more than $750 per adult accommodated. The province or municipality where the project occurred was also required to make a small contribution – if only because housing was provincial jurisdiction – expected to be in the form of free land, to help in keeping monthly rental rates low. Tenants were to be selected by the welfare department on the basis of need.[26]

Other initiatives of the NEC in the area of unemployment and youth and women lacked any creativity. While the NEC deserves credit for drawing attention to joblessness among women, and for documenting the extent of the problem, Nancy Christie observes that "its recommendations were to say the least flaccid. With trying regularity, it advanced a standard program of domestic training; one of its most creative suggestions was that women could create new employment niches for themselves by growing and selling seeds." In this regard, the commission proved to be no further advanced than the conventional thinking that women's unemployment, both in terms of the causes and the solutions, was a social rather than an economic problem.[27]

Taking the various aspects of the NEC's mandate for short-run measures and putting them into a coherent framework was no simple task. One aspect of the NEC's duties could not be justified on any other terms than political crisis management. The relief camps were closed in July 1936 and the NEC scurried to put in place a farm-work program as an alternative for what it politely described as a potential "urban overcrowding" problem. The resulting Farm Improvement and Employment Plan expanded upon previous initiatives to provide farms with a small cash payment in order to place unemployed workers into temporary agricultural work during the winter. It was, according to James Struthers, both "clever and cynical"[28] at the same time: there was little economic rationale for such a program save being a relatively inexpensive way to prevent a concentration of unemployed in cities fomenting unrest. Purvis was quite candid about this is an address to the Canadian Club: "During the Winter of 1936, over 53,000 single homeless men and women, chiefly in the Western Provinces, were placed at work away from the subversive influence of irresponsible agitators."[29]

UNEMPLOYMENT RELIEF AND INSURANCE

Whatever the NEC may have lacked in policy innovation, it made up for in political intrigue. At the centre of the matter was dominion-provincial relations and the agent provocateur was Mackintosh.

In its *Interim Report* of July 1937, the NEC accepted that responsibility for the administration of unemployment relief should remain in the hands of the provinces and municipalities; however, by the time that its *Final Report* was drafted just four months later, it was prepared to recommend that the dominion government assume complete jurisdiction over both the administration and financing of relief. When Sutherland informed King that the NEC was prepared to recommend the unthinkable, King spared no hyperbole. To him, it was an "unfriendly and cruel" act of backstabbing, "more disturbing than anything I have seen in public life" (at least in peace time), "the greatest embarrassment I have had in public life," and, what was perhaps worst of all, a potential cause of electoral defeat.[30] At issue for King was not just the hoary matter of dominion-provincial relations, but the suggestion that the dominion should assume greater expenditures when he was anxious to balance the budget in time for the next election. As he had feared several months earlier, established in order to save money, the NEC had suddenly become "a spending body."[31]

King quickly identified the villain in the piece: "This is really a scheme of Mackintosh's of Queen's, who may be a good professor of economics, but knows nothing about politics."[32] Mackintosh, according to this view, had persuaded Purvis to adopt the recommendation and then, together with Tom Moore, had formed a "united front" that cowed the other commissioners, save Sutherland, into acquiescence. (When Neil McLean wavered, insisting that he needed more time to consider the matter, Purvis issued a firm rebuke: "all Commissioners were assured a full month in which to study the original draft and to make up their minds on their individual views. It would seem to me that after a continuous eighteen months of the general relief and employment problem involved, this amply provided for mature consideration."[33])

But as King investigated the matter further, he learned of a wider "Queen's conspiracy," beginning with his "amazement" to learn that Rogers supported the NEC's position.[34] The cause of Rogers's corruption was also clear: "I am inclined to believe that Rogers himself has been working too completely with Mackintosh and seeking to form his own view too strongly in the past, to be able to really eradicate himself from the position to which the Commission and he have been brought."[35] W.C. Clark was next to be implicated. Ian Mackenzie reported to King that "Purvis and Mackintosh also stated that the Finance Department had approved the financial proposals of the original report." Mackenzie dismissed this claim, asserting, "I am certain Mr. Dunning never heard of this." However, King realized that it was likely the deputy minister, and not the minister, who was being consulted.[36] The final blow came when O.D. Skelton also expressed his approval of the NEC's initiative. King then experienced a minor epiphany:

> This ... caused me to see the whole picture in one minute which was that these men, all of whom are Queen's University, Department of Economics, have come together, and have been working jointly to seek to bring about a change in constitutional relations which will lead to a centralization of powers and away from the present order of things.
>
> The Rowell Commission will be doing the same thing; with Skelton's son as Secretary, and with Clark, will be working toward the same end. I told Council, quite frankly, this was my sizing up of the whole situation, and that these University men who had this inside opportunity, thought they had more in the way of wisdom than the rest of us put together. I said I thought our hand had been forced by Purvis' behaviour, and though Rogers sought to defend him, to an extent, by saying that he, himself, had been responsible in part for the Commission taking up unemployment insurance. The impression, I think, created on the Cabinet was that Rogers had played with the Queen's people rather than the Government in this whole matter. Doubtless, from the best of intentions and the belief that the Department of Economics, at Queen's, knows more about these matters than any corresponding group in Canada.[37]

The commissioners had every reason to anticipate King's reaction. In February 1937, when Purvis had first raised the issue of reform to the Unemployment Relief Act to allow for grant-in-aid of up to three years' duration, Sutherland suggested that the government would be "shocked and terrified" by such a proposal. She added that "I have gathered that in some ways we are not in too high repute with some of the Members of the Government," and that the usefulness of the commission would be minimized "by our proposing measures we have reason to believe are not in accord with Government policy."[38] Having complied with the narrow terms and conditions of its mandate for eighteen months, the NEC waited until its *Final Report* to challenge the direction of the dominion government's policy.

Several factors might account for this sudden change in direction between the *Interim* and *Final* reports. It would be pleasing to think that the main factor was the force of argument. The call for a unified system of unemployment insurance, unemployment relief, and the Employment Service under dominion jurisdiction as the most effective vehicle for addressing the hardships that individuals faced was compelling. There were important differences in unemployment insurance and relief – the former was a contributory plan based on an insurance principle that would, with limited government funding, be actuarially sound. On the other hand, relief, though limited to those who had previously been in the labour market, was largely for those who were not covered by insurance or whose benefits had been exhausted. Nonetheless, a common administration, including the Employment Service, promised significant economies when compared to the "patchwork" system of provincial relief programs. Moreover, there were "decisive advantages in a nation-wide system, including the pooling of risk across a larger population, the capacity to respond more effectively to regional shifts in employment, and addressing the unique issues faced by transient workers."[39]

The veracity of the argument notwithstanding, there was also much at stake for Purvis personally. He may not have been responsible for the grand expectations that accompanied his appointment, but he certainly did very little to dispel them. His reputation as a man of action – as "Job Maker Purvis" – no doubt compounded his sense of impatience with the government's failure to act on many of the recommendations. Part of the motivation for issuing an *Interim Report* had been to draw public attention to the NEC's activities and the number of recommendations that were awaiting government approval. The HIP gained cabinet approval, with the government committed to guarantee loans up to a maximum of $50 million, and the announcement of its implementation in October 1937 was greeted with much fanfare in the press. The program proved to be popular because of its simplicity and the extensive publicity campaign that accompanied it. As a testament to Purvis's energy and business savoir faire, the program's administration and publicity was entirely funded by private money solicited from the construction and financial firms who were expected to benefit most directly from its implementation. In its first twelve months, 30,772 loans were made under the program, and Purvis estimated that it had supported $60 million to $75 million in cash expenditures and work for 50,000 men at virtually no cost to the government.[40]

But the other parts of the housing initiative never reached fruition. To encourage greater new-home construction under the Dominion Housing Act, the department of finance met with lending institutions and offered to assume a greater proportion of the losses on smaller loans, in order to encourage greater lending outside larger urban areas. Clark's "personal, candid" response was that most of the suggestions for facilitating mortgage lending in rural and remote communities had already been tried and proved futile, but that he was still "willing to keep on cultivating stony ground."[41] Purvis and Mackintosh then met with a cabinet subcommittee and, in cooperation with the department of finance, drafted legislation that was forwarded to Rogers on 25 March 1937. But no action was taken by cabinet. The low-rental housing plan suffered a similar fate. The NEC entered into an initial experiment in Windsor, where Mackintosh and Clark worked closely with a local organizing committee.[42] The NEC's recommendation was forwarded to Rogers on 10 February 1937, but, in the face of cabinet inaction, its *Final Report* reiterated the need to act "while conditions are favourable" rather than to delay and risk competing for labour and capital inputs when the economic recovery was further advanced.[43] When the National Housing Act (1938) was finally passed, Part II, dealing with low-income housing, did not offer any government subsidies. The program eventually fell victim to wartime restrictions on access to building materials and was cancelled in March 1940 without projects in Winnipeg, Montreal, and Halifax reaching fruition.[44]

With a host of other recommendations awaiting cabinet approval, the NEC was in danger of passing into history with little to its credit other than having been a vehicle for reducing relief grants to the provinces and the HIP's modest contribution to job creation. Public support for the NEC was clearly waning. The *Windsor Daily Star* referred to the housing initiative as a mere a "stop-gap" measure with little else to support it, while the *Financial Post*, despite its earlier boosterism, was forced to acknowledge that the HIP had "not proved an Aladdin's lamp in solving the unemployment problem." Purvis was not prepared to go without a fight. Rumours of discontent on the NEC and of Purvis's imminent resignation mysteriously appeared in newspapers in July 1937, with the *Montreal Standard* described him as "crusading vigorously, reckless of the dismay that he is causing in ministerial circles ... he is the bear whom the Mackenzie King cabinet is holding by the tail."[45]

A third and more important factor in the NEC's turnabout was that the political scene would play out in the context of a sudden and unexpected downturn in the Canadian economy. Until the summer of 1937, it was plausible to argue, as Mackintosh had, that a recovery was under way and that no extraordinary government measures should be undertaken that might interfere with this "natural" path back to full employment. Since the 1933 trough in the Depression, economic conditions had undergone steady, if rather painfully slow, improvement. However, a sharp downturn in the United States spilled over into Canada by the fall of 1937. The fragile recovery was quickly halted, and prospects for a bad crop year heightened the sense of gloom. This undermined the fundamental assumption of the NEC concerning the international forces driving the recovery and the justification for the absence of more radical job-creation initiatives. Having made its best effort to affect some useful policy measures within an extremely restricted mandate, the NEC saw the onset of a renewed economic downturn threatening to destroy what little progress had been achieved.

Conspiracy or not, King faced a major political problem. The government could hardly denounce the recommendations of its own commission, but, at the same time, he was adamant that the dominion government not assume additional financial commitments. When King learned of the intentions of the NEC on 20 December 1937, he immediately called Rogers and directed his minister to seek a change to the draft report. Rogers refused, but the confrontation was defused when Purvis and Mackintosh, at Rogers's request, consulted with Justice Newton Wesley Rowell of the newly appointed Royal Commission on Dominion-Provincial Relations. Purvis agreed to revise the NEC's report to limit its recommendation for dominion responsibility over unemployment relief to administration only, and to refer the financial question to the royal commission for consideration.[46] Then, over Mackintosh's complaints of "political pressure," the commissioners, with the exception of Sutherland, revised the *Final Report* by replacing two offending paragraphs. An evening meeting passed the amended report, with Sutherland recording her dissenting opinion.

Figure 7.1 Index of employment in Canada, 1929–1939

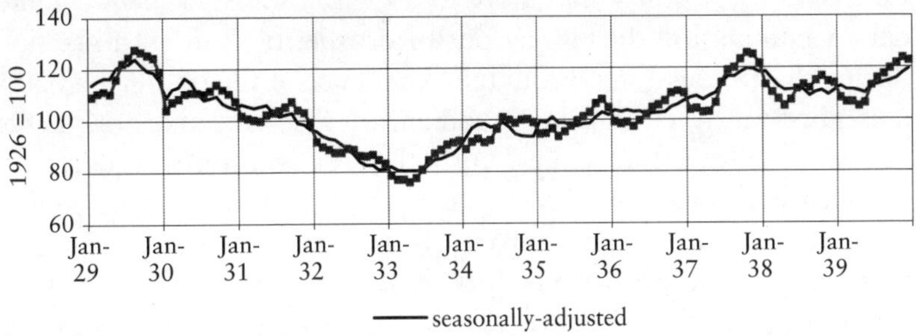

Source: Index Numbers of Employment as Reported by Employers … at the First of Each Month, January1926=100. *Canada Year Book*, 1928–1940 (Ottawa, 1929–1941).

THE NEC AS KEYNESIAN?

To the extent that unemployment insurance under dominion jurisdiction was to become a major pillar in Canada's post-WWII social-security legislation, the NEC's *Final Report*, as Struthers maintains, "marked a watershed in the Canadian welfare state."[47] This being the case, it contributed to the development of "Keynesian politics" by envisioning a larger role for the state in the management of the economic lives of Canadians.

It is also possible to argue, as Neatby does, that the NEC's *Final Report* "marks a significant advance in the analysis in Canada of the role of government fiscal policy."[48] In Section II, drafted by Mackintosh, the NEC addressed for the first time the issue of long-range planning and explicitly endorsed the principle of counter-cyclical fiscal policy. "The Commission holds that this country, the fortunes of which are so inextricably bound up with those of the great industrial countries of the world, must be prepared to meet business fluctuations, whether large or small, which may arise from circumstances over which it has no control."[49] To its credit, it recommended that haphazard and hastily designed make-work projects be replaced with public-expenditure programs that would provide the infrastructure for private development in tourism, forestry, mining, and other economic pursuits.

But the application of this principle to the circumstances facing Canada during the Great Depression stopped well short of advocating deficit-financed government expenditures. The NEC's criticisms of Canadian fiscal policy had more to do with excessive spending and debt accumulation during periods of prosperity than with inaction during the Depression: "From the experience of the past eight years, it is abundantly clear that Canadian governments did not, in the period of buoyant revenues, curb their expenditures and reduce sufficiently their debts."[50] Moreover, as Leonard Marsh pointed out, the *Final Report*, though apparently Keynesian in perspective "on first reading," stopped well short of arguing for any form of state economic planning. Recovery was only to be achieved through private, not public, investment:

> The Commission, unlike Mr. Keynes, appears to hold the view that only private and not public enterprise will have the desired effects. Even the low-rent housing programme proposed does not call for a large out-and-out expenditure by the Government, and the Home Improvement Plan much less so. Their purpose is to entice private capital into this field where it has been 'particularly timid.' Government expenditures are approved specifically only on tourist development, roads to mining areas, forestry preservation, clearance for land settlement, etc. – notably projects which will not compete with private enterprise ... it is still necessary to explain the readiness with which it is taken for granted that government taxes have "restrictive and harmful effects" on "private expenditures in productive industry" (p.36), without reference to the various forms and extent, the ways in which they are spent, and their ultimate incidence.[51]

Mackintosh was amply conversant with Keynes's *General Theory*. In a brief review of the book for the *Queen's Quarterly* he provided a terse summary that identified the three fundamental equations in a Keynesian model – the determination of consumption, investment and the interest rate – but stops short of either criticizing or endorsing the main argument. "Mr. Keynes' new book will not be unscathed by criticism," he concluded, "but it will affect profoundly the trend of economic thought."[52] (Perhaps of significance is the fact that he devoted relatively more space to a review of the League for Social Reconstruction's *Social Planning in Canada*, which appeared in the same issue.) His reluctance to urge more active government intervention in the Depression reflected his adherence to the orthodox view that "maladjustment in prices and costs" lay at the heart of the economic problem, and that increased government spending was only appropriate "when essential readjustments have been completed." It was more appropriate for both governments and business to avoid "the dislocation of labour" by "restraining excessive and misdirected investment and in facilitating Canadian readjustment to changed world conditions of prices and costs."[53]

Alvin Hansen, one of the leading American advocates of Keynesian policy, reviewed the NEC's *Final Report* for the Province of Manitoba and argued that it failed to reflect the shift in thinking on the timing of government expenditures over the business cycle. Where the NEC adhered to the role of "priming the pump" during the latter stages of a slump, when private investment might be expected to respond because costs had readjusted and older capital stock had been liquidated, the more important role of public expenditure was to offset the slump in private spending at the early stages. "Compensation, not pump priming, is then the purpose."[54] There is no escaping the fact, as Struthers emphasizes, that the hallmark of the NEC was its rejection of public works and activist fiscal policy in general.

Before the NEC can be dismissed as highly orthodox in its economic thinking, however, its rejection of public works as a short-run vehicle for alleviating unemployment needs to be placed in the appropriate context. The underlying premise that informed the NEC's recommendations – at least until the fall of 1937 – was that economic recovery was already under way, and that it was important to avoid government actions that might interfere with renewed private investment. Moreover, in arguing against public works, to many at the time the sine qua non of Keynesianism, Mackintosh cited a most unlikely authority: Keynes. In a series of articles that appeared in the London *Times* in January 1937, Keynes warned that the British re-armament program endangered economic recovery if it was not accompanied by a contraction in other government expenditures.

> We are approaching, or have reached, the point where there is not much advantage in applying a further general stimulus at the centre. So long as surplus resources were widely diffused between industries and localities it was no great matter at what point in the economic structure the impulse of an increased demand was applied. But the evidence grows that – for several reasons into which there is no space to enter here – the economic structure is

> unfortunately rigid, and that (for example) building activity in the home counties is less effective than one might have hoped in decreasing unemployment in the distressed areas. It follows that the latter stages of the recovery require a different technique. To remedy the condition of the distressed areas, ad hoc measures are necessary ... We are in more need today of a rightly distributed demand than of a greater aggregate demand; and the Treasury would be entitled to economise elsewhere to compensate for the cost of special assistance to the distressed areas. If our responsibility in this direction could be thus disposed of we could concentrate with a clear mind on our central problem of how to maintain a fairly steady level of sustained prosperity.[55]

That Keynes would call for a reduction in public spending at a time when the unemployment rate in Britain was over 10 per cent was the source of much debate at the time, and this debate has continued in the academic literature that seeks to interpret his writings. However, Keynes's argument clearly resonated with Mackintosh, who took to the pages of the *Canadian Banker* to endorse this perspective: "Mr. Keynes, among others, pointed out that when the rearmament boom was added to the building boom there was a grave danger that without skilled management a serious crisis might develop."[56] Moreover, various aspects of Keynes's argument are reflected through Mackintosh's memorandum "On Public Works," written less than a month after Keynes's articles appeared in the *Times*: that the Canadian economy was already on the road to recovery; that specific sectoral programs might be warranted, but a general stimulus to aggregate demand would merely result in an unwarranted increase in public debt; and that the priority at the time was to overcome the rigidities in the labour market to ensure the new employment opportunities, when they occurred, could be filled. But there is no doubt that Mackintosh was opportunistic in extending Keynes's argument to Canada. The recovery was much further advanced in Britain, and there was no comparing the magnitude of British spending on armaments to the small economic stimulus that was expected in Canada. The best that the NEC could point to was an increase in railway orders of $30 million and $75 million in spending under the HIP.

A more compelling explanation for the NEC's willingness to justify rather than challenge the narrow terms of its mandate on

public spending is offered by Struthers. He points out that the preoccupation with avoiding greater government debt drew more inspiration from the staple thesis than from Keynes. The argument that Mackintosh had stressed in his treatment of the *Economic Problems of the Prairie Provinces* concerned the dangers inherent in staple industries with highly variable income and fixed overhead costs. The need to avoid assuming additional government debt at a time when Canada's traditional export industries faced depressed international commodity markets trumped any argument for public works as a form of economic stimulus. What was crucial was "To avoid excess borrowing and the piling up of fixed charges."[57] Thus, when Keynes met the staple thesis for the first time, it was the staple thesis that won the day.

THE ART OF POLICY MAKING

Mackintosh's service on the NEC would provide him with invaluable experience for his future career as a public servant. Unlike his earlier activities with the department of labour, the Combines Investigation Act, and the Advisory Board on Tariff and Taxation, in which he gave a relatively detached assessment of a particular economic question, the NEC involved him much more directly in the "art" of policy making, or the political process of seeking to persuade politicians of the appropriate course to pursue. Handed a mandate that left little room for creative initiative, Rogers, Purvis, and Mackintosh sought to produce some substantive economic reforms out of a process designed largely to legitimatize the government's unwillingness to undertake any major economic initiatives. This inevitably led to political conflict that gave Mackintosh his first taste in the rough-and-tumble of hard-nosed politics, with no less formidable an adversary than Mackenzie King. While it is neither possible nor appropriate to declare a clear winner in the process, Canadian economic policy was nudged towards a more enlightened path, taking a small, hesitant step closer to adopting a Keynesian economic framework.

In 1946, Mackintosh looked back on his association with Purvis on the NEC as his most formative policy experience in terms of his own personal development.[58] The two men developed a deep respect for each other. Mackintosh spoke of Purvis's "magnificent and eager spirit," while Purvis acknowledged that the work of the NEC was "inconceivable" without Mackintosh: "The Commission's effort

would have been quite unthinkable without your great part in it. I think you already know how much I have appreciated that fact. You were an everlasting source of strength in what, after all, was a fairly difficult atmosphere." He added that "I look forward to seeing you soon so that we can talk over our battles and inspect our scars!"[59] The two men would indeed meet again. During World War II, while Mackintosh was working with the department of finance, Purvis resumed his role as an "industrial statesman" as head of the British Supply Council, where he was responsible for the procurement of war supplies in the United States (and was made a member of the Privy Council for his efforts). By chance they would meet on the train on 11 August 1941, the night before Purvis left for the United Kingdom "on his last and, as it proved, quite unnecessary trip" – the airplane crashed and Purvis was killed.[60]

But in 1938, there was little opportunity to reflect on the outcome of the NEC's deliberations. Mackintosh had already committed himself to work with the Rowell–Sirois Royal Commission and, instead of returning to Queen's to devote his full attention to academic work, he figuratively (and literally) moved up the street in Ottawa, from the NEC offices in the Jackson Building on the corner of Slater Avenue and Bank Street to the offices of the Royal Commission on Dominion-Provincial Relations at Bank Street and Wellington Avenue.

8

The Royal Commission on Dominion-Provincial Relations: Ottawa, 1938–1939

I urge that ... [*The Economic Background of Dominion-Provincial Relations*] be read not only with the veneration due a classic – which it is – but also with a certain malice aforethought. No reprinting was necessary to ensure either the book or its author a prominent place in the history of Canadian economic thought. Therefore read it with a subversive intent. Dr. Mackintosh's reputation is not at stake; yours is.

J.H. Dales, 1964[1]

Mackintosh did not have to wait long for a second opportunity to address the issue of unemployment relief and the broader matter of federal-provincial finances in Canada. While the National Employment Commission was completing its *Final Report*, he was solicited to join the research staff of the newly-struck Royal Commission on Dominion-Provincial Relations. Despite being embroiled in the political machinations surrounding the NEC at the time, and exhausted by from regular treks between Ottawa and Kingston, Mackintosh accepted the appointment and, in doing so, would contribute to the most comprehensive review of Canadian public finance since Confederation.

The royal commission was established because it was amply clear to all concerned that a new fiscal arrangement was required between the dominion and provincial governments. The division of responsibilities and taxation powers outlined in the British North America Act was no longer appropriate to the changed economic conditions, a point driven home by the effective bankruptcy of the western provinces during the Great Depression. (In 1937, spending on poor relief alone in Saskatchewan was 50 per cent greater than the province's revenue.) There was also awareness that the country had reached a pivotal point in its economic history. Looking back, it had passed through a period in which the prairie wheat economy had lent a unity to the country's economic and political development. However promising this was for claims to economic nationhood, the experience of the Great Depression demonstrated how vulnerable the Canadian economy remained. The institutional arrangement that had contributed to economic growth in the early part of the decade was no longer suitable: the old "National Policy" was now outmoded and the commission self-consciously set out on the task of designing a new national policy, at least insofar as public finance was concerned, for the "post-wheat" era.

History would scuttle such an ambition. The onset of World War II not only placed government priorities elsewhere, but precipitated further economic changes that were unimaginable a few years earlier and thus circumscribed the commission's contribution to a postwar vision of the Canadian economy. In redefining the role of the state in directing economic activity, some long-overdue reforms that were advocated – a national unemployment-insurance program and a dominion compulsory contributory pension plan did eventually form part of the recommendations – but when the Dominion-Provincial Conference convened in 1941 to consider the commission's broader objective of rearranging government financial relations, it ended in spectacular failure. The first day of the conference left O.D. Skelton feeling "rather ashamed of my country" with "easily understood and blatant demagogic 'arguments'" triumphing over economic logic.[2] While the second day would restore some of his faith, no substantive agreement was reached, and it would not be until 1947 that peacetime dominion-provincial tax-sharing agreements would be forged.

The historical analysis of the commission, however, did not lose its validity, and remains its enduring legacy. Some of the research output was disappointing, but it is difficult to dispute Mackintosh's assertion that, taken together, "the analysis in the *Report* and in its many appendices will stand for many years as perhaps the most substantial contribution to applied social science which has been made in this country."[3] Of particular note in this regard was his own report on the *Economic Background of Dominion-Provincial Relations in*

Canada, which remains the best single history of the Canadian economy in the period between Confederation and the Great Depression, and the definitive statement of the staple thesis of economic development applied to Canada's post-Confederation history.

THE COMMISSIONERS AND THE RESEARCH STAFF

The Royal Commission on Dominion-Provincial Relations, announced in August 1937, was charged with examining "the economic and financial basis of Confederation and of the distribution of legislative powers in the light of the economic and social developments of the last seventy years." In particular, it was expected to offer recommendations for resolving the fiscal impasse that hamstrung dominion-provincial relations because of the growing imbalance between the provinces' responsibilities and their financing capacity to meet them. Newton Wesley Rowell (chief justice of Ontario) was appointed to head the commission, with Thibaudeau Rinfret (justice of the Supreme Court), John Dafoe (*Winnipeg Free Press*), R.A. MacKay (Dalhousie University political scientist), and H.F. Angus (UBC economist) completing the roster of commissioners.

The commission was soon fraught with problems. Justice Rinfret, ostensibly representing Quebec, resigned due to illness in November 1937 and was replaced by Joseph Sirois, a law professor at Laval. A few months later, when Justice Rowell suffered a stroke (thus depriving the commission of its sole Ontario appointee) and with MacKay in the hospital with appendicitis, O.D. Skelton grew anxious over the capacity of the commission to fulfil its mandate. He expressed his concern to King on 1 June 1938: "It is not proving as strong and coherent a body as was hoped for, and without the Chief Justice it will lack direction except from Mr. Dafoe, who does not appear to have as much constructive energy as he used to have. If a constructive and helpful report is to be prepared within any reasonable time, it would seem essential that some additional appointment to the Commission, even if of a temporary character, should be made." The name he put forward was a familiar one: "[W.C.] Clark tells me this morning that he is suggesting to Mr. Dunning the appointment of Dr. Mackintosh in such a capacity. He is familiar with the evidence and hearings through his work in charge of the main piece of economic research for the Commission, and his appointment would thus give continuity. He is level-headed, takes a sane Dominion point of view, and would give leadership and coherence to the organization. Exception might be taken to the appointment of a further professorial member, but I at least have not been able to think of any judge, lawyer or businessman who would meet the exigencies of the case."[4]

Recommending Mackintosh as a commissioner, following so shortly after the drama of the NEC, was surely an audacious act. Nor did the possibility of giving renewed life to the Queen's conspiracy go unnoticed by King. As he recorded in his diary, "I objected to McIntosh [sic] (of Queen's) being added to the staff, and suggested the present commission working together submitting general views through Clark and Skelton via Skelton's son (the Secretary) so that the Govt. can direct where obviously wise to do so. I do not favour adding another man to the Commission." He reported that "Skelton seemed to take kindly to my suggestion."[5] Though King made no reference to the NEC, O.D. Skelton, in his own diary, left no doubt that King was not in a forgiving mood: "Sandy [Skelton] and Clark think it is necessary to get an economist, push Mackintosh but PM turns thumbs down on account of his stubborn attitude on Purvis Employment Committee."[6] A month and a half later, Skelton would repeat his appeal for a temporary replacement, but to no avail. The commission soldiered on in the absence of Justice Rowell, with Sirois succeeding as chair.

The commission faced other problems. After it began public hearings in January 1938, Alberta and Quebec declined to participate on the grounds that a dominion-appointed royal commission had no authority to investigate independently questions of provincial finance. Ontario would later withdraw from the proceedings, arguing that there had been a breach of faith when Ottawa altered aspects of the Income War Tax Act prior to the commission's *Report*. None of the three provinces presented a formal brief, although both Alberta and Ontario did make presentations at the hearings.[7]

The disarray among the commissioners and its public hearings meant that the research staff assumed a more significant role in determining the outcome of the proceedings. To this end, an extraordinary group both – in terms of quantity and quality – was assembled, drawn primarily from Canadian universities. Over sixty individuals assisted in some aspect of the research work, the largest such group assembled to date by a royal commission. Economists were well represented among those who contributed to published background studies: Mackintosh and Frank Knox (Queen's); D.C. MacGregor (Toronto); W.J. Waines and Pete McQueen (Manitoba); Stewart Bates (Dalhousie); George Britnell (Saskatchewan); J.J. Deutsch (from the Bank of Canada); and S.A. Saunders (who had completed his PhD under Innis at Toronto and persevered as an independent scholar).[8] Others drawn from Canadian universities were: Donald Creighton (history, Toronto); Albert Edward Grauer (sociology, Toronto); Alex Corry (political science, Queen's); Esdras Minville (social scientist, Montreal's l'École des hautes études commerciales); and Brooke Claxton (lawyer and McGill professor). Rounding out the roster were: J.B. Rutherford of the Dominion Bureau of Statistics: H.C. Goldenberg, economist, lawyer, and government consultant; Wilfrid Eggleston, an Ottawa journalist (and fellow student of Sandy Skelton during their days at Queen's); Léon Gouin (Montreal lawyer, whose father and grandfather had both been premier of Quebec); and C.T. Kraft (independent scholar). The commission also received the special assistance of several civil servants. Notably, there was only one woman among the sixty individuals providing research support: Margaret Mackintosh.[9]

The research was directed by the commission's secretary. Alexander Douglas (Sandy) Skelton obtained his BA from Queen's, attended Oxford University as a Rhodes Scholar, and then became the first director of research at the Bank of Canada. Since his early undergraduate days, Sandy Skelton had worked hard and played even harder. "He had had a somewhat tempestuous career as a Queen's student and was an adventurous, even reckless, spirit, constantly in all sorts of pranks and scrapes. He was a boxer and football player, immensely strong and agile. He was fearless and loved a fight, the rougher the better."[10] Jean Easton Mackintosh, his second cousin and good friend from their undergraduate days at Queen's, could attest to his reckless nature. She recalled his appearance through the window of her dormitory room one night to steal her away for a midnight canoe trip on Lake Ontario. Needless to say, his father was constantly given cause to worry about his son's "impulses and desire to do things differently from other people."[11]

Folklore about Sandy Skelton abounds: he rescued an orphaned bear cub and reared it in his home until the neighbours complained, and he kept pregnant mares for female hormones.[12] His proclivity for late-night partying presented certain challenges for his work. As David McQueen recounts: "A difficulty for Skelton was that often, the next morning, he had to consult closely with Prime Minister Mackenzie King, whose puritanical views were well known. To mask the residue of the night before, Skelton resorted to Sen-Sen breath fresheners, until one day the PM looked up from the spreadsheet they had been examining and said, 'See here, Skelton – I don't mind if you drink, but will you please stop sucking those dreadful lozenges!'"[13] His penchant for the provocative extended to his activities for the commission. After Tim Buck, head of the Communist Party of Canada, completed his appearance at the Ottawa hearings, Skelton invited him for lunch at Ottawa's exclusive Rideau Club. Informed of his son's lunch date, O.D. Skelton could only wonder who would be fired first, "S[andy] ... from Rideau Club or Buck from Communist Party."[14] But despite these eccentricities, Alex Corry observes that "Sandy was as close to a Renaissance figure as our age provides. He was versatile, imaginative, always testing his powers in extravagant ways. Acknowledging no masters, he was equally irreverent to the pretentious and the great, yet generous to his friends, deeply sympathetic to the unfortunate and to underdogs."[15]

Sandy Skelton's larger-than-life persona notwithstanding, it is easy to grasp how his background led to a life in academia and government. Not so with John J. Deutsch, the assistant director of research. Born in a small, German-speaking farm community in Quinton, Saskatchewan, Deutsch was the eldest in a family of seventeen (some reports say nineteen) children, making quite plausible the allegation that he "had been away from home so long that he couldn't remember the names of his younger brothers and sisters."[16] He completed his high-school degree at Campion College, a Jesuit institution in Regina, while teaching mathematics and physics there. In 1932 and 1933, he registered as an extramural student at Queen's, but his third-class standing in both economics and commerce courses suggests that he was not a ringing success. In 1933, he moved to Kingston, taking courses at Queen's while teaching middle and high school at Regiopolis College in order to pay for his university expenses. Described as a "very serious student, and high-minded gentleman,"[17] he graduated from Queen's in 1935 with a commerce degree, and the dramatic improvement in his academic performance earned him a position in the Bank of Canada's research division.[18] His dedication to work might be inferred from one item saved among in his papers. Scribbled on the back of a program for a production of

Verdi's *Il Trovatore* at Massey Hall in 1935 are references to papers by Hayek, Leontieff, and other economists; one hopes that these notes were added after, rather than during, the performance.[19]

Pete McQueen was another notable recruit, persuaded to accept the appointment in part at Mackintosh's insistence that the research staff needed greater western representation.[20] Corry describes McQueen as "a brilliant economist and famous raconteur ... [a] fabricator and retailer of stories. His tastes were broad, irreverent, blasphemous, salacious. He gathered them and spread them around. The only test of fit was that they had to be really funny. And they were."[21] McQueen and Sandy Skelton proved a potent combination. Mackintosh remarked once that he knew McQueen had arrived in Ottawa because Skelton had failed to show up for work the next day.[22] On another occasion, Skelton was reported to be "in a big row with Dr. McKinnon of the Chateau [Laurier], from whom he rescued Pete McQueen in hospital after a stand up row and many ups and downs ... McKinnon threatened a libel suit for damages to his professional reputation."[23]

Mackintosh agreed to join the research staff after the completion of the NEC's *Final Report*. His task was to help identify the background reports required, to supervise those dealing with regional aspects of economic development, and to produce a larger study of the economic conditions since Confederation. His only stipulations were that he would not begin working until the conclusion of the NEC and that he could work initially from Kingston by relying on Deutsch as a liaison with the staff assembled in Ottawa. Otherwise, he joined the staff at the regular remuneration of $25 per day.

Corry emphasizes the solidarity within the group. "Working in close physical contact, we often ate meals together and had many evening sessions together, enjoying one another's company. The problem each of us was working at involved, in most instances, breaking new ground. We exchanged thoughts and discoveries, and were led to face up to the central issues before the Commission about which we argued. I became friends with a number of men who were already notable authorities, or were moving surely towards that status."[24] This is not to suggest that there was no discord, for Sandy Skelton complained to his father about the problems of dealing with "academic prima donnas."[25] Nor is there any mistaking the fact that this was a boys' club and that a locker-room mentality prevailed at times, with debate filled with "obsessive sexuality" and "artistry in profanity." Corry detected a distinctive prairie flavour to the ribald verbiage. "George Britnell, a former student of McQueen's at the University of Saskatchewan and able economist, admired McQueen greatly and modelled himself on him in every respect. They brought with them habits established in their long association. So when they discussed economics in a group, they always found room for argument and were soon reviling one another as 'ignorant bastards,' 'stupid buggers' and more generally, in the picturesque idiom of the Saskatchewan vernacular." The more staid members of the group "found McQueen and Britnell startling variations in the species, almost like creatures from another world"; as Creighton observed, "If you are in a group and these western chaps are there, it is remarkable how quickly someone is accused of sexual irregularity."[26]

The dedication to public service among men that could certainly have made more money in private industry had its unique cultural expression: conspicuous displays of consumption were replaced by conspicuous displays of counter-culture and the rejection of acquisitiveness. What counted was not who was the best-dressed, but who wore the shabbiest clothes, and not who had the most expensive car, but who could keep the one in the greatest state of disrepair on the road. Again, it was Sandy Skelton who epitomized this culture. "He drove an old rattletrap of a car with unreliable brakes, and within eighteen months he had had half a dozen accidents." The celebration of substance over style was thus elevated to its own standard, and this spirit was also later in evidence at the Five Lakes Fishing Club, the Gatineau Hills retreat where senior civil servants gathered in an atmosphere free of the strictures of the Ottawa civil service.

One name noticeably absent from the research staff was Harold Innis. Sandy Skeleton had, in fact, first appealed to Innis to oversee the historical work – "We are counting on you greatly" – but Innis declined, and it was only then that Mackintosh could be "coerced into serving in this capacity.[27] Innis's presence, however, was not entirely lacking, as he agreed to act as an "anonymous critic" in reviewing the background studies: "If I can be of any use of course I have no objection to lending a hand. It would probably be simpler from all points of view to hand them on as anonymous."[28] In this role, he also served as a "circulating library" by passing material on for comments to his Toronto colleagues, Vincent Bladen, Alexander Brady, R. MacGregor Dawson, and Wynne Plumptre. But on his own account, Innis served up a staccato supply of criticism of the background studies. Goldenberg's *Municipal Finance in Canada* was "a very unsatisfactory study on a very important subject." As for Kraft and Eggleston: "This volume is too largely descriptive with the result that it appears to be loosely written and without adequate research or interpretation ... A weak volume!" Saunders, his former graduate student, was not spared: "This is a very uneven volume – some excellent analysis and some resort to statistics of limited value." His assertion that the volume lacked perspective was expressed in characteristically Innisian style: "too much about potato and not enough about sulphite pulp." Corry's treatment of divided jurisdictions was deemed "suggestively stimulating but not conclusive. It has the advantage of 'horse sense' but it is limited because of its narrow range." Knox's contribution was interesting, but failed to "give sufficient attention to the importance of the United States price polices and their effects on Canada," and Waines's study was pessimistic when "every possible optimistic element" was warranted.[29]

In light of these criticisms, Sandy Skelton had reason to be concerned. "I am quite disturbed by your letter," he confessed to Innis. "I know a lot of our studies are third rate, lamentably lacking in analysis and failing completely to grasp the main issues or, at any rate, to see them in a comprehensive way. Naturally I feel a good deal of responsibility for this myself. I am at the moment fighting a rearguard action against publication of more than four or five of them, and hope to make up for some of the deficiencies in the main body of the report."[30] Innis replied with words of reassurance: "Do not worry about my criticisms. As far as you are concerned the planning of studies strikes at the heart of the federal problem – you cannot escape the regional factor in choosing individuals and I do not see how you could have done better. I think your line is thoroughly sound – publish the best and make the report protection against criticism which would be levelled at you if you had published the weakest as well."[31] At the same time, however, Innis felt unconstrained in writing the most damning critique of the commission's *Final Report*.

THE MYTH OF CANADA'S RISE TO NATIONHOOD

If one research study was singled out for praise, it was Mackintosh's *The Economic Background of Dominion-Provincial Relations*. Written over a very short period – the first draft was completed in August

1938 and the final text revised in spring 1939 – it drew upon his own published work, the contributions of his research assistants, and other background studies.[32] Oddly, Mackintosh confessed to Jacob Viner that the opportunity to write a history of Canadian economic development "was not a task for which I had a great zest for I was already tired out when I undertook it … I wish I had more leisure and greater energy to put on this work. It was originally supposed to be Innis' job but he refused to put his head in the noose. I feel fairly sure of my analysis, but the form and point of report leaves me quite unsatisfied."[33] Despite these reservations, he produced the classic statement of the staple thesis applied to Canada's history since Confederation.

He begins by restating the staple thesis: the "fundamental considerations" of Canadian economic history were the capacity to borrow foreign capital and technology in order to support the export of raw materials to more advanced economies. Since most of the borrowing was assumed by governments, the economy faced the challenge of meeting its external debt payments from highly volatile export earnings. He thus reiterated the fundamental insight derived from Innis's *Fur Trade* and his own *Economic Problems of the Prairie Provinces*: "the economic difficulties in which new countries so frequently find themselves are those that occur when fluctuating incomes are coupled with the rigid expenditures occasioned by heavy debt charges."[34] He then proceeds to apply this framework to four specific periods: Confederation, the "national policy" initiatives of the latter nineteenth century, the wheat-boom era, and the Great Depression.

Confederation was the outcome of a "dramatic realignment in the world economic order," which began in the 1850s as the era of "wood, wind, and water," gave way to "steam, rail, and steel." Britain's shift to free trade left its North American colonies "cast adrift" with the loss of preferential access to traditional export markets. With an outflow of European savings to be tapped, each colony sponsored railway construction in an effort to compete with American ports for traffic from the interior and to secure markets for their fledging manufacturing industries. As Mackintosh observes, "each colony developed its own exports, planned its own transportation and settlement projects, and did its own borrowing – economically separate and isolated units with common problems of railway financing and access to US markets." Confederation offered the promise that "the whole, economically as politically, would be found to be greater than the sum of the parts because of broader financial power and greater borrowing power; hope for inter-provincial trade."[35] The latter meant overcoming the geographical barriers that divided British North America into five distinct regional economies – the Maritimes, Ontario, Quebec, the prairies, and BC – because of high transportation costs.

What followed was Canada's "national policy," based on three "basic economic decisions" designed to create an integrated national economy. Imitating US initiatives, Rupert's Land was purchased as a western frontier for agricultural settlement under dominion administration; an all-Canadian railway was built from east to west in order to overcome the imposing barrier of the Laurentian Shield; and greater tariff protection was given to support fledgling manufacturing industries in central Canada, as well as to generate revenue for government-subsidized construction projects. Prairie settlement, therefore, was to be the stimulus to growth, while transportation and tariff policies were to ensure that the associated benefits would be captured within the domestic economy. Despite the apparent coherence, these were by no means parts of a grand strategy "adopted in full consciousness of their implications," but in large measure decisions based on "political expediency." The immediate results proved disappointing. Even with favourable terms of trade for Canadian exports, rapid expansion did not occur throughout much of the remainder of the nineteenth century. Construction of the Grand Trunk Railway from central Canada failed to secure much of the carrying trade from the American Midwest; the greater promise of the American land frontier delayed settlement of the Canadian prairies, such that it was generally a period of net emigration from Canada; and the hopes of the Maritime provinces – that its ports would handle much of the Canadian export trade and that its coal would attract manufacturing – were largely unrealized.[36]

It was not until the fortuitous "conjuncture" of events after 1895 that the expectations of Canada's national policy were realized. Rising world commodity prices and a decline in ocean freight rates opened up European markets to Canadian wheat, while the pulp-and-paper industry expanded based on exports to the United States. At the same time, lower interest rates facilitated capital imports to finance investment in railways, agriculture, and manufacturing. The associated population growth fostered the expansion of a domestic market and tariff protection, aided by deflecting demand to domestic firms in the clothing, iron and steel, and lumber industries. The chief beneficiaries in this regard were Ontario and Quebec, where manufacturing, financial services, and distribution facilities pushed the population of both Montreal and Toronto to over five hundred thousand.[37] Halifax, in contrast, struggled to maintain its influence in the Maritime region. Canada's claim to "nationhood" in economic if not political terms was thus largely forged during the wheat boom: "the driving force behind the new period was wheat and the wheat-growing region. It gave an economic unity to the country not hitherto experienced and built up a degree of interdependence between its different regions which was in sharp contrast to the isolation of the separate economic regions which had united in 1867 ... The forms into which investment flowed were manifold. Expanding industries provided markets for subordinate and contributory industries, which in turn built up markets for others. As communities grew in population and wealth, large investments were made in such national and community equipment and services as railways and public utilities, roads, schools, and other institutions. Yet it is quite clear that the focus of the great expansion is to be found in the growing export trades."[38]

The soundness of this expansion was to be judged according to Canada's capacity to generate sufficient export revenue to meet the cost of servicing capital imports. "Investment is induced by prospective, not actual, profitability. It is justified or condemned after the event. Specifically (because investment was based on external borrowing) the justification in the case of Canada would have been the achievement of a surplus of 'exports' (goods and services) over 'imports' sufficient (when capital imports were no longer available) to pay the interest and dividends annually payable abroad."[39] The heavy fixed charges assumed by the dominion government could be easily met as long as expansion continued and export prices remained high. Mackintosh suggests that impending difficulties were forestalled by Word War I. "Not only did the accident of War facilitate an otherwise difficult international readjustment for Canada. The enlarged demand for Canadian products and the great rise in prices turned many an investment from a loss into a gain but for some the test was merely postponed."[40] Following the economic downturn immediately after the war, expansion continued anew in the latter half of the 1920s, as healthy export markets and credit available on easy terms fuelled an investment boom. But the harbingers of future problems were apparent: the expansion in wheat exports had slowed, pulp and paper prices were falling, and newer durable goods industries, such as automobile manufacturing, were also vulnerable to fluctuations in demand. The optimism of the period resulted in much "misdirected investment," with unwarranted expansion of productive capacity.[41]

The day of reckoning came with the collapse of export markets during the Great Depression. Since the driving force to the economy was the income earned in export industries, it led to a severe contraction in domestic investment – so much so that net investment was negative through the early years of the 1930s. The sharp reduction in export earnings made it difficult to meet the heavy fixed payments associated with foreign borrowing.[42]

Mackintosh thus constructed a powerful myth of Canada's rise to economic nationhood based on the unity created by the wheat economy. Prairie settlement served as the basis for the creation of an integrated transnational economy, but the heavy dependence on the export of staples left the Canadian economy vulnerable to severe dislocation because of the volatility of export earnings and the fixed nature of the cost of servicing foreign borrowing.

The harshest critic of the draft to the *Economic Background* was S.A. Saunders, Mackintosh's colleague on the research staff. He wrote a twenty-page commentary, expressing his frustration that some of the other studies, including his own, were not receiving due consideration.[43] The substance of his critique was that it understated the degree of integration, and common interests, of the Maritimes with other regions. In his treatment of the period leading up to Confederation, Mackintosh was faulted for not recognizing the degree of intercolonial trade, the potential importance of Maritime ports to Ontario, and the common concerns with transportation, as well as trade relations, with the Colonial Office and with the United States. Similarly, he disputed the emphasis placed on the development of the West to the neglect of the position of the Maritime provinces in the creation of a national economy. This bias was deemed important to the interpretation of the present status of the Canadian economy: "As the report now stands, considering the negative attitude taken towards the economic relations of the Provinces at the time of Confederation, it seems to me to confirm the views of those in the Maritimes who claim that Confederation was a mistake, and of those in the West who claim that they paid the piper without calling the tune."[44]

Saunders, however, expressed a minority view among those commenting on the manuscript. "This is really a very fine bit of work," wrote Duncan MacGibbon. "Without sacrificing other qualities, Professor Mackintosh has managed to give a sense of continuity and development and to make Canadian economic history interesting. In his general interpretation I differ from him in two or three respects which do not in any sense destroy the value of his monograph."[45] W.C. Keirstead offered some minor criticisms but concluded by asking Skelton to "Kindly tell Mackintosh how highly I value his contribution. *The one man for this job*. I was impressed with the way Dr. Mackintosh did keep all the factors in mind and with the objectivity and comprehension of his reasoning. He is a disciple of the great Marshall in method if not in doctrine. The language is clear and simple."[46] But the most important praise came from Innis, who declined to make substantive comments on Mackintosh's manuscript on the grounds that "It would be gilding the lily … I thought throughout how fortunate you were in getting him to do it."[47]

The argument of the *Economic Background* has also stood up remarkably well over the passage of time. In 1964, John H. Dales launched a challenge to the view of the national policy as a grand strategy for development, both in terms of the degree of coordination among its three elements of land settlement, tariffs, and railways, as well as with the impact of economic activity.[48] A generation of scholars subsequently took up this challenge. Edward J. Chambers and D.F. Gordon, in an argument that questioned the veracity of the staples thesis generally, contended that wheat exports contributed only modestly to per-capita income in Canada in the early 1900s, while others examined the impact of railway construction and the Homestead Act on the pace of western settlement.[49] On the whole, the argument has largely survived this revisionist scholarship; indeed, it is Mac Urquhart's work on constructing estimates of Canada's income national accounts prior to 1926, undertaken in the 1980s, that has lent the greatest support to Mackintosh's interpretation.[50]

THE VINER–MACKINTOSH EXCHANGE ON THE REGIONAL BURDEN OF THE TARIFF

An intriguing aspect of Mackintosh's involvement in the Rowell–Sirois Commission was a debate that he engaged in with Jacob Viner over the regional implications of Canadian tariff policy. The issue was of secondary importance to the deliberation of the commission, as both men agreed on the substantive point that income transfers between provinces were necessary. Nonetheless, it highlighted important aspects of economic analysis and the appropriate application of theory to immediate policy concerns.

The context for the exchange was the government of Manitoba's presentation to the commission. To its credit, Manitoba did much to shape the agenda of the commission by arguing that dominion government policies had placed an unequal share of the cost of national development on the Prairie provinces. In making its case, it enlisted the assistance of two of North America's leading economists, Viner and Alvin Hansen, to oversee the research in support of the province's position.[51]

Viner's stature within the discipline bears emphasis. Born in Montreal in 1892, he obtained his BA from McGill in 1914 (undoubtedly Stephen Leacock's greatest, if only, contribution to economics) and his PhD under the supervision of Taussig at Harvard in 1922. Although he was in the same graduating class as Mackintosh, they did not overlap at Harvard, since Viner had been teaching at the University of Chicago since 1916, where he quickly became "the brightest star in the galaxy" of young and talented economists. His first paper on "Some Problems in the Logical Method in Political Economy" (1917) was indicative of his future contributions in economic theory and the history of economic thought, while publication of his doctoral thesis on *Canada's Balance of International Indebtedness* (1924) and other books established his reputation as the discipline's foremost international trade theorist. Moreover, his review of Keynes's *General Theory* in 1937 offered an incisive criticism, despite the fact that Viner was not altogether hostile to the concept of state economic management. As editor of the *Journal of Political Economy*, he exercised considerable influence over the direction of the discipline, an influence that extended to Canada. Many prominent Canadian economists chose to pursue graduate work under his direction, among them Pete McQueen, Frank Knox, and, later, Mac Urquhart. Because of his own high regard for Viner, Mackintosh appealed to Innis when Leacock's retirement in 1936 opened up the position of head of McGill's department of economics: "How about suggesting to your friends at McGill that they offer the chair to Jake Viner?"[52]

Viner's personality is also worthy of note. Lionel Robbins, the British economist, provides a compelling description of Viner: "The short alert figure with his candid and penetrating eyes, now brimming over with fun, now sober with deep reflection, his quick wit, his delight in argument and the general sense of intellectual vitality that informed even his casual remarks ... [His] zest for the exchange of ideas and the pursuit of the thought wherever it led him which made any session with him an exciting and strenuous adventure."[53] But he could also be "prickly," so much so that his fellow students at Harvard "black-balled" him from membership in the Political Economy Club. Between Mackintosh and Viner, however, there was a deep mutual respect, and their paths would cross later during the international discussions leading up to the Bretton Woods conference.

Part IV of Manitoba's presentation to the commission, written by H.C. Grant and C.B. Davidson of the University of Manitoba, sought to estimate "the added burden that national tariff policy places on the agricultural industry of Western Canada."[54] By increasing the price of consumer goods and agricultural inputs, without any effect on export prices, the tariff had reduced incomes of farmers in the prairie region. The magnitude of the tariff burden was estimated by comparing prices in areas of Minnesota and Manitoba within thirty miles of the international border. Applying these price differentials to a typical annual farm budget of roughly $1,000, Grant and Davidson found that the tariff increased the average farm's cost in Canada by roughly $110 annually. Given that there were some 290,000 farms in the prairie region, the report concluded that the annual tariff burden on farm income in the three Prairie provinces was in the order of $30 million a year.[55]

While Mackintosh maintained that his *Economic Background* was not designed to address the Manitoba argument, there seems little doubt that he was enjoined to address it.[56] He dismissed the effort to calculate the tariff burden on the grounds that there was inadequate statistical information for the purpose, choosing instead to focus on the implicit assumptions underlying the Manitoba brief.[57] His critique rested on two propositions. First, the protective tariff was in place by 1879 and remained largely unchanged until the downward revisions in the 1930s. By increasing the price of consumer goods and of agricultural inputs, the tariff encouraged the expansion of protected manufacturing industries chiefly located in Ontario and Quebec, and discouraged the expansion of export-oriented prairie agriculture. By driving up the cost and thereby reducing the return on wheat farming, agricultural land of marginal productivity would not be brought under cultivation, and total prairie farm income and population would be lower. Second, inter-regional mobility of factors of production would tend to equalize per-capita incomes across the country: labour and capital would move into the manufacturing sector and out of agriculture until returns to labour and to capital were equalized between regions. Only the owners of immobile factors of production – in particular, land – would have benefited or lost due to the tariff, with the return on urban real estate in manufacturing regions increased and the return on farm land reduced.

Under these conditions, it did not follow that prairie farmers were unduly harmed. Since the tariff had been in place prior to the bulk of western lands being taken up, settlers would have incorporated the higher cost of inputs and consumer goods into their decision to settle. In this important *ex ante* sense, one could not argue that individual settlers, as land holders, were harmed. "The lands had been homesteaded, sold, and bought under fairly constant tariff conditions. Those conditions had been discounted in the prices of land from the outset; not with complete accuracy, of course, but presumably with the degree of approximation with which other economic conditions had been evaluated."[58] He reiterated this view under the adage that "an old tax is no tax": the impact of the tariff on costs of production and expected returns was known prior to the decision to invest or not. The impact of the tariff, therefore, may have reduced the rents earned on western land and, by virtue of discouraging marginal land from being settled, may have reduced total prairie farm income. Per-capita income in the Prairie provinces, however, remained unchanged.

This was a highly innovative argument, dubbed by J.H. Young the Mackintosh–Deutsch analysis after Mackintosh generously acknowledged Deutsch's contribution, and it became a landmark interpretation of the regional effects of tariffs.[59] In many important respects, the model developed by Chambers and Gordon some thirty years later merely gave it more formal expression (but without due attribution).[60]

So forceful was Mackintosh's argument that Viner felt obliged to defend the Manitoba position in a supplementary brief to the commission. In reading the preliminary draft of the *Economic Background*, Viner told Mackintosh that he found "most of it excellently argued, and excellently presented, and that I read it with both pleasure and profit."[61] This did not prevent him, however, from providing seven pages of criticism and corrections, many of which Mackintosh conceded to and incorporated in his final version. While

Viner accepted the theoretical validity of the argument, two areas of dispute were left unresolved. The first was with respect to the appropriate counterfactual as the basis for measuring the tariff burden. For Viner, it was what *aggregate income* in an area would have been in the absence of a protective tariff; for Mackintosh it was only the *per-capita income* that individuals would have received. Second, Viner challenged the argument on empirical grounds, stating that the level of tariff protection did not remain substantially unchanged over the period in question; that the owners of factors of production did not incorporate the costs imposed by the tariff into their decisions; and that factors of production were insufficiently mobile to equalize rates of return between different regions. This exchange did much to clarify the nature of the debate on the regional impact of tariffs, but also served as a fascinating discussion of the application of the assumptions of economic theory to an important policy issue. Ironically, it was the economic historian (Mackintosh) who appealed to formal reasoning, while the theorist (Viner) based his argument on factual grounds.

The eighty-five days of public hearings of the commission ended on the same issue on which they began. Premier Bracken and Finance Minister Garson, accompanied by their economic advisors, appeared in Ottawa to restate the Manitoba position about the costs that federal policy had imposed on the prairie provinces. Quite apart from the substance of their case, it afforded a unique opportunity for discussion among economists. Frank Knox and Mackintosh were invited to attend the hearings, and afterwards, together with Sandy Skelton and Manitoba's economic advisors – Viner and Hansen – they took the occasion to debate and discuss the nuances of Canadian economic policy long into the evening.

REPORT OF THE COMMISSION

Whatever the strengths and weaknesses of some of the background reports produced by the research staff, McQueen's prediction that "the group of us would be valuable as a group – many times more valuable than the sum of our isolated values" proved true in the commission's *Report*.[62] It was organized in three parts: Book I provided a detailed analysis of Canadian public finance, economic policy, and the economy generally; Book II outlined the rationale for the commission's recommendations; and Book III added statistical information, including an attempt to construct consistent provincial income accounts. Corry maintains that it was "the work of several people"; indeed, so frequently did members of the research staff gather at the home of Donald Gordon, Bank of Canada secretary and soon to become deputy governor, during the summer of 1938, that his son could claim that the report was written on the family's kitchen table. Nonetheless, Mackintosh credited Sandy Skelton with principal authorship. "Though many others helped, and helped decisively, Skelton was the architect of the investigations and the framer of the issues ... It is difficult to think of anyone who could have brought to this enormous task the energy and concentrated talent which he put into it."[63]

The *Report* complemented Mackintosh's economic history by outlining the evolution of public finance. It argued that the division of powers at the time of Confederation was appropriate to an economy based on western continental expansion: the dominion government exercised control over the key policy tools (transportation, immigration, inter-regional and international commerce) and major revenue sources (customs and excise duties).[64] Significant regional diversity persisted, based on wheat, forestry, base mining, hydroelectricity, and the automobile industry – "economically, Canada can be compared to a string of beads, and they are not all pearls"[65] – yet a national economy had been forged because of greater inter-regional trade and the emergence of a sizable domestic market. The end of the wheat boom, however, undermined the "unifying effects" of western settlement through "a complete breakdown in the strongest dynamic factor marking east-west integration"[66] and rendered obsolete the system of public finance. The weaknesses of the division of powers, apparent in the growth in social-welfare spending under provincial jurisdiction without a concomitant increase in revenue, became all too evident with the effective bankruptcy of the prairie provinces during the Great Depression and the "friction and waste" of competing policies in an effort to respond to the crisis.[67] The commission thus called for a rearrangement of public finance appropriate to the changed economic conditions in a post-wheat-boom period.

The logic of its recommendations rested on two premises. First, while governments had collectively assumed "the responsibilities for the alleviation of individual distress and for the provision of rising standards of public welfare and education," the dominion government had implicitly accepted a greater role. "The Dominion, by its large-scale intervention in the economic life of the country, and as a corollary of its conscious policy of selected stimuli, protection, and control, has unconsciously committed itself to many responsibilities for the maintenance of economic welfare. On the other hand, it has created a claim for itself to tax whatever surplus incomes and fortunes are accumulated within the framework of these policies."[68] Second, this evolution towards a stronger central government was appropriate, because only the dominion government had the capacity to stabilize economic activity, since this required coordinated trade, monetary, and fiscal policy.[69]

Accordingly, the commission offered two alternatives. Plan I recommended that the dominion government control the most important fiscal levers, while ensuring that the provinces had adequate resources to provide a minimum national standard of social welfare and education services. On the revenue side, the dominion would be given the exclusive right to impose personal income taxes, corporate income taxes, and succession duties – the most volatile revenue components – in return for national adjustment grants to the provinces to meet their financial requirements. In addition, the dominion would assume all provincial debts, to be repaid over time, on condition that all future provincial borrowing be in Canadian dollars only. On the expenditure side, the dominion government would be solely responsible for a contributory and compulsory old-age pension plan, and for the unemployed, through the provision of unemployment insurance and unemployment relief. This latter was justified in terms of efficient administration and as an appropriate alignment of incentives: since the dominion government was chiefly responsible for maintaining and promoting full employment, it should bear the cost of unemployment relief. The alternative (Plan II) would be to leave fiscal arrangements unchanged, but have the dominion assume sole responsibility for unemployment relief – essentially the recommendation of the NEC.

Plan I, in recommending an expanded role for the state in social security, was in fact redefining the citizen-state relationship associated with "Keynesian politics."[70] However, it went a step further: a rearrangement of taxation and expenditure responsibilities removed the impediments to the dominion government's ability to manage aggregate demand. Keynes's views had gained wide currency among members of the research staff. Deutsch, for instance, was well acquainted with Keynes's arguments,[71] while Mackintosh and McQueen were planning to collaborate on the writing of an introductory economics textbook that would incorporate the new macroeconomic literature. The project was put on hold and never reached fruition, but an indication of what they had in mind can be gathered from McQueen's 1940 review of *A Social Approach to Economics*, written by Harold Logan and Mark Inman. He labelled the Logan–Inman book as a Canadian version of Frank Taussig's legendary introductory text, but added that "as great as is Taussig, the time has come for a new university course in principles." Such a course needed to incorporate the basic lessons of macroeconomics emerging in England, and primarily at Cambridge. Students "need a familiarity with the concepts of national income, capital goods and consumer goods, and saving and investment," according to McQueen, and he cited Dennis Robertson work on money and saving, James Meade's treatment of income, and Joan Robinson's discussion of the relation between investment and income as "examples of good exposition of these basic notions."[72]

Moreover, when Alvin Hansen, in his capacity as an advisor to the government of Manitoba, placed before the commission a Keynesian-inspired interpretation of the factors contributing to the Great Depression, McQueen was sufficiently impressed to write a commentary on Hansen's presentation for the *Manitoba Arts Review*. McQueen expressed his acceptance of the Keynesian view that the "true causes of depression in capitalist countries lie deeply imbedded in the nature of investment activity" and were not strictly a monetary phenomenon.[73] When the investment boom of the 1920s came to an abrupt halt, there was a "rush to gold" as a liquidity preference increased, prices fell, and the expected return on investment projects declined. This triggered a deflationary spiral as reduced investment curtailed the flow of wages and profits, causing aggregate demand to fall yet further. While the monetary disturbances of the 1930s – deflation, disparities in relative prices, and a cessation in lending – were seen as "secondary phenomenon," this did not preclude the use of monetary policy as a means of addressing the downturn. Canada, however, chose to pursue a policy of "sound money" rather than allow a depreciation of the Canadian dollar to stimulate exports.

The *Report*'s commentary on economic policy during the Great Depression also reflects an awareness of Keynes's writings. It offered two possible alternatives that the dominion government might have pursued. The road not taken involved "risky and unorthodox monetary measures" and expansionary fiscal policy to counteract the decline in export earnings. "The effects of the rapidly shrinking purchasing power of the exporter could have been lessened by the creation on a sufficient scale of purchasing power connected with the financing of temporary government deficits by borrowing the otherwise unused savings of individuals and by the expansion of bank credit ... The view that unbalanced *budgets*, financed by the expansion of bank credit and the issue of fiduciary currency, were desirable in certain contingencies, was regarded as rank heresy."[74] Instead, the government stuck to a policy of "sound finance," by restricting credit expansion and maintaining the external value of the dollar (depreciation was described as an "international immorality" with dire consequences) in order to maintain confidence in public credit, and to protect incomes in "sheltered areas" by reducing imports and supporting the price of wheat. With respect to fiscal policy, it noted that "relief and public welfare overshadowed all other government activities during the depression; aggregate expenditures of all Canadian governments on every other service, apart from net debt charges and defense, declined."[75] No conclusion was offered as to which policy might have had a greater impact on national income, but it did argue that the latter approach exacerbated regional income disparities.

However much Keynesian ideas were "in the air" or were reflected in the text, the *Report* included not a single reference to Keynes. This may have been motivated by the desire to avoid any association with the New Deal in the United States, but more properly it argued that "the commission's task is not to say what policy should be followed, but, within the scope of its terms of reference, to recommend adjustments in the federal financial system which will make it possible to follow some policy."[76] Similarly, the *Report* states that it is "not our function to map out a program for controlling employment," but did go so far as to endorse a "cautious and conservative policy" of adjusting the timing of public-works projects to counteract a downturn in private spending.[77] "The planning of public works and developmental expenditures, and intelligent and co-ordinated use of credit and foreign exchange, trade, transportation and taxation policies, are powerful instruments with which to combat unemployment and to reduce fluctuations in income. The Dominion is the only Government that can use these instruments effectively."[78]

END OF AN ERA

Whether due to the limitations of its mandate or the intrusion of World War II near the end of its deliberations, the commission's analysis was appropriate to an era that was clearly over. This had one immediate implication for the reception of its recommendations: the proposed fiscal rearrangement had little hope of securing provincial agreement, because recommendations were based on revenue and expenditure estimates derived from the depression period, and were not appropriate to a time of prosperity.[79] Unfavourable to wealthier provinces, the constitutional amendment needed to implement the recommendations never had much likelihood of being made. With its main recommendations rejected at the dominion-provincial conference in 1940, the Rowell–Sirois Commission would have to be satisfied with laying out the framework for wartime financial arrangements and subsequent tax rental agreements.

That it offered little vision of the future of the Canadian economy did not, however, detract from the significance of its historical work. Handed the "seemingly prosaic task" of examining dominion-provincial finances, Dales suggests that it became necessary for the members of the research staff to find "their bearing in a strange new world," and the result was impressive: "the makers of the Report and its supporting studies succeeded in writing a history for their own times."[80] Mackintosh's *Economic Background* was again singled out for special praise. Writing twenty-five years after its publication, Dales hailed it as a landmark study that "will long stand as a major contribution to our knowledge of ourselves; it is a taut piece of writing and shows no trace of the aimless empiricism that had characterized so much of the early work in the field."[81] In a similar vein, Canada's great political theorist, C.B. Macpherson, observed that "Social and historical thought is to a peculiar degree formed by the very forces it seeks to interpret." As with the economy generally, Canadian scholarship initially relied upon borrowed techniques, but a "characteristically Canadian social science," in the guise of the staple thesis, emerged in the interwar period. "Neither Marshall's *Principles* nor Taussig's *Principles*, nor, later, Keynes's *General Theory*, could be applied directly to a country where the price system, though no doubt ultimately dominant, was complicated and distorted by significant national peculiarities." For Macpherson as well, the effort to understand the pattern of Canadian economic life reached its high-water mark in Mackintosh's "masterly volume."[82] That this volume would be written under the auspices of a royal commission says much about the nature of the economics discipline in Canada. Certainly no academic department in the country could have rivalled the collection of social scientists and the fertile setting for discussion and debate. As a collective project, it summarized the work of a generation of scholars and represents the zenith of its work.

The completion of the *Economic Background* was also the end of an era in a personal sense for Mackintosh. Fifteen years after arguing the need to redress the "constitutional bias" in Canadian history, Mackintosh's *Economic Background* would do just that. With this task complete, it brought to a close his most prolific period of academic scholarship. Once again, however, there was little opportunity for Mackintosh to reflect on his accomplishments. The pace of work that he had maintained since 1936, juggling his teaching and administrative duties at Queen's with his policy work in Ottawa, was remarkable. But it was not to abate in intensity. In September 1939, he retreated for a weekend of fishing in the Gatineau Hills with W.C. Clark, and, in this serene setting that the two men had chosen as a refuge from the pressures of Ottawa, they awaited the announcement that the country was at war.

9

"The Economist's War": Ottawa, 1939–1943

Ladies and Gentlemen, it is a great pleasure to me to be asked to introduce Professor Mackintosh to speak on "Coordination of the Economic Effort for War." Among those of us who pretend an interest in economics there was a general feeling of uneasiness as to the role of economists in Ottawa until Professor Mackintosh was appointed. We now say among ourselves after any major pronouncement has been made that Mackintosh did that or Mackintosh wrote that and we refuse to believe him when he says he didn't. His denial is an indication to us that reasons of state make it necessary. We give his denial public lip service because we know how dangerous it would be if the enemy should learn that he is as important as he is. In these days of fifth columns one cannot be too careful. In his interest I must not say more. Professor Mackintosh.

H.A. Innis, 1941[1]

Dr. Mackintosh, this is important, isn't it?

Mackenzie King, 1941[2]

In describing World War II as an "economists' war," Paul A. Samuelson underscored the strategic importance of converting the economy from civilian to military purposes and the role that economists could play in this task.[3] For Mackintosh, this provided a unique opportunity to exorcise a lingering unease. However much his decision not to enlist during World War I was based on a conviction that it was an unjust war, it left him with the sense that he had not met his civic obligation. In World War II, he was the first and most important economist recruited from outside the civil service, and when he departed seven years later, Donald Gordon would state, in the rhetoric of the day, "I salute you as one whose wartime effort is second to none."[4]

Mackintosh joined the department of finance on 11 December 1939, two months after Canada's declaration of war on Germany.. "The work of this Department has so increased during the past few months," stated W.C. Clark, "that it has become necessary for me to have some person appointed to assist me in dealing with the financial and economic problems arising out of the war."[5] To no one's surprise, Mackintosh was the person. J.L. Ralston, minister of finance until July 1940, observed that Mackintosh was "by long odds the best man, and indeed probably the only man, who could come into the Department and immediately ease the burden on my Deputy."[6]

Mackintosh was the perfect complement to Clark. Over the course of their long association, dating back to 1914, each had "acquired respect for the ability and tolerance for the peculiarities of the other." Mackintosh admired Clark's "amazing capacity for rapid, almost frantic work" and looked past his colleague's legendary disorganization. "The desk piled high in disorder, the brief case carried home protesting at the volume of papers bundled into it, the variable hours for meals, these all indicated Clark's optimistic hope of getting more done than any human could manage to accomplish. He was behind schedule on most things but on the crucial ones he just managed to meet the dead-line. Whether it was business or social contacts he always tried to crowd more into an hour than could possibly be accommodated." He also tolerated Clark's argumentative bent. "He rose to an argument. When he no longer argued, one knew he was tired or ill. Indeed he had a habit, which could be annoying at times, of arguing vehemently and even indignantly against a proposal, on which he was not too well briefed, only to accept it willingly in the end if it was effectively defended. Having accepted it, he embraced it. Younger men were sometimes intimidated, strangers sometimes bewildered but the method though wearing had some pedagogical soundness."[7] Mackintosh's concise and ordered thinking, his careful attention to detail, and his persuasive pen would translate Clark's ideas into effective policy proposals. To this he would also add many on his own initiative.

Under Section 40 of the Civil Service Act, Mackintosh was appointed as a temporary employee, with the title of "Special Assistant to the Deputy Minister of Finance." His affairs at Queen's were quickly put in order: his teaching was covered by John Deutsch for one term, followed by Harold Poole once Deutsch himself returned to Ottawa, and then by the permanent appointment of C.H. (Connie) Curtis, a Queen's graduate and PhD candidate at Chicago.[8] Frank Knox assumed administrative duties as department head, while Smails and Walker shared the responsibility of director of the commerce program. Mackintosh also resigned his positions as a director of the Empire Life Insurance Company, and as editor of the *Canadian Banker*. He also had a major family concern with which to deal, for in 1939 his daughter, Alison, was born. He thus moved into the Château Laurier until Jean and Alison joined him in October 1940, whereupon they rented a small house at 17 Belvedere Crescent, in the Rockcliffe Park colony of senior civil servants. He reported for work in good health, still five feet eight inches tall, but now weighing some 166 pounds. His annual salary of $7,500 was roughly equivalent to his university pay and consistent with his conviction that no one should benefit financially from government wartime service.

Mackintosh expressed the task at hand in matter-of-fact terms. The objective was "to develop full use of resources and devote as much as possible to the war." This meant determining Canada's economic capacity, putting the mechanisms in place to channel the necessary capital and labour into military purposes, and "making all parts of the plan appropriate to each other and ensuring that in tone and scope the parts fit together."[9] Yet this simple description masked the scope of the problem and the immense difficulties in regulating Canada's foreign exchange, financing government expenditures, procuring the raw materials and capital goods for the military, curtailing private consumption, ensuring that the labour market matched the supply of available skills to wartime demands, and regulating wages and prices to achieve the "delicate balancing act of distributing the cost of fighting the war." In meeting these challenges, Canada (and Mackintosh) left an enviable record.

FISCAL POLICY: HOW TO PAY FOR THE WAR

Prior to Clark's appointment as deputy minister of finance in 1932, economic policy was, according to Mackintosh, "carried in the Minister's head, or in the case of Mr. W.S. Fielding, very frequently in his hat."[10] Over the next few years, Clark recruited a small but able staff of senior officials – including Kenneth Eaton, Harvey Perry, David Johnston, George Lowe, and, of course, R.B. Bryce – with the capacity to offer the minister competent advice on economic matters. In joining this group, Mackintosh was enlisted to work on the department's central task of setting out fiscal policy to enable the prosecution of the war.

Canada's pre-war budget of April 1939 – deemed by Bryce to be "one of the first clearly Keynesian budgets in any country"[11] – came only after considerable debate. In contrast, the exigencies of war removed any resistance to large increases in government spending. In a remarkable series of wartime budgets, dominion expenditures rose from $681 million in 1939 to $5.322 billion in 1943, accounting for over 48 per cent of national income at the height of the war effort (Table 9.1). "Fortunately," states Bryce, in reference to the first war budget of September 1939, "we were able to get the minister's approval of a general approach that adopted and extended the Keynesian type of analysis, and policies based on it, that Dunning had used in the April 1939 budget." Justifiably proud of his own contribution, especially in drafting the budget speech with its "somewhat Keynesian flavour," Bryce had an influence that did not go unnoticed. Wynne Plumptre sent his congratulations: "I should rather like all my students to read the Budget Speech, given a fortnight ago, the authorship of which I suspect." Similarly, Monteath Douglas of the Bank of Montreal wrote to Bryce that "I seem to detect your hand at work in Ilsley's speech, and would therefore like to tell you that it strikes me as one of the most interesting and stimulating documents that ever came out of Ottawa. If you gentlemen can handle the problem of financing our end of this war with the same vigour and clarity as you have conceived it, you will be an example fit to be enshrined forever in all the text books."[12]

Unanimity on the need to increase government spending still left open the question of how to pay for the war. In response to the first emergency war budget in Britain, which relied upon a large government deficit to finance the military commitments, Keynes warned in *The Times* of the danger of excess demand leading to inflation. The overwhelming lesson of World War I was that inflationary spending placed the burden of the war on workers, through a sharp decline in real wages. Allowing nominal wage increases to maintain real incomes, however, would leave purchasing power unchanged and undermine efforts to divert resources to the war effort. Higher rates of taxation and personal savings, therefore, were needed to restrict civilian consumption and avoid the upward pressure on prices that would distribute the burden of war unfairly. In *How to Pay for the War: A Radical Proposal for the Chancellor of the Exchequer* (1940), Keynes extended his argument. Such measures as rationing, import controls, and price controls would only be effective if purchasing power was reduced, which, by extension, meant a severe reduction in all incomes, including those of workers. To appease labour groups, he proposed a compulsory savings plan, in which a portion of the increased tax revenue would be repaid to individual workers after the war, a plan which had the dual appeal of dampening spending during the war and increasing it afterwards to offset the possibility of a postwar slump.

Canada adhered to such a "pay-as-you-go" principle from the outset: the war would be financed domestically, chiefly through taxation and borrowing from the public, in order to avoid inflationary pressures. Mackintosh later stated the case in a memorandum to the Prime Minister's Office (PMO):

> The government's declared policy is to pay as we go to the greatest extent practicable. This means heavy reliance on taxation. It implies an attempt to catch the revenue while incomes are large during the war. The difficulty is that taxes take time to devise, and take time to go into operation. Consequently, in the case of a sudden upsurge of income such as we have during war, they can never operate fast enough. The balance must be made up by means of loans, and the important end to achieve, whether taxes or loans are employed, is that the purchasing power and the productive power of the national shall be devoted to war purposes rather than to luxury consumption, or to consumption which can be postponed … In pursuing this policy of taxation, the Government is implementing its declared opposition to profiteering and to inflation.[13]

The relatively modest appropriations for war spending in the September 1939 and June 1940 budgets were financed through monetary expansion (borrowing from the chartered banks). Any inflationary pressure caused by an increase in the money supply was deemed acceptable in light of the unemployed resources that prevailed. However, the framework for increased taxation that was put

Figure 9.1 Gross national expenditure, by expenditure category Canada, 1938–1946 (current dollars – million)

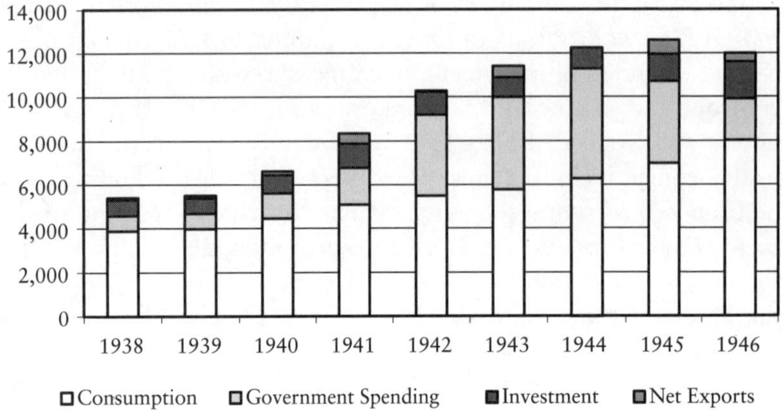

Source: Derived from Statistics Canada, *Historical Statistics of Canada*, series F13-32.

Table 9.1 Federal government budgetary expenditures, 1939–1945 (millions of dollars)

Year	*Defence and mutual aid*	*Veterans benefits*	*Total government expenditure*	*GNP*	*Government expenditure/ GNP*
1939	126	60	681	5,621	12.1%
1940	730	60	1,250	6,713	18.6%
1941	1,268	58	1,885	8,282	22.8%
1942	2,563	62	4,387	10,265	42.7%
1943	4,242	70	5,322	11,053	48.1%
1944	4,000	114	5,246	11,848	44.3%
1945	2,942	402	5,136	11,863	43.3%

Source: Statistics Canada, *Historical Statistics of Canada*, Series H19-34.

in place signalled an intention to rely more heavily on direct taxes, with indirect taxes targeting largely luxury goods. In addition to the familiar increases in excise taxes on tobacco, liquor, and other luxury goods, there was a surcharge of 20 per cent on personal income taxes (under the War Income Tax Act), a 2-per-cent War Defence Tax imposed on all personal incomes above $600 per annum, an increase in corporate income taxes from 15 to 18 per cent, and a new Excess Profits Tax at a rate of 50 per cent on profits above pre-war levels.[14] These relatively modest tax changes did little to reduce private spending, but the accompanying increase in prices was not alarming in light of the deflation during the 1930s.

With the fall of France later in 1940, the urgency of an all-out war effort became apparent and, accordingly, so too the need to divert resources from civilian to military use through fiscal measures. There were two impediments to an effective federal government response. The first was the failure of the dominion-provincial talks in January 1941 to resolve the matter of overlapping tax jurisdictions identified in the report of the Rowell–Sirois Royal Commission. The problem grew more acute, as the war tended to have a beneficial impact on provincial treasuries: revenues increased with higher incomes, while expenditures on relief and social assistance fell. "Generally speaking," Mackintosh noted in a memorandum to the PMO, the provinces were "taking advantage of the situation to be thrifty in their expenditures, and, in nearly all cases, it looks as if war would be a period of very substantial debt reduction in the municipal and provincial fields."[15] Moreover, sharing the burdens of war on an equitable basis was undermined by the variation in provincial income-tax rates. A solution was not found until the tax rental agreements, reached in time for the 1941 budget and formalized in 1942, that would form the basis of dominion-provincial revenue sharing in the postwar period. Walter Gordon, at the time the other special assistant to the deputy minister of finance, proposed that the federal government announce the taxes it planned to impose and invite any province to enter into an agreement to give up its rights to levy personal and corporate income taxes for the duration of the war in return for a fixed payment roughly equal to their current tax revenue. Although the provinces were under no obligation to acquiesce, Gordon was cognizant that, if they declined to do so and continued to impose their own taxes, "the burden of taxation on its residents would be unbearable." When Gordon outlined his proposal to the deputy minister, "Clark, as was his custom, peppered me with questions, but I could see from his excitement that he thought it might be the answer to our problem. He asked Bill Mackintosh to join us and we went through the proposal with him again. We then called on Mr. Ilsley, and after much discussion we agreed to lay the plan before the Cabinet ... This was the essence of the wartime tax agreements." Gordon adds that, when the proposal was placed before the premier of Ontario, "Mitch Hepburn, who was quick and intelligent and accustomed to use rather pungent language when he wished to shock people, listened carefully. He then walked round to me and whispered loud enough for Ilsley to overhear, in language designed to upset him, "Walter, does this mean you've got us by the _____? I replied, also in a whisper, "Yes, Mitch, and we intend to keep on squeezing until you sign."[16]

The second impediment was the sorry state of Canada's national income accounts. Estimates produced by the Dominion Bureau of Statistics (DBS) were based on the value-added method of summing up the net production in each industry. While this was a reliable means of estimating output in goods-producing industries, net output of service industries was crudely based on the number of employees and the dubious assumption that labour productivity was the same as it was in goods industries. More unreliable were estimates for the government sector, which followed Simon Kuznets's approach of treating government like a private firm: tax receipts were interpreted as the payment for government services, with any budgetary deficit or surplus recorded as a profit or loss.[17] Deutsch commented that such estimates of the value of government services were incorrectly based on the manner in which they were financed. As long as governments relied strictly on tax revenue, the estimates were largely correct; however, if all government spending was financed exclusively through borrowing, it would be effectively recorded as valueless.[18] In essence, the DBS's value-added approach gave businesses some guide to the state of affairs in their own industries, but was of little assistance in the design of fiscal policy.

The DBS national-income statistics were recognized by the Rowell–Sirois Royal Commission as defective, of little help in understanding the division of national income among regions, industries, and social classes, or its disposition by consumption and investment categories, "for the proper formulation and administration of the normal economic policies of the Dominion Government."[19] The Bank of Canada and department of finance found it necessary to produce their own national income estimates, and George Luxton was assigned the task.[20] Luxton prepared tentative income and expenditure accounts for 1938 onwards but, without access to adequate data, he struggled to remove the inconsistency between measuring government accounts at market prices and national income on a factor-cost basis, leaving his calculation of government spending as a percentage of national income as, at best, an informed guess.[21]

Mackintosh would be the first to make public use of Luxton's estimates when drafting the 1942 Budget speech. "You will have noticed," he wrote to Luxton, "that without quoting any figures and necessarily without giving any credit, I have used your estimates in a sort of paraphrase in the Budget Speech."[22]

Mackintosh returned from the 1942 Commonwealth talks in London with a report by James Meade and Richard Stone outlining the importance of accurate national-income figures expressed according to Keynesian expenditure categories, for use not just in the planning of fiscal policy but also in enlisting public support for the war effort. Presented for the first time in the 1941 British White Paper on national income and expenditures, government war spending, stated as a percentage of national income, provided an important justification for the sacrifice that citizens were making. In a similar vein, they were useful in appealing to allied governments to increase their own support for the war effort.[23]

Canadian officials needed little convincing. Deutsch had insisted that reliable statistics were "essential for the proper formulation and administration of the normal economic policies of the Dominion Government," and Towers pressed the case with Clark. "I am firmly of the opinion that this is the last time that such an ad hoc estimate should be made," he wrote. "Even if we could place more reliance upon the global figures, they are, by themselves, of little help to the appraisal of the economic situation or to the framing of policies."[24] Clark then informed his minister that "nearly every major problem in the field of fiscal and borrowing policy and economic policy generally could not be solved intelligently without adequate figures of this type. It was also shown how embarrassing it was that in Canada today we have three sets of figures [DBS, Bank of Canada/Finance, and the Bank of Nova Scotia], all compiled in different bases and showing different results and not one of them being of such a character as to enable use to be made of it with confidence."[25] Clark succeeded in obtaining the cooperation of all parties, including a rather recalcitrant DBS, for the development of new income-and-expenditure accounts, but his efforts were frustrated by the inability to secure a suitable individual to undertake the analysis, such as Abba Lerner, the Russian-born, LSE-trained economist who went on to a celebrated academic career.[26] Luxton was eventually assigned the task and appointed chief of planning and development staff at the DBS.[27] With his untimely death, however, it was not until 1946 that Canada's system of national accounts were placed on a similar basis to that used in the United Kingdom and the United States.[28]

With greater freedom of action in the taxation field and the benefit of at least Luxton's informed guesses with respect to the national accounts, the question was how much could be paid for through taxation. In the budget speech of 1942, which Mackintosh took particular pride in writing, Ilsley stated that "we too have now come to the stage where the choice between guns and butter must affect the average man and woman in Canada. We must accept a temporary reduction in our average standard of living if we are to achieve the necessary standard of fighting. We cannot hope to live as well as most of us are used to living and fight a total war at the same time."[29]

The practicable limits of taxation were, according to Mackintosh, to be defined on the principles of equity, the preservation of individual incentives, and the appropriate balance between compulsory and voluntary saving. Personal income taxes bore the brunt of the increase. Marginal tax rates were further increased and, by incorporating the previously flat-rate national-defence tax, were given an even more progressive nature. Moreover, Bryce and Mackintosh acknowledged that it was necessary to "go after" the incomes of those of "moderate means" by lowering personal-exemption levels in order to raise revenue and to choke off personal consumption. Prior to the war, a minority of Canadians paid income taxes: in 1939, only 300,000 individuals out of a total labour force of over 5 million filed tax returns, because of the relatively high personal-exemption level, and the money paid accounted for less than 10 per cent of dominion revenue. By lowering the personal exemption level to $600 and increasing marginal tax rates, personal income taxes would constitute nearly one-third of dominion revenue by the end of the war. A married couple with two children, earning $3,000 a year, saw its effective tax rate rise from 3.4 per cent in 1939 to 35.5 per cent by June 1942, while a similar family with an annual income of $10,000 experienced an increase from 9.1 per cent to 51.1 per cent.[30]

Corporate income taxes and the Excess Profits Tax also increased sharply: the minimum corporate tax rate rose to 30 per cent, and the Excess Profits Tax rose to 75 and then 100 per cent, with a refund of 20 per cent to be made after the war. The dominion government also entered the field of succession duties for the first time; higher rates were imposed on interest and dividends to non-residents; and

Figure 9.2 Federal government budgetary expenditures and revenue Canada, 1938–1946 (current dollars – millions)

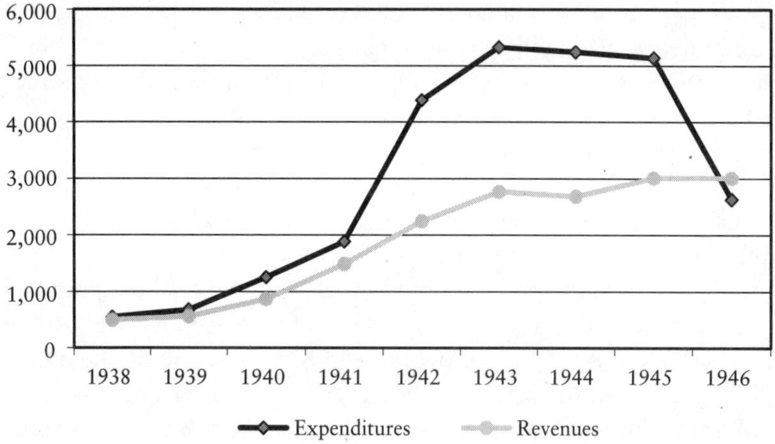

Source: Derived from Statistics Canada, *Historical Statistics of Canada*, series H18 and H34.

Table 9.2 Federal government budgetary revenue, by major source, 1939–1945 (millions of dollars)

Year	*Personal income tax*	*Corporate income tax*	*Excess profits tax*	*Sales tax**	*Total tax revenue*	*Total revenue*	*Tax rev./ expen- ditures*	*Total rev./ expen- ditures*
1939	45	78	0	227	468	562	68.7%	82.5%
1940	104	132	24	373	778	872	62.2%	69.8%
1941	296	186	135	563	1,361	1,489	72.2%	79.0%
1942	484	348	435	628	2,067	2,250	47.1%	51.3%
1943	698	311	429	781	2,437	2,765	45.8%	52.0%
1944	673	276	341	695	2,155	2,687	41.1%	51.2%
1945	687	218	427	684	2,202	3,013	42.9%	58.7%

*Includes excise taxes and duties.

Source: Statistics Canada, *Historical Statistics of Canada*, Series H1-18.

consumption taxes were raised on such "non-essential" items as sugar, cameras, jewellery, photographs, radio tubes, and entertainment events.

The search for greater tax revenue, without causing a one-to-one reduction in personal savings, led to some experimentation. In 1942, Mackintosh referred to the need for a "logical splicing of compulsory with voluntary savings. Since we must continue to use both methods, and not to substitute one for the other, we very much prefer not to use the term compulsory savings or forced savings but to speak of refundable taxes."[31] To this end, a "compulsory saving component" was added to personal income taxes. It was a highly graduated tax that was refundable at the end of the war, including a 2-per-cent annual interest payment.

Another proposal for compulsory savings was to require consumers to buy a five-cent savings stamp for every dollar spent on taxable items. Stamps could then be redeemed after the war. Mackintosh was initially skeptical of the idea on the grounds that it would largely supplant voluntary purchases of war bonds, would be administratively cumbersome, and might be viewed by the public as a "dishonest trick" of imposing a regressive form of taxation.[32] By the time of the 1942 budget deliberations, however, he had reversed his opinion. "My own thought is that the income tax is a pretty unwieldy weapon for getting at the part of the population that is not already saving 10 per cent or more of its income, either through insurance, pension funds, war bonds, &c, and that in order to reach down to this group the exemption limits have to be put at a desperately low level. On the other hand, this group is spending, and it is the spending that we wish to prohibit now, or better still to postpone till some later date. The purchase of a redeemable stamp will not only force people to purchase less now, but it will also enable them to purchase more after the war, and this end can be attained very easily."[33] With the exception of jewellery and cut-glass ware, however, war stamps were introduced as a form of voluntary saving. Humphrey Michell, at McMaster, told Mackintosh that "This war saving certificate scheme is right up Mrs Michell's alley. She delights in buying stamps and her collection of certificates is growing. But every time she fills up another folder with stamps and sends it off to get her certificate, I am struck with the same thought. Why is it necessary to send these folders to Ottawa to get a properly registered certificate in exchange?" Mackintosh could only concede that "After a couple of years in the Civil Service, I am far from assuming that even a Civil Servant can offer a rational explanation for all the things that Governments do."[34]

Since tax revenue covered, at best, half of the government's cash requirements, a substantial increase in personal saving was required, not only to fund war spending but also to keep inflation in check. Reflecting Mrs Michell's concern, the administratively cumbersome War Bond Certificates gave way to the highly-successful series of

Victory Loan campaigns organized by the National War Finance Committee. In his analysis of Canada's war-time fiscal policy, Craig McIvor estimates that the total amount of new cash raised through government borrowing operations during the war amounted to $14.8 billion, with $12.5 billion provided by the general public (individuals and corporations) with the remainder from the chartered banks and Bank of Canada. That this money was raised exclusively from domestic sources was a testament to the success of the propaganda campaign to convince the public of the importance of the principle of pay-as-you-go.[35] Despite the substantial increase in the government's debt during the war, the proportion payable in foreign markets steadily declined.

Canada's pay-as-you-go approach to wartime finance was an unqualified success. McIvor concludes that "in obtaining from taxation an amount of cash which approached one-half of its total wartime cash deficiency, the accomplishment of the government was one which compares very favourably with the records established by any of the other major belligerents."[36] This was complemented by the Victory Loan campaign, which relied almost exclusively on the Canadian public to finance the remainder of spending. Second, the rationalization and improvement in the structure of taxes was tantamount to, in Slater's words, a "virtual revolution," which created a modern system of taxation that persisted after the war.[37] The temporary agreement that the provinces would vacate the fields of personal and corporate income taxation in return for fixed payments from the federal government allowed a more uniform application of direct taxation across the provinces, while shifting the burden from indirect to direct taxes vested the tax system with a strong progressive element.

THE ECONOMIC ADVISORY COMMITTEE (EAC)

Mackintosh's second major task was in helping to coordinate the economic aspects of the war effort. In harnessing the physical resources for war, much mention has been made of the powerful Advisory Committee on Economic Policy (commonly referred to as the Economic Advisory Committee, or EAC), formed in September 1939, just days after Canada entered the war.[38] Its initial membership was composed of an impressive array of senior civil servants from the relevant branches of the federal government: Clark (finance); Graham Towers (Bank of Canada), H.D. Scully (Commissioner of Customs), Hector McKinnon (chairman of the Wartime Prices and Trade Board), G.S.B. Barton (deputy minister of agriculture), Charles Camsell (deputy minister of mines and resources), L.D. Wilgress (director of the Commercial Intelligence Service), R.H. Coats (Dominion Statistician), Lt-Col. Henri Desrosiers (associate deputy minister of national defence), Norman Robertson (external affairs), and a representative of the ministry of munitions and supply (after some delay, R.A.C. Henry). Bryce, who served as secretary, described it as "the first general-purpose, inter-departmental committee of top-level officials established in Ottawa."[39] It was given the wide-ranging power, "of its own motion or upon request of any Minister of the Crown, to investigate report and advise upon questions of economic and financial policy and organization arising out of Canadian participation in the war." It became commonplace for ministers to refer questions to the EAC before presenting material to the cabinet War Committee or to the cabinet directly. During the first year of the war it would meet over forty times, often late into the evening.[40] "The key to the EAC's effectiveness," according to Bryce, was that "after consideration of a complicated subject, effective action was taken. As a senior committee of top public servants, it could draw upon an impressive range of experience and knowledge and deal directly with problems that transcended the usual department responsibilities. Between them, Clark and Mackintosh produced many of the committee's reports and played a dynamic role in its discussions."[41]

Despite the talent assembled, the EAC was hardly an effective committee during the first few months of the war. When Mackintosh joined it as an ex officio member in December 1939, he quickly assumed the lead in steering it towards a more important role. After sitting through several meetings over the course of two months that dealt with such matters as the impact of imported canned pineapple on the domestic fruit industry, or listening to delegations from the silver-fox and canned-lobster industries pleading for relief from export controls, he grew increasingly impatient. Retreating to his office, he drafted a memorandum to Clark on 7 March 1940, in which he expressed "a growing conviction that the Economic Advisory Committee must move forward to a new stage in its function. Up to the present, it is not clearly distinguishable from an ordinary, inter-departmental committee in much of its work. Without reducing the usefulness of the Committee in this respect, it is desirable that its functions should be more specifically along the line of coordinating economic policy."[42] With Clark's blessing, he then circulated a longer memorandum to the members of the EAC, arguing that it should limit its deliberations to larger policy issues and leave to subcommittees matters arising on an ad hoc basis.[43]

To facilitate this approach, he further recommended that periodic reviews of economic conditions be undertaken to assist in identifying areas of concern. On 27 March 1940, he produced an "Economic Survey of the First Six Months of the War" and, with Bryce, a dense twenty-four-page "Economic Survey of the First Year of the War" on 16 September 1940. Together, these reports laid out the economic background to the war, the changes as hostilities unfolded, and the areas requiring immediate attention.

At the outset of the war, the Canadian economy had yet to recover from the Great Depression, let alone the cyclical downturn in 1938–39: the unemployment rate was estimated to be 12 per cent, while prices remained 17 per cent below their 1929 levels. The situation was exacerbated by a growing wheat surplus and the loss of other export markets in Europe. Output and employment had increased during the first six months of the war in response to government military contracts, but there was still considerable unused capacity, and Mackintosh suggested that national income could rise in the order of 20 to 25 per cent without any significant upward pressure on productive capacity – and, thus, on prices. Economic growth accelerated during the next six months, as greater government spending and private investment fuelled by war contracts got under way, while consumption (as measured through retail sales), had risen by 10 per cent over the first year of the war. Employment, accordingly, had also increased rapidly. Between July 1939 and July 1940, the number of employed workers had risen by 395,000 (or 9 per cent of the labour force), including some 180,000 drawn into the armed services. The number of unemployed had fallen from 352,000 to 238,000, and the "employables" on relief had declined by 54,000. This implied that some 200,000 people who had been outside the labour force had been drawn into employment.[44] The cost of living, in contrast, had increased by only 4.4 per cent, a fairly modest rate given the depressed state of prices at the beginning of the war.

The first year of the war, therefore, had been prosecuted with relatively little strain of the country's resources. Government contracts had been placed with relative ease, while the labour supply proved reasonably elastic, drawing upon the reserve of unemployed and on new entrants into the labour force. Yet Mackintosh and Bryce warned of the urgency of preparing for the stage at which the economy approached full employment. They identified three areas, existing or anticipated, requiring immediate attention: the conservation of foreign exchange; better coordination among wartime agencies, in order to secure the necessary materials for the war effort without undue increases in inflation; and labour market planning. A fourth concern – wages policy and industrial relations – would emerge as labour markets tightened.

Foreign Exchange

The need to conserve the country's foreign-exchange reserves was recognized from the outset of the war. The triangular pattern of Canadian trade – with most exports to Great Britain in the form of wheat, munitions, and other foodstuffs, and the majority of imports from the United States – depended upon converting the sterling received from the UK in order to meet payments in US dollars. But with imports from the US expected to increase with Canada's military production and the general economic recovery, and anticipation that the UK would be unable to maintain sterling convertibility, Canada would accumulate a sterling surplus that could not be used to purchase US goods. This situation would be compounded by the loss of exports to non-sterling countries in German-occupied parts of Europe.

The Foreign Exchange Control Board (FECB) was thus established to control the nation's gold and other monetary reserves by approving all foreign currency transactions. In an effort to stabilize Canada's international balance of payments and maintain the Canadian dollar at a 10 per cent discount to the US dollar, it immediately placed restrictions on the imports of commodities such as raw sugar, soy beans, and bananas, and on the export of capital. Further fiscal measures were adopted in the June 1940 budget to limit the inflow of consumer goods; however, these had a relatively modest impact, given that some two-thirds of Canadian imports from the US were capital goods, which were expected to increase as military production expanded. When Louis Rasminsky, working for the FECB on behalf of the Bank of Canada, offered a pessimistic forecast of

Canada's foreign-exchange situation, the need for further restrictions became apparent.[45] It fell to Mackintosh, in his capacity as finance's representative in the FECB, to advise on additional courses of action to further conserve foreign exchange. He enumerated several non-fiscal measures: restrictions on non-essential civilian imports; increased gold production; improvements in Canada's tourism balances with the US; increased exports to non-sterling countries; the sale of gold reserves in the United States; the acquisition and sale of US securities held by Canadians; limitations on international dividend and interest payments in US dollars; and an increase in the amount of gold received in settlement of the UK debt.[46] He singled out "a fairly drastic curtailment of the automobile and allied industries" as "a clean and effective mobilization of resources for war." The automobile sector was targeted, because of its peculiar nature in Canada: largely designed as an export platform for US companies, parts were shipped from the US to Canada for assembly, in order to take advantage of Canada's preferred tariff treatment in the sterling bloc (the Commonwealth, excluding Canada, Newfoundland, and Hong Kong). Under this arrangement, Canada was the world's third-largest exporter of automobiles, but since the cars were destined for Commonwealth countries, the loss of export revenue was of little immediate concern, since the revenue would merely have exacerbated the growing sterling reserves.[47] Restricting the trade in automobiles and parts thus had the double virtue of saving foreign exchange and making available facilities that were easily converted to armaments production. The War Exchange Conservation Act of December 1940 consolidated the host of restrictions to date and further prohibited a wide range of imports from non-sterling countries, required import permits for raw materials, and extended excise taxes on a wider range of consumer durables to stop Canadian production from expanding to take the place of imports. It imposed a war exchange tax of 10 per cent on all imports from non-sterling countries and an excise tax on cars, ranging from 20 to 80 per cent, depending upon the import content, and announced that no US dollars would be made available for tourists travelling to the US.[48] Special depletion allowances were also introduced on new investments that increased non-sterling exports.[49]

Foreign tourism – or more specifically, motorists crossing the Canada–US border – was targeted because of the large impact on Canada's international balance of payments. Mackintosh experienced his share of frustration with various committees during his time in Ottawa, but saved his greatest exasperation for the Inter-Departmental Advisory Committee on Travel and the Tourism Industry, struck in August 1940. As a member of the committee, he encouraged it to provide leadership to the "voluntary tourist" movement, just as the NEC had attempted to do, by producing a bulletin or newsletter that kept local committees informed of activities in other parts of the country. After six months of inaction, Mackintosh resigned from the committee. "To speak frankly," he wrote to P.J.A. Cardin, minister of transport,

> it was quite clear to me, and I think to other members of the Committee, that Mr. Dolan [chair of the committee and chief of the Canadian Travel Bureau] resented the existence of the Committee as an interference with his management of the Government's programme for promoting tourist traffic. As far as I know, the Committee has no knowledge of the programme for the coming year for which an appropriation of $500,000 has been asked. I do not know whether any effective programme has been worked out or whether the proposal is simply to increase the amount of advertising carried in United States publications. As a result, I find myself in an ambiguous position from which I must ask to be relieved.[50]

The committee was disbanded and re-formed in November 1941 as the Tourism Development Committee. Mackintosh expressed "a good deal of reluctance in accepting membership on this Committee, as I have already served on three successive versions of the same committee. That the experience was relatively unpleasant is not important, but that I felt myself to be an ineffective member of an ineffective committee was important." Nonetheless, he indicated "a qualified acceptance of the appointment until I see whether the new Committee seems likely to succeed where its predecessors failed." When gasoline rationing was imposed a month later, he faced a new obstacle in the guise of Canada's Oil Controller, who was actively discouraging American motorists from travelling north. This was one battle he chose not to fight. His final contribution was to suggest that "we would get more tourists this year if we did not do any advertising by this Government because the type of advertising that

Figure 9.3 Canada's trade with the US, 1938–1945 (current dollars – millions)

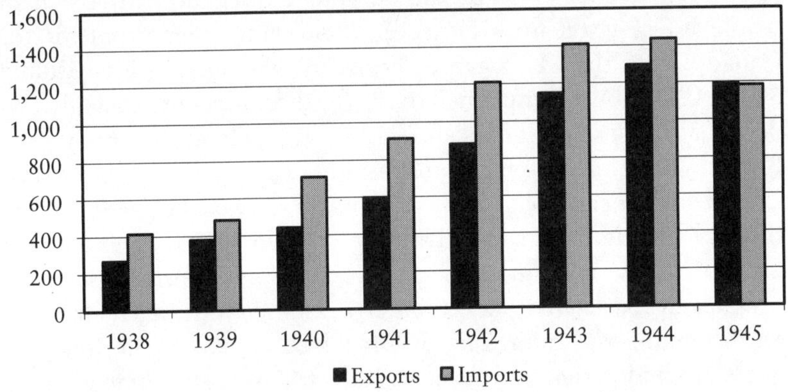

Source: Derived from Statistics Canada, *Historical Statistics of Canada*, series G389-400.

Figure 9.4 Canada's trade with the UK, 1938–1945 (current dollars – millions)

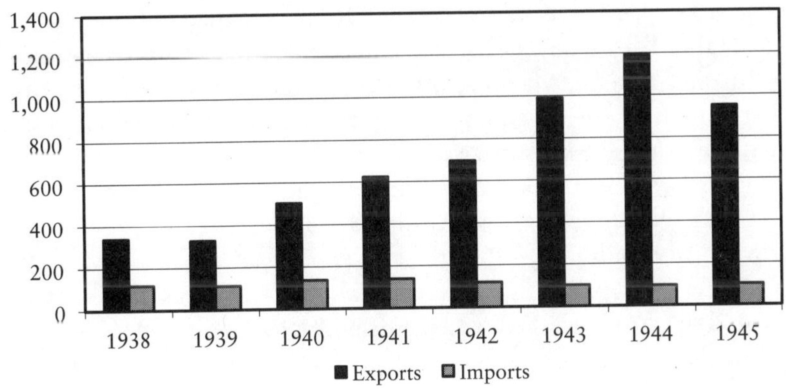

Source: Derived from Statistics Canada, *Historical Statistics of Canada*, series G389-400.

we are going to be able to do will … discourage rather than encourage tourist travel this year."[51]

Despite all of the measures adopted, it was clear that Canada was incapable of solving the foreign-exchange problem on its own. By December 1940, the situation became grave when, as anticipated, the UK announced that it was suspending the payment of gold to meet its outstanding international debt. The US lend-lease agreement addressed the UK's immediate financial needs by providing war materials to the UK and its allies, to be paid for after the war. (Roosevelt likened this to lending your garden hose to the man whose house is on fire.) However, it brought other problems for Canada, since the UK began diverting its war orders to the United States. C.D. Howe complained that: "It is becoming increasingly evident that our present financial relations with Great Britain and the British Dominions are most unsatisfactory in operation, as against United States Lease-Lend arrangements. In spite of the agreement on the part of Britain to keep existing production capacity in Canada occupied, there is an increasing tendency to attempt to procure all supplies in the United States, under Lease-Lend arrangements … I am beginning to doubt the wisdom of accumulating sterling balances in London that will never be paid."[52] A solution came with the Hyde Park Declaration of February 1941, in which the US undertook to purchase war materials from Canada, while materials exported to Canada for use in the production of munitions for the UK would be charged to the UK under the lend-lease arrangement. The subsequent reversal in Canada's foreign-exchange situation was dramatic. The Hyde Park agreement, coupled with rationalization of Canadian-American defence production and buoyant wheat exports, left Canada with an embarrassing surplus on its balance of trade with the United States in 1943.

Left unresolved was the accumulated debt of the sterling area to Canada, which reached $700 million during 1941 and eventually rose to $1.7 billion by November 1942. Considering there was little prospect of repayment, it became abundantly clear that Canada would need to bear the costs. To dispose of some if the sterling surplus, the EAC endorsed finance's proposal that Canada undertake more direct war spending in Britain – such as on Canada's air squadron there – rather than financing British spending. Then, in December 1941, an interest-free loan on the outstanding sterling balances was extended to Britain as well as a "billion dollar gift." Mackintosh drafted the text announcing that Canada would give the UK, "free of charge and without obligation, munitions of war, foodstuffs, and other supplies up to the amount of $1,000 million. This gift to the common cause of defeating the Axis, together with other provisions, to which the Prime Minister referred, will be sufficient, it is estimated, to provide for all United Kingdom requirements up to March 31, 1943."[53] When this money was spent in less than a year, mutual-aid agreements based on a combination of loans and gifts were provided to Britain throughout the duration of the war.[54]

The Fight Against Inflation

As the country entered the second year of the war, Mackintosh and Bryce asserted that a different economic stage was looming: as full employment approached, competition for resources would become more acute, making it necessary to curtail domestic consumption in order to make sufficient resources available for military use. The economic machinery, however, was deemed ill-equipped for this challenge.[55]

There was no shortage of government agencies responsible for some aspect of the conduct of the wartime economy, with three centres of authority. The department of munitions and supply, created by parliament in September 1939 and implemented in April 1940 under the direction of C.D. Howe, was charged with ensuring that the necessary resources were available for war industries and with placing large contracts for armaments, foodstuffs, and materials with private firms. Second, the War Industries Control Board, composed of individual commodity controllers (of things such as metals, oil, power, machine tools, ship repairs, and motor vehicles), exercised broad powers to ensure that supplies were available to war-related industries. Third, the Wartime Prices and Trade Board (WPTB), chaired by Hector McKinnon, with Kenneth Taylor as secretary, was responsible for civilian supplies and for curtailing domestic consumption so as not to compete with war industries for necessary resources.[56] Canada's military commitments had, to date, been met with relative ease. Munitions and supply had "little occasion as yet to take restrictive action or to order priorities for war supplies"; the WPTB had found it necessary to exercise only "light control" in a number of areas; the transportation controller exercised authority over ocean shipping, but had not given consideration to railway or motor-vehicle traffic; and the department of labour had no special programs in place to address the expected shortage in skilled labour. Yet Mackintosh and Bryce concluded that the "multiplicity of organizations, in conjunction with impending scarcities of labour, materials, directing personnel and equipment makes the need for coordination of extreme urgency."[57]

The immediate requirement was to ensure the procurement of supplies for war industries. The EAC endorsed the formation of a Wartime Planning Board, under the direction of munitions and supply, to undertake an analysis of the economic requirements of Canada's defence industries, to identify the materials, power, and manufacturing and transportation facilities needed, and to accord military needs priority over all other claims on resources.[58] Mackintosh was reluctant to give munitions and supply a free hand in directing the allocation of resources. As he confided to Bryce Stewart, deputy minister of labour: "The Cabinet Committee was inclined to think that more definite authority should be given to someone to deal with the matters which our Inter-Departmental Committee discussed. Apparently, the proposal is to give blanket authority to the Minister. This is, I think, all to the good except in so far as it leads other Ministers to feel that they can act with impunity in the field of labour, and leave it to the Minister of Labour to take drastic remedial action." He added that "There are quite a lot of people who don't know the meaning of the word 'co-ordination.' There used to be a patent medicine widely advertised in France as permitting the user to commit the worst excesses with impunity. I should think there would be quite a wide sale for it in this particular town."[59] Finance was particularly frustrated with the failure of munitions and supply to share information with other agencies; thus when the US government requested information on Canada's procurement procedures in August 1940, Mackintosh seized upon it as an opportunity for finance to extract more information for its own purposes. "The attached request from the United States Minister," he wrote to Clark, "would seem to Bryce and myself to provide the smooth stones with which we can slay Goliath. It is suggested that the Minister be asked to speak to Mr. Howe to arrange officials of this Department be given facilities for getting answers to these questions."[60]

Of equal concern to Mackintosh was the growing indication that "a consumption boom is getting under way," which would test the government's capacity to control prices strictly through fiscal measures.[61] To concede that inflation could not be controlled and that wages had to be adjusted accordingly, he decried as "sheer defeatism."[62] As inflationary pressures mounted during the first months of 1941, Grant Dexter of the *Winnipeg Free Press* observed the split between the WPTB and finance over the severity of the threat of inflation, and the policy steps required: the WPTB favoured fiscal measures to offset potential price increases, while finance insisted that stricter and more widespread price controls were in order. Mackintosh accepted that it was possible to rely primarily upon fiscal measures to reduce purchasing power through taxation, such that households would be left with only enough money to buy available output at current prices; however, imposing higher income taxes alone was a "blunt and rigid instrument," leaving an undue burden to fall on lower-income groups. This would, in turn, result in agitation for higher wages and defeat the objective of restricting purchasing power. Complementary action, therefore, was required by the WTPB, to avoid unwarranted price increases on specific goods, and by munitions and supply, so that there were no shortages of specific materials and labour required for war industries.

The alternative was to rely more heavily upon production restrictions in consumption industries to free up resources for military purposes. This would require the WPTB to undertake "sweeping measures to prevent price increases resulting from enforced shortages" and for munitions and supply "to curtail quantities and varieties coming on the market and to do this in accordance with a general policy and not merely in accordance with particular shortages as they emerge."[63] In a personal letter to Frank Knox, he reported that "I have been pressing for a long time for production restrictions, but, so far, have only succeeded in having them apply to motor cars ... I think through the rationing of production and of dealers, we can indirectly ration consumers to a considerable degree. Where, however, there is a tendency to develop queues, it will, doubtless, be necessary to get into the terrific administrative problems of consumer rationing."[64] But he was frustrated by the lack of cooperation from the WTPB and munitions and supply with the efforts of finance.

> It is elementary that policies in these three fields must be co-ordinated if they are to be successful. Current discussions suggest that there is a lack of understanding of what fiscal policy the Government requires because there is no understanding of what that fiscal policy is. Thus, the Prices Board suggests to the Minister that drastic action in respect of prices would be unnecessary if a more drastic fiscal policy were adopted, while the Minister is of the opinion that unless the Prices Board acts decisively his fiscal policy is jeopardized. In the field of commodity

Figure 9.5 Monthly cost-of-living index, Canada, 1939–1945 (1935–1939 = 100)

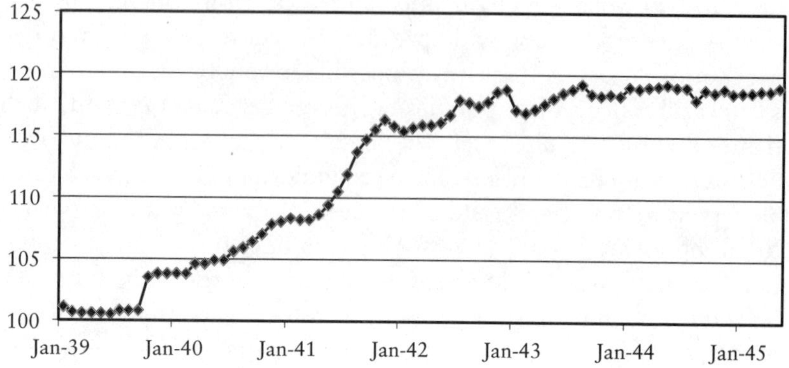

Source: Derived from Canada, Dominion Bureau of Statistics, "Index Numbers of Living Costs in Canada," *Canada Year Book*, 1939–1946.

> controls, there is some indication that Munitions and Supply have no understanding that anything more is required of them than to conserve scarce materials for war needs, and the only liaison, other than through Cabinet, is through Mr. Berkinshaw's membership on the Price's Board.[65]

The introduction of price ceilings in October 1941 gave an apparent victory to finance but, according to Dexter, conflict persisted. "The Bank of Canada, Cliff Clark and Bill Mackintosh, with much less emphasis on Bill, are for the concrete, unyielding ceiling. The Wartime Prices and Trade Board were for the selective ceiling and when this was beaten they desired leeway of 10 per cent or so to adjust prices to prevent undue hardships, breakdowns and perhaps, chaos. As you know, the Bank of Canada has been of the view that the McKinnon Board was not competent to do this job, and Towers has resisted every indication of adjustment in prices."[66] The matter was decisively resolved with the appointment of Donald Gordon to replace McKinnon as head of the WPTB in November 1941 and with Mackintosh's addition to the committee in March 1942.[67]

Regardless of where the credit lay for the attack on inflation, the cost-of-living index, after rising by 17 per cent from the beginning of the war until October 1941, rose by less than 3 per cent until the end of the war, the best record among Allied nations.[68]

Labour Supply

Also alarming to Mackintosh and Bryce was the lack of labour-market planning. In 1940, there was no general shortage of labour, but the expansion of wartime manufacturing industries resulted in a regional and occupational redistribution of employment.[69] Mobilizing additional labour resources required greater geographical labour mobility, as well as training programs to overcome the mismatch between the skills of available workers and demand in job vacancies. As the demand for labour increased, the skills among the available pool of workers – including both youths and women, drawn into the labour force for the first time, and long-term unemployed – were wanting. "Considering the deterioration in employability among the unemployed and the uneven expansion of employment, industrially and geographically, we are unlikely to have an irreducible residue of less than 100,000 'unemployed,' leaving 48,000 to 78,000, almost wholly unskilled, as our reserve of experienced wage-earners of whom another 20,000 to 40,000 will have been drawn upon in the past six weeks." As they put the case, "While labour shortage is not general, it is sufficiently specific and near at hand to make provisions for efficient mobilization and control of labour supply the most urgent of all requirements."[70]

In its advice to the cabinet, the EAC echoed the view that "the impending crisis in the matter of labour supply is acute and of the gravest importance." Among its recommendations were training programs in specific trades that were needed in war industries, the active recruitment of women for industry and for work auxiliary to the armed services; and the withdrawal of skilled and semi-skilled workers from non-essential industries. A cabinet committee struck to consider these proposals endorsed the need for increased training, agreed that the recruitment of women for "light work" connected with war industry should be encouraged in the event of a shortage of male workers, and concurred that "in work other than war industries there appear to be positions where women could be substituted for men, thus adding to the manpower reserves for industry or armed forces." However, it rejected more direct controls over the movement of labour within non-war industries, on the grounds that "the situation at present is not sufficiently acute to warrant interference with the personal and civil rights of individuals."[71] To implement these proposals, the cabinet created the Inter-Departmental Committee on Labour Co-ordination by order-in-council on 25 October 1940. In one of the rare instances that Mackintosh claimed personal credit for a government initiative, he wrote to Norman Robertson that he and Sandy Skelton were chiefly responsible for the committee's formation.[72] It was assigned the authority, under the direction of the department of labour, to ensure an adequate supply of skilled labour, by ascertaining the expected demand for labour, by coordinating dominion and provincial training programs, and by overseeing Employment Services in affecting all job placements. "Basically," Mackintosh wrote, "the Co-ordinator would operate like a General Staff putting plans in practical shape and getting them carried out in proper co-ordination by the operating units of governments and industry."[73]

As a member of the committee, Mackintosh quickly set to work drafting its agenda. In typical fashion, he outlined the need to gather information on the demand for skilled and unskilled labour in war-related industries, and on the reserve of skilled and unskilled workers registered with Employment Services or on relief rolls. Subsequently, it was necessary to ascertain the extent of training programs throughout the country, whether they be in provincial technical schools or within firms, and to define the possibility for increased training opportunities. Then the committee needed to plan the duties and operations of "field men" to direct the necessary actions of matching training positions to anticipated needs and ensuring that Employment Services placed available labour into job vacancies. In an effort to estimate "the quantitative and qualitative reserves of labour now existing," Mackintosh lamented that a "statistical approach to this problem would be of no value because it is a field in which statistics do not exist" and, moreover, that the department of labour "admits that no review of this type has been made or is contemplated."[74] The best forecasts for the year 1941 estimated that labour demand would increase by 300,000, with roughly 120,000 entering into the armed services and 180,000 into war and ancillary industries. The need for unskilled labour could be supplied from a large untapped reserve, while the expected demand for 75,000 skilled workers could be met through provincially-run vocational schools and "plant schools" designed for the training of returning soldiers and older married men. If necessary, provisions for the training of skilled workers would be included in government military production contracts.[75]

The introduction of compulsory military training for men made the encroachment upon individual rights in the civilian labour market less offensive, and regulatory controls were extended and consolidated with the establishment of the National Selective Services (NSS) in March 1942. Through a series of orders-in-council, the NSS required compulsory registration for unemployed men in order to assess the available labour force. Permits were required for all people seeking or entering into employment; advertising of job vacancies was prohibited, to avoid the "poaching" of labour from another employer; the movement of workers out of agricultural industries, as well as into specific occupations and industries, was prohibited without a permit; and employers were required to provide and justify separation notices. By September 1942, consistent with the rules governing conscription for the armed forces, a "greater degree of compulsion" was exercised in directing the flow of workers to particular jobs, with all men capable of serving in the Armed Forces obliged to register and be assigned to particular jobs.[76] The government had thus largely usurped the role of the labour market in matching workers to available jobs.

Whether through planning or ordinary market forces, the labour market performed admirably during the war. Between 1939 and 1944, total employment increased by 1,135,000. There were 243,000 fewer workers in agriculture and an increase of 608,000 in non-agricultural jobs and 770,000 in military service. The demand for workers was met through an additional 660,000 individuals drawn into the labour force (civilian and military) and the remainder met from the ranks of the unemployed. Accordingly, the unemployment rate fell from 11.4 to 1.2 per cent.

Mackintosh's work on the civilian labour supply was sufficiently compelling that Sandy Skelton recommended he be promoted into the ranks of the cabinet. With the press attacking the government for its lack of a coherent manpower policy within the selective services, he urged that King consider Mackintosh as not the deputy minister, but the minister. King quickly dismissed the idea: "I told Sandy," he wrote in his diary, "that there were political aspects to a suggestion of the kind which would have to be considered; to bring in a Minister meant a by-election. No sooner would it start than Meighan or some other Conservative would be in the field. If the government lost the seat it would be a serious matter … [Skelton] used the expression [that Mackintosh was] of the Norman Rogers' tradition.

Figure 9.6 Employment in Canada, by sector, 1939–1945

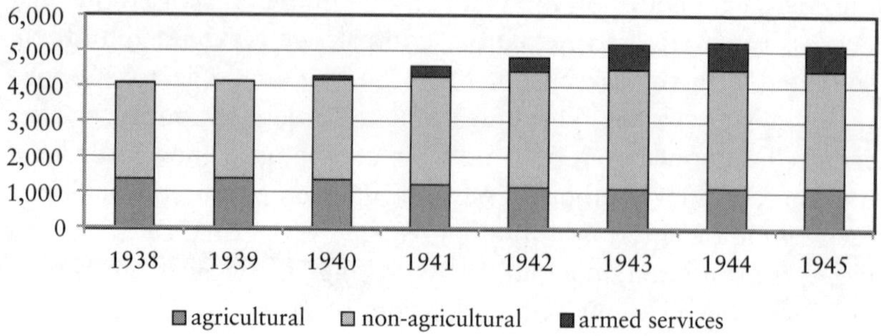

Source: Derived from Statistics Canada, *Historical Statistics of Canada,* 2nd ed., series D 127.

Figure 9.7 Labour force and unemployment rate: Canada, 1939–1945

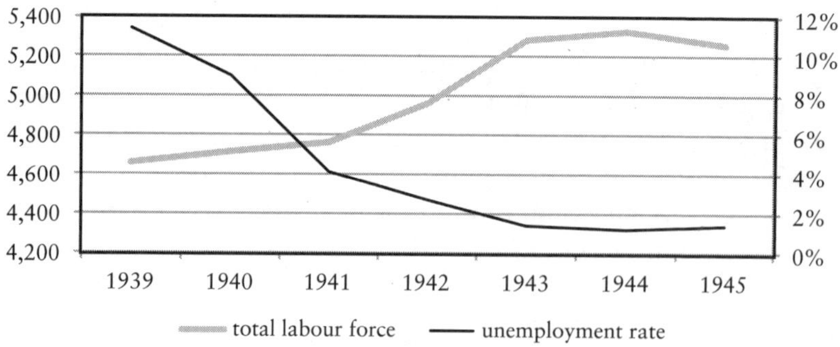

Source: Derived from Statistics Canada, *Historical Statistics of Canada,* 2nd ed., series D 124-133.

This convinces me that I am right in what I surmised, namely that this is another case in point of the intelligentsia trying to run a government on their own lines."[77]

Wages and Industrial Relations

Given the obvious desire to manage capital-labour relations in order to prevent any interruption in war production, the government's approach to industrial relations was both slow and haphazard. When the War Measures Act gave greater federal authority over labour relations, coverage of the antiquated Industrial Disputes Investigations Act (IDIA), with its unique provision for compulsory conciliation prior to a strike or lockout, was extended to all war-related industries, as well as to any other industries upon the consent of the two parties (Privy Council Office Order-in-Council 3495 or PC 3495).[78] In addition, PC 2685 laid out the "Principles for the Avoidance of Labour Unrest during the War," which included statements in support of the rights to join a union and to free collective bargaining. "In this rather piecemeal fashion," notes Stuart Jamieson, "a labor code of sorts had developed on a nationwide basis."[79] However, it was far more notable for what it lacked. In contrast to the Wagner Act, passed in the United States in 1935, there were no provisions for the certification of union bargaining agents or compulsory union recognition that obliged the employer to deal with a certified bargaining agent. As unemployment fell and labour markets tightened, the upsurge in labour militancy exposed the inadequacy of the government's policy.

On the wages front, early long-term contracts issued by the War Supply Board allowed for pay increases tied to the rate of inflation. The EAC endorsed the idea of cost-of-living bonuses, but feared that the government was establishing an undesirable precedent for all workers. Without complementary fiscal and labour-supply policies in place, labour incomes would rise faster than wage rates because of higher employment levels and longer hours of work, triggering increased consumption, rising prices, and further wage-rate increases.[80] Thus, in November 1940, when the western coal industry and the United Mine Workers negotiated a settlement that included cost-of-living bonuses, the EAC acknowledged that the time had come for a wage policy embracing all war-related industries.[81] Therefore PC 7440, enacted in December 1940, set out guidelines for boards of conciliation in their wage recommendations. Existing wages were declared to be "fair" if above 1926–29 levels, and a cost-of-living bonus was to be paid with every increase in the price index above 5 per cent.[82]

Mackintosh acknowledged that greater administrative control over wages encroached upon collective bargaining rights, but portrayed the genesis of voluntary wage guidelines as a compromise between two elements, "a militant unionism in the process of organization which was eager to use demands for higher wages as a bait to attract members" and "employers who, because of the Excess Profits Tax and their antagonism to any union organization, were only too willing to outflank the CIO by granting wage increases in advance."

He insisted that there was no legitimate collective bargaining "unless the employing firm is bargaining with its own money." Moreover, he defended the wage guidelines in PC 7440 as a form of "rough justice," to the extent that they provided lower-paid workers with some protection against inflation. They also promised a more equitable distribution of wages within industries: "The indications are that labour has embarked on an organizing campaign, making their attack exclusively on firms holding war contracts ... the result being that wages are getting out of line in various plants in the same branch of industry."[83] He acknowledged that "The rough-and-ready wage policy being worked out under PC 7440 could not be defended by anyone as an ideal theoretical solution. It is, however, tremendously in advance of anything that has been tried in the United Kingdom, any of the British Dominions or the United States."[84]

He also defended the wages policy against criticisms from the other end of the political spectrum. R.J. Deachman, a friend and former Liberal MP, wrote to argue that it was unfair to raise workers' wages at a time when agricultural incomes were fixed or falling. "I should have no objection to breaking a lance with you if it were not that you have ridden off in the wrong direction," responded Mackintosh. "I quite agree with you that it is, and will be, a serious matter if we allow industrial wages to rise greatly while farm income stays down. I do not think, however, that you will persuade the industrial worker of the desirability of your policy simply by telling him that he is better off than the farmer and he shouldn't be."[85] Similarly, Gilbert Jackson, the Toronto economist, favoured a total wage freeze, and suggested that the extension of PC 7440 would be highly inflationary by increasing the country's total wage bill. Mackintosh replied that to freeze wages was an "entirely fanciful" proposal and that the cost-of-living bonus, introduced at a time of extremely tight labour markets, moderated wage increases and did not guarantee the standard of living of workers. Instead, it called upon workers "to share in such sacrifices as the war may make necessary for the whole nation."[86]

With the advent of price controls in October 1941, the voluntary wage guidelines of PC 7440 were replaced by the Wartime Wages and Cost of Living Bonus Order (PC 8253) and extended throughout all industries. Wage rates were based on the level prevailing on 15 November 1941, with a cost-of-living bonus to be added only when the price index rose above 10 per cent. Enforcement machinery was established under the National War Labour Board with the help of nine regional War Labour Boards.[87]

Even if wage controls were deemed a justifiable encroachment upon collective bargaining rights, their imposition did not avert an industrial-relations crisis by 1943. Rising unionization and the government's failure to invoke compulsory union recognition, led to a sharp increase in the incidence of strikes, as many employers refused to negotiate with duly certified bargaining agents. Moreover, strikes in key wartime industries, such as coal, steel, and military-related industries, resulted in negotiated agreements that violated the wage guidelines, leaving observers such as Walter Gordon pessimistic about the ability to maintain wage-and-price controls in their present form. "The best course," he argued, "would seem to be for the government to retreat some distance and then to re-establish its lines again."[88] But the EAC remained steadfast in the face of increasing labour unrest. The tripartite National War Labour Board (NWLB) filed a review of the government's wage and industrial-relations policy in September 1943, and the report was sent to the EAC for its consideration.[89] The EAC agreed that the existing order needed a thorough revision, but reaffirmed the need for strict wage controls on the grounds that stabilization policy could not be maintained if awards continued at the prevailing rate.[90] The EAC did endorse the NWLB's recommendation for compulsory union recognition, on the grounds that "it is desirable and indeed inevitable in any democratic state under a system of private enterprise that collective bargaining should become the rule with few, if any, exceptions." More to the point, it insisted that "only a wholehearted and thorough-going acceptance of compulsory collective bargaining will regain the confidence of labour." With passage of the Labour Relations Regulations (PC 1003), in February 1944, the main components of the U.S Wagner Act were adopted in Canada: the right of workers to organize, the machinery to define and certify bargaining units, compulsory collective bargaining, and the establishment of labour-relations boards for enforcement. In so doing, the basis for the postwar industrial-relations system in Canada was established.[91]

The government also faced labour unrest within its own ranks. The tremendous growth in the size and complexity of the civil service during the war resulted in many ad hoc arrangements in personnel administration. For the six-year period from 1938 to 1943, total appointments under the Civil Service Act rose from 6,406 to 56,342, with over fifty different agencies in the public service hiring staff and setting their own pay scales. Dissatisfaction among employees with seemingly arbitrary treatment was compounded by wartime policies: promotions and job reclassifications were suspended; a maximum salary of $3,000 was imposed, so that some qualified for cost-of-living bonuses, while other did not; temporary wartime appointments recruited from private industry were typically paid more than permanent employees; and there was inadequate compensation for overtime work.[92] The resulting morale problems prompted the creation, in May 1944, of the National Joint Council of the Public Service of Canada (NJC) as an employer-employee consultative body. Despite the government's comparison of the NJC to Whitley Councils in the British public service, it differed in two important respects that limited the power of workers: the absence of compulsory arbitration in the event that the two sides (the government and staff associations) failed to reach an agreement left the government with an effective veto over any recommendations; and rates of pay were, with one exception, excluded from consideration.[93] The NJC thus reflected the "sovereign employer" theory that "the Queen does not negotiate": any parallel to private-sector collective bargaining in the civil service would be infringing upon the authority of parliament. This left the NJC with a purely advisory role over aspects of working conditions.

Mackintosh was appointed chair of the NJC, later describing himself as the "the only inoffensive acceptable person," but claimed no credit for its creation ("it was a responsibility that was thrust upon me and not the result of any planning on my own part."[94]) Reflecting upon the NJC a decade later, he held that it was unrealistic to expect it to engage in collective bargaining. "In considering the exclusion of actual wage bargaining from the Council you must bear in mind that it was set up at a time when there was a wage and salary ceiling and that there were very serious rivalries and overlapping among staff associations, it being very difficult to get them to agree on fair representation. Furthermore the experience and capacity of the staff associations varied greatly and was not in any case extensive. In terms of the content of 1944 it would have been illogical if not impossible to make the Joint Council a salary-negotiating body."[95] Indeed, the NJC was to consist of six staff and six government representatives, but the rivalries among staff associations in the Post Office necessitated that the number of staff representatives be expanded to nine, since no agreement could be reached on a single representative from among Post Office employees. The distrust among staff associations spilled over into the NJC's proceedings. As one representative explained to Mackintosh "we represent two distinct movements which cannot be reconciled, the Amalgamated Civil Servants and the Federated Association of Letter Carriers, and the Federated Association of Letter Carriers is out to fight them to the last ditch. We have been at it for twenty-six years now, and there is no possibility of compromise."[96]

Despite the general exclusion of salary matters from its deliberations, the first issue addressed by the NJC in August 1944 was whether some postal clerks should receive a pay increase. The staff side made the case that basic pay in the civil service was effectively frozen in May 1940, eighteen months before similar controls imposed in the private sector.[97] When the NJC recommended that the moratorium on reclassifications be lifted, that full cost-of-living bonuses be paid to those within the $2,100 to $3,000 salary range, and that statutory increases in salaries for those making more than $3,000 be resumed, Fred Whitehouse, the representative of the Association of Canadian Postal Employees, extended his personal thanks to Mackintosh: "I am convinced that this first action of the National Joint Council will impress all civil servants, and they, too, will be convinced that the Council will really function in the interests of civil servants which will, no doubt, bring about ultimately that much desired spirit of understanding and co-operation between the Official and Staff Side of the Government Service." His enthusiasm was no doubt tempered two months later; after consideration by the Treasury Board, Ilsley refused to act on the recommendations.[98]

Upon his resignation in 1946, the NJC expressed its "keen regret": "Dr. Mackintosh filled the post as chairman admirably, that his wise counsel was a major factor in initiating the work of the Council under promising auspices, and the activities to date have been made much more effective by reason of his sound guidance." Clark described the tribute as "only too well deserved. I wish there was another Mackintosh to take your place." Mackintosh responded that "I do not count [the NJC] one of my great successes, though on the whole, the relations have been kept from going sour."[99] The NJC would eventually lead to the formation of the Public Service Alliance of Canada.

THE MANAGED ECONOMY

The rapid transformation of the Canadian economy allowed as much as 45 per cent of productive capacity to be harnessed for the war effort. When imposed on a pre-war economy that rested heavily upon primary industries, the creation of wartime industries was, in Mackintosh's view, nothing short of an industrial revolution. Not only did government directly oversee close to half of the economy through its war-related purchases, personal consumption was subjected to rigid price and quantity controls, private investment to procurement restrictions, and merchandise trade to foreign exchange, export permits, and import restrictions. On the supply side, labour markets came under increasing regulations, wage controls were imposed, and industrial relations were recast. What made these changes all the more extraordinary is that they were undertaken as a learning-by-doing experiment, based on a series of pragmatic steps to find "adequate solutions to problems as they arose." By whatever means, the result was to define a new role for the state in the construction of a managed economy, many aspects of which – including a modernized tax structure, industrial-relations regulations, and tentative steps towards national income accounting – persisted into the postwar period. In effect, it entailed creating from the ground up the government infrastructure to complement, and in many cases supplant, market mechanisms for allocating resources.

Such policy was only possible because of the broad public support for government economic management. The success of "pay-as-you-go" fiscal policy and strict controls over prices and wages were only effective because they were embraced as fair in distributing the burdens of war across social classes. Having personally witnessed the social unrest during the Winnipeg General Strike at the end of World War I, Mackintosh was intent to "avoid the gross inequities and the disorganizing effects of inflationary increases in prices and incomes."[100] While PC 1003 and the NJC laid the groundwork for unionization in private and public sectors respectively, there is no escaping the fact that the government's industrial-relations policy during the war represented a serious encroachment on collective bargaining rights by limiting the scope of wage negotiations. Mackintosh termed it a "regrettable limitation." However, he maintained that organized labour was in a stronger position due to wartime stabilization policy than it would have been riding the roller coaster of the business cycle. Although McIvor cautions against placing confidence in the cost-of-living index during the war, the evidence suggests that the distribution of the burden of war finance was favourable to both farmers and workers. Between 1939 and 1945, the index of the farm price of agricultural products rose from 91.8 to 176.5 (1935–39 = 100), at a much greater rate than farm operating costs (99.5 to 123.5). Similarly, the index of average wage rates in ten major groups of industries rose from 105.3 to 147.8, well in excess of the cost-of-living index (101.5 to 119.5).[101]

Striking the "delicate balance" in the distribution of the cost of the war among social classes was, for Mackintosh, essential to maintaining the goodwill and social institutions on which Canadian society rested.

10

International Reconstruction: Ottawa, London, Washington, and Bretton Woods, 1941–1946

Said Halifax to Keynes,
"I think it's rather funny
That we've got all the brains
And they've got all the money."

Said Keynes to Halifax,
"I agree that it is rummy
That though we have *our* brains
We still can't get *their* money."

Said Ilsley to himself
"'Twould seem the dice are weighted
But as far as brains and pelf,
Perhaps they're both inflated."[1]

Canada's interest in the international institutions governing postwar reconstruction was governed by the single principle of multilateralism. Canadian officials adopted the consistent refrain that international monetary and trade reform had to avoid bilateral or regional trade and currency blocs. Canada was not unique in endorsing a multilateral world, but it was certainly among the most vociferous in doing so, because a heavy reliance on exports left it with more at stake in ensuring that world markets remained relatively open in the postwar period.[2] It also occupied a unique position in the realignment of world power that accompanied America's economic ascendancy and the United Kingdom's descent: Canada enjoyed the preferential access to British markets that the imperial system afforded, and yet was one of the few Commonwealth countries remaining outside of the sterling currency area. If sterling convertibility was not ensured, the only plausible alternative was a greater dependence on continental trade and, by extension, closer economic relations with the United States. In the postwar period, Mackintosh insisted that "collaboration with the United States, or with the hemisphere, if either is based on exclusiveness, can only be the last resort of economic policy for Canada."[3]

Canadian officials thus attempted to mediate what would prove to be difficult Anglo-American negotiations over postwar economic arrangements. Talks took place under the auspices of Article VII of the US–UK lend-lease agreement, in which, as consideration for the financial support provided by the United States during the war, the United Kingdom agreed to address postwar economic relations. Discussions centred on a monetary agreement to ensure exchange-rate stability (leading to the formation of the International Monetary Fund), an investment agreement directed primarily at the reconstruction and rehabilitation of Europe (the International Bank for Reconstruction and Development), and a commercial agreement designed to lower trade barriers (the aborted International Trade Organization). A related concern was providing financial support to Britain in the immediate postwar period. That the terms of Article VII included a commitment "to the elimination of all forms of discriminatory treatment in international commerce" meant that the negotiations would be extremely difficult. With the United States intent on "destroying" the pre-war British imperial system based on preferential tariffs and the sterling currency area, and the United Kingdom seeking whatever leverage available to preserve a measure of its international power, conflict was inevitable. Keynes declared at an early stage that it would be "madness" for Britain to abandon elements of its imperial system in order to embrace a freer movement of trade and currency until it had sufficient time to recover some of its lost export markets and reduce its international debt incurred in fighting the war. The United States, in contrast, held what Mackintosh repeatedly referred to as "theological convictions" with respect to "the iniquity of the British preferences," while showing little interest in radical reductions in its own high tariff structure.[4]

Much has also been made of the personalities involved in Anglo-American negotiations, with the combination of Harry Dexter White's "instinctive prejudices against the ruling class of a decaying empire" and Keynes's legendary intemperance resulting, at times, in what James Meade described as a "strident duet of discord" and a "crescendo of abuse."[5] If people did matter to the outcome, Canada was well-served. Mackintosh, Louis Rasminsky, Graham Towers, and other officials exercised a technical expertise and diplomatic aplomb that was widely recognized and eagerly sought. Dennis Robertson referred to the "very compact and able Canadian team" engaged in discussions with American officials. For Keynes, "the Canadians have been more successful than any other interviewees [with the Americans] in getting to grips, partly because they are not unduly nervous about how to handle the American Treasury and partly because they are exceptionally well informed on these matters," and he was sufficiently impressed by Towers to recommend him as governor of the Bank of England. To these plaudits, Lionel Robbins, a LSE economist working for the British government during the war, added his own: "How refreshing these Canadians are. My own private view is that if they rather than UK officials had led for the Commonwealth, policy all around would be much more effective and much more intelligent. What a wonderful flowering it is which has produced Robertson, Wrong, Pearson, Mackintosh, and Rasminsky."[6]

For his part, Mackintosh would represent Canada in London on four occasions and in Washington numerous times, was the effective head of the Canadian delegation at Bretton Woods, and served in various auspices at the United Nations. This work brought him into contact with Keynes, Robertson, Robbins, Meade, Richard Stone, Wilfred Eady, Cameron Cobbold, and other British economists in the Treasury, Board of Trade, and Bank of England. In Washington he would encounter radical "proto-Keynesian" economists, including White and Canadian-born Lauchlin Currie (two members of the "Freshman Brain Trust" in Washington recruited by Jacob Viner) and a younger generation of Keynesian economists. Among them were Frank Coe, Charles P. Kindleberger, John Kenneth Galbraith, Edward Bernstein, Alvin Hansen, and Walter Salant (to whom Keynes remarked, "Well, I have to tell you that you are more Keynesian than I am"[7]). It would also result in a long friendship between Mackintosh and Rasminsky, based on a deep mutual respect and admiration.[8] They were the two most important officials representing Canada in international trade and currency talks and, as a fitting testament to their contributions, Rasminsky would be nominated as Canada's executive director of the International Monetary Fund and Mackintosh as the executive director of the International Bank for Reconstruction and Development.

Yet despite their efforts, Canada failed to achieve the goal of multilateralism to forestall Canada's increased economic dependence on the United States.

PRELUDE: THE CANADA–US JOINT ECONOMIC COMMITTEES

Canada's initial foray into the area of postwar planning occurred with the creation of the Canada–United States Joint Economic Committees (JECs) in June 1941. Struck at the behest of Canada's department of external affairs, the principal task of the JECs was to facilitate the integration of North American resources in the production of defence requirements, as expressed in the Hyde Park Declaration; secondarily, they were also given a broader mandate to explore avenues to minimize postwar dislocation.[9] R.A.C. Henry, special advisor to the minister of munitions and supply, was to chair the Canadian committee but, upon his illness, the duty fell to Mackintosh. The Canadian side also included G.C. Bateman (metals controller, munitions and supply), Georges Bouchard (assistant deputy minister, agriculture), Sandy Skelton (Bank of Canada), H.L. Keenleyside (assistant undersecretary of state, external affairs), H.F. Angus (external affairs) as liaison officer, and J.J. Deutsch (Bank of Canada) as secretary. The American committee was chaired by Alvin Hansen (Federal Reserve Board) and included W.L. Batt (War Production Board), E. Dana Durand (Tariff Commission), White (Treasury), A.A. Berle (assistant secretary of state), L.D. Stinebower (state department) as liaison officer, and Kindleberger (Federal Reserve System) as secretary. Other economists who participated at times on the American side including Frank Coe, Walter Salant and three Canadian-born men, Lauchlin Currie, John Kenneth Galbraith, and Jacob Viner.

From the outset, Mackintosh was skeptical about the role the JECs could play, a sentiment shared by White. Convinced that communications between Ottawa and Washington on matters of defence production should be channelled through the appropriate departments, Mackintosh maintained retrospectively that the creation of the JECs was "based on a false assumption, namely, the desideratum was a fresh contact between the two governments. On the contrary, the problem was the rapid multiplication of contacts and the inability of External Affairs and the State Department to exercise an effective coordinating influence ... Any hope that the Joint Economic Committees could achieve this co-ordination seems to me completely unreal."[10] Indeed, one month before the announcement of the JECs, much of their role was usurped by the joint US–Canadian Materials Coordinating Committee designed to integrate the supply of raw materials for military production. Mackintosh confessed privately to C.H. Herbert of the WPTB that "I cannot say that I am bursting with ideas for its activity," and when Sandy Skelton outlined an ambitious agenda for the committees that covered all aspects of Canadian–US economic integration, Mackintosh responded that he found that the "full implications of such a programme are somewhat terrifying."[11] Despite these misgivings, the JECs were very active during the first year: the Canadian committee met twenty times, and there were ten joint sessions, leading to recommendations on export-control regulations, the allocation of shipping space for Canadian exports overseas, reciprocal tariff reductions on agricultural goods, restrictions on civilian consumption, and liberalizing travel across the border.[12] With the recommendation in October 1941 that a Joint War Production Committee coordinate the procurement of military goods and assign production between the two countries (to complement the Materials Production Committee), the JECs' immediate mandate was met, and it turned its attention to postwar planning.

To this end, a bold statement was issued on 5 December 1941: "To achieve a just and durable peace in an economically interdependent world, the signatory governments recognize their common responsibility to collaborate with one another in promoting full employment, increasing production, expanding markets, improving standards of living, and fostering social security and economic stability throughout the world."[13] In forwarding the JECs' recommendation to Mackenzie King, Mackintosh outlined in dire terms the implications for Canada of American isolationism or a retreat by the United Kingdom behind the imperial trade and currency barriers:

> Unless the United States follows post-war an expansive employment and trade policy and contributes substantially to international investment, the United Kingdom will face an acute shortage of US dollars and may be persuaded or indeed forced

> to try to use its bargaining power as an import market to achieve a series of discriminatory trade and clearing agreements with the object of ensuring that those countries dependent on its markets for the sale of their agricultural products and raw materials shall equally purchase their requirements in that market. In such circumstances, Canada, who has been dependent on selling the sterling proceeds of her exports for US dollars to pay the United States for imports and interest, would face a painful dilemma. She could not continue her wartime practice of selling her exports for sterling which was unusable. She would have to obtain her imports from those markets which took her exports or she should have to find other exports which could be sold in the markets from which she desired to import ... It is only by promoting and participating in a collaboration between the United States and the United Kingdom, with the threefold object of developing co-ordinated policies for maintaining employment, ensuring relative freedom of trade, and contributing to productive international investment, that Canada can find after the war the large world economy necessary to her tolerable existence.[14]

Bryce describes the JECs' declaration as "an international New Deal ... made possible by the zeal of a selected group of early Keynesian economists." But he also points out its major shortcoming: issued just one day before the attack on Pearl Harbor, it was largely ignored on both sides of the border.[15]

The committees pressed on, however, and, in August 1942, issued a *Tentative Draft of a Joint Report on Canadian-United States Relations in the Post-War Period*, which sketched out economic relations between the two countries and the implications for postwar collaboration.[16] Economic integration prior to the war had been modest, because tariff protection limited merchandise trade to a handful of commodities (US exports of capital goods, fruit, cotton, coal and oil, and Canadian exports of newsprint and metals); indeed, reciprocal tourism flows tended to exceed commodity flows in value. Financial integration, in contrast, had increased, with New York largely replacing London as the source of most Canadian foreign borrowing. The war increased the coordination of military production, but controls over exports, imports, foreign exchange, and labour mobility otherwise drove a greater wedge between the two economies.

This dictated attention to a few issues of a purely bilateral nature, especially the orderly conversion of the wartime industries to peacetime purposes. Arguing that "a war economy is essentially a metals economy," expanded capacity in iron, steel, nickel, magnesium, copper, lead, zinc, and aluminum, as well as the chemical and machine tools industries had to be addressed, without incurring a substantial decline in output and employment. The draft report recommended reducing tariff barriers to increase North American integration "on a selective basis," coordination of anti-depression policies through the timing of possible joint development projects (such as the construction of the Alaska Highway), irrigation, and soil and forest conservation. On the financial side, it recommended that Canada remove its foreign-exchange controls "cautiously," but as quickly as possible, while the United States should support Canada's monetary reserves until the reconstruction of Europe restored traditional Canadian export markets.

But the report's emphasis was on defining a set of common objectives for "world economic collaboration." To re-establish economic relations in a fractured world economy required financial and material support for reconstruction and, in the longer-term, the restoration of trade and investment flows through reductions in tariff barriers, stabilization of commodity prices, economic development in "backward areas," and exchange-rate stabilization. It acknowledged the United States leadership role by virtue of its financial and economic power, and its need to make available the foreign exchange to allow European countries to rebuild. Canada too was expected to be a net lender to Europe, but faced its own unique problems. The war had brought increasing industrialization but also the loss of many traditional export markets for agricultural goods such as tobacco, wheat, and other foodstuffs; moreover, it was anticipated that Canada's "awkward" foreign-exchange position would persist and likely worsen, with further accumulation of sterling reserves and the persistence of a current-account deficit with the United States.[17]

When the draft report evoked little response, both sides acknowledged that the usefulness of the JECs had run its course. Over the opposition of munitions and supplies and some officials in external affairs, Mackintosh argued for their disbandment: "There was no disposition on the part of External Affairs or the State Department to use the Committees. Virtually everything that was done was initiated by the Committees themselves ... In a number of cases the intervention of the Committees was not welcome."[18] Keenleyside added that there was a lack of attention to postwar problems on the part of both governments, leaving the JECs with little policy direction, and, as such, their work was being largely ignored.[19] Kindleberger's impression from the American vantage point was that production people on both sides "asked not to be bothered … Our role was largely one of effecting introductions."[20] Nor did Mackintosh find much support for postwar planning among both governments. "Washington has, on the whole, been more backward on definite moves [for postwar planning] than either London or Ottawa … they are extremely nervous about the whole situation. Of course, individuals in Washington are very eager to discuss and promote various ideas, but one has no assurance that he is talking to any responsible part of the administration."[21] He was reluctant to engage further in bilateral talks when "Nearly all the broader problems of collaboration, both wartime and postwar, proved to extend beyond Canada-US relationship."[22] He so informed Hansen that "we have gone far enough to encounter the difficulties of postwar planning on a bilateral basis. Indeed, the discussions have led us to the conclusion that a major object should be to escape the necessity of working on a bilateral basis … The fact that wartime collaboration does, and must increasingly involve all the United Nations, whether on an equal or unequal footing, reduces greatly the effectiveness of bilateral committees such as ours."[23] With other initiatives already under way, the role of the JECs ended.

THE FUND, THE BANK, AND BRETTON WOODS

By the fall of 1941, White, on behalf of the US Treasury, and Keynes, as an "unofficial advisor" with Britain's chancellor of the exchequer, were simultaneously crafting plans for a supranational bank to facilitate international currency stability. Common to their thinking was the need to provide short-term credit facilities to avoid exchange-rate volatility: with many European countries expected to run significant trade deficits in the period of reconstruction, a pool of reserves larger than that afforded by the gold standard was needed to allow them to finance these debits without resorting to the "race to the bottom" in competitive currency devaluation that occurred in the 1930s. It was also necessary to avoid "blocked balances": currency had to be freely convertible, so that a debt with one country could be paid out of the surplus with another. Both were a precondition to liberalized trade on a multilateral basis.

Anglo-American discussions under the terms of Article VII began in August 1942, but were placed in abeyance until after the November US elections. Britain thus took the opportunity to invite the dominions and India for an "informal exchange of views," and Hume Wrong (external affairs), Rasminsky, and Mackintosh (nominally in his role on the JEC) flew to London to represent Canada. The novelty, and discomfort, of flying across the Atlantic in the "chilly belly" of a Lancaster bomber – regular transatlantic passenger air service had begun only a few years earlier – was compounded by their flight being delayed two days by weather conditions. They arrived in London on 23 October 1942, the opening day of a two-week conference. To add to the experience, the scheduled meeting on the last day was cancelled, given the "imminent departure of the Canadian delegation." However, as it would work out, there was no need to rush to get to the airport. A disruption in air travel would leave them scrambling for the first available plane or ship, and it was nearly a month before they could arrange passage back to Canada.[24]

This was Mackintosh's first opportunity to see Keynes in action, and Keynes was on his best behaviour; indeed, Rasminsky reported that he was rude only once.[25] The meetings covered a range of topics, including postwar commercial relations, the stabilization of primary commodity prices, reconstruction investment, the regulation of international cartels, and national income accounting. However, they centred on Keynes's detailed presentation of his "Proposal for an International Clearing Union." The Clearing Union was to be, in effect, an international central bank, through which payments for all transactions would eventually clear. Short-term credit would be extended to countries through overdrafts, common in the British banking system: a country with a debit imbalance with another country could run an overdraft up to the limit of their predetermined quota. The creditor country, in turn, would have to accept payment in the form of a credit balance with the Clearing Union, which it could use in payment for any other international transactions. Equipped with its own currency – the bancor – the Clearing Union would have a form of monetary reserves independent of gold – as long as countries were willing to accept bancor as a payment for its exports. There was no limit on the bancor reserves that could be created. Moreover, as a unit of account, changes in a country's bancor holdings was a ready indicator of its balance-of-payments situation.

In return for overdraft privileges, a member country was obliged to maintain its exchange rate within a limited range and to undertake, when deemed necessary by the Clearing Union, the appropriate domestic policy to address a current account imbalance. Pressure on debtor countries came in two forms: interest payments on the overdraft and a limitation on the size of the overdraft relative to the country's quota. A country's right to devalue its currency without the permission of the Clearing Union was limited to 5 per cent a year after it had used over 25 per cent of its quota. There was also pressure on creditor countries to take remedial action. Largely in response to the perception of the United States as an irresponsible creditor nation during the 1930s – when its protected domestic market prevented other countries from correcting a current-account deficit by exporting more – credit balances were also subject to interest payments. Nor could a creditor accumulate bancor above its quota, forcing it either to forgive debts or to accept exports in return.

Rasminsky and Mackintosh were each struck by the elegance and simplicity of the overdraft system, but pointed out the obvious bias against creditor countries that would make the proposal unacceptable to the United States: expected to be the largest, if not the only, creditor country in the immediate postwar period, it faced an open-ended liability, since member countries could vote to raise quotas.[26] Rasminsky also suggested that interest charges on credit balances and the limitation on holding credit balances above a country's quota would be a hard to explain to the US Congress. As he later quipped, "it is not generally considered to be good banking to have the debtors control the bank."[27] Moreover, there were insufficient safeguards against a country adopting a policy of devaluation. Mackintosh offered the scenario in which a country deliberately maintained a high debit balance in order to give it the freedom to devalue, a point that Keynes conceded, and he subsequently amended his proposal to place further limitations a country's unilateral right to devalue its currency.[28]

Apart from the details, the overriding significance of the Clearing Union proposal was that Keynes firmly embraced a multilateral approach to postwar monetary and commercial arrangements. As late as September 1941, he was still adhering to the view that, given the scale of its anticipated postwar current-account deficit, Britain's only short-term path was to pursue bilateral trade arrangements wherein it used access to its market for foodstuffs as leverage to open up export markets for its manufacturing industry.[29] After attending a meeting of the Council on Foreign Relations in January 1942, Rasminsky had observed that the "bilateralist views are losing ground in the UK and that even Keynes now is shifting his ground because he feels that attempts at UK bilateralism will lead to serious political friction with the United States."[30] Given the opposition within British circles towards freer trade and currency movements, Rasminsky declared the 1942 Commonwealth talks as the intellectual high point of the discussions leading up to the Bretton Woods agreement. "I think it would be very difficult to overestimate the importance of the conversion of Keynes to multilateralism," he stated. "The forces operating on the other side were very strong. If Keynes had not come down on the side of multilateralism we might have had quite a different situation after the war."[31] Keynes for his part described the 1942 London talks as "an outstanding success – really a model of what sensible, constructive international discussion should be."[32]

Six months later, in April 1943, Rasminsky, Mackintosh, and Deutsch, accompanied by Wynne Plumptre from the Canadian legation, were in Washington to work through the details of White's American Stabilization Fund proposal with White and Edward Bernstein.[33] The original "White Plan" had a "mixed bag of currencies" totalling $5 billion, created by member countries that deposited an amount of gold, national currency, or securities equal to their assigned quota. A country that experienced a balance-of-payments deficit could borrow any currency it required, up to the amount of its quota, to meet its obligations. Countries could only devalue their currency in situations of "disequilibrium" and with the permission of the fund, over which the United States would effectively exercise a veto. It would be, in Bryce's words, "a small, powerful organization controlled by the US."[34]

White also initially equipped his fund with its own currency – the Unitas – but this was little more than a bookkeeping device, because its value (equal to US$10) was tied to gold. In appearance, then, the "White Plan" merely constituted a restoration of the gold standard, since all exchange rates would be stated in their gold equivalent and the credit facilities limited by the contributions based on gold equivalents. But it did prevent countries from unilaterally altering their exchange rates and placed obligations on them to undertake specific steps to adjust their balance-of-payments position. Creditor countries were also forced to make adjustments through the manner in which "scarce currencies" were treated. If the United States (or any other country) amassed large credits to the point that its currency became scarce, other countries could apply a range of protective and discriminatory measures "with impunity" against this country in an effort to redress the imbalance. Because it gave debtor countries such power, the British initially doubted that US officials understood the implications of the clause. Following White's assurance that the purpose of the ill-drafted clause was a lever to ensure that the United States government would take appropriate measures to prevent the development of such crisis conditions, Keynes remarked that "this American olive branch in the interests of international co-operation was worth everything else in the scheme put together."[35]

As they worked through the plan on a clause-by-clause basis, Rasminsky, with input from Mackintosh, identified four major flaws. First, a reserve of $5 billion was too small to address the anticipated current-account deficits in the postwar period. (When Bernstein insisted that it would be adequate based upon the net balance-of-payments positions of countries in the 1936–38 period, Rasminsky replied that "One of the objects of the fund should be to avoid what happened during 1936–38."[36]) Second, there was confusion over how the fund might use its reserves and credit facilities. From an accounting perspective, if the fund sold a country's currency for purposes other than current-account transactions, the virtue of the clearing-union proposal as a device for automatically revealing the country's balance-of-payments position would be lost. More vexing was that the fund could make decisions regarding the buying and selling of a currency or take action in the event of a country's currency becoming scarce, without the country's approval. White acknowledged that "You have given us something to think about" and agreed that the appropriate clauses would need to be rewritten.[37] Third, the fund would set a country's exchange rate upon its entry, since, as White argued, to do otherwise would result in "interminable bilateral discussions." Mackintosh noted that in practice such discussions would be unavoidable: larger countries would have little avenue for exiting the fund once in, so that an acceptable exchange rate was an obvious precondition for entry. The Canadians were thus invited to propose alternative wording.[38] Finally, the distribution of voting rights gave the US an effective veto over all decisions (the US would have roughly 25 per cent of voting rights, and a four-fifths majority was required for most important decisions). Mackintosh suggested that, apart from the political concern of reassuring the US Congress, this was a clumsy means of attempting to protect creditor countries from unlimited demands by debtor countries. Canada, for instance, could not adjust its exchange rate without the approval of the United States. He thus proposed, as a more "rational and very much more palatable" solution, giving all creditor countries, and not just the United States, greater voting power on some matters. White conceded that these were "excellent points," which he would incorporate into the subsequent draft of the fund proposal.[39]

Publication of revised Clearing Union and Stabilization Fund proposals left Canadian officials with a decision about how to proceed. There were several possibilities, at least in theory. One was to press for tripartite talks, but Mackintosh told Clark as early as May 1942 that he doubted the likelihood of "forcing ourselves into the discussions," and that some other avenue had to be found, for "if these discussions go on without our intervention, we will have very little opportunity later to influence decisions."[40] A second possibility was to acquiesce to the British view by supporting a unified Commonwealth position.[41] Yet as much as Canada shared an interest in ensuring that the United States behave as a responsible international creditor, it had more in common with the American position, by virtue of the expectation that it would be a net international lender in the postwar period. Third, Canada might seek to continue its de facto role as a mediator, but the fear was that an "unsatisfactory situation" was developing, in which the Americans and British might not talk at all to each other, but would instead seek to rally the support of other countries behind their respective plans.[42] As such, it was deemed "tactically wise" to produce a "Canadian Plan" – first suggested by Plumptre – that merged elements of the Stabilization Fund and Clearing Union proposals as the best way of advancing discussions, rather than working from one proposal or the other. This would also be politically expedient, by allowing third countries, and not just Canada, to enter into discussions without having to choose sides. Mackintosh also added the curious rationale – both in a brief for Ilsley and later in a letter to Keynes – that, in light of the isolationist tendencies of the US Congress and the financial conservatism of the American banking system, Canada's entry into discussions might facilitate the acceptance of a currency plan. "The United States Treasury does not command a great deal of support in the country or in Congress," he argued. "Canada has, on the other hand, an almost embarrassingly high position in banking and financial circles in the United States and is not without reputation in Congress where we at least have no taint of the New Deal about us."[43]

Rasminsky was at work on a "Canadian Plan" as early as March 1943, and produced his preliminary "General Observations of Canadian Experts" and "Summary of Proposals" by 20 May 1943.[44] Either the White plan or the Keynes plan could be "made to work," in that they combined access to short-term credit with pressure on countries to make long-term adjustments to remedy an adverse balance-of-payments situation, and were multilateral in the sense that credits accrued with one country could be used to pay the debits with another.[45] The fundamental differences were that the open-ended obligations on creditor countries meant that the Clearing Union had little prospect of being accepted in Washington, while the lack of exchange-rate flexibility in White's fund would meet with objections in the United Kingdom. Rasminsky thus proposed a US-style contributory fund of roughly twice the size, enlarged by greater contributions and by agreed-upon lines of credit, to create a more active institution. In terms of national sovereignty, it struck a compromise between US rigidity and UK flexibility with respect to the right to devalue currency and maintain exchange controls; it also eliminated the US veto by providing less-objectionable safeguards for creditor countries.[46]

Having received authorization to engage in further discussions with the United States, Mackintosh informed White that a Canadian delegation would be ready by 15 June to present the "Canadian Plan" to a number of countries invited to Washington to discuss White's fund proposal.[47] While Towers, Clark, Rasminsky, Deutsch, and Plumptre were in Washington for this purpose, Mackintosh was in London for Commonwealth talks on commercial policy. After an informal meeting with British officials, he was sufficiently concerned about the British reaction to the Canadian Plan that he cabled Norman Robertson, advising him to postpone its release until after there was an opportunity to reflect on the outcome of the London meetings. "United Kingdom fears the finality and finished quality (flattery) of our plan may prevent adequate discussion of their points.

They would also like to be satisfied in conference on United States attitude before abandoning their position ... [David] Waley of opinion that United States would feel that our draft represented what British would be willing to concede and refuse to be persuaded that it did not."[48] Rasminsky, however, would present the Canadian Plan in Washington the next day, with White's blessing.[49]

The British were not amused, and Rasminsky was "somewhat sore and bewildered" by the reception of the Canadian plan in London.[50] "We were much upset by the Canadian draft," Keynes told Dennis Robertson. "It all seems a great misfortune. The Canadian redraft is, of course, a great improvement so far as it goes. All the changes are for the better, and the drafting has been improved or made much clearer in many points of detail. But this makes one all the sorrier that it has been put in so definitely at this stage. For at a later date and with some further changes it might have been so easy for Canada to take the really decisive part of producing a mediated scheme. Really a most awful pity."[51] Keynes insisted that he did not object to Canada "using its good offices" to produce a synthesis of the two proposals, but that the time was not right: "I am sure it would be a mistake to produce anything of the sort until the compulsion of public opinion from all parts of the world has convinced Washington that some considerable measure of compromise ought to be attempted."[52] Yet Keynes's displeasure surely had less to do with the strategic timing of its release than with the content, which had much more in sympathy with the Stabilization Fund, and he thus dubbed the Canadian plan as "off White."[53] "Whether, in addition to upsetting us, the document will please the Americans remains to be seen. There is such a large ingredient of copy-cat that, from that point of view, Harry White ought to be pleased and flattered. But whether he will be completely pleased by having all his skeletons dragged out of their cupboards is not so obvious. In particular, the treatment of scarce currencies becomes horribly unambiguous."[54] When the British delegation in Washington a few weeks later received rather "casual treatment," they reiterated the view that the Canadian plan was a mistake, in that it undermined the negotiating strength of the Commonwealth. Clark sought to reassure Robbins of the British delegation that the apparently rude behaviour of the Americans should not be construed as ill-intent. "They're like this and they'll never be any different. But there is no sinister intention. We know Harry very well."[55]

The Canadian plan was in many respects a victim of its own success. Rasminsky's wording was "clear, precise and persuasive,"[56] where White's was garbled, and the modification of the White plan along several of the lines suggested – increasing the size of the aggregate quotas, with all quotas paid up immediately; that initial exchange rate be set with a country's consent and the right to devalue up to 10 per cent, restricting the use of funds to meet "an adverse balance on current account"; and the right to draw on up to 50 per cent of one's quota per year – made further discussion of the Canadian plan unnecessary.[57] Even Keynes was ready to concede that the approach of the White plan was the only politically acceptable one. After White's revision to the Stabilization Fund proposal and the somewhat volatile Anglo-American discussions in September/October 1943, enough common ground was established to produce a "Joint Statement of Experts." Mackintosh would offer Canada's endorsement of the "Statement of Principles" to Keynes during the London talks in 1944, arguing that a multilateral accord was necessary to "bring the United States whole heartedly into a full acceptance of its responsibilities."[58]

Complementing the fund was to be a separate organization for international investment. Keynes had proposed that the Clearing Union could play a number of supplementary roles, including using bancor to finance international reconstruction and development. But even before the idea was first presented at the Commonwealth talks in 1942, Mackintosh insisted that the Clearing Union was no panacea and should not be encumbered by extra activities.[59] Instead, it was White's International Bank for Reconstruction and Development (IBRD) that formed the basis for discussion. Keynes welcomed the idea, deeming an international flow of long-term financing important for economic development as well as for enhanced monetary stability, but he was unsparing in his criticism of the garbled drafting, referring to White as a "perfect ass" for his "Sumerean" writing and, during face-to-face negotiations, describing aspects of the scheme as "plain loony."[60] A second draft did little to remedy the situation. At the London Commonwealth talks of 1944, Keynes described White's proposal as "one of the oddest documents he had ever set eyes on ... it began at the extreme of wrong thinking and then laboured back in search of some degree of sanity." Mackintosh was forced to agree, but did so in more delicate terms, stating that he read the first version of the American proposal with "extreme dismay" and finding the second draft plagued by a lack of clarity.[61]

Keynes's substantive criticism of White's IBRD proposal was that it failed to differentiate between the roles of creditor and debtor nations in promoting overseas investment. Keynes specified two guiding principles: that debtor countries could share some of the risk (if not contribute some of the capital) and that "it would be highly retrograde for an international body to support the principle of tied loans ... [and] that any international institution must be free of that taint." He anticipated that most foreign lending would be intergovernmental and that, without some exceptional support, it would be difficult for some nations to float loans at reasonable interest rates on American financial markets. Mackintosh suggested that, if Canada emerged as an inexperienced foreign lender after the war, it would welcome "a sound international institution" to facilitate lending into areas outside of the United States. Keynes and Mackintosh agreed that the most appealing aspect of White's proposal was the emphasis on the bank's role in guaranteeing loans, rather than being a lender itself.[62] Keynes's redraft of White's bank proposal, written on the boat to Bretton Woods, served as the basis for an agreement.

With enough common ground established, the United States invited forty-four countries to Bretton Woods, New Hampshire, in July 1944, in order to consider the formation of an International Monetary Fund and an International Bank for Reconstruction and Development. A preliminary drafting conference was held in Atlantic City during the last two weeks of June, after which special overnight trains carried the delegates to Bretton Woods. A total of 730 people attended – more than anticipated and too many to accommodate in the hastily reopened Mount Washington Hotel. Despite the panoramic setting of the White Mountains, with their numerous holiday attractions, it was, as Mackintosh unnecessarily insisted, "definitely a working conference," which produced "concrete and workmanlike results."[63] There were two principal commissions, one on the fund, chaired by White, and the other on the bank, led by Keynes. (A third commission on "Other Means of International Financial Cooperation" played a negligible role in the conference.) Each commission, in turn, had four committees, in which delegates worked through several issues still outstanding – such as the size of each country's quota, the percentage of subscriptions that had to be paid in gold, the degree of flexibility that a country could exercise in adjusting its exchange rate, and the penalties that could be imposed on countries with a credit balance. The conference had to design the procedures and draft language to capture the principles enunciated in the Joint Statement, as well as to deal with the numerous amendments proposed but left unresolved in Atlantic City. Rasminsky, who headed the drafting committee, noted that in some instances there were as many as eleven alternative wordings proposed for the same clause. "The pressure of work has been unbelievable," said Keynes.

> It is as though, in the course of three or four weeks, one had to accomplish the preliminary work of many interdepartmental and Cabinet committees, the job of the Parliamentary draftsmen, and the passage through several Houses of Parliament of two intricate measures of major dimensions, all of this carried on in committees or commissions, numbering anything up to 200 persons in rooms with bad acoustics, shouting through microphones, many of those present, often including the Chairman, with an imperfect knowledge of English, each wanting to get something on the record which would look well in the Press down home, and one of the most important delegations, namely the Russian, only understanding what was afoot with the utmost difficulty and expense of time ... We have all of us worked every minute of our waking hours practically without intermission for what is now four weeks ... How people stood it is a miracle.[64]

The Canadian delegation, led by Ilsley, included parliamentarians St Laurent, D.C. Abbott, Lionel Chevrier, Walter Tucker, and J.A. Blanchette, as well as Towers and Clark; but the "continuous work" was done by Rasminsky, Mackintosh, Deutsch, and Plumptre. Robbins suggested that only the Americans, British, and Canadians had the technical expertise to appreciate the details to an agreement. "The debate on technicalities continues. We are experiencing much difficulty in reaching a satisfactory formulation of the clauses relating to capital transfer and multilateral clearing. When I say 'we' in this respect, I mean essentially ourselves and the United States. Although 44 nations are here assembled, with the single exception of the Canadians, there are no other delegations who really have sufficient technical knowledge to grapple with these arcana."[65] Rasminsky – who was also the reporting delegate on Commission I – continued to mediate between the Americans and British, both in

Atlantic City and Bretton Woods.[66] Mackintosh's participation at Atlantic City was limited, because his departure from Ottawa was delayed until June 26.[67] At Bretton Woods, however, he would chair the important committee on the "Operations of the Fund," after a Soviet delegate, P.A. Maltin, declined the responsibility because of a lack of fluency in English.

The final outcome of the Bretton Woods conference was deceptively simple. The International Monetary Fund (IMF) was to be a $8.8-billion fund created through the contribution of member countries, according to their relative importance in trade, monetary reserves, and national income. Contributions were to be paid up immediately with, under most circumstances, gold accounting for 25 per cent, with the rest in the country's own currency. Countries could then draw upon this fund, up to the amount of their quota, to meet payments on their current account. In return for this, member countries had to agree to maintain their exchange rate as initially agreed to with the fund and to maintain full convertibility of their currency. They could unilaterally devalue it by up to 10 per cent, but anything more required the agreement of the fund.

With respect to the bank, the largest amount of time was spent redrafting clauses in an effort to reflect the appropriate balance between the demands of European countries for reconstruction and those of other countries for development. In its final form, the IBRD would have a capital stock of $10 billion to be used for long-term lending. It would engage in three types of transactions: direct loans of up to 18 per cent of its subscriptions in "tied loans," where the money could be used only for purchasing the goods of the lending country; loan guarantees; and loans from funds raised by the bank by issuing debentures on the private market. Canada's contribution to the bank of $3.75 billion ranked it as the seventh-largest donor. While the fund itself was relatively small, it was anticipated that most of the bank's activities would involve guaranteeing loans, rather than through direct lending on its own account. The borrowing country would approach the bank with a private investment project for which it was seeking financing. Upon its approval of the project, the bank would guarantee the principal and interest on the loan, and then securities would be issued on private capital markets. Such loan guarantees would allow projects to be undertaken that might normally not be able to secure financing. The bank would finance its activities by charging a fee of 0.5 to 1 per cent on the outstanding principal on the loan.[68]

At the closing plenary session of the Bretton Woods conference, Keynes was given the honour of moving the "Final Act." The Soviet Union and Canada were then called upon to second the motion. It was Mackintosh who rose to speak on behalf of the Canadian delegation. He began by paying homage to Keynes: "All of us, I am sure, find it wholly fitting that the motion to accept the Final Act should be presented by the delegate of a country which has played so great and honourable a part in the world's monetary and financial history. We find a happy fitness also in that delegate being Lord Keynes. Throughout the Conference, as indeed throughout his life, he has showered his ideas upon us and has occasionally nourished some of ours. His sudden insights, his revealing phrases, and, if I may say so, his passionate striving for what is reasonable and emancipating in human affairs, have contributed greatly to the progress and wisdom of our deliberations." He hailed the outcome of the conference as "a great and even historic achievement ... The Final Act is evidence of what can be achieved when men forsake the conflict of creeds, and endeavour, in the phrase of a great American [Oliver Wendell Holmes, Jr] "to think things, not words."[69]

The Bretton Woods agreement had to be ratified by individual countries and, when it was brought to the Canadian House of Commons, both Rasminsky and Mackintosh appeared before the Standing Committee on Banking and Commerce. Rasminsky's testimony took up the better part of a day and a half, and he found the process "exhilarating"; in contrast, Mackintosh's experience was a rather sobering reminder of the nature of parliamentary politics. Summoned at the last minute, he appeared as a witness at ten in the evening; the first question put to him was by a Social Credit member, who wanted to know if the rise of Hitler could be attributed to the Great Depression. "I have read that" was the response. When pressed on the matter, Mackintosh showed great patience given the late hour: "I am afraid, Mr. Blackmore, I would be wasting the time of the committee in offering myself as an expert witness on why Hitler rose. The committee could tell me much more about that than I could tell them." The question was then posed a third time: "But suppose we assume that this is the case, would not the cause of the depression have a major bearing on the war?" Mackintosh could only acknowledge the tautology: "On your assumption, I think it would." The committee chairman would thank Mackintosh and the other members of the committee "who have exercised such great restraint."[70] The bill was then approved by the committee and passed by the House the next day.

TRADE: TARIFF REDUCTIONS AND IMPERIAL PREFERENCES

While monetary talks proceeded at a rapid pace towards an agreement, commercial negotiations occurred fitfully and did not reach a satisfactory conclusion. Both the United States and Britain expressed the desire for a multilateral convention, but there was no consensus on what the "rules of the game" should include, how they might be achieved, and, more importantly, how much conviction there was concerning such an objective. Dissent prevailed within each camp as well as within the Commonwealth. In contrast, the direction of Canadian policy was clear. As expressed by Mackintosh: "We need both the UK and the US as customers but we need them both under multilateral arrangement where neither can apply undue pressure on us. There would be no net gain in any move which would merely substitute one market for another. A multilateral convention is also our best chance of re-entry into the European market from which we would probably be excluded under regional arrangements."[71] Canadian officials thus adopted a clear stance on commercial policy at the outset and "stuck to their brief" throughout.

Since the early twentieth century, Canada had a three-column tariff structure, with special treatment for low- and high-tariff countries. This had evolved by granting lower rates to areas within the British Empire, a practice formalized in the Ottawa Agreement of 1932, with the "binding of bound preferences" that prevented members from negotiating alternative rates with countries outside the imperial system. At the same time, high rates were imposed on countries with high rates of protection, such as the United States. For Mackintosh, the severe dislocation that would be imposed on Canadian manufacturing with the removed of preferential tariffs was a problem "worth facing" in return for a multilateral accord, for "without ... the expansionist world economy for which everyone wished, Canada would find it almost impossible to function."[72] In suggesting an across-the-board cut in tariffs in the order of 50 per cent in most-favoured-nation rates, he acknowledged that this would not completely eliminate preferential duties but make the "residual preferences defensible," and that a reduction in high US tariffs was a reasonable quid pro quo. As he put it, "To insist that the mote of discrimination be taken out of the UK eye while the beam of prohibitive tariffs in the US is left to Congress is not sensible."[73]

Mackintosh first advanced Canada's position at the London Commonwealth talks in 1942, and found it largely in agreement with the principles enunciated in Meade's "International Commercial Union" – deliberately named to parallel Keynes's International Clearing Union proposal. Mackintosh likened Meade's commercial union to a "club," freely open to all countries, with "most-favoured-nation" treatment extended to members of the club, and "most-unfavoured-nation" treatment of countries that remained outside.[74] Import quotas and other quantitative restrictions would be permitted only during the transitional period, some latitude would be extended in the event that a country encountered a balance-of-payments problem, and allowances would be made for infant industries. Mackintosh voiced support for the protection of infant industries on the grounds that "A great many of the potential signatories to such a Convention are, in fact, new countries anxious to diversify their economies and build up industries for which they are especially suited."[75]

When Commonwealth talks resumed in London in June 1943, the focus was on the British *aide-mémoire* outlining the principles governing its approach to commercial negotiations with the United States. The British delegation was led by Sir Arthur Overton of the Board of Trade and included Meade, Percival Leishing, and R.J. Shackle. (The participation of the latter two allowed Keynes to describe the British initiative as an effort to "unleash" and "unshackle" international trade.[76]) Mackintosh, accompanied by Hector McKinnon, J.S. MacDonald, and Yves Lamontagne, reported that, despite a significant difference of opinion within the British government, it held to the position outlined in Meade's proposal for the commercial union. Other Commonwealth countries were less receptive to the British *aide-mémoire*. Australia was intent on pursuing a bilateral trade deal with the United States before entering into a multilateral convention, while the position of the South African delegation "was not easy to define but it appeared to support a bilateral position." Mackintosh responded that "the interlocking of preferential arrangements made multilateral action the only feasible one in reality and that by accepting the bilateral form we should greatly weaken our position by frittering away our bargaining power vis-a-vis the United States." Overton and Liesching would confide after the meetings that they considered Canada's attitude of "decisive importance," since Britain was ready to press ahead with or without the support of the rest of the Commonwealth.[77] Mackintosh would later meet over lunch with Keynes at the House of Lords, at which time he reiterated Canada's qualified support for the British proposals.[78]

Anglo-American talks in September 1943 resulted in a joint statement of principle – with the treatment of imperial preferences left unresolved – and two short Canadian-American meetings followed in New York in January and February 1944.[79] Canada agreed to entertain bilateral talks only to the extent that they contributed to the creation of a multilateral convention, and Mackintosh reported that the US was receptive to such an approach.[80] Canada also objected to the two-price policy in American agriculture – a practice also followed in many European countries – in which domestic producers received a price higher than the world price, because of import restrictions. While government subsidies for domestic agriculture were acceptable, a two-price system distorted consumption, production, and international competitive conditions. In contrast, the Canadian Wheat Board subsidized domestic producers through a licensing and quota system, but Canadian consumers paid the world price. The American delegation was sympathetic to the argument, but insisted that Congress would not support a change in agricultural policy.[81]

At the third series of Commonwealth talks in 1944, Mackintosh found a disturbing shift of direction, with Britain's insistence that the transition period, during which countries would be free to pursue bilateral and discriminatory trade policies, be extended to five years, and where tariff reductions would only begin to be phased in after three years.[82] Mackintosh objected that countries would begin the conversion to peace-time industry immediately, and that the gradual elimination of tariffs would do little to support industries that were not going to survive in the long run. He urged an immediate cut in tariff rates, but a tolerance of quantitative trade restrictions in the transition period. He also continued to insist that a series of bilateral negotiations of tariff reductions was too arbitrary and too slow a process to achieve a multilateral convention.[83] "Special expedients" extended during the transition period, he warned, would have a permanent effect on trade patterns, and however great countries perceived their bargaining power in bilateral negotiations to be, the stakes to be divided were small. He thus urged the need for a multilateral convention, with dramatic cuts in barriers to trade.[84]

It would be over a year before commercial talks between the US and UK would resume, and, after the Audit Room talks at Cambridge in May 1945, Mackintosh and McKinnon met with officials at the Board of Trade for an update. McKinnon's draft report reflected his frustration with the state of affairs: "At first, we were generally puzzled – and not a little disturbed – by what appeared to be an unreadiness or a reluctance of the part of the United Kingdom authorities to come to grips with the admittedly troublesome subject of Commercial Policy ... We came finally to regard it as really the outward indication that the United Kingdom officials *had nothing new to tell us* regarding the basic proposals respecting Commercial Policy."[85] Mackintosh would "tone down" the report on redraft, but expressed dismay that the last round of Anglo-American talks were "very much Hamlet without the Prince," largely limited to establishing a timetable for further discussions.[86]

Little progress was made towards reaching a commercial agreement until the US insisted on addressing the matter prior to negotiating the loan to Britain in October 1945. An agreement was then quickly reached – with the issue of preferences unresolved – based upon an American proposal for an International Trade Organization. The commercial accord would also embrace agreements on the regulation of primary commodity markets and on the regulation of cartels, along with an employment accord. Keynes first advanced the idea of stabilizing commodity prices as a function of the Clearing Union: it would finance the holding of buffer stocks in key raw materials by international commodity boards. Having determined the long-run supply price, a commodity board would buy or sell to offset short-run price fluctuations. When the idea was presented at the 1942 Commonwealth talks, both Rasminsky and Mackintosh were unconvinced that the regulation of commodity prices was the appropriate role of the Clearing Union, but even after separating buffer stocks from how they were financed, Keynes's proposal ran afoul on several grounds. Depending on the rules by which commodity boards were governed, buffer stocks were depicted as a "speculator's paradise" by American officials, a view to which the Bank of England also subscribed.[87] When discussed during the 1944 London Commonwealth Talks, a more protracted issue was raised of the relationship between short-run price stabilization and quantitative restrictions, whether they be export quotas or limitations on domestic production. Whichever the case, the determination of the long-term supply price would invite division between producing and consuming countries. Robbins had referred to the "residue of suspicion" from the conference to establish the Food and Agriculture Organization at Hot Springs, Virginia, in 1943, where many exporting countries were skeptical that the role of buffer stock and the regulation of commodity prices generally was to support the income of producers, given Britain's status as the world's largest food importer.[88] In this vein, it was perhaps American protection of its agricultural industries that led to the "curious intellectual resistance" that Robbins found among US officials to the idea of buffer stocks. Mackintosh suggested that a buffer-stock authority would need to concern itself with only historical prices, and that any effort to establish a "just price" that balanced the interests of producers and consumers would be "doomed."[89]

Buffer stocks aside, there was still a role for an international convention on commodities. As Mackintosh made the case, commodity agreements were going to exist in the postwar period, so the choice was really between a series of ad hoc arrangements between private and government institutions, or an international agreement with clear rules of conduct. The later might be achieved through the creation of an international body with a set of principles to which member countries would comply, and with the power to approve and review agreements entered into by member countries. He reported, however, that Canadian–American discussions on this topic had been brief and unproductive. He found that, while American officials were very concerned with an anticipated emergency situation in the supply of cotton, sugar, vegetable oil, and possibly wheat, they had little interest in discussing the regulation of commodity markets in the long term. He suggested as a possible compromise that the establishment of an international organization to deal with the disposal of wartime stockpiles of commodities might be an avenue to the acceptance of a buffer-stock scheme.[90]

Nor was much progress made on the regulation of international cartels. Prompted by American concerns that "private international cartels" were usurping the role of governments in making international commercial policy, three methods were proposed for dealing with them: legal prohibition as advocated by the United States, a complaints procedure similar to what was in place in most of the dominions, and the simple registration of agreements.[91] Canadian and British officials could do little more than listen politely, confess to having done little thinking on the topic, and then lament that an international accord was unlikely to be reached. Mackintosh observed that it was difficult for Canada to seek to ban an international practice such as price fixing when no similar prohibition existed in its domestic policy (since it first had to be demonstrated that the practice was detrimental to the public interest). He described Canada as being on the "fringe" of international cartels, where subsidiaries of American firms were themselves not party to a particular agreement but were bound by the dictates of the head office that was. Britain was even less predisposed to regulating the practices of international firms, only committing itself to cooperate in the registration of international firms and to gather more information on their practices. With such a "radical difference" in American and British approaches, Mackintosh argued that the United States had no place in dictating to other countries that they pursue more vigorous domestic policies, but did accept that practices such as non-competition agreements to divide up world markets were legitimate grounds for an international government accord.[92]

While no one questioned the value of an international employment agreement intended to coordinate efforts to ensure full employment, there was little consensus on how this might be achieved without encroaching unduly on national sovereignty. At the end of the 1944 Commonwealth talks, for instance, there was some consternation when the Australian delegation proposed "ferocious penalties" for countries that failed to maintain full employment. Mackintosh later remembered overhearing Keynes murmur, paraphrasing Charles Kingsley, "Be good, sweet maid, and *very* clever."[93]

The principles outlined in the "Proposals for Consideration of an International Conference on Trade and Employment," formed the basis for the Havana Charter in 1948 to establish the International Trade Organization (ITO) as a specialized agency of the United Nations. Commenting on the draft agreement to the charter in 1947, Mackintosh expressed his disappointment with the lack of bold initiatives to address the scope of the problem of restoring world trade.

The elimination of quantitative restrictions on imports allowed for several exceptions, tariff reductions were to proceed through a series of bilateral negotiations that would not necessarily be binding on signatories to the convention, and state trading monopolies were given sweeping exceptions. Yet while he deemed the draft agreement to "fall far short of an ideal," he continued to support the creation of the ITO as a vehicle for setting some minimum standards and as a working agency to achieve more radical trade reforms.[94] But when the United States refused to seek congressional ratification for the ITO Charter, the organization was effectively dead. An international agreement on trade was thus limited to the more narrowly defined General Agreement on Tariffs and Trade (the GATT) reached in Geneva in 1947.

THE AUDIT ROOM MEETINGS AND CANADA'S LOAN TO BRITAIN

Regardless of the outcome of the Bretton Woods conference, Britain expected to face an acute shortage of monetary reserves when the war ended. By 1943, its accumulated balance-of-payments deficit was nearly £6 billion and the annual deficit for 1945 was expected to exceed £2 billion. With its exports at less than 30 per cent of the pre-war level, a deterioration in its international terms of trade, and many of its overseas assets liquidated, it faced a long transition period before there would be any prospect of balancing its current account and paying down some of its debt. The limited size of the proposed IMF meant that direct financial assistance from the United States and Canada would be required if Britain could realistically be expected to liberalize its international trade and currency movements.[95] It was the British hope that both of these creditor countries would be willing to pay a certain price to ensure that Britain embrace multilateral agreements.

The prospect of a Canadian loan to Britain in the postwar period (Stage III) arose in the context of discussions over Canada's assistance during Stage II, or the period between the surrender of Germany and the defeat of Japan. Keynes and Wilfred Eady, of the British Treasury, travelled to Ottawa at the conclusion of the Bretton Woods conference to appeal for more Canadian support under the Mutual Aid Program. Compared to the intensity of Bretton Woods, the meetings in Ottawa were relaxed and congenial. Keynes, accompanied by Lady Keynes,[96] took up residence in the Moorish suite of nine rooms in the Château Laurier, and the first order of duty was to host a party to celebrate the two hundred and fiftieth anniversary of the Bank of England with a small party that included Rasminsky, Mackintosh, Clark, Bryce, and Donald Gordon. Several meetings on various aspects of the Mutual Aid program followed throughout the first two weeks of August, with Keynes at his persuasive best, acknowledging Canada's generosity but adding that "one good deed leads to the expectation of another," and Bryce reported that "Canadian ministers felt they needed to be cautious about taking decisions under his spell."[97] Upon his departure on August 15, Keynes could claim important short-term and long-term victories: Canada's commitments for additional funding in Stage II in the order of $600 million and "having produced a considerable effect … [p]utting the Canadian civil servants and Ministers into a mood of wanting to find a way to meet us in so far as they can without involving themselves in political and parliamentary difficulties."[98]

Keynes's visit to Ottawa three months later – following lengthy talks in Washington and in the midst of the conscription crisis – did not proceed as happily. Several points of contention arose over past payments related to items such as the air training schemes, but more troubling to Canadian officials was the scale of military activities planned by Britain and the appeal for a substantial increase in Canada's Mutual Aid contribution to finance it. As Skidelsky describes the matter in his biography of Keynes, "[Ottawa] was now being asked to help underwrite a British effort that was appropriate to a great power but that Britain could no longer afford on its own."[99] Keynes proposed that munitions and war services be pooled, with each country giving freely and charging the items used to Mutual Aid. Bryce expressed his irritation with this arrangement, which was clearly of no benefit to Canada. "Keynes's repeated efforts to sell us this 'gimmick' demeaned him in the eyes of our ministers (and Clark and me)."[100] The meetings left Keynes depressed and Canada anxious about a drift in British policy towards greater protectionism in the sterling bloc.[101]

The tenor of the discussions prompted Towers to prepare a lengthy memorandum, "A Proposal for Maintaining Canada's Exports to the Sterling Area during the Postwar Transitional Period." He insisted that Canada had to do everything it could to maintain its level of exports in a three-year transitional period (Stage III), targeting an annual value of exports that was half the wartime level, but twice what it was before the war. To achieve this level, he forecast that Britain would need to absorb one-third of Canada's exports, but that it had already indicated that it would discriminate against Canadian goods "on currency grounds ... If the UK and the rest of the sterling area operate along these lines after the war, then the outlook for Canada is bleak indeed. Yet there is no point in our merely remonstrating with them or drawing attention to the bitter feeling that will be generated in this country against the United Kingdom if, after the assistance we have given them in the past five years, the return we get is discrimination against our exports." Towers thus proposed that Canada extend Britain credit of $1.2 billion for the purchase of Canadian goods during the transitional period on two conditions: that Canada be treated on the same terms as sterling-area countries, both in terms of currency and trade; and that sterling be convertible to Canadian dollars for the purpose of meeting current-account payments to Canada. He conceded that the terms of repayment of the loan would need to be flexible: "The plain fact of the matter is that our bargaining position is not strong and we shall have to go a long way to meet the United Kingdom if we are to overcome their reluctance to go into our debt on a considerable scale."[102]

Towers's memorandum prompted much discussion among key ministers and senior officials in the Bank of Canada (James Coyne, Donald Gordon, and Rasminsky), department of finance (Clark and Bryce), external affairs (Robertson and Wrong), and department of reconstruction (where Mackintosh was now located), including a long meeting on New Year's Day, 1945. There was general endorsement of Towers's argument that a high level of exports was necessary "if we are to have a sporting chance at full employment" and that Canada's only leverage with the United Kingdom was the veiled threat of closer relations with the United States and a fracturing of Commonwealth relations. Mackintosh was already on record in support of generous treatment based upon self-interest: Canada "should be prepared to invest in a valuable customer and finance her purchases through her period of difficulty, for the purpose of maintaining our position in the market."[103] Revisions to Towers's memorandum resulted in a policy statement on "Post-war Commercial Policy Prospects," which would form the basis of Canada's approach to the loan negotiations. Three telegrams drafted by Towers, Mackintosh, and Clark, were then sent to the British on 23 February 1945. During

Stage II, Canada would extend the Mutual Aid agreement throughout 1945 on the scale requested, but only on the condition that there be no discrimination against Canadian exports. During Stage III, Canada offered to extend credit to the sterling area for purchase of Canadian exports, thus effectively financing both sides of Canada–UK trade.[104]

The Canadian High Commission in London reported that the telegrams "created an excellent impression at the official level and are warmly welcomed. They are regarded as realistic, constructive, imaginative, and generous."[105] Meade and Robbins advised the cabinet that a bilateral policy would not only put further financial assistance from Canada in jeopardy but test the patience of sterling countries over repayment of Britain's debts. At the cabinet meeting to consider the Canadian financial proposals, Vincent Massey reported that opposition was anticipated from Lord Beaverbrook and from Mr R.S. Hudson. "When the Cabinet came to consider the draft reply which had been prepared by the Treasury and the Dominions Office, the Prime Minister glared around the table, said in his grimmest voice, 'I think this is the very least we can do to meet the Canadian Government's wishes,' and went on with the next item of business. Neither Lord Beaverbrook nor Mr Hudson were able to open their mouths."[106]

A Canadian delegation was then invited to London, and Mackintosh, Towers, and McKinnon flew from Montreal to London. They arrived on 16 May, in time to attend the reopening of the National Gallery the next day.[107] Keynes explained the circumstances in extending the invitation to the gallery event: "At the beginning of the war all the masterpieces in the National Gallery were taken and buried deep in air-conditioned chambers in the middle of a mountain in Wales. This week fifty of the major masterpieces are being brought back to Trafalgar Square and (though it is not mentioned on the card) the King and Queen are expected to be present at 3 o'clock on Thursday to re-open the Gallery. As perhaps you know, Vincent Massey is Chairman of the Trustees of the Gallery (of whom I am also one), and I know he would welcome your presence, if you can manage it."[108] They then took a train to Cambridge late Friday afternoon for the Whitsun weekend. The meetings were made more noteworthy because the Canadian secretary, Douglas LePan, provided a vivid account of the Cambridge weekend in both a written vignette and his official minutes.[109] There they received the full

King's College experience, from the rather spartan accommodation in the college residence ("Even Bill Mackintosh and Hector McKinnon, who had rather simpler tastes, were hardly enthusiastic"), to a formal lunch in the Combination Room, hosted by Keynes and Lady Keynes, with his Cambridge economics colleagues John Clapham, Dennis Robertson, and Austin and Joan Robinson in attendance. LePan recalls Keynes and Mackintosh drinking port and madeira "conversing rather dourly about Edgeworth and Marshall, as though economics were indeed the dismal science." Also on the agenda were two evenings at the Arts Centre, an excursion on Saturday to see Ernest Milton in Dickens's *Dombey and Son*, and on Sunday a concert by a French quartet.[110]

On Saturday morning, the two groups gathered in the Audit Room at King's College. On one side was Keynes, amid officials from the Treasury (Hopkins, Eady) and the Bank of England (Cobbold); on the other side was Mackintosh ("his bald head glistening and his small-town boyhood sometimes showing through his experience and composure"), flanked by Towers, McKinnon, and LePan. Although Mackintosh was nominally the head of the delegation, the primary duties fell to Towers, "whose incisive mind, fluent but precise speech, and dedication to the constructive solution of the British economic problem made him a fitting match for Keynes."[111] Keynes would hold forth for more than a day and a half, giving the Canadian delegation a full preview of his argument for the US loan negotiations in Washington in September 1945. After reviewing Britain's wartime finances and its expected balance-of-payments deficits during the postwar period (forecast to be between £6 billion and £9 billion over the first three years), he outlined its options in the transitional period in emotive terms. "Starvation Corner" was "a disagreeable option of last resort": in the event that no American and Canadian financial support was forthcoming, Britain would be forced to maintain its wartime rationing and import controls, postpone domestic spending projects, and further retreat from overseas activities in order to husband scarce foreign exchange. He acknowledged that "This is not a well-chosen moment for a declaration of our financial independence from North America." The second option was "Temptation," in which large and generous terms on Canadian and American loans to settle lend-lease and Mutual Aid debts would give Britain sufficient monetary reserves to liberalize its trade and currency. Under the third scenario, "Justice," Canada and the United States would recognize the undue burden that Britain had carried during the war by forgiving some of its accumulated debts, and converting a portion of the loans to unconditional grants. Under these latter terms, Britain could embrace world multilateral trade and "the sweet breath of justice would be felt to be blowing" by the people of the United Kingdom.[112]

Keynes continued in the Sunday-afternoon session, finally coming to the "modest" contribution to be asked of Canada: elimination of $600 million in book debt associated with Mutual Aid, the option on a loan of $500 million, and continuation of the existing $700-million interest-free Canadian-dollar loan.[113] Mackintosh was the first to respond, expressing his pleasure with the objectives outlined by Keynes, and then turned to Towers, who suggested that a US loan of $8 billion, with flexible terms of repayment, would be easier to obtain. To this, both Keynes and Eady were adamant that a loan by itself would not be acceptable, as "the United Kingdom would always be at the mercy of the United States financially; it would continually be in the position of coming cap in hand to Washington for concessions or modifications." Mackintosh then urged that offering a short transition period would give the UK the greatest leverage in negotiations, while Towers reminded Keynes that failure to achieve a multilateral trade-accord agreement would mean that Canada would be forced into closer economic relations with the United States, to the detriment of the Commonwealth.

LePan was "spellbound" by Keynes's "stunning performance," which displayed "all of his marvellous gifts – intellectual, forensic, social, cultural, personal – outspread like a spangled train." His argument "often soared and fluttered and hovered, was bright with fancy, was variously inflected." Keynes was simply "the most extraordinary creature I have ever listened to … [There is] something mythical and fabulous about him." LePan noted that Towers shared his admiration for Keynes – "Towers was clearly stimulated and invigorated by him, and felt deep and fundamental sympathy for him" – but was dismayed by Mackintosh's reaction. "Between [Keynes] and Mackintosh sympathy was much more imperfect. Once that weekend and several times in later years, Bill Mackintosh told me that he considered Keynes 'a spoiled brat.' I never felt in a position to pursue what lay behind this remark. To argue seemed useless, my own attitude was so different."[114]

Mackintosh's view of Keynes reflects the same ambivalence of Meade who would observe Keynes's brilliance one day and the next bemoan his ill behaviour; of Lionel Robbins, who would write effusively about Keynes's "genius" and his petulance in the same paragraph; or that of Bryce, who admired his former Cambridge mentor but recorded his embarrassment with his behaviour during his visit to Ottawa in November 1944. Mackintosh's attitude was, no doubt, coloured by his general dislike for Oxbridge pretense, and one can only admire his restraint on at least one occasion. As they strolled through the Fellows' Gardens at King's College, Mackintosh declared, "How beautiful it is," to which Keynes replied, "Yes, it is beautiful, isn't it? And we want to keep it, you know. That's why you are here."[115] Mackintosh's response, if he had one, is not recorded. He later acknowledged his difficulty in understanding Keynes (this "brilliant but somewhat complicated creature"), but when he sent Keynes a note of thanks, he did so in the most gracious terms: "May I assure you of the enjoyment and enlightenment we got from our visit. It was most encouraging to find such close agreement on objectives and the main obstacles. I think there would not have been such appreciative understanding on either side had it not been for your stroke of imagination in assembling us for the most enjoyable weekend at Cambridge. For that and other things, thank you very much indeed."[116]

Towers, McKinnon, and Mackintosh would spend the next two weeks in London talking to officials in the Treasury, Board of Trade, and the Bank of England. Mackintosh met with Keynes in his Treasury office on 28 May and received the commitment that Britain would not discriminate against Canadian goods during Stage II. They then left London on 2 June, arriving in Ottawa the next evening.[117]

With Japan's surrender on August 13, Canada's Mutual Aid and the US lend-lease came to an end. Keynes sailed on the SS *Pasteur* to Quebec City and then flew to Ottawa to brief Canadian officials on his instructions for the financial negotiations in Washington. In informing Mackintosh (now in the guise of acting deputy minister of finance) of the visit, the British High Commissioner in Ottawa added that "the authorities at home greatly appreciate the helpful and sympathetic attitude which you have been adopting towards this whole problem and in particular Lord Keynes asked me to send you a personal message saying how much your helpful attitude is recognized and appreciated at the present time."[118] In the "nightmarish" negotiations that followed, Keynes was mistaken in thinking that the United States would provide a large unconditional gift in recognition of its moral obligation to accept a portion of Britain's cost in prosecuting the war. The agreement reached in December 1945 fell well short of Keynes's expectations. It included a loan of $3.75 billion, at an interest rate of 2 per cent, to be repaid after 1950, and credit for $650 million due to lend-lease. In return, the UK agreed to the full convertibility of sterling within one year. The only important concession that Keynes could achieve was a waiver clause, stating that the debt could be repaid in goods. Writing from London, LePan reported that Cameron Cobbold of the Bank of England and Eady found the US waiver clause to be a "derogation of the United Kingdom's dignity," whereby it could default on the agreement and retain "its status as a gentleman of good standing." It was only after Keynes convinced them that they were "standing on a punctilio which the hard circumstances of the case would not allow the United Kingdom to indulge" that they would relent and support the agreement. Just the same, when LePan suggested that Keynes had been forced to accept what he had earlier described as a policy of Temptation, "Eady smiled wryly and agreed."[119]

In December, Keynes would return to London via Ottawa to outline the settlement to Canadian officials. It would be Mackintosh's last occasion to meet with him, as Keynes would be dead four months later at the age of sixty-three. In his stead, Eady and Cobbold arrived in Ottawa in February 1946 to settle Canada's long-term loan. Negotiations proved amicable and relatively straightforward given the basis for agreement established earlier.[120] Eady would later reflect upon his time in Ottawa as "the most delightful of our experiences."[121]

"THE UNITED NATIONS IN A DIVIDED WORLD"

Despite the heroic efforts to reconstruct the international economy around such institutions as the IMF, IBRD, and ITO, the objective of a postwar, multilateral world was not achieved. Some twenty years later, Robbins would reflect on the period in a letter to Mackintosh: "I cherish the most vivid memories of our collaboration during the War, when we all worked together like a band of brothers – as Maynard Keynes said – hoping against hope that we could do something to improve the world. I don't think we did any harm but I have often asked myself to what extent have we registered any very notable success."[122] The decision of the Soviet Union not to ratify the Bretton Woods accord was one of the first indications of the onset of the Cold War and the inability of the United Nations to cope with growing East-West tensions. The IMF, as well as the Canadian and American loans, proved incapable of coping with the magnitude of Britain's current-account deficits, and it was forced to suspend convertibility and eventually to devalue the pound sterling in 1949. The IBRD proved too small for the scale of the rehabilitation of Europe (which fell largely to the Marshall Plan to finance) and would be of little immediate assistance to the developing world.[123] Agreement on a broad commercial pact floundered when the United States failed to ratify the ITO, leaving the more narrowly defined General Agreement on Tariffs and Trade to govern international trade. Meanwhile, imperial preferences persisted until 1961. Given the limitations of the IMF, IBRD, and GATT, Mackintosh could only take solace in the form, rather than the substance, of a step forward in international collaboration on international monetary and trade relations.

Nor did Canada's place as a rising middle power – an international creditor exercising a significant degree of economic independence from the United States – materialize. As Towers had warned, the persistence of the sterling area would force Canada into a closer relationship with the United States. Few could have predicted the degree of Canada's dependence upon trade with the United States, and even fewer foresaw the flow of US foreign direct investment into Canada. Facing its own balance-of-payments crisis in 1947, because of restrictions on sales to the sterling area and rapidly rising imports from the United States, by March 1948 Canada was on the brink of a free-trade agreement with the United States.[124]

Mackintosh's last service to Canada on the world stage was at the United Nations. In April 1946, he travelled by train to New York and settled in at the Biltmore Hotel for ten days in meetings of the Economic and Employment Commission (EEC) held at Hunter College. He was elected chair of the EEC, a permanent advisory committee to the Economic and Social Council (ECOSOC) on the continuing work needed to ensure economic expansion. In September he attended the first meeting of the General Assembly held in New York and the third session of the ECOSOC at Lake Success, NY.[125] The experience left him with significant misgivings. He found the UN to be clumsy and over-organized, with a proliferation of "large and unwieldy" agencies and commissions, and watched with discouragement as the ECOSOC bogged down in political wrangling to the neglect of substantive matters.[126] His more damning indictment was the lack of a "common spirit and understanding," particularly with respect to the inability to overcome the breach with the Soviet Union. In a world "rife with a new assortment of old sins," only "dusty answers" had been offered as a solution. Yet he remained steadfast in believing that there was no alternative to the UN and that the only answer was to continue to try to build it into a more effective organization.[127]

In many respects, the work of Mackintosh and others in shaping postwar institutions reflected White's view of the "US a coming nation and the UK a going one"[128] and facilitated the transfer of world power from London to New York. But no amount of planning could avoid the fact that the health of the postwar economy rested on the United States exercising its power in a responsible fashion. Just two months after the Bretton Woods accord, Mackintosh lamented that "In economic as well as in political thinking, the United States is veering toward imperialism. They do not seem to understand that the one real empire in the world has been rapidly transformed over the past generations, and that the attempt of other countries to establish empires was close to the root of the two wars. What we have to find now is the way to internationalism which does not involve a re-creation of imperialism."[129]

11

Domestic Reconstruction, the White Paper, and the Green Book: Ottawa, 1941–1946

Some people, having overweening ambitions, no doubt hope that their words will be immortal. I am highly gratified if some of mine have stood up as long as nine years.

W.A. Mackintosh to C.D. Howe, 7 April 1954[1]

The experience of the Great Depression and the early stages of World War II each contributed to the adoption of Keynesianism in Canada. The former lent support for the emergence of Keynesian politics, a broad social consensus that the state had a role to play in ensuring that the conditions of the 1930s did not recur, while the improvisation that characterized the economic organization for war and the experimentation in social policy provided important lessons in the federal government's management of aggregate demand. Planning for the postwar period pushed Canada a step further down the road to Keynesianism by applying what was learned during the war to the planning of a peacetime economy. In the United States, Paul Samuelson warned against any complacency in assuming that pent-up demand would be sufficient to ensure full employment in the absence of government stabilization policy. "Deferred demand is a fair-weather friend. When the forecast says squalls, deferred demand is all too likely to be deferred some more."[2] What was required was not simply "reconversion" of wartime industries to peacetime purposes, but "reconstruction" of the economy as a whole, with a clearly defined role for the state.

The approach that emerged was in part based upon long-term planning and, more specifically, upon a better understanding of how to manage aggregate demand in an economy characterized by a large dependence on international trade and which operated within an uneasy division of state powers between the dominion and provincial governments. The short-term, political need was to undertake long-overdue reform of social policy. Narrowly defined, as far as the Liberal government was concerned, this meant countering the growing popularity of the Co-operative Commonwealth Federation (CCF), while in a broader sense it meant addressing the public demands for expanded social security. Mitchell Sharp's insistence that the CCF was "pushing against an open door,"[3] contrasts with Mackintosh's view (as reported by Grant Dexter) of the state of King's government in November 1943. It was "comprised of burnt out men" with "no disposition to stand up to the CCF" in order to contest the field of social policy. "Bill Mackintosh put the thing to me the other day. He finds that over the past year the Cabinet has lost its constructive power. It can say 'No' and can carry on feuds but it doesn't seem to have the gumption to go out and fight the CCF or to undertake new policies ... But, says Bill, the tragic part of it is that the government is letting the CCF carry all before it, without a word of challenge. The whole case of international co-operation, of trade, of monetary policy – of all that is essential if we are to have a brave new world – plus private enterprise goes down for lack of defence."[4]

The absence of a clear political direction from the cabinet left a void for the bureaucracy to fill, and Mackintosh seized on the opportunity to articulate a coherent vision of the postwar economy. When the Canadian government's 1945 White Paper on *Employment and Income with Special Reference to the Initial Period of Reconstruction* signalled the federal government's acceptance of responsibility for stabilizing economic growth, Canada became among the first countries to formally embrace Keynesian economic policy. The *Proposals of the Government of Canada* (commonly referred to as the Green Book), prepared for the Dominion-Provincial Conference in the same year outlined the social-policy initiatives which would, in time, form the basis of Canada's modern social-security system. The common denominator of both documents, and of the majority of proposals for postwar economic policy, was Mackintosh as the principal draftsman.

RECONSTRUCTION, THE JAMES COMMITTEE, AND THE ECONOMIC ADVISORY COMMITTEE (EAC)

Canada's planning for the postwar domestic economy began as early as 1941. Largely at the instigation of Ian Mackenzie, minister of pensions and public health, the cabinet's Committee on Demobilization and Re-establishment created the Advisory Committee on Reconstruction (the James Committee) in September 1941. The advisory committee was designed to gain the advice of experts from outside government circles and to raise public awareness of reconstruction issues, and its intent, as seen by some, was "to counteract the bureaucratizing tendency which is powerful in Canada today. The bureaus, boards, and departments in Ottawa should not be left to do all the thinking on national policies."[5] The committee was composed of Cyril James (principal of McGill University, and an economist) as chair; Tom Moore (president of the Trades and Labour Congress of Canada and Mackintosh's fellow commissioner on the NEC); D.G. McKenzie (formerly vice-president of the United Grain Growers' Grain Company and recently appointed chair of the Board of Grain Commissioners); J.S. McLean (president of Canada Packers); R.C. Wallace (principal of Queen's, and a geologist); and Edouard Montpetit (secretary-general of the University of Montreal, and an economist). Leonard Marsh (the McGill social scientist) was hired as research advisor, and O.J. Firestone (the Canadian economist who had studied at McGill, the University of Vienna, and the LSE) was added to the research staff. Three ex-officio members were drawn from the government ranks, including Mackintosh in his capacity as chair of the Canadian side of the Canada-US Joint Economic Committees (JECs). In March 1942, a separate secretariat was established for the James Committee, reporting to Mackenzie.

The James Committee launched into its task with great vigour, issuing broad public statements about its plans and approach, appearing before both the House of Commons and the Senate Standing Committees on Reconstruction, sponsoring several research studies (a total of eighteen over its thirty-month life) and striking four subcommittees to look at agriculture, employment, construction, and natural-resource conservation.[6] James's ambitious agenda immediately prompted concerns within the civil service. When he appealed to Mackenzie King for permission to visit the Royal Institute of International Affairs in London to discuss reconstruction work, it raised the hackles of Hugh Keenleyside (external affairs representative on the JECs). He wrote to Arnold Heeney (secretary of the Privy Council) complaining that the

> members of the Joint Economic Committee were under the impression that Principal James and his Reconstruction Committee would devote their attention to problem of *internal* rehabilitation ... [T]hat James should proceed to England primarily for the purpose of discussion with Chatham House [the Royal Institute of International Affairs, an independent policy body], would also be a mistake. In the first place Chatham House is suspect among the more serious British officials, and secondly, in spite of Chatham House's semi-official character, the dispatch of Principal James on such a visit would be about equivalent of the British Government sending Arthur Greenwood to Canada to talk to the CIIA (this might not be a bad idea, but it is certainly not a step that the British Government would take). Although he has not seen this memorandum, Dr. Mackintosh agrees with my views in regards to the problem raised by Principal James' letter.[7]

King permitted James to go, but with the understanding that he was not representing the government of Canada.

More provocative was James's ill-conceived political step of commissioning a study by Maxwell Cohen, "Review of Machinery of Economic Control Set Up under the War Measures Act in Relation to Post-war Administration Exigencies." Cohen's report was highly critical of the EAC as a "competing Cabinet," guarded in secrecy, and offering advice that "may not have been as realistic as the demands of total war should have made it." Cohen alleged that the slow rate of industrial conversion to wartime purposes, "with its radical effects upon living standards may be due, in part, to the kind of technical advice that the Economic Advisory Committee may have been giving to Cabinet." He also criticized the department of finance for implementing fiscal policy that "still attempts to operate, on one side with fixed prices and wages, and on the other with voluntary loans, war savings and heavier taxation, and their resulting inequalities. Such devices, to reduce purchasing power and to divert resources thus freed for certain use in war production, as compulsory savings, with family allowances, capital levies to draw off saved cash that can and will be used to buy consumer goods, and other methods have not yet been suggested publicly as likely to be used in the near future."[8] Cohen's report was inflammatory not only because it sought to air publicly many of the internal divisions within government circles, but because it largely articulated the perspective of the department of munitions and supplies (where he had been employed in its economics branch), based on speculation and inference in the absence of any factual basis for how policy was actually constructed.[9]

These tensions were further aggravated by James's personality. David Slater, who would encounter James after the war in academic circles, does not mince words in saying that James, "supercilious in mien and manner, engendered hostility among those he should have impressed ... All doubted his judgment. He and Marsh were a contrast in Englishmen, the one a pretentious climber who had worked his way to the Principalship of McGill through American academic posts, the other a brilliant, industrious and modest scholar with a strong social conscience. James also suffered from not being 'one of the boys' of the intellectual elite that formed in Canada between the wars. He was pushy and manipulative."[10] To Mackenzie King, James was simply "an ass of a fellow."[11] For his part, Mackintosh maintained a cordial working relationship with James, although he was not particularly impressed with his work as an economist.[12]

These factors notwithstanding, the source of the conflict that would emerge between the James Committee on the one hand, and politicians and the civil service on the other, was the ill-defined role of such an external committee in the policy process. Raising for public discussion the general role of the state in a postwar economy was of unquestioned benefit; however, the implementation of specific policy proposals was hardly a realistic expectation for an extra-governmental committee.[13]

The government's first step to "rein in" the James Committee was to assign responsibility for reconstruction planning to the EAC under a subcommittee headed by Mackintosh. In November 1942, the "Interim Report on the James Committee" was forwarded to the EAC for its assessment. It rejected the recommendation to place responsibility for reconstruction under the control of a "Ministry of Economic Planning" and a special cabinet committee – a step that presumably would have enhanced the authority of both Ian Mackenzie as minister and James – on the grounds that it could not achieve the degree of interdepartmental cooperation required. The EAC further reserved for itself the responsibility for investigating and assigning tasks to specific departments: "an outside or non-departmental committee of the type of the Committee on Reconstruction can perform valuable functions in assisting with the development and promotion of postwar plans, but ... the experience of the United Kingdom and the United States points to the general conclusion that postwar planning must be the responsibility of the Government itself and that the bulk of the preparatory and advisory work must be done within the ordinary Government Departments and agencies."[14] When the cabinet accepted the advice of the EAC, Grant Dexter interpreted the change in the following terms: "Originally ... the social security committee under Cyril James functioned under Ian Mackenzie's department. But as things got hotter, the brain trust insisted on taking it away from Ian and James, and so it was transferred ... to Willie, thus letting Clark, Towers, et al. in on the ground floor."[15] The James Committee would continue in its advisory capacity, reporting directly to the prime minister rather than the cabinet, with its recommendations then forwarded to the EAC for evaluation. James, perhaps ingenuously, wrote to Mackintosh that "The whole scheme seems to be excellent, but I am somewhat vague as to the precise division of work between the new [EAC] committee and my present committee – as well as by the need for a close and continuous liaison between the two if they are to work effectively in harness. These problems cannot, as the Report emphasizes, be defined in any cut and dried fashion at this stage, but I should like to have a chat with you at some convenient time."[16] Clark was equally satisfied and encouraged Mackintosh to have "a frank discussion with [James] on the division of work. We can probably arrange to allot the field in fairly satisfactory way – leaving no duplication in some fields and duplication in other fields where the outside point of view as well as the bureaucratic one are desirable."[17]

But James's ambitions were hardly curtailed, and he again raised the ire of the government when he ventured into the murky field of dominion-provincial relations. In a letter to the prime minister in January 1943, James explained that his committee had been carrying on discussions with western provincial ministers concerning the conservation and utilization of raw materials. "In view of all the changed circumstances, and particularly of the recent change in the status and functions of the Committee on Reconstruction, I should like to know whether in your opinion it seems desirable to proceed with these arrangements. If you approve, I shall naturally discuss with Dr. Mackintosh the general details of the agenda that will come up for discussion."[18] King replied that "I am inclined to think that it is unwise to proceed further in discussing these questions with Provincial representatives until there has been a full opportunity for you and your Committee to consider, with Dr. Mackintosh and the Economic Advisory Committee, the general lines to be followed in the field."[19]

Things came to a head with the Marsh Report prepared for the James Committee and the intrigues surrounding its public release on 16 March 1943. Following the Beveridge Report in Great Britain, Marsh set out to provide a similar blueprint for a comprehensive social-security system in Canada by first defining the level of income required for a minimum standard of living, and then outlining the necessary components of social assistance, including contributory unemployment and disability insurance, maternity leave, old-age pensions, and the public provision of family allowances, unemployment relief, and public-works programs. The Marsh Report was widely acknowledged to be a clarion call for a comprehensive welfare state and established Marsh's reputation as the "Canadian Beveridge," but its shortcomings as a policy document left it vulnerable to criticism. Walter Gordon, for one, made great sport of how hastily the report was written and its open-ended implications for the government's budget. Mackenzie, who took the brunt of the criticism, was "like the monkey that sat on the lawnmower. You can hear him screaming two blocks away."[20] Mackenzie saw the public release of the Marsh Report as a deliberate act to undermine the work of the Reconstruction Committee, claiming that, in Dexter's words, he was "hijacked by the bloody brain trust of the East Block; that the plan of Clark and the others is to make a laughing stock out of the whole business"[21] When informed that the report had been made public, Mackintosh was unruffled, because he saw it as being rather benign: "As I understand the intention of this report, it is to review the measures of social insurance and related fields which are at present in operation in Canada, and suggest what it would be necessary to add to them if a complete social security system was contemplated ... Any work which the Reconstruction Committee undertakes on the actual planning of social security measures will be done in coordination with the Economic Advisory Committee."[22] But whether due to "U-boat activity" on the part of the bureaucracy or not, there is little question that significant damage was done to the credibility of the James Committee.[23]

What misgivings that existed about the James Committee prior to the Marsh Report were compounded with the announcement of Mackenzie's proposed bill on health insurance. It revisited the hoary issue of dominion-provincial finance by proposing provincial administration with dominion cost-sharing through grants-in-aid, upon certain standards being met. Since this approach to the division of jurisdiction and costs had been rejected in the Unemployment Insurance Act, the EAC was reticent to recommend another large social-security program without federal-provincial funding arrangements being first resolved. Moreover, the bill was unlikely to secure provincial cooperation, since the dominion was offering to pay only one-sixth of the cost, with the remainder split between individuals (bearing half the cost) and the provinces (responsible for making up any shortfall in personal contributions).[24] Undeterred, James continued to seek to extend the range of his committee's activities. In April, just one month after the release of the Marsh Report, he sought permission to travel to Newfoundland, to strike a new subcommittee on housing and community planning, to hire seven additional staff members, and to give Marsh a substantial raise (from $4,000 to $6,500) and the title of "special assistant."[25] When approached by Heeney for advice, Mackintosh was unsupportive: "My arrangement with the Reconstruction Committee is that they will continue the work presently being carried on by their sub-committees, very few of which have as yet prepared recommendations that they would not undertake new studies without consultation. In this connection, they have consulted me only in respect to one enlarged activity, namely, that of a reorganized sub-committee on housing which I have approved after considerable discussion with C.A. Curtis [Mackintosh's Queen's colleague] who has been named Chairman." Nor did he support giving Marsh more money. "I would think … that $6,500 would represent quite a substantial margin above his salary at McGill. While I think that, during the war, there is room for some margin where people are transferred to temporary government appointments, I have been inclined myself to take the attitude that the government salary should not leave more than a moderate amount for the additional cost of living in Ottawa. I recognize that Marsh is a hard and capable worker, and I would like to see him treated generously; on the other hand, I should think you should be careful that the salary was defensible in terms of his ordinary occupation."[26]

In June Heeney alerted Mackintosh to James's intent to create an independent subcommittee on industrial reconstruction composed of "big" industrialists, raising its own money and conducting its work in secret. "I think the potential for political mischief, if nothing worse, involved in this procedure, is very serious," Heeney warned.[27] Walter Gordon expressed a similar concern to Mackintosh: "I noticed in the paper this morning that Dr. Cyril James advised the Senate Committee on Reconstruction and Social Security that his committee has undertaken to obtain certain facts from private industry and I am wondering if that means that they are taking over from you the job which we discussed some time ago. Obviously you cannot have two sets of people approaching private industry on the same general subject and if the James Committee are going to do this you could not very well follow along behind it." Mackintosh's response expressed his frustrations with James, but he remained largely nonplussed: "he has organized, or has given his blessing to the organization of, an industrial sub-committee made up of a galaxy of bankers and industrialists most of whom except for J.S. McLean and J.S. Duncan, are from Montreal."[28] Concern over the number of subcommittees and the amount of spending by the James Committee surfaced within the cabinet, and James was "deeply disturbed" over the increasing restrictions imposed. He argued that his committee was created to have "liberty of action very much in excess of normal civil service procedure," but Heeney merely responded that the need to justify public expenditures was not limited to the James Committee.[29]

The "Final Report" of the James Committee thus came as an anticlimax. It was referred to the EAC, which issued its recommendations on 17 November 1943. The report was described as "preliminary in scope and educational with few formal and specific recommendations," but was applauded for the "number of valuable comments on the roles which governments, private enterprise, labour and agriculture must play in a successful program ... The main emphasis ... is on the objects of full employment and social security, coupled with a program of planned development of natural resources." As far as the immediate postwar transition period was concerned, the EAC warned that the report relied too heavily on the experience of the last war in expecting pent-up demand for consumer and capital goods to result in boom conditions; instead, the EAC cautioned that, with rapid military and non-military demobilization, the potential for unemployment was high unless labour was efficiently transferred between sectors. The EAC commented specifically on the proposals for a National Development Board, a Construction Reserve Commission, dominion-provincial relations, and the social-security initiatives outlined by Marsh, but since each of these items had already been reviewed by the EAC, there was no need to offer further recommendations. Instead, it limited its recommendations to the report's publication, because of its "educational value" – perhaps a rather dismissive characterization – adding that it might be criticized as too conservative in approach in some circles.[30] With this, the activities of the James Committee came to an end.

There were various explanations offered for the demise of the James Committee – cabinet politics, with Mackenzie seeking to carve out a greater role for himself and for social-welfare initiatives; interdepartmental disputes over control of reconstruction work; a jealous civil service seeking to "torpedo" an extragovernmental committee; the politics of social security and interpretations of the Marsh report as either too radical or too conservative; and James's obnoxious personality and personal ambitions – but it is probable that they all played a role. For his part, however, Mackintosh maintained a consistent position. He did not object to giving the James Committee liberty of action as long as it did not stray into areas of external relations and dominion-provincial finance, but treated it as an advisory body that should play no role in actual policy formation. If he was at fault, it was for being too lax in his oversight of the James Committee. Yet lost amid all the kafuffle over the committee's autonomy were the substantive contributions it made to postwar planning: the proposal for a single government ministry to oversee reconstruction work, which was eventually adopted; the National Development Board to consider demobilization and public initiatives in the event that emergency employment opportunities were required; and the Construction Reserve to provide a "shelf" of public-works projects. Though the ideas were not altogether new, or the proposals worked out in the form of concrete policy, they managed to push along reconstruction planning at a time when government officials were preoccupied with other matters. It now fell to Mackintosh and the reconstituted EAC to pull together the various strands of reconstruction work into a coherent plan of action.

THE RECONSTITUTED ECONOMIC ADVISORY COMMITTEE

With the administrative reorganization in January 1943 that delegated authority over reconstruction planning to the EAC, its Subcommittee on Postwar Reconstruction (composed of Mackintosh, Bryce, Rasminsky, Sandy Skelton, Deutsch, J.R. Baldwin, and Jean Chapdelaine) began meeting in earnest. Mackintosh augmented the staff by recruiting T.L. Avison ("on loan" from Sun Life Assurance Company), Steven Trachtenberg (an MA student at the University of Toronto), and Malcolm (Mac) Urquhart. They would be joined by Marsh, Firestone, and the rest of the staff of the James Committee when it was disbanded. Avison remained in reconstruction work for the remainder of the war, while Trachtenberg's service was interrupted by a two-year bout of tuberculosis, during which time he was replaced by D.C. Rowat.[31]

The relationship between Urquhart and Mackintosh would be an enduring one. Born on an Alberta homestead in 1913, Urquhart had attended Normal School and taught school for five years before entering university. He graduated from the University of Alberta in 1940 as the Governor General's Gold Medalist and then spent two years in the doctoral program in economics at the University of Chicago. After a year of teaching at MIT, and with Jacob Viner's enthusiastic recommendation, he joined the department of finance in Ottawa, after much encouragement by Mackintosh.[32] Urquhart's gifts were immediately recognized in Ottawa, and Mackintosh jealously guarded against his secondment to other government duties. When the Dominion Bureau of Statistics requested his services to work on the national income and expenditure accounts, Mackintosh refused to transfer him, despite personal appeals by S.A. Cudmore and Bert Marshall, arguing that "it is going to be very important not only that we have national income statistics, but that we should have some people at this end who can integrate them with the Budget and other phases of government policy."[33] When Mackintosh took up the position of director general of research in the department of reconstruction, he insisted on taking Urquhart with him. He was equally adamant at the end of the war in recommending Urquhart for an appointment at Queen's, where he would enjoy a long and distinguished career.

In preparation for the first meeting, Mackintosh sent Bryce a four-page memorandum on "Post-War Economic Problems," with eighteen items listed. As was not unusual when dealing with Bryce, he received back a nine-page response with twenty-one items enumerated, and before the two men were finished, the list had grown to twenty-seven.[34] The purely domestic problems to be addressed were then winnowed down to a workable grouping: demobilization, monetary and fiscal policies for the postwar transition, public capital spending, social security, and dominion-provincial relations.

The immediate issue was the rate at which demobilization would occur and the capacity of the economy to absorb men back into civilian life. At Mackintosh's request, George Luxton prepared labour-force estimates in order to establish the scope of the problem: after deducting the unemployable, retired, and institutionalized, the potential labour force was estimated to be 8.5 million in March 1943, while total employment stood at 5.1 million, with roughly one-third in war-related industries. Of those remaining outside of the labour force, there were 55,000 employable men, 880,000 farm women, 1,564 non-farm women, and 570,000 students.[35] "It is not certain that a crisis will arise," reported the EAC, "but the fairly rapid demobilization of some one and a half million persons, or nearly one-third of the gainfully occupied population, from the armed services and war industries, when viewed against the inability of the durable goods industries to start peacetime production without some months of preparation, renders it sufficiently probable that the Government must put itself in a position to act."[36] Robert England (Mackintosh's fellow student at Queen's, who was hired by the government at the beginning of the war) was at work on a report for the General Advisory Committee on Demobilization and Rehabilitation to address the repatriation and discharge of men in the armed services. Deutsch was assigned the task of analyzing the educational background and postwar plans of men returning from overseas, and an appeal was made to the Unemployment Insurance Commission to extend coverage to war veterans.[37] Mackintosh would later praise the Demobilization Committee for designing a Veterans Act which, through generous war-service grants and rehabilitation allowances, provided a model that the United States would imitate.[38]

The expansion of manufacturing during the war – from a third to over one-half of the total net value of commodity production – posed a significant challenge in the conversion of war plants to peacetime purposes.[39] A review of the rate of termination of war-industry contracts was undertaken by S.C. Scobell of munitions and supply, Urquhart set to work on a study of postwar industries and their employment impact, and Eric Adams of the Foreign Exchange Control Board identified emergency measures in the event of a postwar slump. A number of incentives for private investment were proposed, from double-depreciation allowances, the easing of corporate income taxes, the Bank of Canada's commitment to lower interest rates, the manner in which Crown assets and inventories were disposed, and export development.[40] Long-range planning also entertained the possibility that pent-up consumer demand and a shortage of materials would lead to inflation, rather than unemployment, as the major economic concern. To this end, it was proposed that wartime taxation, supply and production controls, and price controls be unwound gradually, while public investment would give way in favour of housing and other private investment.[41]

As a vehicle for implementing policy, the EAC proposed a National Development Board, which had been recommended earlier by both the EAC and the James Committee, to place members of the Armed Forces into employment or retraining programs. In the draft legislation prepared by Mackintosh and Bryce, it was to monitor the transition of veterans into the economy and to coordinate and plan dominion capital expenditures by "inducing departments to make long term detailed plans and, at the other end, be ready to explain to the Minister of Finance the advantages of one project against another because of their different effects on employment and their other economic results."[42] This was to be complemented by a Construction Reserve Commission to coordinate all large public construction jobs, in the event that such might be needed to offset a slump in private spending as wartime contracts were terminated.[43] A public investment board would manage and provide technical assistance to the "shelf" of government projects, beginning with dominion-only items, and broadening to include a wide range of projects. Bryce's "rough checklist" identified mapping of land use and natural-resource potential; forestry development and mineral development; hospitals in small and rural areas; rural electrification; highway modernization and farm and home modernization; airport development; rural-centre development; capital projects for tourism and recreation industries; construction of public buildings; shipbuilding;

drainage and irrigation; development of northern Canada; housing; urban improvement and redevelopment; and censuses of housing and durable goods.[44] "While it is suggested that the project be subjected to further study, the intention is that the proposal be perfected, not discouraged. The Economic Advisory Committee is of the opinion that early action along these general lines is urgent."[45]

The EAC also pressed for initiatives on social security. Mackintosh argued that "a crystallizing of public opinion and a heightened social consciousness demands that an effort be made to meet [persistent problems] more effectively than in the past. Most of the field of social insurance belongs in this group. Contributory old-age pensions were no less desirable before than after the war and the war has not changed the nature of the problem. What has probably changed is the attitude of the public. Nutritional and housing programs, long run plans for agriculture and industry, regulation of monopolies, industrial and scientific research, education – these are all groups of persistent problems for some or all of which government will wish measures devised."[46] With the scope of initiatives and guiding principles having been laid out in the Marsh Report, it remained to draft viable policy in the areas of unemployment relief and insurance, housing,[47] national health insurance, price support for farm and fisheries products, and, most significantly, family allowances.

The concept of family allowances was not new in Canada, having been debated in the House of Commons as early as 1929. But in addition to the constitutional problems encountered, the idea had been opposed on the left (such as by the Canadian Trades and Labour Congress) on the grounds that it would depress wages, and on the right by groups such as the Social Services Council, which argued that, by transferring money to mothers, it was inimical to the basic principles of marriage.[48] Although the idea of family allowances was endorsed by the CCF at a policy convention in July 1942 and was recommended by the Marsh Report in January 1943, more pivotal to its adoption was the support of the department of finance for family allowances as an alternative to a general wage increase. Avison, Rowat, and Trachtenberg were assigned the task of shaping a proposal. Initial payments of between $5 and $8 a month per child, depending on the age of the child, when compared to an average monthly wage of a single-earner household of $145, was deemed an effective means of supporting the standard of living among lower-income families.[49]

"The government as a whole isn't too enthusiastic on social security," wrote Dexter in December 1943, and he observed the frustration among senior civil servants, including Mackintosh.

> Coming to the brain trust, I've talked with Towers and Clark and Mackintosh. I think they are discouraged. They have done a good job on health insurance. The new post-war housing policy has been thoroughly worked out. [Clifford] Curtis did the main job here. Clark is completely sold on family allowances as the only effective way to deal with slum clearance. You have to give the boys the money to buy the houses that you intend to build for them. The difficulty in past housing schemes was to meet the needs of the lowest and largest income group. The revised family allowance scheme, however, is a graded one – by size of families and by age groups. But the brain trust can't get the cabinet to act, to come to grips with post-war problems.[50]

Responding to Clifford Curtis's pessimistic view of the prospects for re-election of the King government, Mackintosh wrote: "Your statement that the prospects for the Government are somewhat depressing sounds almost hopeful in the light of the degree of demoralization which has taken place at the centre. It is certainly an amazing example of disintegration."[51]

The King government eventually did respond and put in place many of the initiatives originating in the James Committee and the EAC. Slater expresses the common view that King's interest in social security only followed a series of electoral defeats to the CCF in by-elections in the summer of 1943. Walter Gordon provides a similar depiction of the gradual subsiding of the intransigence of the cabinet. "With his intense preoccupation with political survival, King was always reluctant to embrace new ideas and new policies. He preferred to move slowly or, it often seemed, not to move at all. And yet in fairness, he was persuaded by Clifford Clark, supported by Bill Mackintosh, to introduce some important social legislation towards the end of World War II, including unemployment insurance and family allowances."[52] The government would bring forth an impressive list of legislation during the 1944–45 session. The creation of the Industrial Development Bank as a subsidiary of the Bank of Canada was designed to extend loans or equity investment in industrial enterprises to meet the short-term financial needs. The

Export Credit Insurance Corporation was established to insure companies against the risk of loss in contracts for exports. The National Housing Act, in anticipation of the shortage of materials and spike in demand during the immediate postwar period, extended loan guarantees to home owners and construction companies. Price floors on agricultural and fisheries products and the Farm Loan Improvement Act provided support to primary commodity producers. Aid to veterans was provided in measures that helped them obtain vocational training, university education, and settlement assistance. The centerpiece, however, was the Family Allowance Act – described by Bryce as "the most radical, expensive, unlikely and popular legislation of the 1944 postwar program."[53]

DEPARTMENT OF RECONSTRUCTION AND THE WHITE PAPER

As planning for the postwar period accelerated, the cabinet placed responsibility under a single Department of Reconstruction, headed by C.D. Howe. Slater describes the role of the new department as a compromise between purely coordinating the efforts of other bodies versus directing all reconstruction work. It was to plan and coordinate activities, but the power to direct other ministries was assigned to a newly established cabinet Committee on Reconstruction. Moving reconstruction work from the EAC to a new department reflecting the urgent need for action, a difference in emphasis (industrial reconversion versus social security), and change in leadership within the cabinet. Again, the common denominator was Mackintosh. "While the work of reconstruction involves an adventure into the unknown," wrote Howe to Mackintosh, "I have a feeling that those of us who undertake the work will have a great field of service to Canada. I sincerely hope you will join us."[54] R.A.C. Henry, deputy minister of the new department, reported to Howe that: "Dr. MacIntosh [*sic*] stated that he did not desire to assume any responsibilities which were administrative in character, or responsibilities which would tie him down indefinitely to Government service, but he thought that he could be helpful in some phases of the reconstruction work, and, with the consent of the Minister of Finance and Dr. Clark, the Deputy Minister of Finance, would be quite willing to do so. His suggestion was that … he might act in the capacity of Economic Advisor, although the question of title is a matter which does not concern him greatly."[55] A further condition for the transfer was that Mackintosh continue his role in international talks and with the department of finance on the budget, and that Urquhart, Margaret Mary Guthrie (his secretary), and most of the staff from the EAC come with him. With these conditions met, Clark agreed to "loan" Mackintosh to the department of reconstruction as director general of research, effective 1 December 1944.[56]

Mackintosh's team undertook a number of industry studies, surveys, and forecasts of economic and employment conditions, and made an inventory of public work projects. Three months into his sojourn in the department of reconstruction, however, Mackintosh was apparently disconsolate. Dexter records that

> Bill Mackintosh – my favourite – fed up with being a civil servant. He has no bump for organization and no temperament for the rough and bruising career of a civil servant. Prefers educating young men with open minds to trying to split open the solid craniums of cabinet ministers in order to get ideas in. Is convinced that there is no such thing as an open-minded minister. All hopeless. Why waste life in trying to reason with them. So, he goes home to Kingston, stars in his eyes, the moment the big show is over. Meantime he essays daily an intellectual form of volleyball – bouncing ideas off Mr. Howe's battleship steel headpiece. Some of 'em bounce pretty far. But perhaps I am exaggerating. He finds that Howe agrees but does he know what he is agreeing with.[57]

In part, Mackintosh's frustration stemmed from the failure of the government to put forward a coherent vision, and political platform, in response to the growing popularity of the left. As Dexter observed:

> If the CCF was a sound outfit, Bill wouldn't mind it unduly. He is not a partisan. But he knows the CCF very well and finds them to be an impractical, doctrinaire lot, without a grasp of what is required. The great need now is for postwar planning in the international field. This should be stressed and, to a large extent, it is going forward. The brain trust hasn't lost its nerve. And the government is encouraging the work. But the government for other reasons is incapable of talking about it. Unless we get off on the right foot after this war, the future will be very dark. Yet if

> the CCF should come into power in 1944 or 1945, it would plunge into a long drawn out and perfectly fruitless business of taking over the CPR or the banks or aluminium. Suppose you could save a quarter per cent on the interest rate by public ownership, of what value would it be in the larger view? Meantime the vitally important tasks, which appear not to interest the CCF, would be neglected. There was much more in this vein.[58]

Dexter may well have been exaggerating, for Mackintosh soldiered on. He approached Howe with the idea of drafting a document that would pull together the various strands of the government's initiatives into a coherent statement mimicking in form a British white paper. Finally obtaining Howe's conditional permission to do so, Mackintosh wrote a draft over a weekend in early March 1945 and obtained feedback from Bryce and Urquhart.[59] Howe remained unconvinced but, on Henry's urging, Mackintosh spent a day working through the text with Howe, St Laurent, and Ilsley in order to secure cabinet approval: "I stood over him, Ilsley and St Laurent like a schoolmaster and made them read and assent to or modify every sentence and clause that set out government views or gave any commitment to policy," he reported.[60] The result of the endeavour was the masterful White Paper on *Employment and Income, with Special Reference to the Initial Period of Reconstruction*, tabled by Howe in the House of Commons on 12 April 1945, just three weeks before an election was called. Save for two notoriously inelegant paragraphs inserted by Howe, it articulated Mackintosh's vision of the postwar Canadian economy.[61]

The White Paper provided a textbook account of an open-economy Keynesian model, modified to reflect the predominance of the export sector in Canadian national-income determination. It began by enunciating the principle of effective demand – "Remunerative employment and income in any economy are provided by the expenditures which are made" – and then adopted the Keynesian classification of expenditure flows: personal consumption, private investment, government spending, and net exports. This was followed by the assertion that "the Government proposes to use appropriate means to influence expenditures in all these channels with particular emphasis on those which are most susceptible to encouragement and control."[62] The factors influencing each expenditure category are outlined in turn. Befitting Canada's status as a small open economy, the export sector is addressed first. "Export trade has been the greatest dynamic force influencing the level of national income and employment in Canada." He looked forward to the time when Canada's dependence on international trade would be lessened and it would be a net creditor nation; however, in the immediate postwar period, it would be necessary to cultivate international trade. To this end, he emphasized the role of new international institutions arising out of the Bretton Woods accord for ensuring the reduction in trade barriers and increased currency convertibility to permit trade to develop on a multilateral basis.[63]

Next in importance was private investment. Though highly geared to the export sector, an anticipated pent-up consumer demand, a neglected housing sector, and the replacement of a largely depreciated manufacturing capital stock were expected to stimulate investment directed towards domestic markets. He echoed the Keynesian view that the "decision to invest private funds in capital goods will depend on the businessman's view of the prospective margin of profit to be made on the investment."[64] To further encourage private investment the traditional tools of tax cuts, expansionary monetary policy, and public lending institutions received secondary importance.

Consumption, in turn, was expected to be bolstered by rising incomes and the savings accumulated during the war. The income-security measures that had evolved during the war – unemployment insurance, family allowances (scheduled to take effect in July 1945), price support for agriculture and fisheries, and the extension of public pensions – were to play an important role in stabilizing consumption expenditures.

While it left no doubt that private spending was to remain the driving force in the economy, the White Paper defined, for the first time in a peacetime economy, an important role for public investment. "The deliberate use of public investment expenditures as a permanent instrument of employment policy has to be undertaken experimentally. There is, as yet, no working model even in other countries. It will be necessary to frame policy to fit the facts of the Canadian economy and administer it in accordance with our federal constitution."[65] The most important feature of this was the "shelf" of public projects, worked out with the provinces and to be undertaken during times of slower economic growth, and longer-term expenditures on the development and conservation of natural resources.[66] Mackintosh provided a clear statement of the role of counter-cyclical government spending to justify such public infrastructure programs. "The Government will be prepared, in periods when unemployment threatens, to incur the deficits and increases in national debt resulting from its employment and income policy, whether that policy in the circumstances is best applied through increased expenditures or reduced taxation. In periods of buoyant employment and income, budget plans will call for surpluses. The Government's policy will be to keep the national debt within manageable proportions, and maintain a proper balance in its budget over a period longer than a single year."[67]

Written with his characteristic speed, clarity, and straightforward language, the White Paper was designed to enhance the layperson's understanding of economic conditions and, in doing so, to dispel fears of a postwar slump. The *Financial Post* recognized it as "one of the most important documents ever put before [parliament]," but its reception was overshadowed by the announcement of Franklin Delano Roosevelt's death.[68] Reflecting on the White Paper twenty years later, Mackintosh insisted that there was nothing particularly radical or novel in the analysis, but that it was merely a statement of the principles underlying the policies implemented during the war.[69] But it was both radical and novel. It was radical to the extent that its content and organization embraced the new framework for macroeconomic analysis based upon Keynesian expenditure categories, as well as a rudimentary overview of the main variables influencing aggregate demand. Although some attention was paid to long-run supply factors, such as labour-force training and scientific research, it was decidedly Keynesian in its emphasis on short-run demand management. Indeed, the title itself is an obvious reference to Keynes's *General Theory of Employment and Income*.

The novelty was in the application of a Keynesian framework to an open economy. As he later commented: "Neither Keynes nor Alvin Hansen, to whose great work in extending and elaborating Keynesian analysis Kenneth Galbraith has recently and rightly paid tribute, ever really faced squarely the case of the open economy and its relations to larger national economies. Still less had attention been given to the added complication of a federal state. Though the White Paper cannot claim to have made any really significant contributions to policy prescriptions for an open economy with a federal government, it was an honest attempt to set out simply and clearly the real context of employment policy in Canada."[70] This wedding of the staple thesis with Keynesianism is reflected at the outset. The stated goal – "to maintain a high and stable level of employment and income" – is qualified with the proviso "the Government is mindful that employment and incomes will be subject to fluctuations in the sphere of international trade, which cannot be wholly and instantaneously offset." The penultimate sentence reiterated the point: "A prosperous world is essential to a prosperous Canada."[71]

Mackintosh was satisfied that the vision expressed had endured the test of time. In writing to Howe nine years later, he commented that: "One of the features in which I took the greatest pride and which I think distinguished the document from some of those put out in other countries was that I meticulously – and, I am sure, tirelessly – pointed out to you, Mr. St. Laurent, and Ilsley every implication and commitment for government policy that was in the document." Howe, in turn, confessed to Mackintosh that "I recall having had some doubt about the wisdom of tabling the White Paper. I should have had more confidence in your good judgment."[72]

ACTING DEPUTY MINISTER OF FINANCE AND THE GREEN BOOK

It was in the nature of Mackintosh's wartime service that he could not reflect for long on the outcome of one task before having to move on to another. One month after the White Paper was presented in the House of Commons, he was dispatched to London for the Audit Room talks. His return flight, after a midnight stopover in Iceland, landed in Ottawa on 4 June, one week before the federal election, where he learned that Clark had fallen seriously ill. "Cliff Clark – appears to be shrivelling," Dexter had observed just a few months earlier. "Getting to look all head and no body. I should think a darn sight more tired and frayed than anyone I've seen."[73] Mackintosh himself confessed to being "a little weary," but there was to be no respite.[74] Informing Principal Wallace that it would be necessary to delay his return to Queen's for yet another year, he assumed, in addition to his work on the international front, the duties of acting deputy minister of finance for six months and took on the framing of the government's proposals on postwar reconstruction for the Dominion-Provincial Conference.

In 1943, Mackintosh and the EAC, like the James Committee before it, could not avoid returning to an old theme: "Amendments to Canada's constitution will be necessary if the vital economic problems that will crowd upon us immediately after the war are to be solved." Anticipating "an insistent public demand for social security and jobs for all who need them," he stressed that constitutional reform was necessary if the dominion government were to exercise the policy levers to address these concerns.[75] J.R. Baldwin insisted in January 1943 that a study of constitutional powers should go ahead simultaneously with preparations for various social and economic recommendations," and this prompted Sandy Skelton's reports on "Dominion Post-War Policy" and "Constitutional Change Necessary to Deal with Post-War Problems." Given Skelton's involvement, it is not surprising that the recommendations in the EAC's report echoed those of the Rowell-Sirois Royal Commission: that the dominion government should have jurisdiction over all contributory insurance programs, but with decentralized administration, and exclusive jurisdiction over income taxes, corporate taxes, and succession duties.[76] The EAC failed to receive any directives from cabinet following its June 1943 recommendations for dominion-provincial reform, but pressed ahead with efforts to outline the appropriate constitutional changes. The reconstruction department would continue this work, largely under the leadership of Skelton.[77] Since the tax rental agreement reached in the early stages of the war would expire following the cessation of hostilities, a dominion-provincial agreement on financial arrangements was necessary if the broad agenda outlined in the White Paper was to be pursued.

The cabinet committee concerned with reconstruction began meeting in February 1944. Equipped with background studies produced by Mackintosh's staff in the reconstruction department, preparations for the conference began in earnest in spring of 1944. The Advisory Committee on Preparations for Dominion-Provincial Conference met on 30 May 1944 with a rather unwieldy membership of thirty ministers and senior civil servants, including Mackintosh. A coordinating committee was established, with Sandy Skelton as secretary, and subcommittees were set up on public investment, financial arrangements, labour, social security, agriculture, and housing. Mackintosh was assigned responsibility for both the public-investment and financial-arrangements subcommittees, but he protested that the work of the subcommittees depended upon knowing the exact terms of an agreement on dominion-provincial cooperation, the very matter which the conference was intended to achieve. His memorandum for the advisory committee provided the framework for both the division of dominion-provincial jurisdiction and cost sharing, and it became the basis for the dominion's position at the conference. He would also inherit primary responsibility for drafting the dominion's proposals. According to Slater, "[Brooke] Claxton suggested that once decisions had been reached in the major items, they should be turned over to Mackintosh and 'glamourized.'"[78]

The outcome was the *Proposals of the Government of Canada* (hereafter referred to as the Green Book), with its eleven accompanying background volumes. Its rationale was based upon the experience of the Great Depression, during which "the Canadian economy did not provide adequate opportunities for employment and enterprise; the deficiencies in the provision for social welfare became strikingly apparent; and the structure of government finance in our federal system developed basic strains and weaknesses. The war came before solutions to these problems were reached." To this was added the assertion of the White Paper that the state must accept the role of stabilizing incomes and employment: "Success in the attainment of high levels of employment, increased welfare, and security, is dependent upon fruitful cooperation between all governments and groups in this country. It is the responsibility of government to pursue policies that create conditions in which the initiative, energy and resourcefulness of individual citizens can achieve rising standards of living."[79] The Green Book addressed three issues that required dominion-provincial cooperation: managing the "shelf" of public investment, social-welfare initiatives, and reform of the taxation system.

The Green Book called for "bold action by the state in those fields in which the public interest calls for public enterprise in national development." This included expenditures on transportation infrastructure, natural-resource conservation and development, and public works, and was to be implemented on a counter-cyclical basis "so that they did not compete with private activity but supplement it and contribute to the stabilization of employment whenever private employment declines." As a corollary, "the Government will budget for a cycle rather than for any one fiscal year, and ... will design both its spending policies and its tax policies throughout the cycle to level out the deflationary valleys and inflationary peaks ... The modern governmental budget must be the balance wheel of the economy." Coordination of public investment with the provinces was to be achieved through federal grants in areas of shared or exclusive provincial jurisdiction, "to induce provinces to time their construction in a manner to assist other employment programs."[80]

Social-welfare legislation was justified not just on humanitarian grounds, but as a means of enhancing national unity by standardizing services across and within provinces, and of contributing to economic stability. With respect to the latter, it was stated that: "A significant volume of social security payments, flowing into the consumer spending stream, will stabilize the economy of the country as a whole and work against a fall in national income."[81] With unemployment insurance, family allowances, veterans' pensions and farm price supports already in place, three "main gaps" in the social security system were identified: health insurance, national old age pensions, and expanded unemployment assistance.[82]

In proposing national health insurance, the Green Book noted that nearly all western countries had adopted some form of health insurance, and that it was no coincidence that the three exceptions – Australia, Canada, and the United States – were all federal states. The Green Book proposal differed from the bill drafted by Mackenzie in 1943 by offering more federal support. The cost of a national system was estimated at $250 million, or $21.60 per person, for complete medical and dental coverage. The dominion government would contribute 60 per cent of the cost – in the form of a basic federal grant of one-fifth the estimated cost of each service, and one-half of the actual cost, to maximum of $12.96 per person – with the provinces required to pay roughly $12 per person. Coverage would be phased in, with physician services from general practitioners and hospital care included immediately, and specialist physician services, dental services, and drug coverage to be added later.[83] Additional federal aid would come in the form of grants for public health, training, research, and hospital construction.

Pension reform entailed expanding the coverage and generosity of the existing Canadian Old Age Pensions Act. At the time, all British subjects aged seventy and older, who had resided in Canada for more than twenty years, were eligible for a maximum pension of $25 per month, based upon financial need. The federal government contributed 75 per cent of the cost, and the provinces were free to supplement the monthly benefit. This was criticized on three grounds: that it led to wide variations across provinces in the percentage of those seventy and older who qualified for benefits (from 28 to 57 per cent) and in average monthly benefits (from $18.63 to $29.41); that the "embarrassment" of the means test should be minimized; and that the maximum benefit subject to federal funding was too low. The Green Book proposal was to make an old-age pension of $30 per month universal for those seventy and over, and to have it be entirely federally funded and administered. The annual cost was estimated at $200 million. There would also be a means-tested pension for those aged sixty-five to sixty-nine, under provincial administration, for which the federal government offered to pay 50 per cent of the cost up to a maximum of $15 per month. The estimated total cost for this program would be $35 to $40 million.

The dominion proposal on unemployment assistance was to extend coverage of the unemployment insurance to all "employables," since the 1941 Unemployment Insurance Act excluded roughly 20 per cent of the labour force from coverage (including farmers and other self-employed, domestics, government and office employees, and youth). The maximum duration of benefits would be extended from one to two years, after which the individual would be deemed "unemployable" and become a provincial responsibility.

The justification for rearranging taxation authority was the same as given by the Rowell–Sirois Royal Commission. The current system of taxation was highly regressive because of its dependence on consumption taxes, it did not provide for minimum standards across the country, and it provided inadequate financial resources – and thus financial autonomy – to the provinces. The dominion tax proposal was similar to the wartime tax rental agreement: it suggested that the provinces vacate the fields of personal and corporate income taxes, as well as succession duties, in return for unconditional dominion transfers. The latter was to be equivalent to $12 per-capita annually (or a minimum of $138 million per year), and would increase at a rate tied to the growth in population and national income.

As David Slater argues, the Green Book must be read as a companion piece to the White Paper in defining the role of a federal state in managing economic activity consistent with Keynesian policy.[84] Where the White Paper outlined the initiatives that could be undertaken by the central government on a unilateral basis, the Green Book addressed measures that required provincial cooperation. Though many of the suggested initiatives repeated earlier recommendations from the National Employment Commission, the Rowell–Sirois Royal Commission, and wartime measures, the Green Book was distinct in terms of the degree of conviction and the overall framework within which various policy initiatives were expressed.

> Broadly what is proposed is that the Dominion Government should take the initiative in the maintenance of employment and income, (1) by achieving the best possible agreements with the United Nations in the field of economic relations, agreements which would encourage and permit the expansion of world trade and full use of our resources; (2) by pursuing fiscal and other policies which will create 'favourable conditions within which the initiative, experience and resourcefulness of private business can contribute to the expansion of business employment'; (3) by so managing its public investment expenditures and making it financially advantageous to provincial and municipal governments so to manage theirs, that they will contribute to the stability and not to the instability of employment; further, to direct those expenditures particularly to the development and conservation of our natural resources, improving thereby the opportunities of the Canadian people and the financial position of the provincial governments who administer them; (4) by maintaining and stabilizing by a comprehensive system of social security, incomes which are largely spent on consumption and by contributing thereby to the health, welfare and productive capacity of the Canadian people and to their employment.[85]

The Dominion-Provincial Conference on Reconstruction began on 6 August 1945 and continued on an intermittent basis until it was disbanded on 3 May 1946. Social-security initiatives, which were conditional upon striking adequate fiscal arrangements, assumed secondary importance. But the dominion government's fiscal proposals garnered little support. The Ontario government's "disentanglement" model – in which there would be no overlapping federal-provincial responsibilities and distinctive taxation powers – and its outright rejection of the Green Book's framework, left little room for achieving a consensus. Mackintosh played a central role in seeking to rescue the talks. As co-chair of the "Financial Arrangements" committee and as a member of the "Economic Committee," established in January 1946, he sought to find common ground between the dominion and provincial governments.[86] But whether due to a conflict of egos among first ministers, the rigidity of the department of finance and Bank of Canada, or King's lack of commitment of the federal government to social security,[87] the Dominion-Provincial Conference on Reconstruction, like the one that considered the recommendations of the Rowell–Sirois Royal Commission, failed to reach an agreement on a new division of taxation powers and spending responsibilities.

Mackintosh took some solace in the subsequent adoption of tax rental agreements that were similar to the Green Book proposals: the federal government assumed a greater control over taxation in return for fiscal transfers. Unconditional rather than conditional grants, however, continued to dominate, while social-security initiatives were postponed, some for several decades. Speaking twenty years later, Mackintosh was still sobered by the failure of the Dominion-Provincial Conference on Reconstruction: "Such limited knowledge as I have does not lead me to rely confidently on cooperative federalism, though it may have some short-run advantages. Government by negotiation will fall far short of democratic and efficient government. Twenty years after, governments cannot escape from their responsibility. Economists have added greatly to our knowledge of how and when. Effective organization, both within and between governments, is still far from adequate."[88]

RETURN TO QUEEN'S

A remarkable aspect of the time Mackintosh spent in Ottawa was the range of activities in which he was engaged: budget deliberations and the design of fiscal policy; leadership of the EAC through two iterations; work on labour supply and industrial-relations policy; domestic reconstruction planning; international talks leading to Bretton Woods, the postwar loan to Britain, and Canada's role in the United Nations; service on innumerable other committees; dozens of public addresses; and drafting of both the White Paper and the Green Book. The pace of work in Ottawa took its toll on the health of many men, such that Mackintosh's resilience did not go unnoticed. "There is one characteristic that I noted about yourself in my contacts with you over the past couple of years," wrote Henry when his own illness necessitated that he step down as chair of the Canadian JEC in favour of Mackintosh, "and that was that you appear to have a faculty of expending a minimum amount of nervous energy per unit of accomplishment."[89]

A host of other matters daily crossed his desk. He showed extraordinary patience in replying to unsolicited policy advice and other offers of assistance. When a former student wrote promoting a bomb "with great killing power" and indicated his willingness to come to Ottawa to give a demonstration, Mackintosh confessed that "my expertness does not extend to bombs." He directed the would-be bomb-maker to the Inventions Board, but warned him that it would "not want a demonstration but the plans."[90] On another occasion he helped a Winnipeg producer navigate import controls in order to obtain American cucumbers, but had to decline a generous gift of thanks. "I appreciate very much your kindly thought in sending to me a package of your pickles, and I do not in any way misconstrue your cordial intentions. However, it is impossible for me in my position to accept any such gift."[91] The pickles were donated to the Red Cross in Ottawa. This rule was apparently flexible, at least in so far as fresh fruit was concerned. Mackintosh accepted a crate of peaches from the BC Fruit Growers' Association after the EAC had granted it some relief from export controls. According to the association's wishes that "you will find one to spare for the 'slide rule' artist," he replied that "I shall assuredly see that Mr Bryce gets his share."[92]

There was little time for personal distractions. He was elected a "privileged member" of the Rideau Club shortly after arriving in Ottawa, but he resigned in March 1943 after rarely setting foot in it. The principal indulgence he accorded himself was the Five Lakes Fishing Club. Clark's long-standing ambition to develop an inexpensive refuge from the demands of Ottawa for senior government officials reached fruition in May 1940. He purchased an option on a property in the Gatineau Hills, with a rustic lodge sleeping up to twenty. Mackintosh was "impressed with its comfortableness and with the extent to which it has been got into first-class repair," bringing "the friendly bureaucrats face to face with the myth of the wilderness." Membership was restricted to forty. Among the original members still alive in 1970 were J.R. Beattie, F.W. Bruce, R.B. Bryce, J.E. Coyne, D.B. Mansur, J.W. Pickersgill, Alfred Rive, David Sim, and J.R. Tolmie. Rasminsky would join in 1941.[93]

His personal life during the war was affected by the death of his mother and the illness of his sister Margaret, which forced her to retire from the department of labour in 1944. He also suffered the loss of Arthur Purvis, his long-time mentor O.D. Skelton, Norman McLeod Rogers, and Pete McQueen. McQueen's death came as a particular shock given the close friendship the two men had developed through their involvement on the executive of the Canadian Political Science Association and the Rowell–Sirois Royal Commission, and during McQueen's summer teaching at Queen's. Mackintosh surely appreciated McQueen's warmth and often irreverent sense of humour. In their last correspondence, six months before McQueen's death, he wrote requesting copies of the budget speech for teaching purposes and added a personal note: "A dog bit me the day after you left, but it seems that winter is over for it is very warm to-day. I have played no golf, but I saw Dr. Boucher yesterday and he was very anxious that he get you out at the first opportunity. You will be about as bad as I am, so you needn't be hesitant about the matter." On 6 February 1941, just nine days after Skelton suffered a fatal heart attack, McQueen was killed in an airplane crash while travelling to a meeting of the Bank of Canada. When Vincent Bladen wrote, fulfilling his "melancholy duty to arrange obituaries," Mackintosh responded: "Poor Pete, no formal article in the Journal can do justice to him. I gather that the man who could really write something worthwhile, George Ferguson, is too much affected by his loss to be able to write anything for some time." Sidney Smith, president of the University of Manitoba, confided in Mackintosh that: "I can say that I have never suffered such a loss of a colleague as I did in the death of Pete McQueen. He was a good friend, and then a fellow worker. In fact, I have not been able to face up to thinking about the reorganization of the staff in Economics until the last few days. It still seems impossible to think that Pete is not some place around the campus. It will be impossible for us to get a man who can fit into a university in Western Canada as did Pete."[94]

Nor was there any doubt that Mackintosh missed academic life. In October 1944, for instance, amid his busy schedule, he "succumbed to the temptation" to take issue with the author of an article on Adam Smith. "I was disturbed to find [your article] reaching a stumbling stop on the reference in the last sentence to the relations between Adam Smith and James Watt," he wrote

> The statement is that in the *Wealth of Nations* Smith referred slightingly to Watt's invention of "a fire engine." My recollection,

> without looking up the *Wealth of Nations* again, is that the fire engine was not Watt's engine at all, but his predecessor Newcomen's atmospheric engine which was used for a generation in pumping the water out of English coal mines. It was commonly called a fire engine to distinguish it from other pumping facilities which use water power. I may be wrong, but I think Watt did not perfect the reciprocating steam engine until just a year or two before the *Wealth of Nations* was published. Further, far from thinking little of Watt, Smith had a considerable hand in his success ... There is nothing in the *Wealth of Nations* to suggest anything but the greatest interest in mechanical invention on Smith's part, but it must be remembered that there was no application of steam to factory development until considerably after the book was written. All the early Industrial Revolution in England took place on the basis of water power.[95]

It had become routine for Mackintosh to send a letter to Principal Wallace each spring, indicating that his duties in Ottawa remained unfinished, but offering the reassurance that he had no intention of delaying his departure from Ottawa once his obligations were met. With the war at an end and the major reconstruction work complete, Mackintosh submitted his formal resignation in July 1946. He informed Howe that "By September 1st, my temporary service with the Government will have extended over nearly seven years, and I am grateful for the opportunity which was given me to share in some measure in the work of those years. It has been a particular pleasure to work, in the last couple of years, in your Department and to experience the loyalty which you have inspired in your officials. I thank you warmly for your consideration and support and for your many personal kindnesses."[96] Howe acquiesced, noting that Mackintosh had been "a tower of strength to the Department of Reconstruction, particularly through the establishment of an Economic Research Branch which other departments of Government recognize as the best and most reliable in the service."[97] Ilsley would later add: "Among my happiest memories is that period of stress when you were acting as Deputy Minister and the only mistakes I was making were when I was not taking your advice."[98] With his contribution to Canada's war effort complete, Mackintosh wrote to Wallace asking that the family's residence in Summerhill be prepared for their long-delayed return to Queen's.

PART FOUR

A Ruling Passion: Queen's University

The "glacial" pace of change in Canada's universities until the middle of the twentieth century ended abruptly amidst the rapidly evolving social and economic conditions of the postwar period. Public awareness of universities was immediately enhanced by the educational needs of returning war veterans, while in the 1950s there was a surge in enrolment associated with economic prosperity, increasing urbanization, and immigration, as well as a shift in the occupational composition of the labour force towards more white-collar employment. The advancement in scientific knowledge and the influx of the baby boom generation in the 1960s only pushed the rate of change to dizzying new dimensions that would dramatically alter the male-centric world of universities.[1] Higher education thus became more important to the public, governments, and the corporate sector as part of a national effort to produce a highly trained labour force to participate in and to foster economic growth.[2]

Caught in the currents of this "new and strange world," Mackintosh confessed that those associated with universities had to first overcome their "bewilderment" with this new national attention. As traditional institutions, more inclined to preserve and transmit knowledge than to create and innovate, universities were prone to retreat in order to defend the values of academic freedom and of a liberal-arts education.[3] For this he did not apologize. Despite their conservative tendencies, he maintained that universities were one of the greatest revolutionary forces of western civilization. In the context of external pressure to produce more graduates with specialized training, he insisted that Canada must indeed invest more resources in universities, but that these institutions must remain centres for independent research and for ensuring the teaching of more "educated people of integrity."[4]

Individual universities thus had to manage quantitative growth, respond to the changing expectations placed upon them, and maintain their integrity as a place of intellectual freedom.[5] Mackintosh addressed these pressures from a variety of perspectives. In his various administrative roles at Queen's, he had a prominent hand in guiding the institution between 1946 and 1961; as president of the National Conference on Canadian Universities and as chairman of the Association of Universities of the British Commonwealth, he contributed to higher-education policy on a larger stage; and as a social and economic commentator, he argued the cause of universities as part of a broader cultural strategy.

12

Queen's after the War: Kingston, 1946–1951

Why Not More Mackintosh?

Globe and Mail, 1950[1]

Mackintosh carried with him an imposing list of titles on his return to Queen's: head of the department of political and economic science, director of the school of commerce, and dean of Arts (he was named dean in May 1943, but the decision was kept private in order to avoid public confusion).[2] He soon added that of vice-principal, which he downplayed as "taking the Principal's place in his absence and the privilege of being buried in the University lot in Cataraqui Cemetery."[3]

The Mackintosh family settled back into the west wing of Summerhill to pick up their life at Queen's, which had been interrupted by some seven years in Ottawa. Their return brought a measure of youthfulness to the university's culture. When Alison first arrived on campus in 1939, "that very black-haired baby in the screened-in pen" in front of Summerhill had not gone unnoticed, especially by Elspeth Wallace, who lived next door.[4] Now seven years old, Alison had an increased range of movement that warranted the billeting of two male students, who provided baby-sitting duties in exchange for room and board.

The university faced a unique challenge: the problems brought on by budgetary restrictions and stagnant enrolment during the Great Depression and the war had been replaced by the equally vexing need to accommodate the large influx of veterans with a depleted, overworked staff and cramped physical quarters. However, wartime experience left Mackintosh well-equipped to deal with such exigent circumstances. As Mac Urquhart observed, "Success resulted mainly from rearrangements designed to get the best possible product from existing buildings and staff – a war-time type of problem again. But the upshot was no mere 'crash' programme. In these university discussions, Mackintosh insisted on bearing long-run considerations in mind. In particular he sought to protect the classroom teacher from encroachments on his time and energy which would endanger not only the future of the university, but that of the individuals themselves."[5]

If his university duties were not demanding enough, a condition of accepting greater administrative responsibilities was that he be allowed sufficient time to attend to some unfinished business and new assignments in Ottawa. He continued as chair of the Unemployment Insurance Advisory Committee, accepted an appointment as director of the Canadian Mortgage and Housing Corporation, and, under different guises, dispensed advice to the departments of national defence, justice, and trade and commerce. Then, in 1950, he would be thrust onto the public stage in an effort to mediate the national railway strike.

The period between 1946 and 1951 thus proved to be a transitional phase for Mackintosh: it entailed a full-time return to academia coupled with part-time work as a policy advisor in Ottawa. It came to a conclusion when he agreed to devote himself exclusively to the affairs of Queen's as its principal.

HEAD, DIRECTOR, DEAN, AND VICE-PRINCIPAL

With some 750,000 men and women demobilized from the military, Canada's generous educational provisions in the War Veterans Allowance package brought many of them to the doors of Canada's universities. Queen's was no exception, with the number of returning war veterans dramatically increasing enrolment from 2,200 in 1945 to 3,200 in 1947. The challenges facing the department of political and economic science and the school of commerce were particularly acute: in 1946–47, ex-servicepeople made up 57 per cent of those registered in the Faculty of Arts, including 86 per cent of those in commerce, where enrolment was up over twofold from the war years.[6]

During his stay in Ottawa, Mackintosh had remained abreast of events at Queen's but had kept his nose out of his department's business unless consulted by Frank Knox or Clifford Curtis in their roles as acting department head, by Rex Smails as acting-director of commerce, or by Principal Wallace. C.E. Walker's death in 1942 and J.C. Cameron's temporary appointment in Ottawa with the department of labour had reduced the permanent staff in the department to seven: Knox, C.A. (Clifford) Curtis, and C.H. (Connie) Curtis in economics; J.A. Corry in political science; and Smails, J.L. McDougall, and L.G. Macpherson in commerce.[7] At Wallace's insistence, the CA courses had been taught by temporary appointments during the war.[8] After canvassing Mackintosh for his opinion, Principal Wallace promoted Corry (to professor), McDougall (to associate professor), and Macpherson (from instructor to lecturer, and then to associate professor).[9] Mackintosh did intercede in order to ensure the future of the industrial relations section, which had been established on a five-year experimental basis in 1937. With Cameron away and Wallace ambivalent about the section's renewal, Mackintosh took an active role in organizing its annual conference and arranging future financing. "Your news regarding the Principal's attitude towards the Industrial Relations Section is disturbing," he wrote to Knox. "I do not know why he is so timid about the Corporations for I am sure that the money is there for the asking." He was not wrong. By the end of 1942, eighty companies had subscribed a total of $18,175.[10] Converted to a department by Wallace, it offered short courses during the war for company personnel officers involved in training, and assisted companies seeking to provide courses to its staff. An institute for local government was also created during the war, to which K.G. Crawford, a graduate of the University of Western Ontario and city clerk in London, Ontario, was appointed. Clifford Curtis deemed that the "time was ripe" to establish the institute and inherit some of the momentum of the Citizens' Research Group with which Crawford was associated. Mackintosh deferred to Curtis's judgment, despite being less enamoured with "the supporters of the Citizens' Research Institute," who were inclined to be more interested in lower taxes than in good government."[11]

Rebuilding the staff complement began in earnest in the fall of 1945. In economics, Urquhart was appointed upon being released from his government duties, and David Slater was added a year later as a temporary lecturer.[12] In political science, Mackintosh had warned Principal Wallace in 1944 that both McGill and Dalhousie sought to lure Corry away, and advised that every effort should be made to retain him, including that, "barring acts of God and the King's enemies, he would be given an assistant after the war."[13] Wallace needed little persuading, and there was a broad consensus in the department that John Edward Hodgetts was the best available person to complement Corry.[14] Pauline Jewett was also appointed as an instructor for 1947–48.[15] In commerce, Smails canvassed to fill three vacancies, but managed to secure only two: J.E. Smyth and W.G. Leonard. Smyth was a chartered accountant who was teaching part-time while completing his master's degree at Toronto. "I have known for some time how highly Ashley and other members of the Department at Toronto regarded Smyth's character and ability," stated Smails, "but it was some time before I could bring myself to attempt to snatch him away from them."[16] Leonard, who had been teaching part-time at Queen's, assumed responsibility for the CA courses on a full-time basis. Further, C.H. Curtis would shift his teaching from economics to assist Cameron in the industrial relations program.[17]

Despite these additions, all hands were on deck when it came to teaching. Faculty members were lecturing for ten or eleven hours a week during the regular academic term. Mackintosh received only modest reprieve because of his administrative duties, spending seven hours a week teaching.[18] Two expedients were adopted to cope with the surge in enrolment. One was to offer large sections of first-year courses: in economics, for instance, all 240 students in Ec 4 (Introductory Economics) were taught by Knox – using the innovation of "lantern slides" – in a single section held in Grant Hall.[19] The other stop-gap measure was to extend the summer session in order to offer the equivalent of two full academic sessions in a single calendar year. Mackintosh was enamoured with neither remedial measure, tolerating the larger class sizes until the enrolment pressures abated after 1948, while insisting that the intensive summer session not be repeated.[20] In his first report as dean, he emphasized that the heavy workload brought on by higher enrolments impinged on research time. "Sheer numbers of students have added greatly to the burden of most members of the staff. Even though no additional hours were spent in the classroom, large classes are a drain on the energy. The mechanics of handling large classes are time consuming. Examinations and written work are in enormously increased volume. It is necessary to try to make headway against these obstacles to study and research."[21] As a long-term objective, he proposed less undergraduate teaching and more specialized graduate courses that would integrate the faculty members' research interests.

Problems encountered by other members of the academic staff also required Mackintosh's attention. The fallout of the Gouzenko spy affair in Ottawa during the early days of the Cold War did not leave Queen's untouched. Israel Halperin of the mathematics department was charged with providing official secrets to the Soviet Union during his wartime service in the Canadian military, but was subsequently acquitted because of lack of evidence. After the report of the Kellock–Taschereau Royal Commission on espionage in 1947, members of the board of trustees sought his dismissal, but Principal Wallace and Chancellor Dunning came to Halperin's defence.[22] Shortly after, Glen Shortcliffe of the French department incurred the wrath of some trustees for his pro-Soviet commentaries on the CBC. He acceded to their request to discontinue his radio broadcasts,[23] but his problems did not end there. He took a one-year leave of absence from Queen's in order to accept a permanent position in the United States, but was refused entry at the border. With Wallace on leave, it fell to Mackintosh to defend Shortcliffe and ensure that he was rehired at Queen's. As the *Toronto Star* reported Mackintosh's view on the matter, he imagined that professors at the university held "about the same political views as the ordinary population. We are not concerned as much with that as with the man's competence as a teacher."[24]

As the excessive demands on teaching time abated after 1948, concerns over salaries were amplified. Complaints that pay at Queen's lagged well behind that at the University of Toronto had persisted since at least 1920, when Skelton raised the matter as dean of Arts. Annual salary increments were cancelled between 1930 and 1936, only to be restored, along with a $500 salary increase for heads and senior professors, as part of Principal Fyfe's parting gift to the faculty in 1937. Wallace pushed through a significant increase in salaries in 1947, but changes of a similar magnitude at the University of Toronto maintained the sizable pay gap between the two institutions.[25]

In light of rising revenues from tuition fees, operating grants, and privately raised funds, heavy teaching loads and low salaries eroded the goodwill that the faculty had maintained through the frugal periods of depression and war. Although this thriftiness was largely

Table 12:1 Queen's Salary Schedules, 1920–1947

Maximum	*1920–26*	*1926–37*	*1937–46*	*1947*	*% change 1947*	*Toronto 1947*	*Difference 1947*
Head	$4,000	$4,500	$5,000	$6,000	20.0		
Professor	$3,750	$4,200	$4,500	$5,500	22.2	$6,500	15.4%
Associate	$3,250	$4,000	$4,000	$4,500	12.5	$5,500	18.2%
Assistant	$2,900	$3,500	$3,500	$3,750	7.1	$4,500	16.7%
Lecturer	$2,450	$3,000	$3,000	$3,000	0.0	$3,500	14.3%
Minimum	*1920–26*	*1926–37*	*1937–46*	*1947*	*% change 1947*	*Toronto 1947*	*Difference 1947*
Head	$3,500	$3,500	$4,000	$5,500	37.5		
Professor	$3,000	$3,000	$3,500	$4,500	28.6	$5,500	18.2%
Associate	$2,600	$3,000	$3,000	$3,750	25.0	$4,500	16.7%
Assistant	$2,000	$2,500	$2,500	$3,000	20.0	$3,500	14.3%
Lecturer	$1,500	$1,500	$1,500	$2,000	33.3	$3,000	33.3%

Source: Derived from QUA, Frank Knox Papers, 2/10.

identified with William McNeill's management, his retirement as treasurer in 1947 gave no sense of optimism for restoring faculty morale, as he sternly resisted salary increases from his position as a trustee. Gibson refers to McNeill as a man with a "passion for saving" and one who "disliked spending money on anything." In an obituary note, Mackintosh more generously referred to his "thriftiness and resourcefulness." However much he opposed many of McNeill's decisions as treasurer, Mackintosh had an enduring affection for him, and especially for his commitment to Queen's. He wrote to Sir William Fyfe shortly after McNeill's death in 1959: "You will be interested to know about Dr. McNeill's will. Aside from an annuity for his housekeeper and some minor gifts, his estate comes to the University ... Taking a dim view of our investment committee, he has provided that none of his securities can be sold for less than the par value. Since all of them are Government of Canada or Ontario bonds, all of them are now at a substantial discount. The whole estate, including his house, will amount to close to $200,000, a veritable monument of thrift, as I doubt if he ever made a capital gain in his lifetime."[26] With Mackintosh's support, Wallace would eventually succeed in obtaining a further $500 salary increase in 1951, but again this fell short of changes instituted at the University of Toronto.[27]

REFLECTIONS ON THE POSTWAR ECONOMY

Mackintosh used his freedom from the strictures of an official Ottawa position to comment on government policies without bearing responsibility for their creation or implementation. He resisted Grant Dexter's standing offer to use the pages of the *Winnipeg Free Press* whenever he felt "impelled to preach from the pulpit,"[28] but maintained a busy speaking schedule, giving talks to such groups as the Personnel Association of Toronto; the Dominion Mortgage and Investment Association; the Canadian Tax Foundation; the Institute of Public Administration of Canada; the Industrial Relations Institute; the Montreal Board of Trade; the National Office Management Association; and the Life Insurance Institute of Canada.[29] He also followed with interest the affairs of the Liberal Party. At the 1948 party convention, Walter Gordon spotted Mackintosh sitting by himself and joined him. As Gordon recalls, "We had an entertaining time commenting on the speeches and especially in telling each other how much more succinctly Mr. King could have made his several points."[30]

The subject that most attracted Mackintosh's attention was Canada's place in the evolving postwar economy and the performance of many of the institutions, both international and domestic, that he had helped to create. At the conclusion of the war, an immediate concern was how to unwind price and foreign-exchange controls without causing undue inflation. Where the United States dismantled price controls quickly, Canada opted to do so more gradually, expecting that, if the rate of inflation was kept lower, the Canadian dollar would move towards parity from the 10-per-cent discount maintained during the war. An initial inflow of US capital strengthened Canada's balance-of-payments position, but this situation was suddenly reversed when a marked increase in imports created a sizable current-account deficit. To prevent depletion of its US dollar reserves, Canada imposed severe restrictions on imports and on travel to the US at the end of 1947.[31]

In this context, a radio broadcast sponsored by the University of Chicago and the National Broadcasting Company presented an exchange on Canadian monetary policy between Mackintosh and Donald Gordon on the one hand and a young associate professor of economics at the University of Chicago, Milton Friedman.[32] There was agreement all around that the Canadian economy was trying to do too much; as Mackintosh put it, "we are trying to consume more, to construct more and to equip more, and to export more in goods and services than we actually can in the present circumstances produce ... And one result of our endeavour to do too much is that United States goods and services have flowed in to fill the void."[33] Nonetheless, he maintained that Canadian policy was helping: import controls on capital goods were postponing investment projects and a large federal budgetary surplus was further dampening expenditures. Friedman replied that "In contrast to you, Mackintosh, I believe that the measures taken to restrict quantitatively imports and exports are bad ways of fighting inflation – just as I believe that in the United States direct controls through rationing and price controls are a bad way. I believe that the appropriate way in both countries to fight inflation is through general measures which serve to restrict the quantity of money and credit in the hands of the people."[34]

Furthermore, Friedman held that the best way to reduce imports was to devalue the dollar: "Is it not better to let every individual decide for himself what items he wants to curtail in the face of higher prices than to have a government official do it in some over-all, across-the-board, rough manner?" He conceded that the anti-inflation program had been more effective in Canada than in the United States because of stricter credit controls, but that import controls would be very difficult to unravel when the time came. Mackintosh's response was succinct: "The easiest controls in the world to get out of are these dramatic limitations which we have imposed on imports. Everybody is against them. Everybody is going to help us get out of them."[35] On that note, the discussion came to an end. Canada did remove its restrictions on imports and foreign-exchange transactions at the end of September 1949, and the Canadian dollar appreciated rapidly to parity with the renewed inflows of American direct investment. With this, Canada had apparently put its house in order with an orderly transition to a post-controls period.

Evidence that European reconstruction was proceeding, albeit at a slow pace, also gave rise to optimism. But any illusion that postwar institutions were facilitating an orderly international transition to peacetime was shattered with the sterling crisis in the summer of 1949, when Britain announced a 30-per-cent currency devaluation. Despite the impressive program of reconstruction – from the United Nations Relief and Reconstruction Agency, the IMF, the International

Bank for Reconstruction and Development, the GATT and the Marshall Plan – Mackintosh interpreted the sterling crisis as a symptom of the inadequacies of these institutions to cope with the scale of the readjustment needed. Specifically, he stated that the "quotas of the International Monetary Fund are, in light of present day prices, ridiculously small," such that "the fund does not speak with a very loud voice," while Canadian and American loans were too limited to fund Britain's current-account deficit.[36]

More disconcerting was the emerging pattern of world trade that threatened to disrupt the economic relationship between North America and Europe. American protectionism prevented Britain from achieving a balance of trade in the dollar zone, thus forcing it into closer trade relations with sterling countries as well as promoting the adoption of many of the austerity measures that Keynes had warned of during the 1945 Audit Room meetings. For Canada, this caused "grave foreboding," for it threatened a "painful contraction and readjustment" if European markets for foodstuff, lumber, and base-metal exports were lost, and would result in greater dependence on bilateral trade with the United States. In uncharacteristic fashion, he ended on the gloomy note that the "full and ultimate crisis is not yet upon us."[37]

The opportunity to tour Australia in the summer of 1951 gave Mackintosh a chance to return to the issue of dominion-provincial finance. The invitation was extended by Sir Douglas Copland, the New Zealand–born economist who had been appointed vice-chancellor of the newly created Australian National University (ANU).[38] "I am apparently to be sent about to all the universities," stated Mackintosh upon receiving his seventy-five-day itinerary, including stops in Sydney, Armidale, Brisbane, Melbourne, Hobart, Adelaide, Perth, and Canberra. He delivered talks on "Political Thought in Universities," "Free Enterprise in Canada," "The Prairie Provinces," "Dominion-Provincial Relations," and "Canada's External Relations" to a variety of groups, including the Australian Institute for International Affairs, the Economics Society, and several student groups. At the behest of L.G. Melville and H.C. Coombs (who, like Copland, had been impressed with Mackintosh during wartime talks in London), he was also feted by the Commonwealth Bank (later the Reserve Bank of Australia) at each stop.[39] Australia was still an expensive and exotic locale, offering such culturally unique events as the tour of a koala sanctuary near Brisbane and a football match in Adelaide ("I have since felt sufficiently far removed from Australia to pose as an expert on Australia football rules"). He also reported to Harold Innis that "I did my best to learn the language but I must say that I failed completely."[40]

The primary purpose of the visit was the last event, a conference on federalism held at the ANU as part of the university's contribution to the country's jubilee celebrations.[41] Mackintosh limited his discussion to observations on the Canadian experience. "I am not by temperament a missionary and I had no great message to give to the Australians," he wrote to Copland afterwards. "You may have the odd visitor who is disposed to deliver his message *ex cathedra*, but I should think that most of them in the social sciences would be prepared to pool their ideas and look for common answers."[42] He argued that federations are difficult to govern because of the historical conditions that account for their creation: "Problems of the federal state are less difficulties of federalism than of the conditions that made federalism necessary ... Federal states will always be hard to govern. That is why they are federal states." The challenge was to accommodate "diversity without disunity" by recognizing the religious, cultural, and ethnic differences and geographical separation that give rise to different demands upon the state. This required the type of social experimentation that different communities desired.[43]

In the Canadian case, the distribution of tax authority and functions at the time of Confederation was designed to create a stronger central government than prevailed in the United States. Mackintosh characterized the limitation on the provinces' powers to direct taxation (largely on real estate) as "on the stern model of a somewhat unreliable young man being given a not too generous allowance with the warning, that if he is extravagant he must go to work to acquire the extra funds." Given the evolution of direct taxation into one of the most important sources of revenue, however, "the stone which the builders rejected had become the head of the corner." Nor had anyone anticipated the growth in provincial responsibilities in the area of social welfare. The logical response was for a transfer of functions to make the federal government responsible for social security rather than providing conditional grants to the provinces for this purpose. But despite the recommendations of the National Employment Commission, the Rowell–Sirois Royal Commission, and the 1945 Green Book to this end, efforts to reallocate authority largely failed. Instead, the practice of tax rental agreements that began during World War II, and was later modified by equalization payments, became a permanent feature of federal finance, leaving Canada with "a compromise, by no means logical, with the hard facts of federalism."[44]

The cost of this compromise was less responsible governance, because reliance on federal conditional grants did not oblige the provinces to bear the political burden of taxing their citizens. But it also meant less effective government. Mackintosh outlined the proposals of the 1945 White Paper ("those things which the federal government could do on its own authority") and Green Book ("a broad programme was set out which would require the co-operation of the provinces and in some instances constitutional change"), designed to coordinate stabilization policy. To facilitate effective fiscal policy, the federal government needed sole authority over taxation to influence private spending without the provinces adopting offsetting actions, and to exercise control over the timing of public expenditures by offering financial incentives to the provinces at the appropriate time. Neither was pursued, in part because the threat of inflation placed greater emphasis on monetary policy. Thus he concluded that "the great danger of federal financial arrangements is that they should become a straitjacket eliminating the experimentation and diversity which is the hallmark of federalism."[45] Despite these sobering reflections on the Canadian state, he informed Clifford Clark that "you can be assured that Dominion-Provincial relations are dead calm as compared to Commonwealth-State relations."[46]

GOVERNMENT WORK

Mackintosh remained at least a participant-observer in federal government affairs. He was appointed the first director of the Canadian Mortgage and Housing Corporation, and continued as chair of the Unemployment Insurance Advisory Committee.[47] He saw the latter committee's role being largely restricted to ensuring the viability of the Unemployment Insurance fund "so that resources may be available for genuine unemployment compensation," with other matters being the responsibility of parliament.[48] When the UI commission began referring policy matters to the advisory committee, he insisted that the latter body had neither the resources nor jurisdiction to start to conduct public hearings; instead, it was up to the commission to investigate matters, make a specific recommendation, and then ask the advisory committee for its judgment. He held that boards and commissions were generally not good administrative units and "are justified only where there are judicial, or semi-judicial functions to be performed, or when the degree of administrative discretion that it exercises amounts to a quasi-judicial function."[49]

In the summer of 1948, he was asked by Brooke Claxton, now minister of national defence, to participate in preliminary planning in the field of "economic defence."[50] With the uncertainty of events in eastern Europe, it was deemed prudent to prepare for war and to draw upon the experience of World War II to assist in the organization. The Industrial Defence Board (IDB) had been established earlier in the year to advise the government on labour and capital requirements, stockpiling of essential materials, and coordination of production with the United States. But almost as soon as the IDB was created, there was concern that its executive powers encroached upon the turf of various departments, including munitions and supply, national defence, and finance. Arnold Heeney (as secretary to the cabinet) informed Claxton that "I was disturbed last week to learn that members of the executive and staff of the Industrial Defence Board were taking into the Board's territory almost every conceivable function which might be defined as economic and that they were putting up to you a most elaborate plan for this purpose ... I felt quite sure that this conception of the Board's function was quite wrong, and that, if it were not corrected at an early stage, confusion all round and soreness in several quarters would be the inevitable result." He advised Claxton that the IDB was chiefly composed of private-sector industrialists "whose goodwill and experience is important to the government," but who did not understand fully their responsibilities.[51]

Among other things, a "War Book" was expected to delineate the role of the IDB in mobilization plans and to outline the responsibilities of various government agencies in the hope of avoiding the conflicts that arose during World War II. Mackintosh was given the task of drafting the chapter on "Economic and Fiscal Measures," an assignment that, according to Hume Wrong, required both tact and experience. "Economic defence planning is an untidy subject because it touches on all phases of economic activities. By establishing the NSRB [National Securities Resources Board] the United States Government has created what looks like a tidy plan for dealing with it, but we can be sure that in this untidy system of government it will not work out that way. I hope that Dr. Mackintosh will be able to develop this summer a Canadian method of operation which will be both tidy and efficient."[52] He thus had the opportunity to restate his arguments for coordinating the war effort.

Mackintosh met with senior government officials during the summer – including Claxton, Clifford Clark, and Donald Gordon – but largely drew upon his wartime experience. "Conditions of full employment, such as obtain at present, changed superficial aspects such as timing, but did not alter the problem fundamentally. In the last war, a good deal of effort had been directed to building up the national economy and then diverting it to war purposes. Under present conditions, this could probably be done in one process – with stockpiling being substituted for expansion of industry." In September he submitted to Claxton his draft of the chapter, and it went to the cabinet defence committee for approval one month later. The chapter was organized around the subheadings of fiscal measures, price control and civilian supply, foreign exchange control, war risk insurance, controls ancillary to war production, industrial mobilization, food production and procurement, export and import controls, and manpower and selective services. His principal recommendations were for a cabinet committee to parallel the role of the Chiefs-of-Staff Committee in the United States, with initiatives relating to "economic warfare" assigned to a single minister to avoid unwarranted delays, and for more-effective price and supply controls under the authority of the minister of finance.[53] Claxton expressed to Mackintosh his satisfaction with the outcome. "I thought the piece you did was fine. In the end the number of keys had to be increased to fit in with the decorations. However, it came out alright and it still has left in it some of the faint echoes of the distinction with which it left your hand."[54]

In the summer of 1950, Mackintosh was back in Ottawa to help reorganize the economic research branch of the department of trade and commerce, in which Sandy Skelton was the deputy minister. Despite all of Skelton's enormous gifts, his personal shortcomings grew more difficult to ignore. As Mackintosh discreetly put it, "There were some incompatible ingredients in his nature or some deficiency which eroded his energy and resolution."[55] Charles Kindleberger stated the problem more bluntly when he described Skelton as a man "who drank two Scotches with lunch and 140-proof Demerara rum in the evening."[56] He was shuffled between government departments, until the department of munitions and supply lost patience with him, and he was eventually given leave to join a British commission investigating the first few years of Nigerian independence. Mackintosh was thus asked to assist with the department's organization. The episode had a tragic dimension, for less than a month later Skelton would take his own life. He had once told Jean Mackintosh that if he ever wanted to die he would dive in the water and just keep swimming. Alex Corry wrote an account of Skelton's death: "Someone took him out in his sailboat on the Bay of Lagos on a day with some breeze. Sandy was sitting in the stern; the skipper was busy with the boat, tacking into the wind. When he turned around, Sandy was gone." His body was never recovered. Skelton's last written words to Mackintosh are poignant under the circumstances: "In the meantime, thanks again Bill and all my best. Remember me to Jean."[57]

Beginning in June 1950, Mackintosh also served on the Committee to Study Combines Legislation, chaired by J.H. McQuarrie (N.S. Supreme Court), and also including G.F. Curtis (dean of law, UBC) and Maurice Lamontagne (economics, Laval). The principal interest of the federal government in reforming combines legislation was the independence and apparent zeal of its commissioner, F.A. McGregor, the same man with whom Mackintosh had worked during the combines investigation in the 1930s. Prior to World War II, McGregor's attention was largely confined to non-competitive practices among small wholesalers and retailers, and the compulsory publication of the results of an investigation was often sufficient for firms to cease their restrictive practices. But as McGregor began investigating international cartels and large manufacturers after the war, he found himself at odds with the attitude of the St Laurent government. Matters came to a head when McGregor resigned over the government's refusal to publish the results of his investigation of the flour-milling industry. The resulting political embarrassment prompted the government's desire to address the administration of anti-combines legislation and the amount of power exercised by the commissioner.[58]

The McQuarrie Committee entertained written submissions and oral presentations in private hearings, but it was not until June 1952 that its report was issued.[59] In recommending that the commissioner's dual role of investigation and subsequent appraisal of the evidence be separated – on the grounds that it was inappropriate to be both "the prosecutor and the judge" – it addressed the government's concern about the commissioner's independence as well as power.[60] The director of investigation and research would remain responsible for the investigation of complaints, while the Restrictive Trade Practices Commission would subsequently hold hearings and report to the minister of justice on the appropriate action to be taken. Stronger remedies were also urged in cases where convictions had been obtained, including the issuance of orders to dissolve a merger or monopoly.

But the committee went farther in arguing for greater research capacity in light of the growth of monopoly power in the economy. In a contemporary analysis, Gideon Rosenbluth and H.G. Thorburn placed the work of the Combines Investigation Act in the context of two important political considerations. First, the act was designed to strike a compromise between, on the one hand, business groups that resisted any encroachment upon their activities and, on the other hand, employees, farmers, small businesses, and the public generally, who were the victims of monopolistic restrictions. Second, it reflected a "cops and robbers" approach: monopolistic practices were exceptional occurrences in which the majority of businesses did not engage, such that matters could be policed by a relatively small staff and lead to criminal prosecution and punishment by fines. The McQuarrie Committee, in contrast, argued that a special research division be established in order that "research in the field of monopolistic situations and practices should become one of the most important assignments of the Investigation and Research Agency."[61] Further, it recommended that there should be great emphasis on the development of remedies other than criminal prosecution, and that closer integration of anti-combines and other government policy in areas such as taxation, monetary policy, and industrial regulation was required. In essence, therefore, the committee argued that monopoly practices were not merely a legal problem, but a more pervasive, economic one.[62]

There was little reaction to the committee's report, given the "modest" nature of its recommendations, beyond the remedying of the government's awkward political situation. Mackintosh conceded that "It is not a satisfactory report by any means, but I do not know what satisfactory recommendations could be made out of the present constitutional position. On the whole I think they are sensible recommendations but that is about as much as one can say for them."[63] His sense of resignation stemmed from an insistence that tariff and combines policy needed to be coordinated. Writing to Stuart Garson he argued that in many instances "the disciplinary effect of tariff reductions or suspension would far outweigh the clumsy workings of the criminal law. If some industries know that the maintenance of tariff protection depended on their being in good standing under the Combines Act, they would be more circumspect in their arrangements."[64] To Maxwell Cohen he suggested: "I do not think ... that we can make a really good Act until those in charge have the courage and the courts have the good sense to approve a more effective use of the trade and commerce clause than we have yet seen."[65]

THE RAILWAY STRIKE OF 1950

In the middle of August 1950, Mackintosh was enjoying a weekend at the Five Lakes Fishing Club with Jean and Alison. He was fishing on the lake most remote from the main lodge, when the sudden appearance of an earnest young man wearing a suit came as more than a mild surprise and certainly contrasted with the rural scenery. In his outstretched hand he carried a handwritten note in an envelope bearing the seal of the prime minister:

> My dear Mackintosh,
> A serious situation has come about here and I would very much appreciate an opportunity of discussing it with you. Could you come back with the bearer of this note for a talk with me?
> Yours sincerely,
> Louis St. Laurent[66]

Mackintosh was dragged out of his rustic vacation retreat and thrust onto the public stage as the government-appointed mediator in a threatened national railway strike. This transition happened all too abruptly for Jean, since, to her horror, he was still dressed in casual attire during a hastily arranged press conference in Ottawa.

Conditions in the railway industry had all the ingredients for a dramatic confrontation. At issue were the contracts between the unions representing 125,000 non-operating employees (those other than locomotive engineers, firemen, conductors, and trainmen engaged in the running trades) and the major companies, including the Canadian National Railways (CNR) and Canadian Pacific

Railway. Having suffered a loss in real wages during the war and facing rising prices in the immediate postwar period, workers were seeking to recover some lost economic ground. In addition, the US rail industry had adopted a forty-hour work week, and Canadian workers were intent on gaining a similar change from their forty-eight-hour week (with an hourly pay increase to maintain the same weekly take-home pay). Although the railways accepted in principle a forty-hour work week, they insisted that its immediate adoption was not economically feasible. In its place, they offered a forty-four-hour work week, but in return wanted changes in work rules to permit greater managerial control.

The fragmented nature of industrial relations in the railways complicated matters. Non-operating employees – ranging from mechanics, machinists, and sectionmen, to office clerks, station agents, and telegraph operators – were represented by fifteen different international and two national unions under a plethora of separate contracts. Bargaining as a single group, the trade unions sought the same improvements in pay and working conditions for all workers, while the railways were adamant that any reduction in work hours would not apply to hotel and water-transport workers.

Talks on a new contract had dragged on since June 1949, with animosity growing between the two sides. The unions' bargaining team was headed by F.H. Hall (International Brotherhood of Railway and Steamship Clerks) and Aaron Mosher (Canadian Brotherhood of Railway Employees and Other Transportation Workers, and head of the Canadian Congress of Labour), while negotiations for the railway companies was led by Donald Gordon, Mackintosh's former student, wartime associate, and friend, who was now the government-appointed president of the CNR.[67] Described by the union side as "the great gladiator" in his service to the Bank of Canada, the Wartime Prices and Trade Board, and now the publicly owned railway, Gordon's legendary brusque demeanour no doubt contributed to the ill will that developed.[68] The existing contracts signed in 1948 were achieved only after the two parties were called to Ottawa to engage in discussions under the auspices of the minister of labour, and Gordon described the terms of that settlement as "an unreasonably generous adjustment which had been embarrassing and, in fact, forced upon the railways." He maintained that the companies had made "one concession after another" leading up to its contract offer of 10 August 1949, but the parties remained far apart over wages, retroactive pay, hours of work, and changes in working conditions.[69]

If the differences between the two parties were not difficult enough to resolve, the central role of rail transportation in the economy added into the mix the federal government's third-party interest in ensuring that there was no disruption of services. With newspapers predicting the "economic paralysis" and "emergency" conditions that would prevail in the event of a work stoppage, the government was widely expected to intercede on the grounds of defending the public interest. A final dimension to the drama was provided by international events. The Korean War began on 25 June, and Canada was committed to send forces to Korea on July 25, just four weeks before the unions' announced strike deadline. With a work stoppage threatening Canada's ability to ship troops and equipment overseas, Prime Minister St Laurent had appealed to the unions to postpone the strike deadline by thirty days, but this request was denied. Thus as mediation was getting under way, the cabinet was preparing to recall parliament in order to respond to a possible strike.

Mackintosh was catapulted into this theatre, arriving in Montreal's Windsor Hotel on Friday evening, 19 August, with the strike deadline set for Tuesday at 6:00 a.m. The crowd of newspaper reporters awaiting the proceedings spared no hyperbole when it came to the hopes pinned on the mediator. "All parties here agree that the selection by Mr. St. Laurent of Dr. Mackintosh as the special commissioner to mediate the dispute was a brilliant choice," said the *Toronto Star*. It cited the endorsement of a government official: "We appointed the best possible man we could find to mediate this dispute. If this fails there is nothing more we can do." According to the newspaper, Mackintosh faced "one of the toughest assignments in Canadian labour history" and he carried "on his shoulders the hopes of a nation threatened with a railway tie-up less than 70 hours away."[70]

After spending Friday evening conferring with officials of the department of labour, the next morning Mackintosh convened a joint meeting with the bargaining committees in one of the hotel's assembly rooms. His demeanour, according to the *Toronto Star*, helped to alleviate the tension. "Both the company and the union men seemed to have chips on their shoulders as they stood around waiting. Dr. Mackintosh stepped into the room … He was less formally dressed than anyone else in the room. He seemed a little solemn, with the self-contained, at-peace-with-the-world look about him that many farmers have. He went around the room shaking hands with everybody. Each got his tight little smile, and a 'Glad you are here.' And each felt that Dr. Mackintosh felt just that way. There was no glad-handing, just a sincere, intelligent Canadian, humbled by the task he had accepted, but expectant that other Canadians would be as sincere and intelligent and helpful as he intended to be." In his opening statement, he assured both sides that he had neither instructions for settling the dispute, nor any prior judgment of his own on the merits of each party's position. He insisted that his role was to assist negotiations and that "nothing that can be done to avoid a strike should be left undone." Moreover, while he emphasized the importance of the international situation and the potential impact of a strike on the domestic economy as well as the long-run health of the industry, he underscored that "Canadians are a resourceful people" and that it would not result in a disaster unless the work stoppage was a prolonged one. His task, then, was to avoid a strike by reaching a settlement that both parties could accept, and this would require compromise on both sides.[71]

On Saturday afternoon, he then met with each side separately. "Tell me your story," he asked of each as he searched for the basis for a possible agreement. The first hint of any movement did not occur until Sunday morning, when the unions' team indicated that it would drop its demand for retroactive pay to April 1949, in return for a larger pay increase effective 1 April 1950, and would be willing to delay the adoption of a forty-hour work week until 1 April 1951. Mackintosh then approached the companies' side to consider a longer contract, in return for a cost-of-living adjustment, that would allow for a forty-hour work week to be phased in. Gordon responded that this would be possible, but that the general terms of the agreement would exclude water-transport and hotel employees. Further talks with each side extended into the early hours of Monday morning, but no concrete proposals were forthcoming.

On Monday morning, with the strike deadline twenty hours away, Mackintosh, accompanied by deputy minister of labour Arthur MacNamara, made his pitch for reaching an agreement. While differences in the monetary terms of the respective proposals were substantial, he believed that they were not insurmountable. More intractable were the unions' insistence that the contract cover all non-operating employees and the companies' demands for changes in work rules. Meeting with the union side, MacNamara outlined the basis for a possible settlement: a base pay increase, a cost-of-living adjustment, and the adoption of forty-hour week to be phased in over a nine-month period starting on 1 October 1951. The unions' committee expressed some openness to this framework, as long as it applied equally to hotel and water employees and the companies withdrew their proposals for altering existing work rules. The companies, on their part, continued to insist that hotel and water employees be excluded, but did agree to a clause for negotiating work rule changes in good faith.[72]

With this sliver of hope, Mackintosh and MacNamara then met with the full union negotiating committee and MacNamara tabled his own compromise proposal, which included a pay increase; a five-day, forty-hour work week, effective 1 September 1950, with a separate arrangement for hotel and water employees to establish a joint committee to bring their work hours in line with comparable employees in other industries; a modest cost-of-living bonus over a three-year contract; and a joint committee and referee to address work rule changes. This elicited the unions' team's "terminal offer," which softened its stance slightly on monetary terms, accepted no special provisions for hotel and water employees, but agreed to a joint committee to address work rule changes. At 3:00 a.m. on Tuesday morning, however, all hopes for a settlement were dashed. The companies rejected the unions' final position, and when Mackintosh so informed the union committee, mediation was at an end. Five hours later, the strike was on.

Amidst exaggerated accounts of the extent of layoffs outside the railway industry – Bell Telephone spoke of rationing long-distance calls in the absence of telegraph service, and the mayor of Timmins claimed that his town faced starvation in the event of a prolonged strike – Mackintosh and MacNamara travelled back to Ottawa by military car to inform Milton Gregg, minister of labour, on the failure of mediation.[73] When the unions offered to reopen talks two days into the strike and expressed their willingness to meet again with the mediator, an editorial in the *Globe and Mail* asked, "Why Not More Mackintosh?"[74] But this was not to be, and renewed negotiations in his absence resolved nothing. Thus on 29 August 1950, with Mackintosh standing along the back wall of the gallery of the House of Commons, the prime minister introduced the "Maintenance of Railway Operation Act," the first federal back-to-work legislation in Canadian history.[75] Royal Assent followed two days later.

Despite the failure of negotiations, Mackintosh was elevated to heroic status in the press. One reporter reflected that "whether he looked tired, cheerful, or just desperately hopeful, he was unfailingly courteous and always kept a sort of smile which just barely appeared, but was there nevertheless. I think we were all cheering him on, and felt deeply regretful even for his sake alone that he couldn't accomplish what was apparently an impossible task at that stage."[76] Gregg endorsed the work of his mediator. "The fact that it was not successful in its immediate results does not detract in any way from the effort and the excellent work that was carried out with the longer distance in view." Speaking for the Opposition, John Diefenbaker could only offer the criticism that "He was appointed too late."[77]

It was a sobering experience for Mackintosh, as it shook his faith in the capacity of collective bargaining to arrive at a negotiated settlement. In his mediator's report, he was forced to admit that expectations for a settlement were unrealistic from the outset: each party charged that the other was seeking a government-imposed settlement rather than a negotiated outcome and both were probably correct. Accordingly, neither made any significant movement but merely formalized positions that they had tentatively accepted at an earlier stage. In the place of responsible negotiations, he found only "childish attitudes, bitterness, refusal to concede any major points," and thus he did not lament the government legislating an end to the strike. As he summarized the outcome to a colleague, "I was singularly unsuccessful but however I managed to keep the situation reasonably clean so that Parliament could deal with it."[78] Gordon was more shaken but was resolved to restore his reputation with workers at the CNR.[79]

That Mackintosh would be a participant in the events leading up to the first implementation of back-to-work legislation in Canadian history was no coincidence. He was a logical choice as mediator, given his contribution to wartime industrial relations that established much of the framework for the postwar period. Consistent with his earlier views on the efficacy of the Industrial Disputes Investigation Act, his defence of the Winnipeg General Strike in support of the right to collective bargaining, and his role with the National Joint Council of the Public Sector Employees, he shared

St Laurent's view that the public interest superseded collective bargaining rights when the two parties did not act responsibly. As St Laurent made the case, "The injury that the insistence on private rights may do to the public weal is sometimes so great that it has to be given serious consideration, because the existence and security of the state is the first and prior consideration for each one of us."[80] However, there is no escaping that fact that this incident set up a pattern in the railway industry in which the expectation of back-to-work legislation placed a chilling effect on negotiations and it began the disturbing trend towards government encroachment on the principle of free collective bargaining.

"HERESY HUNTING"

Mackintosh returned from the events surrounding the railway strike in Montreal only to find more drama awaiting him in Kingston. When Principal Wallace announced that he was retiring, effective October 1951, Mackintosh was the obvious successor, but there was one small bump on the road to his appointment. In striking parallel to the experience of O.D. Skelton some twenty years earlier, Mackintosh's candidacy was questioned by two influential trustees, J.M. Macdonnell and a member of the Richardson family. When Skelton had been touted as a replacement for Bruce Taylor as principal in 1929, W.C. Clark speculated that his former colleague might be "too little a church-goer to be the 'ideal' of one or two other members [of the search committee]."[81] But where both James Richardson and Macdonnell would eventually come to champion Skelton's candidacy, two decades later Muriel Richardson, James's widow, and Macdonnell demonstrated greater resistance, given Mackintosh's shortcomings "on the spiritual side."[82]

The widely held expectation that Mackintosh would succeed Wallace prompted Muriel Richardson (from a distance in Winnipeg) to write to Macdonnell that "I am told there is, within the University, a spirit of resignation. Among the alumni dissatisfaction and concern are openly expressed. The only notes of approval – and these sometimes run to enthusiasm – come from those who were associated with Dr. McIntosh [*sic*] in Ottawa or from 'outsiders' who obviously know more about his record in Ottawa than they do of Queen's University and her requirements." Two months later Macdonnell wrote to Richardson expressing his feeling "that there will be more opposition in the Board than you and I thought likely at first to the appointment of our friend."[83] The two then canvassed for other possible candidates, confident that they had an ally in Charlotte Whitton, another trustee.[84] At the December 1950 meeting of the selection committee, they succeeded in having three other names added for consideration: Hugh Saunderson (dean of Arts at the University of Manitoba), George F. Curtis (dean of Law at UBC), and possibly K.W. Taylor (deputy minister, department of finance). But when no significant support for any of the three emerged, and there was no spirit of resignation but only enthusiasm among students, staff, and alumni for Mackintosh as principal, Richardson saw no need to attend the May meeting of the selection committee, knowing that Mackintosh's appointment was all but a formality. When the staff was informed of the decision prior to the formal announcement, the news was greeted with enthusiasm; indeed, a few months later Macdonnell conceded the "strong staff backing which Mackintosh has."[85]

The delay in announcing Mackintosh's appointment, however, led to much speculation that the appointment was in doubt. Ed Hall, of the University of Western Ontario, informed Mackintosh afterwards that "for a time rumour ... was very disturbing."[86] Walter Gordon too was concerned.

I telephoned you last night," he wrote of Mackintosh,

> because I had been told by what I thought was a reasonably reliable source that Queen's University was about to make a very foolish and fatal mistake and because if this should happen, Toronto University [where he was on the board of governors] wanted you to know that they would do almost anything to persuade you to move here. I was delighted to learn in confidence this morning that the first of these stories is incorrect and that at a recent meeting any opposition to your obvious appointment was soundly defeated and confounded. While I heard this in the strictest confidence, I thought in the circumstances I might write to you and say how very delighted I and all your friends will be in your staying on at Queen's. I can think of no one better suited to head a university and for my money Queen's without Bill Mackintosh would be a poor thing indeed. This does not mean that there are not a great many people here would not turn handsprings (assuming they were at least fifty years younger)

to have you at Toronto but, selfish interests apart, I think most of them feel your proper place is as Principal of Queen's.[87]

Following the official announcement, Gordon added that "I was delighted to hear via the grapevine last week and to read in the paper yesterday that you have won your by-election. My heartiest congratulations to the voters of Queen's at having defeated the theologians, the stuffed shirts (hair stuffed) and the woolly minded."[88] Sidney Smith, president of the University of Toronto, echoed this sentiment in less colourful but equally emotive terms: "I was canvassed about one or two other men, but I always said to my interrogators that they would make a terrible mistake if they did not invite you to succeed to the Principalship. To a unique degree, you are Queen's and Queen's is you. You have the very ethos of the place in your marrow."[89]

The official announcement was made on May 21, Mackintosh's fifty-sixth birthday. The roughly 250 letters and telegrams of congratulation that survive in the Queen's University Archives provide a glimpse of the rich breadth and depth of his lifelong relationships. Amid the expected correspondence from university presidents, trustees, staff, and alumni are letters from old family friends from Madoc, the headmaster of St Andrew's College, expressing pride in its "Old Boy," his undergraduate classmates, former students, fellow economists, and other academics, politicians and bureaucrats, education administrators, journalists, bankers and other corporate executives, Kingston friends and associates, and, given his professed agnosticism, a surprisingly large number from clerics.

Among the messages from Ottawa politicians are those of the prime minister, Louis St Laurent ("delighted at the news") and a future prime minister, Lester B. Pearson ("I know that you will be very happy about this recognition of your work in the University but not, I assure you, any happier than your friends"); several other cabinet ministers, including Stuart Garson ("Canada and Queen's are both lucky to have you as Principal of the University, and your many admirers, of whom I humbly count myself, will all be wishing that you will continue for many years in this capacity"), and W. Ross MacDonald, the speaker of the House of Commons. Included in the dozens of former Ottawa associates who wrote were the governor of the Bank of Canada, Graham Towers ("this appointment is a very nice thing for your friends. Taking me as an example, I detect in myself a very definite feeling of pride in having a friend who is a University Principal … and I am sure you will not begrudge me the pleasure") and the future governor, Louis Rasminsky. J.L. Ilsley added his congratulations: "If your judgment proves to be as good as Head of a University as it was when you were Acting Deputy Minister of Finance, the University is in safe hands. I have often said that the only time I got in trouble when you were advising me in 1945 was when I failed to take your advice." Other notes of congratulations came from Donald Gordon, Wynne Plumptre ("We missed you at the stag weekend at the Fishing Club, but we were delighted to learn that you were frying larger ones in Kingston"), Dana Wilgress, Office of the High Commissioner for Canada in London ("I know that you have resisted the temptation of many attractive offers in the hope of attaining the position to which you have now been appointed"), David Johnson, High Commissioner for Canada in Karachi ("you were destined for the highest post in whatever field you happened to choose"), Mitchell Sharp ("I find it difficult to express on paper my delight at the news of your appointment"), J.W. Pickersgill, ("Your friends – and they are pretty numerous – will rejoice"); and his longest Ottawa associate, Hector McKinnon ("this is great news … I am very, very happy").[90]

Journalists and long-standing friends such as Grant Dexter ("You know how glad I am and how proud of you") and George Ferguson ("bless your old heart") passed on personal words of congratulations, while Austin Cross was unable to contain his enthusiasm when announcing the appointment in the *Ottawa Journal*: "scholar, gentleman and 'great guy' in the bargain … [A] man like 'Bill' Mackintosh means more to our civilization than all the Rita Hayworths and Ingrid Bergmans that ever have been or ever will be."[91] This left Finlay Sim, of the department of trade and commerce bemused: "We heartily endorse all that has been said in both the *Ottawa Journal* and the *Citizen*, although we cannot quite get the idea of the reference to Rita Hayworth or Ingrid Bergman. Any similarity is not even coincidental."[92]

Mackintosh's colleagues at Queen's added their names to the roster of admirers. Graham George asked: "Did you hear the sigh of relief go up from the campus?"[93] Leonard Brockington, the rector, when told of the date of the installation, replied that "I shall certainly be there if I am able to breath and move."[94] John Hamilton of the psychology department wrote, without fear of toadyism, as he had already accepted a position elsewhere, "It was a great pleasure to hear my fondest hopes confirmed. Speaking very confidentially, I can assure you of the wholehearted support your appointment receives from the staff." Alice and Jim Cameron wrote: "You, Jean, probably do not know just how much Bill is respected and admired by his colleagues," and John Orr, Mackintosh's long-time friend and colleague, on news of the appointment merely added "So say we all."[95]

The most poignant image, however, was of J.F. Macdonald, an Arts '99 graduate of Queen's and O.D. Skelton's old friend and colleague, who had left Queen's during Principal Taylor's mishandling the of English department in the 1920s. As the retired Toronto professor sat in his easy chair with the evening paper, he read the news of the appointment. "My shout startled my wife who is not used to shouting from me."[96]

13

The Principal Lecturer: Kingston, 1951–1961

As a university president, you are both minister and deputy minister and also sometimes messenger. For a variety of problems of administration and policy, the staff is always very thin. Though I have not latterly given as much time to it as I should, the most important job is to select, stimulate and make productive a first-rate staff. Finance and buildings, which take up a great deal of time, are really subordinate to this. Your educational ideas ought to come up from the faculty but, in practice, they will not do so without prodding and other stimulus. Some contact with students is desirable though it can be overdone and made superficial …

It is a good job and well worth doing, though I will not deny that at times it is harassing. At times it is like being the parent of a very large family who are alternatively out of sorts or out of shoes and have to be looked after … You will find that you did not have all the qualities for a perfect university president but you would come to realize that no human being has … You need to be interested in building something. You need to be interested in helping people to develop their departments and themselves, and interested in seeing what happens to the ambitions and minds of youngsters between eighteen and twenty-two. They can be very tiresome at times, but there is a sort of repeated miracle of spring among them, in which one has a small share.

W.A. Mackintosh, 1958[1]

Mackintosh inherited responsibility for a university that had, after coping with the spike in enrolment immediately after the war, changed surprisingly little from the time he joined the staff three decades earlier. The numbers of full-time students (2,100) and faculty (120) were modestly larger and still concentrated in the faculties of Arts, Medicine, and Applied Sciences, and the school of commerce, although the schools of nursing and of physical and health education had been added. The academic and non-academic staff continued to operate on a threadbare basis, within the institution's annual budget of $1.5 million. The physical campus remained confined to twenty-two buildings within, or on the perimeter of, a twenty-five-acre site bordered by University Avenue, Union Street, Arch Avenue, and Stuart Street at the southern end of Kingston.

The decade that followed was to be one of the most active in the history of Canadian universities. In light of the burgeoning demand for post-secondary education, universities accepted the obligation to expand and seized upon the opportunity to do so accorded by new provincial funding formulas and enhanced federal monies. Queen's was not immune to the pressures and incentives: it willingly accepted its share of undergraduate students and laid claim to the resources that would enable it to enhance instruction and research. Everything seemed to grow by at least 50 per cent, whether it be the number of students, faculty and other staff, the physical capacity, or the budget.

This quantitative change occurred amid increasing pressure on universities to broaden their social role through a more direct contribution to economic growth. For Mackintosh, the challenge was to manage this growth and transformation in a manner that retained the character of Queen's as an institution committed to academic quality in teaching and research, and with an intimacy that enhanced a student's experience both within and outside the lecture hall. Just as there was an art to advising on government policy, there was also an art to effective university administration. The mixture of social obligation, external pressures, and the institution's own priorities left him reluctant to devise a master plan; rather, he outlined the "emerging pattern" of the Queen's development. When he left the principal's office in 1961, he did so with the satisfaction that "The University is a considerably larger place than when I took over my present post but I flatter myself that none of the traditions have been sacrificed."[2]

THE RHYTHM TO ACADEMIC LIFE

One week into the job, Mackintosh was "extremely busy trying to find out what the material on my desk means."[3] There was a host of daily demands more typically associated with a small college. He was not above responding to student appeals for admission or for grade revisions, or sending an ominous note to a struggling student "to drop by my office for a chat." In responding to a seemingly endless stream of correspondence, he was called upon to explain why, "rightly or wrongly," men were not allowed to entertain women in their residence bedrooms, to decline an offer to purchase a mounted deer's head but to accept the donation of a steel engraving of Queen Victoria ("a gift horse which ought to be looked carefully in the mouth"), to apologize to the Curator of Insects at another university for a faculty member's delinquency in not returning leaf-beetle specimens, to forward unsolicited manuscripts with a suggestion for the editor ("I met this man some years ago. He was mad as a hatter then, and the disability seems to be progressive"), and to defend why "God Save the Queen" was not played at the start of Queen's University concerts ("It is played at many more occasions than it would be in the United Kingdom"[4]). In other instances a more stern reply was forthcoming. When he received a complaint that Queen's was housing a B'nai Brith cell, he wrote: "If the implication of your letter is that we ought not to admit Jewish students to the University, then I must tell you that you are one hundred and thirteen years too late and that we require by our Charter to apply no religious tests."[5] On the public-relations front, it meant picking through newspaper announcements in order to send letters of congratulations to former students upon their promotions, soliciting and acknowledging donations, and even replying to the occasional genealogical inquiry.

These ongoing duties notwithstanding, university life had its own distinctive rhythm, and the demands on the principal varied with the season. The enthusiasm that accompanied the beginning of the fall term magnified the ever-present concern with "town-gown" relations whenever a boisterous evening during initiation week spilled over onto Princess Avenue, or when rough play at football games – not so much on the field as among students and alumni in the stands – led him to concede that winning the intercollegiate championship was "a good thing once in a while."[6] The fall and winter terms were crowded with out-of-town speaking engagements to alumni associations (travelling in the convivial company of Herb Hamilton), at high-school commencement exercises (in Brantford and Belleville, as a favour to his sisters Agnes and Helen respectively, and as far afield as Kirkland Lake), educational conferences (the sometimes "rather dreary chore" of speaking to a group of high-school teachers), to industrial and professional associations, local service clubs, and Canadian Clubs (including Winnipeg, Toronto, Montreal, and New York).[7] The 1956–57 academic year was fairly typical. October took him to Morrisburg to speak to the local Canadian Club, then to Vancouver, where he delivered the convocation address at UBC. In November he attended the commencement exercise at Westdale Collegiate in Hamilton, spoke a week later at Lower Canada College, and left immediately afterwards for a meeting in New York City. In January he gave a talk at the Seigneury Club in Montreal on "Canada's Economic Prospects," and February found him thanking the guest speaker at the Universities Dinner Dance in Ottawa. In March he was back in Ottawa to present a brief to the Royal Commission on Canada's Economic Prospects on behalf of the National Conference of Canadian Universities, attended meetings of the alumni associations in Chatham and London, spoke to the Canadian Club in Toronto on "National Expansion and Human Resources," and flew to New York City for a Queen's party at the Biltmore Hotel arranged by N.R. "Buck" Crump (president of Canadian Pacific Railway and head of the university's fundraising campaign). In April he delivered a speech on "Are Industrial Resources Enough?" at three Canadian Club meetings in Ontario, and was the dinner speaker at the annual convention of the Canadian Institute of Mining and Metallurgy held at the Château Laurier ("dress preferred is white tie"; the "Ladies Programme" included a separate dinner and fashion show). After a brief respite, he delivered a talk on "The Larger Pattern of Canadian Growth" to the Canadian Life Insurance Officers Association in Montreal at the end of May, a week later gave the keynote address at the Canadian textile seminar, and capped off the year on June 10 by giving the presidential address to the Royal Society of Canada in Ottawa. After several speaking engagements in Toronto in 1951–52, he noted that "I shall probably not disturb them again for some time," and, understandably, he confessed at the end of another academic year that "I am somewhat dredged out as far as addresses are concerned."[8]

The "repeated miracle of spring" required preparations for the convocation exercise at Queen's and other universities ("University Presidents do a good deal of taking in each other's washing"[9]). There was no shortage of entertaining visitors throughout the year – hosting the governor of Jamaica for tea, or holding a reception for Sir

Geoffrey Keynes (the younger brother of Maynard) and Lady Keynes (the granddaughter of Charles Darwin) – but the spring was especially busy welcoming honorary-degree recipients such as Robert Oppenheimer, Adlai Stevenson, Prime Minister John Diefenbaker, Thibaudeau Rinfret (chief justice of the Supreme Court), or Lord Tweedsmuir (the former governor general). To international colleagues, Mackintosh proudly insisted that "Your knowledge of Canada is quite incomplete if you have not visited Kingston," and visitors would invariably comment on "the happy spirit prevalent at Queen's."[10] Moreover, Jean and he were good hosts. "I am afraid that the Mackintoshs' hospitality is of a kind that soothes and lulls their guests into feeling that time is really of no importance," observed Walter Gordon. "How you manage to go out or have people in night after night simply amazes me! If I am out two nights running I am completely done in but I suppose university Presidents must, of necessity, be a hardy lot."[11]

The summer afforded some vacation time. The Five Lakes Fishing Club remained an important social outlet for Mackintosh, as well as for Jean and Alison, and a retreat from the demands of the university, just as it had been in the past with respect to government work. Visits were often timed to coincide with friends such as George Wilson and former Ottawa associates, and his correspondence was frequently sprinkled with news from the club. On other occasions the family visited Donald Gordon at his Lake Luster property or George Ferguson's family at Memphremagog. In 1955 he accepted Walter Gordon's invitation for a more ambitious fishing trip to Matapedia, Quebec, as "a harbinger of Spring." ("The fishing may be good, fair or downright bad depending on the water level, the extent of the poaching and the whims of the Almighty – not to mention the fish."[12]) Other holidays were often combined with university obligations. In August 1952, he enjoyed a "short vacation by the sea," with Jean and Alison, travelling in the family's Nash Rambler through Quebec and the Maritimes, stopping to visit David and Molly Mansur in New Brunswick before attending the National Conference of Canadian Universities in Halifax.

Writing to Alex Corry in 1960, Mackintosh acknowledged that "This letter seems heavily weighted with administrative problems but they, with a modest sprinkling of cocktail parties, give an accurate representation of my day to day life."[13] His approach to these administrative problems followed a clear hierarchy: first and foremost, qualified students learning from an engaged academic staff "is the basic work and basic accomplishment of a university and everything else is merely a means to an end." Second, he acknowledged that it was necessary to provide sufficient rewards in order to attract and retain a first-rate faculty: "Salaries and working conditions must be established which will insure that the very best talent will not shun teaching because it is a depressed occupation ... We must have the best recruits for the universities or succeeding generations will pay dearly." Third, it was necessary to acquire the means to enlarge the buildings, laboratories, and libraries in which teaching and research occurred.[14]

STUDENTS

Mackintosh was the first principal of Queen's who could draw upon his own experience as a Queen's undergraduate. What he treasured, and sought to preserve, was a climate for learning based on a close student-professor relationship: "[Queen's] will continue to be one of the smaller universities in Canada, large enough to offer advantages to first-rate scholars, small enough that individuality may emerge in both teachers and taught, where something of the magic of a master may pass to the enquiring student."[15] The role of the instructor was to guide students in their own learning. W.B. Munro, the distinguished Harvard professor of political science, endorsed this approach when commenting on his undergraduate days at Queen's over fifty years earlier: "I got a pretty good training in the art of self-education."[16] Reflecting his own experience with O.D. Skelton as an intellectual mentor, Mackintosh argued that the primary responsibility of the education system was to nurture the student's desire to learn. "In a sense, no one can teach anyone else anything. He can merely provide facilities and opportunities and show him some way by which he can learn for himself. A good teacher can give a student some sense of independent standards and can contribute to the incentives but the learning must be done by the student himself."[17]

Mackintosh maintained that universities were communities composed of alumni, faculty members, and students as "novices who hope to become members."[18] In welcoming first-year students, he sternly reminded them of the freedoms and privileges they were being extended. "Your time is yours and not someone else's. You can invest it or squander it ... You have the assurance that plenty of young men and women before you, with no better ability than you, have found in this university the entrance to a larger and more rewarding life. If this is what you think is important, there are many who are anxious to help. If it is unimportant to you, there are plenty who are waiting to take your place." Upon graduation, he insisted that they were not leaving the university but welcomed them as new members of the academy, equipped with the tools for better understanding the world in which they lived: "You have learned the points on the compass and have a sense of direction."[19]

In an era of mass education at the secondary-school level, his primary concern was with that number of poorly equipped students arriving at the universities' doors. As his father did some six decades earlier, he parcelled out the blame among families, educational institutions, and the community in general. To the Ontario Educational Association, an institution that his father had presided over years earlier, he expressed his disappointment with the intellectual environment of many households. The problem in the 1950s was that many a home was a place where "the television set is more important than even a modest shelf of books and where, if ambition is stimulated at all, it is only a narrow vocational ambition."[20] He found fault with the curriculum in Ontario's public-school system, suggesting that too much time was spent on creative composition at the expense of precise and accurate exposition. As an example, he suggested that universities dispense with the time-honoured exercise of asking incoming students to write an essay on "Why I Came to College" (citing one woman's answer as "I came to be went with and I ain't been yet"); instead, "they might better have them do an exercise telling another freshman how to get from the University to some obscure point north of Princess Street and make them revise it until every ambiguity and redundant word has been eliminated … I am not, of course, deprecating creative writing. I am inclined to think that the emphasis on it leaves two-thirds of the class untouched." Written and oral expression was "not just a mode of communication but an indispensable tool of thought."[21] Education thus began with a strong foundation in literacy: "mastery of language is not an ornamental accomplishment. It is the beginning and substance of all rational thought." He further asserted that "Ninety per cent of the undergraduates resent English courses and ninety per cent of the graduates who have been out at least two years complain that they did not have enough English."[22] In stating his bias in favour of clear, unambiguous, and economical expression, he liked to repeat the story told by Leonard Brockington about "the prisoner at the bar who addressed the Bench with moving eloquence: 'As God is my judge, my Lord, I am not guilty'; to which his Lordship replied, 'He is not, I am, and you are.'"[23]

Mackintosh was thus a stout defender of the liberal arts. As he told a Canadian Club audience: "If Canadians are to have strength, range, vision and perspective, many of them must be truly educated in literature, history, philosophy and the arts. These are not luxuries, but the necessities of national life."[24] He did not denigrate professional training, but it had to be taught in a liberal-arts-and-science setting. He told an audience of engineers that Canada needed "trained, educated persons of integrity ...We need not only more engineers but we need engineers and scientists of wider and deeper knowledge." The same message was delivered with respect to business schools. "It is the function of any Faculty of Commerce to open the eyes of its students to the place of business in the life of mankind and the course of human history ... to create in their students an awareness to the social significance of what they do, to stimulate their powers of imagination, enabling them to discern the ever-widening patterns of human endeavour and human destiny within which they work. More simply and briefly, it is the function of a Faculty of Commerce to educate, not merely to train."[25] Speaking to the Toronto Board of Trade in 1957, he welcomed the greater acceptance within the business community that the best preparation for business was a liberal arts, rather than vocational, education. As he did thirty years earlier, he insisted that the university served private industry "as one only of the activities of mankind." He was also opposed to the teaching of commerce and propaganda about the virtues of free enterprise extending to the high-school level: "Our students do too little questioning and have their attention too much riveted on lucrative jobs and the possibility of establishing homes and financial success. They are no worse than preceding generations but they are somewhat lacking in curiosity."[26]

His efforts to reinvigorate the department of industrial relations was a case in point. There was no shortage of activity within the department, but in Mackintosh's estimation it had strayed from its initial purpose: "While the Department commands the respect and confidence of industry, it has been losing something of its original position as an active force."[27] Specifically, teaching and outside consulting were interfering with its primary role as a centre for research and the dissemination of information, such that he offered additional resources if the department developed a clear program for the next five years.[28] Since the department did not offer any specialization for degree courses, he insisted that it should return to its logical status as a "centre" or "institute." With James Cameron set to retire in September 1960, the centre for industrial relations was returned to the department of political and economic science, under the direction of W. Donald Wood. J.J. Deutsch applauded Wood's appointment when he observed a few years later that "Professor Wood is making an attempt to be of service to labour representatives as well as industry. This is a new departure for the Queen's Centre which had become pretty much identified with management."[29]

The addition of professional schools was to remain secondary in importance in the short term. For instance, Mackintosh was not interested in adding a faculty of education at Queen's, favouring instead a year of specialized teacher training primarily to prevent "methodology and the so-called professional subjects" from encroaching upon the standard arts-and-science curriculum.[30] The one exception came in his efforts to establish a law school (despite his frequent reference to "those obscure regions where lawyers live."[31]) The Law Society of Upper Canada had refused to recognize university law degrees as adequate preparation for admission to the bar; instead, Osgoode Hall provided trade-focused training to complement articling apprenticeships. Mackintosh had loftier ambitions, citing Justice Oliver Wendell Holmes's view that: "The business of a law school is not sufficiently described when you say merely it is to teach law or to make lawyers. It is to teach law in the grand manner and to make great lawyers."[32] Cognizant of the increasing demand for lawyers and the need for greater breadth in education, Mackintosh and Corry entered into negotiations with the Law Society benchers to accept university law degrees and end Osgoode Hall's monopoly over legal training in Ontario. Four months after an agreement was reached, Queen's Law School opened in September 1957. A building was constructed two years later, and the formal opening was held in 1960, complete with Prime Minister Diefenbaker ("your great Saskatchewan statesman" as Mackintosh described him to Corry) in attendance to receive an honorary degree.[33]

In addressing the increasing demand for university education, therefore, he insisted that Queen's "has no desire to spread prolonged education among those who have neither felt the need nor demonstrated the capacity," likening attending university without adequate preparation to "going into a yacht race with torn sails."[34] In two respects Queen's received a modest reprieve from the obligation to meet the demands of mass education at the university level. First, the sparsely populated hills of Frontenac Country were deemed beautiful by all except the university bursar, or so he would quip, proving a blessing in the early 1950s as applications to Queen's lagged behind other Ontario universities and gave it more time to prepare for accommodating a larger number of students.[35] Second, Kingston's small population and relative isolation from larger urban centres meant that only 10 per cent of students lived at home, sparing Queen's "the problem of the indifferent day student who wants to take a partial course or who, without any clear target, would like to attend college."[36] In 1954, he forecast that the pressure would be one of "selection and quality rather than scarcity of students," but anticipated that "the numbers of honours students and graduates will still be thin for a few years yet."[37] The criteria for Queen's rate of expansion was its capacity to provide "first-class instruction" with an emphasis on honours courses, graduate work, and the addition of one or two professional schools.[38] Queen's long-standing system of honours courses in the Faculty of Arts assumed an even greater role given the pressures of "mass education," for it provided more talented students with specialized instruction and closer association with faculty members.[39]

To this end, more bursaries were created to remove the financial barriers to qualified students, while admission standards were nudged upwards.[40] Until 1956, first-year enrolment was limited in medicine and engineering, but otherwise any student with the equivalent of a Grade 13 high-school degree could gain admission. For the 1957–58 academic year, a 60-per-cent average on Grade 13 examinations was required. It was noted that this would have excluded one-sixth of the 1955 entering class, but that the impact on total enrolment was modest given the high failure rate experienced among those who previously entered with a high-school average below 60 per cent.[41] He acknowledged Queen's needed to accept more students, but not at the expense of losing "our special characteristics of compactness, balance, intimacy of instruction and residential life for our undergraduate students. We will take what share we can while preserving and extending the quality of our work."[42]

Figure 13.1 Intramural student enrolment: Queen's University, 1950/1–1960/1

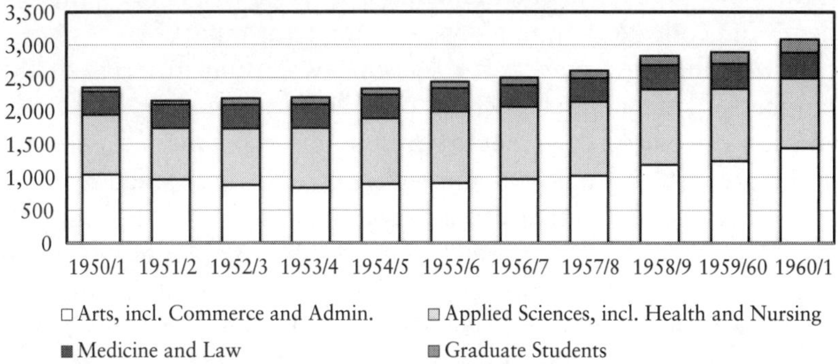

Source: Derived from Queen's University, *Report of the Principal*, 1950–51 and 1960–61.

"DEAR COLLEAGUE"

Just as his experience as a student at Queen's guided his approach to administration, so too did his long history as a member of the faculty. He took his role as principal lecturer literally. He insisted upon continuing to teach, typically reserving Tuesday afternoons for his seminar course on Canadian Economic History (Economics 25). However, he admitted that he found it difficult to maintain his "union card" as a practising economist, confessing to I. Norman Smith, associate editor of the *Ottawa Journal* that "I am always heartened when people remember either that I was once an economist and once an acceptable civil servant and when they remember it with as generous a reference as you do, I find it pleasantly intoxicating."[43] Similarly, he insisted upon continuing to chair the faculty council in order to maintain a close interest in the affairs of his colleagues, but admitted that the duties of the principal removed him from much of the day-to-day life of the faculty.[44] Thus his first important decision upon assuming office was the appointment of Corry as vice-principal. Describing him as "a brilliant teacher, an able and productive scholar, a person whose judgment others seek, and a helpful and lively colleague," he added emphatically that: "There are appointments which on balance seem right. The appointment of Professor J.A. Corry as Vice Principal I know is right." At the same time, he was careful to protect Corry's time as a full-time teacher and researcher, continuing the tradition of the position of vice-principal being an honorary post. "The fact that he remains as a full-time member of the academic staff in daily contact with students and colleagues is, in my view, a great advantage."[45]

In defining the criterion for Queen's expansion in terms of the number of students that it could provide with a quality education, Mackintosh emphasized that this meant not simply more classrooms and more staff, but a deeper and wider scholarship through research and other resources "that can nurture not only knowledge but wisdom." To this end, he set out to improve working conditions and salaries in order to be more competitive with other schools, and particularly with the University of Toronto. The financial hardship of the Depression and the improvisation of the immediate postwar period left working conditions for the faculty behind other institutions in the country. Although Principal Wallace had pushed through some improvements in pay, Mackintosh was "wearily struggling" to narrow the gap in salaries between Toronto and Queen's.[46] A few months into his tenure as principal, he confessed to Claude Bissell, president of the University of Toronto, that "I know that we have fallen rather sadly behind your scale in the past twelve months and I am quite sure that we shall have to make a substantial increase this year."[47] In May 1952 he was true to his word: the salary scale was boosted by some 16 per cent and a 10-per-cent general salary increase given retroactive to the beginning of the calendar year. An additional 5-per-cent average increase was promised for October; however, individual raises would henceforth not be automatic but based on the recommendation of department heads in consultation with the dean. "The main consideration in deciding each case has been merit – effectiveness as a teacher, persistence, resourcefulness and originality in carrying on research and scholarly work, and progress in the professional or scholarly group to which the individual belongs ... I have no illusion that the individual increase approved for 1952–53 represents anything more accurate than very rough justice. I have confidence that over three to five years increases so determined will be fairer and more rewarding than more uniform or more automatic increases." He was confident that the revised salary scales made Queen's relatively attractive compared to other Canadian universities and, in particular, were roughly equivalent to salaries at the University of Toronto.[48]

Parity with the University of Toronto proved to be a moving target. Steady pay increases occurred over the next few years, but by

1957 he was forced to admit that "this cautious approach has been rudely shaken by the new salary scales announced this week at the University of Toronto. These are such to require a fresh look at the whole situation ... The discrepancies which have now been created are too great to ignore."[49] In October 1958, salaries were raised by between 15 and 16.7 per cent, depending on rank, and with the increases offered in his last year as principal he was satisfied that salaries at Queen's were "within a reasonable margin of the current scale at the University of Toronto and compare favourably with those at other institutions."[50]

He also endeavoured to foster more research. The teaching load had returned to a norm of nine hours a week in the fall and winter terms, with summer teaching being voluntary (and paid at a rate of $750 per course). Contract work was encouraged to the extent that it contributed to a faculty member's development as a scholar, while discouraging other forms of consulting was less difficult given Kingston's relative geographical isolation from such opportunities.[51] External research funding increased throughout the decade, although it was largely concentrated in Medicine and Applied Sciences. Research grants from the Canada Council bolstered funding in the Faculty of Arts, while Mackintosh introduced internally funded summer research associateships of $800. On leaving office, he was satisfied that he had redressed the imbalance between teaching and research. "There is no intention of emphasizing research and scholarly work to the exclusion of good teaching but in years past, the bias has been in the other direction and there is a deficiency to be made up. A university without lively scholarship and research work is something less than a university. We are not, however, losing sight of the fact that a university can carry on a great deal of dull routine research and be a thoroughly dull university."[52]

Salaries and research funding apart, Mackintosh was also called upon to defend the academic freedom of members of the faculty. In 1960, Gideon Rosenbluth appeared before a parliamentary committee reviewing Canada's anti-combines legislation and stated, according to a newspaper account, that: "To accept the advice of trade associations on how the Combines Act should be amended is a little like asking burglars to amend the law on theft or basing liquor control legislation on the advice of alcoholics."[53] This prompted several complaints from businessmen and a letter to Mackintosh from a Queen's trustee who found Rosenbluth's words to be "an insult to all businessmen who support and contribute to Queen's University." Mackintosh conceded that Rosenbluth's comments were "inept," but defended him as "an able economist who has done some special studies on Industrial Concentration ... I am sure that there were many useful things in the evidence, which have all been overshadowed by a single careless remark."[54] When another businessman wrote to object to the "nationalistic and socialistic" content of A.R.M. Lower's brief to the Royal Commission on Broadcasting, Mackintosh's response was more emphatic. "Members of University staffs have the same freedom that ordinary citizens have, and are entitled to have views on questions of public policy and to express them. Whether or not I or the graduates of the University agree with the views is irrelevant ... I would, therefore, not think of trying to curb or in any way influence any member of staff in expressing his views on such subjects so long as he was prepared to give careful consideration to them and express them responsibly. I am sure the Royal Commission is fully capable of sorting out and assessing the number of submissions made to it ... I am sure that you would not wish to curb any professor who spoke in favour of the private broadcasting stations and that you will, therefore, agree that similar freedom should be offered to those who happen to favour some measure of public broadcasting."[55] On another occasion when charges of anti-Semitism were levelled (and subsequently withdrawn) in the hiring practices of the medical school, Mackintosh replied that "I would be far from saying that all members of our staff are uniformly right-thinking and completely tolerant, but I would be surprised if anyone could find any element of intolerance in the actions and administration of the University."[56]

Mackintosh was also tangentially involved in the infamous Crowe Affair of 1958. Harry Crowe, a history professor at United College, was teaching at Queen's for a session when he sent a letter to a colleague in Winnipeg that was highly critical of the college's administration, which was dominated by United Church clergy. "I distrust all preachers and think we have abundant evidence that religion is a corrosive force," wrote Crowe. "People don't seem to have principles unless they are prepared to go to Hell." The letter mysteriously ended up on the desk of the principal, Wilfred Lockhart, and Crowe's eventual dismissal became the central focus of academic freedom in Canadian universities. Mackintosh observed that "It would be hard to conceive of more ineptness and wrong headedness being shown by both sides than was the case. I would hope that there were very few university institutions which would be capable of creating such a situation." Other than observing that Crowe had been a capable and assiduous teacher, "I have not gone further in my judgment of the whole case than to conclude that both parties made very grave errors of judgment and good sense."[57] When Frank Underhill appealed to Mackintosh to help find academic positions for several of the faculty at United College who had tendered their resignations, Mackintosh described the actions of United College as "completely outrageous and even if one is determined to be wicked, there is no justification for being unintelligent about it." He added that Queen's would be "very willing" to consider hiring those that had resigned, but advised that it was best to wait in the hope that the mounting pressure on United College would result in some "drastic change." He could not avoid injecting some humour into the situation by citing an anonymous wag who observed that "you cannot dismiss a Crowe without caws."[58]

"FELLOW GRADUATES," TRUSTEES, CORPORATE DONORS, AND GOVERNMENTS

The administrative duty that most occupied Mackintosh's time was the budgeting process, which he described as striking a balance "which will both enable me to live with my colleagues and keep peace with the auditor."[59] In this regard, he benefited from increasing government support. In 1950–51, roughly half of Queen's $1.5-million budget was generated from student tuition, 15 per cent from endowments, and 30 per cent from government grants. The latter required regular trips to Queen's Park in Toronto for a day of "panhandling," and then anxiously awaiting the announcement of annual provincial grants.[60] The Massey Report (Royal Commission on National Development in the Arts, Letters, and Sciences) recommended greater federal funding of universities as part of a broader cultural policy. Money was to be distributed across provinces according to population, and then to individual universities on a per-student basis.[61]

Mackintosh accepted the premise that there were economies of scale in universities and, moreover, that provincial monies were distributed implicitly, if not explicitly, on a per-student basis. As a result, Queen's ability to remain a smaller university of distinction depended upon building up endowment funds, and he thus made no apologies for cultivating close relations between the university and the corporate sector. Through fundraising, responding to inquiries, as a guest speaker, or as a legacy of his former work with the Canadian Bankers' Association and his various roles with the federal government, Mackintosh's corporate contacts were extensive.[62] In 1957, Queen's launched a national fundraising campaign, the National Fund for Queen's University, headed by Crump, and Mackintosh was dragged across the country in the search for money. He found Canadian corporations to be good public citizens, but the same was not true of Canadian subsidiaries of American firms. While some – the Aluminum Company of Canada, Dupont, Imperial Oil, and Ford – gave generously, a number of others, including General Motors, Coca-Cola, Johns-Manville, and Metropolitan and Prudential Life, "simply turn their backs." Mackintosh accompanied Crump to New York in an effort to persuade some of the "recalcitrant" companies, but to little avail. "In the main, however, certain companies run their Canadian business under a purely American pattern and will do nothing in Canada which they would not do in the United States. I said in a speech last year that I was sure it was the missionary ancestors of the directors of some of these companies who put the island native in Mother Hubbard dresses."[63] Upon returning from a visit to Victoria, Vancouver, Banff, Calgary, and Edmonton in the search for corporate funds, he expressed similar frustration with Alberta oil companies. Despite their demands for more engineering graduates, "All our people could do was collect $100 or so from a number of companies who are using our geologists and begging us to turn out more."[64] Regardless of the uneven support from the corporate community, the National Fund eventually achieved its goal of raising $4 million.

By 1960–61, the university's budget had risen to $5.2 million, with the contribution of tuition fees falling to 35 per cent, the relative importance of endowment monies dropping only slightly to 13 per cent, and government grants rising to 44 per cent of the total.

Flush with money from the National Fund, Ontario capital grants, and maintenance reserves cobbled together over time by William McNeill as treasurer, Queen's undertook an expansion program that dramatically increased the physical capacity of the campus. Constructed were: five academic buildings, including Dunning Hall for the school of commerce and business; five student residences,

Figure 13.2 Queen's University revenue sources, 1950/1–1960/1

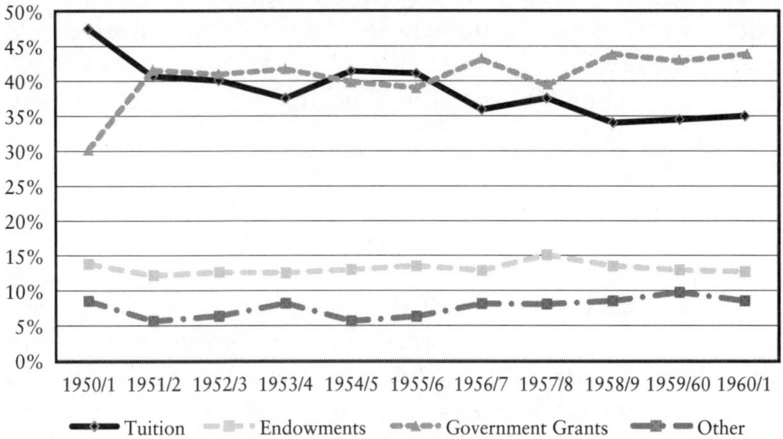

Source: Derived from Queen's University, *Report of the Principal*, 1950–51 and 1960–61.

accommodating roughly a thousand students; Richardson Hall to house senior administration; the Agnes Etherington Arts Centre; and the Engineering Society's student centre. Gibson notes the irony in the fact that Mackintosh, "whose only interest in buildings was altogether what went inside of them," would earn the moniker of "The Building Principal."[65]

The objective was to retain the architectural integrity of the campus and the intimacy afforded by its compact nature. The former was achieved through the use of traditional limestone in construction, and Mackintosh did not let certain details escape his notice: "I went over the Law building plans with Lederman and gave my blessing to them except for the window treatment of the library window. On this he is going to have another go at the architects who, I think, can do better if they try. Their window design reminds me of a child's picture of a house except that the lines are reasonably straight."[66] Maintaining the compactness of the campus posed a greater problem. "West Campus," adjacent to Leonard Field, was developed to accommodate student residences, but elsewhere extending beyond the Union-Arch-University-Stuart perimeter meant encroaching upon private homes. When the university appealed to the Government of Ontario for the right to expropriate, the matter fell on the desk of William M. Nickle, the minister of planning and development and, by probably bad fortune, the MPP for Kingston. Nickle refused to extend general powers of expropriation but only the rights to specific properties, forcing the university to make repeated requests to the province. Gibson, whose admiration of Mackintosh is amply clear, is critical of the manner in which the situation was handled, arguing that the principal's "clannish loyalty" to Queen's was at the expense of appropriate regard for the concerns of local residents. Mackintosh conceded that "There are probably things which I could have done which would have improved matters, though I do not know what they are."[67]

The same cannot be said when it came to planning for the new physics building in 1961. In order to preserve green space on campus, Mackintosh favoured its location on the site of the old Jock Hardy Arena on Arch Street, where Humphrey Hall now stands, but the trustees opted for a site on the lower campus. Mackintosh suddenly found himself in a controversy that was "very distasteful and disturbing." On receiving a flood of letters from students, staff, and alumni (including one from the irrepressible Arthur Lower), Mackintosh informed Corry that "Their information is incomplete and their logic often faulty but the resistance is nonetheless real. I have no rigid views on the site at all except that it is becoming clearer to me that my major responsibility is to provide adequate facilities for first-class work and I have no desire to leave an institution of which people could say, 'It has a second-rate Physics Department but a beautiful view.'" He reported that he was hard at work trying to find an alternative site, and instructed Corry, on sabbatical leave in Spain, to pay no heed: "Don't let this divert you from the sunshine and tangerines." A month later he could report to Corry that "I think we are about out of the fuss over the Physics Building though it still has to be dealt with by the Board in May." A number of houses adjacent to the campus on Queen's Crescent were identified, and Mackintosh spent a weekend as a "real-estate operator," personally negotiating the purchase of properties. The trustees would subsequently give their approval to the new site.[68]

This experience reinforced Mackintosh's approach to managing the trustees. As he counselled Corry: "Let this be a lesson to you. Never let the Board of Trustees make up its own mind." In guiding the board to the correct decision, it was his practice to "neither vote nor watch the vote" when a question was put to the trustees (although whether this was to allow individuals to exercise their judgment free of the principal's intimidation, or to keep the principal from growing angry is not clear).[69] He also employed other strategies. On an otherwise "dry" campus, a drink at the principal's residence became de rigueur at the conclusion of each trustees' meeting. He used this new tradition to good advantage by placing the issues on which he had a stronger conviction near the end of the agenda. After trustees voiced their opinions on matters near the top of the agenda, they would grow restless as the meeting proceeded and, checking their watches to ensure there was sufficient time to visit the principal's residence for the requisite refreshment before catching the last train out of Kingston, would deal summarily with matters at the bottom of the agenda. The machinery of democracy, it seems, needs to be lubricated.

FELLOW PRESIDENTS AND VICE-CHANCELLORS

Mackintosh was front and centre when it came to promoting the national and international interests of universities. In his presidential address to the National Conference of Canadian Universities in 1953, he framed the issues confronting his audience of university administrators. Reluctant to offer stock answers, he could "attempt only a lesser but still useful task of trying to ask the right questions. Asking the right questions may be equally important as pronouncing the answers. Indeed, the ability to ask the right questions is more clearly a mark of maturity of mind than of knowing the right answers."[70]

The first question posed involved the growth and pattern of development of Canadian universities in light of rapid economic growth. He forecast a steady growth in enrolment for a few years, then an acceleration that would bring total numbers to some 60 to 70 per cent above the levels at the time. This demand for higher education was not driven by demographic changes – indeed, he conjectured that the number of eighteen-year-olds in the country (born in 1935 during the depths of the Depression) was lower than in 1939 – but by general economic prosperity, increasing immigration and urbanization, and the growth in white-collar jobs. In light of government funding commitments, the main problem was not one of finance; instead, "We will have to consider the desirable size of universities and the relation of their function to their size." While this raised issues for individual universities – whether there would be a devolution in provincial schools, changes in denominational institutions, or the growth of "city universities" – there were system-wide considerations as to how graduate training and research should develop, be it through a hierarchical organization of research-intensive graduate and primarily undergraduate institutions or some other form. Eschewing the "haphazard development" of higher education in the United States, he asked whether planning should occur at the level of government or of university associations. He insisted that it was the government's role "to ensure that financial barriers to promising students be removed through national scholarships," but otherwise confessed to "a strong bias in favour of variety and experimentation within universities and among them."[71]

He then addressed the relationship of Canadian universities with other countries. On the one hand, he questioned whether graduating training in Canada has gone "a bit far too fast," such that the increasing number of undergraduates doing graduate work at the same institution might be restricting their horizons; on the other hand, he argued that Canadian universities had to do their share in accepting more students from other Commonwealth countries, southeast Asia, and the West Indies.

More disconcerting was a growing emphasis on training at the expense of education, a trend accelerated by new "amazingly complicated" techniques of repetitive learning that could "be mastered by mediocre and quite uneducated minds." He found high-school graduates well trained "but deficient in fundamental education and extraordinarily confused in motives and standards" as they sought to make sense of an increasingly complicated world. He warned universities against retreating to narrow specialization at the expense of the "integration of knowledge." As he stated elsewhere, the reward for students was that "aside from any professional qualifications, they will live in a much larger world, understanding much more experiences and capable of enjoying much that otherwise passes them by."[72] A disturbing aspect of this lack of integration was a broad trend towards anti-intellectualism, defined as the loss of intellectual integrity and honesty. As the world grew in complexity, there was a "futile longing for a simpler world" and a "craving for the absolute," leading to the dogmatic acceptance of simple arguments at the expense of reason – "to claim the absolute authority of the deity or of a philosophy to validate the muddled thinking of humans." Its worst expression was found in the rise of McCarthyism in the United States – "a most repulsive phenomenon and yet evil creatures, ignorant, malicious, vulgar, are not new in the history of mankind."[73] Nonetheless, he concluded on an optimistic note: "I am reasonably confident that if we can find good working answers to these questions which concern the size and pattern of institutions, our relations with people and institutions in other countries, the need for integration in our knowledge, and a courageous rejection of what I have called the craving for the absolute, we will make the next ten or fifteen years in Canadian university life years of progress and achievement."[74]

Queen's, as with other Canadian universities, also belonged to the Association of Universities of the British Commonwealth (AUBC). Mackintosh usually asked Gerald Graham, who had left Queen's to become Rhodes Professor of Imperial History at King's College, London, to represent Queen's in his stead at the AUBC annual meetings; however, he made an exception in 1953 when he was to be named chair of the association for 1953–54, a position he was "greatly honoured" to accept.[75] He spent a month travelling in Great Britain in order to receive honorary degrees from St Andrew's University and the University of Durham, and then attending the annual meeting of the AUBC at Cambridge in July. Afterwards he spent ten days in London at the Mount Royal Hotel, passing one evening with Graham and Irene Spry, and another with Norman Robertson.[76] He declined, however, the opportunity to attend the coronation of Queen Elizabeth in Westminster Abbey.

Mackintosh's selection as AUBC chairman was in part because Canada had been chosen as the location for the 1954 annual meeting of the association in order to facilitate discussions between representatives of American and Commonwealth universities. On 5 September 1954, as sixteen Commonwealth delegates – from Great Britain and Ireland, Australia, New Zealand, South Africa, India, Ceylon, Pakistan, Malta, and the West Indies – descended upon Kingston, Mackintosh reported that "we had discovered human frames concealed by the vice-chancellarian robes."[77] Among them was Sir William Hamilton Fyfe, honorary treasurer of the AUBC and former principal of Queen's. They were followed a day later by executive members of the National Council of Canadian Universities, and a day after that by ten American university presidents. Visitors were accommodated in Adelaide Hall, regular meals and teas were served in Ban Righ Hall, receptions were held in the principal's residence, and the group was treated to a picnic supper at the Chaffey's Locks

Biological Station and a boat tour through the Thousand Islands. The events concluded with a formal dinner on Thursday night in Wallace Hall attended by 220 guests. The logistical challenges were many and varied. To accommodate delegates from India, Ceylon, and Pakistan, Mackintosh appealed to external affairs in Ottawa for guidance on dietary and other arrangements. After consulting with the Ceylon India Restaurant in New York, J.A. Chapdelaine advised that "most Indian delegates, and some Ceylonese delegates, would probably be strict vegetarians and he considered it wise to offer a choice of either a vegetable curry meal or a meat and chicken curry meal. The vegetables used in a vegetable-curry are cauliflower, peas, string beans or eggplant. A wine could also be served with the meal but it is not, by any means, essential as most Indians and Ceylonese are tee-totallers."[78] When the delegates were bundled off on the train to continue discussions at the University of Toronto, there was a sigh of relief from the Queen's organizing committee. Mackintosh was satisfied that "we avoided any major disasters," but there was some unfinished business; a member of the local committee reported that "we finally found Dr. Hall's laundry, and located the rightful owner of the coat Mr. Rowe took from the meeting, got Mr. De Kiewiet's car battery recharged in time for him to start home on Friday, and sent on all President Dodds' underwear which he'd left in his bureau drawer."[79] The matters discussed (first-year curriculum, libraries, shortage of scientists, state funding) took a back seat to the formidable, and at times exotic, challenge of hosting the conference – "such are the obligations of the Commonwealth."[80]

As the Cold War intensified and the launch of the Sputnik satellite heightened western fears that it was falling behind the Soviet Union in scientific knowledge, Mackintosh did not stray from his central message. There was nothing revolutionary in the Soviet approach to education; it was merely an emphasis on the prestige of teachers and scholars, and the dedication of significant resources to universities. To the extent that it was a "disturbed, troubled and frightened generation," he stated that it was not due to the threat of nuclear war – insisting that they were not that far removed from a Hobbesian world in which life was "nasty, brutish, and short." "What frightens people is an uneasy awareness of responsibility – events are not the Acts of Gods or Kings – we are responsible for things that we haven't wit or courage to control."[81] In defining the appropriate response, he returned to a familiar refrain, for he took every opportunity to remind an audience that: "Our greatest need in Canada for the period which is ahead of us is not industrial resources or capital, though these are needed. It is trained, educated persons of integrity."[82]

GOVERNMENT COLLEAGUES, CANADA COUNCIL, AND THE OTHER GORDON COMMISSION

A condition stipulated by the trustees upon Mackintosh's appointment as principal was that he cede all government and other outside work, unless approved by the board. Accordingly, he resigned from his two remaining Ottawa posts – as a director on the Canadian Mortgage and Housing Commission and as chair of the Unemployment Insurance Advisory Committee.[83] He also declined invitations to serve as a director on the board of the Canadian Bank of Commerce and to rejoin the board of Empire Life. "I have, since becoming Principal of the University, held no posts outside the University other than some purely honorary ones in which the University had an interest."[84] These included such positions as patron of the Kingston and District Kennel Club; member of the officers' mess at the Royal Military College and of the HMCS *Cataraqui*; patron of the Kingston Historical Society; and president of the Kingston and District Rod and Gun Club ("I was a bit perturbed to realize that I was not a particularly proficient sportsman, but having looked over your list of honorary presidents, I feel that I would probably rank somewhere in the middle of them"). Mackintosh declined Premier E.C. Manning's request to chair an Alberta Royal Commission on Education, citing a lack of time as well as "serious doubts on my part as to my ability to deal adequately with elementary and secondary education."[85] More controversial was his decision to forego the opportunity to serve on the Royal Commission on Canada's Economic Prospects, headed by Walter Gordon. "He was under great pressure from everyone concerned, including Prime Minister St Laurent," wrote E.C. Gill, a trustee. "The Chairman of the Board of Trustees and I helped him in refusing this request."[86]

This did not end his association with former colleagues in Ottawa. Through the fishing club and other auspices he followed with interest the progress of his friends through the government ranks, dispensed advice on a variety of issues, and welcomed others back into the academic field.[87] He followed the fortunes of the Liberal Party with interest, especially as the jockeying to replace St Laurent as prime minister increased. "There is no sign of Mr St Laurent retiring and the young fellows have settled down to another period of training for the big contest," he wrote to Clifford Curtis in 1954. "So far Walter Harris has not achieved any reputation as Minister of Finance and has even appeared on one or two occasions to be a little naïve."[88] When the big contest did occur, Walter Gordon reported that "While the results of the Convention were successful, it left Mike [Pearson] in a rather exhausted state and because of this he did not do as well as he might have done in the House the following Monday. However, I have no doubt that he will recover from the pasting he received from Diefenbaker and the Press."[89] The Liberal Study Conference held on campus in 1960 brought other familiar faces, including those of Pearson, Pickersgill, George Ferguson, and Paul Martin, Sr.[90] Other old friends he saw when they accepted invitations to speak on campus, including Donald Gordon, Walter Gordon, C.D. Howe, and Sir Saville ("Joe") Garner, the high commissioner for the United Kingdom in Ottawa.

More importantly, he was entrusted with responsibility for the education of many of the offspring of his former Ottawa associates for whom Queen's remained the university of choice. Jean Chapdelaine, for one, credited his association with Mackintosh during the war as the most important factor in sending his daughter to Queen's some sixteen years later: "It is a most pleasant thought for me to know that Claude is one of your wards." Mackintosh responded that "I must say I wake up worried some mornings at the number of the precious progeny of friends of mine who are attending the University. We have and have had quite a roster from Ottawa and External Affairs and, to my great relief, they have almost all done well."[91] The most intriguing inquiry came from Lord Cobbold, governor of the Bank of England, who was encouraging his son, at the time finishing his last year at Eton, to attend Queen's.[92] Singled out for special attention was Donald Gordon's eldest son, Donnie, who was devoting his time to football broadcasts and campus journalism to the virtual exclusion of class attendance. After talking with the son on a couple of occasions and asking an instructor to intervene, Mackintosh counselled the father that "I think you should be patient and not take too serious a view of this for the long pull. I think the boy in a muddled way is trying to find himself, and I have enough confidence in his capacity and stability that I think he will find a way through … I think we can place a long bet on Donald and not worry too much if in the short run he should stub his toe a bit." He was not wrong, for Donnie Gordon would complete his undergraduate degree at Queen's, earn his MA in political economy at the University of Toronto, and enter a PhD program at the London School of Economics. He never finished his doctoral thesis only because he was too busy establishing a notable career as a broadcaster and journalist with such organizations as the CBC and BBC.[93]

There were two exceptions to the prohibition on government work. In 1957, Mackintosh accepted a three-year appointment to the board of the newly formed Canada Council, presumably at the behest of Brooke Claxton, who was its first chair. Mackintosh remained a close friend of Claxton's throughout the latter's difficult term as minister of defence: despite efforts to reform the armed services, his department was rocked by scandal and the perceived poor performance of the military during the Korean War. Forced to admit privately that Claxton had become "something of a liability" to the government, upon his resignation to become president of Metropolitan Life, Mackintosh sent a letter of congratulations: "You can add this to the other letters in the barrel … I do not know any person who has had a more arduous tour of duty nor anyone who worked harder at it." Claxton replied "I appreciate your friendship and support more than I can say."[94] Where the Canada Council was concerned, Mackintosh was expected to represent the views of Canadian universities, but he also defined his role as "to provide a bridge between our hard-faced capitalists and the long-haired enthusiasts of the other wing."[95] With Claxton too ill to attend the August 1959 meeting, Mackintosh informed him that all went well, except for "the insoluble problem of the ballet," and quipped that "I am tempted to suggest propaganda to convince people that this is a decadent form of art and a sinister deviation from our Canadian way of life."[96] It would be his last correspondence with his old friend, who died a year later at the age of sixty-one.

Despite declining the appointment to the Royal Commission on Canada's Economic Prospects, Mackintosh did get to serve on another Gordon commission when Walter Gordon was asked by Ontario's Premier Leslie Frost to head a committee of inquiry "into the relationship of the Provincial Boards and Commissions to the Government and the Legislature" in 1958. As Gordon recounts the story, "when asked whom 'I would like to have serve with me on the committee,' I replied that Bill Mackintosh would be my first choice, together with a lawyer who was familiar with the provincial government machinery. Mr. Frost replied, 'Bill Mackintosh is fine. I have a high respect for him. But, Walter, must the lawyer be a Liberal, too?'" The highlight of its proceedings, according to Gordon, was when Judge W.T. Robb, the chairman of the Liquor Licensing Board, appeared to give testimony. "He is a rather small man but full of confidence. In the course of our questioning about the work of his board, Bill Mackintosh asked what the policy was about granting banquet permits in dry areas. Judge Robb replied that licenses in dry areas were granted only in the case of weddings. Mackintosh in his dry Scottish way then asked, 'And why the discrimination against wakes?' Judge Robb had no reply. It was the only time he was discomfitted."[97] The *Report of the Committee on the Organization of the Government of Ontario* was issued at the end of 1959 and released to the public in January 1960. While not making for the most exciting reading, it is described as a landmark in the history of administrative law in Canada, the first attempt to examine the entire machinery of government within a jurisdiction.[98] Focusing on the relationship of quasi-judicial boards and commissions to the legislature and executive branches, with the aim of improving efficiency without breaching democratic practices, it placed primacy on the principle of ministerial responsibility, warned against the proliferation of boards and commissions, and called for greater legislative control over how such regulatory and quasi-judicial agencies exercised their delegated powers. Frost described the report as "a very excellent one" and acted upon many of its recommendations.[99]

Mackintosh also remained an important commentator on Canadian current affairs, and found ample opportunity to offer his views, although he was disinclined to do so without careful thought. Thus, when asked by a journalist if he favoured Canada's acquisition of nuclear weapons, he simply replied that "My views are not really knowledgeable"; on the matter of whether or not Canada needed a bill of rights, he confessed to not being "completely sure of my own opinion."[100] As he grew older he was more guarded: "I do not confuse the prejudice of age with the wisdom of the ages."[101]

One topic he felt qualified to comment on was the state of the Canadian economy. Since he was the author of the 1945 White Paper that helped shape domestic economic policy and a key participant in the discussions leading to the international institutions that emerged at the end of the war, it would have been excusable if he had adopted a self-congratulatory tone in light of the rapid growth achieved. He was, however, anything but sanguine. In 1952, he took to the pages of *Saturday Night* to warn against complacency in the midst of the economic prosperity. As booming resource markets drove the value of Canada's exports to new heights, the Canadian dollar to a premium relative to the US dollar, and Canada to a more important position on the world stage, he cautioned against relying on imported capital to exploit non-renewable resources at a faster rate than before. "There is indeed a danger that we as a country are being oversold abroad and that our progress may not over the next decade or two keep up with the expectations which have been created. Immense investment is being channelled into the development of wasting assets to be sold in what is temporarily a seller's market."[102] The Canadian economy was certainly more diversified – he likened it to a four-engine airplane that was able to fly on three engines, so that a collapse in one sector, such as wheat, was not as disabling as in the past. But to extend his metaphor, it was still of the turbo-prop variety, too dependent on the export of raw and semi-processed materials.[103] Of equal concern was the economic and political instability associated with the unprecedented inflow of American investment and the level of trade with the United States. Capital was being "forced on us" in areas such as new metallurgical ores and energy that met the priorities of the American economy. He thus advised that "there is special need for caution and good judgement on our part. The United States has often supplied us with initiative and enterprise and capital. More seldom has it contributed sound judgement to our problems."[104]

In large measure, Canada's economic position reflected the failure to achieve the multilateral world that Mackintosh and other officials had sought at the talks leading up to Bretton Woods and the British loan negotiations of 1945. Writing in 1953, he argued that the recovery in the West German and Japanese economies, the growing political gap with the Soviet Union, and increasing food production in Asia had altered the basis for an integrated global economy; nonetheless, the threat to greater unity remained the "fissure" between the dollar and sterling areas.[105] He attributed the recurring crises in the sterling area to the "stubborn facts of economic and political history" associated with the long-term decline in Britain's economic influence. In the early twentieth century, its need to adjust to lost export markets was forestalled by the large amount of income derived from its overseas assets. However, with the liquidation of these assets during World War II and increased competition from West Germany and Japan after the war, its "stark problem of adjustment was laid bare." The retention of preferential tariffs, direct controls over imports and investment, and sterling inconvertibility could not prevent the leakage of expenditures from the sterling zone and a resulting shortage of dollars. Canada's renewed status as a resource exporter was largely a by-product of closer integration with the United States, precisely the eventuality that Mackintosh and Towers had warned of seven years earlier. The dollar-sterling fissure meant that: "There is some danger in the division of the world into economic sectors. The United States and Canada may find themselves split off from the larger world and uncomfortably dependent one on the other. It is true that immediately this may not concern us greatly. The United States offers a great market for materials though the record is that of a fluctuating and not too dependable market. In the long run, however, it offers no substitute for the United Kingdom and Western Europe as markets for our cereals, whose importance I do not need to urge in this year of abundant harvests."[106]

As late as 1954, he continued to argue that the unachieved goals of wartime negotiations were still the correct ones to pursue, although multilateral trade and unimpeded currency flows were "now looked at with more realism but also more informed respect."[107] Responsibility rested primarily with Britain and other sterling-area countries to "put their houses in order," by removing discriminatory tariffs and direct controls to protect domestic manufacturing. However, the United States bore a measure of the blame. The tariff reductions achieved through the GATT were biased in favour of raw and semi-processed materials and only modest in the case of manufactured goods, resulting in a world order in which other countries "produce raw materials to feed the ravening industrial machine of the United States … It does not seem to have been noticed how close this is to the pattern of trade laid down by British colonial policy against which the United States rebelled in 1776 … The system is no more tenable for a great industrial nation such as the United States in the twentieth century than it was for Britain in the eighteenth. There are ominous signs that this pattern of United States tariff policy is being strengthened rather than relaxed." The United States needed to exercise greater leadership by embarking "boldly on the paths of multilateral trade and non-discrimination which the United States has itself prescribed." Capital exports and aid should now be directed to the underdeveloped countries, which would indirectly help Britain and other sterling countries: "Such an outflow can perform the double function of alleviating a dollar scarcity and at the same time giving fresh life and hope to those areas of the world which have been swept by an epoch making revolution. If North America believes in the retreat of imperialism before national autonomy, and believes that other continents can be held in amicable relationship with the North Atlantic, it must be prepared to help in building up workable and profitable relationships based on mutual respect and sound economy. The interest of the United States in enlarging the output of raw materials, and of the foodstuffs on which the production of raw materials depends, is in itself a strong justification for a fresh initiative in directing and enlarging the outflow of capital." The health of the sterling area was important not just for short-term economic growth, but for long-term political goals if the areas of Asia and Africa were to be retained within the western orbit.[108]

A year later, Mackintosh questioned for the first time Canada's pursuit of multilateral arrangements. Writing in *Foreign Affairs*, he interpreted the steep recession of 1954 as the end of the era of postwar transition – spending under the Marshall Plan was nearing an end, and the recovery of the Japanese and West German economies had intensified international competition – and yet there was little prospect of sterling convertibility or trade reform on the horizon. Citing the "number of disturbing problems bearing on Canada's foreign economic relations, especially with the United States," he became more concerned about living "under the shadow of the metropolitan centres to the south." The optimistic wartime aspirations that Canada would expand its manufacturing sector by following an American model of industrialization had not been realized, because the country was caught between the highly protected US market and low-wage competition emerging from European and Asian countries. Trade barriers in the United States had prevented Canadian firms from achieving the necessary economies of scale, while American tax laws gave the subsidiaries of US firms a competitive advantage over domestic ones. Acknowledging that support for trade liberalization was waning in light of US protectionism and that there were "some murmurs of complaint that certain areas of Canadian industry and finance are powerfully affected by United States subsidiaries in which there is no Canadian investment," he stated that

"Canadians are wondering if their liberal trade policy has not become too one-sided to be advantageous to a small country with a big neighbour."[109] Arguing that "the drive for multilateral trade and convertible currencies has had repercussions both favourable and disturbing," he concluded that: "At the end of the Second World War, Canadians struck out on an economic path which they have followed closely to this day with considerable confidence that they were on the right road. Now they are in the mood to take another view ahead."[110]

Rethinking Canadian policy occurred with the Royal Commission on Canada's Economic Prospects. In reviewing the commission's preliminary report, Mackintosh did not quarrel with the analysis: he agreed that, for the foreseeable future, there would be no sharp change in economic direction, with the dynamic source of growth in natural-resource exploitation. He deemed the argument that further trade liberalization threatened Canada's secondary industries to be consistent with the general views of the 1945 White Paper, and he accepted the concern that American foreign direct investment was intensifying Canada's dependence on resource industries and branch-plant manufacturing facilities. But with respect to the nationalist leanings in the policy prescriptions of the Gordon Commission, Mackintosh opposed any restrictions being imposed on the inflow of foreign capital, instead chiding Canadian firms for being too timid and foregoing opportunities seized upon by American firms.[111] Although he declined to review the final report for the *Canadian Journal of Economic and Political Science*, in a personal note to his old friend, he heralded it as "the framework of thinking and the source of ideas for many years to come."[112] Nor could he suspend his self-interest in applauding the commission's emphasis on education: "The vigour of your support of the universities in your Report is likely to result in an academic movement to have you canonized." Gordon reminded him that "I am not too familiar with religious practices but I seem to recall that canonization usually takes place after death. On this premise I suspect there are a good many people who would be willing to see me immortalized in such fashion – including some members of the Boards of Governors."[113]

In his presidential address to the Royal Society of Canada in 1957, Mackintosh returned to many of the same themes. (He was determined to deliver at least the first five minutes in French, and Alison recalls his painstaking rehearsals in front of the mirror at home.) Reviewing Canada's economic history, he emphasized the underlying continuity of its reliance of staple exports. There had been an astonishing increase in speed of development since World War II "but no conspicuous change in pattern ... we are still developing ... great bulk exports albeit with an increased amount of processing and refinement. We are still dependent on markets abroad. We are still the field for investment of great sums of external capital."[114] Foreign direct investment from the United States required Canada to be alert but not alarmed, comfortable in the belief that American firms would be good corporate citizens. Instead, he warned against "second-rate" borrowing of foreign techniques, whether it be in the realm of economics, politics, technology, or culture. "Anti-American, anti-foreign, or narrowly nationalistic policies are likely to be short lived, but broadly national policies founded on the need for the protection and development of what is distinctively Canadian will be persistent."[115] In this regard, he placed his hopes on greater investment in Canada's human resources, an admittedly self-serving argument by a university principal, but also one that was consistent with his lifelong commitment to the importance of education. His unwavering confidence in human capacity allowed him to transcend many of the more immediate debates on Canadian economic policy and the role of economic nationalism to embrace a long-term objective: "Culturally, the goal is intellectual, aesthetic and social excellence, not a national culture *per se*."[116]

STEPPING DOWN ... AND A FEW PACES TO THE RIGHT

Mackintosh was sixty-five years old in 1961, his health "unobtrusively robust," despite the onset of diabetes and a lifetime of cigarette smoking. But he had told the trustees over a year earlier of his intention to retire as principal, a decision he explained in the following terms: "I have for a long time held the view that it was undesirable for anyone to continue in a senior administrative position into the period when he might be biased in favour of peace and quiet rather than fresh enterprise. Even though the fifties have been very full of problems, the sixties will have just as many problems and opportunities."[117] He was confident that his successor, Alex Corry, was well-equipped to meet these challenges.

In many respects, Mackintosh's tenure as principal marked the end of an era at Queen's. The "informal coziness" of campus life extended to its administration, with the principal maintaining a hands-on approach to a variety of duties, whether it be the budget, private fundraising, or relations with students, staff, and the board of trustees. He often mused about the expectations placed on a principal "to act continuously as though you really knew the difference between a bad football coach and a good biochemist" or to offer one's judgment "on everything from style of architecture to the best methods of teaching a language which you yourself do not understand ... Instead of being able to delegate everything to my well organized colleagues, I find that they, in fact, drop all their insoluble problems on my desk."[118] The pace of change was quickening, however, and expansion brought with it greater administrative demands. As much as enrolment had increased during the 1950s, all were cognizant of the expected explosion in demand for undergraduate education in the 1960s, as more of the baby-boom generation made its way to the doors of Canadian universities. When student enrolment in his final year as principal reached 3,100 students, he confessed to Corry that something more sophisticated than the "very crude" method of selecting students based on their Grade 13 average grades would be necessary, but that "I am as far as ever from having a clear notion of how it may be effectively done."[119]

The Crowe Affair further highlighted the change in Canadian universities. Although United College was much smaller than Queen's, Mackintosh recognized that relations between the administration and the faculty grew more complex. "Life would be much simpler had we only a small group of staff with whom one had frequent personal associations and with whom communication was easy. However, when the academic staff rises to more than two hundred, it is not easy to maintain adequate communications without the help of an association, and not easy to get their views of many things such as the pension arrangements, medical care, etc., for there are many considerations other than the overall cost." He described the officers of the Faculty Association at Queen's, formed in 1951, as having consistently been "men of prudence and good judgment," but added that "While we may all think we are not as some other institutions are, there is a strong Biblical condemnation of making formal statements of that sort."[120] Indicative of these changes was Mackintosh's surprise at the number of complaints he received from faculty members over what he admitted were "pretty meager salary increases" contained in the last budget that he oversaw. He informed Corry that "For the first time I have had quite a few protests, perhaps twelve or fifteen, some mild and some angry, about promotions and salary adjustments. I was not prepared for this having had very little of it in the past. Some of it arises from the greater competitiveness of the market and there are one or two instances of low morale as in the Physics Department. While I have normally in the past been pretty resistant to making adjustments after the budget has been struck, I have felt in this case that I had better not leave you any of these sore spots and I have, I hope, fixed them all up amicably." Also indicative of the era, he added that "I am inclined to think that perhaps your first official appearance should be a lecture to your colleagues' wives not to nag them about taking a firm stand on salaries."[121] But he was forced to confess that he found himself talking to trustees and outside groups more often than to staff.[122]

In the wake of the Crowe Affair, an investigation into university governance across the country by the Canadian Association of University Teachers gave Queen's a "clean bill of health," despite the lack of faculty representation on the board, because the principal had its full support.[123] Mackintosh's reluctance to include faculty members on the board of trustees was to avoid tempting the board to comment on purely academic matters: "My timid apprehension is that while I can reserve academic matters for the Senate, the presence of three or five senior academics would inevitably mean that discussions would extend into that area and the first thing we knew the Board of Trustees would be taking academic initiatives. My guess is that something like the Oxford system works well so long as the speed is insufficient to disturb the moss or crack the joints."[124] Yet when it came to selecting his successor, Mackintosh acknowledged that the faculty had no input into – and were belatedly informed of – the decision, and that the best he could do was recommend that a meeting of the faculty association be held immediately after the announcement.[125] The volume and scope of the demands on the principal also forced administrative changes. Mackintosh admitted that, since the beginning of the national fund-raising campaign in 1957, he felt "hemmed in by work" and that his last academic session was a particularly wearing one.[126] Appeals to different public and private funding sources forced him to consider the appointment of a public-relations officer for the first time in 1960.[127]

Despite these changes, Mackintosh remained up to the task. He explained to a trustee that "had an acceptable successor not been available, I would, no doubt, have agreed to stay on but Alex Corry is highly acceptable and will bring fresh ideas to the post."[128] Corry, four years Mackintosh's junior, had gradually assumed more administrative duties during his decade as vice-principal, chairing research and other committees, organizing the meetings of the Learned Society at Queen's in 1960, overseeing the creation of the Faculty of Law and serving as its acting dean. The board of trustees had approved Corry's appointment as principal a year in advance, but had not made it public. With Corry on sabbatical leave in England during the 1960–61 academic year, Mackintosh took "vicarious satisfaction in the pleasure which I hope you and Alice are having. Everyone who has visited London in recent months brings more vivid reports of your convivial and riotous life."[129] With the rumours that Corry was selling his house (in preparation to move into the principal's residence) fuelling speculation of his appointment, Corry's ascension was announced in March 1961.

Mackintosh, in fact, had not just one replacement in mind but a line of succession of two. In 1959, he brought J.J. Deutsch to Queen's as vice-principal of administration to help sort out matters on the financial side. In February 1961 he informed Corry that he was switching offices with Deutsch: "We are assuming that you will not immediately want to appoint a Vice-Principal and that if you did, it might be someone who already has an office in the building."[130] Corry was in agreement, arguing that "four at the top" would be too many, and he speculated on the possibility of appointing Deutsch vice-principal and allowing the post of vice-principal of administration to lapse.[131] Given Deutsch's itinerate nature – since joining the Bank of Canada in 1935, he had served with the Rowell–Sirois Commission, the federal departments of external affairs and finance, Queen's department of political and economic science, the *Winnipeg Free Press*, the Treasury Board, and UBC – both Mackintosh and Corry were relieved to find that he was intending to remain at Queen's for the long haul. "For your very private ear," Mackintosh informed Corry, "John said some things in recent discussions which you might bear in mind. He undoubtedly has noted that this is the second time the Vice-Principal has succeeded the Principal. He seems to want to make clear that he understood that this pattern would not persist. He told me that he felt in another year possibly he would have straightened out the administrative setup and that he ... would be very happy to be simply professor of economics. I was very pleased with this as indicating that he had thought about the matter and, more important, that his plans were to stay here."[132] Deutsch would succeed Corry as principal in 1967.[133]

Other aspects of life in the Mackintosh household were also brought to a conclusion in 1961. Alison had entered high school at the age of twelve, attending Kingston Collegiate Vocational Institute (KCVI), then Havergal College in Toronto for Grade 11, before returning to KCVI, where she was head girl in her final year. Because she was only seventeen upon graduation, her parents preferred that she gain more experience before entering university and suggested a year at Neuchâtel College in Switzerland. Since she had already completed her senior matriculation, the academic demands on her at Neuchâtel were modest, but it was an exciting year in Europe marked by the Hungarian revolution and the Suez Crisis. She embraced the opportunity to explore Switzerland, Spain, Austria, and Italy, including their ski slopes. At the end of her school year, the family spent two months motoring throughout Britain, during which time Mackintosh "was highly successful in avoiding universities and people concerned with public affairs."[134] Alison had then enrolled at Queen's in the fall of 1957 and, in the last convocation over which Mackintosh would preside as principal, she graduated, claiming the Gold Medal in Commerce.

The summer following her graduation, Alison would marry Ieuan Morgan. Ieuan, who had studied chemistry at Oxford, had come to Kingston to work with Canadian Industries Limited, and the two met at a tea party on Halloween in 1957. To celebrate their wedding, a large party was held in the dining room of Leonard Hall, at which Mackintosh was gratified by the large number of friends – including the Rasminskys, Plumptres, Bryces – who travelled from Ottawa and elsewhere for the occasion. One week later, on June 17, a small family wedding was held in Summerhill, attended by John Orr, his long-time colleague, a few family friends, and a half-dozen relatives. For Alison, who was effectively born and raised on the campus, it was a fitting location to bring to a close one chapter in her life.[135]

When Mackintosh assumed his duties as principal, he had done so with a healthy measure of humility. As he reminded himself and others, "It is perhaps indicative of another attitude of the founders that in directing the first principal, a Scots clergyman, to proceed to Kingston and bring the charter with him, they ensured the charter for £600 but left the Principal to travel at his own risk."[136] He left the post with the same attitude. As he wrote to Corry, "There has perhaps been a bit more reference to my leaving than to your accession but some of this results from design as it seemed a good plan to get all the farewells out of the way this spring and leave the fall exclusively to the welcome. I shall try not to let my shadow hang around but having during the past ten years been introduced by a graduate as Principal Wallace, I can't guarantee that you will be free from all such annoying occurrences."[137]

In his final report to the board as principal, Mackintosh provided a succinct commentary on developments at Queen's during the decade under his leadership. Full-time enrolment had risen from 2,093 to 3,030, and the number of faculty member from 122 to 226. Higher provincial operating grants, federal monies, and private funds had pushed the total budget from $1.5 to $5.6 million. With this money, salaries doubled, library facilities were enhanced, sixteen new buildings were in place or under construction, while "in no areas has there been more growth in the past decade than in research and scholarly work." He insisted that Queen's had not "drifted with the tide" but expanded only "so that we might still have diversity and national representation in our students and so that we might train and attract first-rate scholars and scientists to our faculties." Satisfied with the direction taken under his stewardship, he passed control to Corry: "His hand is on the tiller. He has a sound and proven ship, an able and loyal crew ... The wind is fair. The tide is right. The glass is rising. I wish him Bon Voyage." He did so with a "special sincerity and earnestness," adding that "for a while I shall be a passenger."[138] Mackintosh was not leaving the university but "merely moving a few paces to the right," vacating the principal's residence for the adjoining quarters in Summerhill, and remaining as vice-chancellor at the request of the board of trustees.

14

The Royal Commission on Banking and Finance and After: Ottawa and Kingston, 1961–1970

We enjoyed your letter immensely and Karen's drawings. Do you think there is a danger that she is getting too representative? I dig the abstractions myself.

W.A. Mackintosh, letter to Alison, 1970[1]

After some forty years of steady employment, in June 1961 Mackintosh found himself without a full-time job. At the behest of the trustees he continued as vice-chancellor at Queen's, expected to "work part time at a variety of problems, most of which I could not get the time to work at in the past decade." While handsomely rewarded, this work was hardly sufficient to keep him fully occupied.[2]

A compelling opportunity emerged three months after he resigned as principal: appointment to the Royal Commission on Banking and Finance (RCBF). The RCBF was established with the broad mandate "to enquire into and report upon the structure and methods of operation of the Canadian financial system, including the banking and monetary system and the institutions and processes involved in the flow of funds through the capital market."[3] A thorough review of Canadian banking and monetary policy had not been undertaken since the Macmillan Commission in 1933. Like the British Radcliffe Committee and the United States Commission on Money and Credit, the RCBF was expected to reassess the financial system in light of modern monetary thought and the changing role of the state in economic management.

On a personal level, the RCBF was a fitting capstone to Mackintosh's involvement in policy work for the federal government. The year-long hearings of the commission were an ideal stage for his wit and wisdom, his range of interests and expertise, and as a public farewell to many of his past associates. As international figures – such as Dennis Robertson, Lord Cobbold, Marius Holtrop (president of the Central Bank of the Netherlands), Jacob Viner, Paul Samuelson, Allan Sproul, Woodlief Thomas, and Edward Bernstein – and old Canadian friends and colleagues – including Graham Towers, Lou Rasminsky, Stewart Bates, Kenneth Taylor, Wynne Plumptre, and David Mansur – testified before the commission, he took pleasure in debating the interpretation of Canada's recent monetary experience. In writing the commission's *Report*, he would help articulate an approach to Canadian monetary policy which, when combined with his authorship of the White Paper and Green Book, constitutes a comprehensive statement of his views of postwar fiscal, social-welfare, and monetary policy.

PRELUDE

Upon succeeding Graham Towers as governor of the Bank of Canada in 1955, James E. Coyne was an outspoken critic of the federal government's fiscal policy and debt management. He deemed the unprecedented inflow of American direct and portfolio investment as the main contributor to Canada's worsening current-account deficit, because of the associated outflow of profit and interest payments, as well as higher imports of capital goods. Under such circumstances, Coyne held that the government's expansionary fiscal policy was misguided, and he openly stated the bank's tendency towards monetary restraint. The logic to Coyne's approach was hardly orthodox. The higher interest rates associated with monetary tightening were expected to reduce domestic consumption and investment, thereby addressing the current-account deficit by curtailing imports; however, they only served to promote short-term capital inflows into Canada, pushing up the value of the Canadian dollar at the expense of employment and output, while placing further pressure on the long-term cost of servicing international indebtedness.[4] When a group of economists published an open letter to the minister of finance calling for Coyne's dismissal, Mackintosh was annoyed by the "pretentious length" of the letter and provided some "ammunition" for George Ferguson's editorial response in the *Montreal Star*.[5] Indeed, he was sufficiently angered to write to Coyne, his former colleague during the war and a member of the fishing club: "I wanted to say to you it was one of the most ill-mannered, ill-advised and impertinent communications I ever saw. There has been need over the past few years of more reasoned analysis and criticism of both government and banking policy and the economists are at fault in not having supplied more if it, which they had every opportunity to do … I am glad to say that nobody at this university had any share in this letter. In its implication that it was the united voice of economists, it must have reminded a lot of people of the three tailors of Tooley Street."[6]

Mackintosh was initially unconcerned with the bank's monetary policy, viewing it as a short-term response to US monetary tightening; however, the bank's commitment to restricting the money supply persisted in open defiance of the government's expansionary objectives as a recession took hold in the latter part of 1957.[7] In writing to Coyne, Mackintosh was careful not to endorse the bank's policy. "I suspect that if I had time to work matters out, I probably would not agree with the line you are taking and might even say so, but the course which these people have taken I find thoroughly offensive." Coyne replied that

> Having always had a high regard for the intellectual tradition, I have found the personal attacks on me from time to time by academics rather shattering, and certainly very perplexing. I have done my best to stir up objective discussion of monetary policy and other economic matters relevant to the problems of the day … It was very good of you to take the trouble to write. The realization of how heartening such a letter can be at such a time is a reminder of the importance of personal feelings in an otherwise materialistic world … With reference to your last paragraph, I do wish you had time to work matters out. Some day perhaps I will be able to tell you the whole story of the practical problems of the last few years. I would like to think that if you turned your mind to these matters and went over the immediate issues and considerations of actual policy with myself and the others here you would find yourself in substantial measure of agreement with us.[8]

When Donald Fleming, the minister of finance, asked Coyne for his resignation, he refused without first having a public hearing. The

House of Commons then passed a bill declaring his position vacant, but the Senate, in considering the bill, would hold two days of hearings, during which Coyne stated his case. "He seems to be handling himself reasonably well," stated Mackintosh, although he expressed his disappointment that Graham Towers and Jack Bryden, one of the bank's directors, had been drawn into the fray.[9] With Diefenbaker threatening an election on Senate reform, Coyne, having had his opportunity to be heard, resigned.

Quite apart from the substance of the debate on monetary policy, the Coyne Affair underscored the central dilemma in the relationship between the Bank of Canada and the federal government. "It is clearly impossible to have a central bank which combats the Minister of Finance and purports to exercise a veto on his policies," wrote Mackintosh. "On the other hand, a central bank which was merely the creature of the Minister of Finance might as well move back into the basement of the Department."[10] When the federal budget promised a royal commission in the wake of the Coyne resignation, Mackintosh mentioned to J.A. Corry that "there is great speculation as to the membership of the Commission ... Someone from Ottawa told me that ... John Deutsch and I had been the most frequently suggested and the most frequently rejected persons."[11] But Mackintosh was wrong, for a few months later he joined Dana Harris Porter (Chief Justice of Ontario), W. Thomas Brown (investment banker), James Douglas Gibson (former deputy chairman of the Bank of Nova Scotia), Gordon L. Harrold (western grain trader), Paul H. Leman (Alcan executive), and John C. MacKeen (Maritime executive) as "one of the seven wise men to attack the money mess."[12]

HEARINGS

The commission embarked on sixty-five days of public hearings that stretched out over ten months, beginning in Victoria on 12 March 1962 and ending in Ottawa on 21 January 1963. Given the number of lengthy and often repetitive briefs that jumped from topic to topic (110 briefs in all, with the transcript of the hearings and briefs extending to over 17,000 pages), it is understandable that the commission's hearings did not engage the public interest. When one witness asked for spectators to refrain from clapping until after he introduced all the people in his delegation, Mackintosh was obliged to inform him that "We rarely have been bothered by applause."[13]

To the *Toronto Star* reporter who maintained a "lonely vigil" throughout the hearings, the saving grace was the "flashes of humour. Often as not they stem, with an infectious grin, from economist W.A. Mackintosh. Speaking from behind a long cigarette holder, he can send gales of laughter through the solemn gatherings."[14]

Mackintosh took obvious delight in exposing the fuzzy thinking of many witnesses. "I didn't say I was married to the fact," insisted one, who was told that "You didn't say you were divorced." When a municipal official described a modest interest payment given to taxpayers who paid their accounts in advance as a "public service," Mackintosh was left to wonder "When you say this is public service why isn't it just ordinary horse sense?" An official of the Bank of Canada, who stated that "I still do not quite see where we said that moral suasion was a good thing," was told "It must be if it is moral." To a representative of the Canadian Life Insurance Officers' Association who mentioned that companies do not emphasize the net interest rate when promoting insurance, Mackintosh replied, "You don't exactly whisper about the prospective policy dividends." An executive with the Montreal Trust Company, who suggested that "Liquidity is a difficult word to define," was told that "You know what it means when you haven't got it."[15]

Perplexing to Mackintosh was the lack of financial knowledge of many in the industry. W.S. Row, president of Kerr-Addison Gold Mines Limited, asserted that it was "almost inevitable" that gold would be "revalued upwards," leaving Mackintosh to clarify the difference between speculation and knowledge with the quip, "Is this a friendly tip?" Similarly, after listening to P.P. Saunders (president of Laurentide Finance Corporation) explain how interest rates were set, he retorted that "I am not sure that you have not destroyed my growing confidence in your method of doing business." When Jake Froese of the Winkler Credit Union insisted that credit unions did not create money "because we are just dealing with the money we get from our members," Mackintosh noted that this erroneous view was not very different from that expressed years earlier by representatives of commercial banks.[16]

He also drew upon "homespun" metaphors to clarify a witness statement or to cast it into sharp relief. The lack of arbitrage opportunities between Canadian stock exchanges was restated as: "There are no restrictions on fishing, but there are no fish." The relationship between credit constraints and inventory control was refashioned in the following terms: "While one fellow was wanting to reduce his receivables, half a dozen other fellows were wanting to increase their payables ... it is a bit of a hot dinner plate you can't get rid of." An equivocating witness was told that "One horse is black and the other is white – they are not interchangeable." When another indicated that the answer to Mackintosh's question was in the written brief, he was politely reprimanded: "I must have forgotten what play we were producing." David Kirk of the Canadian Federation of Agriculture ran afoul of Mackintosh's wit when he complained that "the labour you get from hired help nowadays tends not to be very satisfactory," only to have his statement placed in context: "They will not sleep in the haystack anymore."[17] On one occasion Mackintosh was too vague when he asked, "In the past in some countries certain eventualities, if not liabilities, have occurred which have affected the Canadian banks. Is this a consideration for the future?" When the witness asked "What do you have in mind, Dr. Mackintosh?" he received a succinct response: "Oh, Cuba would do as an example."[18]

He was also on the receiving end of such repartee. Stewart Bates, his wartime colleague and now president of CMHC, asked Mackintosh to clarify what he meant by "substandard housing" in a question he posed. "You people are always talking about such 'substandard houses,'" Mackintosh answered. "That is where I got the word." Bates then confessed that "I am hoisted on my own petard here, because Dr. Mackintosh was the director of the Corporation before I came near it." Commissioner Brown then interjected, "You will probably find that he invented the term himself."[19] When he compared Jacob Viner's views on fixed exchange rates to "a monastic law on divorce: it is a concession to the wickedness of the people," Viner responded in equally rich language: "Yes. In a way it is like putting a chain and anchor on the leg of your citizens at random, because you are not sure which ones are dishonest and which are honest and can be safely allowed to roam the streets at night." Or when A.H. Emmett, reeve of the District of Burnaby, complained that municipalities were not consulted on issues like increased taxation of cigarettes, Mackintosh chided him that he would still have a chance to express his opinion. "I did," stated Emmett, who then gave Mackintosh a lesson on the demand curve: "I gave up smoking."[20]

This was all good sport and helped to break the tedium of long days of testimony. But it also served the purpose of challenging many assertions that rested upon well-worn myths. For instance, the

Canadian Small and Independent Business Federation referred to the preferential tax treatment of mining companies, while at the same time seeking special consideration for small businesses. Mackintosh interjected "And you say right away that the boy in the back seat needs looking after too? ... There are an awful lot of people talking about the needs of small business who, on questioning, don't really know very much about small business in any practical way of financing or directing. It is a kind of enthusiasm ... There is a tendency to weep over small business. Whatever small business needs, I think, is not tears."[21] In a similar vein, he challenged the arguments regarding barriers to regional development put forth by W.Y. Smith of the Atlantic Provinces Economic Council. When reference was made to Mackintosh's background report for the Rowell–Sirois Royal Commission, he stated "That is the trouble with the Atlantic provinces, they are always bringing up history." Looking forward, Mackintosh expressed skepticism about the capacity of Atlantic Canada to capture European markets ("what commodities?") and of an industrial strategy to pick key industries in which to invest. "What are the characteristics of these cornerstone plants and how can you tell one when you meet them?" he asked. "It is not easy to select industries which generally turn out to be a cornerstone industry. I can see some possibility of the scriptures being reversed – the stone which the builders chose which turned out not to be head of the corner?"[22]

Central to the hearings was the emergence of near banks – trust companies, credit unions, and caisses populaires – and other financial intermediaries. Of these, Mackintosh was "very favourably impressed with the work which the credit unions have been doing." He was intrigued by their evolution along the lines of banking institutions by their offering of chequing accounts and short-term consumer loans, and as building societies through long-term mortgage lending. Asked if they expected to take things a step further and borrow directly from the public rather than the banking system, J.R. Robinson (manager, BC Central Credit Union) acknowledged that: "One is tempted by the extra one per cent or so that exists as between outside and the prime bank rate," but Mackintosh noted that "I take it the assurance of a line of credit helps you resist the temptation."[23] He went on to inquire if the credit-union movement might be a victim of its own success. "This is not a club among neighbours," he said to a representative of the Canadian Co-operative Credit Union Society Limited. "This is a big organization." He asked whether the larger administration and centralized control over reserve funds might weaken the strength that rested on "the fundamental attitude of credit union members." When the problems were not seen as insurmountable, Mackintosh suggested that "you are paraphrasing the biblical text, 'If need be that the offence cometh.' You see certain advantages in being the offender."[24]

He was less enamoured with consumer-loan companies and the novelty of allowing consumer purchases on instalment plans. He questioned the legitimacy of retailers selling without stating a cash price, in favour of monthly instalment payments, in that it rested in part on the inability of the consumer to calculate the effective interest rate. "Not being an astute consumer ... if one cash price was $350 and another was $325, and one charged 16.3 per cent interest and the other charged 15.4 per cent interest, I think I would be inclined to pick it by colour." When the head of the Canadian Consumer Loans Association suggested that instalment payments were introduced in part as a response to the financial hardship of consumers, Mackintosh stated facetiously that he was "just trying to whittle off the compassionate rind that had been part of this." He was equally circumspect in his approach to J. Allyn Taylor's assertion that the Huron and Erie Mortgage Company was reluctant to lend at rates above 8 per cent because of "consumer resistance." Mackintosh replied that "I am not completely carried along with the theory of squeamishness," and added that "So far I do not think anybody has been concerned with the poor fellow who is going to buy the house."[25]

The relevant question, insofar as Mackintosh was concerned, was "whether the present terms of competition ... favour these near banks by allowing the opportunities without the same responsibilities."[26] Specifically, the growth of credit unions led other financial institutions to complain that their tax-exempt status and freedom from some forms of regulation constituted unfair competition. For his part, Mackintosh did not object to the tax-exempt status but did to the rationale provided: "I was not arguing about taxation. I do object, however, to the suggestion that credit unions render a public service and members of the Commission do not." When others complained of the credit unions' use of volunteer labour, he asked, "Don't you think the little people ought to be able to take advantage of being little?"[27]

Since near-bank institutions were not subject to the same regulatory oversight, several witnesses suggested that the chartered banks were being placed at a competitive disadvantage. For instance, Neil J. McKinnon, president of the Canadian Imperial Bank of Commerce, cited the faster growth of non-bank institutions in support of such an argument; Mackintosh responded that "You are saying that a man doesn't grow as much as a boy!" Another witness was asked if he was not underestimating the power of the banks since "[they are] not exactly shrinking?"[28] He issued constant reminders that the chartered banks were, after all, profit-seeking institutions, retained a healthy market position, and should be subject to regulatory control just as were manufacturing industries. When the head of the Canadian Manufacturers' Association argued that the restriction on chartered banks lending above 6 per cent forced small businesses to turn to other financial institutions and borrow at much higher rates, Mackintosh stated that: "The reason why government does not, in normal times, impose a ceiling on the prices at which manufacturers sell is not because there is a touching trust in manufacturers. There is an assumption that externally or internally there will be enough competition to arrive at a reasonable price." The witness replied, "Are you not inviting rather a comparison of our banks and the degree of competition of our banking system, as compared to that of manufacturing industry?" To which Mackintosh answered: "Why not?"[29]

Mackintosh expressed concern about the increasing concentration and "chumminess" among Canada's charter banks. When Mr Lambert, president of Toronto-Dominion Bank explained that no brief had been prepared because other bank presidents did a good job, Mackintosh expressed his impatience by simply asking, in a perfunctory manner, "Which of the other three Presidents did you agree with?"[30] He thus expressed his surprise with the suggestion of C.F. Elderkin, inspector of banks, that consolidation led to greater competition: "I think without being ingenuous, I could reverse the argument you have made." On another occasion he stated that "There would be some concern if the development was towards more and more of [intercompany] linkages other than through the market. We have a chartered banking system with very few units which are very large. They are, of course, competitive to a degree. Their power is limited by not only their own competition but the competition from near banks which come in on the fringe and compete in a particular area. I think that with the spread of control or linkage it is inevitable that the competition might not be so keen." As he told one witness, "I am not concerned about the banks, they look after themselves fairly well." Thus when Duff Roblin, premier of Manitoba, stated that he did not want to appear "uncharitable to the banks," Mackintosh responded that "I don't think charity enters into our banking system."

When attention turned to the macroeconomic implications of the financial system, Mackintosh examined witnesses on the efficacy of fiscal, monetary, and debt-management policy in an effort to clarify how much autonomy Canadian authorities exercised and the leverage that different policy tools provided.

The implications of international capital flows received relatively scant attention. Mackintosh expressed his surprise with the number of witnesses that argued for unfettered access to American capital: "It apparently was the view in imposing withholding taxes [in December 1960] that we did not need American capital. All representations here seem to be that we need an inflow of American capital." When Allan Blakeney, treasurer of Saskatchewan, expressed the view that "we are not fearful of foreign capital," because the cost of servicing the debt was lower today than in World War I or the 1930s, Mackintosh replied that "I don't like either of your precedents ... The weight of interest and dividends in our balance of payments is a very considerable problem." To John Robarts, premier of Ontario, he stated that: "There seems to be lots of opinion that foreign equity investment is disadvantageous at the present time. In the latter part of the 1930s the great complaint was that foreign investment was all fixed term and, therefore, a dead weight not dependent on the economy. We may find in the 1970s that we are back to the earlier concept."[31]

On fiscal policy, he found many witnesses to be "pretty catholic" in their views on cutting taxes and on the capacity of fiscal policy to painlessly achieve rapid economic growth. When Russell Bell, of the Canadian Labour Congress, called for "massive investment" in the public sector as the main driver to achieve a 5-per-cent rate of economic growth, Mackintosh first confessed that "you have undermined my question to some extent by mentioning the universities in this list of items for greater public spending." Nonetheless, he described 5 per cent as "a bit ambitious" and cited "the discipline of foreign markets" as a constraint on domestic expansion, because it would trigger a rise in imports. Encouraging the witness to get "out of the diagram and into reality," he argued that "Economists have invented all sorts of policies for a closed economy but they have not been able to invent a closed economy."[32] In response to those who saw fiscal policy as a technical instrument that could be applied mechanically and without cost whenever an increase in national income was desired, Mackintosh invoked one of his favourite quotations. "This sort of question – and it is a difficult question – always reminds me of a reply which Lord Keynes gave to some people who put forward a pretty hard and exacting stabilization employment policy, and his reply was 'Be good, sweet maid, and very clever.'" Louis Rasminsky struck a similar refrain when he stated that "You could obtain full employment if that is all that you were interested in – and I do not recommend this as a course of action – by having half the population dig ditches and the other half fill them in again, but you certainly would not attain growth." To which Mackintosh asked wryly, "How would you provide a coffee break?"[33]

In Regina, he sparred with Blakeney on the capacity of fiscal policy to achieve full employment, particularly in light of Canada's federal structure. Blakeney stated that the Canadian economy in 1961 was operating well below full employment, and that Ottawa had a leadership role in counter-cyclical spending. Accepting the latter premise, Mackintosh suggested that the implementation of effective policy was not simple in practice. Not only did governments often lack the room to manoeuvre, but recessions were often too short for an adequately-timed response, especially if "you have to have a dominion provincial conference to start it." He then restated the Saskatchewan argument: if money exists for anti-recession spending, it should be the federal government (or a federal-provincial program) that undertakes the spending, because of its greater financial leeway and because the benefits spill over to other provinces. Further, he characterized the view of the provinces as being that "If the federal government would pay 80 per cent … this is a good project; if they will pay only 20 per cent it is a bad project." When Blakeney concurred, Mackintosh merely stated that "I was hoping you were getting up to a more lofty height."[34]

The effectiveness of monetary policy in an open economy rested on the uncertain relationship between the money supply, domestic prices, liquidity, interest rates, and international capital flows. Mackintosh accepted that inflation was one way of "wiping out all sorts of structural and institutional obstacles to change," but deemed it to be "enormously costly and unacceptably ruthless."[35] He pressed Dennis Robertson, the now-retired Cambridge authority on monetary economics, on the impact of monetary policy ("Would it be fair to say that a shift in the interest rate in the short run rather brings about a shift in assets and, in the longer run, will have an influence on savings?") and on national income ("Is this, you might say, a sort of permissive thing, that you can accommodate monetary policy to growth, or can you get some positive push?")[36] In discussions with Woodlief Thomas of the US Federal Reserve System, he observed that "in the evidence before the Radcliffe Committee there seemed to be a sharp division, which is not unusual among economists, some of them asserting with great dogmatism that if you controlled liquidity you need not pay any attention to rates, and others were equally dogmatic that if you can set the structure of rates you don't need to pay attention to liquidity." He then turned to the question of the relationship between the central bank and the private banking system, asking if, when seeking to discourage banks from borrowing from the FRB, "there is no moral suasion, no attempt to preach at them?" Thomas replied that "You need to remind them of the conventions."[37] Mackintosh put the question about the effectiveness of moral suasion to Edward Bernstein in the following manner: "Do you not think [the banks] would reply in the way Vanderbilt, I think it was, replied: '6 per cent talks louder than 4 per cent?'" To Mackintosh, it was more a matter of getting "the hands of the chartered banks in a position where they could twist them."[38]

When one witness advocated non-discretionary monetary policy, in which the money supply would be set to increase at a constant rate, Mackintosh did not reject the idea on theoretical grounds but emphasized the practical difficulties for an open economy. "The bank which is charged with running or administering monetary policy has to look over one shoulder at the debt, and over the other shoulder at the international balance … [T]here is no presumption that a year-by-year increase of 2, 3, 4 or 5 per cent – whatever you think is desirable – will fit into the exigencies. It would be nice to be autonomous, but we are not."[39] Robertson agreed with the contention that Canada's interest-rate policy could not diverge significantly from that in the United States, and Mackintosh posed the same question to Paul Samuelson. "We are accustomed here to think that we have a very open, not to say windy, economy, and putting aside the question of degree, how far in such an economy do you think you can find any criterion for monetary policy other than your international bonds and international flows? In other words, how significant is a domestic monetary policy aside from the external?" Samuelson agreed that "the smaller you are, the more open an economy you have, the less scope you have for independent policy"; however, he added that "I think that if I were a small nation and I were somewhat dependent on staple products ... and I had open to me the option ... of a floating exchange rate, I ought to take up that option."[40]

Apart from the autonomy of the Bank of Canada in setting interest rates, Mackintosh expressed his skepticism about the sensitivity of investment to changes in the interest rate. He acknowledged that the effects of monetary policy on financial variables were visible, but "the amount of real investment seems to me always to be disappointing." (As he paraphrased Keynes, "Well, we have got the horse there. How can we make him drink?") To one witness he stated that, "I think we have to admit that it is fairly difficult to find specifically an unquestionable incident anywhere in Canada when you could say because the [interest] rate was 6½ it did not go and if it had been 6 it would have gone." Similarly, he invoked Keynes's argument of a liquidity trap when suggesting that, during periods of loose money, low interest rates might be ineffective in encouraging investment: "When you come to the bottom of a severe depression it is not merely making credit available to applicants at low rates, it is a series of processes by which un-creditworthy applicants are turned into creditworthy applicants, and that takes more than monetary policy and it can be a peculiarly stubborn problem. The banks, even in depression, have lots of applicants but very few of them are creditworthy."[41] Thomas, however, reminded him that "it is the marginal decisions that are significant."[42]

The hearings came to a conclusion in Ottawa, where the issues surrounding the Coyne Affair were addressed by Robertson, Lord Cobbold, Viner, and others. The specific circumstance during Coyne's term as governor were that the government needed loose money to finance its debt, but the Bank of Canada kept a tight monetary policy. Mackintosh suggested to Robertson that "when you have a higher rate of interest, a premium on your currency, and an undesirably high rate of unemployment, you have not a clear situation." Robertson agreed: "You have a very sticky one." Mackintosh then restated the general dilemma. "there is a basic conflict [between the Bank of Canada pursuing its own monetary policy while acting as the fiscal agent for the government] in that fiscal policy must on occasion adjust itself to monetary policy and on other occasions monetary policy must adjust itself to the exigencies of fiscal policy." On this matter, Lord Cobbold, former governor of the Bank of England agreed that once fiscal policy had gone ahead there was little a central bank could actually do to the contrary.[43] Viner stated unequivocally that the Bank should operate under a written and public mandate from the government. However, when other witnesses referred to vague "directives" issued by the department of finance to the governor of the Bank of Canada, Mackintosh commented that "I am not very sure whether they mean a nod or a notarized document." He raised the issue during Robertson's testimony, noting that the weekly instructions that the Federal Reserve's Open Market Committee gave to the Federal Reserve Bank in New York contained a lot of generalities. "I should think it would," replied Robertson. "I don't suppose they look at it, do they?" To which Mackintosh responded, "You are on the record as having said that, not I."[44] The gravity of the issue as far as Canada was concerned diminished given the attitude of Louis Rasminsky, Coyne's successor as governor of the Bank of Canada, and his unequivocal statement on the autonomy of the central bank. During what Porter described as a "truly magnificent performance over the four days of testimony," Rasminsky maintained that he could "nag" the minister of finance over the deficit, but otherwise had little choice but pursue a complementary monetary policy.[45]

REPORT

The commission's *Report* ran to 566 pages and was accompanied by a second volume of statistical information and an appendix that included twelve background papers prepared by the who's who of a generation of young Canadian economists.[46] Responsibility for writing the report is unclear, but Gibson later commented that "[Mackintosh and I] seemed to be the only two commissioners who felt it necessary to work together late into the evening on our economic thinking."[47] Brown recalled that, "It was in great part [Mackintosh's] stimulating and down to earth thinking that made our Report the acceptable document it appears to have been." He added that: "He always had available that anecdote that would bring heated discussion not just back to the point, but back with a laugh."[48] In a review of the report, Francis Schott of the New York Federal Reserve identified as its most important characteristics the "comprehensive history and analysis of Canada's postwar financial experience" and its great didactic value, which derives from the commission's self-defined role of educating the public. "The reader is taken rather painlessly from the level of the proverbial 'intelligent layman' to approximately that of a graduate student in economics." When these features are added to the "lucid exposition" and "scholarly yet pragmatic appraisal of the financial system," it is fair to state that the document, if not chiefly written by Mackintosh, bears his imprint.[49]

The report begins by observing that, since World War II, Canada had become increasingly urbanized and industrialized, and its economy richer and more diversified. Financial requirements had changed accordingly. The greater demand for borrowing meant that financial intermediation in the economy had grown in scale (the assets of financial institutions rising from $5.5 billion in 1932 to $42 billion) and complexity with the emergence of new types of financial instruments. In order to address these changes, the report provides a clear analytical framework. At the microeconomic level, it dispelled the frequent misperception of chartered banks as having a quasi-public status by applying the theory of the firm to profit-seeking financial institutions; at the macroeconomic level, it considered the relationship between income and saving, and between real and financial activities.[50]

The report is divided into three parts. The first considers the changing needs of primary borrowers in the economy, with chapters covering each of the personal, business, and government sectors, and the sources of lending, including a chapter on foreign capital. Households as a group were deemed to be in a healthy state, with a high rate of saving and most of the debt incurred to purchase houses and durable goods; business investment, which had subsided since the boom of the 1950s, was increasingly funded out of retained earnings; and governments' use of capital markets had grown, but the debt-to-GNP ratio was at a manageable level. The shift in foreign borrowing from debt to equity led to a passing comment on the rising foreign control of Canadian resource and manufacturing firms, but servicing the cost of foreign borrowing was not seen as a significant problem for Canada's balance of payments.

Part 2 (Chapters 6 to 19) then considers how well financial institutions, instruments, and markets met "the legitimate present and prospective needs of lenders and borrowers in an efficient, flexible, non-discriminatory way."[51] Among traditional institutions, chartered banks had grown much larger in size, and their holdings were concentrated among a smaller number, while insurance companies were also larger in size and fewer in number. Despite the concentration of ownership, chartered banks and insurance companies faced more competition with the emergence of credit unions and caisses populaires in the market for short- and medium-term credit, development companies providing medium- and long-term financing for new businesses, trust companies offering mutual funds and pension funds in personal finance markets, mortgage lenders in real-estate markets, and consumer loans companies. These changes were accompanied by a wider range of financial instruments, including government savings bonds, commercial papers, and day loans to investment dealers.

Chapter 6, "a most important and brilliant, chapter" according to David Slater, develops the basis for assessing the performance of the Canadian financial system. Different financial institutions mediate the relationship between ultimate borrowers and lenders by issuing their own financial instruments and by acquiring those of others. Competition among profit-seeking financial institutions "play[s] an important economic role in filling the gap between the preferences of ultimate borrowers and lenders in terms of the desired characteristics of diversity, risk, yield, and liquidity."[52] This framework is applied in separate chapters dealing with the evolution of various types of institutions (chartered banks; Quebec savings banks; caisses populaires and credit unions; trust and mortgage lenders; sales finance and consumer loan companies; special credit agencies for small business, agriculture, and exporters; insurance and investment companies and pension funds) and in chapters on specific markets (for residential mortgages, foreign exchange, bonds, and stocks).

Canada's financial system had generally adapted well to the needs of borrowers and lenders. In response to profitable opportunities, new types of financial institutions had emerged, new financial instruments had been created, and the financial system as a whole was responsive to changes in policy under existing conventions and rules.

The principal recommendations were designed to encourage greater competition within and between types of financial institutions, and to better safeguard the public. To address the emergence of near-bank firms that issued highly liquid, short-term claims that were close substitutions for money, a broader definition of banking institutions was proposed based upon the liabilities created (short-term and demand claims). To place chartered banks and near-banks on an equal footing, all such institutions would be subject to the same regulations, such as minimum cash reserves. Some existing regulations, designed to protect the public, interfered with the competition and often forced borrowers to turn to less-reputable, higher-cost forms of borrowing. Accordingly, it recommended eliminating the prohibition on chartered banks from lending on mortgage securities, the 6-per-cent ceiling on interest rates charged by the banks, and limitations on lending activity by trust and loan companies. Meanwhile, insurance companies would be allowed to hold up to 25 per cent of their assets in the form of corporate securities.[53] To better protect of the public, it recommended that regulations be strengthened in some areas and broadened in scope to cover new institutions. It called for greater supervision of local credit unions by provincial authorities; rules governing the operation of pension funds with respect to solvency and investment diversification; and more stringent standards over corporate disclosure, investment dealers, and stock exchanges as part of a general effort to create a more informed public investor. Consumer loan companies attracted special attention. To "curb the exploitation of ill informed borrowers by certain fringe institutions and lenders," the maximum charge on personal cash lending (in the range of one per cent monthly) should be extended to all such transactions and raised to amounts up to $5,000 rather than the present $1,500.[54]

In general, the commission placed its faith in a competitive financial system to improve efficiency. "We have, in summary, favoured a more open and competitive banking system – carefully and equitably regulated under uniform legislation but not bound by restrictions which impede the response of the institutions to new situations, enforce a particular pattern of narrow specialization, or shelter some enterprises from competitive pressures. We believe that this framework will encourage creativity and efficiency and offer the public the widest possible range of choice of financial services, while reducing the danger of unregulated institutions springing up to serve real needs which others are prevented from meeting. Some institutions may attempt to offer a full range of services and others may choose to specialize in a variety of ways, but the legislation will allow all of them – and such new institutions as are qualified – to adapt to new opportunities and situations created by changing public preferences and needs."[55]

Part 3 (Chapters 20 to 26) considers the relationship between the monetary, fiscal, and debt-management policy on Canada's postwar economic performance and the avenues for the future. The commission accepted that monetary policy could influence the real economy by affecting credit conditions, but that, in isolation from other policy initiatives, it was a weak lever. During short business cycles, lags in the effects of monetary policy reduced its usefulness; during a prolonged boom, there was a practical limit on how high interest rates could be raised without having destabilizing effects on public confidence; and during a prolonged slump, monetary measures offered little stimulus as long as there were few prospects for profitable investment. Direct forms of monetary intervention, such as exchange controls, disrupted the operation of capital markets in the long term, such that they should be used only sparingly and under "emergency conditions."[56] It was only in coordination with debt management and fiscal policies that monetary measures were effective in altering the flow of incomes and expenditures. Monetary policy, therefore, must be applied in concert with fiscal measures, designed in cooperation with provincial governments, which operate more directly on the flow of incomes and expenditures. The challenge was to get "the broad set and timing of policies right to influence aggregate demand in the right direction." This required the experience and wisdom of policy authorities, so that the commission rejected such ideas as Friedman's non-discretionary monetary policy. "Apparently similar circumstances may call for differing policy approaches and the authorities cannot be guided by doctrinaire preferences for emphasizing one policy instrument rather than another."[57]

The range of domestic policy options was also highly constrained by international circumstances. Canada's commitment to international institutions – such as the World Bank, the International Monetary Fund, and the Organisation for Economic Co-operation and Development – derived from the openness of its economy and, as such, its dependence on a healthy state of international finance and trade. With the recent experience of Canada's exchange crisis of 1962 and the abandonment of floating exchange rates, the commission argued in favour of a fixed-exchange regime on the grounds that this imposed a degree of discipline on domestic policy, since it "must be geared more closely to external considerations. The increasingly close links between the capital markets of Canada and other countries, and international financial flows are highly sensitive to changes in interest rate differentials, which can be readily influenced by the monetary authorities. While Canada is bound to be influenced by external developments under any exchange rate system, our links with the rest of the world have more immediate consequences for monetary policy under a fixed exchange rate."[58]

Finally, the report addressed the relationship between the minister of finance and the governor of the Bank of Canada in light of the Coyne Affair. It stated definitively that, while the Bank of Canada required a degree of independence, it was in the final instance a policy arm of the government. In the event of a difference of opinion, it accepted Rasminsky's view that the minister of finance should instruct the bank on what actions to be pursued. But consistent with Mackintosh's faith in people acting in a rational manner, it expected that such a directive procedure would never be used: "As with all relationships, however, that between the Governor of the Bank and the Minister of Finance depends ultimately on the responsibility and good sense of those involved."[59]

The RCBF was a landmark in the assessment of Canada's financial system. Writing in 1977, Ronald Shearer found the 1964 *Report* unique in its scope and depth of analysis, comparing favourably with the contemporary reports of the British Committee and the American Commission on Money and Credit. Its analysis was unique in two important respects. First, the long-standing concern with the "soundness" of the banking system was replaced with a consideration of its efficiency and contribution to economic growth. He notes, however, that the commission's "grand design" for fostering a more competitive banking system was not enacted. Second, it signalled a rejection of the quantity theory of money in favour of what Shearer describes as "an eclectic Keynesian model."[60] Money was not neutral, but had an important potential influence over real variables, such as employment and output. Control of the money supply affected credit conditions, which in turn affected the flow of income. Its eclecticism stemmed in large part from the necessary mix of coordinated monetary, fiscal, and debt management policy appropriate to an open economy. Slater provided more qualified praise. While impressed with the commission's analysis of the role financial institutions play in light of current monetary theory, he questioned whether a "marginal nudging" to foster more competitive financial institutions, coupled with a reliance on traditional instruments of economic policy, provided a sound foundation for the future of Canadian banking and financial policy.[61]

At the same time, the report reflected a continuation of the Canadian tradition of "cautious pragmatism," an approach that reflected the role of Queen's economists in shaping the development of Canadian banking and financial policy. Through the generations of bank employees and executives who had passed through the university's banking courses and the roles of O.D. Skelton, Mackintosh, Knox (and later Slater) as successive editors of the *Journal of the Canadian Bankers' Association,* the department did much to promote a better-informed industry. The influence of Queen's on Canadian monetary inquiries is also apparent in Adam Shortt's voluminous writings on currency and finance, Mackintosh's rejection of Fisher's compensating-dollar proposal presented to the 1923 Select Committee on Banking and Currency, the "Queen's proposal" to the Macmillan Commission in 1933 for a central bank, Frank Knox's work on the balance of payments for the Rowell–Sirois Royal Commission, and C.A. Curtis's chairmanship of the 1949 Royal Commission on Prices. An emphasis on monetary theory per se in many instances gave way to practical considerations deemed specific to Canada's role as a major exporting nation and recipient of both short- and long-term capital inflows. In an earlier era, this led to an acceptance of "sound money" policy under the gold standard, since stable exchange rates took precedence over concerns with the impact of monetary policy on domestic output and prices; in the post-WWII era, it marked the recognition of the potential role of monetary policy on employment and income. To the degree that its "watchwords were pragmatism and flexibility,"[62] the 1964 *Report* reflected Mackintosh's own cautious conversion to Keynesian policy.

RETIREMENT

Shortly after the royal commission's work, Mackintosh completed his term as vice-chancellor of Queen's. Jean and he moved from Summerhill on the university grounds and a built a house on Alwington Place – "a modest enough home, but has a magnificent view of the Lake and in the evening I can watch the navigation lights blinking on Wolfe and Simcoe Islands."[63] It was a long overdue expenditure, given that Mackintosh had championed Canadian housing policy and was the first director of the Canadian Mortgage and Housing Corporation. He was a good neighbour and particularly endeared himself to Pat MacKay, who remembered him as "a great man who invited a little boy to watch Batman with him."[64] Remaining closely attached to the university, he retained his place on the board of trustees and made the one-kilometre walk to campus most weekdays for lunch with colleagues at the University Club.

A variety of tasks kept him busy. Appointed a director of the Bank of Canada in 1964, he was "a constant source of strength and wise advice" to Louis Rasminsky.[65] He continued to serve as treasurer of the Royal Society of Canada, rejoined the board of Empire Life, and also accepted an honorary appointment to the Canadian–American Committee on Trade. In 1967, he prepared a report for the Councils of the Provincial Institutes of Chartered Accountants in Canada, in which he recommended that "the Institutes adopt as their goal, in organization and provision of instruction, the negotiated transfer of all instruction necessary for qualification as a chartered accountant to the universities."[66]

By 1968, however, his health was visibly deteriorating. In February he was hospitalized for two weeks following an attack of angina and a "minimal" stroke; "however they allow me to go about with the instruction not to get tired and with a pocketful of nitroglycerin."[67] A series of small strokes followed that left him slightly disabled in his walk and speech,[68] while the obligation to step down as director of the Bank of Canada upon reaching the age of seventy left him somewhat disconsolate.

In contrast, he continued to derive much pleasure from observing the careers of Alison and Ieuan. They had moved to Boston in 1963, where, to his father-in-law's delight, Ieuan entered the MBA program at Harvard, while Alison found work as a research assistant to Wassily Leontieff on his legendary input-output project, which yielded her a co-authored paper.[69] (She took care not to mention that her father had played a pivotal role in convincing the Dominion Bureau of Statistics not to produce similar input-output tables for Canada.) Upon Ieuan's graduation, they moved to Montreal, where Ieuan returned to work for CIL and Alison, on Leontieff's recommendation, worked with Kari Levitt of McGill University on producing input-output tables for Atlantic Canada, the Dominion Bureau of Statistics now persuaded of their merits.[70] Their itinerant lifestyle then took them to London, Ontario, when Ieuan accepted a job at the University of Western Ontario teaching decision theory and Alison took advantage of the opportunity to enrol in an MA program in economics on a part-time basis; to Chicago in 1969 to allow Ieuan to complete a PhD and Alison to further her studies in economics; and to Quebec City, where Ieuan taught at the University of Laval and Alison took up work with the Government of Quebec, first in the ministry of agriculture and then in l'Office de la planification et de développement, which assumed an important role following the election of René Lévesque's government. Eventually, and perhaps inevitably, they would return to work at Queen's. Iuean joined the school of business, while Alison worked in a variety of teaching and administrative roles in the department of economics and eventually became university secretary.

When their work took them away from Kingston, they were never emotionally far removed from the city, and Ieuan proved to be an exceptional fishing companion on the occasions of their visits. Particularly gratifying to Mackintosh was the arrival of two grandchildren. Karen Sian Morgan was born in Montreal on 21 February 1967. She would fondly refer to her grandfather as "pipe," reflecting his switch away from cigarettes. Owen William Rhys Morgan was born in Chicago on 5 February 1970. His encounter with his grandfather was brief but poignant. Meeting him for the last time during the Christmas holidays, the eight-month-old walked unsteadily across the living room, placed his hand on his grandfather's knee, and, one might imagine, assured his grandfather that his legacy was secure.

Mackintosh would suffer a massive stroke and die without regaining consciousness two days later, on 29 December 1970. Despite his age, his death came as a shock to many. He had been a part of Queen's for so many years, many recalling his daily walk across campus from Summerhill to his office, cigarette in hand, and escorted for part of his trip by the family dog. To former Ottawa colleagues "he had always seemed so permanent and indestructible."[71] A funeral service was held in Grant Hall – the place that he had entered some six decades earlier as a "coltish" seventeen-year-old undergraduate, and where he had been installed as principal – and he was laid to rest in the Queen's University plot in the Cataraqui Cemetery. Among the honorary pall bearers were Douglas Gibson, Robert Bryce, Douglas LePan, George Ferguson, Clifford Curtis, L.G. Macpherson, and Mac Urquhart. Jean would survive him for another thirteen years.

Legacy

Dr Mackintosh is a great economist because he is so much more. He has humour in his heart and poetry in his soul.

W.E. McNeill, 1951[1]

Each of the three aspects of W.A. Mackintosh's contribution to public life was duly recognized during his lifetime. His scholarship was acknowledged with an honorary life membership in the American Geographical Society, election as president of the Canadian Political Science Association, nomination as vice-president of the American Economic Association, and appointment as a fellow of the Royal Economics Society. He was also made a fellow of the Royal Society of Canada in 1929, serving as president of Section II for the social sciences (1950–51) and president (1956–57), and was the first recipient of its Innis–Guerin Medal in 1967. For his government service during World War II, he was made companion of the Most Distinguished Order of Saint Michael and Saint George. In university affairs he was elected president of the National Conference of Canadian Universities (1952–53) and as chair of the Association of Universities of the British Commonwealth (1953–54). He received honorary degrees from Brown (1953), St Andrew's (1953), Durham (1953), and nine Canadian universities (Manitoba, 1942; Laval, 1952; St Francis Xavier, 1953; Toronto, 1954; UBC, 1957; Saskatchewan, 1959; McGill, 1961; Royal Military College, 1962; and Queen's, 1965). In 1971 he was named Companion of the Order of Canada, the first year of the award, sharing the stage with the likes of Gabrielle Roy and Arthur Lismer. Over forty years since his death, then, his place in Canadian history remains secure. Yet looking back over his life, his contribution to scholarship, policy, and university governance requires clarification and reiteration.

SCHOLAR

Born in eastern Ontario near the end of the nineteenth century, Mackintosh's sense of place and time influenced his vision of the world. Observing the struggles of families to eke out a living from the marginal agricultural lands on the Laurentian Shield left him with a profound admiration for the pioneering spirit of the region's early settlers and an equally profound disdain for snobbery and pretence. He was also a child of the wheat boom, and his experience living near the mouth of the St Lawrence River and teaching school in Saskatchewan shaped his understanding of the potential for prairie agriculture to create an integrated, national economy. Also shaping his world view was the outbreak of World War I, which would result in a personal crisis that tested his commitment to public duty against his conviction that it was an unjust war.

Schooled at Queen's, Mackintosh did not shy away from the painstaking primary research akin to that of Adam Shortt, but also acquired O.D. Skelton's gift for casting larger patterns into sharp relief. His 1923 paper on the "Economic Factors of Canadian History" helped to define a research agenda for a generation of political economists. The result was the staple thesis: the export of a succession of key primary commodities, and the particular techniques of production and social organization of each staple, shaped the pattern of economic and social development. The central message was the vulnerability of an economy dependent upon primary commodity exports and foreign borrowing, while the capacity to transform from a pioneer to a mature economy rested, in the first instance, on generating the export earnings to pay for the cost of foreign borrowing and, in the second instance, on the capacity for diversification into manufacturing and service industries.

There has been much thoughtful work on the interpretation of the staple thesis and its contemporary relevance. Mel Watkins distinguishes between Mackintosh's "steady-growth" version and Innis's "dependency" version; Paul Craven provides an intriguing, but undeveloped, characterization of Mackintosh's work as a "whig-staples" variant; and John Richards emphasizes Mackintosh's "pragmatic" approach.[2] In contrast, less informed readings of Mackintosh have him serving as a "launderer" of Innis's interpretation of the staple thesis, a trite exercise in intellectual sloganeering that reveals much less than it obscures, particularly in the absence of any textual reading.[3] An equally creative interpretation forces Mackintosh's work into a linear "stages of development" model that would give "academic legitimacy" to a "continentalist school of post-World War II economic development."[4]

Given the shared nature of the undertaking, the different interpretations of the staple thesis offered by Mackintosh and Innis are overstated. Both emphasized the particular characteristics of the export staple – the geographical background for its exploitation, the existing techniques of production, and the level of international demand – in placing their stamp upon the pace and pattern of economic and social development. Both highlighted the importance of social organization of production in adapting to and, in many cases, in shaping the pattern of growth. Finally, both focussed on the vulnerability of an economy dependent upon heavy international borrowing for the development of an export staple with a highly volatile income stream. The extent to which Mackintosh provided a more optimistic view was largely because of the particular historical period under consideration. His analysis drew on the prairie wheat economy and its potential for transforming a pioneer economy into a more diversified one. An integrated national economy rested upon capturing the linkages to manufacturing and transportation and the creation of a larger domestic market for consumption goods because of the relatively equitable distribution of income generated in the wheat sector. But, just as Innis wrote of Canada moving from "colony to nation to colony" in a different context, Mackintosh wrote of the "fictitious prosperity" of the wheat-boom era: as international wheat markets collapsed during the Great Depression, Canada lacked the export earnings to service its foreign borrowing, and its economic vulnerability of relying on staple exports was laid bare.[5]

Where Innis and Mackintosh parted company was over the role of the academic in public-policy process. Innis's criticism of "present-mindedness," at the expense of understanding the long-term patterns to economic expansion and decline, stood in sharp contrast to Mackintosh's conviction that good policy and good scholarship was part of the same heuristic process. In what proved to be his final scholarly contribution, "Government Economic Policy: Scope and Principles," he praised Keynes's role in wartime policy:

> By no means all that Keynes wrote or said has stood the test of more careful analysis ... yet he profoundly changed economic thinking, particularly in regard to policy. When he rudely broke the hardening crust of economic analysis, many a flower not of his planting broke through. There may be little left of his positive contributions but the fact remains that there will always be a dividing line in thinking about economic policy, pre-Keynes and post-Keynes. Why is this so? In him the creative impulse, the desire to act, overshadowed his scientific interest. His impatience and sense of urgency induced a concentration on short-run economic effects. This led him to many errors in analysis but it also led him to analytical concepts which were much closer to the stuff of which decisions in either public or private policy are made.[6]

It comes as no surprising, then, that Mackintosh's lasting scholarly contribution to the economics discipline came from his policy work. His definitive statement of the staple thesis in the *Economic Background of Dominion-Provincial Relations* was written in the course of his work for the Rowell–Sirois Royal Commission, while his restatement of the staple thesis within a Keynesian aggregate-demand framework applicable to an open economy governed by a federal state occurred in his government White Paper on employment and income.

In his interpretation of the staple thesis, Mackintosh was no less circumspect about the failure of the postwar Canadian economy to realize the potential for development. Writing in 1956, he stated that: "It was assumed by many, if not most people, at the end of the [Second World] war, that the Canadian economy would grow and mature and that, in maturing, it would develop a relatively larger secondary industry than it had had in the past. In other words, that relatively the production of finished goods, particularly consumer goods, would have a greater place. In fact, this has not happened. Primary industry and the service industries have increased more rapidly than have secondary industries and at times secondary industries have found the going hard. One reason for this has been that instead of building a larger economy on the existing base, we have greatly extended the base and in most respects are more of a pioneering country than we were twenty years ago."[7]

POLICY ADVISOR

Mackintosh proudly claimed to have been appointed to an advisory position by every prime minister from Robert Borden to Lester Pearson. His work with the dominion government began with summer research for the department of labour and the Dominion Bureau of Statistics (1917–18), with the Advisory Board on Tariff and Taxation (1926–29), and with the registrar of the Combines Investigation Act (1926), then as a member of the National Employment Commission (1936–38) and as research advisor on the Royal Commission on Dominion-Provincial Relations (1938–39). His wartime work brought a variety of titles – special assistant to the deputy minister of finance (1939–44), director of research for the department of reconstruction (1944–45), and acting deputy minister of finance (1946) – that hardly begin to describe his range of responsibilities. After the war he was a consultant to the departments of national defence (1948) and industry trade and commerce (1950), a member of the MacQuarrie Committee (1950–52), mediator of the national railway strike of 1950, chair of the Unemployment Insurance Advisory Committee (1941–51), director of the Canadian Mortgage and Housing Corporation (1946–51), member of the Canada Council (1957–60), commissioner on the Royal Commission on Banking and Finance (1961–64), and director of the Bank of Canada (1964–70). Equally impressive was the number of positions declined, including director of the International Bank of Development and Reconstruction.

There is an obvious continuity between his scholarship and his policy work. Just as the staple thesis identified the underlying geographical, technological, and international conditions that defined the constraints upon individual and collective human agency, his role as a policy advisor was based on an analysis of the fundamental economic forces that defined the scope of potential government action. Canadian policy had, as far as Mackintosh was concerned, evolved in response to the particular circumstances of its staple-based economy. "Here and there obstinate facts, some peculiar to Canada and some typical of young countries, have forced distinctive policies. Our federal system has created intractable problems and necessitated realistic thinking. In setting the standards of trade or working conditions we have been largely dependent on borrowing, conservative borrowing, while making some modifications in terms of our own economic facts." Monetary policy had followed the conservative path of "sound finance" in order to maintain stable exchange rates, while trade policy was defined by Canada's relationship to the United States and the United Kingdom, with improvisations in the areas of subsidies, anti-dumping duties, and tariff cascading that were "practical if not elegant." Canada's willingness to adopt more active state policy was similarly driven by expediency related to the development of the prairie economy: "In a period when laissez-faire policies were at their peak of respectability the Canadian attitude to the question of public versus private enterprise was purely pragmatic."[8]

Several themes also recur throughout his scholarship and policy work. His interest in industrial relations, beginning with his summer work in the department of labour in 1917, was influenced by his observations on the events surrounding the Winnipeg General Strike. His conviction that capital-labour relations could, and should, be managed led him to champion the creation of the industrial-relations centre at Queen's in 1936, and was of paramount importance during World War II in his efforts to balance the encroachment upon collective bargaining rights against a wage policy that would prevent the inequities and social unrest associated with rapid inflation. Finally, as a mediator in the railway dispute of 1950, his willingness to endorse back-to-work legislation underscores his insistence that workable industrial relations required both parties to act in a responsible fashion, and, where they did not, the state had a right to exercise its constitutional authority. His interest in the fiscal relations of a federal state was based on a general concern with a rational allocation of dominion-provincial spending and taxation powers to ensure appropriate accountability or, as he cited Benjamin Franklin, so that "every tub should stand on its own feet."[9] It assumed heightened importance as he came to embrace a greater role for the state in managing the economy, reflected in the proposals of the National Employment Commission and the Rowell–Sirois Royal Commission for an unemployment insurance program under dominion responsibility, in wartime tax-sharing agreements designed to endow the dominion government with the appropriate fiscal powers to manage aggregate demand, and in the Green Book proposals for a more complete postwar social-security system. His pursuit of multilateral trade liberalization and international monetary reform can be traced to his work with the Advisory Board on Tariff and Taxation in 1926 and culminated in his role leading up to the Bretton Woods agreement. His contribution to domestic money and banking policy, apparent in his editorial work with the *Journal of the Canadian Bankers' Association* and his testimony to the Macmillan Royal Commission in 1932, reached its fullest expression in the Royal Commission on Money and Banking in 1961–63 and his service as a director of the Bank of Canada from 1965 to 1970.

In his approach to public policy, pragmatism was his watchword. Mackintosh had little patience for grand theory ("chess games") or its indiscriminate application ("dogmatism"). What was required was an accumulation of the relevant "facts," their careful analysis, guided by economic principles, and then the exercise of "good judgement" in the application to the issues at hand. He endorsed Keynes's view that economic theory was "a method rather than a doctrine, an apparatus of the mind, a technique of thinking which helps its possessor to draw correct conclusions."[10] This required a clear separation of the tools of the economist from those of the policy-maker: "Policy emerges when the results of economic analysis are combined with political and social considerations and have been subjected to the experience and judgement of the policy maker ... The distinction between principles and policy is elementary but nevertheless important. It is the old distinction between science and art. In acting or recommending action, an economist steps outside of the field of science into that of the practitioner and needs knowledge and experience beyond the limits of his scientific training. Too many economists are anxious to fly straight from a diagram into a statute book ... The one thing that is certain of the future of a country is that it will be somewhat different from anything that has been predicted ... The unpredictable future."[11] He warned that "The country in which the economist has picked up the passwords of the politician and the politician has acquired the jargon of the economist is headed for the bottomless abyss ... The economist must first straighten out the direction of policy by means of his economic analysis and only then come to a consideration of ways and means and of eventualities of the future, having a clear realization that in this part of the field he cannot talk with the dogmatism of science but can only appear as one among a number of practitioners of an art."[12] In Mackintosh, the analysis of the economist and the judgment of the policy-maker were combined in one individual. This did not vitiate his respect for the democratic process, and he never lost sight of the role of non-elected officials in the policy process. He bristled at references to the "brain trust" – true perhaps of Roosevelt's bureaucracy, but not in the Canadian case – telling one minister that "Sir, you don't think we have any brains and you don't trust us."[13]

The zenith of his contribution to economic policy occurred during World War II. It is commonplace in a biography to state that "no one played a more important role" than the protagonist. In this instance, a stronger declaration is required: Mackintosh was the single most important official in Ottawa when it came to the economic organization of the country's war effort. This assertion is supported on quantitative grounds, given the inordinate number of committees on which he served (Economic Advisory Committee, Reconstruction Committee, Labour Supply Committee, Unemployment Insurance Commission, Joint Canada-US Economic Committees, Wartime Prices and Trade Board, several iterations of the Tourism Committee, Foreign Exchange Control Board, and the National Joint Council of the Public Service of Canada) and his involvement in international economic talks leading to the Bretton Woods accord, the Canadian postwar loan to Britain, and the formation of the United Nations. More important, of course, was the quality of his contribution. He was central to the design of domestic fiscal policy, labour-supply and wages policy, social security, and postwar reconstruction, while his contribution to international trade and monetary talks was appropriately recognized when, after Keynes moved the "Final Act" of the Bretton Woods conference, Mackintosh was called upon to second the motion.

Plumptre observed that "To an outsider, one of the most interesting spectacles in the changing drama of war organization is to watch the process of 'survival of the fittest' going on amongst the various individuals and committees with which Ottawa is crowded."[14] Mackintosh was often the fittest in this contest because he was ideally suited to address a variety of problems as they arose, and was the first to admit that, under the pressures of the moment, it was not always possible to give problems the complete consideration that an academic might prefer. One perspective on the wartime work is provided by Frank Knox, who found it difficult to fit into the culture of the federal bureaucracy. "I don't think much of a contribution is to be made in Ottawa unless you are one of the men fairly high up. And that takes more hours, more energy and perhaps also more capacity for quick work on a variety of subjects than I have. I am amused at the way one must be an expert on almost anything at a moment's notice whether he has any title to or not ... Perhaps there is some offsetting virtue in the general competence which these men acquire from dabbling in everything."[15] In this respect, Knox observed that Mackintosh had "a mind superbly equipped to tackle the great variety of puzzles which war threw up."[16] "Dabbling in everything" and doing so effectively meant reducing matters of public policy to the discovery of technical solutions to problems as they arose. For Mackintosh, in most cases good policy came about gradually: "The glaring cases are not too hard to assess but the difficult economic decisions usually come down to the calculus of a little more or a little less."[17] David Slater, who was Mackintosh's student, makes a similar point: "One of his basic theses was that economic policy and economic results accrue from many small actions. Often what is needed and what is possible is to get three, or four, or five things all moving in the right direction; each one seems small and ineffective, but the few together are mutually reinforcing and the total result is far more than the sum of the parts."[18]

His pragmatism and apparently inexhaustible energy no doubt appealed to his political masters, but so too did his capacity to convey an argument in a clear and concise fashion. "He had great skill in picking out the two or three most important issues, and putting them on paper quickly and elegantly," writes David Slater. "He was an outstanding illustration of the adage that the person who 'holds the pen' in Ottawa has great power."[19] Indeed, he elevated the memorandum to a high art form. He explained to his students that good writing generally came only through "practice, criticism, and editing," with his first rule in seeking to gain a person's agreement being to eliminate from the argument all that was irrelevant and nonessential.[20] As Slater recalls Mackintosh's key point, "the principle of writing policy papers was the opposite to detective novels. In the first the plot was revealed at the outset; in the other at the end."[21]

If he was a gifted memo writer, he was equally compelling when translating complex issues for ministerial consideration and for public consumption. As one reporter discovered, he "doesn't indulge in glib off-the handle answers. Ask him a question and he leans back in his chair, looks out the window, draws on a cigarette in the long black holder which is never out of his hand. When he states his carefully thought out opinion, it has an authority and conviction derived from wide experience and a remarkable grasp of theory and reality."[22] Many would draw upon his capacity for a clear, thoughtful answer. Shelia Skelton recalled that "His name was a household word in the Skelton family for as long as I can remember. Often did I hear Dad say to Mother, 'I will speak to Mackintosh about it,' and one knew what respect both had for his opinions and reasons, and the considered answer he would give."[23] Indeed, his demeanor in meetings approached iconic status. J. Douglas Gibson relates the story of when "On one occasion in Ottawa Mr. Ilsley turned to Mackintosh after a long and tough meeting in which Bill had been totally silent and said rather impatiently, "Look here, Mackintosh, how are we going to sort this one out?' And he got a good answer." A similar story was recounted by Corry, with Keynes as the beneficiary: "Speaking of the war-time and post-war discussions and conferences, [Keynes] said 'if Mackintosh had spoken sooner, many of our meetings would have been shorter.'"[24] Indeed, the occasions when Mackintosh's communication skills failed him were so rare as to prompt comment. Mitchell Sharp cites the example of briefing a group of senators on a government bill. "Mackintosh was giving his normal lucid explanation when the senator raised his hand: 'Dr. Mackintosh that is enough, you will confuse the senators.'"[25] But these were exceptions to the rule. When Mackenzie King was having difficulty getting down to writing his memoirs, George Ferguson suggested that he consult Mackintosh. "He believed that he was one of the best persons to talk with," wrote King in his diary. "I agreed and said that of the papers I had read while Prime Minister, I thought his *were* the best prepared of all."[26]

In the course of his government work, Mackintosh emerged as the country's leading advocate of Keynesian policy. His conversion was gradual. Despite admiring the originality of Keynes's arguments in the 1920s and early 1930s, he did not abandon his view that the Great Depression was largely the result of the international economic "maladjustment" in the wake of World War I. Canada's dependence on capital imports and commodity exports left it particularly vulnerable to the international downturn, and the need for sound finance to maintain currency stability ruled out expansionary fiscal and monetary policy to stimulate domestic demand. He maintained this view through his work on the National Employment Commission: although acknowledging in principle the important role that counter-cyclical government spending could play, he insisted that large expenditures on public works would only aggravate Canada's indebtedness and interfere with the "natural" recovery under way in the latter half of the 1930s. For Mackintosh, the impact of Keynes's *General Theory* in 1936 had more to do with the timing than the novelty of the argument. He later wrote that it "was but one of several brilliant books written by Keynes and it is not clear that it was his greatest book. Nevertheless it had the greatest immediate impact mainly because its implications for the economic state were clear and tremendous. It had insight, brilliance in exposition and boldness in conception, but so had his other books. The bitter circumstances of the whole Western world into which it was launched made this particular book strikingly relevant."[27] Yet given Canada's open economy and federal state, the policy prescriptions, at least as far as Mackintosh was concerned, were not immediately obvious. Similarly, in his work for the Rowell–Sirois Royal Commission, he raised questions about the appropriateness of Canadian fiscal and monetary policy and extended the argument for a realignment of dominion-provincial jurisdiction to taxation and spending categories. In this sense, Keynesian "politics," or the unfettered ability to use fiscal policy, was a prerequisite to a managed economy; however, the commission's report stopped short of outlining how fiscal policy might contribute to economic stabilization.

In contrast, the exigencies of managing the wartime economy forced a more concerted effort to understand the demand-side determinants of the economy. David Laidler makes the simple, but often overlooked, observation that the growing acceptance of Keynesian demand management occurred at a time of full employment, when controlling inflation, rather than unemployment, was the principal concern.[28] The massive increase in public spending necessary to meet Canada's military commitments made it abundantly clear that the government could induce full employment; however, the policy challenge was how to curtail other forms of domestic spending within the limitations of the country's productive capacity so as to avoid undue inflationary pressures. In the 1945 White Paper on employment and income, Mackintosh summarized the economic lessons from the war for the postwar period. Once he had accepted the capacity of the state to manage the level of economic activity, it was a short step to embracing a general model of the demand-side determinants of the economy. Since the export sector represented over

40 per cent of the Canadian economy, the suggestion that final demand was the determining factor in national income had intuitive appeal. The policy nihilism of the Great Depression gave way to an understanding of the use of fiscal and monetary policy in an effort to adjust domestic spending to volatility in the export sector. The White Paper and the complementary Green Book proposals for dominion-provincial cooperation on a comprehensive social-security package, are described as tantamount to a defining a "new national policy" for Canada.[29]

Rising inflation at the outset of the 1950s led him to reflect on the consistency of the economic role of the state with liberalism. In his address to the Royal Society of Canada on "Economic Instability and Social Change," he asserts that an important legacy of the Great Depression was "a significant though unmeasured decline in support of and confidence in the values of freedom, the democratic state, and private enterprise."[30] When the war had the effect of enlarging "enormously the scope of the economic policy of the state," he saw no conflict with individual freedom, since "direct measures undertaken to lessen unemployment, if effective, enlarge opportunities."[31] Keynesian policy, he maintained, was equally applicable in periods of excess demand, full employment, and rising inflation, but had different implications for individual freedom, since fighting inflation requires "regimentation" that limits opportunities and restricts enterprise. Changing market incentives – through interest rates, taxation, and credit restrictions – rather than direct controls was thus the appropriate tool in a peacetime economy. Judiciously applied, government involvement need not unduly restrict individual initiative or threaten the private sector, while at the same time ensuring that inflation did not lead to the type of unwarranted income redistribution that occurred in the aftermath of World War I. "If governments are ready to act and can accomplish even imperfect results," he concluded, "social unrest will in part at least be dissipated through accomplishment."[32]

Mackintosh's capacity to persuade based on clear exposition of an argument was, for him, a triumph of reason. He was not naïve about the role of class coalitions or the need for political compromise, and he suffered his share of frustrations – his failure to mediate a settlement to avoid the railway strike of 1950, the repeated inability to reform dominion-provincial relations, and the defeat of multilateral trade after World War II – but it did not shake his faith in human reason and his commitment to building institutions through which responsible citizens could achieve a just result.

UNIVERSITY ADMINISTRATOR

To Mac Urquhart, as to many others, Mackintosh "was fundamentally a University man, convinced of the great importance of a university in our social fabric and ever devoted to the cause of learning, both through education and scholarship."[33] This commitment to education, instilled by his parents and nurtured by Skelton, extended from his early days teaching in rural Saskatchewan, to Brandon College, and throughout his career at Queen's. Education, in the narrow sense, was a matter of facilitating informed decisions by developing the knowledge and tools for applying sound judgment. As he succinctly described his role in higher education to a witness at the hearings of the Royal Commission on Banking and Finance, "I am in the business of believing that people should be widely informed."[34] In a broader sense, it meant equipping students with an understanding of the world in which they lived, and for fostering a commitment to civil society. Education was the foundation to citizenship, responsible institutions, and wise decision making, and thus to the functioning of a liberal democracy.

Kenneth Taylor ranked the "building and maintaining at Queen's a faculty and a curriculum in economics that for sustained quality and balance over a period of close to forty years has not been excelled anywhere in Canada" among Mackintosh's greatest contributions.[35] As director of the School of Commerce from 1923 and as holder of the Sir John A. Macdonald Chair of the department of political and economic science from 1927 – positions that he relinquished only upon being appointed principal in 1951 – he furthered the reputation of Queen's in applied economics. Among his former students were numerous civil servants, businessmen, and bankers.[36] Many went on to do graduate work and to distinguished academic careers, including W. B. Wynne, Earl F. Beach, James Dingwall, Graeme S. Dorrance, Alex N. McLeod, Gail Iverson Ward, Peter McClelland, J.H. Young, and David Slater. His impression on former students was long-lasting. For Gerald Graham, who was also raised in Madoc and studied and taught at Queen's, "from earliest Queen's days no human being had a greater influence on my wayward life. From the beginning – and a very unsophisticated beginning – I had sense enough to appreciate his intellectual distinction; in fact as a youngster I idolized him. There was never any disillusionment as I grew older; no feet of clay ever appeared, not even a toe. He was, and will remain in my mind, one of the really great Canadians of the twentieth century … Perhaps because the impress was so deep, I remember – often to his embarrassment – almost everything he ever said (a minor Boswell to his Johnson). It was not that I made a Boswellian effort; it just happens that one the finest minds I have ever encountered can exercise itself sharply or perfectly. On any plane."[37] Among his colleagues, Frank Knox first met him

> when a young man came through the door of the large economics classroom in Kingston Hall and entered the large enclosure on the platform and began to talk about, to me, a strange subject, economics … Much of the economics I learned thereafter came from him, not only his publications but his lectures and conversation. I have a deep sense of gratitude to him in particular from the department meetings which he led and kept going. They furthered my education in economics and politics, led me to know my colleagues better and, not least by any means, gave a "loner" like me perhaps the most pleasant association of all my Queen's years with my fellow human beings … for such contributions to my human and intellectual growth during the long years we were together at Queen's I shall cherish his memory.[38]

David McQueen was among his last crop of graduate students. "Of all of the teachers I have ever had, he made the most enduring impression on me. This was no so much because of his polished work and his reputation, great as they were, but more because of what he was like when you got a bit closer to him and learned to know him as a person … His combination of toughmindedness and sweet nature is what has most stayed with me in remembering those days – also of course his wonderful, understated wit."[39] Another of his students records for posterity that "I think all of us who studied under him absorbed something of his sense of values."[40]

His subsequent appointment as principal was not just a personal triumph or merely a confirmation of Queen's coming of age through the ascent of its own son, but a reflection of the self-confidence of the Canadian academic community. That George Ferguson was among

Mackintosh's closest friends does not diminish the veracity of his observations on the installation of Queen's twelfth principal. Ferguson arrived for the occasion

> purring with satisfaction and excitement ... [M]y pleasure is not only the personal pleasure of a friend, it is also based on the deep knowledge that Queen's has made an appointment which will lift all Canadian universities, whether they like it or not, to higher standards ... You only had to look around you last Friday to know that this is so. A lot of people go to such a ceremony because it is their duty so to do, or because they feel they will be missed when the roll is called. This was not so on Friday. There was an astonishing number of people who, I *know*, were there for the same reason I was there: it was the best and greatest appointment to a university headship in a generation. A lot of them, of course, were friends of Bill, like me. But I've had a fair number of friends who have 'made good' and I've gone to no trouble to see them launched. I'd have gone to this show in a wheel-chair. If I'd not been invited, I'd have stood outside and cheered ... All this, and much more, has been said to me by others who were there. I never in my life saw such unanimity of pleasure and pride.[41]

Mackintosh did not disappoint. Treating the university as a community of scholars, he subscribed to W.B. Munro's view that "If it can only put scholarly and sincere teachers in the same classroom with capable and ambitious students all other problems seem to solve themselves"[42] Glen Shortcliffe credited him with the "strengthening and expansion of the best intellectual traditions of our University, a task to which he brought not only a vital soundness of judgment at a critical time, but also an imaginative vision of the future tempered only by that sensible caution we have all learned to respect." Knox adds that this emphasis on the goals of learning and scholarship were combined with "a humour and a humanitarian attitude which proved him to be indeed 'a whole man.' The graduates of Queen's in Mackintosh's time remember him not only with respect for his intellectual powers, but with affection. Through the roles many of them now play in our national life, Mackintosh's devoted service to Queen's is proving to be perhaps his greatest service to Canada."[43]

A GENEROUS LOYALTY

Mackintosh's approach to scholarship, policy formation, and university administration was unified not just through hard work and personal integrity, but by his unwavering faith in human endeavour and his commitment to public service. Urquhart, for one, emphasized that Mackintosh's "humanitarianism is reflected in his devotion to the improvement of human affairs through enlightened public policy, and perhaps even more fundamentally, though somewhat less tangibly, in his belief in and commitment to the part that a University may play in benefitting mankind. It appeared equally in his modesty about his own achievements, in his personal kindness to others, in his unfailing courtesy, and his genuine interest in the individual well-being of others." Ironically, it was Mackintosh's very modesty that gave him a special presence. One man's impressions upon meeting him for the first time during an alumni reception are typical: "It was one of the real highlights of my life to have had the opportunity of meeting you," he stated. "I was not long in your presence before I was well aware of the humility that was so dominating in every avenue of your life."[44] His unassuming nature followed from a belief that one should never take oneself too seriously. He was, after all, the man who cited "Mr. Ed" of talking-horse fame when asked about his favourite television show.[45]

"To me he always seemed like the salt of the earth," wrote Douglas LePan, "honest, responsible, tolerant, pithy, and wise."[46] To Eugene Forsey, he was "wise, modest, witty, tolerant, kindly, but with standards of scholarship and conduct which he never relaxed," while Carl Goldenberg added the traits of "able, charming, humble, kind, and the soul of integrity."[47] More often than not, people would add a reference to his "dry, delicious sense of humour," which often included a salty anecdote or two for a bonus."[48] These characteristics won him the trust of bankers, industrialists, farmers, and labour leaders alike. They were also evident in his fierce loyalty to his friends and colleagues, and the vigour with which they reciprocated his trust. His devotion to O.D. Skelton; his enduring friendships with George Wilson, Brooke Claxton, Hector McKinnon, John Orr, and Walter Gordon; his support for Clifford Clark, Norman McLeod Rogers, R.G. Smails, C.E. Walker, Clifford Curtis, Frank Knox, W.H. Wynne, John Deutsch, Mac Urquhart, Alex Corry, and other colleagues at Queen's; his encouragement of the careers of Donald

Gordon and Lester Pearson; his steadfast allegiance to other economists, such as Innis, Sandy Skelton, and Pete McQueen; his defence of the academic freedom of Glen Shortcliffe, Arthur Lower, and Gideon Rosenbluth; the protection he extended to Douglas LePan; his rapport with journalists such as J.W. Dafoe, Grant Dexter, Austin Cross, and George Ferguson; the loyalty he gave to Arthur Purvis, J.I. Ilsley, and C.D. Howe; and the warmth of his personal relationships with wartime associates such as Graham Towers, Louis Rasminsky, and R.B. Bryce – all these relationships were based on deep mutual respect and a shared commitment to the public service.

In the last paper that Mackintosh would write, he paid tribute to O.D. Skelton, the man whom he most admired and emulated, and whose portrait was always prominently displayed in his study. "Some of his work is built into our institutions and laws. But beyond this, where, here and there, people value knowledge as the basis of understanding, prize reason and tolerance as gateways to peaceful accommodation, give high place to personal and professional integrity, and feel a valiant and decent pride in being Canadian, there will be some persisting influence of O.D. Skelton."[49] With these words, Mackintosh wrote his own epitaph.

Notes

PREFACE

1 Dexter, *Ottawa at War*, 499.

2 George Ferguson, cited in Bercuson, *True Patriot*, 230. In his capacity as minister of defence, Claxton was president of the Royal Military College and Royal Roads Military College, and was also a McGill LLD. He admitted that his McGill robes were "pretty gaudy," but Mackintosh advised that "since you are appearing as a college president you should complete the disguise and wear academic dress. The gaudier the better" (QUA, PRO 1250/13/14, Claxton to Mackintosh, 21 September 1951; Mackintosh to Claxton, 24 September 1951).

3 QUA, Mackintosh Papers, 12/1, Mackintosh to Innis, 13 September 1951.

4 QUA, Mackintosh Papers, 11/4, John Orr to Mackintosh, 29 August 1951.

5 Austin Cross, "Dr. W.A. Mackintosh Is Installed as Principal of Queen's University," *Ottawa Citizen* (20 October 1951), 15.

6 *Kingston Whig-Standard* (20 October 1951), 1.

7 Cross, "Dr. W.A. Mackintosh," 15.

8 Mackintosh, "Inaugural Address," in Queen's University, *Proceedings*.

9 *Kingston Whig-Standard* (20 October 1951), 1; *Globe & Mail* (20 October 1951), 1.

10 Mackintosh, "Adam Shortt, 1859–1931," 176.

11 Taylor, "Economic Scholarship in Canada," 7.

12 The Reverend R. Campbell also taught a junior course in Economics and a senior course in Politics prior to Shortt (QUA, Mackintosh Papers, 9/219, "The Teaching of Economics at Queen's Under Adam Shortt, 1889–1906," no author, no date.)

13 Easterbrook argues that "although W.A. Mackintosh, C.A. Curtis and F.A. Knox were to bring a strong analytical interest to bear on Canadian problems, the emphasis on applied economics, particularly at the national level, has remained strong. The ties between Ottawa and Queen's have been close over a long period, and there are few indications that political economy has become less 'political' with the passage of time. Greater interest in the theoretical and statistical aspects of economic inquiry has made for vastly greater competence in the analysis of national problems, but a long-established pattern remains intact" ("Trends," 93).
14 Mackintosh, "Adam Shortt," 175.
15 Ibid., 167, 169; Mackintosh, "Innis on Canadian Economic Development," 186. Shortt's commitment to developing a professional civil service drew the opposition of some Cabinet ministers and ultimately resulted in his being "firmly persuaded" to accept the position as Dominion Archivist (Mackintosh, "O.D. Skelton," 72).
16 LAC, RG19, Mackintosh Papers, 3552/C-00, Mackintosh, "Some Notes for D.D. Calvin," 23 August 1940.
17 Mackintosh, "Adam Shortt," 175.
18 Ibid., 176.
19 Mackintosh, "O.D. Skelton, 1878–1941," 270; "Some Notes for D.D. Calvin."
20 Mackintosh, "O.D. Skelton, 1878–1941," 276.
21 Clark, "O.D. Skelton," 147.
22 LAC, RG19, Mackintosh Papers, 3550/B, Mackintosh to Vincent Bladen, 20 February 1941.
23 QUA, Mackintosh Papers, 8/200, Mackintosh to Wallace, 10 May 1940.
24 Ibid., 11/5, "Presentation of the Canada Council Medals," 22 November 1966.
25 American Economic Association, "Report," 335.
26 Taylor, "Economic Scholarship in Canada," 11.
27 Dales, "Canadian Scholarship in Economics," 87.
28 In personal correspondence, Mackintosh wrote that "I have the feeling that Veblen was a sort of repressed sin for Innis which finally triumphed over the austere dull virtues of Chester Wright" (QUA, PRO, 1251/1/C, Mackintosh to Donald Creighton, 13 November 1957).
29 Innis, "Teaching of Economic History in Canada," 52–68. Mackintosh, "Economics, Prices and the War" and "The Use of Case Material in Economics."
30 Mackintosh, "Economic Factors."

31 Mackintosh, "Innis on Economic Development," 187.

32 Ibid. Although Mackintosh suggested that Innis's nascent interest in staple exports can be found in *The History of the Canadian Pacific Railway*, he was hardly enthusiastic about the book: "The style is compressed and tortured, and many of the generalizations are either obscure or self-evident. Some of the chapters are incredibly dull. It was not a book which Innis himself in later years was concerned to preserve. It displays the inexperienced gropings of a young and industrious scholar towards his life-work. It was not a skillful book, but it reflected solid research and was in no part imitative" (186).

33 Parker, "Harold Innis," 75.

34 Macpherson, "The Social Sciences," 200.

35 Berger, *Writing of Canadian History*, 103.

36 Watson, *Marginal Man*.

37 *Vancouver Sun* (24 July 1935).

38 Underhill, "Conception of a National Interest," 404. Underhill was undoubtedly building on W.C. Clark's metaphor that likened the Canadian economy during the Depression to an ill-designed automobile: "But – if I may state a conclusion dogmatically without attempting proof at this time – the machine, in my opinion, is not incapable of repair ... The brakes need relining and a more powerful system of headlights needs to be installed if we are to drive again at the pace of 1929 ... With such a thorough overhauling and such improvement in control, it will still probably be found that the 'old bus' is still without an equal, still superior to the only competitive model which has yet appeared" (Clark, "What's Wrong with Us?" 2–3).

39 QUA, Mackintosh Papers, 8/199, H.A. Innis to W.A. Mackintosh, 6 October 1942. In thanking Mackintosh for sending a reprint of his paper on "Canadian War Financing," published in the *Journal of Political Economy*, Innis noted that "I am not a subscriber to the JPE which makes the reprint all the more welcome." This is rather astonishing admission, since the journal was one of the two most important in Economics.

40 Easterbrook, "Trends," 97. Easterbrook suggests that "in tone and outlook, in guiding conceptions and dominant interests, differences are sufficiently great to validate the distinction [between Queen's and Toronto]. He cautions, however, that "there is the danger of drawing too sharp a line" between Mackintosh and Innis given the former's path-breaking scholarship and the latter's continual involvement in public affairs" (94n19).

41 Macpherson, "Social Sciences," 206–7.
42 Easterbrook, "Trends," 97.
43 Watkins, "The Dismal State of Economics in Canada," 206.
44 Innis, "Some English-Canadian University Problems," 34.
45 Galbraith, "How Keynes Came to America," 52.
46 Cited in LePan, *Bright Glass of Memory*, 77–8.
47 Mackintosh, "Keynes as Public Servant," 380, 382.
48 Mackintosh, "Canadian Economic Policy," 56, 59.
49 QUA, Biographical File: W.A. Mackintosh.
50 Queen's University, *Report of the Principal, 1960–61*, 11.
51 Ibid., 10.
52 QUA, Biographical File: W.A. Mackintosh.
53 Bruce Hutchison, *Incredible Canadian*, 265–6.
54 Mitchell Sharp, *Which Reminds Me*, 17; Mackintosh, "Inaugural Address," in Queen's University *Proceedings*; Pearson, *Mike*. Vol. 2: 186.
55 Gordon, *Political Memoir*, 35.
56 QUA, Mackintosh Papers (Additions) 1/Death.
57 Personal communication.
58 Gibson, *To Serve*, 309–10. Mackintosh was great fan of Gibson: "Fred Gibson is developing into a person of substantial power in Canadian history" (QUA, PRO 1250/2/PQ, Mackintosh to Beryl Plumptre, 20 April 1959).
59 Grant Dexter, "Dr. Mackintosh Leaves," *Winnipeg Free Press*, 10 August 1946.
60 QUA PRO 1252 12/29.

PART ONE

1 QUA, Mackintosh Papers – Additions, 1/Exemption Certificate. He was probably deemed unfit for overseas service because of an inguinal hernia.

CHAPTER ONE

1 Mackintosh, Sr. "Presidential Address," 30, 31.
2 Al Purdy, *Beyond Remembering*.
3 Mackintosh, "Canada and Its Competitors," 117.
4 Mackintosh, "Review" of G.V. Ferguson, *John W. Dafoe*, 212.
5 Mackintosh, "The Laurentian Plateau," 510–1.

6 Boyce, *Historic Hastings*. Mackintosh would proudly remind people that "I, too, come from a cheese county" (QUA, PRO, 1251/2/UV, Mackintosh to Harold Varty, 29 October 1953).

7 LePan, *Bright Glass of Memory*, 74.

8 Knox, "William Archibald Mackintosh," 69.

9 The three-year-old Agnes Cowie appears in the 1861 Census of Canada West (Enumeration District 4, Fourth Ward, Beverly Township, Wentworth County, Reel 1085). The other members of the Cowie household were John (52) and Helen (54) – both married, of Scottish birth and belonging to the United Presbyterian church – Margaret (23), Glen (19), and Jane (17). It is unclear then who, if anyone in the household, were Agnes's parents. A possibility is William and Isabella Cowie, aged 25 and 21 respectively, listed in the Census records immediately after the members of the household in which Agnes resided. Jane Cowie lived with the Mackintoshes in 1901.

10 William McNeil Mackintosh was likely the victim of a malaria epidemic attributed to the damming of the Moira River for commercial purposes. The 1881 Census records also list "Lizzie McIntosh," the twenty-six-year-old sister of William Mackintosh, Sr, also residing in the household.

11 OA, RG2-114-1 Superannuated Pension Fund.

12 Mrs Maude Pringle Fox, in Pidgen and McKinnon, *Way Back When*, 297.

13 QUA, Mackintosh Papers, 8/206, George Newcombe Gordon to W.A. Mackintosh, 7 August 1942.

14 OA, RG2-42-O-676. In this particular instance, Mackintosh, Sr, refused to extend the temporary permits granted to unqualified teachers in the hope of forcing the local school trustees to create more favourable conditions. A minor furor ensued, largely because the unqualified teacher in question was the daughter of the local reeve.

15 Boyce, *Historical Hastings*, 201.

16 QUA Mackintosh Papers, Box 11, J.W. Dafoe to Mackintosh, Christmas 1941. It is fitting that Mitchell Sharp, who described W.A. Mackintosh's writing as "elegant and economical," modelled his own writing after Dafoe, who, at least in theory, learned his composition under the supervision of Mackintosh, Sr (Sharp, *Which Reminds Me*, 8, 17).

17 Mackintosh, "Review" of G.V. Ferguson, *John W. Dafoe*, 212. As he wrote to Grant Dexter upon Dafoe's death: "Beyond his great work, I always had a personal tie with J.W. for, as he invariably remembered,

we came from the same County, and he knew my father when Dafoe was a small boy in a country school as early as the middle seventies … Some day before you and George get too far with your book, I would like to tell you something of the country he came from, and people from there." (QUA, Mackintosh Papers, 8/202, Mackintosh to Grant Dexter, 14 August 1944).

18 OA, RG2-42-0-6712. William Mackintosh, "Report to Warden and Members of the County Council of Hastings, for 1899," 11.

19 Ibid., 10–11.

20 Mackintosh, Sr's, support for curricular changes to replace Latin with more practical subjects such as "nature study" incurred the wrath of William Houston, the Toronto teacher, journalist, and self-styled intellectual expositor. He took to the editorial pages of the Toronto *Globe* to denounce Mackintosh's efforts as "the most obscuranted and philistinist suggestion that has been made by any educationalist in Ontario or Upper Canada during the forty-four years since I began teaching." W. Houston, "Letter to the Editor," Toronto *Globe* (7 June 1903), 8.

21 William Mackintosh, Sr, "Presidential Address," 30, 31.

22 QUA, W.A. Mackintosh Papers, Additions 1/Correspondence, 1905, George William Ross to William Mackintosh, 31 January 1905. The school inspector was long remembered in the area. In writing to W.A. Mackintosh on the occasion of his ascension to the principalship of Queen's, C.J. Cannon, acting deputy minister of education in Ontario, commented that "It is also pleasant to remember that your father was a Public School Inspector, and I want you to know that when I was inspecting schools in North Hastings some years ago, I heard his name mentioned many times" (QUA, Mackintosh Papers, 11/4).

23 Cox, "Canada's Woman Labour Authority," 21.

24 Both Margaret and Helen served on the executive of the Queen's Alumni Committee.

25 *Globe & Mail* (19 July 1919), 18; (26 September 1935), 5.

26 Among Margaret Mackintosh's publications are "Government Intervention in Labour Disputes in Canada," *Queen's Quarterly* (1924) 31: 298–328.

27 UTA, *Torontonesis* 1902.

28 Hudson, *Fabric of a Dream*, 80.

29 QUA, Mackintosh Papers, 11/4, Bill Dafoe to Mackintosh, Toronto, 22 May 1951.

30 QUA, PRO, 1251/1/C, Howard Connor to Mackintosh, 10 September 1960.

31 Pigden and McKinnon, *Way Back When*, 314.
32 Gossage, *A Question of Privilege*, 166.
33 Scoular, *Not an Ordinary Place*, 28.
34 Upon his death in 1917, the estate of William Mackintosh, Sr, was valued at over $46,000. Most of his assets were held in the form of several mortgages extended to local townspeople and in securities.
35 Gossage, *A Question of Privilege*, 160.
36 Fullerton, *Graham Towers*, 17.
37 QUA, PRO, 1251/1/D, Mackintosh to James S. Duncan, 14 May 1951; Mackintosh Private Papers, "Chronology."
38 St Andrew's College Archives.
39 Knox, "William Archibald Mackintosh," 69.

CHAPTER TWO

1 QUA, The Graduating Class in Arts, *Year Book, 1916* (Kingston, 1916), 86.
2 Calvin, *Queen's University at Kingston*, 266–7.
3 Lim, "Kingston's Chinese."
4 *Queen's Journal* (17 January 1913) 39(20): 4; (24 January 1913) 39(22).
5 Gibson, *To Serve*, 1.
6 Queen's *Journal* (26 January 1914) 40(26).
7 Smails, "The Story of Commerce at Queen's," 7.
8 Among his other fellow students were Oliver Master, who became a prominent civil servant and would frequently cross paths with Mackintosh in Ottawa, H.A. McLeod, elected moderator of the United Church of Canada, W.E. Armstrong and J. Herbert Cameron, who became a high-school Classics teacher in Windsor (QUA, Mackintosh Papers, 11/4, John McNab to Mackintosh, n.d.; QUA PRO 1251/1/L, Mackintosh to Neil M. Leckie, 10 August 1961; QUA PRO 1251/1/Mc, H.A. McLeod to Mackintosh, 26 September 1960; QUA PRO 1251/1/A, Mackintosh to Gordon Aitchison, 10 May 1954).
9 *Queen's Journal* (22 February 1915) 41(34): 6.
10 Ibid., (30 November 1915) 42(15): 6.
11 Ibid., (22 October 1915) 42(4): 2.
12 Mackintosh, "Inaugural Address," in Queen's University *Proceedings*, 8.
13 *Queen's Journal* (1 December 1913) 40(16): 1.
14 Mackintosh, "John Lyle Morison."
15 QUA Mackintosh Papers 12/1.

16 Wilson, "'A Noble Dream.'"
17 Mackintosh, "Bankers' Bookshelf," *JCBA* (July 1931) 38(4). Milgate and Levy, "James Bonar," 260. For a Canadian perspective on Bonar, see MacGibbon's obituary note, "Dr. James Bonar."
18 Daub and Buchan, *Getting Down to Business,* 107.
19 Barry Ferguson, *Remaking Liberalism.*
20 Taylor, "Economic Scholarship in Canada," 7–8.
21 Mackintosh, "O.D. Skelton," 60.
22 LAC RG19, Mackintosh Papers, 3552/C, "Some Notes for D.D. Calvin," 23 August 1940.
23 Ibid.
24 QUA Mackintosh Papers, 9/220, Innis to Mackintosh, 25 March 1941.
25 Ibid., 9/217, J.F. MacDonald to Mackintosh, 18 March 1941.
26 Mackintosh, "O.D. Skelton," 59.
27 In 1917, James A. Richardson complained to Principal Taylor about Skelton's public comments on the government's wartime policy; Taylor would remind Richardson of the importance of academic freedom (LAC, MG30 D33, O.D. Skelton Papers, 1/24, G.Y. Chown to Skelton, 8 January 1917; Skelton to Chown, 9 January 1917).
28 Mackintosh, "O.D. Skelton," 64, 63.
29 QUA, Mackintosh Papers, 9/217.
30 LAC, MG30 D33, O.D. Skelton Papers, 6/2, Clark to Isabel Skelton, 12 February 1941; 7/3, Bryce Stewart to Isabel Skelton, 21 February 1941; 6/2, Knox to Isabel Skelton, 27 February 1941.
31 QUA, Mackintosh Papers, 9/217, Viner to Mackintosh, 13 June 1941.
32 Mackintosh, "Inaugural Address," in Queen's University *Proceedings*, 8.
33 Queen's *Journal* (29 October 1914) 41(5): 1
34 Ibid., (28 April 1915) 41(40): 1; Bindon, *Queen's Men, Canada's Men.*
35 *Queen's Journal* (7 March 1913) 39(34).
36 Grant, *Our Just Cause*, 64. For a full discussion of the Canadian movement for imperial unity, see Berger, *Sense of Power.*
37 As the *Queen's Journal*, (23 October 1913) 40(5): 5, reported on Skelton's address to the YMCA in 1913 on the "Yellow Peril," he opposed Asiatic migration "because of their long prejudice against intermarriage and social integration ... We should be creating for ourselves a problem worse than that of the negro in the United States."
38 Ferguson, *Remaking Liberalism;* Shortt, *Imperial Preferential Trade.*
39 *Queen's Journal* 41(28) (28 January 1915); 41(37) (4 March 1915); 42(17) (6 December 1915); 41(14) (30 Nov 1914); 41(30) (8 February 1915).

40 QUA, Mackintosh Papers, 8/176, "Revolution in Winnipeg." An edited version of this paper, which was never completed by Mackintosh, is published in *Labour/Le Travail* (2007) 60: 171–9.

41 *Queen's Journal* (15 January 1914) 40(23).

42 Urquhart, "W.A. Mackintosh's Scholarly Work."

43 QUA PRO, 1251/1/Mc, Mackintosh to George McKelvey, 12 January 1961. Mackintosh notes that some enterprising students who were able to return to the same school for four years were able to "prove up" on a homestead.

44 SAB, *Saskatchewan. Education Department. Inactive Teachers List: 1912-1938*. Microfilm Reel 32. "Mackintosh, William Archibald." Saskatchewan changed its regulations to grant provisional teaching certificates to students who had completed at least second year in an Arts program and were nineteen years of age or older (Queen's *Journal* (5 March 1914) 40(37).

45 Today the site of the school – Section 11-13-6-W3 – in what is now part of the Regional Municipality of Shamrock, is marked by the original school sign. The schoolhouse was purchased by the Gravelbourg Legion in the 1950s and presently makes up part of the Gravelbourg Lion's Den at 104, 6th Avenue. East. His personal knowledge of the region is evident in Mackintosh, *Prairie Settlement*, 56.

46 SAB, Saskatchewan. Department of Education. School District Files R-177.10/7, file 1207, Wiwa Hills School District No. 1207, J.T. Dales to Department of Education, 3 March 1913; William A. Armson to Department of Education, 2 December 1913.

47 Recollections of Edna Hill, Shamrock History Book Society, *Harvest of Memories*, 400.

48 *Harvest of Memories*, 136–9.

49 Mackintosh, *Agricultural Cooperation in Western Canada*, ix.

50 Urquhart, "W.A. Mackintosh's Scholarly Work," 2.

51 QUA, W.A. Mackintosh Additions/2, University of Saskatchewan, Jubilee Convocation, 29 September 1959.

52 QUA, Mackintosh Papers, 11/5, Wilfrid Eggleston, "Principal of Queen's," *Winnipeg Free Press*, 24 May 1951, 13.

53 Swanson was a Queen's undergraduate who earned his doctorate at Chicago. He taught at Queen's until 1916, when he became head of the department of economics at the University of Saskatchewan. See the obituary note in the *Canadian Journal of Economics and Political Science* (1951) 17: 383–4.

54 Mackintosh, "Social and Political Teachings," 31.

55 Ibid., 38, 41, 45-6.
56 Ibid., 67.
57 Ibid., 70. J.A. Cramb was a noted English imperialist and warmonger; John Burns and John Morley resigned from the British government over its declaration of war; and Karl Liebknecht was a Marxist member of the German Social Democratic Party who opposed the war.

CHAPTER THREE

1 QUA, Mackintosh Papers, Additions/2.
2 *Harvard Crimson*, 12 June 1916.
3 Mackintosh, "William Clifford Clark," 3; LAC MG30 D33, O.D. Skelton Papers, 1/23, W.C. Clark to O.D. Skelton, 15 February 1915.
4 Cited in Mason and Lamont, "The Harvard Department of Economics," 410.
5 Church, "The Economists Study Society," 26.
6 Quoted in Bateman and Kapstein, "Retrospectives: Between God and the Market," 253.
7 Dorfman, *The Economic Mind in American Civilization*, v. 4: 403.
8 Fogel, "Academic Economics."
9 Mackintosh, "The Psychologist and Economics."
10 Ibid., Mackintosh, "The Canadian Wheat Pools."
11 Mason and Lamont, "Harvard Department of Economics," 401.
12 Johnson and Samuels (eds.), *Economic Theory by Taussig, Young and Carver at Harvard*.
13 Heaton, *A Scholar*, 38.
14 Ibid., 67.
15 QUA PRO 1251/1/H, Mackintosh to Heaton, 26 March 1954; QUA, Mackintosh Papers, 6/162, "The Canadian Pulp and Paper Industry and the American Tariff," Ec2k, 5 May 1917.
16 Schorske, "A Life of Learning."
17 Jun, "Academics: From Peking University to Harvard."
18 QUA, Gerald S. Graham Papers, 73-070/1, File: Correspondence, W.A. Mackintosh, 1927–1965, Mackintosh to Graham, 24 February 1927.
19 Fogel, "Academic Economists."
20 Heaton, *A Scholar*, 6
21 QUA, PRO 1251/1/H, Heaton to Mackintosh, 29 March 1954.
22 Mason and Lamont, "The Harvard Department of Economics," 410. Mason, who studied at Harvard in 1919, had vivid recollections of Mackintosh as a graduate student some fifty years later, but left no

record of them (QUA, Mackintosh Paper Additions 1/2, Ruth Smith to Mackintosh, 16 October 1970). Mason was an interesting story in his own right. He worked in a copper mine, a zinc mine, on a cattle ranch, and in an oil field while completing a degree at the University of Kansas by the age of nineteen. He spent a year at Harvard before going to Oxford as a Rhodes Scholar, and then returned to Harvard in various capacities for the next sixty-three years of his life (Vernon and Dunlop, "Edward Sagendorph Mason").

23 QUA, Mackintosh Papers 12/Diary, 18 April 1917; 25 February 1917.

24 Ibid., 16 February 1917.

25 No record of the published version was found despite a search through the relevant volumes of the *Economic World*. That it appeared in print is apparent in an entry in Mackintosh's diary: "Letter from President of American Statistical Association asking me to give a paper on Cost of Production in relation to prices at the Joint Session with the American Economic Association! Truly Mr. Hill would be surprised if he knew Professor W.A. Mackintosh of Brandon College. Referred to my article in Economic World" (ibid., 21 November 1919).

26 Ibid., 2 March 1917.

27 Ibid., 2 April 1917. He was equally intrigued by the event leading up to the Russian Revolution, attending public talks by Leo Wiener, David Starr Jordan, and the Canadian, J.S. Ewart. "Does it mean the freedom of Russia or but another form of despotism?" (ibid., 16 March 1917).

28 This secular view is reflected in his appreciation for a story recounted to him by George Wilson: Sir Henry Jones, when accused by a woman of denying the divinity of Christ, replied, "Madam, I deny the divinity of no man" (ibid., 30 October 1919).

29 Mackintosh Private Papers, "Chronology." Henry Roper notes that Wilson's reading of Tolstoy led him to both celibacy and pacifism (Roper, "The Lifelong Pilgrimage of George E. Wilson").

30 QUA, Mackintosh Papers 12, Diary, 6 April 1917.

31 Ibid., 26–27 February 1917.

32 Ibid., 25 March 1917.

33 Ibid., 2 April 1917.

34 Mackintosh, "O.D. Skelton, 1878–1941," 271.

35 CBA, Brandon College, "Report of the Board of Directors, year ending August 31, 1917," 38; Brandon College, "Report of the Board of Directors, year ending August 31, 1919," 46.

36 Vera Leech, in McKenzie (ed.), *History of Brandon College*, 13.

37 CBA, Brandon College, *General Calendar*, 1917–1918, 63.

38 LAC MG30 D33, O.D. Skelton Papers, 1/1.13, Clark to Skelton, 15 February 1915.
39 Duncan A. MacGibbon in McKenzie (ed.), *History of Brandon College*, 15.
40 CBA, The Baptist Union of Western Canada. *Year Book, 1917*, 38. Stone and Garnett, *Brandon College*, 101.
41 Its earlier faculty members included W. Sherwood Fox (future president of the University of Western Ontario), and among Mackintosh's colleagues was the historian Chester New. The college might have noted with pride that, at the joint meetings of the Canadian Historical Association and Canadian Political Science Association in 1935, both presidential addresses were given by its former faculty members.
42 Horn, *Academic Freedom in Canada*, 82.
43 Rawlyk, "A.L. McCrimmon," in Rawlyk, ed., *Canadian Baptists*, 48.
44 CBA, Brandon College, *General Calendar, 1917–1918*, 9.
45 Stone and Garnett, *Brandon College*, 38.
46 BUA, Brandon College *Quill* (December 1917) 8(1): 12. MacGibbon observed that Brandon's students, drawn from rural backgrounds, tended to be older than typical undergraduates.
47 QUA, Mackintosh Papers 12, Diary, 6 October 1917.
48 Ibid., 16 October 1917.
49 Ibid., 6 October 1917.
50 BUA, Brandon College *Quill* (December 1917) 8(1): 50.
51 LAC RG32, Public Service Commission. Series C-2, 455/1895.05.21, W.A. Mackintosh to R.H. Coats, 3 November 1918.
52 Stone and Garnett, *Brandon College*, 102.
53 BUA, Brandon College *Quill* 9(1): 35; 8(2): 36; 8(2): 16–18.
54 Acland would later put his experience as an editor to better use when he became the King's Printer in Ottawa.
55 LAC, RG32, Public Service Commission. Series C-2, 455/1895.05.21, Mackintosh to R.H. Coats, 30 April, 1918.
56 Ibid., R.H. Coats to Mackintosh, 17 September 1918.
57 Ibid., Mackintosh to R.H. Coats, 30 April, 1918.
58 Ibid., Mackintosh to R.H. Coats, 13 May 1918.
59 Ibid., R.H. Coats to Mackintosh, 19 October 1918.
60 Ibid., Mackintosh to R.H. Coats, 18 November 1918.
61 QUA, Mackintosh Papers 12, Diary, 5 August 1918.
62 LAC, RG32, Series C-2, 455/1895.05.21, Mackintosh to R.H. Coats, 12 May 1919.
63 Mackintosh, "Economics, Prices and the War."

64 Dickinson, *Economic Motives*.
65 Mackintosh, "The Psychologist and Economics," 298–9.
66 Mackintosh, "Economics, Prices and the War," 10.
67 Mitchell, "A Square Deal."
68 Just as J.S. Woodsworth and Salem Bland had done in Winnipeg, A.E. Smith, a Methodist minister, formed a local Ministerial Association and was its delegate to the Trades and Labour Council. In 1920, he was elected to the provincial legislature under the banner of the Brandon Labour Party, leaving the city with the distinction of having elected two religious leaders – one Baptist and conservative (Whidden), the other a former Methodist and radical (Smith) – as their provincial and federal members of parliament. On his federal counterpart, Smith quipped that political faith was contained in the proverb: "Speech is silver, but silence is golden" (Smith, *All My Life*, 41). On Smith, see Mitchell, "From the Social Gospel to the 'Plain Bread of Leninism.'"
69 Mitchell, "A Square Deal," 46.
70 "Mackintosh Wants Special Commission," *Brandon Sun*, 1 April 1919.
71 Mackintosh, "Economics, Prices and the War," 14–15.
72 Mackintosh's primary purpose in visiting the West was to gather information for his doctoral thesis. Skelton published a short note on the "Winnipeg General Strike" in *Queen's Quarterly* 27 (July-September 1919).
73 The text to Bland's address can be found in the University of Saskatchewan Archives, Salem Bland Papers.
74 QUA, Mackintosh Papers 12, Diary, 12 August 1919.
75 Published as "Revolution in Winnipeg," *Labour/Le Travail* (2007) 60: 171–9.
76 Ibid., 174.
77 Ibid., 177.
78 Ibid., 178.
79 Mackintosh, "Adam Shortt, 1859–1931."
80 BUA, Brandon College *Quill* (March 1918) 8(2): 45. Irene Parlby was, at the time, involved with the United Farmers' Movement; two years later she become a cabinet minister in Alberta, and a decade later was among the "Famous Five" women to challenge the definition of "person" to the Supreme Court of Canada.
81 BUA, Brandon College *Quill* (June 1919) 9(3): 54.
82 He maintained an interest in the college's affairs, corresponding with "Susie" Cline and J.R. Evans during the next few years (Diary, 15 October 1919; 8 February 1920). In 1929 he sent congratulations

to Evans upon his appointment as college president and expressed the hope that "when you go touring about looking for men that you may turn up in Kingston some day: I should be most happy to see you" (BUA, Brandon College Administrative Records, BC 1, 5, 1913–1938, File 13, Mackintosh to J.R. Evans, 4 January 1929). Their next meeting, when Evans attended Mackintosh's installation as principal of Queen's, was indeed a happy occasion for both men.

CHAPTER FOUR

1 Cited in Mackintosh, *Agricultural Cooperation*, 20.
2 Ibid., viii.
3 Ibid., vii.
4 QUA, Mackintosh Papers 12, Diary, 9 October 1919.
5 Ibid., 24 October 1919.
6 Ibid., 20 October 1919.
7 Ibid., 17 October 1919.
8 Mason and Lamont, "The Harvard Department of Economics," 410.
9 Carlson, "The Education of an Economist before the Great Depression," 108–9.
10 QUA, Mackintosh Papers 12, Diary, 28 January 1920.
11 Ibid., 6 February 1920; 20 February 1920. Mason was more sympathetic, describing Ripley as looking like "a southern gentleman, sort of an intellectual colonel Sanders of Kentucky Fried Chicken, with a small goatee and a deprecating, ingenuous manner that concealed a sharp but friendly wit" (Mason and Lamont, "The Harvard Department," 403–4).
12 QUA, Mackintosh Papers 12, Diary, 9 January 1920.
13 Ibid., 26 November 1919; 26 October 1919.
14 Ibid., 19 February 1917.
15 Ibid., 13 October 1919. For a biographical note on Hedges see Mitchell, *Encyclopedia Brunoniana*.
16 As a testament to the lifelong friendships that were forged, Mackintosh would send both Merk and Schaeffer a copy of his "Inaugural Address" as principal of Queen's in 1951.
17 QUA, Mackintosh Papers 12, Diary, 20 January 1920.
18 Ibid., 18 October 1919; 18 January 1920.
19 Ibid., 25 October 1919, 14 November 1919. Hyde, of Quebec City, spent most of his academic career as professor of economics at the

University of Virginia (Snavely, "Memorial: Duncan Clark Hyde 1896–1957."

20 QUA, Mackintosh Papers 12, Diary, 18 January 1920.

21 Ibid., 26 October 1919.

22 Ibid., 28 January 1920.

23 HUA, Official Student Records, "William Archibald Mackintosh," UAV 161.272.5.

24 QUA, Mackintosh Papers 12, Diary, 19 June 1919.

25 On Dunning's place in Canadian business history, see Nerbas, *Dominion of Capital.*

26 Hedlin, "Edward A. Partridge." Other popular accounts of Partridge include Knuttila, "That Man Partridge" and Booth, "E.A. Partridge."

27 QUA, Mackintosh Papers 12, Diary, 9 August 1919.

28 Mackintosh, *Agricultural Cooperation*, 20n1. Another footnote pays similar tribute to Partridge: "Cooperation provided a temporary remedy for existing abuses in the grain trade ... Then would come true cooperation based on the ethics of Ruskin" (34n1).

29 Ibid., 4–5. In particular, it was spring wheat that was of particular value, since new milling techniques made it popular for blending with softer wheat varieties.

30 Ibid., 51–2.

31 Ibid., 72–3. Mackintosh was more circumspect about the likely influence of the wheat pools. To meet the emergency conditions during the latter stages of World War I, the federal government established the "Board of Grain Supervisors," followed by the Canadian Wheat Board, to assume complete control over the purchase and sale of wheat for export. The high price received for wheat created widespread support for the Wheat Board, so when it was disbanded farm organizations created wheat pools in each of the three provinces in 1923 to replicate its role. Pool members contracted to sell all their wheat to the pool for five years, and the pool would then be responsible for selling the grain and returning the value of the sales, less expenses. The pool's success, therefore, depended on its ability either to gain a higher world price or to increase the share of the total received by farmers. Since there was little avenue for the former, it was only through improved marketing that the pool could improve the livelihood of the farmer. Mackintosh held that there were only minor opportunities for greater efficiency through lowering administrative costs and the elimination of the middleman, but he did concede that

the pools might stabilize the price received by farmers. The pool essentially insulated the farmer from speculative swings in prices by controlling the flow of grain onto the market, but this required the pool to be a better forecaster of future prices than the grain exchange (Mackintosh, "The Canadian Wheat Pools").

32 Mackintosh, "Review of *The Challenge of Agriculture*," 205.
33 Mackintosh, "Review of *Pooling Wheat in Canada*," 353.
34 Mackintosh, *Agricultural Cooperation*, 87, 88–9.
35 Michell, "Review of *Agricultural Cooperation in Western Canada*," 181–2.
36 Vivian, "Review of *Agricultural Cooperation in Western Canada*," 284–5.
37 *American Economic Review* (1925) 15: 313.
38 Mackintosh, *Agricultural Cooperation*, 149.

PART TWO

1 For a discussion, see Owram, *The Government Generation*.
2 Coats, "Review" of *Statistical Contributions to Canadian Economic History*.

CHAPTER FIVE

1 "Queen's Theological Conference," *Queen's Review* (December 1928), 2(8): 264.
2 Mackintosh, "The General Election of 1921," 316.
3 Gibson, *To Serve*, 31.
4 LAC MG 30 D33, O.D. Skelton Papers, 1/1.33, Skelton to Taylor, 20 April 1923.
5 Mackintosh replaced (or more accurately, displaced) Humphrey Michell, the Oxford-trained economist, who moved to McMaster University, where he spent the remainder of his career.
6 Perry, "The Queen's Connection."
7 Macdonnell, "The Decline of the Arts Faculty," 9.
8 Clark, "University Training for Business – A Reply."
9 Mackintosh, "Psychologist and Economics," 304.
10 Ibid., 305.
11 Mackintosh, "The Curriculum of a Course in Commerce," 95.
12 QUA, *Queen's Tricolor, 1928*, 85.
13 LAC MG30 D33, O.D. Skelton Papers, 1/1.13, Skelton to Taylor, nd.

14 Creighton, *A Sum of Yesterdays*, 375. See also C.A. Ashley's entertaining account of his arrival in Kingston with Smails, "Two Hatless Englishmen."
15 LAC MG30 D33, O.D. Skelton Papers, 1/1.13, Skelton to Taylor, nd. Walker, forty-three years of age when hired, had previously worked at Brandon College and Regina College (Smails, "C.E. Walker, 1880–1942").
16 Smails, "The Department."
17 Creighton, *A Sum of Yesterdays*, 375.
18 Smails, "The Department."
19 LAC MG 30 D33, O.D. Skelton Papers, 1/1.33, Skelton to Taylor, 20 April 1923
20 Mackintosh. "O.D. Skelton," 273.
21 LAC, MG30 D33, O.D. Skelton Papers, 11/11-14. Diary, 17–20 July 1924.
22 Gibson, *To Serve*, 54.
23 QUA, Gibson Papers, Mackintosh to Principal Taylor, 13 August 1924.
24 Knox never completed his Harvard PhD, complaining that his supervisor, Allyn Young, was responsible for so many thesis students that it was difficult to get much of his time (QUA, Frank Knox Papers, 2/2.4(1/2), Knox to A.N. McLeod, 1 February 1945).
25 Upon visiting Wynne at Cambridge, Mackintosh was favourably impressed. "He seems to have ability, ambition and sufficient geniality to make him acceptable to students" (QUA Gibson Papers, Mackintosh to Principal Taylor, 13 August 1924).
26 Ashley, "Two Hatless Englishmen." He would return to Canada in 1930, joining the University of Toronto, where he would eventually replace Innis as chair of the department of political economy.
27 QUA Gibson Papers, Mackintosh to Principal Taylor, 13 August 1924; J. King, "Herbert Heaton." I am indebted to Professor King for drawing my attention to Heaton's background prior to his arrival in Canada.
28 LAC, MG 30 D33, O.D. Skelton Papers, 11/11–15, Diary, 20 August 1924.
29 Mackintosh, "Address to the Institute of Chartered Accountants of Ontario," 2.
30 LAC, MG30 D33, O.D. Skelton Papers, 1/1.33, Skelton to Taylor, 20 April 1923.
31 Ibid.
32 LAC, MG 30 D33, O.D. Skelton Papers, 11/11–15, Diary, 22 March 1925.

33 QUA, Mackintosh Papers, 8/206, Mackintosh to R.B. Taylor, 30 July 1925.

34 LAC, MG 30 D33, O.D. Skelton Papers, 11/11–15, Diary, 24 March 1925.

35 QUA, Mackintosh Papers, 8/206, Skelton to Mackintosh, 6 April 1925; Mackintosh to Skelton, 1 June 1925.

36 Ibid., Mackintosh to Skelton, 1 June 1925. Mackintosh's opinion of Heaton did not improve. He wrote to Clifford Clark that "I cannot say that the imported goods even measure up to my previous expectations. We seem to have acquired essentially a historian with a dash of journalism. One tried hard to retain one's illusions with regard to English education but outside of Cambridge people it seems to be getting more and more difficult" (ibid., Mackintosh to W.C. Clark, 12 March 1926).

37 Wynne would accept an appointment at Williams College, where he enjoyed a productive academic career. During World War II he worked with the Industrial Section of the US National Resources Planning Board (Samuels, ed., "Materials from Economics 5 and 6.") Mackintosh remained a steadfast supporter of Wynne, obtaining his services for the National Employment Commission, the Citizens' Research Institute, and with the research staff of the Rowell–Sirois Royal Commission on Dominion-Provincial Relations. (LAC, RG19, EAC 4663/187-EAC-46), Report on the Advisory Committee on Reconstruction, William H. Wynne, "Development of the Wartime Industrial Economy," Staff Report on Industrial Section of the National Resources Planning Board, June 1943); RG27, 3347, Arthur Purvis to Mackenzie King, 19 January 1937; RG19, Mackintosh Papers, 3589/T-03 Taxes, Mackintosh to D.L. Morrell, 7 February 1941). The devotion of graduates of Queen's to the institution was also apparent in the case of J.S. Prentice who obtained his BA and MA in economics there. Hired for one year as a temporary lecturer in 1927, he wrote to Mackintosh twenty-four years later: "Queen's meant so much to me as a student that I longed to live my life on that campus. But that was not to be." He went to Middlebury College in Vermont, where he eventually chaired a four-person department. "I have little reason to complain of my life in exile" (QUA PRO 1250/13/14, J.S. Prentice, 27 November 1951).

38 QUA, Mackintosh Papers, 6/206, Mackintosh to Clark, 12 March 1926.

39 LAC, MG 30 D33, O.D. Skelton Papers 1/11–15, Diary, 12 November 1925.

40 Gibson, *To Serve*, 60–1.

41 QUA, Mackintosh Papers 8/206, Skelton to Mackintosh, 28 April 1927.

42 LAC, MG30 D33, O.D. Skelton Papers, 11/17, Diary, 17 June 1927.

43 Mackintosh, "Economic Factors," 14, 15.

44 As a case in point, Mackintosh examined the economic and political relations between Canada and Vermont from the Declaration of Independence to the end of the War of 1812. "Geographically and economically ... Vermont was linked to the St. Lawrence. The artificial boundary of the forty-fifth parallel could not disguise the fact that the economic salvation of Vermont depended on the St. Lawrence system as a means of transportation for the bulky products of pioneer industry" ("Canada and Vermont," 30). This would explain Canada's overtures to annex Vermont during the Haldimand negotiations of the 1780s and the delay in Vermont's entry into the American union until 1791.

45 Mackintosh, "Economic Factors," 17.

46 Ibid., 21–2.

47 Ibid., 25

48 Mackintosh, "Laurentian Plateau," 537.

49 Ibid., 541.

50 Ibid., 549.

51 Ibid., 545.

52 Ibid., 546.

53 QUA, Mackintosh Papers, Additions 2/Addresses, "The Challenge of Growth," an address to the Canadian Institute of Mining and Metallurgy, 23 April 1957.

54 Mackintosh, "Laurentian Plateau," 549.

55 LAC, RG36/11, Advisory Board on Tariff and Taxation, 57/0-10-23, Mackintosh, "Some Contrasts in the Economic Development of Canada and the United States," an address delivered to the Statisticians, Economists and Actuaries Group, 1927.

56 Mackintosh, "General Election of 1921," 311.

57 *Queen's Quarterly* (1921) 29: 309–16; (1924) 31: 218–20; (1924) 31: 329–33; (1925) 32: 422–23; (1925) 33: 370–74.

58 QUA, Mackintosh Papers, 5/131.

59 Mackintosh, "Future Trend in Prices."

60 LAC, MG30, D33, O.D. Skelton Papers, 1/1-13, Michell to Mackintosh, 25 June 1923.

61 Ibid., Mackintosh to Michell, 26 June 1923.

62 Ibid., 11/11-11, Diary, 5 July 1923.

63 Friedman, "The Harvard Economic Service."

64 In 1923, Mackintosh wrote that "both Dean Skelton and myself would be glad to recommend Mr. Heasman, not as a brilliant statistician, but as a thoroughly able and hard-working boy capable of good independent work, very reliable and ambitious enough to make good" (LAC RG32. Public Service Commission. Series C-2, 455/1895.05.21, Mackintosh to R.H. Coats, 5 April 1923). A few years later he proposed Ross M. Winter, who had completed work for his MA, as "a thoroughly dependable and intelligent student who is quite capable of doing independent work ... he has the prime requisite of the statistician, gumption. I should expect him to do a very creditable piece of work even in competition with men of more experience" (Mackintosh to Coats, 11 May 1926.)

65 LAC RG32, Public Service Commission, Series C-2, 455/1895.05.21, Mackintosh to Coats, 11 May 1926, 14 May 1926.

66 Ibid., Mackintosh to Coats, 16 April 1927.

67 QUA, Graham Papers, 73-070/1/Correspondence, W.A. Mackintosh, 1927–1965, Mackintosh to Graham, 24 February 1927; LAC RG32, Series C-2, 455/1895.05.21, Mackintosh to Coats, 12 February 1927. Salaries at the DBS ranged from $1,800 to $2,280 for a principal statistics clerk and from $2,400 to $2,800 for a "head" statistical clerk. Coats wrote that he only had a vacancy in the junior position, prompting Herbert Heaton to reply: "I was talking over with Mackintosh the matter you raised on Saturday concerning Caldwell. We both think he would do that work well, and would go farther in it than he is likely to do in teaching. The trouble is that he wouldn't want to start at a salary so much below what he has been getting. That stubbornness may wear off as he gets better" (ibid., Coats to Mackintosh, 26 February 1927; Heaton to Coats, 11 April 1927). Other economists working during the summer for the DBS in the period included Kenneth Taylor (McMaster), Benjamin Hurd (Brandon), and H.R. Kemp (Toronto).

68 Canada. Department of Labour, *Investigation into the Proprietary Articles Trade Association*.. Mackintosh's brief may be found in QUA, Mackintosh Papers, 9/215.

69 QUA Mackintosh Papers, 1/43, "Professor E.H. Morrow Calls Registrar's Report on PATA a Hasty Decision," *Hardware and Metal* (30 October 1926) 38(44): 26–7, 53.

70 Ibid., 1/43, "Editorial," in *Canadian Pharmaceutical Industry* (November 1926) 60(4): 193–4.

71 "The Public and the PATA," *Canadian Forum* (November 1926) 7(24): 38–9.
72 LAC RG79, Advisory Board on Tariff and Taxation, 215/80-13.
73 Among the economists hired during the first few years of the board's existence were Gilbert Jackson (Toronto), H.R. Kemp (Toronto), Henry C. Grant (Manitoba), and W.R. Maxwell (Dalhousie).
74 Bryce, *Maturing in Hard Times*, 27.
75 LAC, RG36/11, Advisory Board on Tariff and Taxation, 57/0-10-6, Mackintosh to Hector McKinnon, 13 July 1927.
76 Ibid., William H. Moore to W.C. [*sic*] Mackintosh, 13 July 1927.
77 Ibid., Mackintosh to Moore, 16 July 1927.
78 Ibid., Mackintosh to Moore, 4 August 1927, 9 August 1927.
79 Ibid., Mackintosh to Moore, 11 August 1929.
80 Ibid., Fridinburg to Mackintosh, 19 October 1927.
81 As he wrote in a memorandum: "Number 563 [Dress goods, etc. in the grey]: It is generally admitted that this item will stand reduction as most of these goods are imported rather than produced in the country. It is further stated that competition in the garment trades and among retailers is such that there is no doubt that the saving in duty will be passed on to the consumer and will not be absorbed by the dyer" (ibid., "Memorandum on Tariff Items 554 to 568a – Wool, Woollen Yarn and Woollen Fabrics," nd).
82 Ibid., Moore to Mackintosh, 19 November 1927; 2 December 1927.
83 "March of Events," *Journal of the Canadian Bankers' Association (JCBA)* (1925) 32: 406.
84 LAC RG36/11, 9/3–15, W.A. Mackintosh, "Confidential Memorandum to the Chairman: Visit to Sydney, Cape Breton," 15 September 1928.
85 *JCBA* (April 1928) 35: 226.
86 "The National Budget," *JCBA* (April 1928) 35: 223–30.
87 Mackintosh received $3,574 from the Tariff Board ($400 per month for roughly nine months' work) between 1927 and 1929 (Canada. House of Commons. *Debates*. 3rd session, 19–20 George V, 1929, vol. 1, 1025; 1930, vol. 3, 2551; Mackintosh Private Papers, Income Tax Returns).
88 Mackintosh Private Papers, Income Tax Returns.
89 LAC, O.D. Skelton Papers, 1/13, Mackintosh to Skelton, 26 June 1923.
90 QUA, Gibson Papers, Mackintosh to Principal Taylor, 13 August 1924
91 Mackintosh Private Papers, Ian S. Wright to W.A. Mackintosh, 9 October 1924.

92 LAC, MG30 D33, O.D. Skelton Papers, 11/15, Diary 25 May 1925.
93 Ibid., 11/16, 22 July 1926.
94 Ibid., 23 July 1926.
95 Newman, "The Ottawa Establishment," 34; Pearson, *Mike*, I: 58.
96 LAC RG36/11, 56/0-10-6, Mackintosh to McKinnon, 3 September 1927.
97 Mackintosh was nominated to the RSC by Skelton, Stephen Leacock, and R.H. Coats (LAC, RG32, Series C-2, 455/1895.05.21, O.D. Skelton to R.H. Coats, 15 February 1929).
98 LAC RG36/11, 56/0-10-6, Mackintosh to Moore, 3 May 1928.

CHAPTER SIX

1 QUA, Gerald S. Graham Papers, 73-070/1, Correspondence, Mackintosh to Graham, 16 February 1961.
2 Innis, "Teaching of Economic History in Canada," 63.
3 LAC, Advisory Board on Tariff and Taxation, RG36/11, 57/0-10-6, Mackintosh to McKinnon, 20 August 1927.
4 See Neil Smith's account of Bowman's role in US foreign policy in *American Empire*. For a discussion of the project, see Wright, *The Professionalization of History*, and Brison, *Rockefeller, Carnegie, and Canada*.
5 Brison, *Rockefeller, Carnegie, and Canada*, 156–8. Mackintosh, a fitful diarist, left a few pages of notes during June, probably in 1930, of meetings with R.W. Murchie, Duncan MacGibbon, Premier John Bracken, and others in Winnipeg as part of a month-and-a-half trip that would also take him to Regina, Saskatoon, Calgary, and Edmonton. He received $4,000 for the project from the SSRC grant and his university salary was reduced by an equivalent amount (Mackintosh Private Papers, Income Tax Files; QUA, PRO, 1250/ Salaries and Status, "Queen's University Salary List as of March 31, 1931"; "Queen's University Salary List, April 1932."
6 Vol. 1 – W.A. Mackintosh, *Prairie Settlement*; Vol. 2 – Arthur S. Morton, *History of Prairie Settlement*, and Chester Martin, *"Dominion Lands" Policy* (1938); Vol. 4 – Mackintosh, assisted by A.B. Clark, G.A. Elliott, and W.W. Swanson, *Economic Problems of the Prairie Provinces* (1935); Vol. 5 – R.W. Murchie, assisted by William Allen and J. F. Booth, *Agricultural Progress on the Prairie Frontier* (1936); Vol 6 – C.A. Dawson, assisted by R.W. Murchie, *The Settlement of the Peace River Country: A Study of a Pioneer Area* (1934); Vol. 7 –

C.A. Dawson, *Group Settlement: Ethnic Communities in Western Canada* (1936); Vol 8 – C.A. Dawson and Eva R. Younge, *Pioneering in the Prairie Provinces: The Social Side of the Settlement Process* (1940); and Vol. 9 – A.R.M. Lower, *Settlement and the Forest Frontier in Eastern Canada* and Harold A. Innis, *Settlement and the Mining Frontier* (1936). Mackintosh gave a preliminary report of the project in "Pioneer Problems" and in "The Economic Problem of Western Canada."

The missing Volume 3, with D.A. McArthur to write the first section and W.A. Carrothers the second, was never published because of McArthur's neglect and then illness. Efforts to complete the volume dragged on until 1944. With news that McArthur's health was improving, Ellen Elliott of the Macmillan Company of Canada wrote to him in January 1942 with the gentle reminder that "Part II by Professor Carrothers has been set up in type for the last five years, awaiting the completion of your own Part I." Eighteen months later, however, McArthur was dead, with no further word on any progress. When Elliott appealed to Mackintosh, he confessed that "Volume III has been a great source of worry, and I made fruitless efforts to get Dr. McArthur either to complete the manuscript or relinquish the work." In a last effort to salvage the volume, Chester Martin and Gerry Riddell were dispatched to investigate the state of the material left by McArthur. A "voluminous" amount of material was found among his papers, but nothing approaching the basis to a manuscript. Riddell was prepared to submit a manuscript of his own, but the Macmillan Company had, by then, lost patience with the project. "[W]e are not at all anxious to incur any further expense," Elliott informed Mackintosh in May 1944. "Publication was subsidized to some extent by the Social Science Research Council, but I do not need to tell you that on the whole scheme we have lost money." Mackintosh reluctantly admitted defeat and agreed that all but 150 copies of the unbound pages to the series that "crammed" Macmillan of Canada's warehouse should be destroyed (LAC, Mackintosh Papers, 3579/McC–0, Mackintosh to Elliott, 2 September 1943; Elliott to Mackintosh, 2 May 1944).

7 *Prairie Settlement*, 44, 185.
8 *Economic Problems*, 1, 32, 20, 4, 8, 14.
9 Ibid., 10.
10 Ibid., 31.
11 Ibid., 33, 32.
12 Ibid., 185.

13 *Prairie Settlement*, 187, xiv, 201. Mackintosh elaborated upon the expected rate of settlement in relation to Canadian immigration policy in "Canada as an Area for Settlement." Although he saw immigration being closely tied to prairie settlement, he was critical of Canadian policy for not exercising greater control over the inflow during periods of high unemployment. He was equally critical of the preference given to immigrants from northern Europe: "it is not desirable that race should form the basis of such selection."

14 UTA A76-0025 006 (06), Biss to Innis, 10 June 1935; Innis, "Review of *Prairie Settlement.*" Biss informed Innis that: "Waines [of the University of Manitoba] feels that Mackintosh books were palpably written from 'Ottawa or somewhere in the East' and not from here." Innis responded that "I suppose there is some point to Waines' criticism of Mackintosh's volume but he seems a little unfair and a bit regional or provincial" (UTA A76-0025 006(03), Biss to Innis, 30 May 1935; LAC Spry Papers, Innis to Biss, nd).

15 *Canadian Journal of Economics and Political Science* (1935) 1: 110–16; 2: 297–9; QUA, Mackintosh Papers 8/206, Skelton to Mackintosh, 4 June 1934.

16 Taylor, "Review," 138.

17 M.J. Bonn, *Geographical Journal* (1934) 84: 531–2; *Geographical Journal* (1935) 86: 547–548; *Australian Geographer* (November 1937).

18 QUA, Mackintosh Papers, 11/15, Isaiah Bowman to Mackintosh, 4 June 1935.

19 QUA PRO 1251/1/C, Mackintosh to Clark, 14 March 1953.

20 "Book Reviews: Economic History," *Queen's Quarterly* (1933) 40: 486; Mackintosh, "Innis on Canadian Economic Development," 189.

21 Wilson, "Review," 575.

22 Mackintosh, "Innis," 188.

23 Innis, "Canadian Frontiers of Settlement: A Review," 105–6.

24 Innis, *Fur Trade*, 393; Mackintosh, "Economic Factors," 25.

25 *JCBA* (July 1933) 40(4). Mackintosh was equally subdued in his review of Innis's *Selected Documents*.

26 Donald, "The Canadian Political Science Association."

27 QUA, A.R.M. Lower Papers, v. 1, Lower to Bladen, 2 September 1938.

28 Innis, "The Penetrative Powers of the Price System," 308.

29 Mackintosh, "Discussion," of H.A. Innis, "Transportation," 202.

30 Published as "Some Aspects of a Pioneer Economy."

31 Ibid., 457.

32 Ibid., 460–1. Mackintosh addressed Keynes's argument about the elasticity of investment to the interest rate. "Having cast out Mr. Hawtrey's contention that the rate of interest influenced the amount of stocks held by dealers as absurd because the speculative risk so far exceeded the interest cost, Mr. Keynes is for similar reasons now doubtful of its close relation to the volume of long-term investment. But where trading in equities as contrasted with permanent investment for income is common practice, the rate of interest used in capitalizing the returns from land and durable capital goods has very important effects on the amount of new investment. The pioneer is always a speculator, always a trader in equities, and I am inclined to think that the rate of interest has more importance in new countries than in old except in so far as it is overshadowed by the importance of innovations" (ibid., 463).

33 Innis, "Notes on Problems of Adjustment in Canada."

34 UTA, Innis Papers. Mackintosh to Innis, 4 January 1936; Mackintosh to Innis, 6 March 1936; Mackintosh to Innis, 12 March 1936; 17 March 1936. Mackintosh was naïve about the bureaucracy at the University of Toronto and the apparent havoc he was wreaking on its bookkeeping, so he consented to cash the cheque ("I am more concerned about being a nuisance") but reiterated that he would keep the money to offset the cost of a visit to Queen's by a Toronto colleague.

35 Innis, *The Bias of Communication*, xxvii.

36 *Canadian Journal of Economics and Political Science* (1940) 6: 563–71.

37 Mackintosh, "The Use of Case Material in Economics," 35.

38 Mackintosh, "An Economist Looks at Economics."

39 Ibid., 313, 315, 320, 321.

40 Ibid., 316.

41 Bladen, *Bladen on Bladen*, 70–1. He adds that "Innis was elected. Whether it helped to clinch the appointment I cannot know. But the generosity and good judgement of Bill Mackintosh deserves to be recorded." One assumes that Bladen correctly recalls the spirit of the conversation but not all of the details, for Innis was elected president of the CPSA one year after Mackintosh.

42 Cited in Watson, *Marginal Man*, 170.

43 Mackintosh, "Adam Shortt, 1859–1931," 164, 176.

44 Smails, "The Department of Political and Economic Science."

45 Mackintosh would write in 1935 that Curtis "has not the natural aptitude for teaching that Knox has but he has good standards, a

steady persistence that brings results ultimately, and energy with which to tackle outside work. In many respects, he has a better reputation outside Queen's (I mean through the country generally) than has Knox though I regard Knox as the more valuable man. He and McQueen are under consideration for the post at Manitoba, though I think he does not know this yet" (QUA Gibson Papers, Mackintosh to Fyfe, 18 March 1935).

46 UOSA, RG2001.1. Murray Correspondence, File A53, Mackintosh to Murray, 13 May 1936. Corry's appointment occurred despite the resistance of J.M. Macdonnell, who favoured the candidacy of George Smith, a historian at the University of Alberta. Since R.C. Wallace had yet to take up the principalship, Macdonnell advises William McNeill as acting principal, to canvas opinions outside of the department. McNeill responded succinctly: "The situation is then that Mackintosh, Head of the Department, backed by Skelton a former Head, and by Dr. W.C. Clark, a former member of the Department, strongly advises the appointment of Corry and with finality rejects Smith. I do not see under these circumstances it is possible to do anything but accept the recommendation. It would be counter to sound principles of administration for me to bring in a recommendation for Smith in view of the expert opinion in favour of Corry" (QUA PRO 1251 2/ File: Correspondence re. Corry's Appointment, McNeill to Macdonnell, 6 June 1936).

47 QUA PRO 1250/13/7, Mackintosh to Wallace, 13 November 1936.

48 *JCBA* (April 1925) 32(3).

49 *JCBA* (July 1937) 44(4): 360–1; (October 1937) 45(1); (January 1938) 45(2): 139.

50 QUA PRO 1250/13/8, James A. Richardson to R.S. McLaughlin, 14 July 1937; Richardson to Wallace, 31 July 1937.

51 Ibid., Mackintosh to A.B. Purvis, 22 July 1937. Margaret Mackintosh also helped to secure all the publications of the International Labour Office (J.C. Cameron to Wallace, 1 February 1939).

52 QUA, Mackintosh Papers, 8/206, Bryce Stewart to Mackintosh, 2 June 1937. Cameron, forty-four, obtained a B.Comm. and M.Comm. from Queen's before joining Canada Packers (Queen's University, Industrial Relations Centre, "Industrial Relations at Queen's," 2).

53 In 1947, F.A. Sherman of the Dominion Foundries and Steel Limited (Dofasco) in Hamilton also declined to support the IR section because its "pro-labour sentiment is far too strong" by virtue of its insistence that "collective bargaining is the one and only answer to good labour

relations" (QUA PRO 1250/13/7, F.A. Sherman to Wallace, 30 June 1943). In 1947, J.S. Vanderploeg, of Anaconda American Brass Ltd., wrote to Principal Wallace objecting to the participation of union leaders C.H. Millard and Madeleine Parent at a conference sponsored by the Queen's IR section: "Frankly, we dislike contributing, however indirectly, to the furtherance of at least some of the ideas of these two individuals." Wallace responded: "It is essential in University that opinions that may be of influence in the community should be heard, in order that critical judgement may be made of them by students and staff. And students and staff are critical; they do not swallow half-baked assertions" (ibid., J.S. Vanderploeg to Wallace, 23 July 1947; Wallace to Vanderploeg, 18 August 1947).

54 QUA, Frank Knox Papers, 1/1.5, Diary, 30 November 1935.

55 Mackintosh Private Papers, McQueen Correspondence, Mackintosh to McQueen, 10 February 1936.

56 Spafford, *No Ordinary Academics*, 56.

57 LAC RG32, Series C-2, 455/1895.05.21. Mackintosh to R.H. Coats, 6 May 1929.

58 Ferguson, "He Was One of Us," 19–20.

59 After much persuasion, McQueen accepted the position of head of the department of political economy and political science at the University of Manitoba (Mackintosh Private Papers, McQueen Correspondence, McQueen to Mackintosh, 1 March 1933; Mackintosh to McQueen, 19 March 1934; QUA PRO 1250/18/16, McQueen to Wallace, 19 March 1940).

60 *Queen's Quarterly* 40 (1933): 264–81, 424–40, 580–99; 41 (1934): 81–98. Mackintosh also collaborated with Knox on *A Survey of the Electrical Equipment Manufacturing Industry of Canada*, and with Robert Owen Merriman on *Trade and Industry*. The latter, published some five years after Merriman's premature death, was Mackintosh's tribute to his former colleague. Merriman served for years as a tutor in economics after completing his BA (1922) and MA (1925) at Queen's (QR (November 1934) 8(8): 230). Despite the good intent, the book was a distinct failure as an introductory survey of economic history.

61 Brecher, *Monetary and Fiscal Thought*.

62 Mackintosh, "Doctoring the Gold Standard"; "Current Events: Banks and Banking," *Queen's Quarterly* (1923) 31: 218–20.

63 Mackintosh, "Doctoring the Gold Standard," 65, 66, 69. His stylized account of the impact on an increase in the money supply anticipated the expectations-adjusted inflation models of the 1970s. There is a

short-term stimulus to output but "the final result ... must always be the same. The increased purchasing power which credit gave is finally cancelled by the rise in prices. Production which had been undertaken at a rate of increase based on increasing purchasing power cannot be equalled by sales and industry goes through one of those periods of readjustments which have such lamentable results" (ibid., 66). His analysis of the "Future Trend of Prices" (1927) reiterated this adherence to the quantity theory of money: the pattern on inflation and deflation in the world was explained in the relationship between the world stock of gold and productive capacity, and in Canada as modified by the rate of capital inflows.

64 *JCBA* (January 1929) 36(2).

65 Mackintosh, "Problems of Reparations." On a more optimistic note, and foreshadowing his involvement in the discussions leading up to the Bretton Woods agreement, he was intrigued by the idea of an international bank as a clearing house for war debts and repayments, and held that there were "tremendous potentialities" for broadening its role to wider banking functions and for the control of gold and other forms of international exchange.

66 *JCBA* (January 1929) 36(2); (April 1929) 36(3).

67 *JCBA* (July 1929) 36(4): 320, 321. Similarly, the United States was acting as "a bully" in proposing to raise the duty on luxury goods and dairy products, identified as particularly harmful to France and Canada respectively (*JCBA* (January 1930) 37(2): 121).

68 *JCBA* (October 1929) 37(1).

69 *JCBA* (January 1930) 37(2): 121.

70 Kindleberger, *World in Depression*, 292.

71 Mackintosh, "Trade Barriers as an Obstacle to Prosperity," 1.

72 Mackintosh, "Central Banks and Business Recovery," *JCBA* (July 1931) 38(4): 360–3.

73 *JCBA* (October 1932) 40(1): 19.

74 *JCBA* (January 1933) 40(2); (October 1933) 41(1): 9; (July 1934) 41(4); (April 1934) 41(3): 291.

75 Mackintosh, "The Progress of Canada's Recovery," 391. As Mackintosh calculated the situation, the average farmer in 1932 harvested 15 bushels per acre. After keeping 1½ acres for seed and paying 4½ acres for taxes and 7 acres for mortgage and other interest payments, he was left with 2 bushels per acre at less at 30 cents per bushel.

76 *JCBA* (January 1933) 40: 154–5.

77 Mackintosh, "The Progress of Canada's Recovery," 394.

78 *JCBA* (October 1930) 38(1). Citing data from the World Economic Conference of 1927, Mackintosh noted that the average tariff rate in Canada (23%) was lower than in the US (37%), Argentina (29%), and Australia (27%), slightly higher than in France, Italy, Germany, and much higher than in the Scandinavian countries ("Canadian Tariff Policy").

79 On anti-dumping legislation, Mackintosh wrote that "The weakness of the new amendment is that where it is almost impossible for a government department to find out costs of production in Canada it is quite impossible for them to discover costs of production of foreign countries. There is, moreover, no machinery for undertaking investigations of this sort" (*JCBA* (October 1930) 38: 15) More generally, he held that the Bennett government's "competitive tariff" changes, designed to equalize the cost of production between domestic and foreign producers, was not only wrong-headed but impossible to implement fairly given the lack of adequate data (*JCBA* (October 1932) 40(1)).

80 Mackintosh, "Trade Barriers."

81 Issue was taken with Keynes's "sophisticated argument" in favour of tariffs and export controls. Keynes maintained that the efficiency loss of protectionism might be justified in the United Kingdom in terms of a better distribution of wealth and a higher standard of living. The Queen's economists held that short-term adjustments to the tariff schedule in support of industries with idle capacity was a crude and ineffective means of reallocating resources (Mackintosh, "Canadian Trade Policy").

82 "Trade Barriers," 5.

83 *JCBA* (January 1938) 45(2): 130; (January 1939) 46(2).

84 Brecher, *Monetary and Fiscal Thought*, Chapter 4.

85 Mackintosh, "Canadian Politics," 331; *JCBA* (January 1929) 36(2): 113; (April 1929) 36(3): 210.

86 Mackintosh applauded the attempt to overcome the divided jurisdiction of the US federal system in order to impose uniform labour standards, but thought that Roosevelt confused this with "a theory of under-consumption and higher wages" ("The Progress of Canada's Recovery," 399).

87 *JCBA* (April 1933) 40(3): 291.

88 *JCBA* (April 1933) 40(3); (July 1933) 40(4); (April 1934) 41(3); (January 1935) 42(2): 173; Mackintosh, "Review of *Problems of Staple Production in Canada*."

89 "Financial Problems of Our Federal System," *Queen's Quarterly* (1933) 40: 587.

90 *JCBA* (1928) 35: 110, 111. Three years later he complained that the "growing tendency in Canada to regard Confederation as a contract to which the provinces are the parties is a doctrine which it is difficult to support by reading the British North America Act or the Confederation Debates ... It would seem questionable how far Ontario could claim to be a party to a contract when the province of Ontario was in fact created by the legislation resulting from the contract. However this may be, the view has been urged by several provincial premiers and is certain to find widespread support" (*JCBA* (1931) 38: 120).

91 *JCBA* (January 1934) 41(2): 189.

92 Mackintosh did not appreciate the significance of changes in the Bank Act at the time for he did not oppose Canada's return to the gold standard in 1926 because the Canadian dollar was at parity with the US dollar and Canada held large gold reserves (*JCBA* (July 1926) 33: 417).

93 Most of the seventeen economists from Canadian universities making submissions "followed more or less closely the lines of argument which were well known among Canadian economists and had been chiefly promulgated by the economists of Queen's University" (Plumptre, "Evidence Presented to the Canadian Macmillan Commission," 60). Two of those opposed to a central bank – Humphrey Michell and W.W. Swanson – formerly taught at Queen's. For a perspective on the creation of a central bank in Canada, see Bordo and Redish, "Why Did the Bank of Canada Emerge in 1935?"

94 LAC RG33-17, v. 2 Royal Commission on Banking and Currency. Proceedings 1933, 6: 3060–1.

95 Ibid., 6: 3057, 3057–8, 3058–59a.

96 Ibid., 6: 3057, 3058, 3052.

97 Brecher, *Monetary and Fiscal Thought*, 88.

98 *JCBA* (October 1939) 47(1): 6.

99 QUA, F.W. Gibson Papers, 1125/5/14, Mackintosh to Principal Fyfe, 2 March 1934. Fyfe agreed to the request under the normal terms that the cost of hiring a replacement be paid out of the salary of the individual on leave. Mackintosh's salary at the time was $4,500. With Smails and Walker sharing the $500 stipend for the director of the commerce courses, and McQueen receiving a salary of $2,800 as a teaching replacement, the small residual covered the premiums on Mackintosh's retirement annuity (ibid., Fyfe to Mackintosh, 5 March 1934).

100 *Toronto Star* (6 September 1934), 26. See his collection of postcards, QUA, Mackintosh Papers, Box 9.
101 QUA Gibson Papers, Mackintosh to Fyfe, 18 March 1935.
102 Lela Rasminsky would recall "the warmth and friendliness of the two of you to two youngsters that we were – not that you were that much older but Bill was already a respected professor" (QUA Mackintosh Papers, Additions, 1/Death, Lela Rasminsky to Jean Mackintosh, 9 January 1971).
103 *JCBA* (January 1935).
104 Mackintosh, "Italy Faces the World." In 1935 he addressed the Canadian Clubs of Toronto ("Italy under Mussolini") and Ottawa ("European Problems in 1935"). The *Globe and Mail* gave an account of the latter under the headline "Duce's Energy Given Praise: But Efforts to Gain 'Prestige' Criticized" (5 November 1935, 11).
105 QUA, Mackintosh Papers, 11/Correspondence, 1935–1966, Bonar to Mackintosh, 10 January 1935; Mackintosh Papers, Additions, 1/ Bonar, James. Since his retirement to England, Bonar had stayed abreast of affairs at Queen's (University of Glasgow Library, Special Collections, MS Gen 518. Letters from James Bonar to G.F. Shirras, 1926-1939; MS Gen 518/64 9 July 1929, MS Gen 518/182 31 August 1931, and MS Gen 518/423, 9 December 1936).
106 QUA, Gibson Papers, Mackintosh to Fyfe, 18 March 1935; Mackintosh Papers, 11/6 "Carnegie Endowment for International Peace."
107 Mackintosh, "Public Affairs: The British Elections."
108 Mackintosh, "Central Europe and the German Appeasement," 407; and "Retrospect and Prospect in Europe."
109 *JCBA* (October 1935) 43(1): 1; *JCBA* (October 1936) 44: 132; "France – 1935," 325.
110 *JCBA* (July 1936) 43: 370–1.
111 Mackintosh, "Retrospect and Prospect in Europe," 90.
112 Mackintosh, "Central Europe and the German Appeasement," 411.
113 Angus, *Summerhill.*
114 Cited in Gibson, *To Serve*, 136.
115 QUA Gibson Papers, D.H. Laird to Fyfe, 24 April 1934.
116 QUA, Mackintosh Papers, 11/1 Mackintosh to Aberhart, 15 September 1936.
117 QUA, Gibson Papers, Macdonnell to Wallace, 17 April 1937; Mackintosh Papers 8/206, P.E. Mackenzie, Chairman, Board of Governors of the University of Saskatchewan to Mackintosh, 29 April

1937; Additions, 1/Correspondence, 1930–1950, 11 May 1937; UOSA, RG2001.1. Murray Correspondence, file B54, Mackintosh to Murray, 6 May 1937; McKenzie to Murray, 11 May 1937; and Murray to Mackintosh, 19 May 1937.

PART THREE

1 Pickersgill, "Mackenzie King's Political Attitudes and Public Policies," 23.

2 Bryce, "The Canadian Economy in the 1930s," 113.

3 Cited in Drummond, *Political Economy at the University of Toronto*, 61.

4 Keynes, *Collected Writings*, v. 14: 98n and Besomi, ed., *Roy F. Harrod's Interwar Papers and Correspondence*. The passage in Robertson's letter to Harrod (9 November 1936) runs as follows: "The Neo-Keynesian formulation seems to me definitely retrograde in various respects. In particular, it divorces money held for 'precautionary motives' from direct connection with the rate of interest, which is supposed to be relevant only to money held for 'speculative motives,' i.e. because it is thought that the rate of interest may change. Thus interest is paid because interest is expected to change! (I have seen an effective criticism by Plumptre along these lines)." Robertson repeats his reference to Plumptre's criticism of Keynes's liquidity preference theory in *Essays in Monetary Theory*, 25.

5 Bryce's lecture notes, along with those of Tarshis, constitute the bulk of Rymes, *Keynes's Lectures, 1932–35*.

6 Bryce, "Keynes as Seen by His Students," in Patinkin and Leith (eds.), *Keynes, Cambridge, and the General Theory*, 41.

7 Kindleberger, *Life of an Economist*, 65.

8 Harcourt, "Lorie Tarshis."

9 Ibid., 1248–9.

10 At the outset of World War II, Bryce informed W.C. Clark that "several young men have spoken or written to me about positions, but I have hesitated to mention them to you until some sort of demand appeared. Also, I know of at least one and possibly several competent young Canadian economists now teaching in the States who could probably be brought back here. In particular, Dr. Lorie Tarshis, of Tufts College, who was at Cambridge at the same time as I was, might be useful in connection with cost of living and price control, wage policy, et cetera, if there is need of an economist specializing in that field" (LAC RG19, R.B. Bryce Papers, 3444/Bryce's Personal correspondence, 1938–39,

Bryce to Clark, 28 September 1939). Bryce wrote to Tarshis on 23 August 1940 indicating that Kenneth Taylor wanted to know if Tarshis was available to work for the Wartime Prices and Trade Board. Some time after, Tarshis informed Bryce that "[I] haven't had any word from Taylor yet. Do you think there is any hope? I'm pretty soon going to have to become an American unless I get something in Canada" (ibid., Bryce to Tarshis, 23 August 1940; Tarshis to Bryce, n.d.).

11 Spafford, *No Ordinary Academics*, 147.

12 Samuelson, "Credo of a Lucky Textbook Author," 157.

13 Harcourt, "An Early Post-Keynesian."

14 Ibid.

15 Ainley, "Mabel F. Timlin"; Dimand, "How Keynes Came to Canada."

16 Johnson, "Canadian Contributions to the Discipline of Economics since 1945."

17 The best overviews are provided by Wolfe, "The Rise and Demise," and Campbell, *Grand Illusions,* chap. 1.

18 Neatby, *Politics of Chaos*, 84; Smiley, "Introduction" to *The Rowell-Sirois Report*; Bradford, "Writing Public Philosophy."

19 Skidelsky, "The Political Meaning of the Keynesian Revolution." For a more general discussion, see Peter Hall, "Introduction."

20 Hall, "Introduction;" see also Christie and Gauvreau (eds.), *Cultures of Citizenship in Post-War Canada, 1940.*

21 Wolfe, "The Delicate Balance"; McInnis, *Harnessing Labour Confrontation.*

22 Skelton, "Government Expenditure in Depression," 376; cited in Owram, *The Government Generation*, 204.

23 Patinkin, *Anticipations of the General Theory?*

24 Hicks ("Mr Keynes and the "Classics") characterized a simple Keynesian model in terms of investment function, in which investment was strictly determined by the level of national income; a consumption (or saving) function, where national income again was the sole determinant; and a liquidity preference function.

25 As Patinkin (*Anticipations*) makes the case, investment was the key component of aggregate demand, and it was through changes in output, not the interest rate, that investment and saving were brought into equilibrium. In this respect, Patinkin is in agreement with James Meade's earlier assertion that it was the investment-savings relationship that was the novel aspect of a Keynesian model.

26 For a review of Canadian fiscal policy in the immediate postwar period, see Wolfe, "The Rise and Demise," and Campbell, *Grand Illusions*.

CHAPTER SEVEN

1 LAC MG 26, Mackenzie King Diary, 11 March 1938.
2 King Diary, 8 April 1936.
3 This point is emphasized by Struthers, *No Fault of Their Own*, 143.
4 Canada, *Interim Report of the National Employment Commission*, 5.
5 *Globe and Mail* (16 May 1936), 1.
6 *Globe and Mail* (21 April 1936), 1.
7 *Financial Post* (7 August 1936), 9.
8 *Financial Post* (25 April 1936), 2.
9 *Financial Post* (23 May 1936), 18; (7 August 1936), 9, 13. Marois, Young, and McLean would play a limited role on the NEC (although McLean produced one frightening memorandum on monetary policy that was politely acknowledged and then ignored by the other commissioners), leaving Purvis, Moore, Mackintosh, and Sutherland handle the majority of the work.
10 The committee produced a report by H.M. Cassidy, *Unemployment Relief in Ontario*.
11 LAC, MG26, W.L.M. King Papers, J4 C137, 496.
12 LAC MG26 King Papers, J1 C3692: 193,524, Purvis to King, 31 March 1936.
13 King Diary, 5 August 1936.
14 During the 1936–37 fiscal year, Mackintosh received $1,786 in salary for ninety-four days of work at a per-diem rate of $19 (LAC RG27 3348/5).
15 LAC, RG27, National Employment Commission, 3374/8, W.A. Mackintosh, "Economic Fundamentals of Recovery. Much of this memorandum is included in Section II, Chapter A of the NEC's *Final Report*.
16 Ibid., 1.
17 Ibid., 8.
18 Ibid., 10.
19 LAC RG27, 3374/12, Mackintosh, Memorandum: "Public Works."
20 Ibid.
21 LAC MG 26 1, King Paper, C3728: 206, 493–512.
22 LAC RG27, 3347/1, W.A. Mackintosh, "House Renovation and Construction as a Source of Employment," 31 August 1936.
23 LAC RG27, 3374/16, Minutes of Fifteenth Meeting, 15 December 1936. He also offered a more refined approach by comparing the index of the value of new residential building (adjusted for deflation

in the construction price index) with the population index over the past five years and reached a number of similar magnitude.

24 LAC RG27, 3547/41. Mackintosh to Purvis, 31 July 1936.

25 The limited-dividend housing corporation had become a popular feature of American social policy (for a review see Cam, "United States Government Activity in Low-Cost Housing"). The corporation under the NEC proposal could not pay more than a 5½-per-cent dividend on paid-up capital.

26 LAC, RG27, 3374/18, Meeting Report 18, 1937, "National Employment Commission, Low-Income Housing Proposal," 3 February 1937. The overall design and specific details of the low-income housing proposal drew upon the work of the Bruce Committee in Toronto and a limited-dividend corporation in Winnipeg, supported by Clark and financed through the provisions of the Dominion Housing Act.

27 Christie, *Engendering the State*, 229.

28 Struthers, *No Fault of Their Own*, 159.

29 LAC, RG27, 3547/3, Arthur B. Purvis, "The Work of Rehabilitation," address to the Canadian Club, Toronto, 29 November 1937, 6. He emphasized the same points when forwarding the NEC's recommendation to Rogers: "The object is to get as many as possible of this transient class out on farms as it is less expensive to do so than to maintain them on relief in the cities, and less dangerous" (LAC RG27, 3352/6, Purvis to Rogers, 27 August 1936).

30 King Diary 22 December 1937; 23 December 1937; 12 January 1938.

31 Ibid., 4 January 1937.

32 Ibid., 21 December 1937, 5.

33 LAC RG27, 3347/7, Purvis to McLean, 30 December 1937.

34 King Diary, 20 December 1937.

35 Ibid., 22 January 1938, 4.

36 King also had his suspicions about what his minister of finance knew, since he viewed Purvis to be Dunning's appointee on the commission (ibid., 20 December 1937).

37 Ibid., 25 January 1938. Rogers often sought out Skelton's advice on government matters (LAC MG30 – D33, O.D. Skelton Papers, 3/4.24, O.D. Skelton to Isabel Skelton, 23 July 1937). King might have inferred Skelton's sympathies a few weeks earlier when he received a telegram sent by Rogers from Miami Beach – where the Rogerses were vacationing with the Skeltons (MG 26, King Papers, J1, C3738 – 219, 418–9).

38 LAC RG27, 3350/20, Sutherland to Purvis, 22 February 1937.

39 The problems with shared jurisdiction were magnified in the case of "transients." When the NEC sponsored a special conference with provincial and municipal representatives, the discussion got off to an unpromising start when no consensus could be reached on a definition of transiency. One delegate defined a transient as "any person who applies for assistance in another province than that in which he has established domicile prior to application for relief," while another deemed a transient to be "a social misfit in any community." Mackintosh attempted to smooth over the matter by suggesting that "The definition might only be considered important in so far as it throws light on the problem." But when he asked for their views on how to address the problem, the response ranged from the need to close provincial boundaries to enhanced efforts to prevent "rod-riding" (LAC RG27 3358/13, "Notes on Conference Called by National Employment Commission to discuss the problem of transiency," 18 August 1936).

40 The government's liability was $12.1 million in the unlikely case that there was a 100-per-cent default rate. When the program was cancelled at the end of March 1940, the government's total liability was $41.1 million but defaults amounted to less than 0.2 per cent of the amount of loans made (LAC RG19 W.C. Clark Papers, 3427/National Housing Act, "Report on the Operation of the National Housing Act and the Home Improvement Loans Guarantee Act," 15 May 1940).

41 LAC RG27, 3356/2, Clark to Purvis, 1 March 1937.

42 LAC RG27, 3354/6, Mackintosh to Purvis, 20 November 1936.

43 NEC, *Final Report*, 9.

44 LAC, RG17, 3427/National Housing Act, "Report on the Operation of the National Housing Act and the Home Improvement Loans Guarantee Act," 15 May 1940. According to one account, Mackintosh and the NEC were the unwitting victims of Clark's trickery. In his review of Canadian housing policy, John Bacher argues that "W.C. Clark waged a determined battle to prevent the construction of a single unit of social housing" and through "a number of ruses," cabinet memorandums, and "astute public evasion of issues," "was able to outwit the small group of well-intentioned and dedicated reformers who wanted a bold social-housing program for Canada" (Bacher, *Keeping to the Marketplace*, 24). The difficulty with this account is the extent to which Clark and Mackintosh worked closely together, and

might be more compelling if some explanation was offered of Clark's zealous struggle against social housing.

45 LAC, RG27 3352/12, newspaper clippings.
46 RG27 3357/7, Purvis to Neil McLean, 18 January 1938.
47 Struthers, *No Fault*, 175.
48 Neatby, "The Liberal Way," 109.
49 NEC, *Final Report*, 21.
50 Ibid., 24.
51 Marsh, "Report of the National Employment Commission," 84.
52 Mackintosh, "Review" of *The General Theory of Employment, Interest and Money*, *Queen's Quarterly* (1936) 43: 228–9.
53 NEC, *Final Report*, 23, 26.
54 QUA Mackintosh Papers, Additions 1/Queen's University-Economics 25, Hansen to Stuart Garson, 31 August 1938.
55 Keynes, "How to Avoid a Slump," *The Times* 12–14 January 1937. Reprinted in *The Collected Writings of John Maynard Keynes* v. 21: 385.
56 *JCBA* (October 1937) 45(1): 11.
57 NEC, *Final Report*, 24.
58 Richard Graybiel, "Economic Expert Genial, Unassuming," *Windsor Daily Star* (22 March 1946), 14.
59 QUA, Mackintosh Papers, Additions/11, Purvis to Mackintosh, n.d.
60 QUA, PRO 1251/1/E, Mackintosh to Robert England, 6 Feb. 1956; *Globe and Mail* 15 August 1941, 1–2.

CHAPTER EIGHT

1 "Introduction," to Mackintosh, *Economic Background*, 3.
2 LAC, MG 30 D33, O.D. Skelton Papers, 5/5-4, Skelton to Brooke Claxton, 24 January 1941.
3 Mackintosh, "Douglas Alexander Skelton."
4 LAC MG 33 D30, O.D. Skelton Papers 5/5-4, Memorandum for the Prime Minister, 1 June 1938.
5 LAC, King Diary, 2 June 1938.
6 LAC, MG33 D30, O.D. Skelton Papers 13/13-3, Diary 4 June 1938.
7 *Report of the Royal Commission on Dominion-Provincial Relations* (Ottawa, 1940), I: 16–17.
8 T.W. Acheson provides a valuable biographical sketch of S.A. Saunders in an "Introduction" to a reprint of Saunders's *The Economic History*

of the Maritime Provinces. Born in New Brunswick and raised in Saskatchewan, Saunders had embarked on a career in banking when he lost his eyesight. Undaunted, he obtained his BA from Dalhousie University. His doctoral dissertation at the University of Toronto established him as the leading authority on Maritime economic history. Unable to secure an academic position, Saunders toiled as an independent scholar until he was offered a position with the Canadian National Institute for the Blind.

9 RCDPR, *Report*, I: 18.
10 Corry, *My Life and Work*, 108–9.
11 LAC, MG30-D33, O.D. Skelton Papers, 11/11-14 Diary 17–20 July 1924.
12 Corry, *My Life and Work*, 109; Kindleberger, *Life of an Economist*, 63.
13 McQueen, "Economic Research at the Bank of Canada, 1935–65."
14 LAC, MG30-D33, O.D. Skelton Papers, 13/13-3, Diary 4 June 1938.
15 Corry, *My Life and Work*, 109.
16 Kindleberger, *Life of an Economist*, 63–4.
17 QUA, John J. Deutsch Papers, 1/2, Leo J. Nelligan letter, 20 April 1935.
18 Ibid., 1/1–3.
19 Ibid., 1/2.
20 Mackintosh Private Paper, Mackintosh to McQueen, 22 October 1937.
21 Corry, *My Life and Work*, 107, 108.
22 Mackintosh Private Papers, Mackintosh to McQueen, 1 February 1938.
23 LAC, MG30 D33, O.D. Skelton Papers, 13/13–3, Diary, 8 December 1938.
24 Corry, *My Life and Work,* 107.
25 LAC MG30 D33, O.D. Skelton Papers, 13/13-3, Diary 25 June 1938.
26 Corry, *My Life and Work*, 108.
27 LAC, RG33 Series 23, Royal Commission on Dominion-Provincial Relations, 53/Innis, Sandy Skelton to Harold Innis, 19 September 1937; Innis to Skelton, 1 October 1937; Mackintosh Private Papers, Mackintosh to Pete McQueen, 22 October 1937.
28 Ibid., 53/Innis, Innis to Sandy Skelton, 3 January 1939.
29 Ibid., Innis to Sandy Skelton, n.d.
30 Ibid., Sandy Skelton to Innis, 5 January 1939.
31 Ibid., Innis to Sandy Skelton, nd.

32 Mackintosh, *Economic Background*. He draws heavily upon his paper "Some Aspects of a Pioneer Economy."
33 LAC, RG33 Series 23, 67/Mackintosh, Mackintosh to Viner, 17 October 1938.
34 Mackintosh, *Economic Background*, 9.
35 Ibid., 14.
36 Ibid., chap. 2.
37 Ibid., 31.
38 Ibid., 23, 26.
39 Ibid., 25.
40 Ibid., 26.
41 Ibid., chap. 5.
42 Ibid., chap. 5.
43 In May 1938, MacGregor, Saunders, and Waines informed Mackintosh that they were "much disturbed" with the "uneven distribution of efforts" on various topics and faulted Mackintosh for not sufficiently coordinating the work. In particular, they were concerned that some of the regional analysis was being ignored, with the result that "too much emphasis will be placed upon the disruptive and not sufficient on the unifying influences in the economy" (LAC RG33 Series 23, 67, W.J. Waines, D.C. MacGregor, and S.A. Saunders to Mackintosh, 4 March 1938.
44 LAC RG33 Series 23, 69/2, S.A. Saunders, "Commentary on Professor Mackintosh's 'Economic Background of Dominion-Provincial Relations.'"
45 LAC RG33 Series 23, 67, "Mackintosh's Memorandum – General Comments," n.d.
46 LAC RG33 Series 23, 53/Keirstead, Keirstead to Skelton, 29 December 1938.
47 LAC RG33 Series 23, 53/Innis," Innis to Skelton, 29 December 1938. Referring to the background reports of the commission's work, J.A. Maxwell stated that: "I hope it does not seem invidious to single out for special commendation" the reports by Mackintosh and Creighton ("Canadian Dominion-Provincial Relations," 586n5).
48 Dales, "Some Historical and Theoretical Comments in Canada's National Policies."
49 On the interpretation of the "wheat boom" period, see Chambers and Gordon. "Primary Products and Economic Growth." Among the numerous responses to this article are: Dales, McManus, and Watkins,

"Primary Products and Economic Growth: A Comment"; Bertram, "The Relevance of the Wheat Boom in Canadian Economic Growth"; Grant, "The Staple Theory and Its Empirical Measurement"; and Lewis, "The Canadian Wheat Boom." On the relationship between government policy, railway construction, and the rate of prairie settlement, see George, "Rates of Return"; Southey, "The Staples Thesis"; Marr and Percy, "The Government and the Rate of Prairie Settlement"; Lewis, "Farm Settlement on the Canadian Prairies, 1898–1911"; and, for a useful summary of the literature, Norrie, "The National Policy and the Rate of Prairie Settlement."

50 Urquhart, "New Estimates of Gross National Product, Canada, 1870–1926." On the rate of growth in manufacturing output, see Altman, "A Revision of Canadian Economic Growth, 1870–1910." On the relevance of the "old" economic history in light of revisionist interpretations, see Aitken, "Myth and Measurement."

51 For an excellent account of Manitoba's involvement in the commission's deliberations, and of the intellectual climate in Manitoba generally, see Ferguson and Wardhaugh, "'Impossible Conditions of Inequality.'"

52 UTA, Innis Papers, Mackintosh to Innis, 4 January 1936.

53 Leitch, *A Princeton Companion.*

54 Province of Manitoba. *Manitoba's Case,* Part IV: 19. Part III of the Manitoba presentation, authored by Arthur Upgren, an economist at the University of Minnesota, took up the complementary argument in terms of monetary policy. Policies resulting in the high value of the Canadian dollar relative to the pound sterling areas had reduced the size and profitability of export industries, such as wheat, and thus lowered incomes in the prairie region. The veracity of this argument was widely acknowledged, but was deemed moot to the extent that, prior to the establishment of the Bank of Canada, there were few monetary controls available to the dominion government, and any departure from the gold standard was never a viable option.

55 *Manitoba's Case,* Part IV, 22.

56 LAC, RG33, series 23, 67. Mackintosh, "Memorandum: On the Relation of the Tariff to Dominion-Provincial Problems," nd.

57 An earlier attempt to quantify the regional effects of dominion policy had been made by Norman McLeod Rogers in his brief to the Nova Scotia Royal Commission in 1934. Kenneth Taylor, on behalf of the province of Ontario, also took issue with Manitoba's calculation of the regional burden of the tariff.

58 *Economic Background*, 85.
59 Young, "A Tribute to John Deutsch," 367. In a memorandum to Mackintosh, Deutsch lays out the kernel of the argument: "During the periods of rapid economic development in Canada, particularly in the West, the tariff (which was fairly stable) was one of the givens, like the existence of the Rocky Mountains. Since it was an expanding economy the transferable productive resources were highly mobile. Hence those resources tended to distribute themselves so that marginal returns were everywhere equal and the fixed resources (i.e., natural resources) tended to take on a value which made the cost of production the same to all producers" (QUA, Mackintosh Papers, 6/153, "Memorandum to Dr. Mackintosh: On Quantitative Measurements of Tariff Burdens and Benefits").
60 Chambers and Gordon, "Primary Products and Economic Growth."
61 LAC, RG33, Series 23, 67, Viner to Mackintosh, 3 October 1958.
62 Mackintosh Private Papers, McQueen to Mackintosh, 18 October 1937.
63 Corry, *My Life and Work*, 107; Mackintosh, "Douglas Alexander Skelton," 90–1. If, in Bryce's view, "Skelton's work habits were irregular – prodigious at times and suspended at other times" (*Maturing in Hard Times*, 215) – this was one of his prolific work periods.
64 RCDPR, *Report*, I: 77.
65 Ibid., I: 186.
66 Ibid., I: 185.
67 Ibid., I: 217.
68 Ibid., I: 245; 217.
69 Ibid., II: 23.
70 Bradford, "Writing Public Philosophy," 4.
71 QUA, J.J. Deutsch Papers, 1/2, "Mr. Keynes and the General Theory of Employment, Interest and Money," manuscript, no date.
72 MacGibbon, "Robert McQueen," 281; McQueen, "The Approach to Economics."
73 McQueen, "Canadian Monetary Policy."
74 RCDPR, *Report*, I: 151–2.
75 Ibid., I: 174.
76 Ibid., I: 201.
77 Ibid., II: 27.
78 Ibid., II: 24.
79 Bryce, *Maturing in Hard Times*, 219.
80 Dales, "Introduction," 1–3.

81 Dales, "Canadian Scholarship in Economics."
82 Macpherson, "The Social Sciences," 181, 185, 199.

CHAPTER NINE

1 UTA, Innis Papers, B72-0003 Box 1012 Folder (43).
2 Cited in Sharp, *Which Reminds Me*, 25.
3 Samuelson, "Unemployment Ahead."
4 LAC, RG32, Public Service Commission, Series C-2, 455/1895.05.21, Donald Gordon to Mackintosh, 19 July 1946.
5 Ibid., Clark to Bland, 4 December 1939.
6 QUA, Gibson Papers, J.L. Ralston to R.C. Wallace, 24 November 1939.
7 Mackintosh, "William Clifford Clark," 13–14.
8 C.H. Curtis obtained his BA and MA in economics from Queen's before taking up graduate work at the University of Chicago (1934–36). He lectured for five years at Mount Royal College in Calgary before returning to Queen's as a lecturer.
9 Mackintosh, "Economic Coordination of the War Effort," 180.
10 Mackintosh, "William Clifford Clark and Canadian Economic Policy," 412.
11 Bryce, *Maturing in Hard Times*, 232. That the budget's Keynesian flavour coincided with Bryce's arrival in the department of finance was no accident. Among his many virtues, Bryce brought with him a host of connections to younger Keynesian economists from his days at Cambridge, England, and Cambridge, Mass.: the Canadian-born Lauchlin Currie and Lorie Tarshis, Alec Cairncross, Walter Salant, John Kenneth Galbraith, Paul Sweezy, and Alan Sweezy, all of whom were drawn into wartime service, either in London or Washington. He also credits Mackintosh's indirect input, since the *Final Report of the National Employment Commission* prompted lengthy cabinet discussions beginning with the Supplementary Estimates of 1938.
12 Bryce, *Canada and the Cost of World War II*, 21; LAC, RG19, R.B. Bryce Papers, 3444/Bryce's personal correspondence, 1938–39, Bryce to Walter Salant, 12 October 1939; Wynne Plumptre to Bryce, 30 September 1939; Monteath Douglas to Bryce, 24 September 1939. See also Bryce's comments in Patinkin and Leith (eds.), *Keynes, Cambridge, and the General Theory*, and in the account by Barnett, *Keynes Comes to Canada*. Ralston had been sworn in as minister of

finance but had no seat; therefore, J.I. Ilsley presented the budget in the House of Commons on 12 September 1939.

13 LAC, RG19, Mackintosh Papers, 3561/D-14, "Memorandum for Mr. Brockington," 30 November 1940.

14 Slater, *War Finance*, chap. 5; Mackintosh, "Canadian War Financing."

15 LAC, RG19, Mackintosh Papers, 3555/D-14, "Memorandum for Mr. Brockington," 30 November 1940.

16 Gordon, *Political Memoir*, 38, 39. Slater suggests that Gordon exaggerates his role in designing tax rental agreements, giving more credit to the Rowell–Sirois Commission and to Mackintosh (Slater, *War Finance*, 48).

17 Kuznets, *National Income*, I; 34.

18 LAC RG19, Clark Papers, 3440/National Income Statistics, 1940–42, J.J. Deutsch, "Memorandum on National Income," 8pp nd.

19 Ibid. Book III of the commission's *Report* provided alternative measures by directly estimating service output, net income in agriculture, and such items as bond interest and dividends, as well as distinguishing between government expenditures and transfer payments.

20 Edward Arthur George Luxton (1914–1945) did undergraduate work at UBC and completed an MA at McGill. He worked for four years as an investment analyst with Sun Life and the International Bond and Share Corporation before winning a fellowship at Harvard in April 1939. Unable to find a suitable academic position – including the temporary job to replace Mackintosh at Queen's – he joined the research department of the Bank of Canada in the summer of 1940. Mackintosh described him as "keen and energetic, with a slight appearance of exuberance about him. I liked him very much, although I had the impression that he might have to be held on the rails occasionally." He was later transferred to the research and statistics branch of the department of labour as assistant director, and then to the DBS as chief of the planning and development staff. He contracted meningitis in 1945 and died at the age of 30 (LAC, RG19, Bryce Papers, 3444/ Bryce's Personal Correspondence, 1940, Luxton to Bryce, 10 June 1940; RG19, Mackintosh Papers, 3580/M-02, "Memo. Re George Luxton," 15 June 1940; QUA, Frank Knox Papers, 2/2.4 (1/2) Correspondence 1940–50, Alex McLeod to Frank Knox, 3 January 1945; Skelton, "Obituary."

21 Moreover, it was necessary to rely upon previous DBS figures as a benchmark and, as Towers warned Clark, "the basis for such

projections is slender, or is simply non-existent." (LAC RG19, 3440/ National Income Statistics, 1940–42, George Luxton, "Variants Comparing National Income with War Expenditure," 12 March 1942; Towers to Clark, 6 January 1942). Luxton's estimates were deemed too cursory to discuss at the Commonwealth talks in London in the fall of 1942, and six months later Bryce described them to be of "doubtful accuracy," such that he insisted that they be cited for domestic use only, with "the strongest sort of qualifications and reservations" (ibid., W.C. Clark to Mr. Robertson, 29 October 1942; Bryce to Clark, 12 April 1943). The reticence of Canadian officials to discuss in detail Canada's national income estimates may have been in part due to earlier criticisms by British officials. Canada's national income calculations were deemed too crude to provide any meaningful measure, probably understated its capacity to fight the war, and overstated its contribution to the war effort (Bryce, *Canada and the Cost*, 57).

22 LAC RG19, Mackintosh Papers, 3551/B-03, Mackintosh to Luxton, 25 July 1942.

23 LAC RG19, Mackintosh Papers 3593/L10-D, London Talks, 1942, 5 November 1942; QUA. Mackintosh Papers, 2/40, "London Talks – Draft Report, Oct. 23 – Nov. 9, 1942." Updating Colin Clark's national income estimates for 1937 (*Economic Journal*, September 1938), placed British government spending at a relatively low level, between 37.8 and 45.4 per cent of national income. Bryce reported that these figures, used in the budget of April 1940, contributed to public discontent and the fall of the Chamberlain government by giving the appearance that the sacrifice being asked of citizens was not matched by the government's preparedness for war (LAC RG19, Clark Papers, 3440/National Income Statistics, 1940–42, "British National Income and Government Expenditures" nd, na; Bryce, "Memorandum for the Minister: Re. Percentage of National Income Being Used for War and Other Governmental Functions – UK, 1940–41, 27 May 1940). Mackintosh did not give Keynes due credit for the development of modern national accounting, for Stone himself traced the methodology to Keynes's *How to Pay for the War.*

24 Deutsch, "Memorandum on National Income"; LAC RG19 Clark Papers, 3440/National Income Statistics, 1940–42, Towers to Clark, 6 January 1942.

25 Ibid., Clark to Ilsley, 13 April 1942.

26 Lerner went on to a celebrated academic career despite the problems he would encounter in securing a permanent position in a North

American university. Bryce knew him from their Cambridge days and promised to keep an eye open for academic or government jobs for him (LAC RG19, R.B. Bruce Papers, 3444/Bryce's Personal correspondence, 1938–39, Bryce to Lerner, 26 December 1939). In 1940 he recommended Lerner to Lothar Richter, who was looking for an economist to do some research work at Dalhousie University. "You have probably heard of A.P. Lerner, of London. He is now at the University of Virginia, temporarily, and was a short time ago very anxious to find some sort of work on this continent. He is undoubtedly one of the most brilliant economic theorists of the younger generation. He told me some time ago he would be interested in doing some applied economics if he got a chance." Bryce added that "He is a wonderful teacher, but his race and opinions make it a little difficult for him to get a position" (ibid., 3444/Bryce's Personal Correspondence, 1940, Bryce to Richter, 30 May 1940).

27 Ibid., RBB, "Notes on Meeting on National Statistics, Thursday, April 9, 1942"; Bryce to Clark, "Re Man to do National Income Work" 27 January 1943; Clark to Donald Gordon, 23 September 1942; Dana Wilgress to Clark, 18 September 1942; Wilgress to Donald Gordon, 18 September 1942; Clark to Towers, 25 April 1942; Wilgress to Clark, 22 April 1942. Bryce touted Lerner as "undoubtedly one of the most brilliant economic theorists of the younger generation," but noted that "his race and opinions make it a little difficult for him to get a position" (LAC, RG19, R.B. Bryce Papers, 3444/Bryce's Personal Correspondence, 1940, Bryce to L. Richter, 30 May 1940).

28 For a full account of the development of Canada's national accounts, see McDowall, *Sum of the Satisfactions* and Barnett, *The Keynesian Arithmetic in War-Time Canada*.

29 Mackintosh sent copies of the budget to several colleagues, including John H. Williams (Harvard, and a former fellow student there), Innis, Hansen, Kindleberger, Viner, Curtis, and Arthur Holcombe (LAC RG19, Mackintosh Papers, 3551/File B-04C, 25 June 1942).

30 Slater, *War Finance*, chap. 5; Mackintosh, "Canadian War Finance."

31 LAC RG19, Mackintosh Papers, 3551/B-04C, Mackintosh to C.C. Luhnow, 15 July 1942.

32 LAC RG19, Mackintosh Papers, 3580/File M-02, Mackintosh to Clark, 30 October 1941.

33 Ibid., 3551/B04-C, Mackintosh, "Memorandum Regarding Budget, 20 May 1942; 3581/N-01, England to Mackintosh, 11 February 1940;

Mackintosh to England, 12 March 1940. In light of the success of a similar British scheme, Mackintosh first promoted the idea in 1940: "I think we may get on to the Savings Programme rather quickly, and I certainly think it is important that it should be put over on a big scale and with a hard-driving, voluntary organization." He later reversed his position, arguing that war stamps were a regressive form of taxation, too costly to administer, likely to interfere with other savings programs and to have the effect of "confusing the public mind by linking buying and saving in one act." He went so far as to suggest that a stamp program might be perceived as a "dishonest trick" to raise the cost of living without a commensurate increase in wages (ibid., 3580/M-02-2, Mackintosh, "Memorandum for Dr. W.C. Clark – Re. Proposal for Forced Savings through Purchase of Savings Stamps with Retail Purchases," 30 October 1941. These arguments apparently prevailed in the 1942 budget discussions, since no such plan was introduced.

34 Ibid., 3581/N-01, Michell to Mackintosh, 13 September 1941; Mackintosh to Michell, 16 September 1941.

35 McIvor, "Canadian War-Time Fiscal Policy." McIvor also provides a useful account of the Bank of Canada's monetary policy.

36 McIvor, "Canadian War-Time Fiscal Policy," 89.

37 Slater, *War Finance*, 55, 40.

38 See, in particular, Granatstein, *The Ottawa Men*.

39 Bryce, *Canada and the Cost*, 32.

40 LAC RG19, EAC, 4660/187-EAC-3 part 3 – Minutes of Meetings, January 1940 – October 1944.

41 Bryce, *Canada and the Cost*, 39–40.

42 LAC, RG19, Mackintosh Papers, 3580/M-02, Mackintosh, "Memorandum to the Deputy Minister," 7 May 1940.

43 LAC RG19, EAC, 4660/187-EAC-1 "General," "Memorandum on the Economic Advisory Committee."

44 Mackintosh, "Economic Co-ordination of the War Effort."

45 LAC RG19, Mackintosh Papers, 3565/F-02, Clark to Mackintosh, 29 June 1940.

46 LAC RG19, EAC, 4661/187-EAC-25: Foreign Exchange, Conservation of (Import Control), "Report of the Economic Advisory Committee on the Formulation of Measures to Preserve Foreign Exchange," 15 August 1940. In October 1940, the EAC recommended the cancellation of the Canada–France and Canada–Poland trade agreements, since both trade pacts extended most-favoured-nation tariff rates

on several luxury goods, and therefore encouraged imports (ibid., 23 Oct. 1940).

47 LAC RG19, Mackintosh Papers, 3565/F-02, "Interim Memorandum on Trade Measures to Conserve United States Exchange, 19 February 1940. In 1939, automobile exports of $23.9 million were 24 per cent of all Canadian exports to the Empire and 22 per cent of the value of production in the Canadian auto industry (ibid., 3589/EAC File T-02 – Trade File nos 1 and 2, W.R. Campbell, Ford Motor Company of Canada to King, 8 March 1940.

48 Ibid., 3551/B-04: Budget material, 1940–41, "Memorandum on Tariff and Taxation Measures to Conserve Foreign Exchange," 28 May 1940.

49 Ilsley backed off raising tax on dividend and interest payments to non-residents after appeals from foreign investors (ibid., 3551/B-04b, Press Release, 10 May 1941).

50 Ibid., 3590/T-06, Mackintosh to P.J.A. Cardin, 19 February 1941. The original chairman, V.I. Smart, died, and was replaced by Dolan. Shortly after Mackintosh's letter of resignation, Dolan made some inflammatory public comments, prompting Mackintosh to advise Clark that Dolan's statements should be repudiated as "not only unauthorized but repugnant to the Government. Mr. Ilsley might do this, or Norman Robertson. The whole question of Dolan's fitness to carry on his activities in the United States should be canvassed with Mr. Cardin … I would think that the Prime Minister should be brought into this discussion" (ibid., "Memorandum for the Deputy Minister," 5 March 1941).

51 Ibid., Mackintosh to T.C. Davis, 25 November 1941; Tourism Development Committee, Minutes of Meeting, 2 March 1942.

52 Ibid., 3589/S-10 Sterling Balances, C.D. Howe to Ilsley, 21 July 1941.

53 Ibid., 3565/F-02, "Draft – WAM," 22 December 1941.

54 LAC RG19, Clark Papers, 3992/Billion Dollar Gift, F.A. Knox, "Memorandum for Dr. Clark: Re. the Rate of Use of the Billion Dollar Gift to the United Kingdom, 30 July 1942.

55 LAC RG19, EAC, 4460/187-EAC-5, W.A. Mackintosh and R.B. Bryce, "Economic Survey of the First Year of the War," 16 September 1940.

56 In addition to the department of munitions and supply, there were finance (fiscal policy); national revenue (import controls, special depreciation rates for war contracts); trade and commerce (export permits, shipping, and British food contracts); transportation (transportation controller); labour (to whom the Wartime Prices and Trade Board reported); agriculture and fisheries (commodity supply boards);

war services (British Food Contracts, Travel Bureau, Bureau of Information; Military Recruitment Training); national defence (recruitment of manpower); Foreign Exchange Control Board; Joint Economic Committee; and the Wartime Prices and Trade Board (Mackintosh, "The Price System and the Procurement of Essential Supplies").

57 Mackintosh and Bryce, "Economic Survey."

58 LAC RG19, EAC, 4660/187-EAC-4, pt.2, "Report of the Economic Advisory Committee on the Establishment of a Wartime Planning Committee," 5 November 1940.

59 LAC RG19, Mackintosh Papers, 3588/S-00, Mackintosh to Bryce M. Stewart, 22 October 1940.

60 Ibid., 3580/M-02, Mackintosh to Clark, 23 August 1940.

61 LAC RG19, EAC, 4660/187-EAC-3-part 3, Minutes of Meeting, 17 September 1940.

62 LAC, RG19, Mackintosh Papers, 3552/C-00, Mackintosh to Clark, "Memo re. R.H. Coats's Letter of March 4," 6 March 1940.

63 Ibid., 3563/D-04, "Memorandum on Fiscal Policy in Relation to Price and Commodity Control," 1 October 1941.

64 Ibid., 3551/B-04b, Mackintosh to Frank Knox, 16 July 1941.

65 LAC RG19, Clark Papers, 3563/D-04, "Memorandum on Fiscal Policy in Relation to Price and Commodity Control," 1 October 1941.

66 Dexter, *Ottawa at War*, 219 (10 November 1941).

67 Problems would persist because of the "unavoidable" overlap between the Wartime Industries Control Board (concerned with assuring war supplies) and the WPTB (dealing with civilian supply and prices). Donald Gordon complained of the encroachment of wartime control over civilian matters (LAC RG19, Clark Papers, 3992/W-2-1, Wartime Prices and Trade Board. General Files, D. Gordon to Howe, 5 August 1942; D. Gordon, "Division of Responsibility between Wartime Industries Control Board and Wartime Prices and Trade Board," 3 August 1942). He also argued that production restrictions on domestic consumer industries would only release less-fit workers in remote geographical areas, thus creating unemployment among those unfit for the armed services or for war industries (ibid., D. Gordon to J.L. Ilsley, 26 March 1943).

68 Sharp, *Which Reminds Me*, 25.

69 In support of this argument, Mackintosh drew upon the comments of William Beveridge in the London *Times* in June 1940: "The practical moral to be drawn from these considerations differs from that

suggested by Mr Keynes. Waste of man-power today does not arise through a deficiency in total demand for labour, and production is not being held up through lack of labour as such. The misfits are of quality or of coordination" (LAC RG19, Mackintosh Papers, 3577/L-04).

70 Mackintosh and Bryce, "Economic Survey," 14.

71 LAC RG19, Mackintosh Papers, 3577/L-04, "Submission of Committee appointed ... to report on the Agenda of the Committee of the Cabinet on Labour Supply considered at meeting of October 1st and 2nd."

72 Ibid., 3554/D-00, Mackintosh to Norman Robertson, 26 September 1941.

73 Ibid., 3577/L-04, Mackintosh, "Memorandum of Co-ordination in the Field of Labour Supply."

74 Ibid., 3577/L-03, "Labour Supply Research Project," 16 June 1941.

75 Ibid., 3577/L-02(2), "Memorandum on War Labour Demand & Supply for the Year 1941."

76 Ibid., 3581/N-04, National Selective Services Advisory Board, "Historical Summary of the National Selective Services Civilian Regulations," 21 March 1945, Reference Papers, Wartime Information Board, Ottawa.

77 LAC, MG26, King Diary, 18 November 1942.

78 Enacted in 1907, the IDIA was designed to prevent work stoppages in the mining industry and some public utilities by requiring a period of compulsory conciliation prior to any strike or lockout.

79 Jamieson, *Industrial Relations in Canada*, 108.

80 LAC RG19, EAC, 4660/187-EAC-3-part 3, Minutes of Meeting, 11 December 1939; 187-EAC-4, pt. 1 "Report of the EAC on Proposal to Insert in the Wage Clauses of Supply Contracts Provision for a Cost-of-Living Bonus," 14 December 1939.

81 Ibid., Minutes of Meeting, 26 February 1940.

82 LAC RG19, Mackintosh Papers, 3577/L-04, Memorandum, W.J. Crouper to Deputy Minister of Labour, "Wartime Wages Policy and Order-in-Council of December 16, 1940," P.C. 7440. Because its coverage was limited to war-related industries and, as such, prevented standardization of wage rates within skill categories, it provided no criteria for determining whether wages in an industry were too high or too low; there was widespread distrust and confusion as to the calculation of the price indexes.

83 Ibid., "Memorandum for Discussion by the Committee in Labour Coordination," n.d.

84 Ibid., 3580/M-02, Mackintosh to Clark, 8 July 1941.

85 Ibid., 3554/D-00, Papers, Deachman to Mackintosh, 20 June 1940; Mackintosh to Deachman, 27 June 1940.

86 Ibid., 3580/M-02, Mackintosh to Jackson, 8 July 1941.

87 Each board consists of an independent chairman appointed by the government and an equal number of employers' and workers' representatives.

88 LAC RG19, Clark Papers, 3992/W-2, Walter Gordon to Donald Gordon, 11 February 1943, 5.

89 LAC RG19 Mackintosh Papers, 3577/L-02, File 2 EAC – National War Labour Board Reports, Parts 1 and 2, 16 September 1943.

90 The EAC also rejected the NWLB's recommendation that wages under 50 cents per hour should be removed from controls. There was general sympathy for the plight of low-wage earners, such that the "Fair Wage Policy" was amended in spring 1941 to raise the minimum wage rate to 35 cents and 25 cents per hour for men and women respectively. Yet Mackintosh argued that the removal of wages under 50 cents from controls was a "specious attraction" with "a ruthless disregard for job differentials," and would also assist trade unions in their organizing drives. Satisfied with the provision in the existing wage order to "rectification of gross inequities and injustices," he persuaded the EAC to oppose exempting low wages from control (ibid., 3579/M-01, W.A. Mackintosh, "Memorandum for the Minister: Re: Free Collective Bargaining below Fifty Cents an Hour," 6 October 1943).

91 McInnis, *Harnessing Labour Confrontation.*

92 Hodgetts, McCloskey, Whitaker, and Wilson, *The Biography of an Institution,* chap. 9. The War Measures Act, proclaimed on 1 September 1939, pre-empted the Civil Service Act of 1918.

93 Frankel, "Staff Relations." Oddly, in providing its rationale for the NJC, the government stated that, when it was requiring compulsory bargaining in the private sector, it could not refuse the same to its own employees (LAC RG19, Mackintosh Papers 3596/N08b. "Employee Representation in the Public Service of Canada," 16 February 1944).

94 QUA PRO, 1251/F, Mackintosh to S.J. Frankel, 14 February 1956.

95 QUA PRO, 1251/F, S.J. Frankel to Mackintosh, 10 February 1956; Mackintosh to Frankel, 14 February 1956

96 LAC RG19, Mackintosh Papers, 3596/N08b, John J. Reaves to Mackintosh, 17 October 1944. There were three organizations of civil servants in the post office: the Railway Mail Clerks' Federation, the Federated Association of Letter Carriers, and the Association of Postal Employees.

97 Ibid., NJC of PSC "Report of Staff Side Committee on question referred in relation to rates of pay of Postal Workers."

98 Ibid., Fred Whitehouse to Mackintosh, 10 August 1944. Mackintosh had earlier chaired an inter-department committee struck by cabinet to consider the request of postal employees for a wage increase of 20 to 30 per cent. The wage increase was denied on the grounds that it would create an exception to the prevailing wage policy that would have repercussions for other government and private-sector workers (Ibid., 3555/D-13a – Postal Employees, "Report of the Inter-Departmental Committee to Consider the Representations of the Association of Canadian Postal Employees, 1 April 1943).

99 Ibid., 3596/N08b, V.C. Phelan to Ilsley, 18 November 1946; Clark to Mackintosh, 21 November 1946; Mackintosh to Clark, 25 November 1946. When the war ended, Clark, Mackintosh, and Ilsley were in agreement that cost-of-living increases in the public service should not be maintained once the wage orders for bonuses in the private sector were discontinued. Thus, in May 1946, Mackintosh refused to accept the joint recommendation of the NJC for cost-of-living adjustments, and advised Ilsley to provide specific instructions to this end: "you tell me that you were very reluctant to recommend the continuance of the bonus system and, further, that while the bonus should be increased to cover the five per cent now accruing, you were unwilling to have the government committed to such further automatic increases as would amount to making the system permanent" (ibid., Mackintosh to Ilsley, 24 May 1946). For his part, Bryce offered the opinion that "it would be better to avoid the use of automatic formulas to compensate for higher prices, and to retain a widespread resistance to the increases that many pressure groups will continue to seek" (ibid., Bryce, "Alternative Policies on Civil Service Cost of Living Bonus").

100 Mackintosh, "Economic Co-ordination of the War Effort."

101 McIvor, "Canadian War-Time Fiscal Policy," 88. J.D. Gibson, in a brief prepared for the WPTB, enumerated the main beneficiaries of the growth in national income as one million workers that had formerly not been gainfully employed; those benefiting from higher-paid jobs in war industries; farmers for whom net income had more than doubled; most workers in manufacturing, mining, logging, and construction, who had enjoyed wage increases, upgrading, and overtime pay; and skilled workers who had received wage increases. Bryce commented that "[these estimates] do not point out that increases have gone very largely to those who have worked much harder or learned new skills"

(LAC RG19, Clark Papers, 3440/National Income Statistics, 1940–42, J.D. Gibson, "Distribution of Increased National Income" n.d).

CHAPTER TEN

1 QUA, Mackintosh Papers, Additions/2. Authorship is not identified. Possibly written by Mackintosh, it bears the distinctive style of R.B. Bryce. It appears to elaborate on the poetic efforts of Dennis Robertson; see Gardner, *Sterling-Dollar Diplomacy*, xiii.

2 In 1936, the value of exports as a percentage of national income was 26 per cent in Canada, only 3.6 per cent in the United States, and in the order of 10 per cent in the United Kingdom. See Drummond and Hillmer, *Negotiating Freer Trade*.

3 Mackintosh made an exception in the case of defence requirements. LAC RG19, Mackintosh Papers, 3552/C-00, Mackintosh to E.J. Coil (Director, National Economic and Social Planning Association, Washington), 20 September 1940.

4 Mackintosh, "Canadian Views," in Acheson, Chant, and Prachowny (eds.), *Bretton Woods Revisited*, 40.

5 Cited in Skidelsky, *John Maynard Keynes*, III: 318.

6 *Collected Writings of John Maynard Keynes*, edited by Donald Moggridge (25: 284), Keynes to R.H. Brand, 9 June 1943; Howson and Moggridge (eds.), *Wartime Diaries*, 233.

7 Skidelsky, *John Maynard Keynes*, III: 121. On the pre-Keynesian ideas circulating in Harvard in the 1930s, see Laidler and Sandilands, "An Early Harvard *Memorandum*" and "Memorandum Prepared by L.B. Currie, P.T. Ellsworth, and H.D. White." An interesting question remains about the extent to which White was associated with the American communist movement, and whether such an association influenced his work with the Treasury. Skidelsky (*John Maynard Keynes* III: 242) suggests that White admired Soviet economic planning, saw the Soviet Union as the greatest obstacle to German anti-Semitism, and envisioned a postwar US-Soviet pact with a convergence between the two countries towards social democracy. White, as well as Currie and Coe (who became the first managing director of the IMF), were called to appear before the US House Committee on Un-American Activities. On Currie's life, see Sandilands, *The Life and Political Economy of Lauchlin Currie*.

8 Rasminsky was born in Montreal, grew up in Toronto, studied politics and economics at the University of Toronto (where he was a classmate

of Wynne Plumptre), and did graduate work at the London School of Economics. He left the LSE without completing a thesis in order to accept a job with the Economic and Financial Section of the League of Nations in Geneva in 1930. His talents came to the attention of several officials in Ottawa, including Clark, Towers, and Skelton ("It struck me that he had the most vigorous and clear-cut intellectual equipment I had met in a young man for years"), and they were anxious to recruit him despite "the prejudice in question" – Rasminsky was Jewish. After a decade in Geneva, he was finally persuaded to accept an advisory position with the Bank of Canada's Foreign Exchange Control Board in April 1940 (Muirhead, *Against the Odds*, 22, 50). Even the less-than-effusive Frank Knox offered his endorsement: "A very pleasant chap and, from what I could judge, a very competent chap. The Board is probably fortunate to be able to get someone with the experience of the League of Nations Statistical Service behind him." (LAC, RG19, Mackintosh Papers, 3551/B-04, Knox to Mackintosh, 17 July 1940).

9 Ibid., 3570/J-01, PC 4500, 20 June 1941.

10 Ibid., 3570/J-01, "Memorandum on the Joint Economic Committees of Canada and the United States," 7 October 1943.

11 Ibid., 3570/J01(1), Mackintosh to Herbert, 20 June 1941; Memorandum, Alex Skelton, 2 July 1941.

12 Ibid., 3570/3.

13 Ibid., 3570/4, Resolution No. 6.

14 LAC RG19, Clark Papers, 3977/E-3-2, Mackintosh to King, 17 December 1941.

15 Bryce, *Canada and the Cost of World War II.*

16 Canada, Department of External Affairs, Joint Economic Committees, Canada – United States. *Tentative Draft.*

17 At the fourth joint meeting, held in Montreal in November 1941, discussion of the "Report on Long-Run Collaboration" received input from Coe, Salant, and Galbraith. Coe and Salant questioned (wrongly, as history would prove) the basic assumption of the report that American dollars would be scarce in the postwar period, while Galbraith objected that the treatment of pre-war economic relations between Canada and the United States was "made without reference to the volume of employment." He argued that it was the level of national income and employment that dictated trade and monetary policies, such that the emphasis should be on domestic policies to create full employment and that international policy would fall into place (RG19, Clark Papers, 3977/E-3-2, Minutes of fourth joint meeting,

Montreal, 7–9 November 1941). The draft was cognizant of the revolutionary changes in the economic role of governments precipitated by the war (77), but Hume Wrong expressed his disappointment with "an unexpressed assumption in the draft that the most desirable economic framework after the war will involve as great a return as possible to a free capitalist system. Passages could be cited from the draft to a contrary sense, but at several points I seem to detect a nostalgia for the return of laissez-faire and an apologetic note when the continuance of wartime measures of State control is proposed" (LAC, Mackintosh Papers, 3571/J-01-11, Wrong to Mackintosh, 24 August 1942).

18 Ibid., 3569/J01-8, Mackintosh, "Memorandum on the Joint Economic Committees of Canada and the United States," 7 October 1943; J.B. Carswell to Carl Goldenberg, 17 September 1943; 3571/J-01-11, Plumptre to Mackintosh, 29 April 1942. There were rumours of conflict on the American committee between Hansen and Berle (ibid., 3572/J-01-14, Excerpt from *Newsweek*, 7 June 1943).

19 Ibid., 3569/J-01-8, H.L. Keenleyside, "Memorandum for the Under-Secretary" 2 September 1943.

20 Kindleberger, *Life of an Economist*, 64.

21 LAC, Mackintosh Papers, 3572/J-01-14, Mackintosh to A.G. Grauer, 15 March 1943. Mackintosh cited frictions with Munitions and Supply, which jealously guarded its responsibility for organizing military production and resented interventions by the JECs (ibid., 3571/J-01-8, J.B. Carswell to Mackintosh, 15 December 1941; Mackintosh to Bateman, 6 January 1942). The low priority given to the Canadian committee was reflected in the inconvenient office space it was assigned in the Victoria Memorial Museum (now the Canadian Museum of Nature) after being displaced from temporary quarters in the Centre Block (ibid., 3571/J-01-6, J.J. Deutsch to C. Boucher, 23 October 1941; Mackintosh to Robertson, 9 December 1941).

22 Ibid., 3569/J-01-8, Mackintosh, "Memorandum on the Joint Economic Committees of Canada and the United States," 7 October 1943.

23 Ibid., 3571/J-01-6, Mackintosh to Hansen, 17 August 1942. Feeling "more than a little personal responsibility" for the relative ineffectiveness of the committees, Mackintosh did not formally pull the plug on the JECs until February 1944 (ibid., 3569/J-01-8, Mackintosh to Hansen, 17 February 1944).

24 LAC RG19, Clark Papers, 3989/T-2-9-2, Wrong to Robertson, 21 October 1942; Muirhead, *Against the Odds*, 86. The discomfort of

travelling "in the chilly belly of a Lancaster bomber" is emphasized by Plumptre, *Three Decades of Decision*, 24.

25 Muirhead, *Against the Odds*, 86.

26 Clark received a copy of the Clearing Union proposal in September 1942 from Sir Frederick Phillips, the senior British Treasury official in Washington. It was discussed by a subcommittee of the EAC, composed of Mackintosh, Rasminsky, Robertson, Towers, and Clark, before the Canadian delegation left for England (LAC RG19, Clark Papers 3981/M-1-7-1, Mackintosh, "International Clearing Union," n.d.). Bryce also prepared comments that largely endorsed Keynes's proposal without seeing it as terribly innovative ("Notes on Memorandum Proposing an International Credit Union," 10 October 1942).

27 Cited in Van Dormael, *Bretton Woods*, 97. Rasminsky was struck by the extent that Britain had assumed a "debtor mentality." Mackintosh noted that one member of the British Treasury wanted any creditor country accumulating bancor to be expelled, and that the Australian delegate wanted all debits in bancor forgiven (Rasminsky, "Canadian Views," 35).

28 LAC RG19, Mackintosh Papers 3593/10-D, PET (42) 3rd Meeting – Tuesday 27 October 1942. Keynes's proposal initially allowed for a country to use 25 per cent of its quota and to depreciate its currency at 5 per cent per year; following the Commonwealth talks this was changed to a one time 5-per-cent depreciation after two years.

29 See Moggridge, *Maynard Keynes*, chap. 26.

30 LAC RG19, Clark Papers, 3977/E-3-1, Report on Second Special Meeting of the Economic and Financial Group, Council on Foreign Relations, New York City, 24 January 1942. Alex Cairncross provided a similar account of Keynes's conversion in a letter to Bryce: "Keynes continues to exercise a powerful influence in the Treasury. Thanks to James Meade and others, this influence is on the whole a healthy one and he seems to have got over his original dislike of the Americans. There was a time when, after his return from Washington, he advocated views about the future of world trade similar to those which you ascribe to [Geoffrey] Crowther. But I think that he has now reconverted to a more liberal view – strangely enough, by arguments which I first heard from him (e.g., that discrimination is apt to exacerbate political relations between friendly powers). I can imagine that the Americans (who have suddenly become more Manchester – or should I say more Hull? – than Manchester ever was) were not too pleased at

the Brave New World of Bilateral Trade Agreements sketched for them by Crowther" (LAC RG19, Bryce Papers 3444/Correspondence, 1940; Alec Cairncross to Bryce, 30 November 1941). Crowther, editor of the *Economist*, was working in the Ministry of Supply. Meade suggested to Rasminsky that Keynes's conversion to multilateralism came while writing the first draft of the Clearing Union proposal, designed to argue in favour of retaining bilateral arrangements (Muirhead, *Against the Odds*, 81).

31 Rasminsky, "Canadian Views," 34. The chief opposition came from Hubert Henderson and Cobbold in the Bank of England (Skidelsky, *John Maynard Keynes*, III: 201). At a meeting in 1945, Bryce observed that Cobbold "spoke, almost lovingly, of the sterling area, its banking origins and subsequent evolution, its vital role in the war during foreign exchange control, and its immediate problems" (Bryce, *Canada and the Cost of World War II*, 298).

32 Skidelsky, *John Maynard Keynes,* III: 248.

33 LAC RG19, Clark Papers, 3981/M-1-7-2, "Canada – United States Discussion of Stabilization Fund Proposals," United States Treasury, 21–26 April 1943. The White Plan was received by Clark on 24 December 1942.

34 Bryce, *Canada and the Cost of World War II*, 232.

35 LAC RG19, Mackintosh Papers, 3592/11-D, ASD (Money) (44) 7th Meeting, 13 March 1944.

36 LAC RG19, Bryce Papers, 3447/1, "Canada – United States Discussion of Stabilization Fund Proposals," United States Treasury, April 21–26 1943," 3.

37 Ibid., 14–15, 19.

38 Ibid., 19–22.

39 Ibid., 39–43.

40 LAC, RG19, Clark Papers, 3989/T-2-9-2, Mackintosh to Clark, 26 May 1942.

41 When word of pending Anglo-American discussions on a full-range of postwar issues reached Clark in August 1943, he questioned whether Commonwealth discussions were merely to facilitate bilateral talks between "the two great powers." He asked Mackintosh, "Are we now supposed to be in the bag?" Mackintosh reassured him that Canada had encouraged direct US–UK talks as a means of setting the agenda for wider international discussions, and that there was no doubt in anyone's mind that Britain spoke only on its own behalf and not for

the Commonwealth (ibid., Clark to Mackintosh, nd; Mackintosh to Clark, nd; Clark to N. Robertson, 2 August 1943).

42 Ibid., 3981/M-1-7-1, Telegram, Canadian High Commissioner in London to the Secretary of State for External Affairs in Ottawa, 30 May 1943.

43 LAC RG19, Bryce Papers, 3447/1, Mackintosh, "Memorandum for the Minister: Proposed Steps in the Future Discussion of the Clearing Union and Stabilization Fund Proposals," 2 June 1943, 5. Nor would a Canadian plan attract the instinctive negative reaction that a British proposal would. Upon receiving the text of Keynes's speech to the House of Lords (in which Keynes insisted that the intent of the Clearing Union plan was not "to make the United States the milch cow of the world in general and of this country in particular," Mackintosh sent a letter of congratulations on a speech that was "not only, as everyone would expect, a model of lucidity and persuasion, but also extremely helpful in tone. It can do nothing but good in the United States." He also informed Keynes of the intent to present a "Canadian Plan" on the grounds that American financial circles "have a fantastically high regard for our fiscal and economic policy and take a very dark view of the United States Treasury" (LAC RG19, Clark Papers, 3981/M-1-7-1, Keynes to Wrong, 19 May 1943; LAC RG19, Mackintosh Papers, 3555/D-03b, Mackintosh to Keynes, 5 June 1943).

44 BCA, Rasminsky Papers, LR 208-12, Rasminsky to Mackintosh, 20 May 1943.

45 Viner characterized the differences between the Clearing Union, with a larger pool of reserves and greater flexibility for adjusting exchange rates, as more suitable to the transition period, while the more conservative Stabilization Fund was appropriate to more stable times (Robbins in Howson and Moggridge (eds.), *Wartime Diaries*, 72).

46 LAC RG19, Bryce Papers, 3447/1, Mackintosh, "Memorandum for the Minister: Proposed Steps in Future Discussions of the Clearing Union and Stabilization Fund Proposals," 2 June 1943; LAC RG19, Mackintosh Papers, 3555/D-03b, "Tentative Draft Proposals of Canadian Experts for an International Exchange Union," 9 June 1943.

47 LAC RG19, Clark Paper, 3981/M-1-7-2, Plumptre to Mackintosh, 29 May 1943; Mackintosh to Plumptre, 3 June 1943.

48 LAC RG19, Bryce Papers, 3447/1, Mackintosh to Robertson, 14 June 1943.

49 When the Canadian Plan was made public about a month later, following a question in the House of Commons, White welcomed its release (LAC RG19, Clark Papers. 3981/M-1-7-1, Clark to White, 10 July 1943; White to Clark, 24 July 1943).
50 Robbins in Howson and Moggridge (eds.), *Wartime Diaries*, 15 June 1943, 72.
51 Keynes to Robertson, 11 June 1943 in Keynes, *Collected Works*, 25: 298.
52 LAC RG19, Clark Papers, 3981/M-1-7-1, Keynes to Hume Wrong, 19 May 1943.
53 Van Dormael, *Bretton Woods*, 88.
54 Keynes to Robertson, 11 June 1943, in Keynes, *Collected Works*, 25: 298.
55 Robbins in Howson and Moggridge (eds.), *Wartime Diaries*, 16 June 1943, 73.
56 Bryce, *Canada and the Cost of World War II*, 234.
57 Horsefield, *The International Monetary Fund*, I: 39.
58 LAC RG19, Mackintosh Papers, 3592/L-11-D, ASD (Money) (44) 8th Meeting, 15 March 1944.
59 LAC RG19, Clark Papers, 3981/M-1-7-1, Mackintosh, "International Clearing Union," point 16.
60 Moggridge, *Maynard Keynes*, 730–1.
61 LAC RG19, Mackintosh Papers, 3592/D-03, Article VII Discussions with Representatives of the Dominions and India, ASD44 (Bank), 14 March 1944.
62 Ibid., ASD44 (Bank), 14 March 1944.
63 LAC RG19, Deutsch Papers, 3597/D03C(1), Mackintosh, "The United Nations Monetary and Financial Conference," 18 September 1944.
64 Keynes, *Collected Works*, 26: 106–7.
65 Robbins in Howson and Moggridge (eds.), *Wartime Dairies*, 181. Robbins was struck by the "very poor showing made by the Europeans," and deemed L.G. Melville of the Australia delegation to be "excruciatingly dingy-minded" (160).
66 In Atlantic City, Keynes told the Canadian delegation that he proposed to amend the clause on exchange-rate adjustments to allow countries greater flexibility. Rasminsky chastised the British for retreating from their earlier position, and Robbins recorded that: "I was not surprised when Rasminsky ... kicked off by saying that if we wanted to make the position of the Americans as difficult as possible we could not have chosen a better method than to put up the modification we had in

mind for the exchange clause. We had already wrung from them last autumn such extensive concessions in this respect, that they had been under continuous public criticism ever since. In his view, it was quite hopeless to expect them to accept. This, of course, harmonises completely with what Dennis [Robertson] and I have said all along; but it was obviously something of a shock to the others. Rasminsky is so competent and disinterested that it would be difficult not to take him seriously" (Robbins in Howson and Moggridge (eds.), *Wartime Diaries,* 158). White would acquiesce, and the changes were incorporated into the Final Act, but Rasminsky would not let the occasion pass without again rebuking the British for, in Robbins's words, "departing from the excellent compromise reached at Washington last October" (ibid., 175).

67 LAC, RG19, Mackintosh Papers, 3588/S-13, Guthrie to Trachtenberg, 27 June 1944; QUA Mackintosh Papers, 8/202, Mackintosh to Deutsch, 22 June 1944.

68 Eady recounts the important role played by Keynes in securing support for the Bank in private financial circles. "New York took much more kindly to the Bank. I remember a wonderful occasion with Keynes. The subscriptions to the Bank were not legitimately saleable in New York though there was pressure on the New York authorities for this to be done. With Keynes we met a considerable number of the chairmen of Insurance Companies. At the conclusion of a little speech of gratitude, Keynes asked the Chairman, 'Will you sell these bonds?' The Chairman took some time in replying and then he said, 'Lord Keynes we will sell these bonds and what is more, Lord Keynes, we will buy these bonds.' I told Keynes that was really one of the greatest triumphs of his work at the Treasury" (QUA, PRO 1251 I/E, Wilfrid Eady to Mackintosh, 23 October 1957).

69 "Verbatim Minutes of the Closing Plenary Session," United Nations Monetary and Financial Conference Journal, no. 23 (July 23, 1944). This passage is frequently misattributed to Ilsley (viz. Van Dormael, *Bretton Woods*, 212). Plumptre wrote to correct the minutes, noting that, since Ilsley was absent at the closing plenary session, it was Mackintosh who spoke for the Canadian delegation (LAC, RG19, Deutsch Papers, 3597/D03C, Plumptre to Kelchner, 26 August 1944).

70 Canada. House of Commons. Standing Committee on Banking and Commerce. *Bill No. 238*, 106, 152.

71 LAC RG19, EAC 4664/187-EAC-58, 14 December 1943; cited in Mackenzie, "White Paper."

72 LAC RG19, Mackintosh Papers, 3981/L11, "A series of discussions between representatives of the UK, the Dominions and India on the economic and financial questions arising out of Article 7 of the Mutual Aid Agreement with the United States, February 23–March 21, 1944," ASD (Trade) 44 5th Meeting – March 3, 1944.

73 LAC RG19, Clark Papers, 3991/U-3-2-4-C, Mackintosh to Clark, 4 Oct 1941.

74 LAC RG19, Mackintosh Papers, 3981/L11, ASD (Trade) 44 9th Meeting – March 10, 1944. On the technical matter of tariff reduction (ad valorem versus specific duties, valuations, ceilings, and floors), Mackintosh endorsed Viner's idea that rates would be reduced through a series of annual adjustments. Britain opposed horizontal tariff cuts because they did not fairly address the differences between high and low tariff items and favoured instead gradual reductions (LAC RG19, 3592/L11–E, "Methods of Tariff Reduction," no author, 7 May 1943; "Report of the Advisory Committee on Economic Policy on Trade Policy" (Dominion Office Telegram of 22 April 1943); ASD (Trade) 44 6th Meeting – March 7, 1944; Viner, "Objectives of Post-War International Economic Reconstruction."

75 LAC RG19, Bryce Papers, 3447/1, Mackintosh, "Report of the Canadian Representatives at the 'Post-War Commercial Policy Discussions' Held in London between June 15th and June 30th, 1943," 16 July 1943. This point was reiterated at the 1944 talks (ASD 44: 1st Meeting, 23 February, 1944; ASD 44 2nd Meeting, 15 March 1944).

76 LAC RG19, Mackintosh Papers, 3592/L-11E, "Post-War Commercial Policy Discussions," PCP (43) First Meeting, 15 June 1943); Skidelsky, *John Maynard Keynes*, III: 323.

77 LAC RG19, Mackintosh Papers, 3592/L-11E, PCP (43), 9th Meeting, 25 June 1943; Mackintosh, "Report of the Canadian Representatives." He added that the South African representative, J.E. Holloway, "made a long and not always relevant statement, in which he rightly complained of his difficulty in avoiding a network of platitudes."

78 LAC RG19, Mackintosh Papers, 3593/L11-F, Mackintosh, "Memorandum of Meeting at Treasury – June 23, 1943"; "Memorandum of Conversation with Keynes. Lunch – House of Lords, June 22, 1943"; "Memorandum of correspondence with Keynes, 22 June 1943."

79 LAC RG19, Clark Papers, 3989/T-2-9-2, "Informal Exploratory Conversations Between Officials of the United States and the United Kingdom Regarding the Formulation of an Agenda for Discussions

Looking Toward the Implementation of Article VII of the Mutual-Aid Agreement between the United States and the United Kingdom," 16 October 1943; "Informal Exploratory Conversations between Officials of the US and Canada … Jan. 3–7, 1944 (Washington) and Feb. 12–13 (NY)," 14 February 1944.

80 Mackintosh favoured bilateral talks only on reducing trade barriers that might lower the effective rate of protection on goods for which the United States was the chief supplier in return for the elimination of preferences in ten years (ibid., Mackintosh, "Memorandum re Special Trade Agreement Possibilities," 14 December 1943).

81 LAC RG19, Mackintosh Papers, 3981/L11, ASD (Trade) 44 2nd Meeting – 25 (3pm) February, 1944.

82 Mackintosh, Hector McKinnon and J.J. Deutsch represented Canada. With the release of the "Joint Statement" on the fund and bank, discussions focused on commercial policy (ibid., 11th Meeting – 17 March 1944).

83 Ibid., 3rd Meeting, 20 March 1944; 4th Meeting, 2 March 1944.

84 Mackintosh cabled Robertson with his concern about a drift in British policy towards bilateralism. Robertson recommended a six-month "hoist" of further negotiations pending the November American elections (LAC RG19, Clark Papers, 3989/T-2-9-2, Telegram, Robertson to Wrong, 8 May 1944).

85 Ibid., 4369/U-3-11, Hector B. McKinnon, "Commercial Policy, London, May, 1945," draft sent to Mackintosh, 8 June 1945.

86 Ibid., "Commercial Policy, London, May, 1945 – "Mackintosh" written in hand on top, 13 June 1945.

87 Skidelsky, *John Maynard Keynes*, III: 339; Moggridge, *Maynard Keynes*, 680.

88 LAC RG19, Mackintosh Papers, 3981/L11, ASD (Commodities) (44) 1st Meeting, 1 March 1944; Robbins in Howson and Moggridge (eds.), *Wartime Diaries*, 30–6.

89 LAC RG19, Mackintosh Papers, 3981/L11, ASD (Commodities) (44) 4th Meeting, 13 March 1944.

90 Ibid., 1st Meeting, 1 March 1944; 4th Meeting, 13 March 1944.

91 Ibid., ASD (Cartels)(44): 2nd Meeting, 14 March 1944.

92 Ibid., 1st Meeting, 8 March 1944; 2nd Meeting, 14 March 1944.

93 Ibid., 5th Meeting. 21 March 1944; "Canadian Views," 40.

94 Mackintosh, "Planning the International Trade Organization."

95 At the 1944 London Commonwealth talks, Mackintosh agreed with Keynes's contention that, had the Stabilization Fund been larger, there

would have been no need for tackling separately the problem of Britain's wartime debt (ibid., ASD (Money) (44) 8th Meeting, 15 March 1944).

96 Lydia Lopokova, Lady Keynes, added an element of theatre. On the runway in Ottawa, "Sumptuously wrapped in brown fur coat and hat, Lydia rushed towards Malcolm MacDonald [British high commissioner in Ottawa], whom she had never met, flung her arms around him, and before he could say a word, exclaimed in a loud voice, "Oh, my dear High Commisar, how are you? I dreamed zat I was lying in bed, and zat you were lying in my arms." She also interrupted talks among the British delegation "in a state of near nudity" (Skidelsky, *John Maynard Keynes*, III: 359).

97 Bryce, *Canada and the Cost of World War II*, 195, 196.

98 Keynes, *Collected Works*, 24: 76–97, 100. Keynes was struck by North American prosperity during the war and the availability of consumer goods and more specifically conditions in Ottawa: "If one ever had to emigrate, this should be the destination, not the United States."

99 Skidelsky, *John Maynard Keynes*, III: 207–8. Keynes and Eady based their request from Canada in Stage II (FY 1945–46) on planned British military spending at two-thirds of its 1944 level. Anticipating a purchase of $2.1 billion in Canadian goods, it requested that $1.2 billion be financed through Mutual Aid. Canadian officials refused to make any immediate commitment but indicated that they expected Mutual Aid to be less than $600 million in 1944.

100 Bryce, *Canada and the Cost of World War II*, 206.

101 Canada's concern about postwar discrimination by the sterling area was piqued by the comment by R.S. Hudson, UK minister of agriculture, that Britain will have none of "multilateral nonsense" (LePan, *Bright Glass of Memory*, 66–7). Keynes wrote to Clark to reassure him that Hudson represented "an attitude of mind" that prevails in parts of the public, press, and politicians that would be dispelled once Britain had something concrete to offer in return (Moggridge, *Maynard Keynes*, 783).

102 LAC RG19, Clark Papers, 4369/U-3-11, "Post-War Commercial Policy Aspects: A Proposal for Averting a Breakdown in International Trade Relationships," 25 November 1944.

103 Cited in MacKenzie, "'The Path to Temptation,'" 197.

104 LAC RG19, Clark Papers, 4369/U-3-11, Telegrams 45, 46, and 47.

105 Ibid., Hudd to Robertson, 28 February 1945.

106 Ibid., Vincent Massey, 4 May 1945, No. A. 160.

107 Ibid., Stephen L. Holmes to Clark, 4 May 1945.
108 Ibid., Keynes to Mackintosh, 15 May 1945.
109 LePan, *Bright Glass of Memory*. Douglas Valentine LePan (1914–1998) was born in Toronto and educated at the University of Toronto (BA) and Oxford (BA, MA). He taught briefly at Toronto and Harvard (where he was a friend of John Kenneth Galbraith) before serving as an artilleryman in the Canadian army. He then worked for the department of external affairs (1945–59) and taught at Queen's (1959–64) and Toronto (1964–1979). LePan won the Governor General's Award for both poetry (*The Net and the Sword*, 1953) and fiction (*The Deserter*, 1964). He was a last-minute replacement at the Cambridge meetings for Frederic Hudd, who was hospitalized with a sciatic condition (LAC RG19, Clark Papers, 4369/U-3-11, Clark to Holmes, 4 May 1945).
110 LePan, *Bright Glass of Memory*, 74, 76.
111 LePan, *Bright Glass of Memory*, 77; Bryce, *Canada and the Cost of World War II*, 222. Clifford Clark was also expected to attend, but when he suffered a collapse on May 8, Mackintosh headed the delegation on behalf of the department of finance.
112 LAC RG19, Clark Papers, 3439/U-11-3, LePan, "Minutes of Conversations Held in King's College, Cambridge, from Saturday, May 19th to Monday, May 21st between the Canadian Financial Delegation and Representatives of the United Kingdom Treasury."
113 Ibid.
114 LePan, *Bright Glass of Memory*, 57, 78, 77–8. Skidelsky (*John Maynard Keynes*, III: 393, 394) offers a peculiar interpretation of LePan's fascination with Keynes: "Although Keynes' homosexuality had long been purely sentimental, he could still exert a formidable charm on the young when stimulated to do so ... He seemed to sense that LePan – secretly at the time – shared his tastes." LePan was married from 1948 until 1971 and had two children. It was his 1990 publication of gay love poems that brought to public attention his bisexuality. How tenable was LePan's career at external affairs throughout the Cold War is an open question; in 1957, Mackintosh invited LePan to visit Queen's with an appointment in the department of English in mind (QUA, Mackintosh Papers, Additions/2, LePan to Mackintosh, 11 January 1957).
115 LePan, *Bright Glass of Memory*, 96.
116 QUA PRO 1251/1/F, Mackintosh to C.R. Fay, 1 February 1961 (see also Mackintosh, "Keynes as Public Servant"); LAC RG19, Mackintosh Papers 3577/L-00, Mackintosh to Keynes, 5 June 1945.

117 LAC RG19, Clark Papers, 3439/U-11-3 "Commercial Policy, London, May, 1945; Mackintosh's redraft on 13 June 1945.

118 Ibid., Munro to Mackintosh, 28 August 1945.

119 Ibid., LePan, "Memo to High Commissioner," 23 January 1946. On Keynes's invitation, Towers flew to Washington during the negotiations, where he sought to persuade Keynes on the value of the US waiver on repayment (Bryce, *Canada and the Cost of World War II*, 289).

120 There was a large loan outstanding from 1942 and British obligations under the Air Training program. The UK wanted all claims save the 1942 loan forgiven, plus $1.25 billion interest-free for fifty years. Eventually Canada agreed to eliminate Air Training debt ($460 million), and insisted that the 1942 loan obligations be honoured. For a detailed account of the negotiations, see MacKenzie, "The Path to Temptation."

121 "I remember with delight my experiences with you all in Ottawa, and my simplicity at not understanding how Graham Towers had learnt nearly everything I had said to Clark in a few minutes. He pointed out to me that it was a long walk from the Hotel to his house but that a telephone worked much more quickly" (QUA PRO 1251/1/E, Wilfrid Eady to Mackintosh, 23 October 1957).

122 QUA. Mackintosh Papers, 11/Correspondence 1935–66, Robbins to Mackintosh, 17 May 1966.

123 A point emphasized by Deutsch in "Canadian Views."

124 In March 1948, Deutsch and McKinnon reached a draft free-trade treaty with the United States, but King broke off talks, to the regret of Lester Pearson, because of the perceived political risks (Hilliker, *Canada's Department of External Affairs*, II: 39).

125 LAC RG49, Department of External Affairs, 2392/5-281-1. "Report of the Canadian Delegation to the Third Session of the Economic and Social Council of New York," September 11–October 3, 1946.

126 Mackintosh noted that "While our efforts at International Conferences gained us the respect of the majority of nations, they consider us as rather unusual and it might perhaps be worthwhile trying to make a number of converts beforehand" (Canada. Foreign Affairs and International Trade Canada. Documents on Canadian External Relations, v. 12 – 528 CH /Vol. 2103. Minutes of an Interdepartmental Meeting, 20 July 1946. He confided to Isadore Lubin, the American member of the ECC, that he was extremely doubtful about the ESC's potential for significant change (QUA, Mackintosh Papers, 7/180, 2 July 1946).

127 Mackintosh, "The United Nations," 221.
128 Cited in Skidelsky, *John Maynard Keynes*, III: 187.
129 LAC RG19, Deutsch Papers, 3597/D03c, Mackintosh to Herbert, 29 September 1944.

CHAPTER ELEVEN

1 QUA PRO 1251/1/H, Mackintosh to CD Howe, 7 April 1954.
2 LAC RG19, Mackintosh Papers, 3584/R09–3, "Summary of an Interim Report on Wartime Planning for Continuing Full Employment," by Paul Samuelson for the National Resources Planning Board, 28 July 1942.
3 Sharp, *Which Reminds Me*, 21.
4 Dexter, *Ottawa at War* (1 November 1943), 446.
5 Brady, "Reconstruction in Canada."
6 Subcommittee reports covered a range of issues, including "The Function of Education in Reconstruction for Canada," (by Wallace), "War Effects on the Location and Expansion of Canadian Industry" (Marsh), "Principles on Which a National Public Works Programme Should Be Based," and "Population Trends Underlying the Potential Agricultural Development in Canada" (W.B. Hurd). For an exhaustive, careful, and insightful account of the James Committee, see Bright, "Planning to Plan."
7 LAC RG19, Mackintosh Papers, 3583/R09-1, Lord Astor to James, 4 November 1941; James to Mackenzie King, 19 November 19, 1941; Hugh Keenleyside, Memorandum for Mr Heeney, 22 November 1941.
8 Ibid., 3583/R09-3, Maxwell Cohen, "Review of Machinery of Economic Control Set Up under the War Measures Act in Relation to Post-war Administration Exigencies," Committee on Reconstruction, nd, 12. There is no evidence that the report was ever released to the public. For a review of Cohen's career, see MacDonald, "Maxwell Cohen at Eighty."
9 Mackintosh scolded Heeney on more than one occasion for mentioning the EAC in public communications, or for referring public inquiries to the EAC on the grounds that the EAC operated under a "confidential relationship with the Cabinet. It has never had, and ought not to have, direct contact with individuals and organizations outside the Government" (LAC RG19, Bryce Papers, 3446, Mackintosh to Heeney, 1 February 1943).
10 Slater, *War Finance*, 185.
11 LAC MG 26, King Diary, 8 August 1943.

12 In a lukewarm review of James's *Economics of Money, Banking and Credit* (New York: Donald Press, 1929), Mackintosh wrote that "Not all parts of his book, however, are equally well digested" (*JCBA* (1930) 38(1)).

13 See Bright ("Planning to Plan") for a summary of the factors contributing to the tensions surrounding the James Committee and the interpretations offered by various authors. A compelling argument with respect to the contradictions in relying upon an extragovernmental task force for policy advice is provided by Young, "Reining in James."

14 LAC RG19, EAC, 4660/187-EAC-4(2), "Report of the EAC on the Reconstruction Committee's Recommendations regarding Ministerial Responsibility for Reconstruction Planning," 30 November, 1942; LAC RG19, Mackintosh Papers, 3583/R09-3, Committee on Reconstruction, "Interim Report Regarding Certain Aspects of Government Machinery for the Planning of Reconstruction Policies," 2 October 1942.

15 Dexter, *Ottawa at War*, 405

16 LAC RG19, Mackintosh Papers, 3583/R09-3, James to Mackintosh, 28 September 1942.

17 Ibid., Clark to Mackintosh, n.d.

18 Ibid., 3584/R09, James to King, 13 January 1943.

19 Ibid., King to James, 16 January 1943.

20 Dexter, *Ottawa at War*, 405.

21 Ibid., 406. Christie provides an insightful commentary on the politics surrounding the Marsh Report and adds to the intrigue surrounding its early release when she asks: "What prompted Mackenzie King to personally intervene on 17 February 1943 to have Leonard Marsh's research findings on social insurance published rather than the long-awaited recommendations of the James Committee?" (Christie, *Engendering the State*, 274).

22 LAC RG19, Mackintosh Papers, 3584/R-09, Heeney to Mackintosh, 17 March 1943; Mackintosh to Heeney, 10 February 1943.

23 Dexter, *Ottawa at War*, 406.

24 LAC RG19 EAC 4660/187-EAC-4(2), "Report of the Economic Advisory Committee on the Proposal to Establish a National System of Health Insurance," 20 January 1943. Writing to Clark in 1941, Mackintosh deemed public health insurance to be of secondary importance to a public pension plan (LAC RG19, Mackintosh Papers, 3580/M-02, Mackintosh to Clark, 21 November 1941).

25 Ibid., 3584/R-09, James to Mackintosh, 4 February 1943; King to James 6 March 1943.

26 Ibid., Heeney to Mackintosh, 9 April 1943; Mackintosh to Heeney, 12 April 1943; Heeney to James, 8 September 1943.

27 Ibid., Heeney to Mackintosh, 2 June 1943.

28 Ibid., W. Gordon to Mackintosh, 1 April 1943; Mackintosh to Gordon, 12 April 1943.

29 Ibid., H.F. McDonald to Mackintosh, 13 April 1943; Heeney to Mackintosh, 16 April 1943; Heeney to Marsh, 4 June 1943; James to Heeney, 2 July 1943; Heeney, to James, 3 July 1943. A meeting of the Subcommittee on the Postwar Problems of Women was cancelled by the EAC in order to "maintain careful control over expenditures," although a subsequent meeting was permitted to go ahead (ibid., Heeney to James, 28 July 1943). C.A. Curtis, who was heading the Housing Committee, was also circumspect about the James Committee. As he wrote to Mackintosh, "I asked two or three times how much of the Dominion's money they had given away but no one got around to doing it. However in light of the potentialities that were present I think that the general conclusions are really not too bad. At the same time I had to swallow hard on some of them" (ibid., C.A. Curtis to Mackintosh, 9 December 1943). There was clearly some friction between Curtis and Marsh, the latter informing Mackintosh that "the Housing Report is just finished except for some typing and a couple of Appendices. I still have to clear it with Curtis, and have arranged a conference with him. I suppose it is no secret to you that I have had to assume practically the whole burden of writing the text" (ibid., Marsh to Mackintosh, nd).

30 LAC, RG19 EAC 4660, EAC, "Report of the Economic Advisory Committee on the Report of the Advisory Committee on Reconstruction."

31 Avison worked in Sun Life's British Securities Section of the Investment Division. At the age of thirty-one, he was highly regarded, and had been sought earlier to work on the national income accounts. He entered at a salary of $4,500, enough to compensate him for his work in Montreal with Sun Life and as a lecturer at Sir George Williams College. He joined Mackintosh's staff in February 1943 and remained until the company petitioned his release, effective October 1945 (LAC RG19, Mackintosh Papers. 3580/M-02-2, Mackintosh to Clark, Memorandum Re. T.L. Avison, 9 March 1943; 3588/S-13, E.A. Macnutt to Clark, 16 August 1944). Trachtenberg came recommended by

Vincent Bladen and Harold Innis. He entered at Grade IV with a salary of $1,800. Shortly after arriving in Ottawa, however, he contracted tuberculosis and was confined to a sanatorium in his home town of Winnipeg from November 1943 until September 1945. Upon his recovery he rejoined the department of finance, where he would spend the rest of his career (ibid., 3580/M-02-2, Mackintosh to Clark, "Memorandum Re. Samuel Trachtenberg," 13 March 1943; 3588/S-13, Bladen to Mackintosh, 9 April 1943; Trachtenberg to Mackintosh, 22 November 22, 1943; Mackintosh to Trachtenberg, 24 November 1943).

32 Ibid., 3580/M-2, Mackintosh to Clark, Memorandum Re. Malcolm C. Urquhart, 23 February 1943.

33 Ibid., 3588/S-13, Mackintosh to George Luxton, 6 September 1944; Cudmore to Clark, 26 October 1944; Marshall to Mackintosh, 27 October 1944.

34 LAC RG19, Bryce Papers, 3446, Bryce, "Memorandum for Dr. Mackintosh: Your List of Post-War Economic Problems," 27 January 1943; Mackintosh to Bryce, 11 February 1943.

35 Ibid., George Luxton, "The Magnitude of Civilian and Service Demobilization," 3 March 1943.

36 LAC RG19, EAC, 4660, "Draft Report of the EAC on the 2nd part of the Interim Report of the Reconstruction Committee (Oct. 2, 1942), Proposal for the Establishment of a Construction Reserve Commission," 6 January 1943.

37 LAC RG19, Bryce Papers, 3446, Subcommittee of Economic Advisory Committee on Postwar Reconstruction, Minutes for 11 March 1943.

38 Mackintosh, "The White Paper," 12.

39 QUA, Mackintosh Papers, 2/39, Stewart Bates, "Location and Effects of Wartime Industrial Expansion in Canada, 1939–44," 1 November 1945.

40 Ibid., 2/41, "Memorandum on Approach to Post-war Problems for Discussion with Department of Munitions and Supply," 9 September 1943. Mackintosh served as the representative of the Reconstruction Department on the Wartime Industries Control Board (ibid., 5/145, Mackintosh to Howe, 15 December 1944).

41 J.D. Gibson reported on "Post-War Decontrol" (28 July 1943), while Scott of the Bank of Canada provided an "Outline for Study of Financial Institutions in Relation to Post-War Requirements" (LAC RG19, Bryce Papers, 3446). Firestone's report on "The

Construction Industry in Relation to Post-war Economic Policy," prepared for the James Committee, was forwarded by Mackintosh to Trachtenberg for comments. In the latter's view, it provided a comprehensive statement of steps to be taken by industry, labour, and government, towards a three-billion-dollar "shelf" of public capital projects, but "in general I would think that some of these recommendations stand little chance of being implemented either prior to or during the immediate post-war period." He recommended that Mackintosh's group needed to incorporate the report's findings into a broader study of public spending and its economic impact (LAC RG19, Mackintosh Papers, 3584/R-09, Trachtenberg to Mackintosh, 3 September 1943).

42 LAC RG19, Bryce Papers, 3446, Mackintosh, "Draft of National Development Board," marginal notes by Bryce, 6 April 1943.

43 The EAC reiterated its endorsement of the recommendation of the James Committee (LAC RG19, Mackintosh Papers, 3583/R-09-3, Committee on Reconstruction, "Interim Report Regarding Certain Aspects of Government Machinery for the Planning of Reconstruction Policies," 2 October 1942).

44 LAC RG19, Bryce Paper, 3446, Bryce, "Rough Check List of Possible Emergency Employment Projects for Immediate Post-war Use," 28 March 1943

45 LAC RG19, EAC, 4660/187-EAC-4(2), "Report of the Economic Advisory Committee: Proposal for the Establishment of a Construction Reserve Commission in the Second Part of the Interim Report of the Reconstruction Committee," 20 February 1943

46 QUA, Mackintosh Papers, 2/41, "Memorandum on Approach to Post-war Problems for Discussion with Department of Munitions and Supply," 9 September 1943.

47 A report on housing policy, which reflected many of the initiatives undertaken by the NEC, was provided by Clifford Curtis under the auspices of the James Committee. "Summary of Findings and Recommendations of the Housing and Community Planning Subcommittee" (LAC RG19, Mackintosh Papers, 3584/R-09). Mackintosh preferred "as far as possible, to have the building demand held off so that it may serve as a stabilizer after the war" (ibid., 3567/H-02, Mackintosh to J.M. Macdonnell, 12 November 1940). Stewart Bates and an EAC working group to study basic commodities prices were chiefly responsible for the design of income support for producers (LAC RG19, Bryce Papers, 3446, Minutes of Second Meeting, 29 March 1943).

48 LAC RG19, Mackintosh Papers, 3577/L-04, Margaret Mackintosh, Memorandum for the Deputy Minister, "Family Allowances in Canada," 16 July 1941. For a discussion of the politics surrounding the issue of the family allowance in Canada, see Christie, *Engendering the State*, chap. 7.
49 Ibid., 3584/R-09, "Meeting of Sir William Beveridge with the EAC and Advisory Committee on Reconstruction on 24 May 1943," 31 May 1943.
50 Dexter, *Ottawa at War*, 451.
51 QUA Mackintosh Papers, 6/148, Mackintosh to C.A. Curtis, 7 September 1943.
52 Gordon, *Political Memoir*, 325.
53 Bryce in Slater, *War Finance*, 216; Slater, "Colour the Future Bright."
54 QUA, Mackintosh Papers, 8/202, Howe to Mackintosh, 16 October 1944.
55 LAC RG32, Public Service Commission, Series C-2, 455/1895.05.21, Memorandum, R.A.C Henry to Howe, 14 October 1944.
56 Ibid., W.C. Ronson to J. Driscoll, 29 November 1944; Clark to Howe, 9 November 1944; QUA, Mackintosh Papers, 8/202 Mackintosh to Howe, 25 October 1944.
57 Dexter, *Ottawa at War*, 499 (1 March 1945).
58 Ibid., 446–7.
59 Bryce's comments can be found in LAC RG19, Clark Papers, 3977/E-3-5(2). The third draft, written on 27 March 1945, was circulated to R.A.C Henry, Norman Robertson, Clark, Graham Towers, Oliver Masters, Donald Gordon, Sandy Skelton, John Baldwin, and Arnold Heeney. Urquhart provided labour-force projections for 1946, based on the assumptions of longer schooling, earlier retirement, women remaining in the labour force, and population forecasts. He estimated a labour force of 4.9 million and a Gross National Product of $9.2 billion, roughly double that of 1939 (QUA Mackintosh Papers, 2/42, M. Urquhart, "Postwar Labour Force," 2 February 1945).
60 QUA PRO 1251 2/M, Mackintosh to Donald Mansur, 19 April 1954.
61 Canada. Department of Reconstruction. *Employment and Income, with Special Reference to the Initial Period of Reconstruction. Ottawa, 1945.*
62 Ibid., 4.
63 Ibid., 9.

64 Ibid., 11.
65 Ibid., 16.
66 Ibid.
67 Ibid., 21.
68 Slater, "Colour the Future Bright," 195.
69 *Employment and Income*," 19.
70 Ibid., 14–15,
71 Ibid., 1, 23.
72 QUA PRO 1251 1/H, Howe to Mackintosh, 2 April 1954; Mackintosh to Howe, 7 April 1954.
73 Dexter, *Ottawa at War*, 499.
74 QUA, Mackintosh Papers, 8/205, W.S. Brooke to Mackintosh, 10 July 1945. Brooke writes, "I remember you said that you were a little weary last winter."
75 LAC RG19, EAC 4660/187-EAC-4(2),"Report of the Economic Advisory Committee on Constitutional Problems in Post-War Economic Policy," 7 June 1943.
76 Ibid., J.R. Baldwin, "Constitutional Problems of Reconstruction," 16 January 1943; Sandy Skelton, "Dominion Post-War Policy" (12 April 1943); "Constitutional Change Necessary to Deal with Post-War Problems"; and "Report of the Economic Advisory Committee on Constitutional Problems in Post-War Economic Policy."
77 QUA Mackintosh Papers, 3/76, Sandy Skelton, "Dominion-Provincial Relations Post-War," 19 February 1945.
78 Slater, "Colour the Future Bright," 207; QUA, Mackintosh Papers, 3/74, "Advisory Committee on Preparations for Dominion-Provincial Conference – Minutes, 30 May 1944; Mackintosh, "Memorandum of Suggestions for the Agenda and Procedure" 15 May 1944; 5/142, "Working Committees and Terms of Reference for Preparations of Dominion Brief to Conferences," 29 June 1945.
79 Canada, *Proposals of the Government of Canada,* 5.
80 Ibid., 7, 8. The Public Investment Committee was responsible for four subcommittees – Resource Development, Public Projects, Housing, and Agriculture and Combined Resources – which provided background reports (QUA Mackintosh Papers, 5/145, "Dominion Proposals on Public Investment," n.d; Committee on Public Investment of the Sub-Committee on Resources Development, Part 2 (July 1945); 5/142, "Interim Report of the Sub-Committee on Public Projects to the Dominion-Provincial Committee on Public Investment, July 11, 1945";

5/143, "Recommendations of the Sub-Committee on Agriculture and Combined Resources Committee on Public Investment. Dominion-Provincial Conference, 1945 – 12 July 1945."

81 Canada, *Proposals of the Government of Canada*, 28.

82 Ibid., 27.

83 Ibid., 30–3.

84 Slater, "Colour the Future Bright."

85 Canada, *Proposals of the Government of Canada*, 52.

86 QUA, Mackintosh Papers, 3/69, Heeney to Claxton, 21 January 1946. Bryce provided spending and revenue estimates under a range of economic scenarios ("a prosperous year" and a "very good year") in a memorandum entitled "Possible Projection of Canadian Budget, Fiscal Year 1948–49" (QUA, Mackintosh Papers, 3/70, Bryce to Mackintosh, 29 November 1945).

87 For one view, see Finkel, "Paradise Postponed." See also Owram's discussion in *Government Generation*, chap. 12.

88 Mackintosh, "The White Paper," 21.

89 LAC RG19 Mackintosh Papers, 3571/8, R.A.C. Henry to Mackintosh, 23 December 1941.

90 Ibid., 3554/D-00, Telegram from Alton F. Dingee to Mackintosh; Mackintosh to Dingee, 26 December 1940.

91 Ibid., 3554/D-0, Mackintosh to David Dydon, 24 February 1941.

92 Ibid., 3577/L-00, A.K. Loyd to Mackintosh, 4 September 1940; Mackintosh to Loyd, 9 September 1940.

93 QUA Mackintosh Papers, Additions 1/Five Lakes Fishing Club; Warhaugh, *Behind the Scenes*; Granatstein, *The Ottawa Men*, 14–16.

94 LAC RG19, Mackintosh Papers, 3550/B, Bladen to Mackintosh, 8 December 1941; Mackintosh to Bladen, 11 February 1941; 3588/S-00, Sidney Smith to Mackintosh, 19 March 1941.

95 Ibid., 3554/D-00, Mackintosh to S.G. Dobson, 27 October 1944.

96 LAC RG32, Public Service Commission, Series C-2, 455/1895.05.21, Mackintosh to Howe, 5 July 1946.

97 QUA Mackintosh Papers, 11/1, Howe to Mackintosh, 9 July 1946. Henry added his own word of thanks: "I need hardly tell you what a keen disappointment it is to me to have you leave us, although I fully sympathize with your decision. I recognize how very much this department owes to your ability and sound thinking, and personally you have been of great assistance to me" (ibid., 11/1, Henry to Mackintosh, 9 July 1946).

98 QUA Mackintosh Papers Additions 1/Correspondence, 1930–1950, Ilsley to Mackintosh, 7 June 1948.

PART FOUR

1 Owram, *Born at the Right Time.*
2 Axelrod, *Scholars and Dollars*, 3–6.
3 QUA Mackintosh Papers, Additions, 2/Addresses, "The Challenges and Traditions of Our Universities," 10 February 1959.
4 QUA Mackintosh Papers, Additions, 2/Addresses, "Canadian Universities in the National Life," Canadian Society of New York, 24 May 1954; "The Challenge of Growth," Canadian Institute of Mining and Metallurgy, 23 April 1957; Address to the Twenty Club, Montreal, 7th Quinquennial Dinner, 30 April 1960.
5 In defining academic freedom, Michiel Horn draws the important distinction between the university's autonomy from outside interference and the faculty's right to pursue teaching and research of their own design (*Academic Freedom in Canada*, 6). Mackintosh's interpretation was consistent with both meanings of the term.

CHAPTER TWELVE

1 *Globe and Mail*, 24 August 1950, 6.
2 QUA, Gibson Papers, R.C. Wallace to Mackintosh, 13 May 1943; Mackintosh to Wallace, 18 May 1943.
3 QUA, Mackintosh Biography File.
4 QUA Mackintosh Papers, Additions 1/Death, Elspeth (Wallace) to Jean Mackintosh.
5 Frank Knox, "William Archibald Mackintosh."
6 Gibson, *To Serve*, 249; "Report of the School of Commerce and Administration," and "Report of the Faculty of Arts," in Queen's University, *Report of the Principal, 1946–47.*
7 The decrease in staff was outstripped by the decline in enrolment, such that Knox stated in April 1942 that "our marginal productivity here is going to be pretty low." Knox feared further staff reductions might be necessary, but may well have been overstating the case as a rather awkward way of asking Mackintosh if some temporary work in Ottawa might exist. Mackintosh replied that Principal Wallace had no intention of reducing the staff and had refused to release J.A. Corry

from wartime service after failing to secure George Grant as a possible replacement. Nonetheless, while questioning the "propriety of bringing more Queen's people into the Department [of Finance]" he arranges some part-time summer work for Knox. C.A. Curtis and Smails also undertook part-time government work, with Curtis noting the "quantitative inadequacy of the good people in Ottawa" (QUA, Mackintosh Papers, 6/148, C.A. Curtis to Mackintosh, 14 January 1942; C.A. Curtis to Mackintosh, 16 November 1943; Knox to Mackintosh, 19 April 1942; Mackintosh to Knox, 28 April 1942).

8 Personal politics may also have played a role in the case of C.D. Wade. When he sought promotion to a permanent position. Knox stated emphatically that Wallace would never promote him and, when asked to intervene, Mackintosh advised Wallace that it was necessary to make the junior accounting positions more attractive. Wallace refused to budge, forcing Mackintosh to inform Wade that "I have never had much voice in the matter of determining salaries" and that "Much as I would dislike to see you leave the University, I think you ought not to neglect consideration of alternative posts" (ibid., Knox to Mackintosh, 27 April 1941; Mackintosh to Wallace, 24 March 1941; Mackintosh to Wade, 16 December 1940; Smails to Mackintosh, 25 November 1940). Three years later, Smails reported that relations between Wade and the rest of the department were "getting pretty strained." Wade resigned in favour of a job with the United Mine Workers of America in Glace Bay, Nova Scotia, leaving Mackintosh to "shudder to think what he is going to learn about human nature in the next few months with the UMWA. There are a lot of things that the Left Book Club did not explain" (ibid., Smails to Mackintosh, 20 July 1944; Mackintosh to Smails, 1 September 1944; Mackintosh to Smails, 27 November 1940).

9 Mackintosh was enthusiastic about promoting Corry, saw no rush in promoting Cameron, deemed Macpherson "highly competent," and McDougall "well worth promotion," despite a lacklustre reputation as a teacher due to some "undesirable mannerisms." Wallace had his own reservations about McDougall's teaching, but promoted him nonetheless (ibid., 6/148, Mackintosh to Wallace, 30 April 1941; Wallace to Mackintosh, 5 May 1941).

10 Ibid., Knox to Mackintosh, 7 March 1941; Mackintosh to Knox, 10 March 1941; QUA PRO 1250/13/9, "Subscribers to Industrial Relations Section in 1942."

11 Ibid., C.A. Curtis to Mackintosh, 9 February 1944; Mackintosh to Curtis, 15 February 1944.

12 Slater was a Winnipeger who gained an interest in economics from Pete McQueen while studying commerce at the University of Manitoba. He abandoned his studies in order to enlist in the Canadian Armed Forces in 1942. Upon being demobilized he obtained his economics degree from Queen's in 1946 and was immediately employed as a temporary lecturer for two years. He then departed for graduate studies at Chicago, and, after a brief stint at Stanford, was given a permanent appointment at Queen's in 1952. He would eventually become dean of the School of Graduate Studies and Research at Queen's University and president of York University before moving to the department of finance in 1973, and later chaired the Economic Council of Canada. Due to a series of mishaps and distractions, Slater would not receive his PhD from Chicago until 1957 (Grady, "David W. Slater").

13 QUA Mackintosh Papers, 6/148, Mackintosh to Wallace, 7 June 1944; Wallace to Mackintosh, 9 June 1944. Corry would later turn down an offer from the University of Toronto.

14 Mackintosh, Corry, and Urquhart were all enthusiastic about Hodgetts, as were Innis and Bladen of Toronto (ibid., Corry to Mackintosh, 24 March 1945; Mackintosh to C.A. Curtis, 5 February 1945; Mackintosh to Corry, 29 January 1945; Corry to Mackintosh, 27 January 1945. Gordon Robertson and James Aitchison were also considered for the position (ibid., Mackintosh to Corry, 4 October 1944). A year later, Corry inquired about D.C. Rowat, who was working with Mackintosh in Ottawa. Mackintosh deemed him to be "bright and intelligent" but too early in his graduate work to merit consideration (ibid., Corry to Mackintosh, 6 February 1946; Mackintosh to Corry, 13 February 1946).

15 Jewett obtained her MA from Queen's in 1945, held a fellowship at Radcliffe (1945–6), and was an instructor at Wellesley College (1946–7). She had completed the residency requirements for her PhD at Harvard.

16 Ibid., R.G. Smails to Mackintosh, 25 February 1946.

17 Bryce Stewart, as deputy minister of the department of labour, prevailed upon the university to release Cameron in March 1941 in order that he could serve as executive assistant to the Interdepartmental Committee on Labour Coordination and as chairman of several Conciliation Boards. C.H. Curtis's duties were shifted temporarily

from economics to the industrial relations section, and the arrangement was made permanent in 1944 (QUA PRO 1250. 13/7, Cameron to Wallace, 25 January 1944; Cameron to Wallace, 17 June 1943).

18 QUA Mackintosh Papers, 6/148, Knox to Mackintosh, 3 February 1946.

19 QUA PRO 1250/7/14, Mackintosh to Gordon J. Smith, Treasurer, 15 April 1948. There were two one-hour lecturers per week, with twelve tutorial sections conducted by senior students.

20 QUA, Frank Knox Papers, 2/4-2/2, Knox to Marvin Farrell, 21 December 1948; Knox to Urquhart, 12 February 1949.

21 "Report of the Faculty of Arts" in Queen's University, *Report of the Principal, 1946–47*, 35. Corry, for instance, taught for thirteen consecutive months with only a one-week break (Gibson, *To Serve*, 260).

22 Gibson, *To Serve*, 284.

23 Gibson faults Wallace for failing to defend Shortcliffe vigorously enough because he was "jittery" about possible repercussions on an endowment-fund campaign (ibid., 291).

24 *Toronto Star*, 28 September 1949, 29.

25 Gibson, *To Serve*, 268–71.

26 Ibid., 264, 263; Mackintosh, "William Everett McNeill"; QUA, Graham Papers, Mackintosh to Fyfe, 26 May 1959.

27 Gibson, *To Serve*, 268–71.

28 QUA PRO 1251 1/D, Grant Dexter to Mackintosh, 10 April 1947. Dexter reminded hum "how seriously we take our 'Bill' in this newspaper" (QUA Mackintosh Papers, Additions 1/Correspondence, 1930–1950, Dexter to Mackintosh, May 1949).

29 QUA PRO 1251/1/A, Mackintosh to H.L. Armstrong, 9 June 1947; Mackintosh to W.M. Anderson, 18 March 1948; Mackintosh to J.C. Adams, 4 March 1950; G.R. Arnott to Mackintosh, 11 January 1951; W.J. Adams to Mackintosh, 16 April 1951; 1/C, Mackintosh to Robert Cooper, 25 May 1950.

30 Gordon, *Political Memoir*, 48.

31 Mackintosh, "A Note on the Canadian Dollar."

32 Friedman, Gordon, and Mackintosh, *Canada and the Problems of the World.*

33 Ibid., 4–5.

34 Ibid., 4.

35 Ibid., 10. In response to Friedman's characterization of Canadian loans and relief payments to Europe as "misplaced altruism," Gordon objected that it was a self-interested, long-run policy. Not only was it

designed to "prevent the spread of communism," he expected a rejuvenated European economy to be a major customer for Canadian exports: "Canada is the only country other than the US to develop a European recovery plan. Canada's contribution is far greater than any other country in proportion to its income."

36 Mackintosh, "Canada's Stake in Anglo-American Solidarity"; "Canadian Dollar," 53.

37 A review of Canada's historical dependence on trade with Europe is provided in Mackintosh, "Dependence on Export Markets Overseas."

38 Copland's career had many parallels with Mackintosh's, including scholarly work on primary commodities and government advising during World War II. He later served as the Australian High Commissioner to Canada (Harper, "Copland").

39 QUA Mackintosh Papers, 11/2, Mackintosh to L.G. Melville, 11 May 1951; Melville to Mackintosh, 18 May 1951.

40 Mackintosh's round trip from Kingston to Sydney cost $1,400 (ibid., Mackintosh to W.S. Hamilton, 26 September 1951; Mackintosh to V.A. Edgeloe, 14 October 1953; J.K. Gifford to Mackintosh, 12 May 1952; QUA, Mackintosh Papers, Additions 1/2, Mackintosh to Innis, 13 September 1951).

41 QUA Mackintosh Papers, 11/2, Mackintosh appealed to J. Harvey Perry in preparing for the visit. "One of the things which I am supposed to know something about when I get there is federal finance and I find that my knowledge and documentation stops about 1946" (ibid., Mackintosh to Perry, 23 May 1951).

42 Ibid., Mackintosh to Copland, 19 September 1951.

43 Mackintosh, "Federal Finance," 105.

44 Ibid., 86, 89, 91.

45 Ibid., 100, 104.

46 QUA PRO 1250/13/14, Mackintosh to Clark, 11 September 1951.

47 QUA Mackintosh Papers, 5/113-116; 3/80-94. He also served on the National Advisory Committee on Manpower, formed in 1951, by virtue of his role on the UI Advisory Committee.

48 In his annual report for 1949, he complained that "some significant and unintended drain on the Fund through the payment of benefits to married women who have really withdrawn from employment but who represent themselves as unemployed for the purpose of drawing benefit" (ibid.).

49 LAC RG50, Unemployment Insurance Advisory Committee, 50/U05/12, Mackintosh to MacNamara, 9 February 1943; 51/3 Mackintosh to

W.C. Macdonald, MP, 18 July 1941; 51/17, Mackintosh, "Draft Letter to Unemployment Insurance Advisory Committee" n.d, n.a

50 QUA, Mackintosh Papers, 8/195, Heeney to Mackintosh, 10 June 1948. Upon Claxton's appointment as minister of defence, Mackintosh sent a note of congratulations: "There is certainly great need for an enlightened policy and for a background of experience in linking our Defence policy up with our United Nations obligations" (QUA PRO 1251/1/C, Mackintosh to Claxton, 13 December 1946).

51 QUA, Mackintosh Papers, 8/195, Heeney to Claxton, 19 July 1948.

52 Ibid., H.H. Wrong to Heeney, 16 July 1948.

53 Ibid., Mackintosh to Claxton, 15 October 1948.

54 QUA PRO 1251/1/C, Claxton to Mackintosh, 18 October 1948.

55 See Mackintosh, "Douglas Alexander Skelton."

56 Kindleberger, *Life of an Economist*, 63.

57 Corry, *My Life and Work*, 110; QUA, Mackintosh Papers (Additions) 1/3, Sandy Skelton to Mackintosh, 14 June 1950.

58 Rosenbluth and Thorburn, "Canadian Anti-Combines."

59 As the committee's deliberations stretched out into 1952, Mackintosh found it difficult to devote to it sufficient time and was "rather worried as to the outcome of our prolonged inquiry." The committee gathered in Ottawa for an extended weekend in February to revise the draft report (QUA PRO 1251/1/C, Mackintosh to George Curtis, 4 January 1952; 1/Mc, MacQuarrie to Mackintosh, 9 February 1952).

60 Canada. Department of Justice. *Report of the Committee*, 29.

61 Ibid., 43–6. 50.

62 Rosenbluth and Thorburn ("Canadian Anti-Combines") argue that the government did little to expand the scope of the anti-combine's office. Their review of the administration of the act between 1952 and 1960 indicates that staff, expenditures, and the number of publications did increase, but the amount spent was about the same as that spent by the Newfoundland Bait Service.

63 QUA PRO 1251 1/F, Mackintosh to O.J. Firestone, 23 April 1952. Firestone replied that the responses to the report "have so far been surprisingly mild, most of them speaking favourably about the modesty of the recommendations. However, second reactions may be a bit more critical on matters of detail. In our department (trade and commerce) the feeling is that the report represents a constructive step forward" (ibid., Firestone to Mackintosh, 19 April 1952).

64 QUA PRO 1251 1/G, Mackintosh to Garson, 26 June 1952.

65 QUA PRO 1251/1/C, Mackintosh to Maxwell Cohen, 7 November 1952.

66 QUA Mackintosh Papers, 6/150.

67 Just three years earlier, Mackintosh was chiefly responsible for Gordon being awarded an honorary degree from Queen's. "I used to boast that we belong to the same fishing club and now I can add that we belong to the same university … You will present yourself suitably dressed, which means a dark suit or morning clothes but without the gardenia" (QUA, PRO 1251/1/G, Mackintosh to Gordon, 8 April 1947; Mackintosh to Gordon, 15 April 1947).

68 Jean could attest to Gordon's lack of aplomb. Once, while at the fishing club, she had difficulty getting the very youthful Alison to sleep, prompting Gordon to assume the uninvited child-rearing initiative, which amounted to trying to terrify Alison into compliance. His efforts were unsuccessful.

69 Gordon is cited in QUA, Mackintosh Papers, 6/150, Mackintosh, "Memorandum re. negotiations conducted by Dr. W.A. Mackintosh, as Mediator in railway dispute, Montreal, August 19–22, 1950."A majority report of a conciliation board, issued in May 1950, recommended a seventeen-cent-per-hour increase and a forty-four-day work week. It was characterized by Gordon as "impartial and fair," while F.H. Hall of the unions' committee dismissed its "ill-founded and unwarranted conclusions" (QUA, Mackintosh Papers, 6/150, Hall to Humphrey Mitchell, 11 May 1950).

70 *Toronto Star*, 18 August 1950, 1, 2; 19 August 1950, 19.

71 QUA, Mackintosh Papers, 6/150, "Memorandum re. negotiations conducted by Dr. W.A. Mackintosh, as Mediator in railway dispute, Montreal, August 19–22, 1950."

72 Estimates that Mackintosh received from the department of labour placed the cost of the railways' final position at $102.7 million and the unions' at $115 million (ibid., Mackintosh to MacNamara, 28 August 1950).

73 The government estimated a more modest impact of the strike. In addition to the 125,000 striking workers, 40,000 non-striking railway employees and 15,000 workers in other industries had been laid off. A further 30,000 layoffs in the automobile industry were also anticipated (ibid., "Railway Labour Dispute Bulletin 3," 26 August 1950).

74 *Globe and Mail*, 24 August 1950, 6.

75 *Globe and Mail*, 30 August 1950, 4. On the history of back-to-work legislation, see Price, "Back-to-Work Legislation."

76 *Globe and Mail*, 31 August 1950, 24. Hall and Mosher gave a qualified endorsement of Mackintosh's efforts: "Failure of the talks to bring about an agreement was by no means the fault of the administrator, who was a very able and conscientious man. It was evident, however, that in the mind of the government and of Dr. Mackintosh the term 'mediation' was synonymous with the word 'compromise.' In fact, the first thing that Dr. Mackintosh said to the railways and our committees was that the Prime Minister wanted an agreement between the parties and to effect one there would have to be compromise on both sides" (*Globe and Mail,* 24 August 1950, 12).

77 *Toronto Star*, 30 August 1950, 3.

78 QUA, Mackintosh Papers, 11/2, Mackintosh to D.B. Copland, 10 October 1950. Mackintosh's involvement in the railway dispute also marked a precedent in terms of the trend away from judges in the role of mediating labour disputes (*Globe and Mail*, 4 October 1950, 25).

79 In a personal letter to Mackintosh he stated: "I realize, of course, that some harm has undoubtedly been done mostly with regard to my relationship with the rank and file However, I am convinced that it is not of a character which cannot be repaired and I have a number of plans afoot which will in due course re-establish my position on a satisfactory basis – at least I hope so" (QUA, Mackintosh Papers, Additions 1/Correspondence, 1930–1950, Gordon to Mackintosh, 30 September 1950).

80 *Ottawa Citizen*, 20 August 1950; cited in Price, "Back-to-Work Legislation," 98. Price suggests that the use of legislation to end work stoppages reflected the state's perception that Canadian unions were too weak to "woo" into a formal tripartite arrangement, yet too powerful to contain within the existing collective bargaining framework.

81 LAC MG30 D33, Skelton Papers, 3/31, Clark to Skelton 22 June 1929.

82 Gibson, *To Serve*, 303. Gibson could only speculate that Richardson's objections were also based on Mackintosh's agnosticism (QUA, Gibson Papers, 5/14, Gibson to Agnes Richardson (Mrs William Benedickson), 30 July 1979).

83 Ibid. and QUA, Gibson Papers, 5/14 Richardson to Macdonnell, 14 July 1950; Macdonnell to Richardson, 1 September 1950.

84 "A few of us, who regard the most-mentioned candidate to date as less than adequate for the position, are going to be 'on the spot' unless we can bring forward at least one candidate whose qualifications merit

general appraisal" (ibid. and QUA Gibson Papers 5/14 Richardson to Whitton, 26 October 1950).

85 Ibid., Richardson to Macdonnell, 19 April 1951; "W.A. Mackintosh's Appointment as Principal."

86 QUA, Mackintosh Papers, 11/4, Ed Hall to Mackintosh, n.d.

87 Ibid., Walter Gordon to Mackintosh, 21 December 1950.

88 Ibid., Walter Gordon to Mackintosh, 22 May 1951.

89 QUA Mackintosh Papers, 11/4, Sidney Smith to Mackintosh.

90 QUA Mackintosh Papers, 11/4.

91 *Ottawa Journal*, 22 May 1951.

92 QUA Mackintosh Papers 11/4, Sim to Mackintosh, 25 May 1951.

93 QUA Mackintosh Papers, 11/4, Graham George to Mackintosh.

94 QUA PRO 1250/13/14, Brockington to R.C. Wallace, 9 July 1951.

95 QUA Mackintosh Papers, 11/4, Hamilton to Mackintosh, Cameron to Mackintosh, Orr to Mackintosh, 29 August 1951.

96 QUA Mackintosh Papers, 11/4, Macdonald to Mackintosh, n.d.

CHAPTER THIRTEEN

1 QUA PRO 1251/2/R, Mackintosh to Gordon Robertson, 8 April 1958.

2 QUA PRO 1251/1/L, Mackintosh to Neil M. Leckie, 10 August 1961.

3 QUA PRO 1251/1/G, Mackintosh to Eric R. Gold, 10 September 1951.

4 QUA PRO 1251/2/T, Mackintosh to Nancy Townsend, 8 February 1960; Secretary to Mackintosh to Miss N. Tobin, 1 May 1956; Mackintosh to H.L. Tracy, 9 September 1957; 1/K, J.N. Knull to Mackintosh, 9 January 1957; 2/PQ, Mackintosh to J. Steadmond, 7 October 1960; 1/I, Mackintosh to Mrs. R.S. Detlor, 27 October 1960.

5 QUA PRO 1251/2/NO, Mackintosh to Hubert Osborne, 28 April 1954.

6 One local retailer complained that "If our city boys behaved as some of these lads did last night, they would be placed under arrest." Mackintosh could only appeal to the chief commissioner of the Liquor Control Board to enforce the twenty-one-year age limit on the purchase and consumption of alcohol (QUA PRO 1251 1/Mc, R.M. McRae to Mackintosh, 22 September 1960; 1/L, Mackintosh to the Chief Commissioner of the Liquor Control Board of Ontario, 18 November 1955). Rowdiness at football games was a "never ending problem," so much so that the occasions when fans were well behaved prompted letters of praise (Mackintosh to Gordon Porter, 2/P,

4 November 1955; 1/G, Mackintosh to Patricia Gervan, 23 November 1955; 2/S, Mackintosh to E.R. Stuart, 28 November 1955; 2/W, Mackintosh to J.A. Walker, 17 November 1960; 1/Corry, 1951–61, Mackintosh to Corry, 31 October 1960; 2/No, Mackintosh to Grattan O'Leary, Editor, *Ottawa Journal*, 4 November 1955).

7 QUA PRO 1251/1/Corry, 1951–61, Mackintosh to Corry, 15 September 1960; 1/B, Mackintosh to R.G. Beck, 20 April 1961; 1/C, Mackintosh to Brooke Claxton, 22 April 1955.

8 QUA PRO 1251 passim; 1/C, Mackintosh to Robert Chisholm, 13 February 1952; 1/U, Mackintosh to Industrial Relations Alumni Group, 14 May 1960.

9 QUA PRO 1251/1/B, Mackintosh to R.G. Beck, 20 April 1961.

10 QUA PRO 1251/1/K, Mackintosh to C.P. Kindleberger, 12 December 1958; 1/A, Dr. T. Alty, Carnegie Corporation, Cambridge, Mass., to Mackintosh, 19 November 1953. After visiting Queen's in 1953, Lord Gilbert Campion wrote: "You are very fortunate in having captured and retained the air of academic peace and dignity which Oxford used to have forty or fifty years ago and is now rapidly losing" (ibid., 1/C, Campion to Mackintosh, 14 March 1953).

11 QUA PRO 1251/1/G, Walter Gordon to Mackintosh, 29 February 1960; 10 April 1957.

12 Mackintosh joined Gordon and Douglas Stuart, the American ambassador to Canada ("who is good fun" said Gordon) for a week of fishing. The plan was to fish for salmon from dawn to dusk. "It is a great way to get a rest but limits the amount of time and energy left for carousing," Gordon told him. Mackintosh responded that "I accept with great pleasure and very warm gratitude. I have on occasion by various means caught a trout and a bass but I have never risen into that level of the hierarchy where salmon are killed. However, some of those whom I have heard boast of proficiency in the art encourage me to think that it might not be beyond my talents." (QUA PRO 1251/1/G, Walter Gordon to Mackintosh, 19 April 1955; Mackintosh to Walter Gordon, 22 April 1955).

13 QUA PRO 1251/1/Corry, 1951–61, Mackintosh to Corry, 8 December 1960.

14 Mackintosh, "Queen's Faces the Future"; "Better Teachers Not a Luxury, Says Mackintosh," *Globe and Mail*, 12 March 1957, 12; QUA Mackintosh Papers, Additions, 2/Addresses, "The Challenge of Growth," an address to the Canadian Institute of Mining and Metallurgy, 23 April 1957.

15 Mackintosh, "Queen's University at Kingston," in QUA Mackintosh Papers, Materials from West Campus, Box 1.
16 QUA PRO 1251/2/M Munro to Mackintosh, 18 November 1954.
17 Ibid., Mackintosh to James B. McClinton, 16 June 1959.
18 QUA Mackintosh Papers, Additions, 2/Addresses, Universities Dinner Dance, Ottawa, 22 February 1957.
19 QUA Mackintosh Papers, Additions, 2/Addresses, "To the First Year Students," 29 September 1954; Address to Class of 1955.
20 QUA PRO 1251/1/Mc, Mackintosh to James B. McClinton, 16 June 1959. Mackintosh rejected the use of television as a medium of instruction as not being "Queen's stock in trade" (2/UV, Mackintosh to M.J. Veehaler, 19 September 1957).
21 Mackintosh, "Inaugural Address," in Queen's University *Proceedings*, 11; QUA Mackintosh Papers, Additions, 2/Addresses, "To the First Year Students," 29 September 1954; QUA PRO 1251/1/Mc, Mackintosh to Mary McCallum, Ontario Educational Association, 24 March 1952.
22 QUA PRO 1251/1/H, Mackintosh to C.R. Howey, 17 February 1960.
23 QUA Mackintosh Papers, Additions 1/RMC Convocation, 29 September 1962.
24 "Better Teachers Not a Luxury, Says Mackintosh," *Globe and Mail*, 12 March 1957, 12.
25 QUA Mackintosh Papers. Additions 2/Financial Campaign, 1957, "The Fight of Our Universities", 2/Addresses, "National Expansion and Human Resources" Canadian Club, Montreal, 25 February 1957; Fall Convocation address, University of British Columbia, 25 October 1957.
26 QUA PRO 1251/2/UV, Mackintosh to M.J. Vechsler, Consul and Trade Commission of Canada, Detroit, 27 May 1955
27 QUA PRO 1250/13/11, Mackintosh to Cameron, 19 September 1955.
28 QUA PRO 1250/13/11, Mackintosh to Cameron, 19 September 1955; Cameron to Mackintosh, 27 January 1956; Report on the Work of the Department of Industrial Relations, 24 January 1956. When C.H. (Connie) Curtis was singled out for criticism by Cameron for his excessive involvement in conciliation work for private income, Curtis responded by placing blame for the department's direction on its long-standing pro-management bias. "The work in Industrial Relations was originally sponsored by a small group of companies concerned, in the face of a growing and militant trade union movement, with management's lack of experience in collective bargaining." As these companies

developed their own industrial-relations departments, the Queen's department became more focussed on internal work and began teaching credit courses, but both largely directed towards personnel management. "For some years I have been protesting that hostility to trade unions is a thoroughly unsound foundation on which to formulate the policy of the Department … I am satisfied that my isolation from what has been going on in the Department is largely a result of my outspoken criticism of what I regard as unsound policy. It is partly a result, too, of my insistence that I would associate [as?] freely with trade union people as with employers." He would reiterate this view a few years later, arguing that "it is impossible to establish a programme that both labour and management would be prepared to accept as a bona fide 'neutral' undertaking … I find it difficult to justify the existence of a 'centre' of Industrial Relations with such a narrow [pro-management] outlook" (QUA PRO 1250/13/11, C.H. Curtis to Mackintosh, 10 April 1956; C.H. Curtis to Mackintosh, 1 April 1960).

29 QUA PRO 1250/13/11, Mackintosh to Corry, Deutsch, Duncan, Curtis, and Macpherson, 18 January 1960; Deutsch to Corry, 7 June 1963. A graduate of Queen's, Woods held a PhD from Princeton and had been in charge of industrial-relations research for Imperial Oil. He faced resistance in extending the centre's work and competing for scarce space within the department from Clifford Curtis who, as head, was "doubtful if there is a place for the present Industrial Relations section as an entity even if designated as an Institute within the Department, or the Business School" (QUA PRO 1250/13/11, C.A. Curtis to Mackintosh, 19 February 1960; Wood to Curtis, 10 April 1963; C.A. Curtis to Wood, 17 April 1963).

In 1954, he promoted the introduction of geography within the department of political and economic science, and Donald Q. Innis, the son of Harold and Mary Q. Innis, was hired to this end. The results, however, were disappointing. Mackintosh wrote to Clifford Curtis that "the hope has been held out to Innis that he might by stages develop a department but the initiative has not been very apparent … I find him very uncommunicative. As far as I know, he does his teaching conscientiously though there has been criticism that he does not make himself heard" (QUA PRO 1250/18/16, Mackintosh to C.A. Curtis, 14 January 1957).With endowment funds for a chair, geography was established as a separate department under the leadership of Richard Ruggles.

30 QUA PRO 1251/2/S, Mackintosh to Roy G. Sharp, 26 September 1957; 2/NO, Mackintosh to Dean R.O. Earl, 22 August 1958.

31 QUA PRO 1251/1/B, Mackintosh to Stewart Bates, 1 December 1959.

32 Mackintosh, "Inaugural Address," in Queen's University *Proceedings*, 11.

33 Walters, "'Let Right Be Done.'" Diefenbaker proved to be a gracious guest, but the ceremony was marred by a student shouting "Heil!" during the prime minister's address. In response to a complaint, Mackintosh answered that students were not representatives of the university but part of the interested public. "Even if we had the desire, we have no means by which we can enforce uniformity of conduct upon them" (QUA PRO 1251/1/Mc, Mackintosh to Cora McCulloch, 26 March 1958). Censuring the unpredictable William McAdam "Billy" Nickle proved a different matter. As the local Progressive Conservative member of the provincial legislature and the minister of planning and development, Nickle's support for the university was important, but Mackintosh found that "some of his speeches are startling." So when Nickle asked that a portrait of his father be unveiled during the Law school ceremonies, Mackintosh arranged for Diefenbaker to do so, but was determined to prevent Nickle from making a speech. Mackintosh informed Corry that "he may have been annoyed that he was not asked to speak. This, I assure you, was no accident" (ibid., 2/Corry, 1951-61, Mackintosh to Corry, 31 October 1960).

34 QUA PRO 1251/1/F, Mackintosh to Senator W.A. Fraser, 23 August 1961.

35 "The beauties of Frontenac County are a joy forever but not to a university treasurer" (Mackintosh, "Inaugural Address," in Queen's University *Proceedings*, 11).

36 QUA PRO 1251/2/T, Mackintosh to H.A. Tanser, 28 January 1960.

37 QUA PRO 1251/1/C, Mackintosh to Clifford A. Curtis, 17 December 1954.

38 QUA PRO 1251/2/W, Mackintosh to Frank Wallace, 4 October 1955.

39 One of his measures of the university's performance in teaching, and a greater source of pride, was the number of Woodrow Wilson fellowships and National Research Council awards obtained by its students (QUA PRO 1251/2/Corry, 1951–61, Mackintosh to Corry, 7 April 1961).

40 QUA PRO 1251/2/M, Mackintosh to *Montreal Star*, 11 November 1955.

41 QUA PRO 1251/2/T Mackintosh to H.A. Tanser, 28 January 1960.

42 QUA PRO 1251/1/Mc, Mackintosh to Joyce MacKinnon, 25 September 1958; Mackintosh to James B. McClinton, 16 June 1959; 2/M, Mackintosh to *Montreal Star*, 11 November 1955.

43 QUA PRO 1251/2/S, Mackintosh to I. Norman Smith, 15 September 1960. Mackintosh attended the 1952 meetings of the American Economic Association in Chicago, where he served as a discussant on a paper by W.W. Rostow. In 1954 he acquiesced to S.D Clark's request to review Vernon Fowke's manuscript on the "National Policy and Wheat Economy" (Mackintosh to S.D. Clark, 18 June 1954) and in 1958 chaired the opening session of the Economic History Association when it met in Toronto (Mackintosh to W.T. Easterbrook, 8 Sept. 1958). He declined to participate in editing a book of readings on the Canadian economy for Macmillan of Canada on the grounds that he had little to contribute (Mackintosh to R.H. Strachan, April 1958). *The Canadian Economy: Selected Readings* was published in 1961 under the editorship of Deutsch, Burton S. Keirstead, Kari Levitt, and Robert M. Will. He also declined an invitation from Leon Dupriez (a wartime associate) to participate in a colloquium with Simon Kuznets, H.H. Habakkuk, H. Singer, Carlos Gini, A.K. Cairncross, and E.D. Domar at the International Economics Association meetings in Louvain, Belgium, in 1953 (Mackintosh to Leon Dupriez, University de Louvain, Belgium, 7 April 1953). He did serve on the Universities Advisory Committee of the Economic Development Institute, a college run by the International Bank for Development and Reconstruction, under the direction of A.K. Cairncross, to help train senior officials of the bank's member governments who held important economic posts in underdeveloped countries (Eugene R. Black, President, IBRD to Mackintosh, 18 May 1955). Between 1953 and 1955, he participated in a series of town-hall meetings in New York City on Canadian-American relations sponsored by the Council on Foreign Relations. His own contribution was published as "The People and Their History."

44 Among the students attending his last class was Peter D. McClelland, who won the Knox Scholarship at Harvard and went on to a distinguished career at Cornell (QUA PRO 1251/1/Mc, Mackintosh to McClelland, 6 April 1961). Mackintosh also followed with interest the progress of recent graduates in economics and commerce. In the early 1950s, Gerald Taber completed his MBA at Harvard, J.H. Young was at Cambridge, and Gail Ward was studying at the London School of Economics under the supervision of James Meade. E.A.G. Robinson appealed for more Canadian graduates to be sent to Cambridge: "Before the war we had a remarkable series of Canadian research students who played a very great part in the life of our faculty in Cambridge in the great formative years in the 30s. Some of them are

playing equally important parts, I think, in Canadian affairs today. We have not had since the war more than a very few research students from Canada. We would dearly like to have one or two of the caliber of Wynn Plumptre and Bob Bryce. Do encourage one of your men to think about coming to Cambridge." Mackintosh was forced to admit that "we are going through a decidedly thin period ... we have actually fewer honours graduates in economics then we had in the thirties and it will be a few years before we forge ahead once more" (QUA PRO 1251/2/R, Robinson to Mackintosh, 11 December 1953; Mackintosh to Robinson, 22 December 1953).

45 QUA PRO 1251/1/Corry, 1938-50, "Press Release: Re. Appointment of J.A. Corry as Vice Principal."

46 QUA PRO 1251/2/W, Mackintosh to George Wilson, 23 April 1957.

47 QUA PRO 1250/19/16, Mackintosh to Claude Bissell, 9 January 1952.

48 Ibid., Mackintosh to Members of the Academic Staff, 17 May 1952.

49 Ibid., Salary letter, 20 May 1957

50 Ibid., Salary letter, 23 May 1960. Modest pension benefits were put in place in 1950, with retirees receiving $400 a year. This was later revised to provide supplementary pension benefits of $480 a year until the individual qualified for the old-age pension upon reaching the age of seventy (QUA PRO 1251/2/W, Mackintosh to Wilson, 23 April 1957). He also deemed the provisions for sabbatical leaves at Queen's to be more generous than at most Canadian universities (QUA PRO 1250/19/16, Mackintosh to J.T. Macfarlane, 21 November 1960; Mackintosh to W.F.G. Daechsel, 22 July 1960).

51 QUA PRO 1251/1/L, Mackintosh to Irénée Lussier, 16 July 1958.

52 Mackintosh, Queen's University, *Report of the Principal*, 1967–58, 14. Mackintosh did express to Corry his frustration that department heads were using research associateships as an extra salary inducement in recruiting staff" (QUA PRO 1251/1/Corry 1951-61, Mackintosh to Corry, 15 August 1961.

53 Cited in Gibson, *To Serve*, 342.

54 QUA PRO 1251/1/H, Cameron Hillmer to Mackintosh, 6 July 1960; Mackintosh to Hillmer, 7 July 1960. Mackintosh deemed Rosenbluth to be a "first-class" person (1/C, Mackintosh to Clifford A. Curtis 17 December 1954).

55 QUA PRO 1251/1/D, Mackintosh to F.C. Doak (Quebec Telephone), 12 November 1956.

56 QUA PRO 1251/1/H, Mackintosh to Mrs Louis Horlick, 25 March 1955.

57 QUA, PR, Mackintosh to F.C. Lawson, 5 January 1960
58 LAC, MG30 D204, Frank Underhill Papers, v. 6, Underhill to Mackintosh, 6 December 1958; Mackintosh to Underhill, 8 December 1958. For a full account of the Crowe Affair see Horn, *Academic Freedom in Canada.*
59 QUA PRO 1251/2/W, Mackintosh to H.D. Woods, 12 March 1952.
60 QUA PRO 1251/1/G, Mackintosh to W. Gordon, 4 December 1956.
61 Canada, *Royal Commission on National Development in the Arts, Letters and Sciences, 1949–1951.* Report (Ottawa, 1951), chap. 12.
62 QUA PRO 1251/1/H, Mackintosh to H.J. Hamilton, 8 March 1960. His correspondents over the period include Cyrus Eaton; Arthur W. Rogers (Canadian Bankers' Association); A.J.E. Child (Canada Packers); Herbert H. Lank (Dupont of Canada); A.H. Lemmon (Dominion Mortgage); R.M. Fowler (Canadian Pulp and Paper Association); J. Roy Gordon (the first Canadian president of INCO and also a Queen's graduate); I.K. Johnston (Imperial Bank of Canada); Clarence Fraser (Bell Telephone Company of Canada and a long-time supporter of the industrial-relations centre); W.O. Twaits and D.S. Simmons (Imperial Oil); Hugh G. Hilton (Steel Company of Canada); James E. Neilson (Foster Wheeler of St Catharines); H.T. Airey (Noranda Mines); H.H. Roggs (Canadian Westinghouse Company); A.G. Montieth (Westinghouse, NY); Lewis Sillcox (New York Air Brake Co,); Harry H Edmison (Argus Corp); Melville I Pierce (Western Leaseholds); B.S. Vanstone (Bank of Toronto); W.A. Wecker (General Motors of Canada); M.L. Urquhart (McIntyre Porcupine Mines and a former student); and R.D. Armstrong, who moved from the Canadian National Railways to Chrysler Canada ("I do not know why motors cars are more interesting than diesels but I assume the future holds attractive promises of which I am very glad") (QUA PRO 1251 passim).
63 QUA PRO 1251/2/P, Mackintosh to M.M. Porter, 14 October 1958.
64 QUA PRO 1251/2/P, Mackintosh to Eric Harvie, 29 July 1958.
65 Gibson, *To Serve*, 371.
66 QUA PRO 1251/1/Corry 1951-61, Mackintosh to Corry, 30 July 1959.
67 Gibson, *To Serve*, 382–7.
68 QUA PRO 1251/1/Corry 1951–61, Mackintosh to Corry, 6 February 1961; Mackintosh to Corry, 10 March 1961; Mackintosh to Corry, 7 April 1961. "The change of decision on the Physics Building went through without any difficulty. While Alex MacRae made a long

speech about the indignity of changing one's mind, most of the other Trustees were glad to be out of it and the decision is now made in favour of the Queen's Crescent site. I think everybody is satisfied" (Mackintosh to Corry, 9 June 1961).

69 QUA PRO 1251/1/Corry 1951–61, Mackintosh to Corry, 15 February 1961.

70 Mackintosh, "Presidential Address," *Proceedings*, 12.

71 Ibid., 14; QUA Mackintosh Papers, Additions, 2/Addresses, "The Universities and National Life," Canadian Club, Ottawa, 17 February 1953.

72 Mackintosh, "Presidential Address," 15; QUA PRO 1251/1/B, Mackintosh to A.B. Brown, 18 April 1960.

73 Mackintosh, "Presidential Address," 16. Frederick Merk appealed to Mackintosh in the case of Sigmund Diamond, "another of the academic victims of our McCarthyism." Diamond had been offered a position at Harvard when an FBI report indicated that he had been involved in a communist discussion group at Johns Hopkins. When he refused to serve as an informer, his appointment was withdrawn and he was blacklisted. As Merk stated the case, "No academic administration would take the risk of a McCarthy visitation" (QUA PRO 1251/2/M, Merk to Mackintosh, 13 May 1954).

74 Mackintosh, "Presidential Address," 16.

75 QUA PRO 1251/1/Corry, 1951–61, Mackintosh to Corry, 9 November 1960. Like Mackintosh, Graham grew up in Madoc, studied at Queen's, and earned his PhD at Harvard. He taught at Queen's from 1936 to 1946 before becoming the Rhodes Professor of Imperial History at the University of London (1949–1970). Corry commented that Graham had trouble fitting into "the world in London in which [Edward] Peacock moved," a reference presumably to financial, rather than academic, circles.

76 QUA PRO 1251/1/S, Irene M. Spry to Mackintosh, 25 August 1953; 2/NO, Mackintosh to Norman Robertson, 19 January 1953.

77 QUA PRO 1250/4/9, Mackintosh to T.H. Matthews, 17 September 1954.

78 QUA PRO 1250/4/9, Chapdelaine to Mackintosh, 9 August 1954. They would adopt the suggestion of a mulligatawny soup and chicken, mushroom curry with rice, vegetable, and dal.

79 QUA PRO 1250/4/9, Mackintosh to T.H. Matthews, 17 September 1954.

80 QUA PRO 1250/4/9, Mackintosh to Thompson, 21 July 1954.

81 QUA Mackintosh Papers, Additions, 2/Addresses, Twenty Club, Montreal, 7th Quinquennial Dinner, 30 April 1960.

82 Ibid., "The Challenge of Growth," Canadian Institute of Mining and Metallurgy, 23 April 1957.

83 Milton Gregg (minister of labour) appealed to J.M. Macdonnell to permit Mackintosh's continued service, but was refused. Mackintosh was not disconcerted: "The situation is that I find myself, as you will understand, very hard pressed by a great many new duties and particularly by the difficult problem of university finance, so that quite apart from the feelings of my Board of Trustees, I had thought it necessary to eliminate my Government commitments. Further, after having looked after that Committee for ten years, I feel that there would be at least the conventional virtue in a new broom, and I should be glad to be relieved of it" (QUA PRO 1251/1/G, 11 March 1952). Upon submitting the UI Advisory Committee's report on changes to the UI Act, Mackintosh requested his "honourable dismissal" from the committee (ibid., Mackintosh to Gregg, 2 May 1952).

84 QUA PRO 1251/1/E, Mackintosh to Harry Jackman, 31 January 1958; QUA Gibson Papers 5/14, E.C. Gill to Muriel Richardson, 14 March 1956.

85 QUA PRO 1251/1/A, Anders O. Aalborg to Mackintosh, 27 November 1957; Mackintosh to Aalborg, 29 November 1957.

86 QUA Gibson Papers 5/14, E.C. Gill to Muriel Richardson, 14 March 1956.

87 He sent congratulations to Lionel Chevrier upon his appointment as president of the St Lawrence Seaway Authority ("Though I admit that the St Lawrence runs faster at Cornwall, it is much wider at Kingston, so don't forget to visit this end of the river occasionally"); to Douglas Abbott on his move to the Supreme Court of Canada ("I am sure there is plenty of hard work connected with it, although it always seems a leisurely occupation. After your years in the Department of Finance, I would think the Supreme Court would seem for the first few weeks like a slow-motion picture"; to Elgin Armstrong, on becoming deputy minister of national defence ("It does not seem so long ago that we struggled with Veterans Postwar Benefits and you were the only person out of whom I could get hard facts and sensible judgment"). He dispensed advice to Claude Isbister (assistant deputy minister of finance) on his becoming chair of the department of economics at Dalhousie University; to Justice John D. Kearney (Board of Transportation

Commissioners) on an application filed by the Railway Association of Canada for freight rate increase; and to W. Arthur Irwin on personnel matters in the National Film Board. Others he welcomed "at least part way back into the academic field" as a university chancellor, a post requiring "the sort of fellow who gets the ulcers which the President eludes." Bertie Charles Gardner, chairman of the Bank of Montreal, became chancellor at McGill in 1952. A.E. Grauer, with whom Mackintosh worked on the Rowell–Sirois Royal Commission, became the chancellor of UBC in 1957. Mackintosh described Grauer as "one of these rare people who had reached a very high position in business and still retained his humane approach to affairs." He died in 1961 at age fifty-five. C.D. Howe would also again benefit from Mackintosh's advice in 1957, on this occasion regarding the duties of vice-chancellor, as Howe awaited the formal announcement of his appointment at Dalhousie. Mackintosh had little contact with Howe until the mid-1950s. In their limited correspondence, Howe praised Mackintosh's RSC presidential talk as "a first-class outline of Canada's development over seventy-five years" and accepted the invitation to speak at the school of commerce on Foreign Capital Investment and its Economics and Social Consequences," in June 1958. Mackintosh described him as "refreshingly relaxed and happy and prepared to give time to universities and public service" (QUA PRO 1251/1/C, Mackintosh to Lionel Chevrier, 5 July 1954; 1/A Mackintosh to Douglas Abbott, Department of Finance, 5 July 1954, 1/I, Claude Isbister to Mackintosh, 31 March 1958, Mackintosh to Isbister, 25 June 1958, and Irwin to Mackintosh, 11 February 1953; 1/K, Kearney to Mackintosh, 27 August 1952); 1/G, Mackintosh to A.E. (Dal) Grauer, 17 April 1957 and Mackintosh to Mrs. Dal Grauer, 31 July 1961; 1/H, C.D. Howe to Mackintosh, 16 November 1957; C.D. Howe to Mackintosh, 6 February 1958).

88 QUA PRO 1251/1/C, Mackintosh to Clifford A. Curtis, 17 December 1954.

89 QUA PRO 1251/1/G Walter Gordon to Mackintosh, 30 January 1958.

90 QUA PRO 1251/1/Corry 1951–61, Mackintosh to Corry, 15 September 1960. Mackintosh added that "Frank Underhill was one of those present and for awhile seemed likely to emerge as the grand old man of liberalism. However, I think they tired a little of his witticisms before this week was over."

91 QUA PRO 1251/1/C, Chapdelaine to Mackintosh, 6 January 1961; Mackintosh to Chapdelaine, 13 January 1961. The list included the children, nephews, or nieces of Claude Isbister, Hugh Keenleyside,

Senator W.A. Fraser, and Senator S.S. McKeen (QUA PRO 1251, passim).

92 QUA PRO 1251/1/C, Cobbold to Mackintosh, 23 June 1954; Mackintosh to Cobbold, 17 November 1954. Leonard Marsland Gander, the wartime correspondent for the *Daily Telegraph*, also sent his son to Queen's (2/M, Marsland to Mackintosh, London, 13 July 1953).

93 QUA, PRO 1251/1/G, Mackintosh to Donald Gordon, 16 March 1950. On the turbulent relationship between Donald Gordon and his son, see Schull, *The Great Scot.*

94 QUA PRO 1251/1/C, Mackintosh to Clifford A. Curtis, 17 December 1954; Mackintosh to Claxton, 5 July 1954; Claxton to Mackintosh, 8 July 1954.

95 QUA PRO 1251/2/T, Mackintosh to Thomas W.M. Cameron, 22 April 1957.

96 QUA PRO 1251/1/C, Mackintosh to Brooke Claxton, 28 August 1959. He was also an honorary patron of the Royal Winnipeg Ballet, despite "some skepticism of the value of the relationship to those who are promoting the extension of ballet in this country" (2R, Mackintosh to Kathleen M. Richardson, 14 September 1959).

97 Gordon, *Political Memoir*, 70. The third member of the commission was R.C. Magone, former deputy attorney general of Ontario. Mackintosh received $2,100 in remuneration (Ontario, Legislative Assembly, *Journals*, 26 February 1960, 93).

98 Willis, "Report of the Committee"; Ontario, Committee on the Organization of Government in Ontario, *Report.*

99 QUA PRO 1251/1/F, Frost to Mackintosh, 26 January 1960. When Lorne Cumming left as chair of the Ontario Municipal Board to become deputy minister of municipal affairs, Mackintosh sent a letter of congratulations: "In our report, we properly avoided consideration of personalities but the plain sense of our recommendations was that it was a mistake to load so much municipal affairs on to the Ontario Municipal Board for the sole reason that the ablest and most competent person was the Chairman of the Board. I am glad that the government has found it possible to put him in the Department and I hope that whatever else is needed to make this one of the strongest branches of government will be done" (ibid., 1/C, Mackintosh to Cumming, 22 January 1960).

100 QUA PRO 1251/1/L, D. Leiterman to Mackintosh, 16 May 1961; Mackintosh to Sol. M. Linowitz, 27 September 1955.

101 QUA Mackintosh Papers, Additions, 2/Addresses, Ontario School Inspectors' Association, 30 March 1959.

102 Mackintosh, "Shoring up the Foundations." The article is based on an address given to the Canadian Club in Winnipeg. Coincidentally, it appeared on the day of Innis's death, and a review by B.K. Sandwell of Innis's *The Strategy of Culture* appears immediately following Mackintosh's article. The juxtaposition reinforces just how far the two men had drifted apart in terms of intellectual pursuits.

103 Mackintosh, "The Canadian Economy."

104 Mackintosh, "Shoring up the Foundations," 32–3.

105 Mackintosh, "The Fissure in NATO." In a letter to Clive Davidson of the Canadian Wheat Board, Mackintosh commented that "The degree to which our Asiatic markets are widening is very impressive and I am inclined to think that the inclusion of the food-producing areas of Manchuria and Eastern Europe within the Iron Curtain and the crop of rice production in Southwestern Asia are among the really revolutionary events of our time" (Mackintosh to C.B. Davidson, 26 January 1953).

106 Mackintosh, "Shoring up the Foundations," 33–4.

107 In a personal correspondence, he confessed that "I have no faith in proposals for immediate convertibility. It is essential as a firm target but my technical knowledge is deficient as to steps by which it might be reached" (QUA PRO 1251/2/V, Mackintosh to Imre de Vegh, 10 March 1953).

108 "The Fissure in NATO," 279; "Shoring Up the Foundations," 34–5.

109 Mackintosh, "Canadian Economy and its Competitors," 121, 116, 122, 127.

110 When Hector McKinnon, head of the Tariff Board, read the *Foreign Affairs* article, he was prompted to write to Mackintosh: "I have one word of comment for your ear: Although this Board, in making the recommendation embodied in the Reports, was not consciously undertaking the 're-examination' which you prophesized would come, it is amazing to what extent our proposals do just that" (QUA, PRO 1251/1/Mc, McKinnon to Mackintosh, 22 July 1957).

111 Mackintosh, "Review of Canada's Economic Prospects."

112 He also expressed his admiration of the "distinguished writing" for which Douglas LePan was chiefly responsible (QUA PRO 1251/1/D, Mackintosh to J.H. Dales, 12 February 1958; 1/G, Mackintosh to Walter Gordon, 27 January 1958).

113 QUA PRO 1251/1/G, Mackintosh to Walter Gordon, 8 February 1957; Gordon to Mackintosh, 13 February 1957.
114 Mackintosh, "These Seventy-Five Years," 59.
115 Ibid., 68. Elsewhere he stated that "there is at present in this country quite a strong wave of nationalism which is to a considerable degree irrational, which usually means that it is based on certain feelings which we have about our history. It is, however, quite capable of being directed to rational and desirable ends" (QUA, Mackintosh Papers 11/6, "The Larger Pattern of Canadian Growth," Address to the Canadian Life Officers Association, Seigniory Club, 29 May 1956).
116 Mackintosh remained optimistic about the future of the Canadian economy, suggesting that it was in the midst of a "Kondratieff cycle" or long wave of growth, which, if properly managed could provide the basis for economic transformation. He added the appropriate caveat that economic forecasting is "always hazardous and usually distasteful. It is frequently futile. It is occasionally good clean sport … one faces the hard and unavoidable fact that in business and economic policy, as in plunging off a diving board, one has, with knowledge or without knowledge, with his eyes open or his eyes closed, to take a view of what lies ahead and base his decisions on it" ("The Canadian Economy," 242).
117 QUA PRO 1251/1/L, Mackintosh to Neil M. Leckie, 10 August 1961.
118 QUA Mackintosh Papers, Additions, 2/Addresses, CMA Conference on Management Development, Opening Address, 26 May 1955.
119 QUA PRO 1251/1/Corry, 1951-61, Mackintosh to Corry, 19 September 1960; 15 August 1961.
120 QUA PRO 1251/1/L, Mackintosh to F.C. Lawson, 5 January 1960.
121 QUA PRO 1251/1/Corry 1951–61, Mackintosh to Corry, 9 June 1961.
122 QUA Mackintosh Papers, Additions, 2/Addresses, Faculty Association, November 1953.
123 QUA PRO 1251/1/Corry 1951–61, Corry to Mackintosh, 12 February 1961.
124 QUA PRO 1251/1/Corry 1951–61, Mackintosh to Corry, 15 February 1961. On the paternalism that prevailed at Queen's, see Horn, *Academic Freedom in Canada*, 254.
125 QUA PRO 1251/1/Corry 1951–61, Mackintosh to Corry, 15 February 1961; Corry to Mackintosh, 24 February 1961.
126 QUA PRO 1251/1/L, Mackintosh to Oscar Lundell, 17 May 1959; 1/Corry 1951–61, Mackintosh to Corry, 2 May 1961; Corry to Mackintosh, 24 February 1961.

127 QUA PRO 1251/1/Corry 1951–61, Mackintosh to Corry, 8 December 1960.

128 Ibid., Mackintosh to Neil M. Leckie, 10 August 1961.

129 Ibid., Mackintosh to Corry, 8 December 1960.

130 Ibid., Mackintosh to Corry, Mackintosh to Corry, 6 February 1961.

131 Ibid., Corry to Mackintosh, 12 February 1961.

132 Ibid., Mackintosh to Corry, 15 February 1961.

133 Upon Deutsch's installation. Mackintosh stated that "he will be by a wide margin the best University Principal in the country" (QUA, Graham Papers, 1/File: Correspondence, W.A. Mackintosh, 1927–1965, Mackintosh to Graham, Christmas card, 1967.

134 QUA PRO 1251/1/C, Mackintosh to Alan Creighton, 26 August 1957. On Mackintosh's suggestion, Corry's daughter, Madeline, would also study in Neuchâtel (1/F, Mackintosh to Neil C. Fraser, 17 September 1957).

135 QUA PRO 1251/1/Corry 1951–61, Mackintosh to Corry, 22 June 1961.

136 Mackintosh, "Queen's University at Kingston."

137 QUA PRO 1251/1/Corry 1951–61, Mackintosh to Corry, 9 June 1961.

138 QUA Mackintosh Papers, Additions, 2/Addresses, Installation Banquet, 1961.

CHAPTER FOURTEEN

1 Mackintosh Private Papers.

2 QUA PRO 1251/1/D, Mackintosh to Neil M. Leckie, 10 August 1961. It was widely understood that Mackintosh would assist Corry with financial aspects of the principal's office. His salary as principal and vice-chancellor had risen from $15,000 to $30,000 between 1951 and 1961; as vice-chancellor, he received $19,500 annually. Separating the offices of principal and vice-chancellor required parliament to pass a bill altering the university's charter (QUA, Mackintosh Papers, 1/Appointment as Principal, "Changes at Queen's," *Kingston Whig-Standard*, 24 April 1961).

3 Canada, Royal Commission on Banking and Finance [RCBF], *Report* (Ottawa, 1964), 569. He declined various offers, including one to participate in a biography of C.D. Howe, on the grounds that "at my age, one does not lightly become an indentured servant even for a few years" (QUA PRO 1251/1/B, Mackintosh to Frank H. Brown, 17 February 1961).

4 Clarence Barber offered a frank assessment of Canadian policy between 1955 and 1957. The restrictive monetary policy pursued until the middle of 1957 (the peak of the boom) was "about right," but afterwards "unbelievably bad." He characterized the latter period as one of tight money and loose fiscal policy when the opposite should have been the case (Clarence Barber, RCBF, *Hearings* (Winnipeg, 9 April 1962) 9: 857; Barber, "Canada's Unemployment Problem"; cf. Smith and Slater, "The Economic Policy Proposals of the Governor of the Bank of Canada."

5 QUA, PRO 1251/1/Corry, 1951–61, Mackintosh to Corry, 8 December 1960.

6 QUA, PRO 1251/1/C, Mackintosh to Coyne, 8 December 1960. For H. Scott Gordon and other critics of the Bank of Canada, the overriding objection was not with the substance of monetary policy or whether it contributed to the recession of 1957, but with how the bank described its policy and failed to provide it with an adequate analytical foundation. Gordon and Read complained that the bank had not taken responsibility for its monetary policy by claiming that high interest rates in the period were caused by the greater demand for credit rather than reductions in the money supply, and that beginning in August 1957 it misrepresented its monetary policy as expansionary (Gordon and Read, "The Political Economics of the Bank of Canada").

7 As Mackintosh wrote in a personal correspondence in 1955, "My inclination is to expect that the hardening of interest rates will be a temporary measure. Quite independently of the election, the Americans are notorious for running from one side of the boat to the other, and, further, the evidence seems to be that as rates of long-term Dominions rises to 3.50 or better, they will later recede" (QUA PRO 1251/1/C, Mackintosh to H.E. Cochran, 7 December 1955).

8 Ibid, Mackintosh to Coyne, 8 December 1960; Coyne to Mackintosh, 10 December 1960.

9 QUA PRO 1251/1/Corry, 1951–61, Mackintosh to Corry, 11 July 1961. During the Senate hearings, Mackintosh's letter to Coyne would make its way into the public record.

10 QUA PRO, 1251/1/B, Mackintosh to J.T. Brydon 16 February 1961.

11 QUA PRO 1251/1/Corry, 1951–61, Mackintosh to Corry, 22 June 1961.

12 *Toronto Star*, 3 March 1962, 8.

13 RCBF, *Hearings* (Ottawa, 16 October 1962) 48: 5838

14 Jack MacArthur, "The Lonely Vigil of Don Hanright," *Toronto Star*, 13 July 1962, 13. At times Mackintosh played to those attending the hearings. When C.F. Elderkin, Inspector of Banks, misspoke in asserting that many banks stocks had appreciated from a par value of $100 to as much as $7,000, Mackintosh corrected his figure to $700, noting "some of our audience was feeling richer than they actually were" [RCBF *Hearings* (Ottawa, 21 January 1963) 64: 8556].

15 Ibid., (Ottawa, 16 July 1962), 29.

16 Ibid. (Ottawa, 14 September 1962) 38: 4531 (Ottawa, 24 September 1962) 44: 5403; (Winnipeg, 10 April 1962), 10: 1031.

17 Ibid. (Ottawa, 11 July 1962) 26: 2785; (Toronto, 13 April 1962) 12: 1192c; (Ottawa, 11 July 1962) 26: 2798; (Ottawa, 15 & 16 January 1963) 61: 8192; (Ottawa, 12 July 1962) 27: 2909; (Vancouver, 13 March 1962) 2: 84–5; (Ottawa, 10 July 1962) 25: 2607; (Ottawa, 9 July 1962) 24: 2410; (Ottawa, 21 September 1962) 43: 5270.

18 Ibid. (Ottawa, 18 January 1963) 62: 8324.

19 Ibid. (Ottawa, 19 September 1962) 41: 5084; (Ottawa, 17 October 1962) 49: 6028.

20 Ibid. (Vancouver, 13 March 1962) 2: 113

21 Ibid. (Toronto, 17 April 1962) 14: 1523–4.

22 Ibid. (Fredericton, 5 June 1962) 20: 2072, 2073, 2076,

23 Ibid. (Edmonton, 19 March 1962) 5: 465; (Vancouver, 4 March 1962) 3: 236.

24 Ibid. (Ottawa, 13 July 1962): 28: 3095, 3103, 3261.

25 Ibid. (Ottawa, 25 October 1962) 53: 6611; (Ottawa, 25 September 1962) 45: 5600; (Ottawa, 16 October 1962) 48: 5989.

26 Ibid. (Vancouver, 16 March 1962) 4: 322.

27 Ibid. (Montreal, 15 May 1962) 16: 1685.

28 Ibid. (Ottawa, 18 January 1963) 63: 8405; (Vancouver, 4 March 1962) 3: 180; (Toronto, 16 April 1962) 13: 1407); (Winnipeg, 9 April 1962) 9: 831.

29 Ibid. (Ottawa, 18 September 1962) 40: 4880–1.

30 Ibid. (Montreal, 15 May 1962) 16: 1632; (Ottawa, 21 January 1963) 64: 8546, 8466; (Ottawa, 18 January 1963) 63: 8530.

31 Ibid. (Ottawa, 12 July 1962) 27: 2876; (Regina, 23 March 1962) 8: 596. When Robarts made reference to the Rowell–Sirois Royal Commission, Mackintosh could not resist interjecting: "I am even encouraged at finding the government of the Province of Ontario seeing something worthwhile in the Rowell–Sirois Report" (Ottawa, 30 October 1962) 56: 7168–9.

32 Ibid. (Ottawa, 24 October 1962) 52: 6535, 6540; 6550; 6512–3, 6573.

33 Ibid. (Ottawa, 9 Jan 1963) 59: 7512. Mackintosh was intrigued by Sweden's labour-market policy, and particularly the impact of centralized wage setting on labour-market adjustment. Since Sweden did not allow wages to fall in declining industries, uniform wages tended to cause unemployment and place the costs of labour-market adjustment "at the feet of the government" in the form of unemployment insurance payments and retraining. He suggested that this approach required "a pretty strong and pretty sophisticated bureaucracy in the labour movement," as well as broadly accepted social consensus "to confront the economy with the prospect of unemployment in order to achieve a rearrangement, some reorientation of industry" (ibid. (Ottawa, 12 September 1962) 36: 4366; (Ottawa, 24 October 1962) 52: 6529, 6532).

34 Ibid. (Regina, 23 March 1962) 8: 590–1, 642–4

35 Ibid. (Ottawa, 9 January 1963) 59: 7525.

36 Ibid. (Ottawa, 20 September 1962) 42: 5142, 5112.

37 Ibid. (Ottawa, 19 July 1962) 32: 3761, 3844.

38 Ibid. (Ottawa, 13 September 1962) 37: 4413; (Ottawa, 9 January 1963) 59: 7621.

39 Ibid. (Vancouver, 16 March 1962) 4: 278.

40 Mackintosh maintained that, with respect to flexible exchange rates, "Are not the penalties fairly heavy?" [ibid. (Ottawa, 19 October 1962) 50: 6336, 6337, 6339, 5340].

41 Ibid. (Fredericton, 6 June 1962) 19: 2063; (Ottawa, 30 October 1962) 56: 7096; (Ottawa, 9 January 1963) 59: 7557; (Ottawa, 20 July 1962) 34: 4055.

42 Ibid. (Ottawa, 19 July 1962) 32: 3761. At times, Mackintosh emphasized this point. When replying to John Robarts's assertion that municipalities found it difficult to borrow because of high interest rates: "All [that is] at stake here is some margin. Periods of tight money have recently been fairly short. It is not a matter of good and bad boys but of too many boys trying to get through a bottleneck at once ... We have a tremendous number of clients that think they ought to be freed from any penalty of high interest rates; it is only somebody else who needs to be restrained."

43 Ibid. (Toronto, 16 April 1962) 13: 1420; (Ottawa, 20 September 1962) 42: 4038. Mackintosh opposed the creation of an independent economic council to advise the government on banking policy. "It is very

difficult under our form of government to have a Minister publicly advised as to policy and then ask him to explain why he is not following it," and that the same difficulty applied if an independent body nominated economists as members of the board of the Bank of Canada. He added that "I am not quite sure how to define a professional economist, since I have probably lost my own union papers in the matter," ibid. (Winnipeg, 9 April 1962) 9: 877.

44 Ibid. (Ottawa, 27 September 1962) 46; (Ottawa, 10 July 1962) 25: 2576; (Ottawa, 20 September 1962) 42: 5197.

45 Ibid. (Ottawa, 9 January 1963) 59.

46 Among those writing background papers were Athanasios Asimakopulos, John Helliwell, Harry Johnson, Grant Reuber, Ronald Shearer, Paul Wonnacott, and John H. Young.

47 QUA, Mackintosh Papers, Additions/1, J. Douglas Gibson, Remarks at Queen's University Dinner, 2 February 1979. The two men formed a mutual-admiration society dating back to their wartime service in Ottawa. Gibson hailed Mackintosh as "the best economist Canada has produced" and Mackintosh viewed Gibson's promotion through the ranks at the Bank of Nova Scotia as a sign of the maturation of Canadian banking. "I have become bullish on Canadian banks since you and Bill Hackett have moved into the management," he told Gibson in 1954, and upon Gibson's promotion four years later he wrote: "This is a fine thing for the Bank of Nova Scotia and a fine thing for Canadian banking. I am sure that all your fellow economists will hold their heads a little higher and be a little less suspicious of the Canadian banks, as some of them have sometimes been. Having begun visiting the head offices of the banks more than thirty-five years ago, I know that some of your predecessors would have been more than a little startled" (QUA PRO 1251/1/G, Mackintosh to Gibson, 11 January 1954; 4 December 1958).

48 QUA Mackintosh Papers, Additions/1/Death, Brown to Jean Mackintosh, 30 December 1970.

49 Schott, "Review," 709.

50 RCBF, *Report*, 2.

51 Ibid., 8.

52 Ibid., 424.

53 Ibid., 562–3.

54 Ibid., 562.

55 Ibid., 564.

56 Ibid., 564.

57 Ibid., 566.
58 Ibid., 565.
59 Ibid., 566.
60 Shearer, "Porter Commission," 36.
61 Slater, "The Report of the Royal Commission on Banking and Finance." See also Slater, "General Economic Policy" and "Economic and Financial Evolution in Canada."
62 Shearer, "Porter Commission," 37.
63 QUA, Gerald S. Graham Papers, 73-070/1/6, Mackintosh to Graham, 18 October 1965.
64 QUA, Mackintosh Papers, Additions/ 1/Death, MacKay to Jean Mackintosh, 30 December 1970.
65 Ibid., Rasminsky to Jean Mackintosh, 30 December 1970.
66 QUA Mackintosh Papers, Additions/2, W.A. Mackintosh, "Report to the Councils of the Provincial Institutes of Chartered Accountants in Canada on Education Plans," (20 March 1967), 19.
67 QUA, Gerald S. Graham Papers, 73-070/1/6, Mackintosh to Graham, 17 March 1968.
68 QUA PRO 1250/12/29, J.J. Deutsch to J. R. Gordon.
69 Leontief, Morgan, Polenske, Simpson, and Tower, "The Economic Impact –Industrial and Regional – of an Arms Cut."
70 McDowall, *Sum of the Satisfactions*, 160.
71 QUA Mackintosh Papers, Additions, 1/Death, Jack Pickersgill to Jean Mackintosh.

LEGACY

1 QUA Mackintosh Papers, Biographical File.
2 Watkins, "The Staple Thesis Revisited," "The Innis Tradition," and "Canadian Capitalism in Transition" (the first two papers are reprinted in *Staples and Beyond: Selected Papers of Mel Watkins* (Montreal and Kingston: McGill-Queen's University Press, 2006); Craven, *Impartial Umpire*, 163; Richards, "The Staples Debate."
3 Drache, "Rediscovering Canadian Political Economy" and "Harold Innis and Canadian Capitalist Development."
4 Williams, *Not for Export*. Gordon Laxer (*Open for Business*) picks up the theme and turns Mackintosh into the "intellectual mouthpiece for continentalism." Much of this is written by authors who should know better. Stephen Clarkson writes, with no apparent familiarity with Mackintosh's writings, that the concept of continentalism "entered

partisan, but not academic, discourse as a nationalist epithet to castigate the position of such economists as W.A. Mackintosh and Harry Johnson who believed that increasing economic and political integration with the United States was both unavoidable and desirable." A footnote lends a curious justification for this interpretation: "Mackintosh believed that Canada was a nation created in defiance of geography. For him the continent meant Canada plus the United States" ("'Apples and Oranges,'" 5). When thrice removed from the original sources, the argument borders on the burlesque. In Melissa Clark-Jones's rendering, there are two clearly delineated camps of economic nationalists and continentalists. Mackintosh serves double duty with respect to the latter, as both one of the chief intellectual proponents (back in bed with Harry Johnson) and as its chief bureaucratic proponent in the Cold War period (despite having left Ottawa in 1946), with an even stranger bedfellow, C.D. Howe (*A Staples State*). In this incarnation, Mackintosh is an advocate of free trade and import substitution (a curious combination that many might deem contradictory) and shares the blame for Canada's high unemployment in the 1980s. The entire argument becomes so banal that any meaningful discussion of the development process becomes lost in the effort to assign crude labels. The counter-poising of Mackintosh to Walter Gordon (as the standard bearer of the nationalist view) is intriguing in light of Gordon's frequent and unambiguous declaration that "I am a Mackintosh fan" (QUA PRO 1251 I/G, Gordon to Mackintosh, 31 August 1959).

5 Mackintosh, "Some Aspects of a Pioneer Economy," 460.

6 Mackintosh, "Government Economic Policy."

7 Mackintosh, "Address to the Institute of Chartered Accountants of Ontario," 4. Despite these reservations, he could not help observing the "astonishing progress in making great inroads on the Canadian Shield, that country of granite and muskeg which has divided Canada like a wedge from the St Lawrence to the Arctic. While other changes have been similar to those of the past, this is revolutionary" (QUA Mackintosh Papers, 11/6, "The Larger Pattern of Canadian Growth," Address to the Canadian Life Officers Association, Seigniory Club, 29 May 1956).

8 "Government Economic Policy," 317.

9 JCBA (October 1937) 45(1): 17.

10 Cited in "Government Economic Policy," 315.

11 Mackintosh, "'Discussion' of W.W. Rostow," 32.

12 Ibid., 33.
13 Cited in Sharp, *Which Reminds Me*, 27.
14 Plumptre, "Organizing the Canadian Economy for War," 15.
15 QUA, Frank Knox Papers, Knox to Alex Elliott, 10 June 1944.
16 Knox, "William Archibald Mackintosh," 71.
17 Mackintosh, "Preface" to Clarence L. Barber, *The Cost of Public Welfare Expenditure to Canadians.*
18 Slater, "Strategies of Economic Policy-Making."
19 Slater, *War Finance*, 22.
20 QUA Mackintosh Papers, Additions, 1/Death, Alex Elliott to Jean Mackintosh, 6 March 1971.
21 Slater, *War Finance*, 22, 23.
22 Richard Graybiel, "Economic Expert Genial, Unassuming," *Windsor Daily Star*, 22 March 1946, 14.
23 QUA Mackintosh Papers, Additions, 1/Death, Mrs A.R. Menzies to Jean Mackintosh, n.d.
24 QUA Mackintosh Papers, Additions, 1/Gibson, J. Douglas Gibson, Remarks at Queen's University Dinner, 2 Feb. 1979; QUA Mackintosh Papers, Material from West Campus, 1, Corry to Jean Mackintosh, n.d., including the text of his obituary note for the *Queen's Review*; H.R. Jackman would repeat the same story in the context of Empire Life committee meetings (QUA Mackintosh Papers, Additions, 1/Death Jackman to Jean Mackintosh 31 December 1970).
25 Sharp, *Which Reminds Me*, 17. Grant Dexter makes a similar point when he was bemused by a rare instance when Mackintosh's pen failed him in drafting legislation.
26 LAC, King Diary, 23 March 1949.
27 Mackintosh, "Economic Instability and Social Change."
28 Laidler, "Skidelsky's Keynes: A Review Essay,"
29 Slater, *War Finance*, 245. Slater depicts the development of Canadian social-security policy over the next two decades as "a slow-to-grow and ramshackled version of the original vision [in the Green Book]," ibid., 279.
30 Mackintosh, "Economic Instability and Social Change," 1.
31 "Economic Instability," 5.
32 Ibid., 10.
33 QUA, Mackintosh Papers, Materials from West Campus/2, M. Urquhart, "A Tribute to W.A. Mackintosh."
34 RCBF, *Hearings* (March 16, 1962 – Vancouver) 4: 327.
35 "Economic Scholarship in Canada," 12.

36 Among those who later served as Queen's trustees were Arthur Childs of Burns Foods and W. Earle McLaughlin, the president of the Royal Bank of Canada. Mackintosh is also credited with having identified Donald Gordon as a man of exceptional promise, based upon his performance as an extramural student in the Queen's banking courses (Schull, *The Great Scot*, 25).

37 QUA, Mackintosh Papers, Additions, 1/Death, Graham to Jean Mackintosh, 4 March 1971.

38 Ibid., Knox to Jean Mackintosh, 31 December 1970.

39 Ibid., David McQueen to Jean Mackintosh, 31 December 1970.

40 Ibid., Wally Muir to Jean Mackintosh, n.d.

41 QUA, Mackintosh Papers, 11, G.V. Ferguson to Mackintosh, 21 October 1951.

42 QUA PRO 1251/1/M, Munro to Mackintosh, 18 November 1954.

43 Knox, "William Archibald Mackintosh," 71–2.

44 QUA PRO 1251/1/G, Dickson Glass to Mackintosh, 14 March 1957.

45 Herb Hamilton, *Queen's! Queen's! Queen's!*

46 LePan, *Bright Glass of Memory*, 74.

47 QUA, Mackintosh Papers, Additions, 1/Death, Forsey to Jean Mackintosh, 1 January 1971; Goldenberg to Jean Mackintosh, 5 January 1971.

48 Ibid., Joan Marble Prescott to Jean Mackintosh; B.F. Trotter to Jean Mackintosh.

49 W.A. Mackintosh, "O.D. Skelton," 77.

Bibliography

PRIMARY SOURCES (AND ACRONYMS AND ACCESSION NUMBERS USED)

Bank of Canada Archives (BCA)
Brandon University, S.J. McKee Archives (BUA)
  Brandon College Administrative Records
  Brandon College Quill, v. 8, 9 (1917–1919).
Canadian Baptist Archives (CBA)
  Brandon College Papers
Harvard University Archives (HUA)
  Official Student Records, "William Archibald Mackintosh."
  Official Student Record Card: W.A. Mackintosh.
Library and Archives Canada (LAC)
  Advisory Board on Tariff and Taxation (RG36)
  Department of External Affairs (RG49)
  Department of Finance (RG19)
    R.B. Bryce Papers
    W.C. Clark Papers
    J.J. Deutsch Papers
    Economic Advisory Committee
    W.A. Mackintosh Papers
  National Employment Commission (RG27)
  Public Service Commission (RG32-C-2)
  Royal Commission on Banking and Currency (RG33-17)
  Royal Commission on Dominion-Provincial Relations (RG33-23)
  Unemployment Insurance Advisory Committee (RG50)
  W.L. Mackenzie King Papers (M26)
  O.D. Skelton Papers (MG30 D33)

Irene (Biss) Spry Papers (MG30 C249)
Frank Underhill Papers (MG30 D204)
Mackintosh Private Papers (MPP)
Ontario Archives (OA)
Department of Education (RG2-42)
Gordon Committee (RG65-35-1)
Vital Statistics (RG80)
Princeton University Library
Jacob Viner Papers (MC138)
Queen's University Archives (QUA)
Biographical File: W.A. Mackintosh
J.J. Deutsch Papers
Frederick W. Gibson Papers
Gerald S. Graham Papers
Frank Knox Papers
A.R.M. Lower Papers
W.A. Mackintosh Papers
Principal's Office Records
Yearbook/Year Book/Tricolor (title varies), various years
St Andrew's College Archives (SAC)
Saskatchewan Archives Board (SAB)
Saskatchewan. Department of Education. School District Files
Saskatchewan. Education Department. Inactive Teachers List: 1912–1938.
University of Glasgow Library, Special Collections (UGL)
Letters from James Bonar (MS Gen 518)
University of Saskatchewan Archives (UOSA)
President's Office. W.C. Murray Papers
University of Toronto Archives (UTA)
Department of Political Economy Records (A1976-0025)
H.A. Innis Papers (B1972-0003 and -0025)
Innis Family Papers (B1979-0056 and B1991-0029)
Torontonensis 1902

Newspapers

Brandon Sun
Globe & Mail
Financial Post
Kingston Whig-Standard

Ottawa Citizen
Toronto Star
Vancouver Sun
Windsor Daily Star
Winnipeg Free Press

PUBLISHED WORK BY W.A. MACKINTOSH

1916 "The Social and Political Teachings of Count Leo Tolstoy," Department of Political and Economic Science, Queen's University.

1918 "On Humor and the Humorous," *Brandon College Quill* 9(2) 16–18.

1919 "Economics, Prices and the War," *Queen's Quarterly* 26: 452–8; also appeared as *Bulletin of the Departments of History and Political and Economic Science in Queen's University*. no. 31.

1922 "The General Election of 1921," *Queen's Quarterly* 29: 309–15.

1923 "Economic Factors in Canadian History," *Canadian Historical Review* 4: 12–25.

1923 "The Psychologist and Economics," *Queen's Quarterly* 30: 297–305.

1923 "Banks and Banking," *Queen's Quarterly* 31: 218–20.

1923 "Doctoring the Gold Standard," *Journal of the Canadian Bankers' Association* 31: 60–9.

1924 *Agricultural Cooperation in Western Canada*. Queen's University Studies. Toronto: Ryerson, 1924 (based on his PhD thesis, Harvard University, 1921).

1924 "Canadian Politics," "The Situation in the United States," and "A World Problem," *Queen's Quarterly* 31: 329–33.

1925 "The Return to Gold," *Queen's Quarterly* 32: 422–3.

1925 "The Canadian Wheat Pools," *Queen's Quarterly* 33: 115–42; also published as a *Bulletin of the Departments of History and Political and Economic Science in Queen's University*, no. 51.

1925 "Economic Conditions in Europe," *Queen's Quarterly* 33: 370–4.

1926 "The Laurentian Plateau in Canadian Economic Development," *Economic Geography* 2: 537–49.

1927 "Adam Smith on Education," *Queen's Quarterly* 34: 392–7.

1927 "Some Contrasts in the Economic Development of Canada and the United States," *The Institute Bulletin (Professional Institute of the Civil Service of Canada)* 6(7): 5–9.

1927 "Canada and Vermont: A Study in Historical Geography," *Canadian Historical Review* 8: 9–30.

1927 "From Mine to Coin," *Queen's Review* 1: 14–16.

1929 "The Use of Case Material in Economics," *Contributions to Canadian Economics* 2: 34–44.

1930 "The Curriculum of a Course in Commerce," *Papers and Proceedings of the Canadian Political Science Association* 2: 95–8.

1931 "Introduction" to *Statistical Contributions to Canadian Economic History*. Toronto: Macmillan Company of Canada.

1931 "Gold and the Decline in Prices," *Proceedings of the Canadian Political Science Association* 3: 88–122.

1932 "The Pioneer Problems of the Prairie Provinces of Canada: General Outline." In *Pioneer Settlement*, edited by W.L.G. Joerg. New York: American Geographical Society, Special Publication no. 14, 1–11.

1932 "The Economic Problem of Western Canada," Proceedings of the Fourth Annual Meeting of the Canadian Society of Agricultural Economics.

1932 *A Survey of the Electrical Equipment Manufacturing Industry of Canada*. Kingston: Department of Economics, Queen's University (with F.A. Knox).

1933 "Canadian Tariff Policy," *Canadian Papers, 1933*. Prepared for the Fifth Biennial Conference of the Institute of Pacific Relations, Banff, Alberta. Toronto: Canadian Institute of International Affairs.

1934 *Prairie Settlement: The Geographical Setting*. Canadian Frontiers of Settlement, v.1. Toronto: Macmillan Company of Canada.

1935 *Economic Problems of the Prairie Provinces*. Canadian Frontiers of Settlement, v.4. Toronto: Macmillan of Canada. With the assistance of A.B. Clark, G.A. Elliott, and W.W. Swanson.

1935 "The Progress of Canada's Recovery," *International Affairs* 14: 389–401.

1935 "The British Elections," *Queen's Quarterly* 42: 530–4.

1936 "Some Aspects of a Pioneer Economy," *Canadian Journal of Economics and Political Science* 2: 457–63.

1936 "Trade Barriers as an Obstacle to Prosperity," *Annals of the American Academy of Political and Social Sciences* 186: 1–5.

1936 "Retrospect and Prospect in Europe," *Queen's Quarterly* 43: 85–94.

1937 "An Economist Looks at Economics," *Canadian Journal of Economics and Political Science* 3: 311–21. Presidential address delivered at a joint meeting of the Canadian Political Science Association and the Canadian Historical Association.

1937 "Canada as an Area for Settlement," in *Limits of Land Settlement: A Report on Present-day Possibilities*, edited by Isaiah Bowman et al. New York: Council on Foreign Relations.

1938 "Central Europe and German Appeasement," *Queen's Quarterly* 45: 401–12.

1939 *The Economic Background of Dominion-Provincial Relations*. Appendix 3 to the Report of the Royal Commission on Dominion-Provincial Relations, Ottawa.

1939 *Trade and Industry*. Toronto: Ryerson (with Robert Owen Merriman).

1939 "Crisis in Wheat," *Queen's Quarterly* 46: 348–59.

1940 "Reciprocity: A Review Article," *Canadian Journal of Economics and Political Science* 6: 611–20.

1941 "Economic Co-ordination of the War Effort" in *Canadian War Economics*, edited by J.F. Parkinson. Toronto: University of Toronto Press, 180–6.

1941 "The Price System and the Procurement of Essential Supplies," *Canadian Journal of Economics and Political Science* 7: 338–49.

1941 "Price and Wage Ceilings – Why?" *The Canadian Chartered Accountant* (December), 385–96.

1942 "Canadian War Financing," *Journal of Political Economy* 50: 481–500.

1947 "Planning the International Trade Organization," *The Round Table: The Commonwealth Journal of International Affairs*, 37(148): 390–6.

1947 "The Problem of the United Nations," *Queen's Quarterly* 54: 90–9.

1948 "Trade and Fiscal Policy," in *Canada Looks Ahead: A Series of Addresses and Papers Presented at the National Summer Conference of the Young Liberal Federation of Canada, McMaster University, Hamilton, Ontario, September 1 to 5, 1947*, edited by Charles Clay. Ottawa: Tower Books.

1948 *Canada and the Problems of the World*. University of Chicago Round Table/NBC radio broadcast, with Milton Friedman, Donald Gordon, and W.A. Mackintosh. University of Chicago Press.

1948 "Dependence on Export Markets Overseas," in J. Douglas Gibson, ed., *Canada in a Changing World*. Toronto: Macmillan of Canada.

1949 "Canada and the World Economy in the Making," *Lloyd's Bank Review* n.s. 12: 12–29.

1949 "Canada's Stake in Anglo-American Solidarity," *Foreign Affairs* 28: 18–29.

1950 "Government Economic Policy: Scope and Principles," *Canadian Journal of Economics and Political Science* 16: 314–26.

1950–51 "A Note on the Canadian Dollar," *International Journal* 6: 50–3.

1951 "Economic Instability and Social Change," *Transactions of the Royal Society of Canada* 45, series 3, sec. 2, 1–12.

1952 "Federal Finance," in *Federalism: An Australian Jubilee Study,* edited by Geoffrey Sawer. Melbourne: F.W. Cheshire for the National University of Australia.

1952 "Discussion," of W.W. Rostow, "Economic Theory and Public Policy," *American Economic Review, Papers and Proceedings* 42: 32–3.

1952 "Shoring up the Foundations of Our Boom," *Saturday Night* (November 8) 68: 32–5.

1953 "The Fissure in NATO: North American and Sterling Area Trade," *Foreign Affairs* 31: 268–79.

1953 "The People and Their History," in Lester B. Pearson, et al., *Canada: Nation on the March*. Toronto: Clark, Irwin and Co., 15–34.

1954 "Queen's Quarterly, 1893–1954," *Queen's Quarterly* 60: 460–1.

1955 "Preface" to Clarence L. Barber, *The Cost of Public Welfare Expenditure to Canadians*. Toronto: Gilbert Jackson.

1955 "The Canadian Economy and its Competitors," *Foreign Affairs* 34: 117–27.

1957 "These Seventy-Five Years: Presidential Address," *Proceedings of the Royal Society of Canada*, series 3, 51: 53–62.

1957 "Canada's Economic Prospects: A Review of the Recommendations Contained in the Preliminary Report of the Gordon Royal Commission on Canada's Economic Prospects," in *The Canadian Chartered Accountant* (March)

1959 "Canadian Economic Policy from 1945 to 1957: Origins and Influences," in H.G.J. Aitken, et al., *The American Economic Impact on Canada*. Durham, NC: Duke University Press, 51–68.

1961 "Fifty Years of Financial Growth in Canada," *The Canadian Chartered Accountant* 79(1): 84–8 (July).

1966 "The White Paper on Employment and Income in Its 1945 Setting," in S.F. Kaliski, ed., *Canadian Economic Policy Since the War*. Montreal: Private Planning Association of Canada, 9–21.

n.d. "Introduction" to "Preliminary Report on Studies in the History of Business Conditions in Canada," Department of Economics, Queen's University and McMaster University.

Editor, The Ryerson Business Studies

1923 "Editor's Introduction" to John D. Falconbridge, *The Law of Negotiable Instruments in Canada: A Handbook*. Toronto: Ryerson Press.

1926 "Editor's Preface" to R.G.H. Smails and C.E. Walker, *Accounting Principles and Practice*. Toronto: Ryerson Press.

1931 W.A. McKague, *Investment*. Toronto: Ryerson Press.

1932 "Editor's Introduction" to E.L. Stewart Patterson, *Canadian Banking*. Toronto: Ryerson Press.

1953 "Preface" to A.B. Jamieson, *Chartered Banking in Canada*. Toronto: Ryerson Press.

Published Speeches, Addresses, etc.

1938 "Unemployment and Relief: A Summary," Queen's University, Department of University Extension, *Conference on Public Administration for Municipal Officers*. Kingston.

1940 "Wage Policy in War Time," *Proceedings of the Industrial Relations Conference of the Industrial Relations Section, Queen's University* (Kingston: Queen's University).

1943 "International Aspects of Post-War Problems," *Engineering Journal*, 26: 676–8. Text of a speech delivered to a joint meeting of the American Society of Mechanical Engineers and the Engineering Institute of Canada.

1946 "The United Nations and a Divided World," *Queen's Review* 20: 221–4.

1952 "The Troubles of Prosperity," Canadian Club of Toronto, 28 January 1952.

1953 "Presidential Address," *Proceedings: National Conference of Canadian Universities, 1953*. Ottawa: National Conference of Canadian Universities, 1953.

1955 "The Canadian Economy," *Business Quarterly* 20: 242–6.

1956 "Address to the Institute of Chartered Accountants of Ontario," Kingston, 18 June 1956.

1957 "Forward," to Rudolf Pechel, *Freedom in Struggle: Being the Ninth Series of Lectures Under the Chancellor Dunning Trust, Delivered at Queen's University, Kingston, Ontario, 1957*. Toronto: Ryerson Press, 1957.

1959 "The Prospect for Queen's," *Queen's Review* (1959) 33: 2–3, 27.
1962 Address at Memorial Service for Edward Robert Peacock, held at Upper Canada College, Toronto, 5 December.

Journal of the Canadian Bankers' Association/Canadian Banker

1924–1939 "The March of Events." As editor, Mackintosh provided a ten-page overview of world events in each quarterly issue. He also presumably was the author of several unsigned short editorial pieces, as well as the book-review section, "The Banker's Bookshelf."

The following articles between 1924 and 1939 acknowledged his authorship.

1927 "The Future Trend of Prices," 34: 146–58.
1927 "The Future Trend in Prices: A Rejoinder," 34: 293–300.
1928 "Samuel Rogers: Banker," 35: 376–80.
1929 "The Problems of Reparations," 36: 221–38.
1930 "Economic Prosperity in the British Empire: A Critical Review of Prof. Leacock's New Book," 38: 40–6.
1931 "Central Banks and Business Recovery," 38: 360–3.
1935 "The Recovery of Britain," 42: 230–40.
1935 "France – 1935," 42: 321–33.
1935 "Italy Faces the World," 42: 503–13.

Biographical and Obituary Notes

1932 "Adam Shortt," *Canadian Banker* 38: 247–50.
1938 "Adam Shortt, 1859–1931," *Canadian Journal of Economics and Political Science* 4: 164–76.
1940 "Norman McLeod Rogers," *The Canadian Journal of Economics and Political Science* 6: 476–8.
1941 "Robert McQueen, Scholar and Friend," *Manitoba Arts Review* 2(3): 22–3.
1941 "Adam Shortt." In *Some Great Men of Queen's*, edited by Robert Charles Wallace. Freeport, NY: Books for Libraries Press, 1941, 115–33.
1941 "O.D. Skelton," *Canadian Journal of Economics and Political Science* 7: 270–8.
1941 "O.D. Skelton," *Canadian Banker* 48: 277–9.

1942 "C.E. Walker, 1880–1942," *Queen's Review* 16(1).
1947 "Keynes as a Public Servant," *Canadian Journal of Economics and Political Science* 13: 379–83.
1947 "John Maynard Keynes, 1883–1947," *Canadian Banker* 54(1): 50–4.
1951 "Douglas Alexander Skelton (1906–1950)," *Canadian Journal of Economics and Political Science* 17: 89–91.
1953 "William Clifford Clark and Canadian Economic Policy," *Canadian Journal of Economics and Political Science* 19: 411–13.
1953 "William Clifford Clark: A Personal Memoir," *Queen's Quarterly* 60: 1–16.
1953 "Innis on Canadian Economic Development," *Journal of Political Economy* 61: 185-94.
1953 "John Lyle Morison," *Queen's Review* (13 February).
1958 "Charles Avery Dunning, 1885–1958," given at memorial service in Grant Hall, Queen's University, 26 October (Kingston: Jackson Press).
1959 "William Everett McNeill, 1876–1959," *Transactions of the Royal Society of Canada* 53: 105–9.
1959 "Sidney Earle Smith, 1897–1959," *Transactions of the Royal Society of Canada* 53: 129–33.
1965 "O.D. Skelton," in Robert L. McDougall, ed., *Canada's Past and Present: A Dialogue, Our Living Tradition*, Fifth Series (University of Toronto Press, in association with Carleton University Press, Toronto, 1965), 59–77.

Book Reviews (Selected)

1922 *The Challenge of Agriculture. The Story of the United Farmers of Ontario*. Edited by Melvin H. Staples. Toronto: George N. Morang, 1921. In *Canadian Historical Review* 3: 203–5.
1923 "Survey: Economics," *Queen's Quarterly* 30: 451–4.
1927 Marion I. Newbiggin, *Canada, the Great River, the Lands and the Men* (London: Christophers, 1927). In *Canadian Historical Review* 9: 142–4.
1927 *Canada Year Book, 1926* (Ottawa: Dominion Bureau of Statistics, 1927); and *Statistical Year Book of Quebec, 13th Year, 1926* (Quebec: L.A. Proulx, 1926). In *Canadian Historical Review* 8: 268–9.

1929 Harald S. Patton. *Grain Growers Co-operation in Western Canada.* Cambridge: Harvard University Press, 1928. In *Contributions to Canadian Economics* 2: 102–3.

1930 Harold Innis, ed., *Selected Documents in Canadian Economic History, 1497–1783* (Toronto: University of Toronto Press, 1929). In *Journal of Political Economy* 38: 724–5.

1931 H.A. Innis, *The Fur Trade in Canada: An Introduction to Canadian Economic History* (New Haven: Yale University Press, 1930). In *Canadian Historical Review* 12: 65–7.

1932 "Economics," *Queen's Quarterly* 39: 733–7.

1933 "Economic History," *Queen's Quarterly* 40: 486–8.

1935 C.R. Fay, *Imperial Economy and Its Place in the Foundation of Economic Doctrine* (Oxford: Clarendon, 1934). In *Canadian Journal of Economics and Political Science* 1: 123–4.

1935 *Encyclopaedia of the Social Sciences*, 15 volumes, edited by R.A. Seligman and Alvin Johnson (New York: Macmillan, 1930). In *Canadian Journal of Economics and Political Science* 2: 253–5.

1936 John Maynard Keynes. *The General Theory of Employment, Interest and Money* (Toronto, Macmillan of Canada). In *Queen's Quarterly* 43: 228–9.

1936 League for Social Reconstruction, Research Committee. *Social Planning for Canada* (Toronto: Thomas Nelson and Sons). In *Queen's Quarterly* 43: 231–3.

1937 Walter P. Davisson. *Pooling Wheat in Canada* (Ottawa: Graphic Publishing, 1927). In *Canadian Historical Review* 8: 353–5.

1939 James B. Hedges. *Building the Canadian West* (New York: Macmillan). In *Annals of the American Academy of Political and Social Science* 208: 216–17.

1948 Koppel S. Pinson, ed., *Essays on Anti-Semitism*. New York: Conference on Jewish Relations. In *Queen's Quarterly* 55: 93.

1948 G. V. Ferguson, *John W. Dafoe* (Toronto: Ryerson, 1948). In *Queen's Quarterly* 55: 211–13.

1948 Henry C. Simons, *Economic Policy for a Free Society* (Chicago: University of Chicago Press, 1948). In *American Economic Review* 38: 636–40.

1949 John Jewkes, *Ordeal by Planning* (London: Macmillan, 1948). In *Canadian Journal of Economics and Political Science* 15: 261–3.

1965 J.S. Mill, *Principles of Political Economy with Some of Their Applications to Social Philosophy*, edited by V.W. Bladen and

J.M. Robson. Toronto: University of Toronto Press, 1965. 2 vols. In *Dialogue: Canadian Philosophical Review* 4: 252–4.
1967 Merrill Dennison, *Canada's First Bank: A History of the Bank of Montreal, Vol. II*. In *Canadian Banker* 74(3): 23–7.

Articles by Members of the Department of Economics, Queen's University

In 1933 and 1934, four papers appeared in the *Queen's Quarterly* written by "members of the Economics Department, Queen's University."

1933 "Financial Manipulation: A Project of Reform." 40: 264–81.
1933 "The Proposal for a Central Bank." 40: 424–40.
1933 "Financial Problems of Our Federal System." 40: 580–99.
1934 "Canadian Trade Policy in a World of Economic Nationalism." 41: 81–98.

SECONDARY SOURCES

Acheson, A.L.K., J.F. Chant, and M.F.J. Prachowny, eds. *Bretton Woods Revisited: Evaluation of the International Monetary Fund and the International Bank for Reconstruction and Development*. Toronto: University of Toronto Press, 1972.

Acheson, T.W. "Introduction" to S.A. Saunders, *The Economic History of the Maritime Provinces*. Saint John, NB: Acadiensis Press. 1984.

Ainley, Marianne Gosztonyi. "Mabel F. Timlin, 1891–1976: A Woman Economist in the World of Men." *Atlantis: A Women's Studies Journal* (1999) 23(2): 28–38.

Aitken, H.G.J. "Myth and Measurement: The Innis Tradition in Economic History," *Journal of Canadian Studies*, (1977) 12(5): 96–107.

Altman, Morris. "A Revision of Canadian Economic Growth, 1870–1910 (A Challenge to the Gradualist Interpretation)," *Canadian Journal of Economics* (1987) 20: 86–113.

American Economic Association. "Report of the Dinner Meeting in Celebration of the Fiftieth Anniversary of the Founding of the American Economic Association," *American Economic Review* (1935) 26: 317–40.

Angus, Margaret. *Summerhill: Queen's University at Kingston*. Kingston: Queen's University, 1997.

Ashley, C.A. "Two Hatless Englishmen," *Queen's Quarterly* (1971) 78: 373–80.

Axelrod, Paul. *Scholars and Dollars: Politics, Economics, and the Universities of Ontario, 1945–1980*. Toronto: University of Toronto Press, 1982.

Bacher, John C. *Keeping to the Marketplace: The Evolution of Canadian Housing Policy*. Montreal: McGill-Queen's University Press, 1993.

Barber, Clarence. "Canada's Unemployment Problem," *Canadian Journal of Economics and Political Science* (1962) 28: 88–102.

Barnett, Enid. *Keynes Comes to Canada: The War Budget of September 1939*. Kingston: Harbinger House, 2000.

– *The Keynesian Arithmetic in War-Time Canada: Development of the National Accounts, 1939–1945*. Kingston: Harbinger House, 1998.

Bateman, Bradley W., and Ethan B. Kapstein. "Retrospectives: Between God and the Market: The Religious Roots of the American Economic Association," *Journal of Economic Perspectives* (1999) 13: 249–57.

Bercuson, David. *True Patriot: The Life of Brooke Claxton, 1896–1960*. Toronto: University of Toronto Press, 1994.

Berger, Carl. *The Sense of Power: Studies in the Ideas of Canadian Imperialism, 1867–1914*. Toronto: University of Toronto Press, 1970.

– *The Writing of Canadian History: Aspects of English Canadian Historical Writing Since 1900*. 2nd ed. Toronto: University of Toronto Press, 1986.

Bertram, G.W. "The Relevance of the Wheat Boom in Canadian Economic Growth," *Canadian Journal of Economics* (1973) 4: 545–66.

Besomi, Daniele, ed. *Roy F. Harrod's Interwar Papers and Correspondence*. Ann Arbor: University of Michigan Press, 2003.

Bindon, Kathryn M. *Queen's Men, Canada's Men: The Military History of Queen's University, Kingston*. Kingston: Queen's University, 1978.

Bladen, Vincent. *Bladen on Bladen: Memoirs of a Political Economist*. Toronto: University of Toronto Press, 1978.

Booth, Harold. "E.A. Partridge, That Man Partridge, A Prairie Radical," in *Tales of the Red Fox*. Sintaluta: Sintaluta and District History Book, 1985.

Bordo, Michael D., and Angela Redish. "Why Did the Bank of Canada Emerge in 1935?" *Journal of Economic History* (1987) 47: 405–17.

Boyce, Gerald E. *Historic Hastings*. Belleville: Ontario Intelligencer Limited, 1967.

Bradford, Neil. "Writing Public Philosophy: Canada's Royal Commissions on Everything," *Journal of Canadian Studies* (Winter 1999/2000) 34(4) 136–67.

Brady, Alexander. "Reconstruction in Canada: A Note on Policies and Plans," *Canadian Journal of Economics and Political Science* (1942) 8: 460–8.

Brecher, Irving. *Monetary and Fiscal Thought and Policy in Canada, 1919–1939*. Toronto: University of Toronto Press, 1957.

Bright, Steven J. "Planning to Plan: Cyril James, the Ottawa Mandarins and the Committee on Reconstruction, 1941–1943." Royal Military College, MA Thesis. Kingston, 2005.

Brison, Jeffrey David. *Rockefeller, Carnegie, and Canada: American Philanthropy and the Arts & Letters in Canada*. Montreal: McGill-Queen's University Press, 2005.

Bryce, R.B. *Canada and the Cost of World War II. The International Operations of Canada's Department of Finance, 1939–1947*, edited by Matthew J. Bellamy. Montreal: McGill-Queen's University Press, 2005.

– "The Canadian Economy in the 1930s: Unemployment Relief under Bennett and Mackenzie King," in *Explorations in Canadian Economic History: Essays in Honour of Irene M. Spry*, edited by Duncan Cameron. Ottawa: University of Ottawa Press, 1985.

– *Maturing in Hard Times: Canada's Department of Finance Through the Great Depression*. Montreal: McGill-Queen's University Press, 1986.

– "The White Paper in Retrospect." In *Papers Presented at the Mackintosh Symposium on the Occasion of the Opening of Mackintosh-Corry Hall*. Kingston: Institute for Economic Research, Queen's University, Discussion Paper no. 178, 1974.

Calvin, D.D. *Queen's University at Kingston: The First Century of a Scottish-Canadian Foundation, 1841–1941*. Kingston: Trustees of the University, 1941.

Cam, Gilbert. "United States Government Activity in Low-Cost Housing," *Journal of Political Economy* (1939): 47: 357–78.

Campbell, Robert M. *Grand Illusions: The Politics of the Keynesian Experience in Canada, 1945–1975*. Peterborough: Broadview Press, 1987.

Canada. Department of External Affairs. Joint Economic Committees – Canada and the United States. *Tentative Draft of a Joint Report on Canadian-United States Relations in the Post-War Period*. Ottawa: 1942.

Canada. Department of Justice. Committee on Combines Legislation. *Report of the Committee to Study Combines Legislation and Interim Report on Resale Price Maintenance*. Ottawa, 1952.

Canada. Department of Labour. *Investigation into the Proprietary Articles Trade Association: An Alleged Combine of Wholesale and Retail Druggists and Manufacturers, Established to Fix and Maintain Resale Prices of Proprietary Medicines and Toilet Articles. Interim Report of Registrar*. Ottawa, 1926.

Canada. Department of Reconstruction. *Employment and Income, with Special Reference to the Initial Period of Reconstruction.* Ottawa, 1945.

Canada. Dominion Bureau of Statistics. *Canada Year Book,* 1928–1945. Ottawa, 1929–1946.

Canada. Dominion-Provincial Conference on Reconstruction. *Proposals of the Government of Canada* ["Green Book"]. Ottawa, 1945.

Canada. Foreign Affairs and International Trade Canada. Documents on Canadian External Relations, v. 12 – 528 CH /Vol. 2103.

Canada. House of Commons. Standing Committee on Banking and Commerce. *Bill No. 238. An Act for Carrying into Effect the Agreement for an International Monetary Fund and an International Bank for Reconstruction and Development. Minutes and Proceedings of the Evidence and Report to the House*. Ottawa, 1945.

Canada. National Employment Commission. *Interim Report of the National Employment Commission*. Ottawa: J.O. Patenaude, 1937.

Canada. National Employment Commission. *Final Report*. Ottawa: J.O. Patenaude, 1938.

Canada. Royal Commission on Banking and Finance. *Hearings and Index*. Ottawa, 1962.

Canada. Royal Commission on Banking and Finance, *Report*. Ottawa, 1964.

Canada. Royal Commission on Dominion-Provincial Relations. *Report*. 3 vols. Ottawa, 1940.

Canada. Royal Commission on National Development in the Arts, Letters, and Sciences, 1949–1951. *Report*. Ottawa, 1951.

Canada. Statistics Canada. *Historical Statistics of Canada,* 2nd ed. Ottawa, 1983.

Carlson, Valdemar. "The Education of an Economist before the Great Depression: Harvard's Economics Department in the 1920s," *American Journal of Economics and Sociology* (1968) 27: 101–12.

Cassidy, H.M. *Unemployment Relief in Ontario, 1929–1932*. Toronto: Dent, 1932.

Chambers, E.J., and D.F. Gordon. "Primary Products and Economic Growth: An Empirical Measurement," *Journal of Political Economy* (1966) 74: 315–32.

Christie, Nancy. *Engendering the State: Family, Work, and Welfare in Canada*. Toronto: University of Toronto Press, 2000.

Christie, Nancy, and Michael Gauvreau, eds. *Cultures of Citizenship in Post-War Canada, 1940–1955*. Montreal: McGill-Queen's University Press, 2003.

Church, Robert L. "The Economists Study Society: Sociology at Harvard, 1891–1902." In *Social Sciences at Harvard, 1860–1920: From Inculcation to the Open Mind*, edited by Paul Buck. Cambridge: Harvard University Press, 1965.

Clark, W.C. "University Training for Business – A Reply," *Queen's Quarterly* (1923) 30: 319–34.

– "What's Wrong with Us?" *The Institute Bulletin* (Professional Institute of the Civil Service of Canada), 10(10): 2–3.

– "O.D. Skelton," *Proceedings of the Royal Society of Canada* (1941), 141–7.

Clark-Jones, Melissa. *A Staples State: Canadian Industrial Resources in Cold War.* Toronto: University of Toronto Press, 1987.

Clarkson, Stephen. "'Apples and Oranges': Prospects for Comparative Analysis of the EU and NAFTA as Continental Systems." European University Institute, Robert Schuman Centre for Advanced Studies, Working Paper, 2000–3.

Coats, R.H. "Review" of *Statistical Contributions to Canadian Economic History*, edited by W.A. Mackintosh (Toronto: Macmillan of Canada, 1931) in *Canadian Historical Review* (1932) 13: 55–8.

Corry, J.A. *My Life and Work: A Happy Partnership.* Kingston: Queen's University, 1981.

Cox, Corolyn. "Canada's Woman Labour Authority," *Saturday Night* (24 July 1943).

Craven, Paul. *Impartial Umpire: Industrial Relations and the Canadian State, 1900–1911*. Toronto: University of Toronto Press, 1980.

Creighton, Phillip. *A Sum of Yesterdays: Being a History of the First One Hundred Years of the Institute of Chartered Accountants of Ontario.* Toronto: Institute of Chartered Accountants of Ontario, 1984.

Dales, J.H. "Canadian Scholarship in Economics." In *Scholarship in Canada, 1967*, edited by R.H. Hubbard. Toronto: University of Toronto Press, 1968.

– "Introduction," to W.A. Mackintosh, *The Economic Background of Dominion-Provincial Relations*. Toronto: Carleton Library edition, 1964.

– "Some Historical and Theoretical Comments in Canada's National Policies," *Queen's Quarterly* (1964) 71: 297–316.

– J.C. McManus, and M.H. Watkins. "Primary Products and Economic Growth: A Comment," (1967) 75: 876–80.

Daub, Mervin, and P. Bruce Buchan. *Getting Down to Business: A History of Business Education at Queen's, 1889–1999*. Montreal: McGill-Queen's University Press, 1999.

Dexter, Grant. *Ottawa at War: The Grant Dexter Memoranda, 1939–1945*, edited by Frederick W. Gibson and Barbara Robertson. Winnipeg: Manitoba Historical Society, 1994.

Dimand, Robert. "How Keynes Came to Canada: Mabel Timlin and Keynesian Economics." In Mathew Forstater and L. Randall Wray, eds., *The Continuing Relevance of the General Theory: Keynes for the 21st Century*. London: Palgrave Macmillan, 2008.

Dickinson, Zenas Clark. *Economic Motives: A Study in the Psychological Foundations of Economic Theory, with Some Reference to Other Social Sciences*. Cambridge: Harvard University Press, 1924.

Donald, W.J.A. "The Canadian Political Science Association," *Journal of Political Economy* (1913) 21: 762–4.

Dorfman, Joseph. *The Economic Mind in American Civilization. Volume 4, 1918–1933*. New York: Viking Press, 1959.

Drache, Daniel. "Rediscovering Canadian Political Economy," *Journal of Canadian Studies* (August 1976) 11: 3–18.

– "Harold Innis and Canadian Capitalist Development," *Canadian Journal of Political and Social Theory* (1982) 6: 35–60.

Drummond, Ian M. *Political Economy at the University of Toronto: A History of the Department, 1888–1982*. Toronto: Faculty of Arts and Science, University of Toronto, 1983.

– and Norman Hillmer. *Negotiating Freer Trade: The United Kingdom, the United States, Canada, and the Trade Agreements of 1938*. Waterloo: Wilfrid Laurier Press, 1989.

Easterbrook, W.T. "Trends in Canadian Economic Thought," *South Atlantic Quarterly* (1959) 58: 91–107.

Ferguson, Barry. *Remaking Liberalism: The Intellectual Legacy of Adam Shortt, O.D. Skelton, W.C. Clark, and W.A. Mackintosh*. Montreal: McGill-Queen's University Press, 1993.

– and Robert Wardhaugh, "'Impossible Conditions of Inequality': John W. Dafoe, the Rowell-Sirois Royal Commission, and the Interpretation of Canadian Federalism," *Canadian Historical Review* (2003) 84: 551–84.

Ferguson, G.V. "He Was One of Us," *Manitoba Arts Review* (1941) 2(3): 19–20.

Finkel, Alvin. "Paradise Postponed: A Re-examination of the Green Book Proposals of 1945," *Journal of the Canadian Historical Association* (1993) 4: 120–42.

Fogel, Robert W. "Academic Economics and the Triumph of the Welfare State," Association of American Universities: Washington, DC, 2000.

Frankel, S.J. "Staff Relations in the Canadian Federal Public Service: Experience with Joint Consultation," *Canadian Journal of Economics and Political Science* (1956) 22: 509–22.

Friedman, Walter A. "The Harvard Economic Service and the Problems of Forecasting," *History of Political Economy* (2009) 41: 57–88.

Fullerton, Douglas. *Graham Towers and His Times.* Toronto: McClelland and Stewart, 1986.

Galbraith, John Kenneth. "How Keynes Came to America," in *Economics, Peace, and Laughter* [a collection of his own papers]. Boston: Houghton Mifflin, 1971.

Gardner, Richard N. *Sterling-Dollar Diplomacy in Current Perspective: The Origins and Prospects of Our International Economic Order.* New York: Columbia University Press, 1980.

George, Peter. "Rates of Return in Railway Investment and Implications for Government Subsidization of the CPR," *Canadian Journal of Economics* (1968) 1: 740–62.

Gibson, Frederick W. *To Serve and Yet Be Free: Queen's University, Volume II, 1917–1961.* Montreal: McGill-Queen's University Press, 1983.

Grady, Patrick. "David W. Slater: An Economist for All Seasons," in *The State of Economics in Canada: Festschrift in Honour of David Slater*, edited by Patrick Grady and Andrew Sharpe. Ottawa: Centre for the Study of Living Standards, 2001.

Gordon, H.S., and L. M. Read. "The Political Economics of the Bank of Canada," *Canadian Journal of Economics and Political Science* (1958) 24: 465–82.

Gordon, Walter. *A Political Memoir.* Toronto: McClelland and Stewart, 1977.

Gossage, Carolyn. *A Question of Privilege: Canada's Independent Schools.* Toronto: Peter Martin, 1977.

Granatstein, J.L. *The Ottawa Men: The Civil Servant Mandarins, 1939–1957.* Toronto: Oxford University Press, 1982.

Grant, Dwight. "The Staple Theory and Its Empirical Measurement," *Journal of Political Economy* (1974) 82: 1249–53.

Grant, W.L. *Our Just Cause: Facts about the War for Ready Reference*. London: Royal Colonial Institute, 1914.

Hall, Peter A., ed. *The Political Power of Economic Ideas: Keynesianism Across Nations*. Princeton: Princeton University Press, 1989.

Hamilton, Herb. *Queen's! Queen's! Queen's!* Kingston: Alumni Association of Queen's University, 1977.

Harcourt, G.C. "An Early Post-Keynesian: Lorie Tarshis (or: Tarshis on Tarshis by Harcourt)," *Journal of Post-Keynesian Economics* (1992) 4: 609–19. Reprinted in Harcourt, ed., *Post-Keynesian Essays in Biography*. Basingstoke: Macmillan, 1993.

– "Lorie Tarshis, 1911–1993: In Appreciation," *Economic Journal* (1995) 105: 1244–55.

Harper, Marjorie. "Copland, Sir Douglas Berry (1894–1971)," *Australian Dictionary of Biography*. Melbourne: Melbourne University Press, 1993. 13: 496–500.

Harvard University. *Courses of Instruction Offered by the Faculty of Arts and Science for the Academic Year 1916–17*. 2nd ed. Cambridge, 1916.

– *Harvard Crimson*, 12 June 1916.

Heaton, Herbert. *A Scholar in Action: Edwin F. Gay*. New York: Greenwood Press, 1968.

Hedlin, Ralph. "Edward A. Partridge," Manitoba Historical Society Transactions, 1958–9.

Hicks, John. "Mr. Keynes and the 'Classics': A Suggested Interpretation," *Econometrica* (1937) 5: 147–59.

Hilliker, John. *Canada's Department of External Affairs, Volume 1: The Early Years, 1909–1946*. Montreal: McGill-Queen's University Press, 1990.

Hodgetts, J.E., William McCloskey, Reginald Whitaker, and V. Seymour Wilson. *The Biography of an Institution: The Civil Service Commission of Canada, 1908–1967*. Montreal: McGill-Queen's University Press, 1972.

Horn, Michiel. *Academic Freedom in Canada: A History*. Toronto: University of Toronto Press, 1999.

Horsefield, J. Keith. *The International Monetary Fund, 1945–1965. Twenty Years of International Monetary Cooperation. Volume I: Chronicle*. Washington: IMF, 1969.

Howson, Susan, and Donald Moggridge, eds. *The Wartime Diaries of Lionel Robbins and James Meade, 1943–1945*. New York: St Martin's, 1991.

Hudson, Brenda M. *Fabric of a Dream: A Settlement Story of Madoc and Elzevir Townships*. Belleville: Mika, 1979.

Hutchison, Bruce. *The Incredible Canadian: A Candid Portrait of Mackenzie King – His Works, His Times, and His Nation*. Toronto: Longman, Green and Co., 1952.

Innis, H.A. *The Bias of Communication*. 2nd ed. Toronto: University of Toronto Press, 2008.

– "Canadian Frontiers of Settlement: A Review," *Geographical Review* (1935) 25: 92–106.

– *The Fur Trade in Canada: An Introduction to Canadian Economic History*. Toronto: University of Toronto Press, 1999. First published in 1930.

– "Notes on Problems of Adjustment in Canada," *Journal of Political Economy* (1935) 43: 800–7.

– The Penetrative Powers of the Price System," *Canadian Journal of Economics and Political Science* (1938) 4: 299–319.

– "Some English-Canadian University Problems," *Queen's Quarterly* (1943) 50: 30–6.

– "Teaching of Economic History in Canada," *Contributions to Canadian Economics* (1929) 2: 52–68.

Jamieson, Stuart. *Industrial Relations in Canada*. 2nd ed. Toronto: Macmillan of Canada, 1957.

Johnson, Harry G. "Canadian Contributions to the Discipline of Economics since 1945," *Canadian Journal of Economics* (1968) 1: 129–146.

Johnson, Marianne, and Warren J. Samuels, eds. *Economic Theory by Taussig, Young, and Carver at Harvard*. Bingley, UK: Emerald, 2010.

Keynes, John Maynard. *The Collected Writings of John Maynard Keynes*, edited by Donald Moggridge. London: Cambridge University Press, 1992.

Kindleberger, Charles P. *The Life of an Economist: An Autobiography*. Cambridge, Mass: Basil Blackwell, 1991.

– *The World in Depression, 1929–1939*. London: Penguin, 1973.

King, Jack B. "Herbert Heaton: A Scholar 'Exiled' from Australia," *History of Economics History* (2006) 43: 56–70.

Knox, Frank. "William Archibald Mackintosh, 1895–1970," *Royal Society of Canada. Proceedings and Transactions* (1971) 4th series, 9: 67–72.

Knuttila, Murray. "*'That Man Partridge': E.A. Partridge, His Thought and Times*." Regina: University of Regina, 1994.

Kuznets, Simon. *National Income and Its Composition, 1919–1938, Volume I*. New York: National Bureau of Economic Research, 1941.

Laidler, David. "Skidelsky's Keynes: A Review Essay," *European Journal of the History of Economic Thought* (2002) 9: 97–110.

Laidler, David, and Roger Sandilands. "An Early Harvard Memorandum on Anti-Depression Policies: An Introductory Note," and the "Memorandum Prepared by L.B. Currie, P.T. Ellsworth, and H.D. White (Cambridge, Mass., January 1932)," *History of Political Economy* (2002) 34: 515–32 and 533–52.

Laxer, Gordon. *Open for Business: The Roots of Foreign Ownership in Canada*. Toronto: Oxford University Press, 1989.

Leitch, Alexander. *A Princeton Companion*. Princeton: Princeton University Press, 1978.

Leontief, Wassily, Alison Morgan, Karen Polenske, David Simpson, and Edward Tower. "The Economic Impact – Industrial and Regional – Of An Arms Cut," *Review of Economics and Statistics* (1965) 47: 217–41.

LePan, Douglas. *Bright Glass of Memory: A Set of Four Memoirs*. Toronto: McGraw Hill, 1979.

Lewis, Frank. "The Canadian Wheat Boom and Per Capita Income: New Estimates," *Journal of Political Economy* (1975) 83: 1249–57.

Lewis, Frank. "Farm Settlement on the Canadian Prairies, 1898–1911," *Journal of Economic History* (1981) 41: 517–35.

Lim, Andrea Rae. "Kingston's Chinese: The Formation of an Enclave, 1891–1980," MA Thesis, Department of History, Queen's University, Kingston, 2005.

MacDonald, R. St J. "Maxwell Cohen at Eighty: International Lawyer, Educator, and Judge," *The Canadian Yearbook of International Law 1989*, v. 27. Vancouver: UBC Press, 1989.

Macdonnell, J.M. "The Decline of the Arts Faculty," *Bulletin of the Department of History and Political and Economic Science in Queen's University*, no. 44 (1923).

MacGibbon, D.A. "Dr. James Bonar," *Canadian Journal of Economics and Political Science* (1941) 7: 283–4.

MacGibbon, D.A. "Robert McQueen, 1896–1941," *Canadian Journal of Economics and Political Science* (1941) 7: 278–83.

MacKenzie, Hector M. "'The Path to Temptation': The Negotiation of Canada's Reconstruction Loan to Britain in 1946," Canadian Historical Association *Historical Papers* (1982) 17. 196–220.

– "The White Paper on Reconstruction and Canada's Postwar Trade Policy." In *Uncertain Horizons: Canadians and Their World in 1945*, edited by Greg Donaghy. Ottawa: Canadian Committee for the History of the Second World War, 1997.

Mackintosh, Margaret. "Government Intervention in Labour Disputes in Canada," *Queen's Quarterly* (1924) 31: 298–328.

Mackintosh, William (Sr) "Presidential Address," *Minutes of the Thirty-First Annual Convention of the Ontario Teachers' Association, 1892*. Toronto: Hill and Weir, 1892.

Macpherson, C.B. "The Social Sciences." In *The Culture of Contemporary Canada,* edited by Julian Park. Toronto: Ryerson, 1957.

Manitoba. *Manitoba's Case: A Submission Presented to the Royal Commission on Dominion-Provincial Relations. Part IV: The Effects of Federal Tariff Policy on Western Canadian Economy.* Winnipeg, 1937.

Marr, William, and M. Percy, "The Government and the Rate of Prairie Settlement," *Canadian Journal of Economics* (1978) 11: 757–67.

Marsh, Leonard. "Report of the National Employment Commission," *Canadian Journal of Economics and Political Science* (1939) 5: 80–6.

Mason, Edward S., and Thomas S. Lamont, "The Harvard Department of Economics from the Beginning to World War II," *Quarterly Journal of Economics* (1982) 97: 383–433.

Maxwell, J.A. "Canadian Dominion-Provincial Relations," *Quarterly Journal of Economics* (1941) 55: 584–610.

McDowall, Duncan. *Sum of the Satisfactions: Canada in the Age of National Accounting*. Montreal: McGill-Queen's University Press, 2008.

McInnis, Peter. *Harnessing Labour Confrontation: Shaping the Postwar Settlement in Canada, 1943–1950*. Toronto: University of Toronto Press, 2002.

McIvor, R. Craig. "Canadian War-Time Fiscal Policy, 1939–45," *Canadian Journal of Economics and Political Science* (1948) 14: 62–93.

McKenzie, A.E. ed. *History of Brandon College, Inc.* Brandon: Brandon College, 1962.

McQueen, David. "Economic Research at the Bank of Canada, 1935–65," *Canadian Business Economics* (1997) 5(2–3): 89–95.

McQueen, Robert. "The Approach to Economics," *Canadian Journal of Economics and Political Science* (1940) 6: 79–85.

– "Canadian Monetary Policy," *Manitoba Arts Review* (Spring 1939) 1(3): 22–38.

Michell, Humphrey. "Review of *Agricultural Cooperation in Western Canada*," *Canadian Historical Review* (1925) 6: 181–2.

Milgate, Murray, and Alistair Levy. "James Bonar (1852–1941)." In *New Palgrave Dictionary of Economics* 1st ed., edited by John Eatwell,

Murray Milgate, and Peter Newman. London: Palgrave Macmillan, 1987.

Mitchell, Martha. *Encyclopedia Brunoniana*. Providence: Brown University Library, 1993.

Mitchell, Tom. "From the Social Gospel to the 'Plain Bread of Leninism': A.E. Smith's Journey to the Left in the Epoch of Reaction After the Great War," *Labour/Le Travail* (1994) 33: 125–51.

– "'A Square Deal for All and No Railroading': Labour and Politics in Brandon, 1900–1920," *Prairie Forum* (1990) 15: 45–64.

Moggridge, Donald E. *Maynard Keynes: An Economist's Biography*. London, Routledge, 1992.

Muirhead, Bruce. *Against the Odds: The Public Life and Times of Louis Rasminsky*. Toronto: University of Toronto Press, 1999.

Neatby, Blair H. "The Liberal Way: Fiscal and Monetary Policy in the 1930s." In *The Great Depression: Essays and Memoirs from Canada and the United States*, edited by Victor Hoar. Toronto: Copp-Clark, 1969.

– *The Politics of Chaos: Canada in the Thirties*. Toronto: Macmillan, 1972.

Nerbas, Don. *Dominion of Capital: The Politics of Big Business and the Crisis of the Canadian Bourgeoisie, 1914–1947*. Toronto: University of Toronto Press, 2013.

Newman, Peter C. "The Ottawa Establishment," *Maclean's* (22 August 1964).

Norrie, K.H. "The National Policy and the Rate of Prairie Settlement: A Review," *Journal of Canadian Studies* (1979) 14: 63–76.

Ontario. Committee on the Organization of Government in Ontario. *Report*. Toronto: Queen's Printer, 1959.

Owram, Douglas. *Born at the Right Time: A History of the Baby Boom Generation*. Toronto: University of Toronto Press, 1996.

– *The Government Generation: Intellectuals and the State in Canada, 1900–1945*. Toronto: University of Toronto Press, 1986.

Parker, Ian. "Harold Innis: Staples, Communications, and the Economics of Capacity, Overhead Costs, Rigidity, and Bias." In *Explorations in Canadian Economic History: Essays in Honour of Irene M. Spry*, edited by Duncan Cameron. Ottawa: University of Ottawa Press, 1985.

Patinkin, Donald. *Anticipations of the General Theory? And Other Essays on Keynes*. Chicago: University of Chicago Press, 1982.

– and J. Clark Leith, eds. *Keynes, Cambridge, and the General Theory*. London: Macmillan, 1977.

Pearson, Lester B. *Mike. The Memoirs of the Right Honourable Lester B. Pearson. Volume 2: 1948–1957*, edited by John A. Munro and Alex I. Ingles. Toronto: University of Toronto Press, 1973.

Perry, J. Harvey, "The Queen's Connection," *Canadian Banker* (1993) 100: 14–18.

Pickersgill, Jack. "Mackenzie King's Political Attitudes and Public Policies: A Personal Impression." In *Mackenzie King: Widening the Debate*, edited by John English and J.O. Stubbs. Toronto: Macmillan of Canada, 1978.

Pigden, Garnet, and Ardith McKinnon. *Way Back When ... Reflections on Madoc Village and Madoc Township*. Madoc, 1975.

Plumptre, A.F.W. "The Evidence Presented to the 'Canadian Macmillan Commission,'" *Canadian Journal of Economics and Political Science* (1936) 2: 54–67.

– "Keynes at Cambridge," *Canadian Journal of Economics and Political Science* (1947) 13: 366–71.

– "Organizing the Canadian Economy for War," in J.F. Parkinson, ed., *Canadian War Economics*. Toronto: University of Toronto Press, 1941.

– *Three Decades of Decision: Canada and the World Monetary System, 1944–1975*. Toronto: McClelland and Stewart, 1977.

Price, Adam Robert William. "Back-to-Work Legislation: An Analysis of the Federal and Ontario Governments' Increased Propensity to End Strikes by *Ad Hoc* Laws, 1950–1978," MA Thesis, Queen's University. Kingston, 1980.

Purdy, Al. *Beyond Remembering: The Collected Poems of Al Purdy*. Vancouver: Harbour Publishing, 2000.

Queen's University. *The Proceedings on the Occasion of the Installation of William Archibald Mackintosh as Twelfth Principal of Queen's University, Kingston, Ontario. 19 October 1951*. Kingston: Queen's University, 1951.

Queen's University. *Queen's Journal*, v. 39–42. Kingston, 1913–15.

Queen's University. *Report of the Principal of Queen's University to the Board of Trustees. 1946–47–1960–61*. Kingston, 1947–62.

Queen's University. Industrial Relations Centre. "Industrial Relations at Queen's: The First Fifty Years." Kingston, 1987.

Rawlyk, G.A. "A.L. McCrimmon, H.P. Whidden, T.T. Shields, Christian Education and McMaster University." In *Canadian Baptists and Christian Higher Education*, edited by G. Rawlyk. Montreal: McGill-Queen's University Press, 1988.

Rymes, T.K. *Keynes's Lectures, 1932–35: Notes of a Representative Student*. Basingstoke: Macmillan, 1989.

Richards, John. "The Staples Debate," in *Essays on Honour of Irene Spry*, edited by Duncan Cameron. Ottawa: University of Ottawa Press, 1985.

Roper, Henry. "The Lifelong Pilgrimage of George E. Wilson, Teacher and Historian," *Collections of the Royal Nova Scotia Historical Society* (1986) 42: 139–51.

Rosenbluth, Gideon, and H.G. Thorburn. "Canadian Anti-Combines Administration, 1952–1960," *Canadian Journal of Economics and Political Science* (1961) 27: 498–508.

Samuels, Warren J., ed. "Materials from Economics 5 and 6, Money and Banking and Public Finance, Taught by Walter B. Smith and William H. Wynne, Williams College, 1930–31," *Research in the History of Economic Thought and Methodology* (2006) v. 24B: 109–82.

Samuelson, Paul A. "Credo of a Lucky Textbook Author," *Journal of Economic Perspectives* (1997) 11: 153–60.

– "Unemployment Ahead (I.) A Warning to the Washington Expert," *New Republic* (11 September 1944): 297–9.

Sandilands, Roger. *The Life and Political Economy of Lauchlin Currie: New Dealer, Presidential Advisor and Development Economist.* Durham: Duke University Press, 1990.

Schorske, Carl E. "A Life of Learning," American Council of Learned Societies, Occasional Paper No. 1, 1987.

Schott, Francis H. "Report of the Canadian Royal Commission on Banking and Finance: A Review," *Federal Reserve Bank of New York Monthly Review* (August 1964): 151–6.

– "Review of Report of the Royal Commission on Banking and Finance," *Journal of Finance* (1964) 19: 709–12.

Schull, Joseph. *The Great Scot: A Biography of Donald Gordon.* Montreal: McGill-Queen's University Press, 1979.

Scoular, William. *Not an Ordinary Place: A St. Andrew's Century.* Aurora, ON: St. Andrew's College, 1998.

Shamrock History Book Society. *Harvest of Memories: RM 134 and Shamrock*. Shamrock, SK, 1990.

Shearer, Ronald A. "The Porter Commission Report in the Context of Earlier Canadian Monetary Documents," *Canadian Journal of Economics* (1977) 10: 34–49.

Sharp, Mitchell. *Which Reminds Me: A Memoir.* Toronto: University of Toronto Press, 1994.

Shortt, Adam. *Imperial Preferential Trade from a Canadian Point of View.* Toronto: Morang, 1904.

Skelton, Alexander. "Obituary: Edward Arthur George Luxton, 1914–1945," *Canadian Journal of Economics and Political Science* (1945) 11: 478–9.

Skelton, O.D. "Winnipeg General Strike," *Queen's Quarterly* 27 (July-September 1919).

Skidelsky, Robert. *John Maynard Keynes, Volume 3. Fighting for Freedom, 1937–1946*. London: Viking, 2000.

– "The Political Meaning of the Keynesian Revolution." In *The End of the Keynesian Era: Essays on the Disintegration of the Keynesian Political Economy*, edited by R. Skidelsky. London: Macmillan, 1977.

Slater, David W. "Colour the Future Bright: The White Paper, the Green Book and the 1945–1946 Dominion-Provincial Conference on Reconstruction" in *Uncertain Horizons: Canadians and Their World in 1945*, edited by Greg Donaghy. Ottawa: Canadian Committee for the History of the Second World War, 1997.

– "Economic and Financial Evolution in Canada," *Canadian Banker* (Autumn 1964): 5–22.

– "General Economic Policy in the Report of the Royal Commission on Banking and Finance," *Canadian Banker* (Summer 1964): 7–22.

– "The Report of the Royal Commission on Banking and Finance," *Canadian Journal of Economics and Political Science* (1965) 31: 421–9.

– "Strategies of Economic Policy-Making: Canada-United States," *The Empire Club of Canada Addresses*. Toronto: The Empire Club Foundation, 1982.

– *War Finance and Reconstruction: The Role of Canada's Department of Finance, 1939–1946*. Ottawa: David W. Slater, 1995.

Smails, R.G.H. "C.E. Walker, 1880–1942," *Canadian Journal of Economics and Political Science* (1943): 9: 75–6.

– "The Department of Political and Economic Science at Queen's, 1878–1959," unpublished, 1960.

– "The Story of Commerce at Queen's," *Queen's Review* (1953) 28: 448–55.

Smiley, Donald V. "Introduction" to *The Rowell-Sirois Report: An Abridgement of Book I of the Royal Commission Report on Dominion-Provincial Relations*. Toronto: Macmillan, 1978.

Smith, A.E. *All My Life*. Toronto: Progress Books, 1949.

Smith, D.C., and D.W. Slater. "The Economic Policy Proposals of the Governor of the Bank of Canada," *Queen's Quarterly* (1961) 68(1): 196–211.

Smith, Neil. *American Empire: Roosevelt's Geographer and the Prelude to Globalization*. Los Angeles: University of California Press, 2003.

Snavely, Tipton R. "Memorial: Duncan Clark Hyde, 1896–1957," *Southern Economic Journal* (1957) 24: 87–9.

Southey, Clive. "The Staples Thesis, Common Property and Homesteading," *Canadian Journal of Economics* (1978) 11: 547–59.

Spafford, Shirley. *No Ordinary Academics: Economics and Political Science at the University of Saskatchewan, 1910–1960*. Toronto: University of Toronto Press, 2000.

Spry, Irene (Biss). "Review of *Prairie Settlement: The Geographical Setting; Economic Problems of the Prairie Provinces*," *Journal of Political Economy* (1935) 43: 705–9.

Stone, C.G., and F. Joan Garnett. *Brandon College: A History, 1899–1967*. Brandon: Brandon University, 1969.

Struthers, James. *No Fault of Their Own: Unemployment and the Canadian Welfare State, 1914–1941*. Toronto: University of Toronto Press, 1983.

Tarshis, Lorie. *The Elements of Economics: An Introduction to the Theory of Price and Employment*. Boston: Houghton-Mifflin, 1947.

Taylor, K.W. "Economic Scholarship in Canada," *Canadian Journal of Economics and Political Science* (1960) 26: 6–18.

Timlin, Mabel F. *Keynesian Economics*. Toronto: University of Toronto Press, 1942.

Underhill, Frank. "The Conception of a National Interest," *Canadian Journal of Economics and Political Science* (1935) 1: 396–408.

Urquhart, M.C. "New Estimates of Gross National Product, Canada, 1870–1926: Some Implications for Canadian Development," in *Long-Term Factors in American Economic Growth*, edited by S. Engermann and R.E. Gallman. NBER Studies in Income and Wealth, v. 51. Chicago: University of Chicago Press, 1986.

Urquhart, M.C. "W.A. Mackintosh's Scholarly Work." In *Papers Presented at the Mackintosh Symposium on the Occasion of the Opening of Mackintosh-Corry Hall*. Queen's University, Institute for Economic Research, Discussion Paper no. 178, 1974.

Van Dormael, Armand. *Bretton Woods: Birth of a Monetary System*. London: Macmillan, 1978.

Vernon, Raymond, and John T. Dunlop. "Edward Sagendorph Mason (22 February 1899–29 February 1992)," *Proceedings of the American Philosophical Society* (1994) 138: 342–5.

Viner, Jacob. "Objectives of Post-War International Economic Reconstruction." In *American Economic Objectives*, edited by W.-L. McKee and L. Wiesen. New Wilmington, PA: Economic and Business Foundation, 1942.

Vivian, Henry. "Review of *Agricultural Cooperation in Western Canada*," *Economic Journal* (1925) 35: 284–5.

Walters, Mark D. "'Let Right Be Done': A History of the Faculty of Law at Queen's University," *Queen's Law Journal* (2007) 32: 314–88.

Warhaugh, Robert A. *Behind the Scenes: The Life and Work of William Clifford Clark*. Toronto: University of Toronto Press, 2010.

Watkins, Mel. "Canadian Capitalism in Transition." In *Understanding Canada: Building on the New Canadian Political Economy*, edited by Wallace Clement. Montreal: McGill-Queen's University Press, 1997.

– "The Dismal State of Economics in Canada." In *Close the 49th Parallel: The Americanization of Canada*, edited by Ian Lumsden. Toronto: University of Toronto Press, 1973.

– "The Staple Thesis Revisited," *Journal of Canadian Studies* (Winter 1977) 12(5): 83–94.

– "The Innis Tradition in Canadian Political Economy," *Canadian Journal of Political and Social Theory* (1978) 6: 12–34.

Watson, Alexander John. *Marginal Man: The Dark Vision of Harold Innis*. Toronto: University of Toronto Press, 2007.

Williams, Glenn. *Not for Export: Towards a Political Economy of Canada's Arrested Industrialization*, 2nd ed. Toronto: McClelland and Stewart, 1986.

Willis, John. "Report of the Committee on the Organization of Government in Ontario," *University of Toronto Law Journal* (1961) 14: 103–7.

Wilson, George. "Review of *The Fur Trade in Canada*," *Dalhousie Review* (1931) 10: 575.

Wilson, Ian E. "'A Noble Dream': The Origins of the Public Archives of Canada," *Archivaria* 15: 16–35.

Wolfe, David A. "The Delicate Balance: The Changing Economic Role of the State in Canada." PhD thesis, University of Toronto, 1980.

– "The Rise and Demise of the Keynesian Era in Canada, 1930–1982," in *Readings in Canadian Social History, vol. 5: Modern Canada,* edited by Michael S. Cross and Gregory S. Kealey. Toronto: McClelland and Stewart, 1984.

Wright, Donald. *The Professionalization of History in English Canada*. Toronto: University of Toronto Press, 2005.

Young, Robert A. "Reining in James: The Limits of the Task Force," *Canadian Public Administration* (1981): 24: 596–611.

Young, J.H. "A Tribute to John Deutsch, *Canadian Public Policy* (1976) 2: 365–7.

Index